LITERACY AND HISTORICAL DEVELOPMENT

Literacy and Historical Development

A READER

EDITED BY HARVEY J. GRAFF

SOUTHERN ILLINOIS UNIVERSITY PRESS
Carbondale

10 09 08 07   4 3 2 1

Library of Congress Cataloging-in-Publication Data
Literacy and historical development : a reader /
edited by Harvey J. Graff.
     p. cm.
 Includes bibliographical references and index.
 ISBN-13: 978-0-8093-2782-9 (pbk. : alk. paper)
 ISBN-10: 0-8093-2782-1 (pbk. : alk. paper)
 1. Literacy—Europe—History. 2. Literacy—North
America—History. 3. Printing—Social aspects—
Europe—History. 4. Printing—Social aspects—North
America—History. I. Graff, Harvey J.

LC156.A2L58 2007
302.2'244094—dc22   2007011084

Printed on recycled paper. ♻
The paper used in this publication meets the minimum requirements of American National Standard
for Information Sciences—Permanence of Paper for
Printed Library Materials, ANSI Z39.48-1992. ∞

FOR LS @ OSU AND ICRPH

CONTENTS

List of Figures and Tables   ix
Acknowledgments   xi

Introduction
                                    HARVEY J. GRAFF   1

1. *Literacy, Myths, and Legacies: Lessons from the History of Literacy*
                                    HARVEY J. GRAFF   12

2. *Literate and Illiterate; Hearing and Seeing: England, 1066–1307*
                                    MICHAEL T. CLANCHY   38

3. *Some Conjectures about the Impact of Printing on Western
   Society and Thought: A Preliminary Report*
                                    ELIZABETH L. EISENSTEIN   82

4. *The Importance of Being Printed*
                                    ANTHONY T. GRAFTON   106

5. *Printing and the People: Early Modern France*
                                    NATALIE ZEMON DAVIS   126

6. *Oral Culture and the Diffusion of Reformation Ideas*
                                    ROBERT SCRIBNER   161

7. *The Literacy Myth? Illiteracy in Scotland, 1630–1760*
                                    RAB HOUSTON   183

8. *First Steps in Literacy: The Reading and Writing Experiences of
   the Humblest Seventeenth-Century Spiritual Autobiographers*
                                    MARGARET SPUFFORD   207

9. *The History of Literacy in Sweden*
                                    EGIL JOHANSSON   238

10. *Growth of Literacy in Colonial America: Longitudinal Patterns,*
    Economic Models, and the Direction of Future Research
    FARLEY GRUBB   272

11. *Dimensions of Illiteracy in England,* 1750–1850
    ROGER S. SCHOFIELD   299

12. *"We Slipped and Learned to Read": Slave Accounts*
    of the Literacy Process, 1830–1865
    JANET CORNELIUS   315

13. *Sense and Sensibility: A Case Study of Women's*
    Reading in Late-Victorian America
    BARBARA SICHERMAN   334

14. *Sponsors of Literacy*
    DEBORAH BRANDT   357

15. *"Welcome to the Jam": Popular Culture, School*
    Literacy, and the Making of Childhoods
    ANNE HAAS DYSON   379

Bibliography of the History of Literacy in Western
    Europe and North America   417
Contributors   441
Index   445

FIGURES AND TABLES

Figures

4.1. Renaissance printing-house 107
7.1. Parishes with surviving Covenants 186
9.1. Threefold interplay of forces in "the world of the 'Hustavla'" 245
9.2. Deaneries in Swedish dioceses with at least one Church examination register 252
9.3. Parishes in Swedish dioceses with a Church examination register 254
9.4. Family of Jacob Eriksson in the Church examination register 256
9.5. Reading ability in Tuna, in Möklinta, and in Skellefteå 263
9.6. Reading ability in Skanör 263
9.7. Reading ability in the diocese of Västerås 266
9.8. Reading and writing traditions in Sweden 268
10.1. Patterns of regional literacy growth in rural colonial America 281
10.2. Supply-and-demand model of colonial literacy decline and growth 286
11.1. Males and females unable to sign at marriage, England and Wales 303
11.2. Males and females unable to sign at marriage, England 305
11.3. Males unable to sign at marriage, Bedfordshire 308
15.1. "Welcome to the Jam," 396
15.2. "Welcome to the Jam," 401

Tables

7.1. Adult male illiteracy in Scotland, 1638–43 187
7.2. Male and female illiteracy in Scotland, 1650–1760 190
7.3. Male and female illiteracy in regions of Scotland 191
7.4. Occupational illiteracy of males and females in Scotland 192
7.5. Occupational illiteracy of males and females over time 194
7.6. Illiteracy of male craftsmen and tradesmen, and labourers and servants over time 194
7.7. Male and female illiteracy in different communities of residence over time 195
7.8. Occupational illiteracy of males in different communities of residence within Scotland 196
7.9. Occupational illiteracy of females in different communities of residence within Scotland 197

7.10. Illiteracy of male craftsmen and tradesmen, and labourers and servants in different regions of Scotland 198

9.1. Reading marks and Catechism knowledge in Tuna, 1688–91 257

9.2. Reading marks in Tuna, 1688–91, related to age 258

9.3. Catechism knowledge in Tuna, 1688–91, related to age 258

9.4. Reading marks and Catechism knowledge in Tuna, 1688–91, related to age 259

9.5. Reading marks and Catechism knowledge in Tuna, 1688–91, related to ages 6–13 260

9.6. Reading ability in Tuna, 1691, in Möklinta, 1705, and in Skellefteå, 1724, related to year of birth 263

10.1. Studies of colonial adult male literacy, 1650–1840 274–75

10.2. Studies of European adult male literacy, 1633–1840 276–77

11.1. Illiteracy by occupational group, 1754–84 to 1815–44 309

12.1. Decade of birth of ex-slaves, by source 326

12.2. Decade when learned to read, by source 326

12.3. Regional location of slaves when they learned to read, by source 326

12.4. Postslavery careers of ex-slaves, by source 327

12.5. Levels of literacy attained while slaves, by source 327

12.6. Owner- versus slave-initiated learning, by source 327

12.7. Contexts for owner-initiated teaching, by ex-slave source 328

12.8. Contexts for slave-initiated teaching, by ex-slave source 328

ACKNOWLEDGMENTS

I want to express my gratitude to a number of individuals and institutions who helped to bring this book to publication:

the Departments of English and History at The Ohio State University, especially Valerie Lee and Nan Johnson, not only for bringing me to OSU and Columbus but also for bringing me back—in part, at least—to literacy/literacy studies;

the College of Humanities, the Department of English, the Institute for Collaborative Research and Public Humanities (especially Chris Zacher), the Colleges of the Arts and Sciences at OSU, for support and funding, including permissions fees and manuscript preparation;

Kelly Bradbury, my graduate research assistant for this project, who contributed in many ways; doctoral student Shawn Casey, who read proof carefully; Vicki Graff, who checked tables and figures;

Karl Kageff, Editor-in-Chief, Southern Illinois University Press, and Bridget Brown, Assistant Acquisitions Editor, SIU Press, and the production department at SIU Press, especially Barb Martin, Wayne Larsen, John Wilson, and Paula Durbin-Westby for their interest, assistance, and advice;

the students in my courses on the history of literacy over the years at the University of Texas at Dallas, Simon Fraser University, the University of Texas at San Antonio, and The Ohio State University;

and most recently, my colleagues and students involved in the Literacy Studies Working Group and Literacy Studies @ OSU.

LITERACY AND HISTORICAL DEVELOPMENT

INTRODUCTION

In almost any sphere of discourse or conversation today, it is difficult to avoid the subject of literacy. Literacy's currency is pervasive; the responses to the topic's introduction are often powerful, emotionally and intellectually. Throughout the Western world, perceived and sometimes documented "crises" of literacy are proclaimed; elsewhere, in under-developing areas, "crises" of *il*literacy garner attention. The amount of interest given to the presumed problems of literacy and illiteracy and the depth and breadth of response are revealing. On the one hand, they reflect the value accorded to literacy in modern societies and states, a value that is fundamentally an historical development. And, on the other hand, they reflect aspects of other contemporary crises—economic, political, cultural—all of which are related closely to literacy, whether in assumptions and theories or in actual practice. That concern and fears about the condition of literacy among youth and adult populations today are so grave and so tightly intermeshed with other serious current concerns is an impressive testament. Identification of the centrality we attach to literacy and its presumed significance for advanced, modern, democratic civilization is made easier by these circumstances.

The introduction to the first edition of this collection of essays on literacy and historical development began with those words (Graff, 1981b). Today, little revision is needed. If anything, our concerns and our fears—of *some* children left behind and others incarcerated in penal institutions rather than learning their letters in school—are even greater. "The value of literacy for achieving fulfilling, productive, expanding, and participating lives of freedom in modern societies is undoubted and unquestioned. At the same time, however, literacy does not seem to be well understood, popularly or academically," I continued (see also Graff and Duffy, 2007). Among students of literacy, especially historians, constructive change is under way. Demonstrating the foundations of that understanding is among the most important purposes of this collection of studies. "Contemporary understanding can be best advanced, in this case, as in many others, through a perspective grounded in history." In fact, as a field of inquiry, literacy studies strive to be critical, historical, comparative, and interdisciplinary (see Graff chapter below). Historical studies are especially important in research, interpretation, and understanding of literacy. Toward that goal, nine of the fifteen chapters are new to this edition.

The study of literacy is prominent among the historical subjects that have attracted significant interdisciplinary attention and is an established interest of a number of historians and other interdisciplinary scholars across the social sciences and the humanities (see for example Graff, 1979, 1987a, 1987b, 1993b, 1995a, 1995b, 2001, 2003). As it happens, literacy and history have much in common. Both are prone to perceptions of crisis and decline—precipitous declines that are sometimes claimed to threaten civilization as we know it. Both are susceptible to mythologization and are hard to define and measure. New interdisciplinary histories of literacy challenge those charges, among other presumptions about literacy that have been influential in many academic disciplines, in public debate, and among policy makers (see chapter by Graff, in this book; see also E. Hirsch, 1987; Gagnon and Bradley Commission, 1989; Stearns 1991, 1993; Graff 1979, 1987a, 1987b, 1989, 1993b, 1995a, 1999a, 2001, 2003; Graff and Duffy, 2006; Griswold et al., 2005; Kaestle et al., 1991; Barton, 1994; Barton and Hamilton, 1998).

The history of literacy is an instructive example of interdisciplinary history with respect to its founding and the course of its development. It followed a path common to new histories (see in general for what follows, Graff, 1987a, 1987b, 1993b, 1995a, 1999a, 2001; Kaestle et al., 1991). On the one hand, pioneering social and cultural historians of the 1960s and 1970s confronted a diffuse historical literature that made easy (if poorly documented) generalizations about the distribution of literacy across populations and also (even if vaguely) the great significance of literacy's presence, absence, or degree of diffusion. On the other hand, they confronted a social science literature, some of it with theoretical aspirations, generally derived from modernization approaches that placed literacy squarely among the requisites for progress by individuals and by groups. The historical writing rested on a thin base of mainly anecdotal evidence, with little concern about its accuracy or representativeness. The social science writing included modernization theories with stages and threshold levels, macrosocial correlations from aggregate data, and, occasionally, contemporary case studies. Writings in both areas treated literacy—whether conceptually or empirically—uncritically and as unproblematic. Literacy's key relationships, they assumed, were simple, linear, and direct, and its impact was universally powerful. At the same time, most scholarly writing neglected the subject of literacy even when it was highly relevant.

As illustrated in this book, the new literacy studies that emerged in the 1970s and 1980s were critical of earlier work and questioned the received wisdom that tied literacy directly to individual and societal development, from social mobility (a positive relationship expected) and criminal acts (a negative relationship) to revolutions in industry (positive), fertility (negative), and democracy (positive). Skeptical about modernization models and with at least some of the conclusions taken from aggregative data, researchers who came from an impressive number of nations, disciplines, and specializations were wary about imprecise formulations, sweeping levels of generalization, and their weak or inconsistent evidential basis. Critical and revisionist in intellectual orientation, a generation of scholars sought to test old and newer ideas, hypotheses, and theories with reliable and relevant data (on new literacy studies in general, see Street, 1995). Specifically, this often meant identifying measures of literacy that, ideally, were direct, systematic, routinely generated, longitudinal, and comparable—quantitative indicators all—and building machine-readable databases to promote their use and enhance their accessibility to other researchers. In Sweden, this meant church registers; in France, marriage and military records; in Britain, marriage and census records; and in North America, manuscript census records (see chapters below by Graff, Houston, Johansson, Grubb, Schofield).

The dream of a precisely comparative history remains elusive. Literacy studies have taught us to make comparisons more carefully, often restricting their range. As a recognizable field of literacy studies emerged, literacy's significance as an important variable for many subjects across the realms of social science and other interdisciplinary histories was accepted. Its relevance expanded just as expectations of its universal powers were qualified and contextualized (for important overviews, see Graff, 1987a, 1987b; Houston, 2002; Vincent, 2000).

Earlier expectations (and theories) that literacy's contribution to shaping or changing nations, and the men and women within them, was universal, unmediated, independent, and powerful have been quashed. Literacy—that is, literacy by itself—is now seldom conceptualized as independently transformative. To the contrary, we now anticipate and recognize its impact to be shaped by specific historical circumstances as context-dependent, complicated rather than simple, incomplete or uneven, interactive rather than determinative, and mediated by a host of other intervening factors of a personal, structural, or cultural historical nature rather than universal. In other words, literacy is a historical variable, and it is historically variable. The chapters in this book confirm this point, including the quantitatively and the more qualitatively based, the economic and the social and cultural approaches. The chapters in this book, in one way or another, also speak to this new understanding, although sometimes from very different perspectives and with different conclusions (compare for example chapters by Clanchy, Eisenstein, Grafton, Davis, Scribner, Spufford, Johansson, Cornelius).

For example, literacy's students understand that the equation or synonymy of literacy acquisition with institutions that we call schools and with the ages we term childhood is itself a fairly recent development. Other arrangements were once common. They included families, workplaces, and peer, religious, and political groups. We recognize that the environment in which one learns to read or write has a major influence on the level of abilities to use and the likely uses of those skills (see chapters by Clanchy, Davis, Scribner, Spufford, Johansson, Cornelius, Sicherman, Dyson).

Social attributes (including ascribed characteristics like gender, race, ethnicity, and class) and historical contexts, which are shaped by time and place, mediate literacy's impacts, for example, on chances for social or geographic mobility (see chapters by Johansson, Grubb, Cornelius, Sicherman, Brandt, Dyson). Literacy seems to have a more direct influence on longer distance migration than on shorter moves (see chapters by Johansson, Grubb). That relationship, for example, carries major implications for the historical study of both sending and receiving societies and for immigrants among other migrants. Literacy's links with economic development are both direct and indirect, multiple, and contradictory (see chapters by Grubb, Schofield). For example, its value to skilled artisans may differ radically from its import for unskilled workers. Literacy levels sometimes rise as an effect rather than a cause of industrialization. Industrialization may depress literacy levels through its negative impact on schooling chances for the young, while over a longer term its contribution may be more positive (see chapters by Graff, Schofield).

Experiences of learning literacy include cognitive and noncognitive influences. This is not to suggest that literacy should be construed as any less important, but that its historical roles are complicated and historically variable (see chapters by Graff, Scribner, Spufford, Johansson, Schofield, Cornelius, Sicherman, Dyson). Today, it is difficult to generalize broadly about literacy as a historical factor. But that only makes it a more compelling subject with implications for today and tomorrow.

Literacy studies have succeeded in establishing a new historical field where there was none. Statistical time series developed for many geographic areas and historical eras limit cavalier generalizations about literacy rates and their strong meanings, whether by demographers, economists, linguists, or literary historians (see chapters by Houston, Johansson, Grubb, Schofield). Three decades of scholarship, represented in this book, have transformed how historians and others conceptualize literacy. Both contemporary and historical theories that embrace literacy are undergoing major revision because of this body of research and recent studies that point in similar directions. The views that literacy's importance and influences depend on specific social and historical contexts, which, in effect, give literacy its meanings;

that literacy's impacts are mediated and restricted; that its effects are social and particular; that literacy must be understood as one among a number of communication media and technologies replace an unquestioned certainty that literacy's powers were universal, independent, and determinative (see especially chapter by Graff).

Literacy's historical students know how recently these ideas about literacy's transforming and developmental powers were central to theories that held sway in major areas of economics, demography, psychology, sociology, anthropology, linguistics, history, and the humanities. The challenge to probe previous understandings with suitable historical data and test the strong theories of literacy attests to the contributions that interdisciplinary historical and comparative social science and cultural studies can make.

The emergence of literacy as an interdisciplinary field for contemporary students opens the way for a richer exchange between historians and other researchers for the mutual reshaping of inquiry past, present, and future that is part of the promise of interdisciplinary studies. Historical studies of literacy, finally, contribute to public discourse, debate, and policy talk nationally and internationally. The many crucial points of intersection include the demonstration that no golden age for literacy ever existed, that there are multiple paths to literacy for individuals and societies, that quantitative measures of literacy do not translate easily into qualitative assessments, that the environment in which literacy is learned affects the usefulness of the skills, that the connections between literacy and inequality are many, and that the constructs of literacy (its learning, the uses of reading and writing, and their relationships and impacts) are usually conceived far too narrowly (see Graff chapter).

Historians of literacy need to bring their criticisms and new conclusions to audiences throughout the academy and beyond. That is one among the purposes of this book. They need to confront the limitations of two generations of study often in numerical records as they continue to build on that achievement. They need to probe the nature of literacy as a historical subject and variable. In part, they can do this by bridging the present gap between the history of literacy and new research on printing, publishing, and readership, on the one hand, and new perspectives in literary studies, writing studies, the humanities, anthropology, psychology, linguistics, and education, on the other hand. Literacy studies join other interdisciplinary research clusters in exploring new approaches to society and culture through narrative, feminist theories, literary theories, critical theory, and many other interdisciplinary connections across the human sciences in the early twenty-first century (see chapter by Graff).

Recent emphases in the historical study of literacy may be summarized:

- Economic history—greater criticism, greater efforts at more precise specification
- Demography—to a lesser extent but more subtly
- Readers and their readings—impacts, difference/differentiation
- Learning literacy(ies)/Using literacy(ies)— levels, limits, contexts, practice, performance; including learning outside of schools in families, workplaces, peer groups
- Ethnographies of literacy in practice
- Deconstructions of literacy as promotion, expectation, ideology, theory
- Multiple literacies and multimedia contexts (including multilingual)
- Reading/textuality/criticism/reader response/literary theory
- Publishing and distribution/circulation/communications
- Religion—influences, impacts, consequences
- Cultures, high, middling, popular, etc.—intersections, interactions, separations
- Reading and writing—creation, expression, performance
- History of emotions
- Political culture/political action
- Gender, social class, race, ethnicity, generation
- Connecting past, present, and future

(Graff, 1995a)

The agendas of new historical studies of literacy may be summarized:
- Historical literacy studies that build upon their own past while also breaking away from it: sharper contextual grounding; time series; linkages, and interrelationships
- Comparative studies
- New conceptualizations of context for study and interpretation including material conditions, motivations, opportunities, needs and demands, traditions, transformations, historical "ethnographies," and micro-histories
- Critical examination of the conceptualization of literacy itself—beyond independent and dependent variables
- Literacy and the "creation of meaning"—linguistic and cultural turns, reading, and so on; for example, history of literacy and transformation of cultural and intellectual history; history of the book, and history of literacy
- Sharper theoretical awareness of the relevance of the history of literacy for many important aspects of social, economic, and psychological theory; history as grounds for testing theories

- Has the tradition of taking literacy as primary object of analysis—"the history of literacy"—approached its end point? From the history of literacy to "literacy in history"?
- Policy issues: social problems, development paths, costs and consequences, alternatives and understandings

(Graff, 1995a)

Uses of this book

Like the earlier edition, this book has several key purposes, whose continuing importance and usefulness mandate its revision. This includes updating the history, broadening the coverage and inclusiveness of studies, illustrating new sources and methods, presenting new forms of interdisciplinary scholarship that draw in part from ethnography, literary theory, and cultural studies. The selection of nine new articles advances these goals (chapters by Graff, Grafton, Scribner, Houston, Grubb, Cornelius, Sicherman, Brandt, Dyson).

This roster outlines the shape and perspectives of major emphases and the broad range of uses of this volume:

- providing a history of literacy in brief compass, from the Middle Ages to the present, an up-to-date survey/overview of the history of literacy in the making of modern Europe and North America, with their implications for efforts to spread literacy to other parts of the world
- providing a strong grounding in the bibliography of the historical study of literacy
- exploring the central (if sometimes contradictory) place of literacy in the development of the modern Western world (and efforts to export ideas and arrangements to other places)
- probing the various interconnections that tie politics, economics, culture, and society and their changes over time and space to patterns of literacy
- introducing new critical conceptual and empirical approaches to literacy, and literacy's social roles and meanings
- introducing exciting and pioneering examples of recent, critical, often interdisciplinary scholarship; providing or encouraging illustrations and comparisons of a range of innovative methods, new primary sources, and noteworthy, often interdisciplinary modes of analysis
- presenting major interpretative problems and their possible resolutions
- illustrating different critical and synthetic questions and interpretations in the history of literacy
- demonstrating substantive and comparative uses of specific case studies

- probing different conceptions of literacy and testing them in historical time, space, and context
- locating literacy among different communication modes, media, and means of understanding/expressing over time, including the critical ongoing roles of orality and visual images (see Scribner chapter)
- focusing on major themes and relationships:
    Literacy and economic and social development (see Grubb, Schofield)
    Institutions for learning, practicing, and using literacy (see Graff, Brandt)
    Literacy, race, ethnicity, class (see Cornelius, Brandt, Dyson)
    Literacy and gender (see Sicherman)
    Readers and reading, cultures and classes (see Sicherman, Dyson)
    Ethnographic and developmental perspectives (see Brandt, Dyson)
    "New literacies" and the "future of literacy," including electronics and cyberspace (see Dyson)
    "Lessons" from the history of literacy (see Graff)
- In sum, providing a foundation for a new understanding of the historical basis for contemporary social issues, arrangement, and problems

Other questions, issues, and themes include "great debates" and presumed transitions that often lie at the center of theories and debates about literacy:

- "Great Divides": oral to written; written to printed; printed to electronic, or classical to vernacular; sacred to secular; restricted to mass; elite to popular
- Impacts of literacy: transformative or selective/constructed:
    individual and/or collective
    Skill/behavioral/cognitive and/or attitude/ideology/discipline
- Roles of schools and institutions including families, workplaces, peer groups
- Literacy's relationships with
    modernization
    literacy and democracy/citizenship
    literacy and equality
    literacy and opportunity/advancement
- Literacy's relationships with "revolutions"
    commercial
    agriculture
    industrial
    urban
    postindustrial/postmodern
- Literacy and literacies

With these perspectives and possible emphases, *Literacy and Historical Development* provides a valuable collection for serious readers concerned about past and present; scholars in literacy studies and the many fields that literacy studies touch, from writing and composition studies to reading research, history of the book, English and literary studies, education, communications, anthropology, sociology, economics, psychology, linguistics, policy studies, children's and family studies, and European and American social and cultural history more generally—and to teachers of both graduate and undergraduate courses in those fields.

With the exception of the first chapter, the order of *Literacy and Historical Development*'s chapters is chronological. My essay, "Literacy, Myths, and Legacies: Lessons from the History of Literacy," provides an extended introduction to the history and historiography of literacy, the major issues, approaches, and points of contention. It also offers a set of lessons for today and tomorrow, rooted in my understanding historical development.

Following that, the story of literacy's history begins in the eleventh century. MICHAEL T. CLANCHY offers an interpretation of the increasing frequency of literacy in medieval England, discusses the meaning of literacy in premodern society, the forces that propelled its expansion, the obstacles, and the interrelations between literate and oral media and culture. He also documents a multilingual environment. (These themes are also articulated in fascinating and instructive detail by Natalie Zemon Davis for early modern France, Robert Scribner for Germany, Rab Houston for Scotland, and Margaret Spufford for England.) Cultural interactions and continuities, as well as changes, patterns of commonality and difference, link these perspectives, as they demonstrate the formative developments of the *early* modern era.

Representing one side of an ongoing debate over the contribution to literacy—and much more—of the invention and diffusion of the technology of printing, ELIZABETH L. EISENSTEIN makes a strong case for the impact of the innovation of movable typographic printing and speculates about the changes that may have followed its advent and diffusion. In an extensive review of Eisenstein's landmark publication *The Printing Press as an Agent of Change* (1979), ANTHONY T. GRAFTON reassesses the era of early printing and late manuscript or scribal cultures. He sketches a revisionist view that endorses neither older understandings of print's power or Eisenstein's revisions. NATALIE ZEMON DAVIS considers print in the lives of the *menu peuple,* or common people, in town and countryside, and their social and cultural relationships to the more educated during the century after the advent of printing.

Tacking similar currents and responding to exceptionally important questions, ROBERT SCRIBNER addresses the links between the rapid spread of the Protestant Reformation and spread of literacy, print, and schooling in Luther's Germany. Reconsidering how we have construed the connections among those factors, he traces a more complex process of transmission than a focus primarily on print permits. Tracing the changing distribution of literacy in Scotland, 1630–1760, RAB HOUSTON illustrates the range of sources and methods for historical literacy studies. He uses them in an effort to probe the accuracy of Scotland's early status, and self-image, as a place of unusually widespread literacy. Branding that image as a "literacy myth," he reconsiders the reasons for Scotland's image and its differing actuality, including the roles of schools and Protestantism. Looking at a similar period of time in England, MARGARET SPUFFORD focuses on individual readers and writers and seeks to understand their motivations and life course consequences. For this testimony and these lives, the power of religious conviction is enormous. Autobiographical sources also have the power to supplement other sources of information about literacy.

EGIL JOHANSSON considers the "transition" to near-universal rates of literacy in preindustrial Sweden. In presenting pioneering case studies, he offers an original perspective on the causes and consequences of changing levels of literacy. Not only are the parish catechetical examination records an exceptional early source that sheds light on *levels* of literacy, they also reveal that the Swedish experience privileged reading over writing and relied on home-based, often maternal transmission of reading. Sweden's achievement owed little to wealth or economic development. FARLEY GRUBB traces what some researchers call the early modern "literacy revolution" from northwestern Europe to colonial North America. Acknowledging colonists' transplantation of European society across the Atlantic Ocean, he compares not only colonial to European patterns of literacy but also regional similarities and differences within North America and their implications for both economic development and economic models to explain them. ROGER S. SCHOFIELD sketches the course of literacy levels in industrializing England, and, in so doing, he also raises serious questions about the causal and temporal connections between the two epochal transformations.

JANET CORNELIUS reopens the intriguing and important question of literacy among slaves in the antebellum American South by turning to the memories of ex-slaves. Despite legal and social proscriptions against their learning to read or write, many slaves did learn literacy. Often rooted in spirituality, the possible uses and value of literacy were many. In her pioneering inquiry into the history of reading, BARBARA SICHERMAN examines a very different part of the American population: late Victorian young women of prosperous families in the Midwest. Underscoring the special importance of print and reading in middle-class women's culture, with her method based in reader-response criticism and concepts of "interpretive communities," she challenges many common ideas about the nature, uses, and significance of reading in late Victorian women's lives.

In a preview of her award-winning study of literacy in twentieth-century America, *Literacy in American Lives* (2001), DEBORAH BRANDT seeks to connect literacy as individual attainment with literacy as economic development. To do this, she focuses on "sponsors" of literacy, the agents or agencies that in one way or another push or pull different persons toward or away from useful or otherwise valued abilities, and some of their changes over the course of the twentieth century. In the final chapter, ANNE HAAS DYSON continues Brandt's emphasis on writing. Through an ethnographic lens, Dyson endeavors to link what she terms "popular culture, school literacy, and the making of childhoods." She portrays African American children appropriating and transforming elements of media-influenced-and-transmitted popular culture as they learn to write in a public elementary school classroom. Challenging students of historical, contemporary, and future literacies, past and present meet, sometimes with an audible clash, in these lives and their learning.

Notes

References to works cited appear in the Bibliography of the History of Literacy in Western Europe and North America at the end of this book.

This introduction draws upon a longer exposition of the historiography and history of literacy, first presented as a Plenary Address to the Conference on Writing and Reading in Western Europe, Valencia, Spain, 1993, and published as "Assessing the History of Literacy in the 1990s: Themes and Questions," in *Escribir y leer en Occidente,* ed. Armando Petrucci and M. Gimeno Blay (Valencia, Spain: Universitat de Valencia, 1995), pp. 5–46; my presidential address to the 25th Annual Meeting of the Social Science History Association, Pittsburgh, Pennsylvania, 2000, published as "The Shock of the 'New' (Histories)": Social Science Histories and Historical Literacies," *Social Science History,* 25(4), 2001, pp. 483–533; and my opening presentation to the international conference, "Egil Johansson, the Demographic Database, and Socio-Cultural History for the 21st Century: Literacy, Religion, Gender, and Social History," Vadstena, Sweden, May 2002, published as "Introduction to Historical Studies of Literacy," special double issue, *Interchange,* 34, 2-3 (2003), "Understanding Literacy in its Historical Contexts: Past Approaches and Work in Progress," ed. Harvey J. Graff, Alison Mackinnon, Bengt Sandin, and Ian Winchester, 117–122, 123–131.

1   LITERACY, MYTHS, AND LEGACIES:
LESSONS FROM THE HISTORY OF LITERACY

Harvey J. Graff

Unlike many discussions, the circumstances that prompted these comments were *not* the proclamation of an imminent "crisis" or "decline." With respect to literacy today—or education, or development—this is unusual. Nevertheless, I fear, that sense accompanies us closely, shadowing our critical and creative work, offering scant illumination, often leading us astray. Consider, on the one hand, today's sirens of "cultural" or "historical" literacy. On the other hand, superficially more germane to our deliberations, there are notions of "functional" illiteracy and "nonfunctional" literacy.[1]

Among the many "signs of our times," they mark our mood as they (often over)heat the crucibles of our deliberations. Contemporary cultural conjunctions, they are also clear culminations of critical historical currents that constitute no less than the origins of the modern world. They incorporate the contradictions of that epochal historical process (Graff, 1987a). Failure to appreciate the provenance of the past, of history, in the present and the possibilities for the future makes us its prisoners, bound to repeat the past, rather than to learn from it and to break its bonds. With respect to literacy, in theory and in practice, this is powerfully the case. Indeed, as a historian, I know of few other topics about which this is so true or so significant—or about which failure to embrace the opportunities for novel learning is so telling.

That is not all that we must embrace. Among those "signs of our times" are tireless but tiresome claims of ubiquitous "crisis" (or "crises") of education higher and lower, of math and science, of the humanities and social sciences, of literacy functional and otherwise, indeed, of cultures and polities and economies, national and international. Not only are these threads densely intertwined, but they are highly relevant to discussions of literacy attainment and standards. Sadly, they typically confuse the conversation more than they provide useful or heuristic contexts for discussion or un-

From Harvey J. Graff, "Lessons from the History of Literacy," in *The Labyrinths of Literacy: Reflections on Literacy Past and Present*, 318–49, © 1995. Reprinted by permission of the University of Pittsburgh Press.

derstanding. In a revealingly self-contradictory essay, "The Storm over the University," the philosopher John Searle (1990, 34) aptly begins his professorial notes for the 1990s: "I cannot recall a time when American education was not in a 'crisis.' We have lived through Sputnik (when we were 'falling behind the Russians'), through the era of 'Johnny can't read,' and through the upheavals of the Sixties. Now a good many books are telling us that the university is going to hell in several different directions at once." As a student of literacy for two decades, I can not recall a time when literacy was not in a crisis.

In that diagnosis, higher education newly joins other levels of schooling. Crises in literacy at least putatively accompany (regardless of their own relationships) those of more elevated learning. Schools and universities readily serve as attractive targets assigned responsibility and blame in difficult, confusing times. Of course, so too does literacy. With revealing contradiction, levels of literacy abilities serve simultaneously as symptoms and symbols, causes and consequences. By themselves, they prove convenient, easy symbols for wholesale criticism rather than central sources of failure or, for that matter, successful transformations (Graff, 1987a; K. Levine, 1985; "Education," 1981). With respect to American schools, the historian Michael Katz (1988, 183) notes, "for about 150 years, education has been proposed as a solution to every major social problem." With respect to the Western world more generally and to literacy, my research establishes a longer historical connection of several millennia and an active association for at least five centuries from the Renaissance and the Enlightenment (Graff, 1987a). This is one among a series of critical historical linkages and legacies we encounter and must challenge. It is also a burden that the institution perhaps—not unlike literacy—cannot bear.

John Searle's (1990, 34) sense of a "crisis" in American higher education shares a basic understanding—a hope, an agenda—with the goals of many: "I believe that, at least in part, the crisis rhetoric has a structural explanation: since we do not have national consensus on what success in higher education would consist of, no matter what happens, some sizable part of the population is going to regard the situation as a disaster. As with taxation and relations between the sexes, higher education is essentially and continuously contested territory. Given the history of that crisis rhetoric, one's natural response to the current cries of desperation might reasonably be one of boredom." (Implicitly, perhaps knowingly, Searle raises the specter of "cultural literacy.") Between the Scylla of desperation and the Charybdis of boredom, consensus and standards are sought. This gives the lie to Searle's attributions of "American uniqueness," along with his resigned pessimism and unimaginative solutions.[2]

Perception of "crisis" thus links Searle's and my concerns. Both are indeed contested territory. Those perceptions in various formulations underlay the post–World War II rise of notions, concepts, programs, and measures of "functional" literacy. Much like Searle's and many others' cavils, as Kenneth Levine observed in 1982, "current notions of functional literacy . . . obscure the identification of appropriate targets, goals, and standards of achievement in the education of adults by promising, though failing to produce, a quantitatively precise, unitary standard of 'survival' literacy. . . . [T]hese varying conceptions of functional literacy encourage the idea that relatively low levels of individual achievement . . . will directly result in a set of universally desired outcomes, such as employment, personal and economic growth, job advancement, and social integration."[3]

More impressive but unremarked is the frequency and commonality of literacy (and schooling) "crises." Not only are they ubiquitous during recent decades but their presence across an expanse of historical time encompassing centuries commands attention; their recognition may lead to fresh perspectives. In resisting the temptations to boredom cited by Searle, we discover a rhetorical discourse of "crisis" and "decline" seldom far from historical consciousness, or at least from expression. This discourse increased its presence and certainly its visibility/audibility from the time of the "Age(s) of Progress" and those of "Enlightenment," although it long predates them. Its sources and its uses are many and diverse. The relationships of this discourse to and implications for literacy and for schools are enormous, especially in difficult, critical periods of historical transformation, among which we must include our own.

My overarching point is *historical.* Historical interpretation offers potentially innovative approaches—*paths,* I call them—in reforming questions and problems, understanding, criticism, and alternative conceptualizations and perspectives.[4] In this approach, *both* continuities and transformations are critical, as are the special circumstances in which they appear or are claimed to develop. Their comprehension, explanation, and resolution require great care and close, contextual investigation. As Michael Katz observes with respect to what he terms "the new educational panic," "by ignoring history, we have replicated the same unsuccessful reform strategies over and over again" (Katz, 1988, 191).[5]

Among literacy's intertwining multiple strands, I distinguish three. Each is claimed to be declining and achieving the status of "crisis." Each of the three (and there are others) is construed, more or less reflexively—but in fact fundamentally *historically*—within the intersecting discourses of literacy and "crisis." Legacies from literacy's history, singly and conjointly, they influence our thinking and actions today. Encompassing uncomfortably a huge and revealing range, they are:

1. "Elementary" or "basic" literacy, typically taken as equivalent to the results from a variety of standardized, "objective" (i.e., "scientific") tests that presume unproblematically (however inadequately) to measure quantitatively and comparatively "schooled" and/or "functional" *reading and writing abilities* (e.g., high school competency, National Assessment of Educational Progress, Armed Forces Qualifying, "skills," etc., tests).

2. Recurrent association, direct and strong to the point of virtual equivalency or synonymy, and unproblematically, of the presumed condition of literacy—including but never limited to basic literacy, but in close connection with visible personal moral, attitudinal, and behavioral characteristics—with the *condition of civilization* (read: morality, order, democracy, progress, productivity, among other things). The association typically implies a great danger to those vested characteristics and the social order itself.

3. The more recently proliferating *many "literacies"* in addition to or "beyond" "traditional" alphabetic literacy—from those of science and numeracy, to the spatial understanding that some geographers term "graphicacy," to the loudly touted and seemingly highly vulnerable "cultural literacy," "historical literacy," and "moral literacy." Some among the lengthening lists are long established in presumption but much more novel discursively or semantically: ecological literacy, "teleliteracy" and other media literacies, food literacy, emotional literacy, sexual literacy.[6]

The extent to which the newly proliferating literacies signify little more than a semantic "name game" or a feature of the politics of literacy and education or professional specialization raises hard questions. This is central to contemporary considerations of "functional literacy" among the many literacies proclaimed. An enormously important set of critical developments, whose potentially revolutionary consequences for learning and teaching are largely unappreciated, thus far remain prisoner to scholarly, cultural, and pedagogical fragmentation. Major new advances in the study of human learning processes, cognition, and development have much to tell us about schooling and learning. If there are indeed, as I am convinced, a number of distinct "literacies," the manner in which their elements overlap or coincide has, at least in the abstract, the revolutionary potential for reconstructing primary, and perhaps higher, education in order to develop and practice those distinct but not completely differentiated abilities.[7]

These three threads stand out among the many. They stand out more clearly than they (co)exist together or separately as significations of literacy and as essential elements of education. Not only does each of them represent a case claimed for "crisis" and "decline." They also illustrate how hard it is to deal with literacy, discursively and critically as well as practically. More disparate and different than proverbial apples and oranges, it is not clear which of the three may be horses and which may be carts. No one leads directly to another; none is interchangeable with the others. Recognizing this implicitly contending plurality is only a halting first step, albeit a necessary one. Beset with numerous conceptual complications, literacy is an exceptionally slippery subject *and* object whether the goal is theoretical, critical, or practical. These three strands only begin to suggest the pervasive powers of deeply rooted and widely shared assumptions and presumptions about literacy.

The nature of the relationships imputed or expected among the three strands underscores the point. The broad appeals of the discourse, indeed, the mentality, of "crisis" and "decline" heighten sensitivity. In this respect, our own epoch has many precedents from which we may learn if we are attentive, patient, and bold. Those connections are fragile, fragmentary, partial; neither necessary nor sufficient. At best they are coterminous, often but not always culturally and socially hierarchical; at worst, they are virtually nonexistent, conceptually and empirically fraudulent. In either case, they can be dangerous—to both human subjects and school subjects, to social and cultural relations, to collective and individual developments—especially when unrecognized and unchallenged. The (sometimes insidious) breadth, power, and attraction of this discourse and its practices is nonetheless established and maintains its hegemony despite the presence of widely differing, even opposing, ideologies and philosophies and practices. In that way these diverging threads are awkwardly but commonly and instructively joined under the title of *Literacy* (capital L).

The hegemony of the rhetoric of crisis and decline among the legacies of literacy is more than ever before challenged, shaken by criticisms social and cultural, political and economic, as well as theoretical and practical (Graff, 1979, 1987a; Botstein, 1990; Winchester, 1990a, 1990b). It has no single or shared resolution or replacement. In the face of confusing challenges and at a time of disconcerting societal and global transformations, efforts evoking "functionalities" and "non-functionalities," "cultural" and "historical" literacy, canons old and new, skills of survival and of humanity speak to the same conclusion: the legacies of literacy must be reconsidered and literacy/literacies reconstructed. That would provide a necessary beginning.

Regardless of rhetoric or misunderstanding to the contrary, the ways in which these contemporary conjunctures emerge are fundamentally *historical.* They stand prominently among the historically produced conceptions, assumptions, expectations, arrangements, and relationships surrounding literacy, learning, education, and schooling. They are the "legacies" and "myths" of literacy.

At least as important, as the three strands illustrate, are the *presumed* connections between basic literacy (reading and writing), on the one hand, and both schooling and education—at various levels—on the other hand. The connections, historically produced and derivative, function as assumption, presumption, expectation, sometimes inflated to the level of "theory," more often as received wisdom/accepted truth. Presumed or perceived to be concrete consequences of human action, including the historical process, they undergird institutional arrangements, everyday practices, policy construction, and terms of evaluation. These relations, for good reason, almost invariably remain unstated, almost unnoticed. Under scrutiny, they appear much less firm, albeit impressively sturdy and long-lasting for "fictions." Both history and criticism demand their explicit formulation in order to (1) identify and trace their shifting but sometimes contradictory, sometimes seminal intersections, and (2) explore and expose their fallacies and fault lines. We owe that much to the young and not so young, as the subjects of our ministrations change—today and tomorrow. That can be accomplished usefully by renewing our own critical connection to the past, in this case the histories of literacy and education.

Lessons from the history of literacy

The history of literacy and its relationship to the history of education—learning and schooling—if harvested carefully, present a rich crop of "lessons" for today and tomorrow.[8] Regardless of the terms of my offering—the menu is selective—they are the fruits of rigorous historical research and interpretation. And, as that kind of product, they are contested terrain with much to argue. For me, the import of the cultivation only heightens the stakes.

Not only is the historiography of literacy sometimes an interpretive battlefield, but so too are large questions about the nature of the relationships tying literacy to learning, schooling, and education on various levels and in varying subject matters. Of this morass, the three literacy-related threads alerted us. Common assumptions of simplicity, directness, or linearity in sequence of teaching or learning and of advancement fall quickly to the quagmire that obstructs the progress of the harvester. In the "lessons" that follow, I emphasize those in which there are important—*but not necessary*—parallels, on the one hand, between the domains of literacy and those of schooling (among a larger universe) and, on the other hand, between historical foundations and developments and contemporary configurations and their "crises." Often constituting lessons more negative than positive, they are no less significant, constructive, or potentially critically liberating.

Lesson 1

Although seldom stated, less often contemplated, present-day conceptions, arrangements, and practices of literacy as well as schooling and learning are *historically founded and grounded.* They are also strong and powerfully resistant to change. Encompassing the domain from basic literacy to higher education, this recognition constitutes necessarily a *first* lesson whose regular neglect by university-based (and other) "experts" only increases the likelihood of failures in communication, understanding, and reform in the means and modes of education. Ian Winchester (1990a, 1990b), for example, refers to the "standard picture of literacy"! We willfully neglect the historical roots and courses of our major goals and the manner in which we seek to achieve them. How often have we seen, at great cost, unsuccessful efforts to transplant the presumed products—often an image—of Western historical development to other parts of the world?

The limits posed by neglect of the (often quietly present) past mark what passes for their historical record as impressively as what is claimed for their achievements. Repetition is least among the costs of failing to learn from history; if only we might repeat the course! More seriously, ignorance of the circumstances in which crucial concepts, notions, arrangements, or expectations were fashioned, the means by which they have been maintained, and their consequences severely limits, if not contradicts, contemporary analysis, diagnosis, and prescription. (Use of the medical metaphor is itself part of this history.) Many more lessons—minor and major, specific and general—derive from the historical cornerstone. The point encompasses ideas, assumptions, and expectations equally with programs, institutions, and administration (Graff, 1987a).

Lesson 2

That subjects such as literacy, learning, schooling, and education are simple, unproblematic notions is a further historical myth. Experience, historical and more recent, to the contrary jointly underscores their *fundamental complexity*—practically and theoretically. Long persisting problems—in learning and using the elements of learning—follow from this legacy. Among them are the many "great debates" surrounding, for example, human language acquisition and usage; literate as opposed to oral, among other communicative modes—and their presumed "consequences"; relations of literacy to hierarchies of power and wealth as opposed to egalitarian democracy; literacy's contributions to developments economic, political, social; and the status of "texts." Even elementary literacy as learned and practiced is quite complex physiologically, neurologically, and cognitively. Its social and cultural dimensions add on numerous layers of complex meanings—among them "continuities and contradictions," as I term them. How little we know about learning—and about teaching, too, especially respecting the level of literacy.

Especially prominent among the central complications of our traditions or legacies of literacy are (1) the extraordinary frailty of conceptions and conceptualizations of literacy, and (2) the contradiction of expected consequences from its acquisition. With respect to the first, presumption of literacy's unproblematic simplicity accompanies "naturally" or "essentially" the assumptions that emphasize its strong, uniform, universal, unitary, unwavering nature and impact. With respect to the second, "strong" theories of literacy directly and linearly associate rising levels (sometimes once a specified "threshold" is achieved) with large-scale impacts, especially the advancement of both individuals and societies. Termed in various formulations the "consequences," "correlates," or "implications" of literacy, the dizzying number and variety of imputed effects span the individual and societal, including the psychological, cognitive, attitudinal, social-relational, behavioral, symbolic, motivational, participatory, and productive. Literate persons, for example, are said to be more empathetic, innovative, achievement-oriented, cosmopolitan, media and politically aware, identified with a nation, aspiring to schooling, "modern," urban in residence, and accepting of technology. Literacy, it is claimed, correlates with economic growth and industrialization, wealth and productivity, political stability and participatory democracy, urbanization, consumption, and contraception.[9] Equally strong traditions of expectations and expert prescriptions surround higher levels of education, sharing with literacy concerns about, for example, moral character, discipline and order, security, and productivity.

Suffice it to say that these wholesale claims rarely stand up to either empirical or conceptual probing historically or contemporarily. The "strong theory" of literacy—despite its hold on popular and policy opinions—turns out to be much weaker, with literacy's impacts seldom so direct, unmediated, abstract, or universal. Constituting much of what I call literacy's central contradictions, these legacies taken together constitute "the literacy myth," a powerful force despite its massive criticism and rejection in some circles. The contradictions nevertheless give the lie not only to "strong" theories but also to proclamations of a "Grand Dichotomy" and "Great Divide" rhetorically erected between literate and nonliterate persons, societies, and civilizations.

Such powerful formulations rest far more on expectations and faith than they do on ambiguous evidence of complex, usually context-dependent relations and more complicated, oblique connections. Great damage is done to individuals and larger collectivities, positively and negatively, in the name of "development" stemming from expectations about mass provision and possession of literacy in worlds developed and underdeveloped. They include what Leon Botstein (1990) evocatively terms "damaged literacy" and Elspeth Stuckey (1991) movingly calls "the violence of literacy." They are also what Kenneth Levine (1985), Jonathan Kozol (1985), and others link with specific programs for "functional" and other out-of-school literacy campaigns. Unfortunately but critically, assertions like Bhola's that "fortunately, hardly anyone today allocates such powers [a *deterministic* role in transforming social realities] to literacy" are contradicted too often; for example, by claims within the same issue co-edited by Bhola ("Adult Literacy," 1990, 138; cf. p. 4). It is neither accurate nor especially helpful to declare sweepingly, "Literacy is rightly seen to act in dialectical relationship with social change, and its emancipatory role in societies is now being well understood." Exaggerating, overvaluing, or inflating consequences expected from shifts in literacy levels among either individuals or larger populations stand among the attendant risks. Notions of literacy as a human right join with those of literacy as "functional," economic or utilitarian, in courting disappointment or even more negative responses due to overloading what might fairly be presumed from changes in literacy levels. History holds powerful lessons in disappointment and misplaced expectations.

Paradoxically, but instructively, the first formulation rests on an epistemology assuming literacy's effects to be universal, unmediated, unitary—monocausal in effect. The second, in contrast, derives from and undergirds a whole series of simplistic dichotomies—from literate/illiterate to written/oral and civilized/barbaric. Confusion about the nature of literacy itself follows, reflected, for example, in questions concerning "quantity" versus "quality," attitudes versus abilities, substance versus "skills" or "tools," or, to paraphrase Ronald Dore, training versus "training in being trained." Self- and other-contradictory, neither position proves itself useful. To the contrary, both underwrite thinking and arrangements whose limits have not only been demonstrated, but which are anachronistic and destructive. What is at issue, of course, is seldom admitted: it is the purpose of literacy and other learning. Those issues are inseparable from their historical course, as are the underlying conceptions of literacy and formulations of its presumed powers.

Lesson 3

Literacy and other levels of learning share not only their unproblematical status, but also the presumption of their central value neutrality (that is often represented, ironically, as beneficial, a "good"). To the contrary, *no mode or means of learning is neutral.* Not only does all "knowledge," however elementary, incorporate the assumptions and expectations, the biases of emphases of its production, association, prior use, maintenance, and preservation. So too do the so-called tools or skills.[10] With them, there are biases with respect to their transmission—the circumstances of learning and practice—and quite likely fundamental biases in their very nature; for example, the newly appreciated textual biases of formal schooling—"school" literacy—and most reading and writing shaped by such formative encounters, tutelage, and generally restricted or regulated practice at relatively early ages. Studies of the "media" of literacy, from script to print and beyond, only begin to suggest the intricately interacting relationships; contemporary confusion about the "future of print" compared to the visuality and aurality of electronic media have an impressively lengthy set of precedents.[11] The history, only partially studied and understood, challenges all presumptions of unmediated, linear relations and impacts.

Studies in cognitive psychology like Scribner and Cole's *Psychology of Literacy* (1981) demonstrate the consequences for literacy of the specific circumstances of acquisition, practice, and use—and of its place in the culture. Raising more questions than they answer, and challenging the legacies of received wisdom, such research joins with other cognitive, linguistic, and historical studies in pointing toward more refined conceptions of skills, abilities, competencies, and knowledge in relatively precise but flexible learning, social, cultural, and communicative contexts.[12]

That alphabetic literacy is one, albeit exceptionally valuable, set of abilities and competencies, among others, slowly influences thinking about schooling and learning, and much else. Here, for example, confusions between long-standing, theoretically touted, and all but boundless *potentials* of literacy when contrasted with more common levels of ability and everyday practices can be excessive and egregious. Here, too, we find contradictions in literacy's and education's history, in part from overvaluing alphabetic literacy *by itself* and slighting (or worse) other "literacies." Enormous implications for teaching and learning, for developing more effective literacies, follow from placing "traditional alphabetic" literacy within its appropriate communicative context along with, say, numeracy and scientific literacy, oral and aural abilities, spatial literacy or graphicacy, visual and aesthetic literacies, and so on. Historians of science suggest that invention and discovery may owe more to visual than alphabetic literacy. How little we know about these "many literacies" sadly corresponds to poor instruction in a limited range of literacy and ignorance of the extent of common elements among different literacies that might support a potentially revolutionary remaking of schooling. It may be difficult to formulate satisfactory notions of literacy(ies) without expanding our understanding of communicative contexts and channels. For such study, history provides a rich laboratory. The challenges of precise comparison across space as well as time, while absolutely mandated, loom large. Any useful notion of literacy or literacies must confront them.

Similarly, we neglect to our loss the extent to which "school" literacy is a very special use of literacy and language. Words are not only taken out of "the context for action," but they are also removed from other, nonschool uses, including much of oral language usage and writing. "School" literacy of course is highly prized, rewarded—but also criticized for its biases and limitations. As David Olson (1977, 75, 86) notes: "To take explicit written prose as the model of a language, knowledge and intelligence has narrowed the conception of all three, downgrading the general functions of ordinary language and commonsense knowledge," much of speech, too. School literacy, predominantly textually based and biased, is often cut off from other modes of verbal communication which are evaluated as inferior regardless of their place in everyday life. Structures of authority are erected on these bases and lines as certain forms of literacy and language abilities support social differentiation, social stigmatization, reinforcement of inequality—and school failure among the young, and not so young. These "literate biases" are another of literacy's legacies, as are the typically inadequate level and form of literacy—of any kind—taken from schools. Neither lower nor higher learning, or students themselves, are served. Yet knowledge of the environment and media of teaching and learning, in relationship to social contexts in which variously literate or nonliterate lives are lived, provides a rich arena for sophisticated study, past and present, that we are only beginning to explore.[13]

Lesson 4

More than excessive are the excesses and damages—massive human costs in domains developed and undeveloped—that follow from the long domination of theoretical presumptions that elevate the literate, the written, (as proposed to the nonliterate) to the power and status of the dominant partner in what Jack Goody calls the "Great Dichotomy" and Ruth Finnegan the "Great Divide." In part the arrogance of the imperial West but more the triumph of Goody's "technology of the intellect" over the intellect and the human spirit themselves, traditions of narrowly construed intellectualism rationalized their reification of light over darkness, civilization over barbarity, developed over primitive, formally schooled over natural, written over spoken, literate over oral.

The urge toward a totalizing universality in literate-based conceptions of the world and the superiority of its "consequences" or "implications" sits proudly, if increasingly insecurely over the gap presumed between the halves of the "great dichotomy." Long-standing historically, with massive contributions during Renaissances, Enlightenments, and nineteenth-century "Eras of Progress," the divide, to late-twentieth-century reinterpretations crossing virtually all the human and biological sciences, threatens to widen into a cavernous earthquake-like fault as intellectual equivalents of tectonic plates shift and reconfigure.

Lesson 5

Hand in hand with simplicity and superiority went presumed ease of learning and expectation of individual, along with societal, progress. Despite our inability to recognize its enormous implications, historical perspective repeatedly reiterates the *difficulties* regularly, perhaps normally, experienced in gaining, practicing, and mastering the elements of alphabetic literacy as well as higher learning. Acquiring even basic elements of abilities that may—or may not—prove necessary and useful in acquiring further skills, information, knowledge, or mentalities is seldom easy, for reasons both obvious and devious. Learning literacy, and whatever lies beyond it, is *hard work*. Granting that should lead to appreciation and value of every learner's struggles and triumph, not the condemnation of the slower pupil (especially when granting the limiting or restricted bias of "schooled" literacy and the hierarchical educational systems erected upon it).

Only in part a matter of instructional media, technology, pedagogy, institutional setting, age, or social circumstances, *motivation*—perception of need, sometimes defensively or fearfully, sometimes with great pleasure and satisfaction—is undoubtedly a greater goad than biological age and social station. Sometimes this is a matter of the individual—the rhetorical focus of our formal efforts—sometimes it is collective, with pushes and pulls incorporating the political, economic, social, or cultural, the radical or the conserving. Historical study and contemporary psychology both show this—a very rare occurrence. Alas, scholars, those of us who live by and depend upon our manipulation of the tools of traditional learning, are perhaps least well placed to appreciate common experiences and include them in revised or reconstructed approaches to learning and teaching.

Lesson 6

Missing from our common operational and legitimizing myths and legacies is the more complicated historical and richly human set of images: of *multiple paths of learning literacy* and much more; the employment of an extraordinary range of instructors, institutions and other environments—including families and workplaces, and beginning "texts"; and the diversity of sometimes conflicting motivations. Missing too is the informality and possibility of elementary and higher learning *without* the lock-step enforced march of age-grading and wholesale psychologies of human cognition and learning based on their simplistic presumptions. In this respect, the early modern "discovery" of children and a "special" state of "childhood" and the last two centuries' efforts to institutionalize them constitute more complicated relationships than usually accorded them.[14]

In contrast, the great reforming dream was to create formal, compulsory, mass public schools as expected sites for virtually universal transmission of a minimal level of literacy along with the tenets of secular morality. This was a literacy presumed nonetheless useful *and* also socially secure, as opposed to literacy gained without the proper leavening agents of carefully crafted learning environments with methods and materials created expressly for their employment. The first dreamers long predated the massive nineteenth-century efforts to construct school systems, which awaited the present century for many areas. Distrust, even fear, of the unwashed masses united them, although for centuries fear of schooled masses dominated over fear of the ignorant or those who learned outside the bounds of formal educational institutions. Before that reversal and the subsequent achievement of mass schooling, and long accompanying its development in many places, looser arrangements continued whose poor press was written by reformers who sought to destroy them. Those arrangements, I suspect, have much to tell us.[15]

While underscoring the relative recency and historical constructedness of the means of mass literacy provision and most of other education—as opposed to notions of their inevitability or destiny—caution and hindsight also demand that we not romanticize nostalgically the "premodern" past. (In higher education, age-grading and notions of the "college-aged," along with major "modernizing" reforms, also took shape in the nineteenth century.) Mass public school systems, despite their great limitations and failings, have undoubtedly increased opportunities and elevated typical educational achievement. The price paid, a high one, included culturally and individually restricted literacy and other learning levels and uses, in contexts that led many pupils to disdain or at least undervalue higher levels of literacy and learning. It also included persistent inequities of opportunity and outcomes, greater rewards for the well-off than for the poor, among much else. Limits of dependence on literacy, itself restricted and likely poorly disseminated, set rigid constraints on the contribution from schools to polity and culture as well as economy. And of course, nearly universal elementary schooling never halted popular cultural practices that included "improper" use of literacy to read scorned or censured writing! This is not to deny that for many individuals exceptional avenues were opened; to be sure, they were never the "common" scholars. Most surprising, perhaps, is how long the legitimacy of mass public schools lasted until its recent erosion.

Among the losses, and ranking high among those we seek to redevelop in recent and new approaches to *adult* literacy, has been the historical condemnation, then obscuring and forgetting that, for a great many persons, traditional alphabetic literacy was acquired in the widest variety of informal, as well as formal circumstances, and at a wide range of chronological ages. These included self-teaching and learning in homes, dame schools, workplaces, fields, class and political domains, cultural settings, carceral institutions, and chance occurrences, at ages sometimes younger but far more commonly older than the limited span of childhood and early adolescence that came to be defined as the "critical period." Modernization of schooling into mass systems rested in part on the denial of previously common paths. Just as importantly and perhaps as powerfully, approved practices respecting institution and age hardened into expectations, policies, and theories (Spufford, 1979; Laqueur, 1976b; Galenson, 1979, 1981a). Impressive is the degree to which novel innovations in flexible and innovative literacy programs and campaigns involve the (sometimes unacknowledged, sometimes unknown) rediscovery or reinvention of historical configurations. We have much more to learn (Arnove and Graff, 1987).

Lesson 7

Literacy as *part of elementary education*—all the formal schooling that most common scholars experienced over the historical long term, until the late and early twentieth centuries—is a form of "foundationism," to use today's buzz word. In close association with the legacies and myths aired so far, this presumption holds that given the availability of written texts and elementary instruction, simple abilities of reading and writing were in themselves fully sufficient for further development of an individual's literacy and subsequent education, and, of course, for the advancement of that individual. In other words, for anyone or everyone, no serious obstacle to achieving a desired degree of literacy or additional learning need trouble those hungry for more. Learning and using literacy, the "foundation," were, after all, easy. No matter that the cognitive and psychological place of reading and writing as foundations is not well understood, or that reading has so long been poorly taught, and that debates over reading methodologies persist with much heat and little light over centuries. Among the corollaries, also shared, is that failure to acquire literacy reflected overwhelmingly on that individual and her or his race, ethnicity, class, and so forth, not on schools, society, culture, or polity. "Blaming the victim," this pattern is called. It, too, has a long, sorry history, in which the victims are not individuals alone but rather social classes or groups defined by race, ethnicity, gender, nationality, age, or other characteristics. Until recently, in the wake of these legacies, tutelage of adults attracted relatively little effort. Ironically, there are indeed long traditions of adult education seldom called into play (K. Levine, 1985; Hautecoeur, 1990).

Among the major complications is massive evidence of unequal opportunities and school beginnings from radically different foundations for children of different classes, races, and ethnicities; and teachers' expectations about the abilities of different young persons all but guarantee their level of accomplishment. Gender figures in complexly, too. Motivations among youngsters vary greatly, both within and across social lines. Competency, proficiency, mastery, and levels of literacy sufficient on which to build further: these qualities are neither easy to achieve or typical products of schooling, nor guarantees of normative advances.

Lesson 8

Just as individuals followed different paths to literacy and learning, societies historically and more recently took *different paths* toward achieving rising levels of popular literacy. When the focus falls on the societal, as opposed to the individual, we learn that in emphasis and in impacts the two are not necessarily synonymous, sometimes quite contradictory. Historically and contemporarily, too, regardless of democratizing rhetoric about individual progress, far greater concern and attention derive from considerations of the collectivity and aim at its improvement, than of individuals within its realm.

Despite massive expectations of one sure road to progress, inscribed in "strong" theories and "standard versions," historical research emphasizes that there is *no* one route destined to culminate in universal literacy *and* its associated "modern" concomitants politically, economically, socially, culturally. In various configurations, private and public, formal and informal, compulsory and voluntary factors, and others, have combined to elevate mass literacy. Similarly, with respect to the contributions of literacy and education, there has been *no* one route to economic development, industrialization, political democracy, or other parcels of the "modernization" complex. In some cases, at some times, literacy worked as causal agent indirectly or directly. In others, it did not. In some circumstances, literacy was influenced by development, an effect rather than a contribution. And in others, the impact on literacy and education was negative—in European early industrialization, for example. Sequencing and timing—chronologically and causally—may be very important, say, in the nature and degree of social unrest during industrialization in different places, or the adaptation of large numbers of immigrants. Still, those relationships seem to vary widely. Often, literacy and higher levels of schooling have served noncognitively, attitudinally, behaviorally, and symbolically in furthering social and economic development. That is no small contribution; it is not, however, the one typically touted (Graff, 1979, 1987a, 1993a; "Education," 1981; "Adult Literacy," 1990).

In general

The great danger, one which twentieth-century education on all levels shares with literacy models, is the simple presumption that economic development in particular depends directly on investment in and high rates of productivity from systems of formal education. Whereas education and the economy are undoubtedly related, sometimes intimately, the nature of those connections is anything but simple, direct, unmediated. The role of the market in schooling at all levels is only one broad example. Only disappointment and today's invidiously negative and self-flagellating international comparisons—and censure of teachers, institutions, and students (in that order)—ensue. Quantity and quality are confused; educational purpose is distorted. The consequent fears of "crisis" and "decline" typically and rigidly narrow the frame of education—including literacy itself—and all but guarantee the repetition of the cycle.[16] The legacies of literacy stand close at hand.

Urban perspectives

Part and parcel of these historical relationships are the twisted links between cities and literacy, a critical subset of the larger connections and a source of major social myths. As hinted above, this history, and its persisting legacies, is contradictory to its very core. That relationship appears at the general level of historical macrosociology. Attend to French scholars Furet and Ozouf: "We had set out with the quiet assurance of the Directory Commissioners, who were convinced that the gathering together of men fostered the contagion of Enlightenment. Indeed, statistically speaking our study bears out their intuition; as a rule, towns improve literacy rates. But what we have discovered in addition is that this is not everywhere, not uniformly, so: the superiority of the towns over the surrounding countryside only becomes really impressive when the regional level of education is wretched; when the *département* as a whole is well-educated, the town-country differential shrinks, and it sometimes even happens that the countryside does better than the towns" (Furet and Ozouf, 1983, 225).

The size of urban places is one pivot on which the connections turn. In their study of France from the sixteenth through nineteenth centuries, Furet and Ozouf found that for places not the *chef-lieu* of their area, at population levels of ten to twenty thousand "literacy begins to mark time, or even slither backwards." More important, "urban literacy rates depended mainly on the nature of the town's functions, economic or administrative, and hence on the socio-occupational makeup of its population."

With industrialization and rapid urban growth, literacy was neither required nor were urban circumstances able to meet the press of numbers and needs. "Certain conditions had to be fulfilled before this new urban population could begin to imitate the cultural behaviour of the traditional city-dwellers: firstly, the occupational composition of the population had to have achieved diversity and equilibrium, mingling the 'middle managers,' clerks and shopkeepers with modern industrial workers and the 'elites' of the older urban society; secondly, the town had to have had time to 'digest' its untrammeled growth and to acquire the amenities—school obviously being one of these—they needed to catch up culturally" (Furet and Ozouf, 1983, 224).[17]

Furet and Ozouf's rhetoric speaks as clearly as their apparent surprise that such central developmental myths of Western (and later worldwide) modernization are disappointed in concrete cases. The myths persist, we know too well.[18] Yet difficult questions relate to the extent that Furet and Ozouf's "certain conditions" were in fact "fulfilled," whether historically or in many parts of the world, developed or underdeveloping, today. The formulation itself requires revision.

Not only do urbanization and literacy levels relate complexly and contradictorily, but so do realities of literacy levels *within* different urban places. Historically and contemporarily, striking and sometimes long-lasting variations and inequalities follow the dividing lines of gender, race, ethnicity, geography, migration streams, language, and other factors. Neither are they "historical survivals" in the West, nor simple signs of "new" or "immature" development elsewhere in the world where the press of numbers, poverty, density, inequalities, and the raw struggle for survival far outshadow Western historical parallels to the point at which comparisons can be more misleading than useful precedents. Needs for survival, adaptation, and familial traditions together limit use of what reformers and developers view as "opportunities" and "amenities," especially by women and the young. Others old and new to cities see the "opportunities" very differently: as alien, potentially dangerous, irrelevant.

Historically and today, cities simultaneously pull their populations toward rising levels of literacy and schooling and push them away. Scholars do not grasp well these relationships. On the one hand, urban places often (but not always) offer greater opportunities for learning literacy both formally and informally. In cities, print is more often present and accessible. On certain levels, too, functional demands for work, daily life, political or cultural participation, and the like lead many to literacy and its practice. None of those connections is surprising to our late-twentieth-century expectations.

On the other hand, cities also obstruct schooling with inadequate, unappealing, overcrowded institutions that have little latitude with which to make schooling more attractive to pupils young or old. Cities for some simply offer fewer and less adequate ways in which to attain survival, thus distracting or foreclosing educational options for them. Demands of living and making a living are hard and occupy many hands. Differences and discriminations of ethnicity, religion, ideology, language, race, class, gender, age, and the like also rebuke and repel. Even in situations in which some schooling is compulsory, urban places make evasion easier. In cities, it is not only easier to secure the message of print from oral sources, directly or indirectly, but both traditional and new communicative modes and media replace its value for many whose own literacy sometimes is "lost" through non-use. Motivation, "seizing opportunities," or "helping one's self" are hardly the issue. Regardless of ideology and myths to the contrary, many low-level jobs require very little in the way of literacy- or school-based skills. Literacy requirements may signify the desire for formal tutelage in noncognitive attitudinal and behavioral lessons. Finally, survival in cities may well depend on an ability to "read the city," a kind of "urban literacy," that bears only a partial relationship to traditional, alphabetic abilities.[19]

Critical literacy

Reflecting notions current at the time and ideas still developing, I wrote abstractly and sketchily for a 1988 conference presentation:

> Those of us who struggle for an alternative approach [to E. D. Hirsch's cultural literacy]—deem it for now, critical literacy—must turn our energies elsewhere. The approach we are seeking requires a broadly based literacy that connects critical thinking with the skills of critical reading and writing in politics, economics, and social relations as well as in a larger cultural sphere, a literacy no longer limited to alphabetic abilities and to a historical basis that is static and acculturative. A critical literacy of course recognizes the significance of common knowledge, but it sees it as a consequence of criticism, as changing and transforming, not as inflexible and timeless. It does not separate "skills" from "content" but strives to link them dynamically. The critical literacy we are seeking must be based not only on a radically revised and more demanding curriculum, but also on an epistemology and theoretical critique that grasps the centrality of ambiguity, complexity, and contradiction to literacy and to life itself (Graff, 1989, 51).[20]

Among the key dements to which I was insufficiently attentive is what Freire eloquently phrased as the relation between the "word" and the "world": "Reading the world always precedes reading the word, and reading the word implies continually reading the world . . . this movement from the word to the world is always present; even the spoken word flows from our reading of the world. In a way, however, we can go further and say that reading the word is not preceded merely by reading the world, but by a certain form of *writing* it or *rewriting* it, that is, of transforming it by means of conscious, practical work. For me, this dynamic movement is central to the literacy process" (Freire in Freire and Macedo, 1987, 35).

Critical literacy today sways uncomfortably between its emancipatory potential and a range of dangers and fallacies, some of which I have noted. Possibilities for individual and collective transformations confront misplaced utopianism and exaggerated expectations. A critical literacy at the core of a radical critical consciousness engaged in revolutionary social reconstruction faces problems of inattention to context, insufficient criticism, and under-theorization—and neglect of history's lessons. Conceptualization of critical literacy is itself often fuzzy, as is the relationship of literacy to other aspects of the radical educational agendas of which it is a part, and of different "literacies" within critical literacy to one another and to traditional alphabetic abilities. Critical literacy also risks semantic and conceptual confusion with and cooptation by conservative "critical thinking" or "critical education." Major dangers stem from overloading concepts and expectations, rending them from contexts theoretical and practical—to the extent of conceiving literacy autonomously or universalistically, in and by itself—and confusing parts and wholes. Half steps backward threaten advances, quite apart from contemporary political and economic "realities" that I must ignore now. These dangers include an unknowing repetition of literacy's history.[21]

My explicit intent, as I conclude, lies not in this negative vein. I under-score these points, these questions of criticism, because I do think that literacy's history has a great deal to teach us, and because I find a general absence of sympathetic criticism in the literature on critical literacy. Paulo Freire's writings and his example are seminal. Freire is seldom accorded the highest respect in the form of rigorous constructive criticism, just as his expositors seldom confront the practical and theoretical complications of "translating" his project to very different societies and polities.[22]

Among those most active in this arena, Ira Shor stands out. Deeply in-fluenced by Freire, Shor strives toward a practical pedagogy aimed at "the desocialized thinking called critical consciousness [which] refers to the way we see ourselves in relation to knowledge and power in society, to the way in which we use and study language, and to the way we act in school and daily life to reproduce or to transform our conditions" (1982, 128). Crucially, Shor conceptualizes and situates critical literacy as one among other "qualities" that constitute critical consciousness. They are power awareness, perma-nent desocialization, self-education/organization, and critical literacy. None stands or is taught alone; each takes its place among the others. Together, they contribute toward curricular practices large and small.

Among proponents of critical literacy, Shor's exposition has a rare, and fresh, specificity descriptively as well as conceptually and theoretically. His critical literacy is recognizable as literacy, no small feat. He writes:

Critical literacy: Habits of thought, reading, writing, and speaking which go beneath surface meaning, first impressions, dominant myths, official pronouncements, traditional cliches, received wisdom, and mere opinions, to understand the deep meaning, root causes, social context, ideology, and personal consequences of any action, event, object, process, organization, experience, text, subject matter, policy, mass media, or discourse; thinking-in-depth about books, statements, print and broadcast media, traditional sayings, official policies, public speeches, commercial messages, political propaganda, familiar ideas, required syllabi; questioning official knowledge, existing authority, traditional relationships, and ways of speaking; exercising a curiosity to understand the root causes of events; using language so that words reveal the deep meaning of anything under discussion; applying that meaning to your own context and imagining how to act on that meaning to change the conditions it reflects (1982, 129).

Shor's project, to condense it unfairly, differentiates rather than universalizes in its critique, approaches, and practices. Attentive to specific contexts of students and their everyday lives, it is impressively sensitive to the age, race, gender, and goals of students and their social and educational conditions. "Desocialization should fit the students as well as the subject matter and the political climate surrounding the classroom. The students' diverse cultures, speech, and thoughts make up the ground on which a desocializing curriculum first plants its feet. Some students are more open than others to transformative learning due to their age or political maturity or to the permissiveness of the local authorities" (1982, 130–31).

The program is explicitly interdisciplinary. Shor refers to "interdisciplinary literacy" as integrating reading, writing, critical dialogue, and cooperative learning across the curriculum while also linking content areas to "collaborative language arts." Ending the "disabling separation" of language studies and academic subjects boosts the practice of literacy in closer connection to students' full range of studies.

Shor calls his program an "activist education." On the one hand, "crossing academic boundaries is curricular action that challenges the dominant structure of education." And, on the other hand, "critical pedagogy is activist in its questioning of the status quo, in its participatory methods, and in its insistence that knowledge is not fixed but is constantly changing" (1982, 188–89). Central to Shor's program for learning and practicing critical literacy is "problem-posing." Literacy dialogically takes its place within an activist education dedicated to studying life in order to change it and to students transforming themselves within history. That is a literacy appropriately critical, attentive if properly critical of its own past and that of others, to their limits as well as their possibilities, and therefore to their future.

Thoughts for the future

In airing a series of key legacies and myths in which the history of literacy resonates and culminates in present-day problems, my goal was to show the benefits of historical perspective. Historical analysis and interpretation, applied carefully and knowingly, often have great power in stimulating fresh views, novel questions, and new understandings. No antiquarian search for "origins" or claims for antiquity of lineage, this is the past alive in the present and shaping the future, not a dead hand hanging over us. It is a "human science" that is relevant and public, in the best sense of those hackneyed and contested terms. In the series of conjunctures discussed here are paths for rethinking literacy, schooling, learning, and education. We might usefully construe them as a significant, perhaps necessary challenge for notions and concepts of literacy and paths toward its attainment.

If we wish to take this challenge from history with the seriousness I think it demands, breaking traditional disciplinary and curricular divisions becomes a major requirement. That would follow from accepting the provenance of the past for grappling better with the present and future and from recognizing the limiting historical legacies from academic disciplines whose foundations were constructed largely during the nineteenth and earlier twentieth centuries but have outlived their usefulness and require fundamental transformation. Among the lessons from the legacies of literacy is not only that no one discipline may claim fairly to understand literacy but also that novel combinations of multi- and interdisciplinary study are now more than ever before needed. To make this claim is certainly not unprecedented. To assert that the discipline (in the several meanings of that word) of history should be central to reconstructing the study of literacy is more novel.

Some recent observers point, in part, to the reorientation I propose and its possibilities. With respect to contemporary cultural currents and current debates about texts, Charles Newman (1985, 129–30) writes: "The electronic media fear nothing so much as the historical sense: its contemplativeness, its revisionism, its circumlocution, the inevitable corrections and abrasions of contrasting perspective. Commodity values are threatened by the historical reflection which has always represented the beginning of fiction's territory—memory resuscitated by the imagination."[23]

Sharing the understanding that today's crises in education and literacy are one of "historical purpose and meaning," the educational critic Henry Giroux and historian Harvey Kaye write with a different end—the college curriculum—in mind. What they articulate might well, with due qualification, stand as a platform for reconstructing literacy(ies):

> We would urge a commitment to *historical* education and the development of humanities and liberal-arts curricula that cultivate perspective, critique, consciousness, remembrance, and imagination. By *perspective* we mean the awareness that the way things are is not the way they have always been nor the way they must necessarily be in the future. *Critique* is more specific, entailing a deliberate notion of unveiling and de-reification in order to comprehend and reveal the social origins of the prominent economic, and cultural orders in which we have lived. *Consciousness* refers to an appreciation of the making of history or, as the Italian political theorist Antonio Gramsci once put it, an awareness of "the sum of effort and sacrifice which the present has cost the past and which the future is costing the present." *Remembrance* acknowledges that while the past is not for dwelling in, it is a reservoir of experience—both of tragedy and hope—from which we draw in order to act. And *imagination* commands that we recognize the present as history and thus consider the structure, movement, and possibilities in the contemporary world that show us how we might act to prevent the barbaric and develop the humanistic (Giroux and Kaye, 1989, A44; see Aronowitz and Giroux, 1988).

That perhaps provides a place to pause, and reflect again.

Notes

References for the works cited appear in the Bibliography of the History of Literacy in Western Europe and North America at the end of this book.

This chapter is based on a series of keynote addresses, public lectures, and articles developed over the course of the 1990s, arguing for a set of clear and useful "lessons" from the historical study of literacy that address key "myths" and "legacies," in my lexicon, from the history of literacy that continue to speak to contemporary concerns. Versions with different focuses and direction were presented at the Bard College Conference on Education for Complexity in the 21st Century, 1991; International Conference on Attaining Functional Literacy: A Cross-Cultural Perspective, Tilburg University, The Netherlands, 1991; New Hampshire Humanities Council Conference on Literacy, Myths, and Lessons, 1991; Tema, Linkoping University, Sweden, 1992; Conference on Adult Literacy: An International Urban Perspective, The United

Nations, New York, 1992; The Literacy Centre, Montreal, 1993; National Literacy Secretariat, Multiculturalism and Citizenship Canada, Ottawa, 1993; American Educational Research Association, Basic Research on Reading and Literacy Group, Atlanta, 1993; Conference on Literacy and Power: Difference, Silence and Textual Practice, Griffith University, Australia, 1993; Institute on Literacies, Language, and Social Justice, Melbourne, Australia, 1993; Australian Reading Association, Melbourne, 1993; and a number of Australian universities during a tour in July 1993. I thank all those who solicited my participation and who responded critically and helpfully. Different published versions acknowledge specific individuals and institutions, a list too long to include. The version printed here reflects those different occasions, audiences, and focuses by incorporating three distinct sets of applications by way of conclusions.

The title reflects rhetorically and substantively my principal books on the history of literacy as well as my historical-based epistemology: Graff, 1979, 1987a, 1987b. Interested readers may also consult, among a large literature, my bibliography, Graff, 1981a; anthology, Graff, 1981b; and Graff, 1987a. Recent works are cited in Graff, 1988, 1993a, and Graff, 1979 (1991). No complete bibliography appears here. The bibliography, however, includes the most important historical work to date and some of the best contemporary writing. It is meant to serve as a guide to the literature.

Unless otherwise specified, usage of the word "literacy" in this chapter refers to basic levels and skills of *alphabetic* literacy—reading and writing. Inflation, exaggeration, and confusion of literacy with various other forms and modes of practice, learning, and schooling is a regular feature—and a great danger—of many discussions of these timely and critical subjects. Our knowledge of the relationships among different modes of literacy, their acquisition, practice, and uses is astonishingly poor. That is one inordinately important set of questions crying out for study today. So, too, is the question of the very expansiveness and inclusiveness of concepts and notions of "literacy" itself. I fear that we too often overload it rather than qualifying more precisely our usage and expectations. That is among the historical legacies and myths of literacy.

Readers should also note that this essay attempts to draw comparisons between literacy and other, "higher" levels and forms of education—whose connections are often far from simple, linear, or direct, despite assumptions to the contrary—and between past and present and future arrangements of schooling and education, levels and uses of learning. This is no easy task. Although I may occasionally seem to violate my own (and no doubt others') dicta, I believe the risks are worth taking. *Caveat lector.* For efforts similar and complementary in spirit if not always in detail and emphasis, see Leon Botstein, 1990; Ian Winchester, 1978, 1990a, 1990b.

1. This obviously is a complicated cultural conjunction. See, as symbol and substance of entanglement and resulting confusion, the fascinating issue of *Daedalus* on "Literacy in America," 1990. Illuminating about many things, on literacy the issue is

more revealing in unintended ways than its title might otherwise lead readers to expect. More directly relevant to deliberations with respect to "functional literacy," see for example, "Adult Literacy," 1990; Hautecoeur, 1990; K. Levine, 1982, 1985. For my earlier critique of the 1975 Persepolis symposium, relevant here, see Graff, 1978. The extent to which common complications with notions of "functionality(ies)" respecting literacy (for example, aired by Levine), among other things, are transcended forms one key criterion for the success of our deliberations.

2. See K. Levine, 1982, 1985; Wagner 1990.

3. K. Levine, 1982, 250, passim. See also, among a large and growing literature, K. Levine, 1985; Hautecoeur, 1990; "Adult Literacy;" 1990. Revealing is the first page of Gabriel Carceles, "World Literacy Prospects at the Turn of the Century," in the latter, and contradictory pronouncements by H. S. Bhola, "Literature on Adult Literacy," also in the latter.

4. I recognize, but will not take up, the epistemological swamp on which I tread—lightly, I hope, for now—in proposing novel uses of the past and of historiography, in pursuing formative, but not deterministic, relationships tying present and future to past. Examples of more sustained approaches on these topics include Graff, 1979, 1987a, 1987b. Once again, *caveat lector!* At this juncture, too, note the implications for curricular and pedagogical revision toward a fundamentally and thoroughgoing historical basis, an experiment well worth the effort, I think, if historians and other "human scientists" (in the Continental sense, that is) began to take themselves and their potential pedagogical and extracurricular contributions more seriously than we typically do. A contextually rooted program, that includes historical context among its major domains, offers, perhaps, one way around the destructive dichotomies (in the debates over the "canons," for example, but elsewhere, too) and other complications that plague educational debates today. The plasticity and flexibility that characterize historical and other contextual approaches to understanding at their best, with traditions of rigorous research methods and practices (old and new), traditional concern for clarity of communication, new attention to both rhetorical and epistemological issues combine to present elements of a program. The vision of history I hold is an interdisciplinary one that ranges widely among the arts and humanities, social and behavioral sciences, and aspects of natural and mathematical science as well.

5. See also Grubb and Lazerson, 1982; Lindblom and Cohen, 1979; Lindblom, 1990.

6. See, of course, Hirsch, 1987, 1988; and the loud debates that persist, among them Graff, 1989. I find Hirsch's conceptualization faulty, epistemological foundations inadequate, and history alarmingly anachronistic. For "historical literacy," see Gagnon, 1989. Nowhere in that book is "historical literacy" defined; perhaps we should appreciate rather than deprecate that omission! Regardless, it is incriminating. Among the former, see the recent issue of *Daedalus* cited above along with earlier issues: "Scientific Literacy," 1983; "Reading Old and New," 1983; Tuman, 1993, among a large and growing literature. Very relevant here are Ian Winchester's recent writings, cited above. See also, alas, Allan Bloom's writings and responses,

what amount in themselves to a sorry "cultural phenomenon." Notions of "cultural" or "historical" literacies, and their as yet "unborn"—legitimate or bastard—siblings cry out for extended criticism. I lack the space for that in this essay.

7. Suggestive here are, for example, Heath, 1983, and her more recent formulations; Scribner and Cole, 1981; and Scribner's more recent studies of nonverbal, nonliterate workplace skills, competencies, or "literacies," among current revisionist research in cognitive psychology formulating and probing multiplicities of "competencies." Her work is joined increasingly by others within that field who are redefining our understanding of intelligences and competencies—and perhaps, in time, of literacies as well. Howard Gardner's work with young children holds important promise too.

8. I make no effort to document what follows. My conclusions derive from almost two decades of reading and research in this field. Interested readers may consult my general works and also Houston, 2002. There are many worthwhile historical studies that merit consultation. Houston, 1985, is an excellent analysis in the tradition of "literacy myths." Ian Winchester's (1990a, 1990b) recent articles treat the implications of new historical—and other—research concerning literacy. For the United States, an important new work is Carl Kaestle et al., 1991.

9. The best known "strong case" is Jack Goody and Ian Watt, 1968, originally published in 1963. By 1968, Goody withdrew from the language of causal consequences to looser formulations. For a critical discussion and bibliography, see Graff, 1987a, esp. Epilogue. Anthropologist Ruth Finnegan's (1988) writings are very important among this literature.

10. The almost cyclical "debate" over "skills" versus "content," which spans the entire educational realm from literacy learning to graduate training, is another version of this. Today's war over undergraduate "core curricula" in such terms is especially silly and wasteful of time and energy. Ian Winchester (1990a, 1990b) relates this issue to the philosophy of science and its revision. There is a large literature on vocational schooling, among the functional and/or utilitarian literacies. For recent years, see K. Levine, 1985, among others.

11. The many works of Walter Ong, Marshall McLuhan, and Elizabeth Eisenstein provide the starting point on these typically misunderstood issues.

12. Charles Lindbloms's (1990) major attack on the kinds of "knowledge" and understandings among social scientists and policy makers represents a clear analogy to the situation with literacy. A fascinating set of examples that stress the import of visual abilities in technological invention appears in several papers by the historian Eugene Ferguson (1977). Some of Peter Burke's (1972) work on artistic orientations in the Renaissance is also complementary.

13. The still novel field of ethnographies of literacy, popularized first by educational anthropologists like Shirley Brice Heath, among others, has tremendous promise. See also Boyarin, 1993; Gowan, 1992; Street, 1993. Historians have just begun to attempt research influenced in these directions. See for example Graff, 1988, 1993a.

14. See Graff, 1995a, 1995b.

15. Suggestive here, for example, are the studies of Laqueur, 1976a, 1976b; and Spufford, 1979. The example of early modern Sweden where exceptionally high levels of reading but not writing literacy and of female literacy were achieved largely without mass institutional schooling is told by Johansson, 1977, 1981, 1985.

16. A neat example of this appears in Barrett, 1990.

17. See also Houston, 2002; Maynes, 1985a, 1985b; Graff, 1979, 1987a, 1993a; Stephens, 1987.

18. The literature on the economics of literacy, including foundational scholarship, for example, by Carlo Cipolla, C. Arnold Anderson, Mary Jean Bowman, Daniel Lerner, Alex Inkeles, Marian Levy, and many others, shows the strong hold of these connections, relatively impermeable but capable of endless qualifications. For one typical case in point, see among his works, Harman, 1974, 11–12.

19. On "reading" cities, see Calhoun, 1969; De Certaux, 1984; Marcus, 1973, 1974; Neuberg, 1973; Kasson, 1984. Obviously, these few paragraphs only begin discussion of very large and difficult subjects. Indeed, my own use of "cities" and "urban places" is hardly adequate to that task.

20. See also McLaren, 1988; Aronowitz and Giroux, 1985.

21. See, in general, for both dimensions and mixture of success and failings in these terms, "Literacy, Culture," 1988; Aronowitz and Giroux, 1985; Edelsky, 1991; Ferdman, 1990; Freebody and Welch, 1993; Freire and Macedo, 1987; Gee, 1990; Giroux, 1988; Lankshear with Lawler, 1987; Lankshear and McLaren, 1993; McLaren, 1988; M. Rose, 1989; Singh, 1989; Shor, 1982; Willinsky, 1990.

22. Compare Freire and Macedo, 1987, for example, with Ferdman, 1990; Giroux, 1988; McLaren, 1988.

23. Some of novelist E. L. Doctorow's essays are also relevant to these issues.

2 LITERATE AND ILLITERATE; HEARING AND SEEING: ENGLAND, 1066–1307

Michael T. Clanchy

Literate and illiterate

In the summer of 1297 some jurors from Norfolk came to the court of King's Bench to attest that Robert de Tony was twenty-one years of age and was therefore entitled to have his wardship terminated. Proving the age of feudal heirs by sworn testimony was a routine procedure at the time, in which each juror attempted to recollect some memorable event which coincided with the birth of the child in question. Jurors might recall, for example, specific gifts or public events or accidents to themselves or their neighbours.[1] Thus in a case in 1304 at Skipton in Yorkshire, Robert Buck, aged 41, remembered being at school at Clitheroe, where he had been so badly beaten that he ran away, and that was twenty-one years ago.[2] Such a cumbersome system was required because births were only rarely recorded in registers. This customary method of establishing the age of individuals by collective oral testimony is a good example of the medieval reliance on memory rather than written record.

The case from Norfolk in 1297 is exceptional in that the proof primarily depended not on the usual personal recollections but on a record of the date of Robert de Tony's birth (4 April 1276), which had been written down in the chronicles of West Acre priory.[3] This record had not been made at the time of Robert's birth, as he was born in Scotland, but a year or more later when he was brought down to West Acre priory, of which the de Tony family were the founders, by his mother. She seems to have been seeking the protection of the priory on her son's behalf and had his date of birth written down there to establish that he was the lawful de Tony heir. Because the circumstances of Robert's birth could not have been known to the Norfolk jurors from personal experience in the customary way, resort had to be made to the West Acre chronicle.

Reprinted from Michael T. Clanchy, *From Memory to Written Record: England, 1066–1307*, 2nd ed. (Oxford: Blackwell, 1993), 224–38, 253–56, 258–71, 272, with the permission of the publisher.

The first juror, William de la Sale of Swaffham, therefore gave evidence that he had seen the chronicle and read it and was thereby certain of Robert's age. Six other jurors agreed with William without exception or addition, that is, they too claimed to have read the chronicle and understood its significance. Three more likewise agreed and added ancillary recollections: Robert Corlu said his younger brother was born in the same year who was now twenty-one; John Kempe said his father had died five years after Robert had been brought down from Scotland. The eleventh juror, John Laurence, agreed with William "with this exception, that he had not read the aforesaid chronicles because he is *laycus*." The twelfth, Roger of Creston, attested the same. A thirteenth juror (why evidence was taken from thirteen men instead of twelve is not explained), Thomas of Weasenham, said that he had neither seen nor read the chronicle, but he had learned of its contents from the prior. Thomas was not necessarily incapable of reading like John and Roger. He may have presented his evidence in this form simply because he had not been present on the day his fellow jurors saw the chronicle.

Thus, of the thirteen men examined, ten swore that they could read the entry in the chronicle, an eleventh may have been able to read, and two were unable to do so. The latter two were described as *layci* (laymen) presumably because they had no "clergy," in the sense of a reading knowledge of Latin. We know that Walter of Bibbesworth took it for granted in the 1250s or 1260s, the time when these Norfolk jurors were growing up, that the gentry usually had experience from childhood of the "book which teaches us *clergie*."[4] Those without this knowledge were "laymen" in the modern sense of being inexpert. The other jurors were "clergy" only in the sense of knowing some Latin. William de la Sale and his fellows were no churchmen. They were knights and freemen of the neighbourhood, approximately the social equals of the heir in question, as required in jury trial procedure.

This case therefore shows that from a random sample of thirteen gentlemen of Norfolk at the end of the thirteenth century, ten could read an entry in a chronicle, two could not, and one's ability is unrecorded. Those who swore that they had read the chronicle were presumably telling the truth, as they risked being cross-examined in the King's Bench, and they had no apparent motive for perjuring themselves since they were not claiming benefit of clergy. The statement that two of the jurors were incapable of reading, together with the unspecific testimony about Thomas of Weasenham, adds credibility to the contrasting testimony of the rest. Although evidence of proof of age was sometimes falsified, there is no reason to reject the essential facts of this testimony. Obviously, no generalizations about levels of literacy can be made from a unique case. On the other hand, the evidence of this case, that the great majority of the jurors examined were capable of reading one line of Latin in a chronicle, need cause no surprise. The procedure for giving juries' verdicts in royal courts, which depended on documents written in Latin and perhaps also in French and English, demanded a higher level of literacy among jurors than that.[5] By 1297 the two who were unable to read at this elementary level are more surprising than the ten who could do so.

Meanings of "clericus" and "litteratus"

The fact that most of these Norfolk gentlemen could read conflicts in appearance only with the medieval axiom that laymen are illiterate and its converse, that clergy are literate. The terms cleric and lay, literate and illiterate, were used in ways which preserved intact the appearances of these fundamental axioms while acknowledging the realities of daily experience, where some clergy were ignorant and some knights knew more of books than brave deeds. Traditional roles had become confused, as Nigel de Longchamp of Canterbury observed with regret in c.1192: "In the church today there are clergy without knowledge of letters, just as there are many knights without skill and practice in arms, who for that reason are called 'Holy Mary's knights' by the others."[6] This discrepancy between theory and practice, between literature and life, did not of course mean that the ideals were immediately altered to fit the facts. On the contrary, the ideals of the learned cleric and the valorous knight became reinforced as fantasies, which had three or four centuries of vigorous life before them in literature and academic treatises.

The axiom that laymen are illiterate and its converse had originated by combining two distinct antitheses:

> *clericus: laicus*
> *litteratus: illitteratus*

The latter antithesis derived from classical Latin, where *litteratus* meant "literate" in something like its modern sense and also (in the most classical usage of Cicero) described a person with *scientia litterarum,* meaning a "knowledge of letters" in the sense of "literature."[7] The former antithesis derived from the Greek *kleros,* meaning a "selection by lot" and hence subsequently the "elect" of God in terms of Christian salvation, whereas *laos* meant the "people" or crowd.[8] Gradually, in the process of Christian conversion those who were specially consecrated to the service of God, the *clerici* or "clergy," became distinct from the mass of the people, the *laici* or "laity." The antithesis *clericus: laicus* was thus a medieval creation, while *litteratus: illitteratus* was of Roman origin. In the half-millennium 500–1000 AD the reduction of the number of learned men in the West coincided with the expansion of Christianity by the conversion of the barbarians. As a consequence *clerici* began to be associated with *litterati,* although the two concepts had originally nothing in common. This association of ideas reflected the fact that outside the Mediterranean area nearly all Latinists were churchmen and most were monks. As academic standards declined, *litteratus,* which had meant "lettered" or "learned" for Cicero, more often came to mean "literate" in the sense of having a minimal ability to read Latin. Such *litterati* were still learned compared with the great majority, who had no Latin or book learning at all.

These first clerical *litterati,* whose sparse knowledge had scarcely anything in common with the Latin scholars either of ancient Rome or of the twelfth-century Renaissance, established a privileged status for themselves in society by despising non-Latinists as an ignorant crowd of *laici.* In reality the *clerici* were unsure of their status, as Europe was dominated not by them but by warriors with a nonliterate sense of values. Charlemagne and Alfred were exceptional in wanting the nobility to be better Latinists; their examples were lauded by the clergy to encourage the others. Dark-Age Europe was far from unique in creating an elite of priests who monopolized writing, yet who were constantly aware of their impotence *vis-à-vis* the dominant warlords. The supposed gulf between cleric and lay, between the elect and damned, was some compensation to the clergy, although not even Pope Gregory VII could make it a reality for long in the terrestrial world.[9]

Thus by constant repetition the pairs of antitheses, *clericus: laicus* and *litteratus: illitteratus,* were coupled in the mind. The terms of each antithesis became interchangeable and ultimately synonymous. By the twelfth century *clericus* meant *litteratus, laicus* meant *illitteratus,* and vice versa. The case from Norfolk has already illustrated *laicus* being used to mean *illitteratus.* The converse (*clericus* meaning *litteratus*) was discussed in detail in the 1170s by Philip of Harvengt, who observed that a person was not called a cleric unless he was "imbued with letters" and hence:

> A usage of speech has taken hold whereby when we see someone *litteratus,* immediately we call him *clericus.* Because he acts the part that is a cleric's, we assign him the name *ex officio.* Thus if anyone is comparing a knight who is *litteratus* with a priest who is ignorant, he will exclaim with confidence and affirm with an oath that the knight is a better *clericus* than the priest ... This improper usage has become so prevalent that whoever gives attention to letters, which is clerkly, is named *clericus.*[10]

Philip, like Nigel de Longchamp and other writers on the state of the clergy, deplored the way real knights and clergy no longer fitted the traditional roles assigned to them. More important in the present context is his observation that a learned knight would be called a *clericus,* because that implies that a person described as *clericus* in a document was not necessarily a member of the clergy. Such a person is just as likely to have been an educated layman.

Philip of Harvengt's comments are best illustrated in England by Matthew Paris's obituary of Paulin Peyver or Piper, a steward of Henry III who died in 1251. He is described as *miles litteratus sive clericus militaris,* "a literate knight or knightly clerk."[11] Matthew thus emphasized that these terms were interchangeable in Paulin's case. Paulin was a cleric only in the learned sense, as he had numerous knights' fees and a wife and legitimate children. Similarly, the Northamptonshire knight Henry de Bray, who was born in 1269 and wrote his own cartulary, noted that his maternal grandfather, Richard, lord of Harlestone, "was called Ricardus Clericus because he was *litteratus.*"[12] The most familiar example of this usage is the nickname "Clerk," or "Beauclerk," given to Henry I. How learned Henry really was is a separate and controversial question; certainly he was described by Orderic Vitalis as *litteratus* and "nurtured in natural and doctrinal science."[13] A *clericus* in common parlance was therefore a person of some scholarly attainments, regardless of whether he was a churchman. As early as the third decade of the twelfth century a polemic of English origin, commenting on the large number of schoolmasters, asked rhetorically: "Are there not everywhere on earth masters of the liberal arts, who are also called *clerici*?"[14] Peter the Chanter summarized the situation in around 1200: "There are two kinds of *clerici* and in both there are good and bad, namely those who are ecclesiastics and those who are scholastics."[15]

The use of *clericus* and *litteratus* as interchangeable terms, both meaning "learned" or "scholarly," is clearest in Jocelin of Brakelond's descriptions of the debates within Bury St. Edmunds abbey over the election of Abbot Samson in 1182 and Prior Herbert in 1200. On each occasion the more scholarly monks argued that they must be governed by *litterati* and not by the ignorant. Their opponents teased them with a new litany, "A bonis clericis, libera nos, Domine!" (From good clerics, good Lord, deliver us)[16] and with puns about learning Latin grammar, "Our good *clerici* have declined so often in the cloister that now they themselves have declined."[17] *Clericus* was a relative term. Thus Jocelin has one monk say: "That brother is something of a cleric [*aliquantulum clericus*], although much learning [*littere*] doth not make him mad."[18] On another occasion Jocelin told of how Hubert Walter, the archbishop of Canterbury, had to admit that Abbot Samson was a better *clericus* than he was, meaning that Samson was the better scholar.[19] The way Jocelin uses *clericus* is explained by Philip of Harvengt, who notes that when we meet a monk of humanity and charity, "We ask him whether he is a *clericus*. We don't want to know whether he has been ordained to perform the office of the altar, but only whether he is *litteratus.* The monk will therefore reply to the question by saying that he is a *clericus* if he is *litteratus,* or conversely a *laicus* if he is *illitteratus.*"[20] It might be added that a monk who aspired to Christian humility would not call himself *litteratus,* even if he were of scholarly inclinations. Thus Adam of Eynsham, in his life of St. Hugh of Lincoln, claims not to know how to satisfy the *litterati* who will cavil at his style and simple narrative.[21] Adam is using here the hagiographer's common device of making his story appear more truthful by being naive.

As *clericus* and *litteratus* both meant learned, it followed that a person of no great book learning was a *laicus,* a "layman," even if he were a monk or a priest. Thus Archbishop Hubert Walter was described by the chronicler of St. Augustine's abbey at Canterbury as *laicus et illitteratus.*[22] Hubert was not of course a layman in the ecclesiastical sense, nor was he illiterate in any modern sense, as he was the chief justiciar and chancellor who did more than any other individual to create the royal archives. The St. Augustine's abbey chronicler was using *laicus* and *illitteratus* as terms of abuse—he also called Hubert a legal *ignoramus*[23]—but he was not using these terms inaccurately. Hubert was a *laicus* in Philip of Harvengt's sense and *illitteratus* in Jocelin's, as he lacked the academic learning of Bologna or Paris. That academic snob, Gerald of Wales, alleged that Hubert's Latin was shaky and that his only school had been the Exchequer.[24]

Like *clericus, litteratus* was a relative term. Whether a particular individual was appropriately described as *litteratus* was a matter of opinion, since essentially it meant "learned." The same man might be *litteratus* in one assessment and *illitteratus* in another. Thus Ralf Nevill, Henry III's chancellor and bishop of Chichester, was certified by a papal legate as *litteratus* when elected dean of Lichfield in 1214, but *illitteratus* by another papal adviser in 1231 when his candidature for the archbishopric of Canterbury was rejected.[25] Conscientious churchmen considered Ralf to be a worldly administrator. Like Hubert Walter, he was no *clericus* or *litteratus* in the ideal sense of being either the elect of God or a scholar. On this occasion in 1231, the successful candidate for Canterbury, St. Edmund of Abingdon, was both. Hubert and Ralf were not the only distinguished churchmen and administrators to be described as *illitteratus.* To their company should be added Roger, bishop of Salisbury, Henry I's chief justiciar, and the controversial Abbot Ording of Bury St. Edmunds.[26] In the exalted view of John of Salisbury, who aspired to Ciceronian standards, all those who are ignorant of the Latin poets, historians, orators, and mathematicians should be called *illitterati* "even if they know letters."[27]

John's contention is taken for granted by Walter Map when he described a boy he had known, who was a paragon and was "educated among us and by us," yet "he was not *litteratus,* which I regret, although he knew how to transcribe any series of letters whatever."[28] Walter would have liked to have described this boy as *litteratus,* since he was one of his kinsmen, but he had to admit that nice penmanship was no substitute for scholarship. He adds that the boy left England and became a knight of Philip of Flanders (1168–91). At his learned court, where many of "the order of laymen" knew "letters" (according to Philip of Harvengt), this boy would presumably not have been numbered among the *milites litterati*.[29] The ability to write well comprised the technical skill of an artist and was not an integral part of the science of letters. Writing is not included among the skills which cause Philip of Harvengt's knight who is *litteratus* to be described as a *clericus.* In Philip's opinion the essential abilities are to read, understand, compose by dictation, make verse, and express oneself in the Latin language.[30] The medieval *miles litteratus* was thus a gentleman educated in the classics; he embodied a recurrent ideal in European culture.

The way the words *clericus* and *litteratus* were used has been discussed in detail here because such examples demonstrate that neither word, when applied to an individual, can be accurately translated by its modern equivalent. A *clericus* was not necessarily either a "cleric" or a "clerk," although he was someone with a reputation for erudition. Likewise a person described as *litteratus* was much more than "literate" in the modern sense. Counting the number of persons called *clericus,* or making lists of knights described as *litteratus,* provides examples of persistent and characteristic medieval ways of thinking, but it throws no light on whether such persons, whether designated cleric or lay by ecclesiastical law, were "literate" in a twentieth-century sense of that word.[31]

The question of the literacy of the laity

Discussions of medieval literacy have been bedevilled by the difficulty of distinguishing between the modern "literate" and the medieval *litteratus.* When a knight is described as *litteratus* in a medieval source, his exceptional erudition is usually being referred to, not his capacity to read and write. Such knights were rare because good Latin scholars have always been rare among country gentry and government officials in England. A few existed even in this period. Thus shortly after the Conquest a Norman called Robert, *miles ille litteratus,* endowed St. Albans abbey with an income to provide books for the church.[32] He probably had a greater interest in books than most of the monks. About a century later, Gerald of Wales tells how a *miles litteratus* appeared as a ghost, demanding to play a game of capping Latin verses with a learned master, for that had been his "social recreation" when he was alive.[33] Similarly Matthew Paris is recording his admiration for the learning and not the elementary schooling of John of Lexington, when he describes him as *miles elegans* (refined) *et facundus* (eloquent) *et litteratus,* or of Roger de Thurkelby, *miles et litteratus.*[34] John was the keeper of the royal seal, whose obituary Matthew was writing in 1257, while Roger was one of the few royal judges who possessed legal wisdom, in Matthew's opinion.

The historian's initial difficulty, when discussing the literacy of the laity, is to avoid anachronisms. Medieval ideas of literacy were so different from those of today that some modern questions are meaningless. To ask, "Were laymen illiterate?" is a tautology: of course *laici* were *illitterati,* because these terms were synonyms. Faced with the question another way round, "Were laymen literate?" a medieval schoolman might have thought that he was being invited to take part in an exercise in elementary dialectic. Asking whether laymen were literates was like asking whether evil was good or black was white. Every bachelor of arts knew that the validity of axioms such as these was not affected by individual cases of moral imperfection or greyness in this imperfect world. The axiom that *clerici* were *litterati* and its converse belonged to the same order of thinking. Contemporaries, like Philip of Harvengt or Jocelin of Brakelond, knew of numerous exceptions in their daily experience, but they saved the appearances of the rules by calling learned knights *clerici* and ignorant monks *laici.* Such axioms cannot be equated with twentieth-century historians' generalizations, which derive from an assessment of a multitude of individual cases. Scholastic axioms derived their validity not from individual experience but from universal rules, which were superior and prior to particular cases because they were part of a divine order of things. When explaining medieval ways of thought, it is correct to say that all laymen were considered illiterate, yet it would be mistaken to conclude from that proposition that in any particular time or place all nonchurchmen were unable to read or write. Scholastic axioms differ from real cases.

Another anachronism is the assumption that the capacity to read and write is a simple and constant measure which readily applies to medieval cases. The automatic coupling of reading with writing and the close association of literacy with the language one speaks are not universal norms, but products of modern European culture.[35] Literacy in this modern sense is so deeply implanted from childhood in every twentieth-century scholar that it is difficult to liberate oneself from its preconceptions, or to avoid thinking of it as an automatic measure of progress. Over the last two centuries medievalists have painfully learned to overcome anachronisms when discussing feudal society or scholastic philosophy. Yet, when they reach elementary education and literate skills, they tend to assume that these problems can be readily understood by applying modern criteria and experience to the medieval past.[36] Past ideas must be analysed in their own terms before they are addressed in modern ones.

As the citations from Walter Map and Philip of Harvengt have already illustrated, reading and writing were not automatically coupled at the end of the twelfth century, nor was a minimal ability to perform these actions described as literacy. Writing was a skill distinct from reading because the use of parchment and quills made it difficult. Likewise the traditional emphasis on the spoken word caused reading to be coupled more often with speaking aloud than with eyeing script. Although the average medieval reader may have been taught to form the letters of the alphabet with a stylus on a writing tablet, he would not necessarily have felt confident about penning a letter or a charter on parchment. Scholars and officials employed scribes, particularly for drafting formal legal documents, just as typists and word processors are employed today. To this rule there are exceptions, of which the most spectacular is the beautifully written will of Simon de Montfort, as it states in its text that it is written in the hand of his eldest son, Henry.[37] Wills were unusually personal documents, intimately associated with the family circle, because their main purpose was to ensure the testator's state of grace at death rather than the worldly disposition of his property; hence Henry was performing a special act of filial devotion in writing his father's will.

Another fundamental difference between medieval and modern approaches to literacy is that medieval assessments concentrate on cases of maximum ability, the skills of the most learned scholars (*litterati*) and the most elegant scribes, whereas modern assessors measure the diffusion of minimal skills among the masses. Consequently, modern assessments of literacy have been primarily concerned with the minimal ability of persons to sign their own names and the development of elementary schools in which this ability is taught as the basic educational skill. In twelfth- and thirteenth-century England the ability to sign one's name was likewise considered important, but it was not directly associated either with writing or with schools. The personal signature or sign manual was not accepted by itself as a lawful symbol of authentication on a document unless the signatory were a Jew. A Christian was required either to sign with a cross, indicating that he was making a promise in the sight of Christ crucified, or more commonly he affixed to the document his *signum* in the form of a seal.[38]

In medieval England possession of a seal bearing the owner's name comes closest to the modern criterion of making the ability to sign one's own name the touchstone of literacy. Although the possessor of a seal might not be able to write, he or she was a person familiar with documents and entitled to participate in their use. Neither the medieval seal nor the modern sign manual on a document indicates that the signatory has anything more than a minimal competence in the skills of literacy. Such a person need not be *litteratus* in a medieval sense nor "educated" in a modern one. If possession of a seal is taken as the medieval equivalent of the modern sign manual as a measure of minimal literacy, the growth of literacy (in this modern sense) can be approximately assessed. Scarcely anyone apart from rulers and bishops possessed seals in 1100, whereas by 1300 all freemen and even some serfs probably had them. Thus the statute of Exeter of 1285 expected "bondsmen" to use them when they authenticated written evidence.[39] How far the expectations of this statute reflected actual practice is a matter for conjecture, although instances can be readily cited as early as the 1230s of smallholders and tenants owing labour services affixing their personal seals to charters.[40] The extent of minimal literacy in this sense among the peasantry by 1300 has been underestimated because historians have been reluctant to allow such competence even to the gentry.

The discrepancies between modern and medieval conceptions of what constituted literacy go deeper than differences in minimal requirements. The variety of languages in which spoken and written thoughts were formulated in medieval England made any capacity to read or write an intellectual achievement. This variety also obstructed the rapid spread of literacy, in the modern sense of the majority of people acquiring a minimal ability to read and write the language they spoke. Elementary instruction in reading and writing started from Latin because that was the traditional language of literacy and sacred Scripture. Those who wrote in vernaculars, whether in Middle English or French, were building novel and complex structures on a foundation of Latin. Neither Middle English nor French was sufficiently standardized, or well enough established as a literary language, to become the basis of elementary instruction in reading and writing until well after 1300. If a person in Edward I's reign or earlier had learned to read in English or French but not in Latin, he could never have become *litteratus,* nor could he have understood the majority of writings circulating in his own lifetime, because these were in Latin. English and French had to have become common business and literary languages before it was practical or desirable to initiate literate skills with them.

Nevertheless by 1300 the supremacy of Latin, and the privileges of the *clerici* and *litterati* who upheld it, was increasingly being challenged, both by writings in vernaculars and by anticlericalism. Boniface VIII introduced his bull *Clericis Laicos* in 1296, directed primarily at Edward I and Philip IV of France, with the provocative words: "That laymen are notoriously hostile to clerics antiquity relates and recent experience manifestly demonstrates."[41] Yet English nonchurchmen were slower than their French counterparts to abandon Latin as the basis of literate skills, probably because of the competition between English and French as alternative literary languages. In general from c. 1300, lawyers and government officials preferred French, while creative writers favoured English. Moreover, in the later Middle Ages an elementary reading knowledge of Latin became a matter of life and death for Englishmen. Any person charged with felony who could read a prescribed verse from the Psalter was theoretically entitled to benefit of clergy and hence escaped the death penalty.[42] Now that middle-class laymen were beginning to assert themselves, they took over the old association of *clericus* with *litteratus* and turned it to their own advantage in order to save themselves from hanging. *Litteratus* was thus reduced from meaning a person of erudition to meaning a person with a minimal ability to read, albeit in Latin. A *clericus* was still a *litteratus,* but he was now neither a churchman nor a scholar: he was anyone who was literate in this minimal sense. By the middle of the fifteenth century, London tradesmen are being described as *litterati.*[43] Consequently, after 1300 it became relatively common to be literate. What had changed, however, was not necessarily the proportion of persons in the population who had mastered reading and writing, but the meanings of words. A *clericus* was now a common clerk, and a *litteratus* was a minimal literate. The literacy of the laity had been achieved, perhaps not so much by the efforts of schoolmasters and the mysterious forces of progress, as is sometimes alleged, as by the method which Humpty Dumpty explained to Alice in *Through the Looking-Glass*: "When *I* use a word, it means just what I choose it to mean, neither more nor less . . . The question is which is to be master—that's all." Verbally at least, the *laici* had mastered the *clerici* and *litterati*; and from that mastery the modern concept of literacy, meaning a minimal ability to read, was born.

Knowledge of Latin among nonchurchmen

To avoid ambiguities, the question, "Were laymen literate?" needs recasting. A more productive question to ask is, "Did nonchurchmen know any Latin?" since Latin was the foundation of literacy in England in this period. The latter question has been progressively answered in the affirmative by scholars over the past fifty years. Starting at the top of the social hierarchy, historians have demonstrated that at least an acquaintance with Latin became increasingly widespread over the two centuries 1100–1300.

Independently of each other in the 1930s, V. H. Galbraith in Britain and J. W. Thompson in California demonstrated that the kings of England from Henry I onwards were instructed in Latin and that Henry I and Henry II were even considered *litterati* by some contemporaries.[44] More importantly, Henry II showed his mastery of written instruments in a series of judgements concerning the charters of the abbeys of St. Albans in 1155, Battle in 1157 and 1175, and Bury St. Edmunds in 1187.[45] He evidently enjoyed presiding over legal wrangles between abbots and bishops in his court, as it gave him an opportunity to scrutinize their charters and demonstrate that he was their master in intellect and legal wisdom as well as in material power. Peter of Blois was probably not exaggerating when he states that among Henry's commonest forms of relaxation were private reading and working with a group of *clerici* to unravel some knotty question: at his court there was "school every day."[46] By "school" Peter did not mean an elementary school, but a circle of learned schoolmen discussing *questiones* as they did at Paris or Oxford. From King John's reign onwards, elementary instruction in Latin was taken for granted: "Henceforth all our kings were taught letters in their youth, and their literacy, as distinct from their culture, has no particular importance."[47]

The example set by the kings inevitably gave the baronage and gentry a motivation to learn some Latin, both to avoid looking foolish at court (where there was school every day), and to have sufficient understanding of the written demands, expressed in Latin, which began to pour from the royal Chancery and Exchequer. For these reasons H. G. Richardson and G. O. Sayles in 1963 widened the range of those who had "a limited knowledge of Latin, a knowledge to be easily and rapidly acquired by any intelligent youth," from kings to the baronage and gentry of twelfth-century England.[48] Their conclusion concerning the baronage is cautious and unexceptionable: "Without rashly generalizing from what may perhaps be called a handful of cases, it may fairly be said that they create a presumption that a man of noble birth will in his youth have had the opportunity of learning something of Latin letters."[49] Richardson and Sayles also suggested that even some of the lesser knights read and wrote Latin. This suggestion is based on the written replies to Henry II's inquest into knights' fees in 1166 and his Inquest of Sheriffs in 1170. The argument is that "the more informal documents, those that have no marks of clerkly skill," were written by the knights themselves.[50] Although the assumption that such men would or could write on parchment is contentious, the lesser conjecture, that many knights read the royal writs themselves and drafted their own replies, is possible.[51]

The strongest argument of Richardson and Sayles for a relatively wide acquaintance with Latin is that royal officials like sheriffs and judges, most of whom were nonchurchmen, had to have a working knowledge of Latin because they performed offices "demanding the use of written instruments."[52] Although such officials usually employed clerks to do their writing, and to read letters aloud to them, they had to understand enough Latin to master the business in hand and not be misled by their clerks or by the litigants' lawyers. At least one of Henry II's lay sheriffs, Richard, sheriff of Hampshire, wrote as well as read in Latin, as his holograph acknowledgement of a debt to William Cade is extant.[53]

The presumption that officials knew some Latin, which applies to officers of the central government by 1200, extends to manorial and village stewards, bailiffs, beadles, and reeves by 1300.[54] On the basis of this evidence M. B. Parkes, in his contribution to the literacy of the laity question, argues that historians should allow for an "extent of pragmatic literacy among the peasantry."[55] His arguments are strengthened by the instances of peasants using seals and charters which have already been discussed. Parkes cites Walter Map, who took it for granted that "serfs [*semi*], whom we call peasants [*rustici*], are eager to educate their ignominious and degenerate children in the [liberal] arts."[56] Walter deplored this because a liberal education was appropriate only for freedom. The question had arisen one day when he and the chief justiciar, Ranulf de Glanvill, were discussing why it was that the clerical judges of Henry II were harsher than the lay ones. Walter's explanation was that the clerics did not behave like gentlemen because they were serfs in origin. Although Walter was only expressing a personal opinion, and his opinions were often perverse and ironical (Walter was a clerical justice himself), his remarks had some basis in fact.

Starting at the top of the hierarchy with kings and descending through barons and knights, historians of medieval literacy have reached the peasants at the bottom and are suggesting that even some of them were acquainted with Latin. N. Orme has surveyed literacy (mainly in the later Middle Ages) from the top of society to the bottom as an introduction to his study of medieval schools.[57] He divides people into seven classes—clergy; kings and princes; nobility and gentry; administrators and lawyers; merchants, craftsmen, artisans; villeins; women. For the twelfth and thirteenth centuries a fourfold classification into kings and princes, nobility or baronage, gentry or knights, and peasantry (both free and unfree) is more appropriate. Neither the clergy nor women were separate social classes, as they derived their place in society from their families. Nor were administrators and lawyers yet a distinct class, as the legal profession (in a literate sense) emerged only in the late thirteenth century.

It might be thought that merchants are worth distinguishing as a group; their families were at the forefront of education in the city-states of Flanders and northern Italy. In England, however, merchant dynasties like those of London took on the social colouring of the landed gentry and were not, in the thirteenth century anyway, a distinct "bourgeoisie." Knightly merchants were as educated as other knights. With lesser merchants, it is doubtful whether literacy in Latin was yet an essential skill, as they worked from memory and tally sticks. Book learning and bookkeeping became crucial to lesser merchants only when they ceased to travel with their wares and sat in offices instead. On the whole, that is a development of the fourteenth century rather than the twelfth, as far as England is concerned. St. Godric, who mastered *mercatoris studium* without any formal education, is probably typical of eleventh- or twelfth-century experience.[58] Financiers, on the other hand, like Osbert Huitdeniers (Eightpence) of London, who employed the young Thomas Becket as a clerk and accountant, needed as much Latin as the judicial side of their business (writing and enforcing bonds for loans) required.[59] But financiers are not a sufficiently homogeneous group to constitute a social class, as many of them were Jews; they were literate in Hebrew and often in Latin as well.

The knowledge of the peasantry (both free and unfree), at the bottom of the social pyramid, remains to be discussed. The suggestion that some peasants were acquainted with Latin is not implausible when the role of the church in village life is considered. Theoretically at least, every adult in England should have known some Latin because of its use in the liturgy. The attitude of the western church towards Latin was ambivalent. The identification of *clerici* with *litterati,* which implied that only Latinists were the elect of God, was counterbalanced by the perennial message of the Gospels insisting that Christian teaching should be conveyed to everybody, and therefore to the crowd of *laici*. Various attempts had consequently been made to translate prayers, Scripture and the church's teaching into vernacular languages. The works of Alfred and Aelfric are obvious examples of such attempts in pre-Conquest England.

By the eleventh century an uneasy compromise seems to have been reached whereby, for the people at large, the irreducible minimum of Christian teaching—namely the Lord's Prayer and the Creed—was to be recited in Latin, while sermons, homilies and the like were expressed in the vernacular. Thus a law of Canute enjoined every Christian to apply himself until he could at least "understand aright and learn the *Pater Noster* and the *Credo*."[60] Although this law does not mean that everybody is to read Latin, they are to recite these two Latin texts by heart. Hence one of the glosses accompanying this law adds that Christ himself first recited the *Pater Noster*. That Latin texts are meant and not English translations is suggested by the use of the Latin names for the texts and also by the glosses which describe the penalties for failing to learn them. If the texts had been in the vernacular, there would presumably have been no problem about learning them.

As it was, most people probably did not find this minimal amount of Latin overwhelmingly difficult because they were accustomed to using their ears to learn, and furthermore, they heard these texts recited whenever they went to church. Assuming that most of the population were minimally conscientious about their religious duties, we are led to the conclusion that most people could recite a little Latin. They had thus taken the first step towards literacy, as paradoxically they could speak *litteraliter.* Those who reached slightly greater competence, in other words, those who understood what they recited and could perhaps also distinguish the letters of the alphabet, would not have been altogether at a loss if they were required to sign their names with seals on Latin charters.

A conjecture of this sort, concerning the level of education of the mass of medieval people, is impossible to prove because evidence of any sort about elementary instruction, and particularly about that of ordinary people, is rare. The biographies of saints sometimes provide glimpses of childhood, but the only detailed description of an English saint of this period of undoubted peasant origins is the life of St. Godric, which was written (in various versions) from his own recollections.[61] Although he features in numerous social histories, because he is the first English example of the Dick Whittington type who made his fortune as a merchant, Godric's story is worth examining again from the point of view of what sort of education he acquired.

Godric was born in Norfolk in c. 1065 of parents who were good, though poor and ignorant. Since he had no wish to remain a peasant, but to exercise his mind, he exerted himself to study.[62] So he strove to learn to be a merchant (*mercatoris studium*), first by selling things locally, then by joining travelling chapmen, and ultimately by becoming an international shipman.[63] As merchants travelled with their wares, he mastered navigation and practical maritime astronomy.[64] Business combined well with religion, as he journeyed to the shrines at Lindisfarne and St. Andrews, and beyond Britain to Rome, Santiago, and Jerusalem.[65] For a while he returned to Norfolk and became steward and general manager to a certain rich man.[66] Godric was a pious but not yet a bookish man, although he had known the Lord's Prayer and the Creed "from the cradle" and he often pondered them on his journeys.[67] At about the age of 40 a kinsman in Carlisle gave him a Psalter, from which he learned the Psalms most diligently, retaining them in his memory.[68] This was an abbreviated version of the Psalter, commonly called "St. Jerome's Psalter." The book must have been quite large, as Godric permanently distorted his little finger by carrying it around, even to bed.[69] After further travels he came to Durham, where he learned more Psalms, "and afterwards he learned the whole Psalter."[70] By staying around St. Mary's church at Durham, where "boys were learning the first elements of letters," he tenaciously applied his memory to "hearing, reading and chanting" and thus became "firm and certain" in the liturgy.[71] Finally he settled at Finchale, near Durham, as a hermit.

Because Godric was self-educated, both the devil and the monks of Durham adopted a patronizing attitude towards him. The twelfth-century devil shared Walter Map's opinion of serfs who had advanced in the world and called Godric a "stinking old peasant,"[72] while his chief biographer, Reginald of Durham, quite often describes him without malice as *laicus, illitteratus* and *idiota*.[73] Technically Reginald was correct, as Godric was not a *clericus* and not *litteratus*. Nevertheless Reginald revealed his own ignorance of the effects of travel on an intelligent man, when he considered it miraculous that Godric understood "French or Romance," even though his mother tongue was English.[74] Reginald likewise considered that it was the Holy Spirit, rather than his native wit, which enabled Godric to understand the Latin conversation of four monks from Durham, who had been sent to cross-examine him.[75] By these means Godric was able to give an impressive exposition of the Scriptures to them (in English), "as if he were an outstanding *litteratus*."[76] The information provided by Godric's biographers about his knowledge was not recorded for its own sake, as it was intended as evidence of his religious devotion and of those miraculous powers which were the indispensable sign of a saint. Nevertheless the various versions of the life are sufficiently circumstantial and consistent to provide a historical record of one man's self-education and rise from the mass.

Godric's life story provides numerous correctives to the modern tendency to assume that schools are the beginning and end of education. He received his instruction in the Lord's Prayer and the Creed "from the cradle," presumably meaning from his parents. He is therefore an example of Christian law being applied in practice, as it was the duty of every parent to teach his child the *Pater Noster* and the *Credo*.[77] Thereafter Godric was self-taught. He learned numeracy and navigation, the *mercatoris studium,* by experience. Literacy obviously presented greater problems. Godric may never have learned to write, and his knowledge of Latin depended primarily on hearing and memorizing. Although he could never become *litteratus* by this method, be could evidently cope with the normal uses of Latin in ecclesiastical circles. Gerald of Wales gives an example of another hermit and traveller, Wecheleu, who had likewise miraculously learned Latin by ear.[78] The fact that such knowledge was considered miraculous suggests, however, that Latin was thought difficult to learn without formal instruction in grammar. Nevertheless even Latin was in its rudimentary stages primarily a spoken language, to which children were introduced by the church's liturgy and prayers in the home.

Although a man like Godric, who had memorized whole portions of the liturgy, could not pass as a Latinist among the *litterati,* he could probably make as good a show of Latin as some clergy. His self-taught Latin became a problem only when he wanted to be accepted as a conscientious churchman and monk. In lay society Godric's lack of a formal education had not prevented him from mastering the *mercatoris studium,* or from becoming a rich man's steward. In the latter capacity tally sticks and a trained memory were more useful than parchments, although if Godric had lived a century later, he might have found it more difficult to conduct business without writing. Yet before deciding that Godric could not have succeeded a century later, it is worth recalling that the greatest of all medieval stewards and business managers, Hubert Walter, was likewise described as *laicus et illitteratus.*[79] Like Godric, he had little or no formal schooling and was ignorant of elementary Latin grammar, if Gerald of Wales is to be believed. A little Latin, like a little literacy in more recent times, could get a man a long way in ordinary business, deplorable as that was in the eyes of scholars.

Hearing and seeing

"Fundamentally letters are shapes indicating voices. Hence they represent things which they bring to mind through the windows of the eyes. Frequently they speak voicelessly the utterances of the absent."[80] In these antitheses John of Salisbury's *Metalogicon* grapples with the basic problems of the relationship between the spoken and the written word. The difference between sounds or voices (*voces*) and things or realities (*res*) was complicated for him, writing in the mid-twelfth century, by the controversy between Nominalists and Realists, between those who argued that universals were mere names and those who claimed they were real things. This philosophical controversy is not our concern here. John's remarks are relevant because, like much of *Metalogicon,* they seem to reflect his own experience as a secretary and drafter of letters as well as exemplifying current scholastic thought.

Numerous charters of the twelfth century are addressed to "all those seeing and hearing these letters, in the future as in the present" or to "all who shall hear and see this charter"; these two examples come from the charters of Roger de Mowbray, who died in 1188.[81] The grantor of another charter, Richard de Rollos, actually harangues his audience, "Oh! all ye who shall have heard this and have seen!"[82] Early charters likewise quite often conclude with "Goodbye" (*Valete*), as if the donor had just finished speaking with his audience.[83] Documents made it possible for the grantor to address posterity ("all who shall hear and see") as well as his contemporaries. In the opening words of the Winchcombe abbey cartulary, "when the voice has perished with the man, writing still enlightens posterity."[84] Writing shifted the spotlight away from the transitory actors witnessing a conveyance and on to the perpetual parchment recording it. By the thirteenth century, when charters had become more familiar to landowners, donors cease addressing their readers, as Richard de Rollos did, and likewise they no longer conclude with *Valete.* Once it was understood that charters were directed to posterity, it must have seemed foolish to say "Goodbye" to people who had not yet been born. In place of such conversational expressions, thirteenth-century charters are more stereotyped; they are often impersonally addressed in some such form as "Let all persons, present and future, know that I, A of B, have given X with its appurtenances to C of D."[85]

A comparable change occurs in wills. Until the thirteenth century the will was an essentially oral act, even when it was recorded in writing. The persons present witnessed the testator making his bequests "with his own mouth"; they "saw, were present, and heard" the transaction.[86] By the end of the thirteenth century a man's final will no longer usually meant his wishes spoken on his deathbed, but a closed and sealed document. The witnesses no longer heard him; instead they saw his seal being placed on the document. When wills were first enrolled, as they were in London from 1258, the formula of probate still put emphasis on the witnesses who had seen and heard. But a generation later, by the 1290s, the London roll often omits the names of the witnesses, presumably because the written will was the preferred evidence.[87] The validity of the will now depended primarily upon its being in a correct documentary form and not on the verbal assurances of the witnesses. This is another illustration of the shift from memory to written record between 1100 and 1300. Wills had been made in writing by the Anglo-Saxons; the novelty lay in their being closed and sealed documents.

Symbolic objects and documents

Before conveyances were made with documents, the witnesses "heard" the donor utter the words of the grant and "saw" him make the transfer by a symbolic object, such as a knife or a turf from the land. William the Conqueror went one better and jokingly threatened to make one donee "feel" the conveyance by dashing the symbolic knife through the recipient abbot's hand, saying, "That's the way land ought to be given."[88] Such a gesture was intended to impress the event on the memory of all those present. If there were a dispute subsequently, resort was had to the recollection of the witnesses. Similar rules applied to the oral "records" of courts, which were retained (in theory at least) in the memory of those present. For example, if the record of the county court were disputed, the aggrieved litigant brought forward two witnesses who each gave evidence of what they had heard and seen. In such a case in 1212 the prior of Ware (in Hertfordshire) defended himself by "one hearing and one understanding," namely Jordan of Warew and Robert of Clopton; Robert also offered to prove the prior's allegation by battle, "as he was present and heard this."[89] In this case some distinction is evidently being made between the knowledge of the two witnesses: Jordan had heard, or at least understood, less of the proceedings than Robert. Likewise at Cheshunt (in Hertfordshire) in a seignorial court in 1220 a litigant challenged the record by "one person hearing and another seeing."[90] Which testimony was thought preferable in this instance, that of the person who heard or of the other who saw, is unclear. These cases suggest that the legal commonplace of making a record by "hearing and seeing" was not a mere formula made meaningless by repetition.

Documents changed the significance of bearing witness by hearing and seeing legal procedures, because written evidence could be heard by reading aloud or seen by inspecting the document. In John of Salisbury's definition, letters "indicate voices" and bring things to mind "through the windows of the eyes." Once charters were used for conveyances, "hearing" applied to anyone hearing the charter read out loud at any time, instead of referring only to the witnesses of the original conveyance. From there it was a short step to substitute "reading" for "seeing," as one of Roger de Mowbray's charters does, which is addressed to "all his own men and to the rest, *reading* or hearing these letters."[91] This phrase plays also with the ambiguity of the word "letters," which in Latin (as in English) means both alphabetic symbols and missives.

A curiously worded grant for St. Mary's priory at Monmouth is addressed to the donors, Richard de Cormeilles and Beatrice his wife, instead of to the recipients.[92] The charter rewards Richard and Beatrice with divine bliss because they have given the tithes of Norton-Giffard to Mary, the mother of God. She is the ostensible grantor of the charter, though the document itself was presumably written by a monk of St. Mary's priory, which was the terrestrial beneficiary. The writer's Latin is eccentric—for example he spells *uxor* (wife) as *hucxor*—but revealing in its phraseology. He includes the phrase *sicut presens breve loquitur* (as the present writing speaks), whereas ordinary usage would have *dictur* (says) or *testatur* (attests) in place of *loquitur*. The writer also makes it clear that the named witnesses, who "saw and heard the gift solemnly exhibited by the book upon the altar," are "subsequent" and therefore secondary to the evidence of the writing itself. In making the writing "speak" and in putting the preliterate witnessing ceremony of seeing and hearing into a subsidiary role, the naive writer of this charter has exemplified John of Salisbury's scholastic definition (which is contemporary with the charter) that letters "speak voicelessly the utterances of the absent," the absent in this instance being the grantor, Mary, the mother of God.

Once property was conveyed in writing, it would have seemed logical for the charter to supersede the symbolic object, such as the knife or turf, which had formerly been used in the witnessing ceremony. As the grant to Monmouth priory shows, that object had sometimes itself been a writing—a book solemnly exhibited upon an altar. Traditionally the book used for this purpose was the text of the Gospels. For example, a gift of a saltpan was made to St. Peter's priory at Sele in Sussex in 1153 "by the text of the Holy Gospel upon the altar of St. Peter, many persons hearing and seeing." The Gospel book was used because it was customary to reinforce oaths with it (as is still the practice in law courts); thus in Edward I's wardrobe there was kept "a book, which is called *textus,* upon which the magnates were accustomed to swear."[93] To replace a Gospel book by a charter in a conveyancing ceremony was a relatively small change in appearance (it was simply substituting one document for another), but a large one in substance. The charter in its text actually "represented" (in John of Salisbury's definition) in a durable record the terms of the conveyance, whereas the Gospel book merely symbolized the solemnity of the occasion for the witnesses. The Monmouth priory charter therefore distinguishes the written grant (*breve*), which "speaks" to the hearers, from the symbolic book (*liber*) which is "exhibited" to the viewers. Nevertheless, although it seemed logical to dispense with symbols and make full use of the potentialities of writing, contemporaries continued with their preliterate habits long after charters had become common. In the rare instances where the conveyance appears to be made by the written document itself (as in the Monmouth priory charter), we should probably assume that the document is serving the ancient function of a symbolic object, rather than being considered primarily for its contents in a modern, literate way.

There are examples of the conveyancing document being presented on the altar like a Gospel book. In a charter of 1193 the abbot of Glastonbury states that "the present charter was placed on the altar of St. Mary by me as an offering, the clergy and people of the same vill [of Street in Somerset] standing round." In his *Life of St. Alban* Matthew Paris portrayed King Offa of Mercia on bended knee before the altar of the saint handing his charter of gift to a monk, who stands facing him vested for Mass, while a servant rings the great bells of the abbey church.[94] Although Matthew showed some of the ancient features of St. Albans in his drawings, like the Roman bricks and the round arches, the form in which he drew Offa's charter is as anachronistic as the bells. It has prominently ruled lines, and the seal looks like the Great Seal (introduced in the eleventh century). These anachronisms may be deliberate, however, as Matthew's purpose was not to teach archaeology but to instruct his contemporaries in 1250 about the endowments of the abbey. Multiple time-frames are also contained in the roundel portraying the principal benefactors of Crowland abbey at the altar of their patron, St. Guthlac. King Ethelbald of Mercia, at the front, is eighth-century, Abbot Thurketel in the centre is tenth-century, and some of the other benefactors are eleventh-century or later. Each one holds open a scroll recording his gift in abbreviated Latin. Thus the scroll of the bearded figure on the extreme left says: "I Alan de Croun give you, Father Guthlac, the priory of Freiston with appurtenances."[95] Scrolls were used iconographically to indicate speech. The Crowland artist, like an artist portraying an Old Testament prophet, turns speech acts into scripture: each benefactor presses forward to lay his scroll on St. Guthlac's altar, as if it were a charter. This roundel is both a work of art and an artifice, which gives written form to gifts for which Crowland abbey had inadequate documentary proof. The benefactors' scrolls are letters which "speak voicelessly the utterances of the absent."

An explicit instance of a conveyance by the charter itself is a gift made by William of Astle in c. 1200 to the Knights Hospitaller. The last witness is Ivo, clerk of Stafford, representing the Hospitallers, "in whose hand I, William, have made seisin with this charter in the church of Alderly."[96] The usual rule was that a conveyance could not be made by a document alone, but depended on the recipient having "seisin" (meaning actual possession of the property). Nevertheless, the exception to this rule in William of Astle's charter may merely prove it, as the charter, conveyed from hand to hand, is a substitute for the usual object symbolizing the transaction. The unfamiliar idea of a writing being interpreted primarily as a symbolic object, rather than as a documentary proof, is most clearly evident when the object written upon is not a parchment, but something else. Thus an ivory whip-handle found at St. Albans abbey had an inscription on it stating that this is the gift from Gilbert de Novo Castello of four mares.[97] The object, a whip, appropriately symbolized the gift of horses; the writing was ancillary. In 1266 an inquiry about the forest of Bernwood in Buckinghamshire attested that John Fitz Nigel held it from the king "by a horn, which is as a charter (*quod est charte*) for the aforesaid forest."[98] An appropriate symbolic object, a hunting horn, was allowed to stand in this case as the equivalent of documentary proof because the tenure dated from before the Norman Conquest, through a gift allegedly made by Edward the Confessor to his huntsman Nigel. The "Boarstall Horn" in Buckinghamshire Record Office, dating in its present mounting from the fifteenth century, may be the same horn as that referred to in the inquiry of 1266.

Most remarkable is a knife preserved at Durham, which symbolizes Stephen of Bulmer's agreement (made in the second half of the twelfth century) with the monks of the Holy Island of Lindisfarne about the chapel of Lowick. Its haft is inscribed, which makes it comparable with the St. Albans whip-handle and the hafts of other inscribed knives no longer extant.[99] Whereas the hafts of these other knives were made of ivory, Stephen's is of hard horn (perhaps a deer's) and the inscriber has had difficulty making much impression on it. He was not perhaps an experienced carver but a scribe, possibly a monk of Lindisfarne, who only had a pen knife readily available. Although the lettering of the inscription is shaky and uneven, it is conceived in a bold monastic hand. Along one side of the knife's haft is written *Signum de capella de lowic* (the sign of the chapel of Lowick) and on the other side *de capella de lowic & de decimis de lowic totius curie & totius ville* (for the chapel of Lowick and for the tithes of Lowick from the whole court and the whole vill). As well as this inscription on the haft, a parchment label is attached (written in a comparable bold monastic hand), which gives fuller details of the agreement. This label cannot be described as a charter, as it is irregular in shape and is written on both sides. A statement on its dorse helps explain the purpose of the knife. It records that Stephen of Bulmer had not come in person to make the agreement at Holy Island, but sent Lady Cecily and Aschetin, the *dapifer*, or steward, in his place. Probably Aschetin brought the knife with him as a symbol of Stephen's consent. It may well have been Stephen's own carving knife; the haft is heavy and shows signs of use and, although the blade is broken near the top, what remains of the knife still measures 13½ cm. It would thus have been an appropriate object for a steward, who probably carved at his lord's table, to bring as durable and substantial evidence that he truly represented his master.

Why go to the trouble of trying to write on a knife, when pen and parchment did the same job more efficiently? Ordinary writing materials were evidently available, as Stephen's knife has the parchment label on it as well as the inscription. The explanation may be that the parties to this agreement had more confidence in the evidence of the knife than in writing. Knives were traditional symbols for conveyances, perhaps going back as far as the discovery of metals, whereas charters authenticated by seals were a novelty (although seals in themselves were ancient). Of particular interest and obscurity is what breaking the knife signified in the conveyancing ceremony. A charter dating from early in Henry I's reign records a gift made by William Fitz Baderon to the monks of St. Florent for their priory of St. Mary's at Monmouth. The gift was "made by a knife," the charter says, but there was a mishap when Bernard, the king's chaplain, "could not break the knife with his hands" and had to "break it beneath his foot" instead.[100] The charter records this mishap presumably because breaking the knife with the hands was an essential part of the conveyancing process, which had not been complied with in this instance. Bernard, the king's chaplain, was curator of the diocese of Hereford, in which Monmouth lay. Why it was his responsibility to break the knife is obscure, as he was neither the donor nor the recipient of the land. Possibly he personified the authority of the bishop or the king. If the symbolism of knives were understood, much might become clearer about preliterate property law in Europe. As well as being traditional, some contemporaries may have thought that a knife was more durable than, and therefore preferable to, parchment and sealing wax. It was true that only the sparsest details of a conveyance could be engraved on the handle of a knife or a whip, but the tradition had been that the true facts of a transaction were engraved on the hearts and minds of the witnesses and could not be fully recorded in any form of writing, however detailed. The symbolic knife would have been retained regardless of whether it had anything written on it, because it preserved the memory of the conveyance.

Only literates, who could interpret the "shapes indicating voices" (in John of Salisbury's definition of letters), were going to be convinced that the writing was superior to the symbolic object. Such objects, the records of the nonliterate, were therefore preserved along with documents. Another example is the knife by which Thomas of Moulton gave the church of Weston in Lincolnshire to Spalding priory, which was deposited in its archive (*in secretario*) according to the charter confirming the gift.[101] This latter knife is no longer preserved. To later archivists, knives and other archaic relics meant nothing unless they had inscriptions connected with them; such things were thrown away as medieval rubbish, because the language of memory which they expressed had no significance for literates.

It is possible that the seals, *signa* in Latin, attached to charters were seen by many contemporaries in a similar way as inscribed "signs." To students of diplomatic today, seals are a method of authenticating documents which preceded the sign manual or written signature. To medieval people they may have appeared rather as visible and tangible objects symbolizing the wishes of the donor. The seal was significant even without the document. Early seals (that is, twelfth-century ones) tend to be disproportionately large compared with the writings to which they are attached. John of Salisbury, writing on behalf of Archbishop Theobald of Canterbury about the safekeeping of seals, says that "by the marks of a single impress the mouths of all the pontiffs may be opened or closed."[102] Just as letters "speak voicelessly the utterances of the absent," seals regulate that speech. Emphasis on the spoken word remained.

The "signs" attached to documents, whether they took the form of inscribed knives or impressed wax or even ink crosses made by the witnesses, all helped to bridge the gulf between the traditional and the literate ways of recording transactions. Preliterate customs and ceremonies persisted despite the use of documents. The doctrine of livery of seisin—the rule that a recipient must have the property duly delivered to him and enter into possession (that is, seisin) of it, whether there was a document of conveyance or not—became fundamental principle of the common law; but there are exceptions to it, like the charter of William of Astle to the Knights Hospitaller which has already been discussed. The treatise ascribed to Bracton insists (in the first half of the thirteenth century) that "a gift is not valid unless livery follows; for the thing given is transferred neither by homage, nor by the drawing up of charters and instruments, even though they be recited in public." Written words were thus entirely inadequate, and even spoken ones were insufficient, without physical symbols: "If livery is to be made of a house by itself, or of a messuage for an estate, it ought to be made by the door and its hasp or ring, by which is understood that the donee possess the whole to its boundaries." It followed also that a gift "may be valid though no charter has been made . . . and conversely the charter may be genuine and valid and the gift incomplete."[103] The physical symbol, the door hasp or ring in Bracton's example, continued to epitomize the whole gift better than any document.

Likewise the drafting rule became general that the past tense should be used in charters for the act of giving: "Know that I, A of B, *have* given," not simply "I give." This emphasized that the ceremonial conveyance was the crucial transaction, whereas the charter was merely a subsequent confirmation of it. This rule became firmly established only in the thirteenth century. Numerous charters of the twelfth century depart from it, presumably because their more amateur draftsmen did not appreciate the relationship between written record and the passage of time. Similarly a generation or two after Bracton the need for the livery of seisin rule was not apparent to ordinary people. Some Derbyshire jurors, who had supposed in 1304 that a charter might suffice without it, were described by a second group of jurors as "simple persons who were not cognizant with English laws and customs."[104] The doctrine of seisin, which had once been a self-evident and commonsense rule, had become with the spread of literacy one of those technical mysteries in which the common law abounded.

The spoken versus the written word

The increasing use of documents created tension between the old methods and the new. Which was the better evidence, for example, seeing a parchment or hearing a man's word? How was the one to be evaluated if it conflicted with the other? A good illustration of this particular dilemma is Eadmer's account of the investiture controversy between St. Anselm, archbishop of Canterbury, and Henry I.[105] Both Anselm and the king had sent envoys to Pope Paschal II; Anselm sent two monks of Canterbury, while the king sent the archbishop of York and two other bishops. The envoys returned to England in September 1101 with papal letters addressed to the king and to Anselm, prohibiting royal investiture of churches and exhorting resistance to them. When the pope's letter to Anselm had been publicly read out, Henry's envoys objected. They claimed that Paschal had given them a purely verbal message that he would treat the king leniently on the investiture question and would not excommunicate him; the pope had added that he did not wish this concession to be put into written form (*per carte inscriptionem*) because other rulers would use it as a precedent. Anselm's envoys replied that the pope had given no verbal message which conflicted in any way with his letters. To this, Henry's bishops answered that Paschal had acted in one way in secret and another in public. Baldwin of Bec, Anselm's chief envoy, was outraged at this allegation and said that it was a calumny on the Holy See.

Dissension then arose in the audience. Those favouring Anselm maintained that credence should be given to "documents signed with the pope's seal" (*scriptis sigillo pape signatis*) and not to "the uncertainty of mere words." The king's side replied that they preferred to rely on the word of three bishops than on "the skins of wethers blackened with ink and weighted with a little lump of lead." They added further venom to the argument by alleging that monks were unreliable anyway, as they should not be engaged in worldly business. Eadmer puts the controversy into dialogue form:

> ANSELM'S MONKS: But what about the evidence of the letters?
> HENRY'S BISHOPS: As we don't accept the evidence of monks against
>   bishops, why should we accept that of a sheepskin?
> ANSELM'S MONKS: Shame on you! Are not the Gospels written down on
>   sheepskins?

Obviously the conflict could not be quickly resolved. In Lent 1102 Anselm set out for Rome and opened on his way another letter from the pope, in which Paschal denied that he had ever given contradictory verbal instructions to the bishops or said that he was reluctant to set a precedent in writing.[106] Who was telling the truth is of course impossible to resolve. Paschal was attempting to make peace and settle the investiture controversy by diplomacy. He may well therefore have said something off the record to the bishops which they had possibly exaggerated. Like all statesmen, the pope obviously had to make a formal denial of such secret negotiations once they became public.

The substance of the story is not our concern here, but the attitudes it reveals towards documentary evidence. Papal letters, sealed with the leaden bull and bearing the symbols and monograms of curial officials, were the most impressive documents produced in medieval Europe, their only rival being Byzantine imperial letters. Yet in Eadmer's story the papal bull is disparagingly described as a sheepskin blackened with ink with a bit of lead attached to it, an extreme example of a document being treated simply as a physical object rather than for its contents. Anselm's supporters were entitled to riposte that the Gospels too were written on parchment—in other words, that Christianity was essentially the religion of a book. At Orléans in 1022 a group of heretics had been burned for disparaging the book learning of the clergy cross-examining them, which they had called human fabrications "written on the skins of animals," whereas the heretics claimed to believe "in the law written in the inner man by the Holy Spirit."[107] The heretics had therefore been arguing that the true written law (*lex scripta*) was not canon law nor Justinian's code, but inspiration retained in the mind alone; real writing was not manmade script on animal parchment. Such an idea may well have derived from the Scripture itself, most probably from St. Paul's Second Epistle to the Corinthians, "written not with ink, but with the spirit of the living God . . . for the letter killeth, but the spirit giveth life."[108] Early in the thirteenth century, St. Francis was to take up this theme as part of his revolt against the spiritually empty book learning of some monks: "Those religious have been killed by the letter who are not willing to follow the spirit of the divine letter, but only desire to know words and interpret them for other men."[109] As so often in his work, Francis blended orthodox and heretical viewpoints in an insight of his own. Literacy was not a virtue in itself. Emphasis on the word inscribed spiritually on the minds of men, as contrasted with letters written on parchment, retained its strength in the Christian message as it did in secular conveyancing ceremonies.

The argument of Henry I's envoys, that their word was better evidence than a papal bull, would not in fact have appeared as outrageous or surprising to contemporaries as Eadmer suggests in his account of the controversy with Anselm. The principle that "oral witness deserves more credence than written evidence" was a legal commonplace. It was cited, for example, by Hubert Walter, archbishop of Canterbury, in a letter to Innocent III in 1200 controverting Gerald of Wales's well-documented claim to be bishop-elect of St. David's.[110] Gerald conceded the point in his reply to the pope, but added that he had brought both documents and witnesses. Behind this principle lay the correct assumption that numerous documents used in legal claims, from the Donation of Constantine downwards, were forgeries. Not all those who relied on the traditional use of the spoken word, rather than parchments, were necessarily therefore obscurantist conservatives. The technology of written record was insufficiently advanced to be efficient or reliable. As a consequence, documents and the spoken word are frequently both used in a way which appears superfluous to a modern literate. To make a record often meant to bear oral witness, not to produce a document. For example, in the civil war of Stephen's reign, Robert, earl of Gloucester, and Miles, earl of Hereford, made a treaty of friendship in writing, in the form of a sealed letter; yet both parties in this document also name witnesses who are "to make legal record of this agreement in court if necessary."[111]

The rule that oral witness is preferable to documents, like the rule that seisin is superior to a charter, shows how cautiously—and perhaps reluctantly—written evidence was accepted. Much important business continued to be done by word of mouth. Bearers of letters were often given instructions which were to be conveyed *viva voce,* either because that was convenient and traditional or because the information was too secret to write down. Twice, for instance, in March 1229 Henry III sent messengers to the count of Toulouse. In their mouths, the king wrote, he had put matters which they would disclose more fully to the count, since the business (presumably concerning a truce with Louis IX) could not be committed to writing because of the dangers of the roads.[112] Similarly in the period of the baronial rebellion, when Henry was in France in 1260, he wrote to the earl of Gloucester instructing him to report on the state of the kingdom by Gilbert Fitz Hugh, the king's serjeant, who would tell the earl more fully *viva voce* about the king's situation.[113] In such negotiations the letter itself did not convey essential information but, like a modern ambassador's letter of credence, was a symbolic object replacing the messenger's ring or other *signum* which had formerly identified him as a confidential agent of his master.

Oral messages were also used to give instructions which later generations would have put in writing. For example, in 1234 John le Franceis and John Mansel were authorized by royal letters of credence to conduct inquiries concerning Jews in certain counties and give instructions to sheriffs *vica voce.*[114] An interesting but non-English case of oral delivery is the poem which the troubadour Jaufre Rudel, lord of Blaye in the Gironde, sent to the Comte de Malche in c. 1150 "without a parchment document" (*senes breu de parguamina*) by the mouth of the jongleur Filhol.[115] The jongleur is thus being used as a kind of living letter. There is, however, a paradox in all such evidence, since historians can only know of the survival of oral ways of conveying information by extant written evidence. Jaufre Rudel's poem, once sent without a script, is written down none the less.

Much business was still done by word of mouth for the obvious reason that documents were bound to be relatively rare until printing made their automatic reproduction possible. The usual way of publishing new laws and regulations was by proclamation. The following instances from the Chancery records of Henry III for 1234 are typical.[116] On 28 August the sheriff of Northumberland and some others were ordered to have it proclaimed (*clamari facias*) that pleas were to be adjourned until the coming of the eyre justices. On 29 August all sheriffs were to proclaim the regulations for supervising hundred courts in accordance with the revision of Magna Carta in 1234. On 1 September the sheriff of Norfolk and Suffolk was to proclaim throughout the two counties that no Jew was to lend money to any Christian in the king's demesne.[117] Matthew Paris suggests that Henry III pursued a policy of legislating by proclamation: in 1248 the people were harassed by diverse precepts promulgated "by the voice of a crier" (*voce preconia*) throughout the cities of England; the king established a new fair at Westminster, for example, in this way.[118] The proclamation to which Matthew gives most attention likewise occurred in 1248, when the king "ordered it to be proclaimed as law by the voice of a crier" that henceforward no man might castrate another for fornication except a husband in the case of his wife's adulterer.[119] The reason for this was that John le Bretun had castrated the Norfolk knight Godfrey de Millers for lying with his daughter.

How extensively or frequently proclamations of this sort were made is not clear. Proclamations were a quick and effective way of conveying information in crowded cities like London, but were obviously less practical in the countryside. Most references to proclamations concern cities. For example, in 1252 Henry III had it proclaimed throughout London that no one should lend money to the abbot of Westminster; or in the preceding year a proclamation had been made against the royal judge Henry of Bath, in London and in the king's court.[120] One consequence for the historian of Henry III's government's use of the spoken word for legislation is that all trace of it is lost, unless a chronicler happened to record it or the Chancery rolls refer to it incidentally. Edward I is considered a great lawgiver partly because the legislation of his time is preserved in the statute rolls. In Henry III's reign less was written down, though a comparable amount of legislative activity probably took place.

Magna Carta became the great precedent for putting legislation into writing. Yet even it was not officially enrolled in the royal archives, although it was proclaimed extensively and repeatedly. Within a few days of King John's assent to it letters were sent to all his sheriffs, foresters, gamekeepers, watermen, and other bailiffs informing them of the agreement between the king and the barons, "as you can hear and see by our charter which we have had made thereon," which they were ordered to have read publicly throughout their bailiwicks.[121] As a result, in theory at least, everyone in England should have heard Magna Carta read out, although it is unlikely that a sufficient number of copies were available.[122] Similarly, when the barons again had the upper hand in 1265, they ordered the terms of Henry III's oath to keep peace with them to be published in the full county court at least twice every year, at Easter and Michaelmas.[123] In 1300 transcripts of Magna Carta and the Charter of the Forest were delivered to every sheriff to read out "before the people" four times a year, at Christmas and Midsummer as well as at Easter and Michaelmas.[124] Nevertheless by 1300 there had been a significant change, as considerable emphasis was now being put on seeing the document as well as hearing it. Sealed transcripts of Magna Carta were sent to all judges, sheriffs, and civic officials and also to all cathedral churches.[125] A precedent for the latter had been made in 1279 when Archbishop Pecham's council at Reading had ordered a copy of Magna Carta to be posted up in every cathedral and collegiate church in a public place "so that it can be clearly seen by the eyes of everyone entering"; in the spring of each year the old copy was to be taken down and a new, fair copy substituted for it.[126] The royal government was sufficiently alarmed to make Pecham have all these copies removed from church doors shortly afterwards.[127]

By 1300 there should have been hundreds of copies of Magna Carta in existence, some transcribed into books of statutes and others circulating in individual exemplars. Not all those who saw them were able to read Latin, but they could be assured of Magna Carta's main points by oral explanations and be confident that the document existed. In modern society similarly it is only lawyers who understand the full texts of legislation; the literate public are generally satisfied with newscasts and press summaries. The copies of Magna Carta which have survived from the thirteenth century are not all identical in their texts, even those of the same redaction, which they would be if they had been printed or photocopied like modern statutes. Not only did scribes make mistakes which were overlooked, they also inserted emendations which in their judgement made better sense of the text. They wrote the words *in capite,* for example, into clause 34 of Magna Carta in order to update it, even though there was no textual warrant for this. "Most scribes were not tremendously concerned to follow their exemplars exactly. The charter mattered, but what mattered to both compilers of statute books and writers of chronicles was its gist, not its exact words."[128] Manuscript culture put the emphasis in any text on its current presentation rather than its archaeological correctness. This was because reading aloud compelled both reader and listener to make immediate sense of the text. Insistence on absolute literal accuracy is a consequence of printing, compounded by photocopying and computing. As Ong points out, the mechanization of letter formation disengages words entirely from speech and living thought; writing takes on an independent existence in typographic space.[129] Operatives of printers and photocopiers can produce texts which have not passed through their minds at all, which was impossible in manuscript culture.

Public readings of documents were done in the vernacular as well as in Latin and might reach a wider audience that way. Thus in 1300, according to the chronicler Rishanger, Magna Carta was read out at Westminster "first in Latin (*litleraliter*) and then in the native tongue (*patria lingua*)."[130] Similarly a year earlier, letters of Pope Boniface VIII about the peace between England and France had been read out in Parliament "in Latin for the literate and in the native tongue for the illiterate."[131] Also in 1299, according to the Worcester annals, royal letters concerning a new perambulation of the forests were "proclaimed in the city of Worcester in the mother tongue (*materna lingua*)."[132] The "paternal" or "maternal" language might mean either English or French. Thus in 1254 the papal excommunication of infringers of Magna Carta was ordered to be published "in the English (*Anglicana*) and French (*Gallicana*) tongues" whenever and wherever appropriate.[133] The use of English and French in this instance was probably a reiteration of existing practice, rather than an innovation, as it is likely that Magna Carta itself had been proclaimed throughout the land in both English and French in 1215.

The distinction the chroniclers wished to emphasize in the citations above was between the language of literacy (Latin) and spoken language; they were less concerned with which vernacular was used. To pedantic Latinists, vernacular simply meant the spoken language. Gerald of Wales hoped that someone would translate his work into French and claimed that Walter Map used to tell him that he (Gerald) had written much, whereas Walter had said much.[134] Although Gerald's writings (*scripta*) were more praiseworthy and durable than Walter's speeches (*dicta*), Walter had the greater profit because his *dicta* were accessible, since they were expressed in the common idiom, while Gerald's *scripta* were appreciated only by the declining few who knew Latin. In fact the distinction Gerald drew here between himself and Walter Map was misleading, as Walter also was a precocious Latinist. Possibly Gerald felt that Walter had been a more successful preacher and *raconteur* in the vernacular than he was. The point of the story from our angle, regardless of whether it is true or not, is that Gerald felt that the spoken vernacular brought greater prestige than written Latin.

Listening to the word

Whatever the language,[135] and whether the record was held solely in the bearer's memory or was committed to parchment, the medieval recipient prepared himself to listen to an utterance rather than to scrutinize a document visually, as a modern literate would. This was due to a different habit of mind; it was not because the recipient was illiterate in any sense of that word. In his account of his claim to be bishop-elect of St. David's, Gerald of Wales describes a private audience in the pope's chamber with Innocent III in 1200, when the pope looked up a register listing all the metropolitan churches of Christendom and went through the rubrics until he found Wales.[136] But when at a subsequent private audience Gerald showed the pope a transcript of a letter of Eugenius III which Gerald had found in another papal register, Innocent handed the transcript to Cardinal Ugolino and told him to read it; "and when it had been read and diligently heard, the pope replied that he was well pleased with it."[137] Gerald's account of the earlier audience depicts the pope browsing through a reference book as a modern literate would do; but when at the subsequent audience the pope needs to absorb carefully the details of a letter, he has it read to him instead of scrutinizing it. Reading aloud in this case is not being done to enable everyone present to learn the contents of the letter, as the only persons at this private audience are Innocent, Gerald, and Ugolino, who is supporting him. Nor, obviously, was Innocent incapable of reading the script of papal registers. Yet he evidently found it easier to concentrate when he was listening than when he was looking; reading was still primarily oral rather than visual.

Indications of the same habit of mind appear in the "auditing" of monetary accounts. Abbot Samson of Bury St. Edmunds "heard" the weekly account of his expenditure, yet he obviously could have consulted such a document (if the account were in documentary form at all), as his biographer Jocelin says that he inspected his *kalendarium* (his register of rents and so on) almost every day "as if he contemplated in it the physiognomy of his own probity as in a mirror."[138] The modern word "audit" derives from a time where it was the habit to listen to, rather than to see, an account. Thomas of Eccleston in his description of the arrival of the Franciscan friars in England in 1224 records that when the superior heard the first annual account of the London friars and realized how little they had to show for such lavish expenditure, he threw down all the tallies and rolls and shouted, "'I'm caught,'" and "he never afterwards wanted to hear an account."[139] In this instance, accounts in writing existed, in the form of both wooden tallies and parchment rolls, yet the superior "heard" them nonetheless. H. J. Chaytor points out, however, that one must be careful of colloquial speech in such an instance as this. For example, modern English uses the phrase, "I have not heard from him for some time," to mean "I have had no letter."[140]

Similarly in law courts, "inspecting" a document might mean hearing it read aloud. Thus in 1219 in an action of warranty of charter in Lincolnshire, William of Well, the defendant, is reported in the plea roll to "have come and claimed a hearing (*auditum*) of his father's charter," and it was duly heard.[141] A generation later, in a similar action in Berkshire in 1248, the abbot of Beaulieu who was the defendant claimed that the plaintiff should "show" him the charter by which he should warrant her.[142] The contrasting emphasis on hearing and seeing in these similar claims only thirty years apart may indicate a general change of attitude developing within this period, if only in the minds of the enrolling clerks; or more likely the two cases show the differing approach to documents of a knight, William of Well, and a monk, the abbot of Beaulieu.

Literary works, especially vernacular ones, were frequently explicitly addressed by the author to an audience, rather than to readers as such. Thus the nun of Barking in her French version of Ailred's life of Edward the Confessor in c. 1163 requests "all who hear, or will ever hear, this romance of hers" not to despise it because the translation is done by a woman.[143] In the *Romance of Horn* by Master Thomas, the author begins by addressing his audience: "Lords, you have heard the lines of parchment" (*Seignurs, oi avez le vers del parchemin*).[144] The parchment is evidently thought of here as a direct substitute for a jongleur; it speaks and is heard, like the charter of Richard de Cormeilles for St. Mary's priory at Monmouth.[145] Likewise in the *Estoire de Waldef* (dating from c. 1190) the author refers to the *Brut* story:

> If anyone wants to know this history
> Let him read the *Brut,* he will hear it there
> (*Qui l'estoire savoir voldra*
> *Lise le Brut, illoc l'orra*)[146]

A modern literate would not say, "he will *hear* it there," but "he will *find* it" or "see it there." The emphasis in such works on hearing does not necessarily mean that their contents stem directly from oral tradition, but that reading continued to be conceived in terms of hearing rather than seeing. Until cheap printing supplied every "reader" with his own book, this emphasis on hearing was understandable.

Latin works too were generally intended to be read aloud—hence the speeches and frequent use of dramatic dialogue in monastic chronicles. Eadmer concludes the first book of his *Life of St. Anselm* with an interval, as in a play: "But here, lest our unpolished speech (*oratio*) weary our readers or hearers by being too long drawn-out, we shall make our first halt in the work."[147] Traditional monastic reading in particular bore little relation to a modern literate's approach to a book. *Lectio* was "more a process of rumination than reading, directed towards savouring the divine wisdom within a book rather than finding new ideas or novel information."[148] The process is well illustrated by St. Anselm's *Meditation on Human Redemption:* "Taste the goodness of your redeemer . . . chew the honeycomb of his words, suck their flavour which is sweeter than honey, swallow their wholesome sweetness. Chew by thinking, suck by understanding, swallow by loving and rejoicing."[149] Reading was a physical exertion, demanding the use not only of the eyes, but of mouth and throat. Writing was a similar act of endurance, requiring three fingers to hold the pen, two eyes to see the words, one tongue to speak them, and the whole body to labour.[150] For these reasons some monks argued that work in the *scriptorium* was an adequate substitute for manual labour.

The system of punctuating and abbreviating words in Latin works was likewise intended primarily to assist someone reading aloud, rather than a person silently scrutinizing the page. N. R. Ker cites the case of a manuscript where the Latin word *neque* (neither), which is written out in full, has been amended throughout to *neq*; he suggests that writing *neque* out in full was likely to mislead an oral reader into stressing the second syllable; writing out the word in full was an error on the scribe's part which has been duly corrected.[151] The earliest printed book, the Gutenberg Bible, reproduced the medieval standard abbreviations as if they were additional letters of the Latin alphabet, which they had indeed become. Occasionally manuscripts have stress-marks on particular syllables to help a reader pronounce the Latin correctly. As medieval Latin was an artificial language without any native speakers, an agreed correct pronunciation—and hence correct punctuation—helped to make sense of it, for both reader and listener.[152] Roger Bacon in 1267 discussed the correct pronunciation of words in the Bible, particularly those with Hebrew or Greek roots. He placed accentuation and punctuation under the heading of music: "because all these things consist in the raising and lowering of the voice and are therefore like some kind of chant, it is obvious that the explanation of all these matters pertains to music."[153] Bacon was correct, as the scholastic art of music centered on the mathematical analysis of sound. But his strident tone suggests that he also knew very well that punctuation articulated the meaning of a statement as much as its sound, and that it therefore belonged to the art of grammar as well as music. Following Isidore of Seville, John of Salisbury (a century before Bacon) had discussed punctuation under the heading of grammar. For him punctuation marks indicate different breathing intervals when speaking, as well as distinguishing the clauses of a sentence.[154]

Ideally a "reader" was expected to look at the text as well as listen to it, but that was the exception and not the rule. In the *Life of St. Margaret* of Scotland the author considered it a point worth remarking that Margaret's daughter, Matilda (Henry I's queen), "desired not only to hear, but also to inspect continually the impress of the letters" of her mother's life.[155] A school manual, not English and later than our period, sums up in a dialogue the medieval meaning of "reading" (*lectio*):

> "Are you a scholar, what do you read?"
> "I do not read, I listen."
> "What do you hear?"
> "Donatus or Alexander, or logic or music."[156]

Donatus's *Ars Minor* and Alexander's *Doctrinale* were Latin textbooks. The term "reading" a subject has been preserved at Oxford and Cambridge;

whereas some undergraduates think that "reading" implies studying books instead of hearing lectures, medieval students understood *lectio* primarily to mean that the master read while they listened. Whole books were published by being read aloud. Gerald of Wales says that he published his *Topography of Ireland* in this way in c. 1188 by reading it at Oxford to different audiences on three successive days. But Gerald's action was not typical, as he boasts that "neither has the present age seen, nor does any past age bear record of, the like in England."[157] The normal way of disseminating scholarly works, as distinct from popular romances, was by the modern method of circulating copies. For instance, Herbert of Bosham assumed in his life of Becket that his readers will be able to study Becket's correspondence, which he omits for the sake of brevity, "because that book of letters is already in the possession of many persons and churches."[158] If Becket is thought too exceptional an example because of his extraordinary popularity, Eadmer mentions in his appendix to St. Anselm's *Life* that he intends to make a new start, because the *Life* has already "been transcribed by many and distributed to various churches."[159] Distributing copies did not, of course, rule out public readings; on the contrary, as more books became available, the practice may have grown even more widespread.

Just as reading was linked in the medieval mind with hearing rather than seeing, writing (in its modern sense of composition) was associated with dictating rather than manipulating a pen. Reading and writing were not inseparably coupled with each other, as they are today. A person might be able to write, yet not be considered literate. As we have seen, Walter Map mentions a boy "who was not *litteratus,* although he knew how to transcribe any series of letters whatever." Literacy involved being learned in Latin, whereas writing was the process of making a fair copy on parchment, which was the art of the scribe. Some authors (notably the great monastic historians Orderic Vitalis, William of Malmesbury, and Matthew Paris)[160] did their own writing, but they are the exceptions, and they distinguished that activity from composition.

Medieval distinctions are well illustrated by Eadmer. He explains that he had to conceal from St. Anselm that he was "writing" his biography. When he had begun the work "and had had already transcribed onto parchment a great part of what I had composed (*dictaveram*) in wax," Anselm asked, "what it was I was composing and copying" (*quid dictitarem, quid scriptitarem*).[161] The process of composing on wax tablets is thus described in Latin by the word *dictitare* (literally, "to dictate'), even though in Eadmer's case he was dictating to himself. The use of "writing" (*scriptitare*) is confined to making the fair copy on parchment. Similarly, when Orderic Vitalis wishes to say that before the time of William the Conqueror the Normans had concentrated on war rather than reading and writing, the phrase he uses is *legere vel dictare,* not *legere vel scribere.* Numerous other examples of using "dictate" where a modern literate would use "write" could be given.[162] Dictating was the usual form of literary composition and the *ars dictaminis,* taught in the schools as part of rhetoric, was the skill governing it. Letter writing was thus an intellectual skill using the mouth rather than the hand. Peter of Blois, a busy secretary of state like John of Salisbury, boasted that the archbishop of Canterbury had seen him dictating to three different scribes on diverse subjects, while he dictated and wrote a fourth letter all at the one time.[163]

Reading aloud and dictating permit the nonliterate to participate in the use of documents, whereas reading and writing silently exclude the illiterate. When the voice is used, the clerk or scribe becomes no more than a medium between the speaker or hearer and the document. Neither the hearer of a book nor the *dictator* of a letter needs to be a master of every detail of the scribal technique himself, just as modern managers are not required to type or to programme computers. Obviously it is helpful if the manager understands how these things are done and has some experience of them, but this experience is not indispensable. For these reasons medieval kings and their officials, such as sheriffs in the counties, did not need to be literate in the modern sense. Lack of literacy did not mean that they were ignorant or incapable of coping with business; they were as literate as the tasks required. As the number of documents increased and habits of silent visual reading became more common, levels of literacy (in the modern sense) presumably increased also; but there is no evidence of a crisis suddenly demanding numerous literates. Because the preliterate emphasis on the spoken word persisted, the change from oral to literate modes could occur slowly and almost imperceptibly over many generations.

The text usually quoted to show that medieval attitudes towards literacy were similar to modern ones is John of Salisbury's quotation in *Policraticus* that "Rex illitteratus est quasi asinus coronatus" (an illiterate king is like a crowned ass).[164] In this passage John is primarily concerned that the prince should have wisdom, which is gained by reading the law of God daily. For that reason, and not for administrative requirements, the prince needs skill in letters. John concedes moreover that it is not absolutely necessary for the prince to be *litteratus,* provided he takes advice from *litterati,* that is, from priests who, like Old Testament prophets, will remind the prince of the law of God. "Thus the mind of the prince may read in the tongue of the priest. For the life and tongue of priests are like the book of life before the face of the peoples."[165] John is obviously thinking here of the spiritual, and not the worldly, value of reading. His discussion emphasizes that an illiterate prince can participate in wisdom through the medium of the priest's voice. The prince is not excluded by being illiterate: "nor is he altogether destitute of reading (*lectionis*) who, even though he does not read himself, hears faithfully what is read to him by others." John thus shows that in his day nonliterates could participate in literate culture; he is not arguing for the absolute necessity of rulers being literate in either the medieval sense of being learned in Latin or the modern sense of having a minimal ability to read and write. Ironically, the king of England at the time, Henry II, was literate in every sense of the word; yet he was not a good king by John's definition, as he refused to listen to the lectures of priests and was responsible for the murder of Becket.

Notes

Abbreviations

Annales Monastici	*Annales Monastici,* ed. H. R. Luard, Rolls Series 36 (1864–69).
Baronial Docs	*Documents of the Baronial Movement of Reform and Rebellion 1258–67,* ed. R. F. Treharne and I. J. Sanders (1973).
Battle	*The Chronicle of Battle Abbey,* ed. E. Searle (1980).
Becket Materials	*Materials for the History of Thomas Becket,* ed. J. C. Robertson and J. B. Sheppard, Rolls Series 77 (1875–85).
Berks. Eyre	*The Roll and Writ File of the Berkshire Eyre of 1248,* ed. M. T. Clanchy, Selden Society 40 (1973).
BIHR	*Bulletin of the Institute of Historical Research*
BM Facs	*Facsimiles of Royal and other Charters in the British Museum,* ed. G. F. Warner and H. G. Ellis I (1903).
Bracton	Henry de Bracton, *De Legibus et Consuetudinibus Angliae,* ed. G. E. Woodbine (1915), reissued with translation and revisions by S. E. Thorne (1968–77).
Carruthers, *Memory*	M. J. Carruthers, *The Book of Memory* (1990).
Chaplais, *Docs*	P. Chaplais, *English Royal Documents: King John–Henry VI* (1971).
Cheney, *Texts & Studies*	C. R. Cheney, *Medieval Texts and Studies* (1973).
Cheshire Facs	*Facsimiles of Early Cheshire Charters,* ed. G. Barraclough, Lancashire and Cheshire Record Society (1957).
Clanchy, *"Moderni"*	M. T. Clanchy, *"Moderni* in Medieval Education and Government in England," *Speculum* 50 (1975), 671–88.
ClR	*Close Rolls: Henry III* (1902–38).

CPatR	*Calendar of Patent Rolls* (1891–).
Eadmer, *Vita*	*The Life of St. Anselm by Eadmer,* ed. R. W. Southern (1962).
Galbraith, "Literacy"	V. H. Galbraith, "The Literacy of the Medieval English Kings," *Proceedings of the British Academy* 21 (1935), 201–38.
Gervase	*The Historical Works of Gervase of Canterbury,* ed. W. Stubbs, Rolls Series 73 (1879–80).
Giraldus	*Giraldi Cambrensis Opera,* ed. J. S. Brewer et al., Rolls Series 21 (1861–91).
Goody, *Literacy*	*Literacy in Traditional Societies,* ed. J. Goody (1968).
Gransden, *Historical Writing*	A. Gransden, *Historical Writing in England, c. 550–1307* (1974).
Jocelin	*The Chronicle of Jocelin of Brakelond,* ed. H. E. Butler (1949).
Kerr, *English MSS*	N. R. Kerr, *English Manuscripts in the Century after the Norman Conquest* (1960).
Legge, *Anglo-Norman*	M. D. Legge, *Anglo-Norman Literature and Its Background* (1963).
Lewis, *Matthew Paris*	S. Lewis, *The Art of Matthew Paris in the "Chronica Majora"*(1987).
Matthew Paris	*Matthaei Parisiensis Chronica Majora,* ed. H. R. Luard, Rolls Series 58 (1872–84).
Monasticon	W. Dugdale, *Monasticon Anglicanum,* ed. J. Caley et al., (1817–30).
Mowbray Charters	*Charters of the Honour of Mowbray,* ed. D. E. Greenway (1972).
Orderic	Orderic Vitalis, *Historia Ecclesiastica,* ed. M. Chibnall (1969–80).
Oxford Facs	*Facsimiles of Early Charters in Oxford Muniment Rooms,* ed. H. E. Salter (1929).
P & M	F. Pollock and F. W. Maitland, *The History of English Law before the Time of Edward I,* 2nd ed. (1898).
Parkes, "Literacy"	M. B. Parkes, "The Literacy of the Laity," in *The Medieval World,* ed. D. Daiches and A. Thorlby (1973), 555–77 [reprinted in M. B. Parkes, *Scribes, Scripts and Readers* (1991), 275–97].
Patrologiae	*Patrologiae: Cursus Completus Series Latina,* ed. J. P. Migne (1844–73).
R & S	H. G. Richardson and G. O. Sayles, *The Governance of Medieval England from the Conquest to Magna Carta* (1963).
RC	Record Commissioners' publications (1805–48).
RS	Rolls Series: *Rerum Britannicarum Medii Aevi Scriptores* (1858–97).

S.   Society serial publications.
Southern,   R. W. Southern, *Medieval Humanism and Other*
 Humanism Medieval   *Studies* (1970).
SPC   *Select Pleas of the Crown*, ed. F. W. Maitland, Selden
                                        Society 1 (1887).
SS   Selden Society publications (1887–).
Statutes   *Statutes of the Realm*, ed. A. Luders et al., Record
                                        Record Commissioners' publications, vol. 1 (1810).
Stenton, *Feudalism*   F. M. Stenton, *The First Century of English*
                                        Feudalism 1066–1166, 2nd ed. (1961).
Stubbs, *Charters*   *Select Charters*, ed. W. Stubbs, 9th ed., ed. H. W. C.
                                        Davis (1913).
Thompson, *Literacy*   J. W. Thompson, *The Literacy of the Laity in the*
                                        Middle Ages, University of California Publications in
                                        Education 9 (1939).
TRHS   *Transactions of the Royal Historical Society.*
Walter Map   *De Nugis Curialium*, ed. M. R. James, C. N. L.
                                        Brooke, R. A. B. Mynors (1983)
Wattenbach, *Schriftwesen*   W. Wattenbach, *Das Schriftwesen im Mittelalter*,
                                        3rd ed. (1896).

1. S. S. Walker, "Proof of Age of Feudal Heirs in Medieval England," *Medieval Studies* (Toronto) 35 (1973): 316–20.

2. *Calendar of Inquisitions Post Mortem* IV, pp. 171–72, no. 239.

3. *Placitorum Abbreviatio*, Record Commissioners' publications (1811), 293 (text incomplete); *Coram Rege Roll for Trinity Term 1297*, ed. W. P. W. Phillmore, British Record S. Index Library XIX (1897), 241–43; G. E. Cokayne, *The Complete Peerage* (2nd ed.) XII part i (1953), 773. No chronicle of West Acre Priory extant.

4. See Michael T. Clanchy, *From Memory to Written Record: England, 1066–1307*, 2nd ed. (Oxford: Blackwell, 1993), ch. 6, n. 1.

5. See Clanchy, *From Memory*, ch. 6, nn. 51–52.

6. Nigellus de Longchamp dit Wireker, *Tractatus contra Curiales et Officiales Clericos*, ed. A. Boutemy (1959), 1:204.

7. H. Grundmann, "*Litteratus-Illitteratus*," *Archiv für Kulturgeschichte* 40 (1958), 17.

8. *Dictionaire du droit canonique*, ed. R. Nax (1935–65) 3, col. 828; 4, col. 328.

9. In general see the contributions by L. Prosdocimi and Y. Congar to *I laici nella societas christiana dei secoli XI e XII*, ed. G. Lazzati and C. D. Fonseca (1968), 56–117.

10. "De Institutione Clericorum," Bk. 4, ch. 110, *Patrologia* CCIII (1855), col. 816; cf n. 30 below. P. Riché, "Recherches sur l'instruction des laïcs du IX au XII siècle," *Cahiers de civilisation médiévale* 5 (1962), 181.

11. Matthew Paris V, 242; N. Denholm-Young, *History and Heraldry* (1985), 32–34.

12. *The Estate Book of Henry de Bray,* ed. D. Willis, Camden S., 3rd series, 27 (1916), 79.

13. Thompson, *Literacy,* 170, n. 40. For a contrary view see Galbraith, "Literacy," 201–2, 211–12.

14. R. W. Southern, "Master Vacarius and the Beginning of an English Academic Tradition," in *Medieval Learning and Literature: Essays Presented to R. W. Hunt* (1976), 268, n. 1, citing *Studia Anselmia* 41 (1957), 65. Cf. R & S, 270, n. 4.

15. J. W. Baldwin, *Masters, Princes and Merchants* (1970) 2:51, n. 57.

16. Jocelin, 12.

17. Ibid., 130.

18. Ibid., 12. *Acts* XXVI, 24.

19. Ibid., 84.

20. *Patrologiae* CCIII (1855), col. 816.

21. Ed. D. L. Douie and H. Farmer (1961) I, p. 43.

22. *Historiae Anglicanae Scriptores Decem,* ed. R. Twysden (1652), col. 1841.

23. "Juris ignarus," ibid., col. 1841.

24. See Clanchy, *From Memory,* ch. 2, nn. 103–5.

25. *The Great Register of Lichfield Cathedral,* ed. H. E. Savage, The William Salt Archaeological S. (1924), 341, no. 713; Matthew Paris III, 207 (citing Roger of Wendover). I owe these references to Dr Jeanne Stones.

26. William of Newburgh, *Chronicles,* ed. R. Howlett, RS 82 (1844), 1:36; Jocelin, 11.

27. *Policraticus,* Bk. 7, ch. 9, ed. C. C. J. Webb (1909), 2:126. Cf. Grundmann, "*litteratus-Illitteratus,*" 52, and Riché, "Recherches sur l'instruction des laïcs," 180–81.

28. Walter Map, Bk. 4, ch. 1, 278.

29. *Patrologiae* CCIII (1855), cols 148–49; Thompson, *Literacy,* 139–41.

30. "Miles legit, intelligit, dictat, versificatur et inter clericos linguam Latinam proferens," *Patrologiae* CCIII (1855), col. 816. Cf. n. 10 above.

31. In general see J. Dunbabin, "From Clerk to Knight: Changing Orders" in *The Ideals and Practice of Medieval Knighthood II,* ed. C. Harper-Bill and R. Harvey (1988), 26–39.

32. *Gesta Abbatum Monosterii S. Albani,* ed. H. T. Riley, RS 28 (1867), 1:57; R. M. Thomson, *MSS from St Albans Abbey* (1982), 1:13.

33. Giraldus 8: 310; R & S, 273, n. 8.

34. Matthew Paris v, 610, 317.

35. H.J. Graff, *The Legacies of Literacy* (1987), 373 ff.

36. These assumptions are discussed by K. O'B. O'Keeffe, *Visible Song: Transitional Literacy in Old English Verse* (1990), 9–10.

37. Facsimile, ed. C. Bémont, *Simon de Montfort* trans. E. F. Jacob (1930), 276–78 (the will is in French and was written in 1258); M. M. Sheehan, *The Will in Medieval England* (1963), 260–61, nn. 128, 131.

38. The symbolism of seals and crosses is discussed in Clanchy, *From Memory,* ch. 9, nn. 53–90.

39. *Statutes of the Realm*, ed. A Luders et al., RC, 1 (1810), 211. See Clanchy, *From Memory*, ch. 2, n. 24.

40. See Clanchy, *From Memory*, ch. 2, nn. 21–2.

41. P. Dupuy, *Historie du differand d'entre le Pape Boniface VIII et Philippe le Bel (1655)*, 14; G. de Lagarde, *La Naissance de l'esprit laïque au déclin du Moyen Age* (1948) 1, ch. 12.

42. L. C. Gabel, *Benefit of Clergy in England in the Later Middle Ages* (1928–29), 68–78. J. H. Baker, *Reports of Sir John Spelman* II, SS 94 (1978), 327–31.

43. Gabel, 82–84.

44. Galbraith's lecture to the British Academy (Galbraith, "Literacy," 201–38) was published in 1936. Thompson's *The Literacy of the Laity in the Middle Ages* (Thompson, *Literacy*, ch. 7) was completed in the same year, but was not published until 1939.

45. *Gesta Abbatum Monasterii S. Albani* I, 150–54; *Battle*, 154–56, 280; Jocelin, p. 51. Cf. Galbraith, "Literacy," 222, n. 46.

46. *Patrologiae* CCVII (1855), col. 198; *Becket Materials* 7:573.

47. Galbraith, "Literacy," 215.

48. R & S, 278 and (more generally) 269–83.

49. Ibid., 273.

50. Ibid., 275.

51. W. L. Warren, *Henry II* (1973), 276–77.

52. R & S, 274.

53. Parkes, "Literacy," 558, n. 20.

54. See Clanchy, *From Memory*, ch. 2, nn. 3–9.

55. Parkes, "Literacy," 560.

56. Walter Map, Bk. 1, ch. 10, p. 12.

57. N. Orme, *English Schools in the Middle Ages* (1973), ch. 1.

58. See n. 63 below.

59. Clanchy, "*Moderni*," 681, and *Becket Materials* 2:361. F. Barlow, *Thomas Becket* (1986), 26–27.

60. I Canute 22, ed. A. J. Robertson, *The Laws of the Kings of England from Edmund to Henry 1* (1925), 170. Cf. n. 77 below.

61. *Libellus de Vita et Miraculis S. Godrici*, ed. J. Stevenson, Surtees S. (1845); T. A. Archer, "Godric," in *The Dictionary of National Biography*, 8:47–49. M. Richter, *Sprache und Gesellschaft* (1979), 80–86.

62. *Libellus de Vita*, ch. 2, p. 25.

63. Ibid.

64. Ibid., ch. 4, p. 30.

65. Ibid., ch. 6, pp. 34, 36.

66. Ibid., ch. 6, p. 35.

67. Ibid., ch. 4, p. 28.

68. Ibid., ch. 9, pp. 41–42.

69. Ibid., ch. 92, pp. 200–201.

70. Ibid., ch. 16, p. 59.

71. Ibid., 59–60.

72. "O rustice decrepite! O rustice stercorarie!" ibid., ch. 38, p. 93.

73. Ibid., ch. 38, p. 94; ch. 47, p. 110; ch. 87, p. 192; ch. 161, p. 306.

74. Ibid., ch. 94, pp. 203–4; ch. 96, p. 206.

75. Ibid., ch. 79, pp. 179–80.

76. Ibid., 179.

77. *Wulfstan's Canons of Edgar,* ed. R. Fowler, Early English Text S. 266 (1972), 6–7. CF. n. 60 above.

78. See Clanchy, *From Memory,* ch. 6, n. 13.

79. See ibid., ch. 6, n. 22, and ch. 2, nn. 103–5.

80. "Littere autem, id est figure, primo vocum indices sunt; deinde rerum, quas anime per oculorum fenestras opponunt, et frequenter absentium dicta sine voce loquuntur," *Metalogicon,* Bk. I, ch. 13, ed. J.B. Hall and K. S. B. Keats-Rohan (1991), 32.

81. *Charters of the Honour of Mowbray,* ed. D. E. Greenway (1972), nos. 92, 347. Cf. Clanchy, *From Memory,* ch. 3, nn. 11–12.

82. Stenton, *Feudalism,* 111, 273, no. 27.

83. E. G. *Oxford Facs,* nos 7, 38, 54, 56, 60, 62, 72, 74.

84. *Landboc sive Registrum de Wincehlcumba,* ed. D. Royce (1892) 1:17.

85. C. A. F. Meekings analyses conveyancing forms in *Fitznell's Cartulary,* Surrey Record S. 26 (1968), cxli.

86. M. M. Sheehan, *The Will in Medieval England,* Pontifical Institute of Medieval Studies: Studies & Texts 6 (1963), 186–87.

87. Ibid., 192; 188, n. 90.

88. P & M, 2: 87, n. 4. In general see J. Le Goff, *Time, Work and Culture in the Middle Ages* (1980), 244–48, 354–60.

89. *CuriaRR* (1922–), 6: 230. See also ibid., 13: 405, no. 1926; and Clanchy, *From Memory,* 77.

90. *SPC,* 124–25, no. 192.

91. *Mowbray Charters,* no. 98.

92. *BM Facs,* no. 16.

93. *Oxford Facs,.* no. 9; Chaplais, *Docs,* 50, n. 2. C. R. Cheney discusses the meaning of *textus* in *BIHR* 56 (1983), 9–10.

94. C. R. Cheney, *Notaries Public in England* (1972), 7, n. 4; Lewis, *Matthew Paris,* 113.

95. For this gift see *Monasticon,* 4:125. For scrolls see F. Garnier, *Le Langage de l'image au Moyen Age* (1989), 2:229–44, 394–400.

96. *Cheshire Facs,* no. 13 (2).

97. H. Ellis, "Observations on Some Ancient Methods of Conveyance in England," *Archaeologia* 17 (1814), 313. I have not been able to trace this whip-handle.

98. *The Boarstall Cartulary,* ed. H. E. Salter, Oxford Historical S. 88 (1930), 170, no. 562; Patent Rolls 1266–72, 15; J. Cherry, "Medieval Horns of Tenure," *Antiquaries Journal* 69 (1989), 113, plate xix.

99. Ellis, "Observations," 313, 315–16, gives examples of inscribed knives. Bulmer's knife is best illustrated in the engraving in J. Raine, *History and Antiquities*

of North Durham (1852), appendix, 135; M. T. Clanchy, "Reading the Signs at Durham Cathedral," in *Literacy and Society*, ed. K. Schousboe and M. T. Larsen (1989), 175–77.

100. J. H. Round, *Calendar of Documents Preserved in France* (1899), 409, no. 1138. Latin text ed. P. Marchegay in *Bibliothèque de l'École des Chartres* 40 (1879), 179, no. 16 (I owe this reference to Dr. J. Barrow). "Bernard the Chaplain" is different from "Bernard the King's Scribe." Breaking is discussed by Le Goff, *Time*, 360.

101. *Monasticon* 3, 217, no. x.

102. *Letters*, ed. W. J. Millor et al. (1955), 1:109.

103. Bracton, fos. 39b–40, 2:124–25; ibid., fo. 11b, p. 50.

104. *Calendarium Genealogicum*, RC (1865) 2:659; P & M, 2:89.

105. *Historia*, 132–40.

106. Ibid., 149–51. R. W. Southern, *St Anselm* (1990), 295, n. 17.

107. *Recueil des historiens des Gaules*, ed. L. Delisle (1869), 10:539; R. I. Moore, *The Birth of Popular Heresy* (1975), 10–15. The author of this account is discussed by B. Stock, *The Implications of Literacy* (1983), 107–15.

108. 2 *Corinthians* 3:3, 6. Cf. Smalley, *The Bible*, ch. 1 ("The Letter and the Spirit").

109. R. B. Brooke, *The Coming of the Friars* (1975), 126.

110. "Testibus et non testimoniis credi oportet," *Giraldus*, 3:14, 21. H. E. Butler, *The Autobiography of Giraldus Cambrensis* (1937), 168, 175–76.

111. See Clanchy, *From Memory*, ch. 2, n. 124.

112. *ClR* 1227–31, 233.

113. Ibid., 1259–61, 281.

114. Ibid., 1231–34, 586.

115. A. E. van Vleck, *Memory and Re-Creation in Troubadour Lyric* (1991), 41.

116. *ClR* 1231–34, 592–93.

117. Ibid., 592; C. Roth, *A History of the Jews in England* (1941), 53.

118. Matthew Paris 5:18, 29.

119. "Voce preconia iussit pro lege acclamari," ibid., 35; *C1R* 1247–51, 139, 394; *CPatR* 1247–58, 387.

120. Matthew Paris, 5:305, 223; *CPatR* 1247–58, 101.

121. J. C. Holt, *Magna Carta* (1965), 345.

122. F. Thompson, *The First Century of Magna Carta* (1925), 94.

123. *Baronial Docs*, 312–15.

124. *Statutes*, 136.

125. *Chronicle of Bury St Edmunds*, ed. A. Gransden (1964), 154; Stubbs, *Charters*, 490–91.

126. "Omnium intrantium oculis," D. L. Douie, *Archbishop Pecham* (1952), 113, n. 2; M. Prestwich, *Edward 1* (1988), 250–51.

127. *ClR* 1272–79, 582.

128. S. Reynolds, "Magna Carta 1297 and the Legal Use of Literacy," *BIHR* 62 (1989), 241.

129. *Orality and Literacy* (1982), ch. 5 ("Print, Space, and Closure").

130. *Willemi Rishanger Chronica,* ed. H. T. Riley, RS 28 (1865), 405.

131. Ibid., 389.

132. *Annales Monastici,* 4:541. For the meaning of *materna lingua,* see C. Clark, "Women's Names in Post-Conquest England," *Speculum* 53 (1978), 224–25.

133. *Annales Monastici* 1 (Burton, Annals), 322.

134. *Giraldus,* 5:410–11.

135. In general see P. Zumthor, *La Poésie et la voix dans la civilisation mediévale* (1984).

136. *Giraldus,* 3:165. R. L. Poole, *Lectures on the Papal Chancery* (1915), 150–51, 194–96.

137. Ibid., 182.

138. See Clanchy, *From Memory,* ch. 3, n. 55.

139. *Monumenta Franciscana,* ed. J. S. Brewer, RS 4 (1858), 1:8.

140. *From Script to Print* (1945), 145.

141. *Rolls of the Justices in Eyre,* ed. D. M. Stenton, SS 53 (1934), 300, no. 630.

142. *Berks. Eyre,* 150, no. 354.

143. Legge, *Anglo-Norman,* 65. Other examples in H. J. Chaytor, *From Script to Print,* 11–12, 144–47. In general see R. Crosby, "Oral Delivery in the Middle Ages," *Speculum* 11 (1936), 90–102.

144. See Clanchy, *From Memory,* ch. 6, n. 63.

145. See n. 13 above.

146. Legge, *Anglo-Norman,* 143.

147. Eadmer, *Vita,* 62.

148. C. J. Holdsworth, "John of Ford and English Cistercian Writing," *TRHS,* 5th ser., 11 (1961), 124.

149. *Opera Omnia,* ed. F. S. Schmitt (1938–61), 3:84.

150. A description repeated by various scribes but originating in the eighth century, Wattenbach, *Schriftwesen,* 495.

151. Kerr, *English MSS,* 51.

152. R. W. Southern explains the punctuation system in Eadmer, *Vita,* xxv–xxiv. Stress-marks are being studied by L. E. Boyle. In general see M. B. Parkes, *Pause and Effect:An Introduction to the History of Punctuation in the West* (1992).

153. "Opus Tertium," ch. 62, *Fratris Rogeri Bacon Opera,* ed. J .S. Brewer, RS 15 (1859), 256. Bacon discusses the pronunciation of Biblical words at ch. 60.

154. *Metalogicon,* Bk. I, ch. 20, p. 46.

155. Thompson, *Literacy,* 171, n. 46.

156. F. M. Powicke, *The Christian Life in the Middle Ages* (1935), 88; C. H. Haskins, *Studies in Medieval Culture* (1929), 83.

157. *Giraldus,* 1:72–73.

158. *Becket Materials,* 3:396.

159. Eadmer, *Vita,* 153.

160. Their holographs are illustrated by Gransden, *Historical Writing,* plates iv, v, x.

161. Eadmer, *Vita*, 150; Carruthers, *Memory*, 195.

162. Orderic, Bk. 3, 2:2. Cheney, *Texts & Studies,* 246–47, gives excellent examples from a letter of the Englishman, Gervase abbot of Prémontré, who died in 1228.

163. Southern, *Medieval Humanism,* 119.

164. *Policraticus*, Bk. 4, ch. 6, ed. C. J. Webb (1909), 1:255; Galbraith, "Literacy," 212–13.

165. *Policraticus,* 255.

3   SOME CONJECTURES ABOUT THE IMPACT OF PRINTING ON WESTERN SOCIETY AND THOUGHT: A PRELIMINARY REPORT

Elizabeth L. Eisenstein

I have found it useful, in any case, to start taking stock by following up clues contained in special studies on printing. After singling out certain features that seemed peculiar to typography, I held them in mind while passing in review various historical developments. Relationships emerged that had not occurred to me before, and some possible solutions to old puzzles were suggested. Conjectures based on this approach may be sampled below under headings that indicate my main lines of inquiry.

A closer look at wide dissemination: Various effects produced by increased output

Most references to wide dissemination are too fleeting to make clear the specific effects of an increased supply of texts directed at different markets. In particular they fail to make clear how patterns of consumption were affected by increased production. Here the term "dissemination" is sufficiently inappropriate to be distracting. Some mention of cross-fertilization or cross-cultural interchange should be included in surveys or summaries. More copies of one given text, for instance, *were* "spread, dispersed, or scattered" by the issue of a printed edition.[1] For the individual book-reader, however, different texts, which were previously dispersed and scattered, were also brought closer together. In some regions, printers produced more scholarly texts than they could sell and flooded local markets.[2] In all regions, a given purchaser could buy more books at lower cost and bring them into his study or library. In this way, the printer provided the clerk with a richer, more varied

Reprinted from Elizabeth L. Eisenstein, "Some Conjectures about the Impact of Printing on Western Society and Thought: A Preliminary Report," *Journal of Modern History* 40 (1968): 7–29, by permission of the University of Chicago Press, © 1968, by the University of Chicago Press and the author. In recent writing, including the afterword for *The Printing Revolution* (Cambridge University Press, 2005), Eisenstein expresses her dissatisfaction with any "impact" model. There she also deals with various controversies that have arisen since *The Printing Press as an Agent of Change* (Cambridge University Press) was published in 1979 and explains her choice of the term *revolution*.

literary diet than had been provided by the scribe. To consult different books it was no longer essential to be a wandering scholar. Successive generations of sedentary scholars were less apt to be engrossed by a single text and to expend their energies in elaborating on it. The era of the glossator and commentator came to an end, and a new "era of intense cross referencing between one book and another" began.[3] More abundantly stocked bookshelves increased opportunities to consult and compare different texts and, thus, also made more probable the formation of new intellectual combinations and permutations. Viewed in this light, cross-cultural interchanges fostered by printing seem relevant to Sarton's observation: "The Renaissance was a transmutation of values, a 'new deal,' a reshuffling of cards, but most of the cards were old; the scientific Renaissance was a 'new deal,' but many of the cards were new."[4] Combinatory intellectual activity, as Koestler has recently suggested, inspires many creative acts. Once old texts came together within the same study, diverse systems of ideas and special disciplines could be combined. Increased output directed at relatively stable markets, in short, created conditions that favored, first, new combinations of old ideas and, then, the creation of entirely new systems of thought.

Merely by making more scrambled data available, by increasing the output of second-century Ptolemaic maps and twelfth-century *mappae mundi*, for instance, printers encouraged efforts to unscramble these data. Hand-drafted portolans had long been more accurate, but few eyes had seen them.[5] Much as maps from different regions and epochs were brought into contact, so too were diverse textual traditions previously preserved by specially trained groups of schoolmen and scribes. It should be noted that cross-cultural interchange was not solely a consequence of augmented output. For example, texts were provided with new illustrations drawn from artisan workshops instead of scriptoria. Here again, different traditions were brought into contact. In this case, words drawn from one milieu and pictures from another were placed beside each other within the same books.[6] When considering new views of the "book of nature" or the linking of bookish theories with observations and craft skills, it may be useful to look at the ateliers of Renaissance artists. But one must also go on to visit early printers' workshops, for it is there above all that we "can observe the formation of groups . . . conducive to cross-fertilization" of all kinds.[7]

Cross-cultural interchange stimulated mental activities in contradictory ways. The first century of printing was marked above all by intellectual ferment and by a "somewhat wide-angled, unfocused scholarship."[8] Certain confusing cross-currents may be explained by noting that new links between disciplines were being forged before old ones had been severed. In the age of scribes, for instance, magical arts were closely associated with mechanical crafts. Trade skills were passed down by closed circles of initiates. Unwritten recipes used by the alchemist were not clearly distinguished from those used by the apothecary or surgeon, the goldsmith or engraver. When "technology went to press," so too did a vast backlog of occult lore, and few readers could discriminate between the two.

The divine art or "mystery" of printing unleashed a "churning turbid flood of Hermetic, cabbalistic, Gnostic, theurgic, Sabaean, Pythagorean, and generally mystic notions."[9] Historians are still puzzled by certain strange deposits left by this flood. They might find it helpful to consider how records derived from ancient Near Eastern cultures had been transmitted in the age of scribes. Some of these records had dwindled into tantalizing fragments pertaining to systems of reckoning, medicine, agriculture, mythic cults, and so forth. Others had evaporated into unfathomable glyphs. All were thought to come from one body of pure knowledge originally set down by an Egyptian scribal god and carefully preserved by ancient sages and seers before becoming corrupted and confused. A collection of writings containing ancient lore was received from Macedonia by Cosimo de' Medici, translated by Ficino in 1463, and printed in fifteen editions before 1500. It seemed to come from this body of knowledge—and was accordingly attributed to "Hermes Trismegistus." The hermetic corpus ran through many more editions during the next century before it was shown to have been compiled in the third century A.D. On this basis we are told that Renaissance scholars had made a radical error in dating.[10] But to assign definite dates to scribal compilations, which were probably derived from earlier sources, may be an error as well.

The transformation of occult and esoteric scribal lore after the advent of printing also needs more study. Some arcane writings, in Greek, Hebrew or Syriac, for example, became less mysterious. Others became more so. Thus hieroglyphs were set in type more than three centuries before their decipherment. These sacred carved letters were loaded with significant meaning by readers who could not read them.[11] They were also used simply as ornamental motifs by architects and engravers. Given baroque decoration on one hand and complicated interpretations by scholars, Rosicrucians, and Freemasons on the other, the duplication of Egyptian picture writing throughout the Age of Reason presents modern scholars with puzzles that can never be solved. In brief, when considering the effects produced by printing on scholarship, it is a mistake to think only about new forms of enlightenment. New forms of mystification were entailed as well.

It is also a mistake to think only about scholarly markets when considering the effects of increased output. Dissemination as defined in the dictionary does seem appropriate to the duplication of primers and *ABC* books, almanacs, and picture Bibles. An increased output of devotional literature was not necessarily conducive to cross-cultural interchange. Catechisms, religious tracts, and Bibles would fill some bookshelves to the exclusion of all other reading matter. A new wide-angled, unfocused scholarship had to compete with a new single-minded, narrowly focused piety. At the same time, guidebooks and manuals also became more abundant, making it easier to lay plans for getting ahead in this world—possibly diverting attention from uncertain futures in the next one. It is doubtful whether "the effect of the new invention on scholarship" was more important than these other effects "at the beginning of the sixteenth century."[12] What does need emphasis is that many dissimilar effects, all of great consequence, came relatively simultaneously. If this could be spelled out more clearly, seemingly contradictory developments might be confronted with more equanimity. The intensification of both religiosity and secularism could be better understood. Some debates about periodization also could be bypassed. Medieval world pictures, for example, were duplicated more rapidly during the first century of printing than they had been during the so-called Middle Ages. They did not merely *survive* among the Elizabethans. They became *more available* to poets and playwrights of the sixteenth century than they had been to minstrels and mummers of the thirteenth century.

In view of such considerations, I cannot agree with Sarton's comment: "It is hardly necessary to indicate what the art of printing meant for the diffusion of culture but one should not lay too much stress on diffusion and should speak more of standardization."[13] How printing changed patterns of cultural diffusion deserves much more study than it has yet received. Moreover, individual access to diverse texts is a different matter than bringing many minds to bear on a single text. The former issue is apt to be neglected by too exclusive an emphasis on "standardization."

Considering some effects produced by standardization

Although it has to be considered in conjunction with many other issues, standardization certainly does deserve closer study. One specialist has argued that it is currently overplayed.[14] Yet it may well be still understressed. Perhaps early printing methods made it impossible to issue the kind of "standard" editions with which modern scholars are familiar. Certainly press variants did multiply, and countless errata were issued. The fact remains that Erasmus or Bellarmine could issue errata; Jerome or Alcuin could not. The very act of publishing errata demonstrated a new capacity to locate textual errors with precision and to transmit this information simultaneously to scattered readers. It thus illustrates, rather neatly, some of the effects of standardization. However fourteenth-century copyists were supervised, scribes were incapable of committing the sort of "standardized" error that led printers to be fined for the "wicked Bible" of 1631.[15] If a single compositor's error could be circulated in a great many copies, so too could a single scholar's emendation.[16] However, when I suggest that we may still underestimate the implications of standardization, I am not thinking primarily about textual emendations or errors. I am thinking instead about the new output of exactly repeatable pictorial statements, such as maps, charts, diagrams, and other visual aids;[17] of more uniform reference guides, such as calendars, thesauruses, dictionaries; of increasingly regular systems of notation, whether musical, mathematical, or grammatical. How different fields of study and aesthetic styles were affected by such developments remains to be explored. It does seem worth suggesting that both our so-called two cultures were affected. Humanist scholarship, belles lettres, and fine arts must be considered along with celestial mechanics, anatomy, and cartography.[18]

Too many important variations were, indeed, played on the theme of standardization for all of them to be listed here. This theme entered into every operation associated with typography, from the replica casting of precisely measured pieces of type,[19] to the subliminal impact upon scattered readers of repeated encounters with identical type styles, printers' devices, and title-page ornamentation.[20] Calligraphy itself was affected. Sixteenth-century specimen books stripped diverse scribal "hands" of personal idiosyncrasies. They did for handwriting what style books did for typography itself; what pattern books did for dressmaking, furniture, architectural motifs, and ground plans. In short the setting of standards—used for innumerable purposes, from cutting cloth to city-planning—accompanied the output of more standardized products.

Here, as elsewhere, we need to recall that early printers were responsible not only for issuing new standard reference guides but also for compiling many of them.[21] A subsequent division of labor tends to divert attention from the large repertoire of roles performed by those who presided over the new presses. A scholar-printer himself might serve as indexer-abridger-lexicographer-chronicler. Whatever roles he performed, decisions about standards to be adopted when processing texts for publication could not be avoided. A suitable type style had to be selected or designed and house conventions determined. Textual variants and the desirability of illustration and translation also had to be confronted. Accordingly, the printer's workshop became the most advanced laboratory of erudition of the sixteenth century.

Many early capitalist industries required efficient planning, methodical attention to detail, and rational calculation. The decisions made by early printers, however, directly affected both toolmaking and symbol-making. Their products reshaped powers to manipulate objects, to perceive and think about varied phenomena. Scholars concerned with "modernization" or "rationalization" might profitably think more about the new kind of brainwork fostered by the silent scanning of maps, tables, charts, diagrams, dictionaries, and grammars. They also need to look more closely at the daily routines pursued by those who compiled and produced such reference guides. These routines were conducive to a new *esprit de système.* "It's much easier to find things when they are each disposed in place and not scattered haphazardly," remarked a sixteenth-century publisher.[22] He was justifying the way he had reorganized a text he had edited. He might equally well have been complaining to a clerk who had mislaid some account papers pertaining to the large commercial enterprise he ran.

Some effects produced by editing and reorganizing texts: Codifying, clarifying, and cataloguing data

Editorial decisions made by early printers with regard to layout and presentation probably helped to reorganize the thinking of readers. McLuhan's suggestion that scanning lines of print affected thought processes is at first glance somewhat mystifying. But further reflection suggests that the thoughts of readers are guided by the way the contents of books are arranged and presented. Basic changes in book format might well lead to changes in thought patterns. Such changes began to appear in the era of incunabula. They made texts more lucid and intelligible. They involved the use "of graduated types, running heads . . . footnotes . . . tables of contents . . . superior figures, cross references . . . and other devices available to the compositor"—all registering "the victory of the punch cutter over the scribe."[23] Concern with surface appearance necessarily governed the handwork of the scribe. He was fully preoccupied trying to shape evenly spaced uniform letters in a pleasing symmetrical design. An altogether different procedure was required to give directions to compositors. To do this, one had to mark up a manuscript while scrutinizing its contents. Every scribal text that came into the printer's hands, thus, had to be reviewed in a new way. Within a generation the results of this review were being aimed in a new direction—away from fidelity to scribal conventions and toward serving the convenience of the reader. The competitive and commercial character of the new mode of book production encouraged the relatively rapid adoption of any innovation that commended a given edition to purchasers. In short, providing built-in aids to the reader became for the first time both feasible and desirable.

The introduction and adoption of such built-in aids, from the 1480s on, has been traced and discussed in special works on printing but has been insufficiently noted in other accounts. We are repeatedly told about "dissemination," occasionally about standardization, almost never at all about the codification and clarification that were entailed in editing copy.[24] Yet changes affecting book format probably contributed much to the so-called rationalization of diverse institutions. After all, they affected texts used for the study and practice of law—and consequently had an impact on most organs of the body politic as well.[25] This has been demonstrated by a pioneering study of the "englishing and printing" of the "Great Boke of Statutes 1530–1533."[26] I cannot pause here over the many repercussions, ranging from statecraft to literature, that came in the wake of Tudor law-printing according to this study. To suggest why we need to look at new built-in aids, I will simply point to the introductory "Tabula" to the "Great Boke"; "a chronological register by chapters of the statutes 1327–1523." Here was a table of contents that also served as a "conspectus of parliamentary history"[27]—the first many readers had seen.

This sort of spectacular innovation, while deserving close study, should not divert attention from much less conspicuous but more ubiquitous changes. Increasing familiarity with regularly numbered pages, punctuation marks, section breaks, running heads, indexes, and so forth helped to reorder the thought of *all* readers, whatever their profession or craft. Hence countless activities were subjected to a new *esprit de système*. The use of arabic numbers for pagination suggests how the most inconspicuous innovation could have weighty consequences—in this case, more accurate indexing, annotation, and cross-referencing resulted.[28] Most studies of printing have quite rightly singled out the provision of title pages as the most important of all ubiquitous print-made innovations.[29] How the title page contributed to the cataloguing of books and the bibliographer's craft scarcely needs to be spelled out. How it contributed to a new habit of placing and dating in general does, I think, call for further thought.

On the whole, as I have tried to suggest throughout this discussion, topics now allocated to bibliophiles and specialists on printing are of general concern to historians at large—or, at least, to specialists in many different fields. The way these fields are laid out could be better understood, indeed, if we opened up the one assigned to printing. "Until half a century after Copernicus' death, no potentially revolutionary changes occurred in the data available to astronomers."[30] But Copernicus' life (1473–1543) spanned the very decades when a great many changes, now barely visible to modern eyes, were transforming "the data available" to all book-readers. A closer study of these changes could help to explain why systems of charting the planets, mapping the earth, synchronizing chronologies, and compiling bibliographies were all revolutionized before the end of the sixteenth century.[31] In each instance, one notes, ancient Alexandrian achievements were first reduplicated and then, in a remarkably short time, surpassed. In each instance also, the new schemes once published remained available for correction, development, and refinement. Successive generations of scholars could build on the work of their sixteenth-century predecessors instead of trying to retrieve scattered fragments of it.

The varied intellectual revolutions of early modern times owed much to the features that have already been outlined.[32] But the great tomes, charts, and maps that are now seen as "milestones" might have proved insubstantial had not the preservative powers of print also been called into play. Typographical fixity is a basic prerequisite for the rapid advancement of learning. It helps to explain much else that seems to distinguish the history of the past five centuries from that of all prior eras—as I hope the following remarks will suggest.

Considering the preservative powers of print: How fixity and accumulations altered patterns of cultural and institutional change

Of all the new features introduced by the duplicative powers of print, preservation is possibly the most important.[33] To appreciate its importance, we need to recall the conditions that prevailed before texts could be set in type. No manuscript, however useful as a reference guide, could be preserved for long without undergoing corruption by copyists, and even this sort of "preservation" rested precariously on the shifting demands of local elites and a fluctuating incidence of trained scribal labor. Insofar as records were seen and used, they were vulnerable to wear and tear. Stored documents were vulnerable to moisture and vermin, theft and fire. However they might be collected or guarded within some great message center, their ultimate dispersal and loss was inevitable. To be transmitted by writing from one generation to the next, information had to be conveyed by drifting texts and vanishing manuscripts.

When considering developments in astronomy (or geography or chronology) during the age of scribes, it is not the slow rate of cognitive advance that calls for explanation. Rather, one might wonder about how the customary process of erosion, corruption, and loss was temporarily arrested. When viewed in this light, the "1,800 years" that elapsed between Hipparchus and Copernicus[34] seems less remarkable than the advances that were made in planetary astronomy during the 600 years that elapsed between Aristotle and Ptolemy. With regard to all computations based on large-scale data collection, whatever had once been clearly seen and carefully articulated grew dimmed and blurred with the passage of time. More than a millennium also elapsed between Eratosthenes and Scaliger, Ptolemy and Mercator. The progress made over the course of centuries within the confines of the Alexandrian Museum seems, in short, to have been most exceptional.[35] To be sure, there were intermittent localized "revivals of learning" thereafter, as well as a prolonged accumulation of records within certain message centers. Ground lost by corruption could never be regained, but migrating manuscripts could lead to abrupt recovery as well as to sudden loss. Yet a marked increase in the output of certain kinds of texts resulted generally in a decreased output of other kinds. Similarly, a "revival" in one region often signified a dearth of texts in another.

The incapacity of scribal culture to sustain a simultaneous advance on many fronts in different regions may be relevant to the "problem of the Renaissance." Italian humanist book-hunters, patrons, and dealers tried to replenish a diminished supply of those ancient texts that were being neglected by scribes serving medieval university faculties. Their efforts have been heralded as bringing about a "permanent recovery" of ancient learning and letters.[36] If one accepts the criteria of "totality and permanence" to distinguish prior "revivals" from the Renaissance,[37] then probably the advent of the scholar-printer should be heralded instead. He arrived to cast his Greek types and turn out grammars, translations, and standard editions in the nick of time—almost on the eve of the Valois invasions.[38]

Once Greek type fonts had been cut, neither the disruption of civil order in Italy, the conquest of Greek lands by Islam, nor even the translation into Latin of all major Greek texts saw knowledge of Greek wither again in the West. Instead it was the familiar scribal phrase *Graeca sunt ergo non legenda* that disappeared from Western texts. Constantinople fell, Rome was sacked. Yet a cumulative process of textual purification and continuous recovery had been launched. The implications of typographical fixity are scarcely exhausted by thinking about early landmarks in classical scholarship and its auxiliary sciences: paleography, philology, archeology, numismatics, etc. Nor are they exhausted by reckoning the number of languages that have been retrieved after being lost to all men for thousands of years. They involve the whole modern "knowledge industry" itself, with its mushrooming bibliographies and overflowing card files.

They also involve issues that are less academic and more geopolitical. The linguistic map of Europe was "fixed" by the same process and at the same time as Greek letters were. The importance of the fixing of literary vernaculars is often stressed. The strategic role played by printing is, however, often overlooked.[39] How strategic it was is suggested by the following paraphrased summary of Steinberg's account:

> Printing "preserved and codified, sometimes even created" certain vernaculars. Its absence during the sixteenth century among small linguistic groups "demonstrably led" to the disappearance or execution of their vernaculars from the realm of literature. Its presence among

similar groups in the same century ensured the possibility of intermittent revivals or continued expansion. Having fortified language walls between one group and another, printers homogenized what was within them, breaking down minor differences, standardizing idioms for millions of writers and readers, assigning a new peripheral role to provincial dialects. The preservation of a given literary language often depended on whether or not a few vernacular primers, catechisms or Bibles happened to get printed (under foreign as well as domestic auspices) in the sixteenth century. When this was the case, the subsequent expansion of a separate "national" literary culture ensued. When this did not happen, a prerequisite for budding "national" consciousness disappeared; a spoken provincial dialect was left instead.[40]

Studies of dynastic consolidation and/or of nationalism might well devote more space to the advent of printing. Typography arrested linguistic drift, enriched as well as standardized vernaculars, and paved the way for the more deliberate purification and codification of all major European languages. Randomly patterned sixteenth-century typecasting largely determined the subsequent elaboration of national mythologies on the part of certain separate groups within multilingual dynastic states. The duplication of vernacular primers and translations contributed in other ways to nationalism. A "mother's tongue" learned "naturally" at home would be reinforced by inculcation of a homogenized print-made language mastered while still young, when learning to read. During the most impressionable years of childhood, the eye would first see a more standardized version of what the ear had first heard. Particularly after grammar schools gave primary instruction in reading by using vernacular instead of Latin readers, linguistic "roots" and rootedness in one's homeland would be entangled.

Printing helped in other ways to permanently atomize Western Christendom. Erastian policies long pursued by diverse rulers could, for example, be more fully implemented. Thus, the duplication of documents pertaining to ritual, liturgy, or canon law, handled under clerical auspices in the age of the scribe, was undertaken by enterprising laymen, subject to dynastic authority, in the age of the printer. Local firms, lying outside the control of the papal curia, were granted lucrative privileges by Habsburg, Valois, or Tudor kings to service the needs of national clergies.[41] The varied ways in which printers contributed to loosening or severing links with Rome, or to nationalist sentiment, or to dynastic consolidation cannot be explored here. But they surely do call for further study.[42]

Other consequences of typographical fixity also need to be explored. Religious divisions and legal precedents were affected. In fact, all the lines that were drawn in the sixteenth century (or thereafter), the condemnation of a heresy, the excommunication of a schismatic king, the settling of disputes between warring dynasts, schisms within the body politic—lines that prior generations had repeatedly traced, erased, retraced—would now leave a more indelible imprint. It was no longer possible to take for granted that one was following "immemorial custom" when granting an immunity or signing a decree. Edicts became more visible and irrevocable. The Magna Carta, for example, was ostensibly "published" (i.e., proclaimed) twice a year in every shire. By 1237 there was already confusion as to which "charter" was involved.[43] In 1533, however, Englishmen glancing over the "Tabula" of the "Great Boke" could see how often it had been repeatedly confirmed in successive royal statutes.[44] In France also the "mechanism by which the will of the sovereign" was incorporated into the "published" body of law by "registration" was probably altered by typographical fixity.[45] Much as M. Jourdain learned that he was speaking prose, monarchs learned from political theorists that they were "making" laws. But members of parliaments and assemblies also learned from jurists and printers about ancient rights wrongfully usurped. Struggles over the right to establish precedents probably became more intense as each precedent became more permanent and hence more difficult to break.

On the other hand, in many fields of activity, fixity led to new departures from precedent marked by more explicit recognition of individual innovation and by the staking of claims to inventions, discoveries, and creations. By 1500, legal fictions were already being devised to accommodate the patenting of inventions and the assignment of literary properties.[46] Upon these foundations, a burgeoning bureaucracy would build a vast and complex legal structure. Laws pertaining to licensing and privileges have been extensively studied. But they have yet to be examined as by-products of typographical fixity. Both the dissolution of guild controls and conflicts over mercantilist policies might be clarified if this were done. Once the rights of an inventor could be legally fixed and the problem of preserving unwritten recipes intact was no longer posed, profits could be achieved by open publicity, provided new restraints were not imposed. Individual initiative was released from reliance on guild protection, but at the same time new powers were lodged in the hands of a bureaucratic officialdom. Competition over the right to publish a given text also introduced controversy over new issues involving monopoly and piracy. Printing forced legal definition of what belonged in the public domain and clear articulation of how one sort of literary product differed from another.[47] When discussing the emergence of a new kind of individualism, it might be useful to recall that the eponymous inventor and personal authorship appeared at the same time and as a consequence of the same process.

The emergence of uniquely distinguished, personally famous artists and authors out of the ranks of more anonymous artisans and minstrels was also related to typographical fixity. Cheaper writing materials encouraged the separate recording of private lives and correspondence. Not paper mills but printing presses, however, made it possible to preserve personal ephemera intact. As an expanding manuscript culture found its way into print, formal compositions were accompanied by intimate anecdotes about the lives and loves of their flesh-and-blood authors. Was it the "inclination" to "publish gossip" that was new in the Renaissance,[48] or was it, rather, the possibility of doing so? The characteristic individuality of Renaissance masterpieces surely owes much to the new possibility of preserving the life-histories of those who produced them. As art historians have shown, the hands of medieval illuminators or stone-carvers were, in fact, no less distinctive. Their personalities remain unknown. Vestiges of their local celebrity have vanished. They must therefore be portrayed as faceless master guildsmen in terms of the garb they wore or the lifestyle they shared with colleagues. What applies to personality may also apply to versatility. Alberti probably was not the first architect who was also an athlete, orator, scholar, and artist. But he *was* the first whose after-dinner speeches, boasts about boyhood feats, and "serious and witty sayings" were collected and transmitted to posterity along with the buildings he designed and formal treatises he composed. He may be displayed at home and in public, as an athletic youth and elderly sage, moving through all the ages of man, personifying earlier archetypes and collective roles. Possibly this is why he appears to Burckhardt in the guise of a new ideal type, *homo universalis.*[49]

Similar considerations are also worth applying to authors. The personal hand and signature of the scribe was replaced by the more impersonal typestyle and colophon of the printer. Yet, by the same token, the personal, private, idiosyncratic views of the author could be extended through time and space. Articulating new concepts of selfhood, wrestling with the problem of speaking privately for publication, new authors (beginning, perhaps, with Montaigne) would redefine individualism in terms of deviation from the norm and divergence from the type. The "drive for fame" itself may have been affected by print-made immortality. The urge to scribble was manifested in Juvenal's day as it was in Petrarch's. But the *insanabile scribendi caeoethes* may have been reoriented once it became an "itch to publish."[50] The wish to see one's work in print (fixed forever with one's name, in card files and anthologies) is different from the urge to pen lines that could never get fixed in a permanent form, might be lost forever, altered by copying, or—if truly memorable—carried by oral transmission and assigned ultimately to "anon." When dealing with priority disputes among scientists or debates about plagiarism among scholars, the advent of print-made immortality has to be taken into account. Until it became possible to distinguish between composing a poem and reciting one or between writing a book and copying one, until books could be classified by something other than incipits, how could modern games of books and authors be played?

Many problems about assigning proper credit to scribal "authors" may result from misguided efforts to apply print-made concepts where they do not pertain. The so-called forged book of Hermes is a good case in point. But countless other scribal works are too. Who *wrote* Socrates' lines, Aristotle's works, Sappho's poems, any portion of the Scriptures? Troublesome questions about biblical composition, in particular, suggest how new forms of personal authorship helped to subvert old concepts of collective authority.[51] Veneration for the wisdom of the ages was probably modified as ancient sages were retrospectively cast in the role of individual authors—prone to human error and possibly plagiarists as well.[52] Treatment of battles of books between "ancients and moderns" might profit from more discussion of such issues. Since early printers were primarily responsible for forcing definition of literary property rights, for shaping new concepts of authorship, for exploiting bestsellers and trying to tap new markets, their role in this celebrated quarrel should not be overlooked. By the early sixteenth century, for example, staffs of translators were employed to turn out vernacular versions of the more popular works by ancient Romans and contemporary Latin-writing humanists.[53] This might be taken into account when discussing debates between Latinists and advocates of new vulgar tongues.[54]

It is also worth considering that different meanings may have been assigned terms such as "ancient" and "modern," "discovery" and "rediscovery," "invention" and "imitation" before important departures from precedent could be permanently recorded. "Throughout the patristic and medieval periods, the quest for truth is thought of as the *re*covery of what is embedded in tradition . . . rather than the *dis*covery of what is new."[55] Most scholars concur with this view. It must have been difficult to distinguish discovering something new from recovering it in the age of scribes. To "find a new art" was easily confused with retrieving a lost one, for superior techniques and systems of knowledge *were* frequently discovered by being recovered.[56] Probably Moses, Zoroaster, or Thoth had not "invented" all the arts that were to be found.[57] But many were retrieved from ancient giants whose works reentered the West by circuitous routes. The origins of such works were shrouded in mystery. Their contents revealed a remarkable technical expertise. Some pagan seers were believed to have been granted foreknowledge of the Incarnation. Possibly they had also been granted a special secret key to all knowledge by the same divine dispensation. Veneration for the wisdom of the ancients was not incompatible with the advancement of learning, nor was imitation incompatible with inspiration. Efforts to think and do as the ancients did might well reflect the hope of experiencing a sudden illumination or of coming closer to the original source of a pure, clear, and certain knowledge that a long Gothic night had obscured.

When unprecedented innovations did occur, moreover, there was no sure way of recognizing them before the advent of printing. Who could ascertain precisely what was known—either to prior generations within a given region or to contemporary inhabitants of far-off lands? "Steady advance," as Sarton says, "implies exact determination of every previous step." In has view, printing made this determination "incomparably easier."[58] He may have understated the case. *Exact* determination must have been impossible before printing. Given drifting texts, migrating manuscripts, localized chronologies, multiform maps, there could be no systematic forward movement, no accumulation of stepping stones enabling a new generation to begin where the prior one had left off. Progressive refinement of certain arts and skills could and did occur. But no sophisticated technique could be securely established, permanently recorded, and stored, for subsequent retrieval. Before trying to account for an "idea" of progress, we might look more closely at the duplicating process that made possible a continuous accumulation of fixed records. For it seems to have been permanence that introduced progressive change. The preservation of the old, in brief, launched a tradition of the new.

The advancement of learning had taken the form of a search for lost wisdom in the age of scribes. This search was rapidly propelled after printing. Ancient maps, charts, and texts once arranged and dated, however, turned out to be dated in more ways than one. Ordinary craftsmen and mariners appeared to know more things about the heavens and earth than were dreamt of by ancient sages. More schools of ancient philosophy than had previously been known were also uncovered. Scattered attacks on one authority by those who favored another provided ammunition for a wholesale assault on all received opinion. Incompatible portions of inherited traditions were sloughed off, partly because the task of preservation had become less urgent. Copying, memorizing, and transmitting absorbed fewer energies. Some were released to explore what still might be learned. Studying variant versions of God's words gave way to contemplating the uniformity of His works. Investigation of the "book of nature" was no longer undertaken by studying old glyphs and ciphers. Magic and science were divorced. So too were poetry and history. Useful reference books were no longer blotted out or blurred with the passage of time. Cadence and rhyme, images and symbols, ceased to fulfill their traditional function of preserving the collective memory. The aesthetic experience became increasingly autonomous, and the function of works of art had to be redefined. Technical information could be conveyed more directly by plain expository prose and accurate illustration. Although books on the memory arts multiplied after printing, practical reliance on these arts decreased. Scribal schemes eventually petrified, to be ultimately reassembled, like fossil remains, by modern research. The special formulas that had preserved recipes and techniques among closed circles of initiates also disappeared. Residues of mnemonic devices were transmuted into mysterious images, rites, and incantations.[59]

Nevertheless, scribal veneration for ancient learning lingered on, long after the conditions that had fostered it had gone. Among Rosicrucians and Freemasons, for example, the belief persisted that the "new philosophy" was in fact very old. Descartes and Newton had merely retrieved the same magical key to nature's secrets that had once been known to ancient pyramid-builders but was later withheld from the laity or deliberately obscured by a deceitful priesthood. In fact, the Index came only after printing, and the preservation of pagan learning owed much to monks and friars. Enlightened freethinkers, however, assigned Counter-Reformation institutions to the Gothic Dark Ages and turned Zoroaster into a Copernican. Similarly, once imitation was detached from inspiration and copying from composing, the classical revival became increasingly arid and academic. The search for primary sources was assigned to dry-as-dust pedants. But the reputation of ancient seers, bards, and prophets was not, by the same token, diminished. Claims to have inherited their magic mantle were put forth by new romanticists who reoriented the meaning of the term "original" and tried to resurrect scribal arts in the age of print. Even the "decay of nature" theme, once intimately associated with the erosion and corruption of scribal writings, would be reworked and reoriented by gloomy modern prophets who felt that regress, not progress, characterized their age.

Amplification and reinforcement: Accounting for persistent stereotypes and increasing cultural differentiation

Many other themes imbedded in scribal writings, detached from the living cultures that had shaped them, were propelled as "typologies" on printed pages. Over the course of time, archetypes were converted into stereotypes, the language of giants, as Merton puts it, into the clichés of dwarfs. Both "stereotype" and "cliché" are terms deriving from a typographical process developed three and a half centuries after Gutenberg. They point, however, to certain other features of typographical culture in general that deserve closer consideration. During the past five centuries, broadcasting new messages has also entailed amplifying and reinforcing old ones. I hope my use of the terms "amplify" and "reinforce" will not distract attention from the effects they are meant to designate. I am using them simply because I have found no others that serve as well. Some such terms are needed to cover the effects produced by an ever-more-frequent repetition of identical chapters and verses, anecdotes and aphorisms, drawn from very limited scribal sources. This repetition is not produced by the constant republication of classical, biblical, or early vernacular works, although it undoubtedly sustains markets for such works. It is produced by an unwitting collaboration between countless authors of new books or articles. For five hundred years, authors have jointly transmitted certain old messages with augmented frequency even while separately reporting on new events or spinning out new ideas. Thus, if they happen to contain only one passing reference to the heroic stand at Thermopylae, a hundred reports on different military campaigns will impress with a hundredfold-impact Herodotus' description on the mind of the reader who scans such reports. Every dissimilar report of other campaigns will be received only once. As printed materials proliferate, this effect becomes more pronounced. (I have encountered several references to Thermopylae in the daily newspaper during the past year.) The same is true of numerous other messages previously inscribed on scarce and scattered manuscripts. The more wide-ranging the reader at present, the more frequent will be the encounter with the identical version and the deeper the impression it will leave. Since book-writing authors are particularly prone to wide-ranging reading, a multiplying "feedback" effect results. When it comes to coining familiar quotations, describing familiar episodes, originating symbols or stereotypes, the ancients will generally outstrip the moderns. How many times has Tacitus' description of freedom-loving Teutons been repeated since a single manuscript of *Germania* was discovered in a fifteenth-century monastery? And in how many varying contexts—Anglo-Saxon, Frankish, as well as German—has this particular description appeared?

The frequency with which all messages were transmitted was primarily channeled by the fixing of literary linguistic frontiers. A particular kind of reinforcement was involved in relearning mother tongues when learning to read. It went together with the progressive amplification of diversely oriented national "memories." Not all the same portions of an inherited Latin culture were translated into different vernaculars at the same time.[60] More important, entirely dissimilar dynastic, municipal, and ecclesiastical chronicles, along with other local lore, both oral and scribal, were also set in type and more permanently fixed. The meshing of provincial medieval *res gestæ* with diverse classical and scriptural sources had, by the early seventeenth century, imbedded distinctively different stereotypes within each separate vernacular literature.[61] At the same time, to be sure, a more cosmopolitan *Respublica litterarum* was also expanding, and messages were broadcast across linguistic frontiers, first via Latin, then French, to an international audience. But messages received from abroad were not amplified over the course of several centuries in the same way. They only occasionally reinforced what was learned in familiar tongues at home.[62]

On the other hand, the fixing of religious frontiers that cut across linguistic ones in the sixteenth century had a powerful effect on the frequency with which certain messages were transmitted. Passages drawn from vernacular translations of the Bible, for example, would be much more thinly and weakly distributed throughout the literary cultures of Catholic regions than of Protestant ones.[63] The abandonment of church Latin in Protestant regions made it possible to mesh ecclesiastical and dynastic traditions more closely within Protestant realms than in Catholic ones—a point worth noting when considering how church-state conflicts were resolved in different lands. Finally, the unevenly phased social penetration of literacy, the somewhat more random patterning of book-reading habits, and the uneven distribution of costly new books and cheap reprints of old ones among different social sectors also affected the frequency with which diverse messages were received within each linguistic group.

Notes

1. Since this enabled scattered readers to consult the same book, it may be regarded as an aspect of standardization, which is discussed in the next section.

2. Early crises of overproduction of humanist works are noted by Denis Hay, "Literature, the Printed Book," in G. R. Elton (ed.), *The New Cambridge Modern History* (Cambridge, 1958), 2:365. The failure of printers to assess their markets shrewdly, which accounts for some of these crises, is noted by Curt F. Bühler, *The Fifteenth Century Book: The Scribes, The Printers, the Decorators* (Philadelphia, 1960), 59–61. Inadequate distribution networks at first were largely responsible. Zainer's firm, e.g., turned out 36,000 books when the population of Augsburg was half that number (Bühler, 56).

3. Hay, 366. By the mid-sixteenth century, "even obscure scholars could possess a relatively large collection of books on a single topic," according to A. R. Hall, "Science," in Elton, 2:389.

4. George Sarton, "The Quest for Truth: Scientific Progress during the Renaissance," in W. K. Ferguson et al., *The Renaissance: Six Essays*, Metropolitan Museum of Art Symposium, 1953 (New York, 1962), 57.

5. These maps are compared and the superiority of manuscript charts to early printed maps is noted by Boies Penrose, *Travel and Discovery in the Renaissance, 1420–1620* (New York, 1962), chap. 16. The logical conclusion—that intelligent, literate sixteenth-century printers did not know what cartographers and mariners in coastal regions did—is, however, not drawn.

6. See R. J. Forbes and E. J. Dijksterhuis, *A History of Science and Technology* (London, 1963), vol. 2, chap. 16, on how "technology went to press" in the sixteenth century. A. R. Hall, *The Scientific Revolution, 1500–1800: The Formation of the Modern Scientific Attitude* (Boston, 1957), 43, states: "Vesalius' cuts are sometimes less traditional and more accurate than his text." The cuts were made, however, by a wood-carver, Stephan of Calcar. (See n. 7 below.)

7. Erwin Panofsky, "Artist, Scientist, Genius: Notes on Renaissance-Dämmerung," in Ferguson et al., 160. This whole essay (which passes over the role of printing) is relevant to the above discussion. Stephan of Calcar's role in Vesalius' work is noted on 162, n. 36.

8. E. Harris Harbison, *The Christian Scholar in the Age of the Reformation* (New York, 1956), 54.

9. G. de Santillana, review of F. Yates's *Giordano Bruno and the Hermetic Tradition, American Historical Review* 70 (Jan. 1965), 455.

10. See Frances Yates, *Giordano Bruno and the Hermetic Tradition* (London, 1964), passim. That ancient Egyptian ingredients *were* present in the third-century compilation is suggested on 2–3, n. 4, and 431.

11. On the "Hieroglyphics of Horapollo" (first printed by Aldus in Greek, 1505, in Latin, 1515) and later developments, see Erik Iversen, *The Myth of Egypt and Its Hieroglyphs in European Tradition* (Copenhagen, 1961), passim. Additional data are given by E. P. Goldschmidt, *The Printed Book of the Renaissance: Three Lectures on Type, Illustration, Ornament* (Cambridge, 1950), 84–85, and Mario Praz, *Studies in Seventeenth Century Imagery* (Rome, 1964), chap. 1. Yates implies that baroque argumentation about *hermetica* ended with Isaac Casaubon's early seventeenth-century proof that Ficino had translated works dating from the third century A.D. But Greek scholarship alone could not unlock the secrets of the pyramids. Interest in arcana associated with Thoth and "Horapollo" continued until Champollion. By then the cluster of mysteries that had thickened with each successive "unveiling of Isis" was so opaque that even the decipherment of the Rosetta stone could not dispel them.

12. Myron Gilmore, *The World of Humanism, 1453–1517* (*Rise of Modern Europe*) (New York, 1952), 189.

13. Sarton, 66.

14. On what follows, see remarks by M. H. Black, "The Printed Bible," in S. J. Greenslade (ed.), *The Cambridge History of the Bible* (Cambridge, 1963), 408–14.

15. The word "not" had been omitted from the seventh commandment (ibid., 412).

16. How important this was is stressed both by Gilmore, 189, and Sarton, 66.

17. The historical importance of new standardized images is spelled out most clearly by William Ivins. K. Boulding, *The Image* (Ann Arbor, Mich., 1961), 64–68, who incorrectly assigns to the invention of writing the capacity to produce uniform spatiotemporal images. His remarks about the "dissociated transcript" do not seem applicable to scribal culture.

18. Ernst Curtius, *European Literature and the Latin Middle Ages,* trans. W. Trask (New York, 1963; 1st ed., 1948), exemplifies erudite humanistic scholarship at its best. Yet his remarks on scribal book production are remarkably fanciful and on changes wrought by printing entirely vacuous (238). His failure to consider how all the issues he deals with were affected by the new technology is shared by most literary scholars and historians of ideas.

19. See S. H. Steinberg, *Five Hundred Years of Printing* (rev. ed., Bristol, 1961), 25.

20. The probable effect of title-page ornamentation on sixteenth-century fine arts and the necessity of taking printing into account when dealing with new aesthetic styles is noted by André Chastel, "What Is Mannerism?" *Art News* 64 (Dec. 1965), 53.

21. This applies particularly to the publisher-printer (or printer-bookseller) as described, e.g., by Elizabeth Armstrong, *Robert Estienne, Royal Printer: An Historical Study of the Elder Stephanus* (Cambridge, 1954), 18, 68. It is also applicable to many independent master printers, to some merchant-publishers (who, literally defined, were not printers at all and yet closely supervised the processing of texts—even editing and compiling some themselves), and finally to some skilled journeymen (who served as correctors or were charged with throwing together, from antiquated stock, cheap reprints for mass markets). The divergent social and economic positions occupied by these groups are discussed by Natalie Z. Davis in "Strikes and Salvation at Lyons," *Archiv für Reformationsgeschichte* 65 (1965), 48, and in "Publisher Guillaume Rouillé, Businessman and Humanist," in R. J. Schoeck (ed.), *Editing Sixteenth Century Texts* (Toronto, 1966), 73-76. Within workshops down through the eighteenth century, divisions of labor varied so widely and were blurred so frequently that they must be left out of account for the purpose of developing my conjectures. Accordingly I use the term "printer" very loosely to cover all these groups throughout this paper.

22. Cited by Davis, "Guillaume Rouillé," 100.

23. Steinberg, 28. A detailed account of the effects of printing on punctuation is given by Rudolph Hirsch, *Printing, Selling, Reading, 1450-1550* (Wiesbaden, 1967), 136-37.

24. The "diagrammatic tidiness" imparted by print to "the world of ideas" is discussed by Walter J. Ong, S.J., *Ramus: Method and the Decay of Dialogue from the Art of Discourse to the Art of Reason* (Cambridge, Mass., 1958), 311. See also his "System, Space and Intellect in Renaissance Symbolism," *Bibliothéque d'humanisme et Renaissance—travaux et documents* 18, no. 2 (1956), 222-40; and his "From Allegory to Diagram in the Renaissance Mind," *Journal of Aesthetics and Art Criticism* 17 (June 1959), 4. Father Ong's somewhat abstruse discussion has recently been substantiated and supplemented by a straightforward study of changes registered on repeated editions of a popular sixteenth-century reference work, which provides detailed confirmation of the above discussion. See Gerald Strauss, "A Sixteenth Century Encyclopedia: Sebastian Münster's *Cosmography* and Its Editions," in C. H. Carter (ed.), *From the Renaissance to the Counter Reformation: Essays in Honor of Garret Mattingly* (New York, 1965), 145-63. See also the

discussion of Robert Estienne's pioneering work in lexicography (in Armstrong, chap. 4), and Davis, "Gulliaume Rouillé, 100–101.

25. The interplay between the printing of existing laws and laws pertaining to (or necessitated by) printing is an instance of complex interaction that deserves special study.

26. H. J. Graham, "'Our Tongue Maternall Marvellously Amendyd and Augmentyd': The First Englishing and Printing of the Medieval Statutes at Large, 1530–1533," *U.C.L.A. Law Bulletin* 13 (Nov. 1965), 58–98.

27. Ibid., 66.

28. G. Sarton, "Incunabula Wrongly Dated," in D. Stimson (ed.), *Sarton on the History of Science* (Cambridge, Mass., 1962), 322–23. Arabic numerals appear for the first time on each page of the Scriptures in Froben's first edition of Erasmus' New Testament of 1516, which also "set the style" for the well-differentiated book and chapter headings employed by other Bible-printers (Black, 419). See also Francis J. Witty, "Early Indexing Techniques: A Study of Several Book Indexes of the Fourteenth, Fifteenth, and Early Sixteenth Centuries," *Library Quarterly* 25 (July 1965), 141–48.

29. Steinberg, 145–53.

30. Thomas Kuhn, *The Copernican Revolution* (Cambridge, Mass., 1957), 131.

31. Ortelius' "epoch-making" *Theatrum orbis terrarum* was published in Antwerp in 1570. (Although Mercator's "milestone" was published in 1569, his new projection remained little known until 1599, when Edward Wright published a set of rules for its construction.) See Penrose, 324–27. Lucien Febvre and H. J. Martin, *L'Apparition du Livre (L'Evolution de l'Humanité)*, vol. 49 (Paris, 1958), 418, point to the fact that Copernicus' *De revolutionibus orbium cælistium* (1543) was not republished in a second edition until 1566 to support the view that printing did not speed up the acceptance of new ideas. In 1551, however, Erasmus Reinhold issued a "complete new set of astronomical tables," based on the *De revolutionibus*. These so-called Prutenic Tables were widely used. See Kuhn, 125, 187–88. The duplication of Napier's logarithms and their use by Kepler in constructing his Rudolphine Tables also seem to me to argue against Febvre and Martin's thesis. See Arthur Koestler, *The Sleepwalkers* (London, 1959), 410–11. J. J. Scaliger's *De emendatione temporum,* which "revolutionized all received ideas of chronology," was published in 1583; R. C. Christie and J. E. Sandys, "Joseph Justus Scaliger (1540–1609)," *Encyclopædia Britannica* (11th ed.; New York, 1911), 24:284. Theodore Besterman, *The Beginnings of Systematic Bibliography* (Oxford, 1936), 7–8, 15–21, 33, argues that Conrad Gesner's *Bibliotheca universalis* (1545), a 1,300-page tome listing 12,000 Latin, Greek, and Hebrew works, does not warrant calling Gesner the "father of bibliography," since Johannes Tritheim's much smaller and restricted *Liber de scriptoribus ecclesiasticus* (1494) preceded it. The "foundations of systematic bibliography were well and truly laid" at any rate before 1600.

32. The issues dealt with by studies such as F. Smith Fussner's *The Historical Revolution: English Historical Writing and Thought, 1580–1640* (London, 1962), and Wylie Sypher's "Similarities between the Scientific and Historical Revolutions

at the End of the Renaissance," *Journal of the History of Ideas* 25 (July–Sept. 1965), 353–68, need particularly to be reviewed in the light of the above discussion.

33. For the most part, I have omitted from this section issues relating to historical consciousness and historiography, since I have discussed them elsewhere; Elizabeth L. Eisenstein, "Clio and Chronos: An Essay on the Making and Breaking of History-Book Time," *History and the Concept of Time* (*History and Theory*, Suppl. 6 [1966]), 42–64. Certain portions of this essay seemed too pertinent to be excluded, however. They have, therefore, been repeated in a slightly altered form and reworked along with fresh material into a different context here.

34. Kuhn, 73, remarks on this "incredibly long time."

35. The strategic position occupied by this unique ancient message center (which apparently swallowed up the contents of its only rival in Pergamum in the first century B.C. to make up for losses suffered in the famous fire) has only recently become apparent to me. Possibly it is well known to specialists in ancient history, "but it still needs to be spelled out in more general accounts." According to Edward A. Parsons, *The Alexandrian Library* (Amsterdam, 1952), xi, the actual use of the museum by scholars over the course of seven (maybe nine) centuries "is still a virgin field of inquiry."

36. Like almost all other Renaissance scholars, Kristeller (P.O. Kristeller, *Renaissance Thought*, vol. 1: *The Classic, Scholastic and Humanist Strains* [New York, 1961], 17), while noting that a selection of the "classics" circulated in medieval times, singles out as the special contribution of Renaissance humanism that "it extended its knowledge almost to the entire range of . . . extant remains." This boils down to the fact that most of what was recovered in the trecento and early quattrocento was not again lost. But it came very close to being lost. The manuscript of *De return natura* found by Poggio Bracciolini in 1417 *has* disappeared. The future of the copy that was made remained uncertain until 1473, when a printed edition was issued. Thirty more followed before 1600. A school of pagan philosophy intermittently revived and repeatedly snuffed out was thus permanently secured. See Danton B. Sailor, "Moses and Atomism," *Journal of the History of Ideas* 25 (Jan.–Mar. 1964), 3–16. Other findings from palimpsests and papyri would come later, as Kristeller notes. They came too late to be inserted into a curriculum of classical studies that was "fixed" (by typography) in the sixteenth century. Hence they are regarded as being somewhat peripheral to the central corpus of classical works.

37. These same criteria, employed implicitly by Kristeller, are more explicitly and forcefully set forth by Erwin Panofsky, *Renaissance and Renascences in Western Art* (Stockholm, 1960), 108, 113. The capacity to view antiquity from a "fixed distance" is, in my view, placed much too early in this study.

38. Burckhardt notes as a "singular piece of good fortune" that "Northerners like Agricola, Reuchlin, Erasmus, the Stephani and Budaeus" had mastered Greek when it was dying out—with the "last colony" of Byzantine exiles—in the 1520s in Italy; Jacob Burckhardt, *The Civilization of the Renaissance in Italy*, trans. S. G. C. Middlemore (New York, 1958), 1:205. The Aldine Press (among others) had already insured its perpetuation, however. All these "northerners," one notes, were

close allies of scholar-printers or (as with the "Stephani," i.e., Estiennes) famous printers themselves.

39. Compare abundance of relevant data in Febvre and Martin, chap. 8, with what is missing in H. Stuart Hughes, *History as Art and as Science* (New York, 1964), 38–40, where the relation between linguistic fixity and nationalism, individualism, capitalism, and the nation-state is discussed. Hughes urges historians to make use of linguistic studies, but linguists, while careful to discriminate between "spoken" and "written" languages, say little about scribal versus printed ones. Judging by my own experience, books on linguistics are most difficult to master and seem to lead far afield. I found the reverse to be true when consulting literature on printing.

40. Steinberg, 120–26. Cases pertaining to Cornish, Cymric, Gaelic, Latvian, Estonian, Lithuanian, Finnish, Pomeranian, Courlander, Czech, Basque, etc., are cited. Of course, other factors may have been at work in other instances than those cited, but the number of instances where sixteenth-century typecasting seems to have been critical is noteworthy.

41. R. M. Kingdon, "Patronage, Piety, and Printing in Sixteenth-Century Europe," in D. H. Pinkney and T. Ropp (eds.), *A Festschrift for Frederick B. Artz* (Durham, N.C., 1964), 32–33, offers a detailed view of how Plantin's Antwerp firm implemented the Erastian policy of Philip II in order to evade payments to a rival firm (none other than Manutius) that had been granted the concession to print Catholic breviaries by Rome. Graham, 71–72, also shows how closely allied Thomas Cromwell was with a circle of law-printers led by Thomas More's brother-in-law, John Rastell—an independent crusader for "Englishing" all law, French or Latin, canon or civil.

42. By pursuing this line of inquiry, one could usefully supplement the theoretical views developed by Karl Deutsch *(Nationalism and Social Communication: An Inquiry into the Foundations of Nationality* [Cambridge, Mass., 1953]) with a more empirical, historically grounded approach.

43. J. C. Holt, *Magna Carta* (Cambridge, 1965), 288–90.

44. Graham, 93.

45. Franklin Ford, *Robe and Sword (Harvard Historical Studies,* vol. 64 [Cambridge, Mass., 1953]), 80, describes this mechanism—not, however, how it was altered. See also his remarks about the "great advance in publicity techniques" and how major parlement remonstrances were being "published" by 1732 in printed form (101).

46. A landmark in the history of literary property rights came in 1469, when a Venetian printer obtained a privilege to print and sell a given book for a given interval of time. See C. Blagden, *The Stationers Company: A History, 1403–1959* (London, 1960), 32. According to Forbes and Dijksterhuis, 1:147, although occasional privileges had been granted previously, the state of Venice was also the first to provide legal protection for inventors in 1474.

47. Raymond Birn, "Journal des savants sous l'Ancien Régime," *Journal des savants* (1965), 29, 33, shows how diverse fields of learning (and a division between "serious" and "frivolous" literature) were clearly defined by the terms of the official privilege

granted this journal to cover a wide variety of different topics of serious concern. Both this article and Fredrick S. Siebert's *Freedom of the Press in England, 1476–1776: The Rise and Decline of Government Control* (Urbana, Ill., 1952), passim, suggest how laws regulating printing raised new issues pertaining to privilege and monopoly, which became an acute source of conflict down through the eighteenth century.

48. P. O. Kristeller, *Renaissance Thought,* vol. 2: *Papers on Humanism and the Arts* (New York, 1965), 11.

49. Burckhardt, 1:149–50.

50. See a witty discussion of these terms by Robert K. Merton, *On the Shoulders of Giants: A Shandean Postscript* (New York, 1965), 83–85.

51. The issue of authorship versus authority is discussed by Marshall McLuhan, *The Gutenberg Galaxy: The Making of Typographic Man* (Toronto, 1962), 130–37. The nature of medieval scribal authorship is brilliantly illuminated E. Ph. Goldschmidt, *Medieval Texts and Their First Appearance in Print* (London, 1943), part 3.

52. See the citation from Glanvill's *Essays* of 1676 cited by Merton, 68 n. Ramus, in the 1530s, had already stated, "All that Aristotle has said is forged," according to H. Baker, *The Wars of Truth* (Cambridge, Mass., 1952), 93.

53. Febvre and Martin, 410. Additional data on the production of vernacular as opposed to Latin works during the first century of printing is supplied by Hirsch, 132–34.

54. Hans Baron's "The Querelle of the Ancients and Moderns as a Problem for Renaissance Scholarship," *Journal of the History of Ideas* 20 (Jan. 1959), 3–22, like many other treatments of this battle of books, passes over the possible role played by printers. Curtius, 251–56, covers the scribal use of terms such as "ancients" and "moderns" but fails to note how they were altered after printing. All of Merton's (tongue in cheek) treatment of the giant and dwarf aphorism is also relevant and points to a vast literature on the topic.

55. Harbison, 5.

56. E. Rosen, "The Invention of Eyeglasses," *Journal of the History of Medicine and Allied Sciences* 11 (1956), 34, n. 99, regards an early fourteenth-century preacher as inconsistent when he is recorded as saying in one sermon, "Nothing remains to be said . . . today a new book could not be made nor a new art" and in a preceding one referring to "all the arts that have been found by man and new ones yet to be found." *Finding* a new art was not, however, necessarily equivalent to *making* one.

57. The Italian word for "invention" has been located only once in fourteenth-century literature—a reference by Petrarch to Zoroaster as the *inventore* of the magic arts (ibid., 192). Thoth (or "Hermes Trismegistus") was responsible for inventing writing and numbering or measurement. Adam had, of course, named all things and (in a prelapsarian state) may have also known all things. A full inventory would include countless other (often overlapping) ancient claimants to the role of originators.

58. Sarton, "Quest for Truth," 66.

59. The most recent study is Frances Yates's *The Art of Memory* (London, 1966), which centers on use made of "memory theaters." According to J. Finegan, *Handbook of Biblical Chronology* (Princeton, N.J., 1964), 57, the term "Amen" encapsu-

lated in the three Hebrew letters aleph, mem, and nun (to which different numbers were assigned) a scheme for remembering four ninety-one day seasons of the solar year. When consulting works on this topic, I find it difficult to decide whether the ingenuity of modern scholars or that of ancient ones is being displayed.

60. H. S. Bennett, *English Books and Readers, 1475-1557* (Cambridge, 1952), 158, notes a "striking difference" between the large number of pagan classics translated into French in the sixteenth century and the greater number of "edifying" devotional works translated into English.

61. How this was done in sixteenth-century England is traced with remarkable clarity by William Haller, *The Elect Nation: The Meaning and Relevance of Foxe's Book of Martyrs* (New York, 1963), passim—an exceptional work that integrates printing with other historical developments. Children's books about Elizabeth I are still being written from bits and pieces drawn from Foxe's massive *apologia*.

62. The most important exceptions are France and Geneva, where by the mid-seventeenth century two differently oriented native literary cultures coincided with a single cosmopolitan one. A sounding board was thus provided for Rousseau, Mme. de Staël, Sismondi, and other Genevans who might otherwise have been as obscure as their German, Swiss, or Dutch counterparts. The reasons for the conquest of the Gallic tongue (which paradoxically linked the most populous and powerful consolidated dynastic Catholic state with the tiny canton that had served as the protestant Rome and with the cosmopolitan culture of civilized Europe) deserve further study. Louis Réau, *L'Europe française au Siècle des Lumières (L'Evolution de l'humanité,* vol. 70 [Paris, 1938]), although devoted to this important topic, slides over issues that need more rigorous analysis. David Pottinger, *The French Book Trade in the Ancien Regime, 1500-1791* (Cambridge, Mass., 1958), 19-23, offers some useful statistics, as does Steinberg, 118. Some further consequences of the spread of French are touched on in Eisenstein, "Some Conjectures," 51, 52. One might note that the reaction to French armies and the rejection of French influence, among Germans and eastern Europeans in the early nineteenth century, necessarily involved disowning the cosmopolitan culture of the Enlightenment as well.

63. R. A. Sayce, "French Continental Versions to c. 1600," in Greenslade, 114, contrasts the deep penetration of vernacular scriptural versions into the literary culture of German- and English-speaking peoples with the shallow effect of French Bible translations. From Pascal to Gide, he notes, Latin citations from the Vulgate appear most frequently when biblical references are evoked. The immense repercussions of the decision taken by the Council of Trent to proscribe vernacular translations and uphold the "authenticity" of the Vulgate are difficult to locate throughout this massive collaborative volume. A clear view of how, when, and where the decision itself was taken is not offered. F. J. Crehan, S.J., "The Bible in the Roman Catholic Church from Trent to the Present Day," 199-237, ostensibly covers this issue but actually obfuscates it.

4 THE IMPORTANCE OF BEING PRINTED

Anthony T. Grafton

Anyone who wishes to know what an early printing-house was like should begin with the *Orthotypographia* of Jerome Hornschuch. The engraving by Moses Thym that precedes Hornschuch's text shows a printer's staff hard at work. In one small room a compositor sets type, a corrector reads copy, a warehouseman sorts paper, a printer and an inker work a hand-press, and a workman lifts wet sheets to dry on a ceiling-level rack. In the background, a girl comes through the door, clutching a mug of beer, the pressman's traditional perquisite; in a corner, an author speaks excitedly to an unidentified companion. In the foreground, dominating the scene, stands the master-printer—a majestic, Prospero-like figure, who seems to be counting on his fingers.[1]

The picture alone reveals some of the complexities and the fascination of early printing and, above all, its unprecedented employment under one roof of intellectuals and craftsmen, scholars and entrepreneurs. Hornschuch's text tells us even more. It was written by and for correctors, the new class of educated printing workers. It demanded that they master a range of skills no earlier job would have required. They had to grasp the mechanics of printing and the intellectual principles of consistent spelling, punctuation, and proofreading. It asked the author as well as the printer to stretch himself. He was required to appreciate the possibilities printing offered for exact and attractive reproduction of his work, to learn to give his printers clean copy, to help them choose an appropriate type-face, and to leave them alone to get on with printing and proofreading his work. Publication as we know it, that drawn-out struggle among author, businessmen, and craftsmen, had come into being.

Early modern historians have long been interested in this strange little world of the printing-house. Eisenstein challenges them to do more. The burden of her book is that the printing-house was more than an important locus of cultural and social change; it was the crucible in which modern

Reprinted from *The Journal of Interdisciplinary History* 11 (1980): 265–86, with the permission of the editors of *The Journal of Interdisciplinary History* and the MIT Press, Cambridge, Massachusetts. © 1980 by the Massachusetts Institute of Technology and The Journal of Interdisciplinary History, Inc.

Figure 4.1. A Renaissance printing-house. From Jerome Hornschuch, *Orthotypographia* (Leipzig, 1608).

culture was formed. But since cultural historians have persistently ignored its pervasive influence, they have given a distorted account of the Renaissance, the Reformation, and the Scientific Revolution.

Eisenstein began to work this thesis out more than a decade ago. She developed it in a series of brilliant polemical articles, all of them distinguished by absolute independence from received ideas, an extraordinary range of interests, and a considerable breadth of knowledge. Now she has stated it in the powerful form of a two-volume study teeming with ideas and information. No historian of early modern Europe will be able to avoid a confrontation with the problems she has raised; for that alone we owe her a great debt.[2]

To be sure, Eisenstein is far too learned and too subtle a scholar to claim that printing by itself brought about the Renaissance, the Reformation, and the Scientific Revolution. Nor does she claim that it affected every area of culture in the same way. Indeed, one of the great strengths of her book is its insistence on the enormous variety and frequent contradictoriness of the developments linked with printing. Yet it is still clear that she sees printing as far more than one among many "factors in modern history." It changed the directions of existing cultural movements as suddenly and completely as a prism bends and transforms a beam of light. If printing did not create the Renaissance, for example, it nonetheless made it undergo a sea change. Printing made an Italian movement of limited scope and goals into a European one. It preserved in unprecedented quantities and disseminated at an unprecedented speed the classical discoveries of humanists, thus preventing their classical revival from being as limited and transitory as those of the Carolingian period and the twelfth century. And it made enough sources of information about the past available to all readers so that men came for the first time to see the ancient world as something clearly different from their own. Without printing, the characteristic Renaissance sense of history and sensitivity to anachronism could never have widely established themselves.

In the field of religion, printing had rather different effects. It spread Luther's message with amazing speed and so preserved it from the suppression that had been the fate of medieval heresies. But that, after all, has long been a commonplace of Reformation historiography. For Eisenstein, the role of printing in preparing the way for the Reformation holds more interest than its role in spreading it. She argues persuasively that the printing press did much to undermine the authority of the Church simply by making available to a wide public biblical texts, with all of their apparent contradictions, as well as by spreading new forms of devotional literature and changing old ones.

For science, finally, printing served still other ends. By making available complete and newly accurate texts of the great ancient works, above all those of Ptolemy and Galen, it created a new foundation of theories, methods, and data on which practitioners of the classical sciences could build more systematically than would ever have been possible in the age of scribes. By making possible the accurate reproduction and systematic improvement of illustrations, it literally revolutionized the collection and checking of data about the natural world. The wide diffusion of classical and modern texts enabled scientists to educate themselves and to become aware of contradictions that had not bothered the less well informed readers of medieval times. And it did more than any other force to create the disciplinary communities and standards that characterize modern science, with its emphasis on collaboration and competition.

The protagonist in each of these movements is the master-printer, a pioneer both as businessman and as intellectual. It was in his shop that artisans came together with intellectuals to create the greatest works of the new science; it was his opposition to authority, something almost inherent in the nature of his calling, that turned networks of printing-shops into the relays along which ran messages of change.

These are only some of Eisenstein's main arguments. No summary can do justice to so rich a book. Every reader will have his favorite pages; my own, perhaps, are those in which she treats the divergence between popular and learned traditions in religious literature after the Reformation and those in which she speculates strikingly about the effects of manuals of "civility" on the relations between parents and children. Every reader will also profit from the many epigrammatic obiter dicta that enrich the book. Eisenstein is often more perceptive than professional students of the fields she treats. She is absolutely right to point out that the Renaissance recovery of classical scientific works was not a retreat to blind worship of authority but the indispensable foundation for the Vesalian and Copernican revolutions—a point on which many historians of science still go wrong. More generally, she is right to hold that historians of ideas, especially in the English-speaking world, have paid far too little attention to the social, economic, and material realities that affected past intellectuals and to point out in particular that the conditions of publication deserve a more prominent place among those realities than even the broadest-minded intellectual historians have accorded them.

For all of the excitement it inspires, however, Eisenstein's book also leaves the reader with a certain uneasiness. It is not surprising that in 700 pages of vigorous argument she has sometimes missed her aim, or that at times she seems to be tilting at windmills rather than real opponents. What is more surprising, and causes more concern, is that many of her errors and exaggerations seem to stem directly from the goals at which she aims and the methods she has chosen.

Eisenstein has decided to do her research not in primary but in secondary sources. She herself describes the book as "based on monographic literature not archival research" (xvi). What she does not explain is why she has abstained so rigorously from studying the thousands of published primary sources on the effects of printing that are available in any major scholarly library. Anthologies of early prefaces and other documents can help to initiate a reader into the field. The colophons of incunabula give us a chance to watch dozens of editors and printers at work, and thousands of such texts are accurately reproduced in the modern catalogs of early printed books. The letters of many of the most influential editors can be read in well-annotated modern editions. And, of course, the early printed books that fill the shelves of the Folger Library, where Eisenstein did much of her reading, are their own best witnesses.[3]

One need not do "archival research" to master these materials; but though Eisenstein has consulted some of them, they have not left much of a precipitate in her book. What a pity, one feels, that she has filled her pages with ungainly chunks of quotation from modern textbooks and articles, with other scholars' summaries and descriptions. Such passages block the lively flow of her prose. It seems a shame that she did not replace them with direct readings of the sources and with well-chosen plates (she uses no illustrations at all). What a pity, for example, that she did not enrich her discussion of the spread of Luther's writings with a quotation from Johann Froben's splendid letter to the reformer:

> The Leipzig book dealer Blasius Salomon gave me a selection of your writings at the last Frankfurt Fair. Since they received much applause from scholars I reprinted them at once. We have sent 600 copies to France and Spain. They were bought up in Paris, and were read and praised by the scholars at the Sorbonne, so our friends have reported to us . . . Calvo too, the Pavian book dealer, a well-educated man and a friend of the Muses, took a considerable number of your writings to Italy in order to retail them in every city. In doing so he is concerned not to make money but to serve the new devotion as best he can. He promised that he would send epigrams applauding you by all the scholars in Italy . . . Moreover we have sent your works to Brabant and England.[4]

Here we see a printer taking on just the sort of innovative role as both entrepreneur and intellectual that Eisenstein's thesis calls for. A rather limited amount of reading—certainly less than a year's work, and she worked for ten—would have enabled her to turn up many passages as revealing as this one and to excise many unnecessary dead patches from every chapter. As the book stands, Eisenstein's few excursions into the documents tantalize the reader without satisfying him. Again and again, the book comes alive as an early intellectual is quoted or an early book or print is discussed; but all too soon we are back in a world of textbook-style generalities.[5]

In some ways, too, the general plan of Eisenstein's structure is as troubling as its foundations are disappointing. She has not told a story but carried on a series of arguments about the importance of printing in a great many fields over two centuries. As a result, she has tended to pull from her sources those facts and statements that seemed to meet her immediate polemical needs, both positive and negative. Sometimes the statements that she quotes are torn so far from their original context that they take on a meaning that their author could not have intended, or are denounced for failing to meet standards that their author could not possibly have reached. Eisenstein criticizes textbooks as if they had been meant to meet the same rigorous standards as monographs. She dissects incidental remarks as if they had been meant to describe complex events and situations in a complete and final way. And she tends, especially in her chapter on the Renaissance, to criticize modern historians in the light of her own interests and knowledge rather than in that of their intellectual contexts. Thus, she does not try to understand *why* Jacob Burckhardt saw the Renaissance as a piercing of a veil that had long hung between men and the natural world; instead, she suggests that his views should be "reformulated" to take into account the role of printing and the continuities between medieval and Renaissance culture that historians have discovered since Burckhardt's time (226). Surely it would be more sensible to try to understand Burckhardt's methods and standards than to criticize him for not living up to ours. These tactics infuse into parts of Eisenstein's book an unpleasant, and certainly unintentional, tone of hectoring.

Yet these attacks on other scholars, however unnecessary, cause less unease than the ways in which Eisenstein sometimes deploys the evidence that they have given her. Facts as well as obiter dicta tend to be pulled out of shape by the force with which she sets upon them. At one point, for example, she argues that the systematic historical study of the ancient world could not come into being until printing had made it possible to have "adequate equipment" for "systematically reconstructing a past civilization" (187). In support of this claim she quotes some lines from a well-known essay by Momigliano, describing the great antiquarians of the sixteenth century. What she does not quote is his description, in the same passage, of the work of earlier antiquarians—in particular, that of Flavio Biondo, whose systematic survey of Roman civilization, *Roma Triumphans,* was completed in the 1450s, well before the existence of printing could have had any impact on the author. "It required at least a century of printing," says Eisenstein, "however before a 'systematic collection' of relics . . . could occur" (187). But what of Biondo's amazingly complete and accurate description of the material relics of ancient Rome, *Roma Instaurata?* That was completed in the 1440s. And it is fully described in another work that Eisenstein knows—Weiss, *The Renaissance Discovery of Classical Antiquity.* I do not think that anyone who has read the works on which Eisenstein relies would agree that her account of them is entirely judicious. And the case of the antiquarians is, unfortunately, not exceptional. It is hard to see how anything but the desire to prove a point could have led Eisenstein to repeat the old canard that the humanists knew almost nothing about the Middle Ages (190–91). The great humanist histories—Leonardo Bruni, *History of the Florentine People,* and Biondo, *Decades*—were precisely histories of medieval Italy, based on wide reading in medieval chronicles and an impressive amount of digging in the archives. These facts are clearly presented in the standard works of Ullman, Baron, and Hay.[6]

These problems of method and approach affect more than isolated points of detail. No craftsman is better than his tools, and at times the defects of Eisenstein's equipment have injured the very substance and structure of her book. Both her lively survey of the change from script to print and her suggestive speculations about its intellectual consequences suffer seriously from her one-sided presentation of the evidence.

Eisenstein wishes to emphasize how radical the break was between the age of scribes and that of printers. To do so she minimizes the extent to which any text could circulate in stable form before mechanical means of reproduction became available. She suggests that almost no reader in any age of manuscripts could have access to a large number of texts. She both argues and implies that the scribal book trade was a casual and ill-organized affair; she dearly holds that no single scribe could produce any large number of books. She relies heavily on De la Mare's pioneering demonstration that Vespasiano da Bisticci, the most famous Florentine manuscript dealer, operated on a far smaller scale than traditional accounts suggest. And she tends to down-play evidence that lay literacy was increasing rapidly even before printing was invented.[7]

I cannot feel that Eisenstein has done justice to the available evidence. She talks a great deal about Vespasiano's backwardness, but not at all about that well-organized and productive scribe Diebold Lauber, who was innovative enough to issue written broadsides listing and advertising his wares. She says very little about the effects of the new educational institutions that popped up like mushrooms in many parts of Europe during the period 1300 to 1500, which must have had a sizeable impact on the level of literacy among members of the lay elite: for example, the ten German universities, all with law faculties, that were founded between 1365 and 1472. And though she criticizes Kristeller for suggesting that a work preserved in three copies "attained a certain diffusion" (211), she says nothing at all about the well-known studies by Soudek and Schucan, both inspired by Kristeller. These two scholars have proved that some of Bruni's translations from the Greek were literally best sellers before printing. Of one of the works studied, more than 200 manuscript copies survive; of the other, more than 300. Many more must have perished. The extant copies belonged to an extraordinary cross-section of the literate, one that included merchants as well as clerics, teachers as well as lawyers and notaries. Such cases make a rather formidable exception to the norms Eisenstein describes.[8]

Nor does Eisenstein say much about the evidence that a private scholar could assemble quite a large and varied library of manuscripts. Niccoli and Salutati had some 800 manuscripts each, which they catalogued carefully and made available freely to other scholars. And even a much poorer man like Poggio, while still a secretary in the Papal Curia, could assemble an astonishingly diverse collection of Latin and Greek texts of every kind. When such men could simply buy manuscripts, they did so. More often they borrowed texts and paid a scribe to copy them. This process had its difficulties—Poggio referred to the scribes who worked for him as "the excrement of the universe"—and collectors were not uncommonly forced to make their own transcripts. Yet the results were libraries far more diverse and rich than one would expect from Eisenstein's account.[9]

Facts like these suggest that the Renaissance might not have been another transitory revival even if printing had not been invented. They suggest that the experience of collectors and readers changed rather less sharply than one might expect with the advent of printed books. And they suggest that earlier scholars may well have been right to hold that it was new forms of education and changes in the nature of governments, rather than the invention of printing, which created the new lay reading public of the Renaissance. At all events, one must regret that Eisenstein's decision to write in so polemical a vein led her to neglect them.

Eisenstein's picture of the printing-house is as bright as that of the scribe's study is dim. These "new centers of erudition," ruled by laymen, became Europe's most active centers of cultural change. We should think in terms of "many print shops located in numerous towns, each serving as an intellectual cross-roads, as a miniature 'international house'—as a meeting place, message center, and sanctuary all in one . . ." (448). In these new circumstances, "the printer's workshop attracted the most learned and disputatious scholars of the day." "Learned laymen . . . were less likely to gather on the church steps than in urban workshops where town and gown met to exchange gossip and news, peer over editors' shoulders, check copy and read proof" (309). Indeed, "Most inhabitants of the sixteenth-century Republic of Letters spent more time in printers' workshops than in 'secluded studies'" (154).

This description certainly fits a few of the great Renaissance print-shops at certain periods: those of Aldo Manuzio in the time of his Academy, Froben in the 1520s, and Christopher Plantin in the 1560s. But I fear that it has little to do with the printing shops that most citizens of the Republic of Letters knew best. Some shops, to be sure, like that of Anton Koberger in Nuremberg, were orderly and well-disciplined operations where the workers arrived and departed at fixed times, while work followed a remarkably regular schedule. But most plants, as McKenzie and others have shown, were typical pre-industrial places of work. Filled with the noise of machinery and the curses of workers when the presses were in operation, noisy with quarrels and dirty, the printing-house was not the sort of place that a gentleman wanted to frequent.[10] And we must not let our prejudices prevent us from seeing that most early modern intellectuals saw themselves as gentlemen. They constantly complained that, as Professor Martinus Crusius of Tübingen put it, "the printers' journey-men hate to set Greek but want plenty of tips; [they're] an ill-behaved, ignorant rabble."[11] Even scholars whose close friends and relations were printers sometimes indignantly denied that they themselves had ever worked for pay in a printing-shop.[12]

The presence of workmen was not all that made many print-shops unattractive. There was also the absence of scholars. Naturally there were shops, especially the famous ones, where master, correctors, or both were learned and original intellectuals. Paolo Manuzio, for example, bargained with his authors in the perfect Ciceronian Latin that befitted the scholar whose commentaries on Cicero were standard works until the nineteenth century. When Commelin printed a school text of the Greek poet Theognis "to keep his workmen busy," he could add interesting text-critical and exegetical notes of his own. Such masters naturally attracted the interest of scholars. But I fear that Eisenstein has extended this model of a printing-shop rather too far. Estienne tells us—admittedly, in a polemical context—that most of his colleagues were ignoramuses who printed whatever works academic con-men offered them, scrimped by refusing to buy good base texts to print from, and hired hacks to write Greek and Latin prefaces under their names, which most of them could not even read. As to the correctors, even Hornschuch admitted that if they were really learned men, "most of them would be off like a shot from this sweat-shop, to earn their living by their intelligence and learning, not by their hands."[13]

Ample evidence suggests that most Renaissance print-shops were much less sophisticated places than Eisenstein would have us believe. Her account conveys little of the variety, fragility, and tiny scale of the majority of printing shops. One thinks of the English printers of the sixteenth century, almost all of whom were small-scale operators of no great skill. One thinks, too, of the starving *petits imprimeurs* of the faubourgs Saint Jacques and Saint Marcel, described so well by Parent, clinging together to survive in companies that grew and disintegrated with amazing speed, like primitive organisms seen through a microscope.[14]

The intellectual level of many printing shops was as low as their finances were unsound. Consider Estienne's gloomy story about a corrector he had met:

> I met one of these fellows who was doing the job of a corrector with such savagery that he ruined every passage where he found the word *procos* (suitors) by putting *porcos* (pigs) in its place . . . "I know," he said, "that *porcos* is the name of a real animal; but I don't think that *procos* refers to animals or anything else in Latin."[15]

Anyone experienced in working with early books knows that many of them were, if not untouched by human hands, at least uninspected by human brains in the course of printing. Take the strange case of Paul the Silentiary's epigram from the Greek Anthology. Since this poem was written in extremely short verses, Aldo printed it in two columns to save space, with the verses in the following order:

1　　2
3　　4
5　　6.

When the Giunti reprinted Aldo's edition of the Anthology, however, they did not bother to read the epigram and reprinted it with column 2 following rather than flanking column 1. The poem thus became incoherent. The proudest editors and printers in Europe—Badius, Gelenius, Estienne, and Wechel—one after another proceeded to reprint the poem in the same unintelligible form, thus providing striking proof that not one of them employed a corrector who knew Greek. Worse printers made even worse blunders. No wonder, then, that some texts deteriorated so far in the course of several editions as to become unintelligible.[16]

After all, printers were businessmen. They had to make money. When, as often happened, this need or the practical difficulties it imposed interfered with scholars' plans, the scholars tended to fly off the handle. Often they were blind to the printer's point of view. Martin Luther, enraged at the bad state of some proofs he had been sent, refused to send any more copy "until I'm convinced that these *Schmutzfinken* and *Geldmacher* are less interested in their own profit than in the books' utility for readers." True, he later changed his mind and sent the proofs. But he never ceased to berate the printers who not only reprinted his works without permission but also made such a bad job of them "that at many points I didn't recognize my own work."[17] Similarly, Nicolaas Heinsius saw the Elzeviers' insistence on printing his works in their favorite small format as the result not of commercial necessity but of an incomprehensible stinginess: "Our printers have been irremediably infected by that wretched custom. They think their books are worthless unless they can be carried around handily by someone who is out for a walk."[18] Given these dashing values and interests, it is not surprising that so many scholars felt that the association with commerce had ruined what could have been the liberal art of printing.[19]

I would not deny that Eisenstein's brilliant picture conveys something of the feel of a great house like Plantin's. It is certainly true that bookshops—which, however, were not always printing-shops as well, especially in the seventeenth century—and the great Frankfurt bookfair were gathering places for intellectuals. It is also true that many of the most original products of early modern scholarship and science—Abraham Ortelius, *Theatrum Orbis Terrarum* (Antwerp, 1570) and Andreas Vesalius, *De Humani Corporis Fabrica* (Basel, 1543)—were the result of unusually close collaboration between innovative scholars and responsive printers. But I do think that she paints a pastel-colored picture of the printing-house and of the connections that it fostered between town and gown. I wonder if, even in those presses that became the meeting-places of learned men, it was not the attraction of the master-printer's scholarship, rather than the nature of his activity, that drew others to him. In that sense, was the attraction of Plantin's printing-house so very different from that of Cujas's study? We ought to remember that when Lipsius and Plantin held their most serious conversations about religion, they left the workplace and went for a long walk in the country.[20]

The exaggerations in Eisenstein's account of the shift from script to print inevitably affect her account of the shift's ramifications for intellectuals. She holds that the writer in an age of scribes had a fundamentally different relation to his public than the writer of a printed book. The scribal author could not hope that his work would be distributed in anything like a stable form, or even under his name. He could not bring out his private idiosyncrasies for public inspection as Montaigne could in his printed *Essays*. Nor could he hope to win lasting fame from works that were so unlikely to be preserved. "The conditions of scribal culture," as Eisenstein remarks in another context, "thus held narcissism in check" (233). Indeed, it is probably wrong even to speak of "publication before printing," as scholars sometimes do.

Here, too, I fear, there is a measure of exaggeration. Surely an author like Petrarch deserves more part in the development of the modern notion of authorship than Eisenstein accords him. He took the greatest care to edit and polish his works before he allowed them to be seen. He cut up and rearranged his letters, not so much to portray himself in a better light as to give what he felt would be a clearer picture of his spiritual development. He even concluded one of the collections of his letters with a formal "Letter to Posterity," in which he speaks to the future reader very much as man to man. True, he feared that some of his works might not survive to find readers, and Eisenstein helps us to grasp the pathos of that fear. Yet he clearly did not find in scribal culture the fearful constraint on self-expression that Eisenstein describes.[21]

In fact, I am not entirely convinced that the process of publication itself changed so radically as Eisenstein holds, especially from the author's point of view. Kristeller showed long ago that publication followed the same course for a fifteenth-century author whether the book in question was to be copied or printed. The author either made or had made a fair copy of his work, called the *archetypum*. This he gave either to a scribe to copy or to a printer to print. The book was said to be "published" (*editus*) "on the day on which the author first allowed the completed *archetypum* to be reproduced by others." In either case, the author's part of the activity of publication remained scribal in character.[22]

If we combine these facts with the findings of students of sixteenth-century printing—with the fact that few authors actually wrote in printing-houses, and the fact that few even came to the printing-house to correct proofs—we may see a less radical shift in the life-experience of writers than Eisenstein suggests. If we take into account the vast amount of time that any early modern writer spent in copying—in taking notes, copying unpublished or rare books, and writing his own works—we may be even more inclined to feel that the pace of change has been exaggerated. Scholars remained scribes for a long time. Some of us still are.[23]

In the end, however, it is less the process of publication than its intellectual consequences which Eisenstein seeks to illuminate. Her book must be tested as a piece of intellectual history. In this regard, too, it not only brings rewards but inspires misgivings.

Eisenstein tries to show that it was printing, not internal developments in Italian culture, that did the most to create the Renaissance sense of history. To prove this point she must refute a number of influential modern interpretations. She must argue, for example, that Panofsky was wrong to suggest that the Renaissance came to see the ancient world "from a fixed distance" and thus to gain a "total and rationalized view" of it. In Eisenstein's words, "That a 'total rationalized' view of any past civilization could be developed before the output of uniform reference guides and gazeteers seems implausible to me" (186). She admits that such "scribal scholars" as Lorenzo Valla had "a growing sensitivity to anachronism." But they lacked a "fixed spatial-temporal reference frame" (187). They had little sense of the chronological order in which ancient texts had been composed or of the great disagreements that had sometimes separated their authors. And to reproach early scholars for making historical or philological errors, as Seznec and others have done, is to forget the inevitably narrow limits of what they could know.[24]

Here, too, I fear, Eisenstein's eagerness to prove her thesis has led her to play down a large amount of contrary evidence. Why Renaissance men developed a new historical sense, I cannot say. But I do know that they began to do so earlier and had far more success at the enterprise than Eisenstein believes.

One finds a new interest in historical and philological questions among Italian intellectuals from the very beginning of the fourteenth century. Take the case of Giovanni of Verona and the two Plinys. Both the *Natural History* of the elder Pliny and the letters of his nephew, Pliny the Younger, which vividly described the uncle's life and death, were widely read in the Middle Ages. Vincent of Beauvais, for example, quoted hugely from both works. Yet both he and other medieval readers attributed both works to the same man, even though the letters made clear that this view was impossible. For some reason, Giovanni read the two Plinys in a new way. He realized that the elder Pliny could not have written a letter about his own death. And he found this discovery so exciting that he wrote a little treatise about it, which began, "It is known that there were two Plinys." The treatise, in turn, found some diffusion in Renaissance manuscripts of the *Natural History*—a fact that suggests that Giovanni's interests and viewpoint were shared by others.[25]

Discoveries of this kind multiplied throughout the fourteenth century. Petrarch, in particular, made his life into a joyous expedition across the *mare magnum* of classical literature. Modern scholars, especially Nolhac and Billanovich, have taught us to follow the stages of his journey in the margins of his many books. And they have proved that he amassed a systematic enough knowledge of the ancient world to solve many technical problems in a way that can still be accepted. He emended corrupt passages in Livy with impressive dexterity. And he did a better job than a whole team of twentieth-century classicists at identifying some of the sources from which the ancient scholar Servius drew his enormous commentary on Virgil.[26]

Later generations were even more sophisticated and knowledgeable. Salutati and Valla discovered and exposed clear chronological errors in the ancient accounts of Roman history. Bruni wrote a perceptive and well-documented life of Aristotle that set the philosopher's life into a general chronological system (that of the Greek Olympiads) and carefully distinguished his ideas from those of his teacher, Plato. Polenton compiled a comprehensive and critical history of Latin literature. He assimilated many of the discoveries of earlier scholars; his section on the Plinys, for example, begins: "Lest anyone be deceived by their identical names, I think I should begin by pointing out that there were two Plinys, uncle and nephew." And he added new ones of his own. He showed that Cicero could not have praised Virgil's sixth Eclogue even if ancient scholars claimed that he had: "Chronology shows that Cicero, who died before the battle of Philippi, could not possibly have praised what Virgil wrote after it." Biondo and Cyriac of Ancona assembled with painstaking care the material relics of the ancient world.[27] Biondo also rightly argued that the ancient Romans must have spoken Latin, not Italian—thus showing a considerable ability to imagine a civilization different from his own.[28] By the end of the fifteenth century such scholars as Angelo Poliziano had arrived at an extraordinarily sophisticated historical understanding of both Latin and Greek culture and had formulated most of the technical methods which modern scholars still use in editing and explicating ancient sources.[29]

Eisenstein is right to say, as others have before her, that printing dramatically affected the nature of scholarship—that it broadened the range of available sources, made it much easier to learn Greek, and made cross-checking and collation of texts far more practicable.[30] But she certainly exaggerates the historical ignorance and ineptness of those whom she demeaningly calls "scribal scholars." By trying to prevent scholars from modernizing the Renaissance unduly, Eisenstein has made the Renaissance less modern than it really was.

Eisenstein's account of the Reformation seems to me altogether more rewarding. She is right to point out that the relationship between printing and the Reformation did not begin with the publication of Luther's first broadside. Printing did offer new careers and a newly widespread power to the reforming literati of Erasmus's generation. It did offer new opportunities to peddlers of indulgences. I suspect that she is also on the right track when she suggests that printing by its very nature worked against clerical authority.

Yet here, too, exaggeration and unimaginative research sometimes harm her arguments. One would not suspect from her account that there was a rather successful Catholic translation of the Bible into German—much less that it appeared in print before Luther's complete Bible and went through some 100 editions, seventeen of them during the sixteenth century.[31] And her account of Simon's contributions to biblical exegesis is less history than travesty. More engagement with the sources, then, could have enriched this already fascinating chapter and made possible a more subtle approach to the problems it raises.[32]

About the Scientific Revolution, finally, Eisenstein makes some of her best points. Her whole second volume is allotted to science. It makes fresher reading than the earlier chapters, perhaps because it is based on more recent research. It rests on a compelling, though incomplete, account of the historiography of science. Many of its arguments carry conviction. In particular, it does seem that the revival and transformation of such descriptive sciences as anatomy, botany, and zoology clearly stemmed, although in different ways, from the new possibilities offered by printing for the checking and correction of data. And her suggestion that the connection between Protestantism and science may have resulted from the relative lack of censorship in Protestant Europe seems plausible.

But even Eisenstein's volume on science suffers from a tendency to exaggeration. She overestimates the instability of manuscript texts and the difficulties involved in gaining access to them. She underestimates the effectiveness of the communications networks that bound intellectuals together across Europe long before 1450—above all, the networks that linked monastic houses and universities. She plays down evidence that does not fit her thesis—for example, Regiomontanus's mastery, derived entirely from manuscript sources, of precisely those problems in astronomy that most exercised Copernicus.[33]

These remarks have been intended only to begin a debate that will probably be long and lively. But they do suggest that Eisenstein's enterprise suffers from two flaws at its heart: inadequate foundation in research and exaggerated claims of explanatory power. Even the most suggestive pages of the book contain too much that is misleading.

Eisenstein considered it more "urgent" to amalgamate her ideas in this form than to do further reading, but I confess that I am not certain why she felt this way. Her views have received extended expression in some of the most influential historical journals in the Western world. Since she began to work in this field, moreover, intellectual historians have begun to show far more interest in the phenomenon and the effects of printing. The best recent American survey of Renaissance and Reformation culture—Eugene F. Rice, Jr., *The Foundations of Early Modern Europe, 1460–1559* (New York, 1970)—begins with a long discussion of printing and its effects. Historians of science have also begun to show more interest in the effects of printing on the formation of scientific disciplines. And a vastly productive and influential group of historians of printing, including both French and American scholars, has done much to give the subject wide publicity and to win younger scholars to its study. In these circumstances, Eisenstein might well have taken the time to carry out case studies using primary sources.[34]

"Books do furnish a room"; whether they do anything else depends on those who read them far more than on those who copy or print them. The story of early modern intellectuals must in the end be a history of ideas, however unfashionable that enterprise has come to be. Like all good histories of ideas, it will have to be based on the primary sources. The role of scribes and printers will certainly form part of that history, and we will owe that in some part to Eisenstein's work. But the story of the medium cannot be substituted for the story of the message.

Notes

1. Philip Gaskell and Patricia Bradford (eds. and trans.), *Hornschuch's Orthotypographia, 1608* (Cambridge, 1972). I follow the excellent analysis in Percy Simpson, *Proof-Reading in the Sixteenth, Seventeenth and Eighteenth Centuries* (London, 1935), 126–30.

2. Elizabeth Eisenstein, "Clio and Chronos," *History and Theory* 6 (1966), 36–64, "The Advent of Printing and the Problem of the Renaissance," *Past and Present* 45 (1969), 19–89, "L'Avènement de l'Imprimerie et la Réforme," *Annales*

26 (1971), 1355–82, and *The Printing Press as an Agent of Change: Communications and Cultural Transformations in Early Modern Europe*, 2 vols. (Cambridge, 1979) (hereafter cited parenthetically).

3. The best place to begin is Hans Widmann, Horst Kliemann, and Bernhard Wendt (eds.), *Der deutsche Buchhandel in Urkunden und Quellen* (Hamburg, 1965), 2 vols., which provides samples of almost every relevant sort of document. For prefaces, see, e.g., Beriah Botfield (ed.), *Prefaces to the First Editions of the Greek and Roman Classics and of the Sacred Scriptures* (Cambridge, 1861); Eugene F. Rice, Jr. (ed.), *The Prefatory Epistles of Jacques Lefèvre d'Etaples and Related Texts* (New York, 1972); Giovanni Orlandi (ed.), *Aldo Manuzio Editore: dediche, prefazioni, note ai testi* (Milan, 1975), 2 vols. (the rich introduction by Carlo Dionisotti is by far the best study in existence of Aldo). The richest single source for colophons is the *Catalogue of Books Printed in the XVth Century Now in the British Museum* (London, 1963–71; rev. ed.), 12 vols. The serious student will also consult older works, above all Ludwig Hain, *Repertorium Bibliographicum* (Stuttgart, 1826–38), 2 vols.; the supplements by D. Reichling (1905–14) and W. A. Copinger (1895–1902). He will go when possible to the greatest of all such lists, the *Gesamtkatalog der Wiegendrutke,* which is now being continued after a hiatus of many years and is up to the letter F. For editors' letters see, for example, P. S. Allen, H. M. Allen, and H. W. Garrod (eds.), *Opus Epistolarum Des. Erasmi Roterodami* (Oxford, 1906–58), 12 vols.; A. Hartmann (ed.), *Die Amerbachkorrespondenz* (Basel, 1942–74), 8 vols. Naturally, many sixteenth-, seventeenth-, and eighteenth-century editions remain indispensable; for example, Pieter Burman (ed.), *Sylloge Epistolarum a viris illustribus scriptarum* (Leiden, 1727), 5 vols.

4. Widmann et al., *Der deutsche Buchhandel,* 1:345.

5. For example, Eisenstein's excellent discussion of Andrew Maunsell, though suggestive, breaks off all too soon (106–7).

6. Arnaldo Momigliano, "Ancient History and the Antiquarian," *Studies in Historiography* (London, 1966), 5–6; Roberto Weiss, *The Renaissance Discovery of Classical Antiquity* (Oxford, 1969), 68–70; B. L. Ullman, "Leonardo Bruni and Humanistic Historiography," *Studies in the Italian Renaissance* (Rome, 1955), 321–44; Hans Baron, "Das Erwachen des historischen Denkens im Humanismus des Quattrocento," *Historische Zeitschrift* 147 (1932–33), 5–20; Denys Hay, "Flavio Biondo and the Middle Ages," *Proceedings of the British Academy* 45 (1959), 97–128.

7. Albinia De la Mare, "Vespasiano da Bisticci, Historian and Bookseller," Ph.D. diss., University of London, 1965. This rich work, which Eisenstein uses in a highly selective way, provides much further evidence both for and against her thesis.

8. For the text of Lauber's broadside, see Widmann et al., *Der deutsche Buchhandel,* 1:15–16. For a discussion of the document, see Widmann, *Geschichte des Buchhandels vom Altertum bis zur Gegenwart* (Wiesbaden, 1975), 1:37; Eisenstein mentions Lauber once in passing (13, n. 28). On universities, see Karl Heinz Burmeister, *Das Stadium der Rechte im Zeitalter des Humanismus im deutschen Rechtsbereich* (Wiesbaden, 1974), 40–51. On Bruni's translations, see Josef Soudek, "Leonardo Bruni and His Public: A Statistical and Interpretive Study of His Annotated

Latin Version of the (Pseudo-) Aristotelian Economics," *Studies in Medieval and Renaissance History* 5 (1968), 49–136; Luzi Schucan, *Das Nachleben von Basilius Magnus "ad adolescents." Ein Beitrag zur Geschichte des christlichen Humanismus* (Geneva, 1973).

9. B. L. Ullman, *The Humanism of Coluccio Salutati* (Padua, 1963), chs. 9–11; B. L. Ullman and Phillip A. Stadter, *The Public Library of Renaissance Florence: Niccolò, Cosimo de' Medici and the Library of San Marco* (Padua, 1972), ch. 2; Ernst Walser, *Poggius Florentinus: Leben und Werke* (Leipzig, 1914), 104–10. For further information on the contents of libraries before the invention of printing, see Pearl Kibre, "The Intellectual Interests Reflected in Libraries of the Fourteenth and Fifteenth Centuries," *Journal of the History of Ideas* 7 (1946), 257–97.

10. On Koberger, see J. C. Zelmer, *C. D. Correctorum in typographiis eruditorum centuria* (Nuremberg, 1716), 15–16. This work remains the richest collection of information on the activities of correctors in the first two centuries of printing; like many other products of eighteenth-century erudition, it is unjustly ignored by modern scholars, whose own works are rarely as rewarding. D. F. McKenzie, "Printers of the Mind: Some Notes on Bibliographical Theories and Printing-House Practices," *Studies in Bibliography* 22 (1969), 1–75; Philip Gaskell, *A New Introduction to Bibliography* (Oxford, 1972), 48–49.

11. Widmann et al., *Der deutsche Buchhandel,* 2:28: "Die Truckergesellen setzen ungern Graeca: hetten aber gern vil Trinckgaelts. Ein loses ungelehrts Gesindlin." Cf. also Angelo Poliziano, *Epistolarum libri XII* (Amsterdam, 1642), 410: "semidocti illi qui librorum excusoribus operam navant" (those ignoramuses who work for printers).

12. Allen et al., *Opus Epistolarum Erasmi,* 9:398 (Ep. 2581); Isaac Casaubon, *De rebus sacris et ecclesiasticis exercitationes XVI* (Geneva, 1655), 38b–39a; also cited by Zeltner, *Correctorum centuria,* 108–9.

13. See the interesting series of letters to Marcantonio Natta in *Epistolarum Pauli Manutii libri XII* (Leipzig, 1603), 3:155–72; Jerome Commelin (ed.), *Theognidis, Phocylidis, Pythagorae, Solonis et aliorum poemata gnomica* (Utrecht, 1659), ep. ded., sig. A 2ʳ: "ne operae, dum majora paramus, cessarent"; Henri Estienne, *Epistola de statu suae typographiae,* in Estienne, (ed. F. G. Roloffius), *Pseudo-Cicero* (Halle, 1737), 362–64; Gaskell and Bradford, *Hornschuch's Orthotypographia,* 27.

14. Ronald B. McKerrow, *An Introduction to Bibliography for Literary Students* (Oxford, 1960; orig. pub. 1928), 281; James Binns, "STC Latin Books: Evidence for Printing-House Practice," *The Library* 32 (1977), 1–27; Annie Parent, *Les métiers du livre à Paris au XVIᵉ siècle (1535–1560)* (Geneva, 1974), 133–35.

15. Henri Estienne, *Artis Typographicae querimonia,* in *Pseudo-Cicero,* 376–77.

16. A. A. Renouard, *Annales de l'Imprimerie des Alde, ou Histoire des trios Manuce et de leurs éditions* (Paris, 1834; 3d ed.), 43. Aldo, too, sometimes made use of incompetent correctors, as well-informed contemporaries complained. See Allen et al., *Opus Epistolarum Erasmi,* 11:288–89 (Ep. 3100); Daniel Wyttenbach, *Opuscula* (Leiden, 1821), 1:360–61. On the deterioration of some other classical texts, see the evidence collected by Estienne, *Epistola de statu suae typographiae,* 338–51.

17. Widmann et al., *Der deutsche Buchhandel*, 2:16, 327.

18. Hans Bots (ed.), *Correspondance de Jacques Dupuy et de Nicolas Heinsius (1646–1656)* (The Hague, 1971), 78. On Heinsius's relations with the Elzeviers, see the exemplary study by F. F. Blok, *Nicolaas Heinsius in dienst van Christina van Zweden* (Delft, 1949), 92–99.

19. See the evidence collected by Zelner, *Correctorum centuria*, 18–20; and Orlandi, *Aldo Manuzio Editore*, 1:170. Luther quoted in Widmann et al., *Der deutsche Buchhandel*, 2:327–28.

20. Certainly some great printers took enormous pride in the excellent work that their craftsmen did and made no bones about working right alongside their men in the shop; Paolo Manuzio added a legend to each of the three volumes of his 1554 edition of Demosthenes, stating that he himself had served as corrector (Zeltner, *Correctorum centuria*, 334). But I would still hold that Eisenstein overstates her case. On Lipsius and Plantin, see B. Reckers, *Benito Arias Montano (1527–1598)* (London, 1972), 102, 156–57—a stimulating book, but one to be used with caution. See Basil Hall, "A Sixteenth-Century Miscellany," *Journal of Ecclesiastical History* 26 (1975), 318–20.

21. Aldo S. Bernardo, "Letter-Splitting in Petrarch's *Familiares*," *Speculum* 33 (1958), 236–41. For the Latin text of "Letter to Posterity" see Petrarch (ed. Giovanni Ponte), *Opere* (Milan, 1968), 886–900; English translation in David Thompson (ed.), *Petrarch: A Humanist among Princes* (New York, 1971), 1–13. Petrarch expresses the suspicion that future readers will "have heard the bare titles" of his works: Petrarch, *Opere*, 886; Thompson (ed.), *Petrarch*, 1. In fact the *Epistula posteritati* remained incomplete and was therefore not included among Petrarch, *Seniles*. But the majority of Petrarch's works did circulate in a very carefully finished form; see Hans Baron, *From Petrarch to Leonardo Bruni* (Chicago, 1968), 7–101. In braving the difficulties of publishing his works—and in believing that they would win him eternal fame—Petrarch was, of course, following a path that the Roman authors he knew best had laid out. See esp. Horace, *Odes,* 3.30 and *Epistles,* 1.20; and Ovid *Tristia*, 4.10. He thus had more reason than Eisenstein suggests to believe that his works would survive pretty much intact. In general, Eisenstein's account fits the histories of technical texts—lexica, grammars, commentaries, and handbooks—and vernacular literary texts far better than it does that of classical or late medieval literary texts, in Greek and Latin, which were valued for the exact same form of their wording.

22. Paul Kristeller, "De traditione operum Marsilii Ficini," *Supplementum Ficinianum* (Florence, 1937), 1:168–81, esp. 169–70, 173. Kristeller's analysis has now been supplemented and slightly revised in its details by Silvia Rizzo, *Il lessico filologico degli umanisti* (Rome, 1973), 303–23; but his general arguments remain valid. Rizzo's work is essential reading for anyone who hopes to understand the relations among intellectuals, scribes, and printers during the fifteenth century. See also the excellent case study by Helene Harth, "Niccolò Niccoli als literarischer Zensor. Untersuchungen zur Textgeschichte von Poggios 'De Avarita,'" *Rinascimento* 7 (1967), 29–53.

23. On authors' participation in proof-correction, which took every form from standing over the printers while they worked to complete neglect, see the evidence collected by Simpson, *Proof-Reading*; Widmann, "Die Lektüre unendlicher Korrekturen," *Archiv für Geschichte des Buchwesens* 5 (1963–64), 774–826; Binns, "STC Latin Books." See also Gaskell, *A New Introduction to Bibliography*, 111. For evidence of the "scribal" efforts of scholars long after the invention of printing, see, for example, *Bibliotheca Universitatis Leidensis, Codices Manuscripti*, 2: *Codices Scaligerandi (praeter Orientales)* (Leiden, 1910); ibid., 4: *Codices Perizoniani* (Leiden, 1946).

24. For the fullest statement of his views, see Erwin Panofsky, *Renaissance and Renascences in Western Art* (New York, 1969). Jean Seznec (trans. Barbara F. Sessions), *The Survival of the Pagan Gods* (New York, 1953).

25. Elmer Truesdell Merrill, "On the Eight-Book Tradition of Pliny's *Letters* in Verona," *Classical Philology* 5 (1910), 175–88; Giovanni de Matociis, *Brevis adnotatio de duobus Pliniis Veronensibus,* ibid., 186: "Plinii duo fuisse noscuntur, eodem nomine et praenominibus appellati . . ."

26. Pierre de Nolhac, *Pétrarque et l'humanisme* (Paris, 1907; 2nd ed.), 2 vols.; Giuseppe Billanovich, "Petrarch and the Textual Tradition of Livy," *Journal of the Warburg and Courtauld Institutes* 14 (1951), 137–208, and *Un nuovo esempio delle scoperte e delle letture del Petrarca. L'"Eusebio-Girolamo-PseudoProspero"* (Krefeld, 1954). I cite only two of Billanovich's most important works. The serious student will find many more studies by him and his students in the journal *Italia Medioevale e Umanistica*. For a particularly revealing case study, see Lucia A. Ciapponi, "Il 'De Architectura' di Vitruvio nel primo Umanesimo," *Italia Medioevale e Umanistica* 3 (1960), 59–99. On Petrarch and Servius, see Eduard Fraenkel, *Kleine Beiträge zur klassichen Philologie* (Rome, 1964), 2:372–73.

27. Ullman, *The Humanism of Coluccio Salutati*, 98–99; H. J. Erasmus, *The Origins of Rome in Historiography from Petrarch to Perizonius* (Assen, 1962), 28–29 (though excellent as an analysis of Valla's argument, this work somewhat overstates Valla's superiority to his contemporaries); Bruni, *Aristotilis vita*, in Ingemar Düring, *Aristotle in the Ancient Biographical Tradition* (Göteborg, 1957), 168–78; Sicco Polenton (ed. B. L. Ullman), *Scriptorum illustrium Latinae linguae libri XVIII* (Rome, 1928), 227, 82. In addition to Weiss, *The Renaissance Discovery of Classical Antiquity*, see Riccardo Fubini, "Biondo, Flavio," *Dizionario biografico degli Italiani* (Rome, 1968), 10:536–59; Bernard Ashmole, "Cyriac of Ancona," *Proceedings of the British Academy* 45 (1959), 25–41; for a contrasting case, see Charles Mitchell, "Felice Feliciano *Antiquarius,*"ibid., 47 (1961), 197–221.

28. John Rowe, "The Renaissance Foundations of Anthropology," *American Anthropologist* 67 (1965), 1–20, reprinted in Regna Darnell (ed.), *Readings in the History of Anthropology* (New York, 1974), 72.

29. See Grafton, "On the Scholarship of Politian and Its Context," *Journal of the Warburg and Courtauld Institutes* 40 (1977), 150–88, with extensive references to older studies.

30. As Eisenstein says, this point had been made before, above all by P. S. Allen, *Erasmus: Lectures and Wayfaring Sketches* (Oxford, 1934), 30–40.

31. Widmann, *Geschichte des Buchhandels*, 1:69.

32. Cf. Eisenstein, 321, with Richard Simon, *Histoire critique du Vieux Testament (Suivant la Copie, imprimée à Paris,* 1680), 1:16–23, 49–50. Whatever Simon was doing—and that is a complex question—he was not "casting in the role of an archivist the prophet who was once believed to have received the Ten Commandments from God on Sinai . . ."

33. See, e.g., M. L. W. Laistner, *Thought and Letters in Western Europe, A.D. 500 to 900* (London, 1957; 2nd ed.), 229; L. D. Reynolds and N. G. Wilson, *Scribes and Scholars: A Guide to the Transmission of Greek and Latin Literature* (Oxford, 1974; 2nd ed.), 82–105. Eisenstein's account quite rightly stresses Regiomontanus's pioneering activity as a publisher (584–88); she lays much less stress on the great originality of his work as an astronomer.

34. For Eisenstein's earlier publications, see n. 2 above. For the history of science, see, for example, Robert S. Westman, "Three Responses to the Copernican Theory: Johannes Praetorius, Tycho Brahe, and Michael Maestlin," in Westman (ed.), *The Copernican Achievement* (Los Angeles, 1975), 285–345. For recent work on the history of printing and the book, see Eisenstein, 29, n. 71; 30, n. 72.

5 PRINTING AND THE PEOPLE: EARLY MODERN FRANCE

Natalie Zemon Davis

Here are some voices from the sixteenth century. "The time has come . . . for women to apply themselves to the sciences and disciplines." Thus the ropemaker's daughter Louise Labé addresses her sex when her collected poems are printed in Lyon in 1556. "And if one of us gets to the point where she can put her ideas in writing, then take pains with it and don't be reluctant to accept the glory." Ten years later in Cambrai, a Protestant linen-weaver explains to his judges about the book in his life: "I was led to knowledge of the Gospel by . . . my neighbor, who had a Bible printed at Lyon and who taught me the Psalms by heart . . . The two of us used to go walking in the fields Sundays and feast days, conversing about the Scriptures and the abuses of priests." And listen to the printers' journeymen of Paris and Lyon in 1572, in a brief they printed to convince Parlement and public that they needed better treatment from their employers: "Printing [is] an invention so admirable . . . so honorable in its dignity, and profitable above all others to the French. Paris and Lyon furnish the whole of Christendom with books in every language." And yet "the Publishers and master Printers . . . use every stratagem to oppress . . . the Journeymen, who do the biggest and best part of the work of Printing." And finally, Pierre Tolet, doctor of medicine, justifying in 1540 his translation of some Greek texts into French, printed for the use of surgeons' journeymen: "If you want a servant to follow your orders, you can't give them in an unknown tongue."

These quotations suggest the several and complex ways in which printing entered into popular life in the sixteenth century, setting up new networks of communication, facilitating new options for the people, and also providing new means of controlling the people. Can this be true? Could printing have mattered that much to *the people* in a period when literacy was still so low? How can one detect its influence? And what do I mean anyway by "popular" and "the people"?

Indeed, these words were ambiguous in sixteenth-century literate usage, as in our own. On the one hand, "the people" could refer to all the natives in the kingdom *(le peuple françoys)* or the body of citizenry and inhabitants

Reprinted from Natalie Zemon Davis, *Society and Culture in Early Modern France* (Stanford: Stanford UP, 1973, 1975), 189–226. Copyright © 1975 Natalie Zemon Davis.

to which a law was promulgated. On the other hand, the word could refer to a more limited but still large population: those who were commoners, not noble; of modest means or poor, not wealthy; unschooled, not learned. For Claude de Seyssel in his *Grand' Monarchie* of 1519, the "little people" lived in both the town and the countryside and were those who worked the land and those who carried on the crafts and lesser mysteries. Recent studies of popular culture in the seventeenth and eighteenth centuries have used "people" in de Seyssel's sense, but have stressed peasants more than city-dwellers. Geneviève Bollème has talked of the *"petites gens";* Robert Mandrou has been concerned with "popular milieus," especially in the countryside.[1]

The connection between these milieus and the printed book has been considered in several ways. First, there are those studies that take "popular literature" as their source material and make a thematic analysis of its contents. Lewis B. Wright's *Middle-Class Culture in Elizabethan England* (1935) is the classic example of such an undertaking for a literate urban grouping comprising merchants, tradesmen, and skilled artisans. Robert Mandrou's subject has been the blue-covered books that were peddled out of Troyes in the seventeenth and eighteenth centuries to villages over a wide geographical area, whereas Geneviève Bollème has examined a large sample of French almanacs. Their goal has been to discover not so much new or continuing patterns of communication, but rather "the outlook of the average citizen" (Wright), or a popular "vision of the world" (Mandrou). Why this confidence in inferring from the book its readers' outlook? Because, so it is argued, the Elizabethan literature was written "for or by the plain citizen"; because the publishers of the *Bibliothèque bleue* stayed in close touch through their peddlers with village needs and tastes.[2]

In establishing the characteristics of a body of printed literature, these studies have been invaluable and even surprising. For disclosing the outlook of a given social group, though, they have some methodological drawbacks. Popular books are not necessarily written by *petites gens.* Master André Le Fournier, author of a 1530 compilation of household recipes and cosmetics for women, was a regent of the Faculty of Medicine at Paris, and he was by no means the only university graduate to engage in such an enterprise. Nor are popular books bought and read only by *petites gens.* The *Grand Calendrier et compost des bergers,* for instance, the archetype of the French almanac, was read perhaps by countryman but surely by king. François I had a copy in the royal collection, and a mid-sixteenth-century edition, now at the Houghton Library, belonged to the king's advocate at Sens.[3] The *Tresor des povres,* a traditional collection of medical remedies, was owned in sixteenth-century Paris by a councillor's wife and a bookbinder.[4]

Finally, it is especially important to realize that people do not necessarily agree with the values and ideas in the books they read. For instance, M.

Mandrou concludes from the fairy stories and saints lives in the *Bibliothèque bleue* that it functioned as escape literature for the peasants, an obstacle to the understanding of social and political realities. Perhaps. But without independent evidence, can we be sure of how a rural audience took its tales of marvels, especially at a period when people might dress up as ghosts to teach children a lesson or might protect peasant rebels by saying they were "fairies" who came from time to time?[5] When a peasant read or was read to, it was not the stamping of a literal message on a blank sheet; it was the varied motion of "a strange top" (to use Jean-Paul Sartre's metaphor for the literary object), set to turning only by the combined effort of author and reader.[6]

Thus we can best understand the connections between printing and the people if we do two things: first, if we supplement thematic analysis of texts with evidence about audiences that can provide context for the meaning and uses of books; second, if we consider a printed book not merely as a source for ideas and images, but as a carrier of relationships. The data to support such an approach are scattered in the pages of the original editions themselves; in studies of literacy and dialects, book ownership and book prices, authorship and publication policy; and in sources on the customs and associational life of peasants and artisans. The theory to assist such an approach can be found in part in the work of Jack Goody and his collaborators on the implications of literacy for traditional societies—especially in their discussion of the relations between those who live on the margins of literacy and those who live at its center. Additional theoretical support exists in the fertile essays of Elizabeth L. Eisenstein on the impact of printing on literate elites and on urban populations in early modern Europe—especially when she talks of "cross-cultural interchange" between previously "compartmentalized systems." Both Goody and Eisenstein have insisted to critics that they do not intend technological determinism, and I am even more ready than they to emphasize the way that social structure and values channel the uses of literacy and printing.[7]

This essay, then, will consider the context for using printed books in defined popular milieus in sixteenth-century France and the new relations that printing helped to establish among people and among hitherto isolated cultural traditions. Were there new groups who joined the ranks of known authors? What was the composition of "audiences"—those who actually read the books—and of "publics"—those to whom authors and publishers addressed their works?*

---

*This distinction is a necessary one but is not made in everyday speech. I follow the terminology of T. J. Clark, *Image of the People: Gustave Courbet and the Second French Republic, 1848–1851* (New York, 1973), 12.

These relations are especially interesting to trace in the sixteenth century. In the cities, at any rate, the basic innovations occurred quite rapidly. By midcentury all the major centers of publication had been established in France: Paris, Lyon, Rouen, Toulouse, Poitiers, Bordeaux, Troyes. Some forty towns had presses by 1550; about sixty had them by 1600. Moreover, economic control in the industry was not yet firmly in the hands of merchant-publishers and commercial booksellers, as it would be after the Religious Wars. Decisions about what was profitable and/or beneficial to print were made also by "industrial capitalists" and artisans, that is, by publisher-printers, like Jean I de Tournes in Lyon and the Marnef brothers in Poitiers; such decisions were even sometimes made by simple master printers publishing their own editions. This diversity may help explain the wide range in the *types* of books that appeared before mid-century. In these decades there proliferated most of the forms to be published in France up to 1700. The same is true of patterns in book ownership. For example, virtually no Parisian artisans other than printers in the generation that died around 1500 owned printed books; by 1560, the percentage of Parisian artisans and tradesmen possessing books in inventories after death had reached the level (not very high, to be sure) that Henri-Jean Martin has documented for mid-seventeenth-century Paris.[8]

This brings me to a last point about method. Rather than thinking diffusely about "the people," I am trying wherever possible to ask how printing affected more carefully defined milieus—namely, cohesive social groups some of whose members were literate. In the countryside this means the entire settled population of a village where anyone was literate. In the cities this means the small merchants and the craftsmen (masters and journeymen), and even semi-skilled workers (such as urban gardeners and fishermen) having some connection with urban organizations such as confraternities or guilds. It means their wives, themselves ordinarily at work in the trades, and even women in the families of the wealthier merchants. It means domestic servants, male or female, who might be living in their households. It does not include the unskilled dayworkers, the *gagedenier* and *manouvriers*, the *portefaix* and *crocheteurs*, the vagabonds and permanent beggars. This floating mass was just illiterate; and however resourceful their subculture, the only reader to whom they listened with any regularity was the town crier ordering them to show up for work cleaning sewage or else leave town under penalty of the whip.

Nor am I including the lower clergy or the backwoods noblemen and their wives, even though they might in the sixteenth century sometimes cluster on the borderline between literacy and illiteracy and as individuals play a role in village life. They are distinguished from the peasants and the urban *menu peuple* not by the criterion of literacy but by their estate and their relations to spiritual and emotional power, to jurisdiction and to property.

I

Let us look first to the peasants. The penetration of printing into their lives was a function not just of their literacy but of several things: the cost and availability of books in a language that they knew; the existence of social occasions when books could be read aloud; the need or desire for information that they thought could be found in printed books more easily than elsewhere; and in some cases the desire to use the press to say something to someone else.

In the countryside we meet a world that sees letters infrequently, whether written or printed. Suggestive of their relevance in the days before printing is a rural festival in Torcy around 1450, where a mock herald—a miller's son—with a mock seal pretends to read to the harvest queen from a blank parchment, whereas in fact he is improvising farcical jokes. Parchment or paper might come into the peasants' life when transactions were being recorded by courts, seigneurs, or rent-collectors, but peasants might equally expect to see these materials used, say, in a humiliating headdress for local offenders. (In the Ile-de-France in the fifteenth century a dishonest chicken-grower is led to punishment wearing a miter with chicks and other fowl painted on it and "an abundance of writing," and in 1511 a lax forest ranger is paraded around in a paper miter decorated with standing and fallen trees.)[9]

Rural literacy remained low throughout the sixteenth century. Of the women, virtually none knew their ABC's, not even the midwives. As for the men, a systematic study by Emmanuel LeRoy Ladurie of certain parts of the Languedoc from the 1570s through the 1590s found that three percent of the agricultural workers and only ten percent of the better-off peasants—the *laboureurs* and *fermiers*—could sign their full names.* In the regions north and southwest of Paris, where the speech was French, the rates may have been slightly higher, and rural schools have been noted in several places. But the pupils who spent a couple of years at such places learning to read and write

---

*Estimates of ability to read based on studies of ability to sign one's name are, of course, approximate. One can learn to read without learning to write and vice versa. Nevertheless, the two skills were most often taught together in the sixteenth century. Statistics on ability to sign, then, give us the order of magnitude of the number of readers. For a discussion of techniques of measuring literacy in the early modern period, see R. S. Schofield, "The Measurement of Literacy in Pre-Industrial England," in J. R. Goody, ed., *Literacy in Traditional Societies* (Cambridge, 1968), 311–25, and F. Furet and W. Sachs, "La Croissance de l'alphabétisation en France, XVIIIe–XIXe siècle," *Annales. Economies, Sociétés, Civilisations* 29 (1974): 714–37.

and sing were drawn from special families (such as that of a barber-surgeon in the Forez, who sent his boys to a school and rewarded its rector with a chapel in 1557) or were intended for nonagricultural occupations (such as the serf's son in the Sologne who went to school "to learn science" because he was "weak of body and could not work the soil").[10]

Surely a lad ambitious to be a *fermier* in the mid-sixteenth century would need to keep accounts, yet not all economic pressures pushed the prosperous peasant to literacy. Charles Estienne's agricultural manual advised the landed proprietor that his tenant farmer need not have reading and writing (one can lie on paper, too) so long as he was experienced and wise in agricultural ways. A peasant in the Haut-Poitou in 1601, designated tax assessor of his village, tried to get out of it by pleading illiteracy. As for sales of land, marriage contracts, and wills, there were itinerant scribes and notaries aplenty who were happy to add to their income by performing these services for the peasants.

The country boys who really learned their letters, then, were most likely those who left for the city to apprentice to crafts or to become priests, or the few lucky sons of *laboureurs* who, at a time when fellowships for the poor were being taken over by the rich, still made it to the University of Paris. One such, the son of a village smith from Brie, became a proofreader in Lyon after his university years, and at his death in 1560 was in possession of a precious manuscript of the Theodosian Code.

But when they came back to visit, such men did not leave books in their villages. "Our little Thomas talks so profoundly, almost no one can understand him" was the observation of Thomas Platter's relatives when he passed through his Swiss mountain home during his student years in the early sixteenth century. One can imagine similar remarks exchanged by peasants in France about a son who had studied books in a strange language or learned his craft in a different dialect. As the peasants' inventories after death* were virtually without manuscripts in the fifteenth century, so they

---

*No study has yet been made of the book holdings of rural *curés* in sixteenth-century France. Albert Labarre examined inventories after death of 23 *curés* of rural parishes in the Amiénois from 1522 to 1561 (fifteen had books, eight had none), but, as he points out, these men were all living in Amiens. Except when the resident *curé* kept a school, we would expect that he would possess little more than a breviary and a missal, and perhaps a book of saints' lives. In his *Propos rustiques* of 1547, Noel du Fail pictured a rural *curé* of earlier decades at a feast-day banquet, not reading aloud, but chatting with parishioners about the text for the day and with the old midwife about medicinal herbs. The education of the rural clergy was, of course, very uneven well into the seventeenth century. Only then do we find French bishops requiring *curés* to own specified books. A. Labarre, *Le livre dans la vie amiénoise du seizième siècle* (Paris, 1971), 107–11; Noel du Fail, *Les propos rustiques,* ed. A. de la Borderie (Paris, 1878),

were almost without printed books in the sixteenth.[11] Why should this be so? Surely a *laboureur* who could afford many livres worth of linens and coffers in the 1520s could afford three sous for a *Calendrier des bergers,* two sous for the medical manual *Le Tresor des povres,* or even two and a half livres for a bound and illustrated Book of Hours, which might be a credit to his family for generations.[12]

Yet just because one can afford books does not mean that one can have ready access to them or need them or want them. A literate *laboureur* in some parts of France during the sixteenth century might never meet a bookseller: his nearest market town might have no presses if it were a small place, and peddlers' itineraries still reached relatively few parts of the countryside.[13] If he did come upon a bookseller, his wares might be in a language the peasant had difficulty reading, since so little printing was done in vernaculars other than French. Only five books printed in Breton during the sixteenth century could be found by an eighteenth-century student of that language, and the first work in Basque came out in 1545 and had very few imitators.[14] Provençal was favored by several editions, mostly of poetry, but the various regional dialects, from Heard to Poitevin, rarely appeared in print at all.

In any case, how much were printed books really needed in the sixteenth-century village? A *Shepherds' Calendar* was a useful, though not always essential, supplement to oral tradition. (Indeed, sometimes as I read the different sixteenth-century editions of the *Calendrier des bergers,* I wonder to what extent contemporary compilers and publishers envisaged a peasant public for them. They appear a cross between a folklorist's recording and a pastoral, a shaped vision of the peasant world for country gentlemen and city people and a way for such readers to identify themselves with the simple wisdom of "the great shepherd of the mountain." The appearance in Paris in 1499 of a *Shepherdesses' Calendar,* a literary contrivance modeled after the earliest *Calendrier* and printed by the same atelier, tends to support this view.)[15] The *Shepherds' Calendar* told which sign the moon was in and its phases, the dates of fixed and movable feast days, and the timing of solar and lunar eclipses. For the most important findings about the year in which the calendar was printed, pictorial devices were given to aid the barely literate. For full use of the various tables, genuine ability to read was required.†

21; T.-J. Schmitt, *L'organisation ecclésiastique et la pratique religieuse dans l'archidiaconé d'Autun de 1650 à 1750* (Autun, 1957), 132–33. J. Ferté, *La vie religieuse dans les campagnes parisiennes, 1622–1695* (Paris, 1962), 186–94.

†The *Shepherds' Calendar* was not published annually. The dates for the new moon could be read off for 38 years; the eclipses were predicted for a century or more. For any year after the year of its printing, the dates of the days of the week, the exact time of the new moon, and the position of the moon in the zodiac had to be worked out from the tables.

Now except for the eclipses, peasants had their own equivalent devices to calculate these results, which they then recorded "in figures on little tablets of wood." These "hieroglyphic Almanacs" were still being made by peasants in the Languedoc in 1655: "On a morsel of wood no bigger than a playing card," said an observer in the Albigeois region, "they mark by a singular artifice all the months and days of the year, with the feast days and other notable things." Why should they then feel the lack of a *Shepherds' Calendar?*

Other parts of the *Calendrier* might have been enjoyable for peasants, such as the recommendations on regimen or the physiognomic signs that warned one who was crafty and who was kind. Yet here, too, rural communities were well supplied with proverbs and old sayings that covered many of these contingencies, sometimes even more aptly than the uniform teaching of the *Calendar*. (Can both Provençaux and Picards have agreed that black curly hair meant a melancholy, lewd, evil-thinking person? Can both Bretons and Gascons have agreed that redheads were foolish, senseless, and disloyal?) The gynecological sections of some *Calendars* (such as Troyes, 1541, and Lyon, 1551) were trifling compared to the wide lore of the village midwife. And let us hope that traveling barbers did not base their bleeding only on the crude illustration of the veins that recurred in these editions.

Similarly, the agricultural advice in the *Shepherds' Calendar* was only of occasional usefulness. Peasants did not really need its woodcuts—a delight though they were to the eyes—to teach them, for instance, that in March it was time to prune the vines. As the old saying went:

> Le vigneron me taille
> Le vigneron me lie
> Le vigneron me baille
> En Mars toute ma vie.

Finally, though I have come upon no example before 1630 of a rural *curé* in possession of a *Shepherds' Calendar,* we can imagine such a priest in the earlier period reading aloud from the extensive religious passages of the book, or even better, showing the villagers the articulated trees of virtue and vice and the pictures of punishments in Hell. This might happen, but could these woodcuts compete with the Last Judgments, the dance of death, the saints' lives, and the Biblical scenes already coloring the walls and filling the windows of so many rural churches at the end of the Middle Ages? And would the seven ways of knowing God and self and the six ways of fulfill-

---

In Noel du Fail's *Propos rustiques,* the village copy of *Calendrier des bergers* is owned by old Maistre Huguet, former village schoolteacher, who reads aloud from it from time to time (15).

ing baptism, wise though they might be, do much to lessen the peasants' dependence on ritual, to move peasant religion toward reading? In short, *Le Grand Calendrier des bergers,* if any of its editions found their way to the village in the sixteenth century, may have jogged the peasants' memory and enriched and perhaps helped standardize its visual store. But it can hardly have brought them much new information or changed significantly their reliance on oral transmission and their relationships with nonpeasant groups.

The festive and musical life of the peasants was also nourished primarily by local tradition and experience and by what the peasants learned from traveling players and saw and heard themselves at fair time in a nearby center. For example, the unmarried youth of the village, organized into Abbayes de Jeunesse, composed chants and playlets to mock the domestic and sexual foibles of older villagers. Thus a mid-sixteenth-century charivari song might be made up on the spur of the moment because a newly wed husband had failed three nights running to consummate his marriage. In the version that has come down to us:

> Quand ils ont sceu au village
> Qua ce mary
> N'avoir non plus de courage
> Q'une soury
> Ils ont faict charyvary
> Pour la riser . . .
> En tres grande diligence
> Un bon garcon
> Du village par plaisance
> Fit la chanson.

In parts of the Auvergne, *reinages* were organized annually in which the right to costume oneself as king, queen, dauphin, constable, and the like was auctioned off to the villager who gave the most wax to the parish church or a local convent.[16] Religious drama also emerged from this nonliterate milieu: in the late fifteenth century, four inhabitants of Triel (Ile-de-France) put on the Life of Saint Victor and got into trouble for taking a statue from the church and using it irreverently as a prop; in 1547, three *laboureurs,* unable to sign their names, contracted with a village painter to make "portraits" for the Life of the child martyr Saint Cyr that they were playing on Sundays in their hamlet of Villejuive.[17]

Farces, moralities, and mysteries were pouring from the presses of Paris and Lyon in the first part of the sixteenth century, but these rural performances used no printed book and probably did not even have a text behind them. So too, it became the fashion in the mid-century to publish so-called *"chansons rustiques"* as part of general collections of songs without music, but there is no evidence that these were aimed at or bought in the villages.[18]

And yet there were a few ways that printing did enter rural life in the sixteenth century to offer some new options to the peasants. The important social institution for this was the *veillée,* an evening gathering within the village community held especially during the winter months from All Saints' Day to Ash Wednesday.[19] Here tools were mended by candlelight, thread was spun, the unmarried flirted, people sang, and some man or woman told stories—of Mélusine, that wondrous woman-serpent with her violent husband and sons; of the girl who escaped from incest to the king's palace in a she-donkey's hide; of Renard and other adventuresome animals.[20] Then, if one of the men were literate and owned books, he might read aloud.

In principle, printing increased significantly the range of books available for the *veillée.* In fact, given the limited channels of distribution in the sixteenth century and the virtuosity of the traditional storyteller, even a rural schoolteacher might have very few books. According to Noel du Fail, a young lawyer from a seigneurial family in upper Brittany who wrote in 1547 a story of a peasant village, the village books were "old": *Aesop's Fables* and *Le Roman de la Rose.* Now both of these had printed editions and urban readers in the late fifteenth and early sixteenth centuries. By the 1540s, however, the learned were enjoying Aesop in fresh Latin and Greek editions or in new French rhyme; and, though still appreciative of the thirteenth-century *Roman,* they were feeling ever more distant from its sense and style, even in the updated version given them by Clément Marot. In contrast, peasants would have had no reason to supplant the early editions that Marot and his publisher disdained as full of printing errors and *"trop ancien langaige."*[21]

Did such reading aloud change things much in the village? *Reading* aloud? We might better say "translating," since the reader was inevitably turning the French of his printed text into a dialect his listeners could understand. And we might well add "editing"—if not for *Aesop's Fables,* whose form and plots were already familiar to peasants, then for the 22,000 lines and philosophical discourses of the *Roman.* In a community hearing parts of the *Roman* for the first time, new relationships were perhaps set up with old chivalric and scholastic ways of ordering experience; some new metaphors were acquired and varied images of women and love added to the listeners' existing stock. Who do you yearn to be, or to love? Mélusine or the Rose? A good question, but it hardly constitutes a connection with the distinctive features of "print culture."*

---

*Noel du Fail was quite particular about the books that he placed in the village. When a pirated edition of his *Propos* came out in Paris in 1548 with other books added to his list, he suppressed them in his new edition at Lyon in 1549. In 1573, however, the Parisian

As early as the 1530s, however, some *veillées* were being treated to a book that was in the vanguard and more disruptive of traditional rural patterns than Aesop, the *Roman de la Rose*, or the *Calendrier:* the vernacular Bible. In Picardy a cobbler reads it to the villagers at the *veillées* until he is discovered by a nearby abbey. Here the literalness of the text was important. The Bible could not be "edited" or reduced to some formulaic magic. It had to be understood, and there were probably no pictures to help. In the Saintonge and elsewhere during the 1550s, Philibert Hamelin, his pack filled with Bibles and prayer books that he had printed at Geneva, comes to sit with peasants in the fields during their noonday break and talks of the Gospel and a new kind of prayer. Some are delighted and learn; others are outraged and curse and beat him. He is sure that one day they will know better.[22]

In the Orléanais a forest ranger buys a vernacular New Testament, a French Psalter, and the Geneva catechism from a bookseller at a fair and goes alone into the forest of Marchenoir to read them. Over in the mountains of the Dauphiné a peasant somehow teaches himself to read and write French and divides his time between plowing and the New Testament. The story goes that when reproached by the priests because he did not know the Scripture in Latin, he laboriously spelled it out until he could contradict them with Latin citations.

Finally, evangelical peddlers begin to work the countryside systematically. A carter, a native of Poitiers, loads up in Geneva with Bibles, Psalters, and Calvinist literature published by Laurent de Normandie and looks for buyers in the Piedmont and the rural Dauphiné. Five craftsmen from scattered parts of France are arrested in 1559 in a village in the Lyonnais with literature from Geneva in their baskets. Even the Inquisitor wonders why they should want to sell such books to *"gens rustiques."*[23]

---

publisher Jean II Ruelle added five titles that may have had some hearing in the countryside: a late-fifteenth-century poetic history of the reign of Charles VII; two medieval romances (including *Valentin et Orson,* which has thematic material relating to the old rural custom of the chase of the wildman or of the bear); an account by Symphorien Champier of the chivalric deeds of the good knight Bayard; and the Miracles of Our Lady. Some of these were part of the *Bibliothèque bleue* of the seventeenth century (du Fail, *Propos,* iv–xii, 138, 187).

On a rainy evening in February 1554, the Norman gentleman Gilles de Gouberville read to his household, including the male and female servants, from *Amadis de Gaule* (A. Tollemer, *Un Sire de Gouberville, gentilhomme campagnard au cotentin de 1553 à 1562,* with an introduction by E. Le Roy Ladurie [reprint of the 1873 ed., Paris, 1972], 285). This chivalric tale had only recently been translated from the Spanish and printed in France.

I think these books would have been received by peasants in the same way as the *Roman de la Rose* and *Aesop's Fables.*

As it turned out, of course, the Calvinist message never won the massive support of the French peasants. Rural Protestantism was to be chiefly the affair either of seigneurs and great noble houses, whose tenants or subjects would then attend Reformed services perforce, or of special regions like the Cévenol, where (as LeRoy Ladurie has shown) initial commitment came from the relatively high concentration of rural artisans, especially in the leather trades.[24] For most peasants, the religion of the Book, the Psalm, and the Consistory gave too little leeway to the traditional oral and ritual culture of the countryside, to its existing forms of social life and social control.

This Calvinist inflexibility is illustrated by the character of a new *Calendrier* that originated in Geneva in the late 1550s and was published in great numbers in the 1560s there, in Lyon, and elsewhere. The engravings for each month still depicted rural scenes, sometimes with great charm. But information on the moon's location in the zodiac either was given not in tables but in *words,* or more often was suppressed altogether (perhaps because it was feared that it would be put to astrological use); and the many saints whose names and pictures marked the traditional *Calendrier* were banished as "superstitious and idolatrous." Instead, the Reformed *Calendrier* listed "historical" dates that would show God's ways to man. Thus Noah's progress in the ark and events in the life of Christ were recorded in their place. On January 26 or 27, 815, Charlemagne died. On February 18, "the feast of fools was celebrated at Rome, to which corresponds Mardi Gras of the Papists . . . successors of the Pagans." March was the month of Martin Bucer's death, July that of Edward IV. Constantinople was taken by Mahomet II May 29, 1453. On August 27, the "reformation according to the truth" took place in Geneva. Under October was remembered Martin Luther's attack on indulgences.[25]

It was an interesting innovation, this slender *Calendrier historial,* which was often slipped in with the Reformed Psalter or New Testament (and even appeared, as they did, in Basque).[26] But how would peasants have responded to it? First, it was harder for the semiliterate to decipher than the Catholic calendar, and it had less astronomical fact. But most of all, no matter how curious the new historical items were, the peasants' year was here stripped beyond recognition, empty even of the saints by which they named their days. Protestant publishers wanted *gens rustiques* to buy these books, but they had not tailored them to a peasant public.*

---

*The *Calendriers historials* were all anonymous and were given their form and content by those that published them. The *Calendrier's* first creator was Conrad Badius, son of a printer in Paris. Of sixteen other *libraires* and *imprimeurs* associated with the editions in Geneva and Lyon in the 1560s, nine of them—and these the most important—were of urban origin.

Still, even if the Bible did not become a permanent fixture in most rural households, merely to think of selling to them on a large scale was something new. Who first opened up the rural markets for the peddlers' books of the seventeenth century? Not a simple printer of rural background; he would remember the illiteracy of his village. Not an ordinary publisher of popular literature; he would worry about meager profits. But zealous Protestants could overlook all that, could face the possibilities of destroyed merchandise and even death for the sake of "consoling poor Christians and instructing them in the law of God."[27]

If printing and Protestantism opened new routes for selling books in the countryside, the press also facilitated the *writing* of a few new books for a peasant public. What happened, I think, was that the printing of "peasant lore," as in the *Shepherds' Calendar* and in books of common proverbs, brought it to the attention of learned men in a new way. These men were discovering the thoughts not of their local tenants or of the men and women from whom they bought grain at market but of The Peasants. And, dedicated to the "illustration" of the national tongue and to the humanist ideal of practical service, they decided that they must correct rural lore and instruct The Peasants. Thus, Antoine Mizaud, doctor of medicine, mathematician, and professor at Paris, writes an *Astrologie des Rustiques* to tell countryfolk without the time to acquire perfect knowledge of the heavens how to predict the weather by sure terrestrial signs. (Mariners, military commanders, and physicians should find it useful, too.) Thus, somewhat later, the royal surgeon Jacques Guillemeau writes a book on pregnancy and childbirth "not for the learned . . . but for Young Surgeons, little versed in the art, dispersed here and there, far away from the cities."

Some new kinds of almanacs appear on an annual basis now, authored by doctors of medicine and "mathematicians," containing bits of possibly novel *agricultural* information, such as when to plant fruits and market vegetables. ("Tested by M. Peron and Jean Lirondes, old gardeners at Nîmes," says one edition, which then tells about the *choux cabus,* artichokes, melons, and other plants that distinguished the seventeenth-century Languedoc garden from its modest fifteenth-century forebear.) Though these almanacs were conceived for a diverse public, they probably were expected to reach some peasant readers—certainly more than were the justly celebrated agricultural

---

The pictures show some attention to agricultural detail: the ox-drawn light plows *(araires)* of the Languedoc figure in some, whereas the horse-drawn heavier plows *(charrues)* of the north appear in others. But some calendars put animal and instrument together in less likely combinations; and a 1566 Lyon edition has placed mowing in the month before reaping—and none provides advice on crops.

manuals of Charles Estienne, Jean Liebault, and others. These latter treatises were intended for landowners, gentlemen farmers, and seigneurs, who would then teach their lessees, tenants, and hired servants what to do.*

The most interesting of these new almanacs, however, was written by Jean Vostet in 1588 and occasioned by the Gregorian calendar reform of six years before. As his patron, the prior of Flammerécourt in Champagne, had said, the ten cut days "had rendered useless the ancient observations of the peasants . . . had ruined their verses and local memory [*leurs vers et mémoire locale*]." So Vostet went through the year's poems and proverbs— culled from sayings and from old manuscript and printed *Calendars* and *Prognostications*—occasionally correcting them when he thought the advice bad or "superstitious" and rewriting them to make up for the lost days. For example, the Bear decides about winter's length no more at Candlemas but on February 12; the hog's acorns are put in doubt not by a rainy St James' day but by a rainy Saint Gengoul's. Instead of it being a good idea to bleed your right arm on March 17, Saint Gertrude's Day, you now should do it two days after the Annunciation. This will keep your eyes clear for the whole year. All this is rather different from the Calvinist *Calendrier historiale,* and not merely because the Protestants refused to accept the pope's reformed calendar until the eighteenth century. (Did Vostet's new sayings catch on?

---

*As Corinne Beutler points out in an excellent review of sixteenth-century agricultural literature, these manuals were addressed to the nobility and landed proprietors, who were then expected to teach their unlettered peasants ("Un chapitre de la sensibilité collective: la littérature agricole en Europe continentale au XVIe siècle," *Annales. Economies, Sociétés, Civilisations* 28 [1973]: 1282, 1292–94). This is clear not only from the introductions to the manuals, but from the assumed public for some of their chapters. Charles Estienne devotes a long section to the kind of *fermier* and *fermière* that the proprietor should hire after he has constructed his farmhouse. Literacy is not a requirement for the tenant, as we have seen, and thus Estienne is not thinking of him as the *reader* of his text *(L'agriculture et la maison rustique de M. Charles Estienne Docteur en Medecine* [Paris: Jacques Du Pays, 1564], chaps. 7–8).

Olivier de Serres, after a preface discussing the limitations of the agricultural understanding of unlettered peasants (an understanding based on experience alone), goes on to a chapter on the different kinds of arrangements by which the Father of the Family may rent out or administer his land. We are long past the time, he writes with ironic wistfulness, when the Father of the Family dirtied his hands working the soil himself. He thinks some of his readers may have to be absent from their property because of service to the king, judicial or financial office, or commercial enterprise. *(Theatre d'Agriculture et Mesnage des Champs d'Olivier de Serres, Seigneur de Pradel* [Paris: Jamet Mettayer, 1600], preface and book 1, chap. 8. Signature at the end of Table in copy at the Bancroft Library: "de Menisson." Marginalia in French, German, and Latin, by different hands, in the chapter on medicinal plants.)

At least in the printed literature they did. We find them in the seventeenth- and eighteenth-century almanacs, but coupled, alas, with the verses they were supposed to supersede.)

Jean Vostet was a man of minor learning, but another book imagined for a peasant public (though actually printed only in Latin during the six- teenth century) was by the eminent jurist René Choppin. It was called *On the Privileges of Rustic Persons,* and Choppin wrote it in 1574 at his estate at Cachan, where he, "half-peasant," was on vacation from the Parlement of Paris. Surveying his fields and flocks, he thought how little jurists had done to recompense the men by whose labor they lived. Why had no one told the peasants of their legal privileges and rights, so they need not be diverted from the plow to wasteful cases in the courts? He would relieve their ignorance in a treatise which, drawing on Roman law, customary law, royal ordinances, and decisions of the Parlements, would answer a host of questions concern- ing peasants—from the status of persons to disputes over pasture.

Was Choppin really trying to make the law accessible to the peasants? Despite the claims of this "semi-paganus" that he wished the "Diligent Husbandman" to read his own law, the promised French translation did not appear till several years after his death. He spoke of the countryfolk with a pastoral nostalgia for their sincerity and an employer's suspicion of their laziness. But especially he visualized peasants as clients or opposing par- ties, and the book was directed to lawyers who would plead for or against them in various courts. It was a genuine contribution to the slow process of unification of French law—though one about which Choppin felt defensive. Writing about rustic things after writing about the royal domain might be thought, as the proverb said, to be going from horses to asses. As for the "asses," it seems unlikely that they read about their privileges. Indeed, we have no *sure* evidence that any of these books addressed to a rural public ever actually reached a peasant audience. Probably some of the almanacs did circulate in the countryside, for they appear in the peddlers' packs in the seventeenth century.

What can we conclude, then, about the consequences of printing for the sixteenth-century peasant community? Certainly they were limited. A few lines of communication were opened between professor and peasant—or rather between bodies of cultural materials, as in the case of some traditional lore that was standardized and disseminated by the press, perhaps with a little correction from above. Expectations were higher by 1600 that a printed book might come into the village and be read aloud at the *veillée,* even where the little spark of Protestantism had burned out in the countryside. But oral culture was still so dominant that it transformed everything it touched; and it still changed according to the rules of forgetting and remembering, watching and discussing. Some printed medieval romances may have come to peasants from the cities, but they cannot have played the escapist role that Mandrou has claimed for them in the seventeenth century. Peasants in the Lyonnais, in the Ile-de-France, and in the Languedoc put on tithe strikes just the same; villages in Burgundy forced their lords to enfranchise about half of their service population; peasants in Brittany, the Guyenne, Burgundy, and the Dauphiné organized themselves into emergency communes, communicated with each other, and rebelled under traditional slogans, ensigns, and captains with festive titles—all neither deflected nor aided by what was being said in print.[28] Indeed, those who wished to control the countryside and bring it to order by means other than sheer force—whether bishop, seigneur, or king—would have to send not books but messengers, whose seals would not be mocked and who would disclose verbally the power behind the papers that they read.

II

In the cities, the changes wrought or facilitated by printing in the life of the *menu peuple* had greater moment. The literacy rate had long been higher among urban artisans and tradesmen than among peasants, but the gap widened—at least for males—in the early sixteenth century. The old choirboy schools still performed their service for the sons of some artisans and petty traders, and more important, the numbers of vernacular schoolteachers and reckonmasters multiplied. For instance, in Lyon in the 1550s and 1560s, some 38 male teachers of reading, writing, and arithmetic can be identified (very roughly one for every 400 males under the age of twenty in the city), quite apart from the masters at the Latin Collège de la Trinité. They marry the daughters of taverners and the widows of millers; they live in houses with pouchmakers and dressmakers; they have goldsmiths, printers, barber-surgeons, coopers, and gold-thread-drawers among their friends. In addition to these teachers, newly established municipal orphanages in some cities provided simple instruction for poor boys, and at times even orphan girls were taught their ABC's.[29]

This press for literacy was associated with technological, economic, and social developments. Printing itself created a populous cluster of crafts (including bookbinding and typecasting) where literacy rates were high. Of 115 printers' journeymen assembled in Lyon in 1580 to give power of attorney, two-thirds could sign their names fully; and the journeymen were already demanding that all apprentices know how to read and write, even those who would be but simple pressmen. In other crafts, such as painting and surgery, literacy was spurred by the desire for a higher, more "professional" status and the availability of vernacular books for training. Even the royal sergeants, a group among the *menu peuple* previously noted only for their skill with the rod, began to live up to a 1499 decree requiring them to read and write.

Literacy was not, of course, distributed evenly among the *menu peuple*. An examination of the ability to sign of 885 males involved in notarial acts in Lyon in the 1560s and 1570s spreads the trades out as follows (masters and journeymen combined):

> Very high: apothecaries, surgeons, printers.
> High: painters, musicians, taverners, metalworkers (including gold trades).
> Medium (about 50 percent): furriers and leatherworkers, artisans in textile and clothing trades.
> Low to very low: artisans in construction trades, in provisioning, transport; urban gardeners; unskilled dayworkers.

In Narbonne, for about the same time, LeRoy Ladurie found that one-third of the artisans could sign their names; another third could write initials; and only one-third were totally foreign to letters. At Montpellier the percentage of craftsmen who could make only marks was down to 25 percent. This range among the artisans contrasts both with the almost complete literacy of well-off merchants of all kinds and with the low rate of literacy among urban women outside the families of lawyers, merchant-bankers, and publishers.[30]

City-dwellers were also more likely than countryfolk to be able to understand French. Towns were, of course, constantly replenished by people from rural areas with their local patois and even by people from foreign lands, and the urban speech itself was not independent of the big patterns of regional dialect. Nevertheless, French was increasingly the language of royal government (after 1539 all judicial acts were to be in French) and of other kinds of exchange; in an important southern center like Montpellier it could be heard in the streets already by 1490.[31] Thus the urban artisan had potentially a more direct access to the contents of the printed book—whose vernacular was French, as we have seen—than a peasant who could read handwritten accounts in Provençal but would have had to struggle over a printed *Calendrier*.

From simple literacy to actual reading is something of a step. Studies based only on inventories after death in sixteenth-century Paris and Amiens suggest that the step was not always taken. In the early years of the century, if an artisan or small shopkeeper in Paris owns a book at all, it is likely to be a manuscript Book of Hours. By 1520 printed books appear, displacing the manuscripts but existing along with the religious paintings, sculpture, and wall hangings that even quite modest families possess. Most artisans, however, had no books at their death. They represent only about ten percent of book owners in Paris and twelve percent of book owners in Amiens (or seventeen percent, if we include barbers and surgeons); that is, well below the proportion of the *gens mécaniques* in the urban population at large. And when they do have books, outside of printers' stock, there are not very many of them. Out of all the editions in the Amiens inventories, only 3.7 percent were in artisanal hands (six percent, if we include barbers and surgeons); and apart from the latter group, the median size of the library was one book![32]

In Amiens that one book was most likely to be a Book of Hours, or perhaps a French *Golden Legend* (the medieval book of saints' lives popular throughout the sixteenth century), or a vernacular Bible. Or else it might be a technical work, such as a pattern book for cabinetmaking or painting. In Paris in 1549, a tanner dies owning a *Golden Legend* and the *Mer des Histoires,* a thirteenth-century historical work still being printed in the 1530s and 1540s; a barber-surgeon leaves behind six French volumes on the art of surgery.[33] Clearly the literate were often without private libraries and, at least on their deathbed, do not appear to have taken much advantage of the varied fruits of the "admirable invention."

There were some economic reasons for this, even though printed books were cheaper by far than manuscripts had been. A twenty-four page sermon on poor relief cost as much as a loaf of coarse bread in the 1530s; an easy little arithmetic, half a loaf. A few years later, a full news account of the seizure of Rhodes could be almost as expensive as a pair of children's shoes; a book of Christmas carols, as much as a pound of candlewax. In the 1540s a French history could cost more than half a day's wages for a painter's journeyman or a printer's journeyman, and almost a whole day's wages for a journeyman in the building trades.[34] In the 1560s the cheapest "hand-size" New Testament in French was not much less. Understandably, some artisans complained that they could not afford to buy it, thus prompting a Protestant polemicist to ask them whether "they didn't have all the Instruments of their craft, however much poverty made it difficult to buy them," and how could they pass up a Book of such utility as the Bible?[35]

In fact, artisans found ways to have access to printed materials without collecting them privately. They bought a book, read it until they were finished, or until they were broke or needed cash, and then pawned it with an innkeeper or more likely sold it to a friend or to a *libraire.* Thus one Jean de Cazes, a native of Libourne, purchased a Lyon Bible in Bordeaux for two écus (an expensive edition), read it, and sold it to someone from the Saintonge before he was arrested for heresy in 1566 at the age of 27.[36] Books were relatively liquid assets and were less subject to depreciation than many other personal items. One kept to the end, if one could afford it, only those

editions that were needed for constant reference or were wanted as permanent family property—thus the Hours, the Bibles, and the workbooks that
show up in the inventories after death. Possibly, too, in the absence of public
libraries, literate artisans and shopkeepers lent each other books from their
small stores as did more substantial collectors (the poet François Béroald
had three leaves of his account book devoted to loaned books); and they may
even have passed on books as gifts more often than we know. Theirs was a
world in which "secrets"—the secrets of the craft, the secrets of women—had
never been private possessions but corporate ones, shared, told, passed on
so they would not be forgotten. What happens when scarce printed books
enter such a world? They flow through the literate segments of the *menu
peuple* rather than remain hoarded on an artisan's shelf.

Books were also shared in reading groups which, as in the countryside,
brought the literate and illiterate together. The traditional winter *veillée*
was not the regular setting, however; for outside the building trades many
craftsmen worked winter and summer, by candlelight if necessary, till eight
or even ten o'clock at night.[37] Gatherings of family and friends for singing,
games, cards, storytelling, and perhaps reading were more likely special
occasions, like feast days. Certain books were designed to be read aloud or
consulted in the shop, such as pattern books for textile design and the French
translation of Birunguccio's *Pirotechnia*, an excellent manual on metallur-
gical processes. So, too, the oft-printed little arithmetics that taught petty
business operations "by the pen" in Arabic numerals and by counting stones
(jetons) "for those who don't know how to read and write" were resources
for apprentices and adults in an atelier even more than for an instructor in
a little school. One *Brief Arithmetic* promised to teach a tradesman all he
needed to know in fifteen days' time and added mnemonic verses to help
him catch on.

Reading aloud in one connection or another must have been especially
common in the printing shop. I am thinking not merely of the discussion of
copy among scholar-printers, authors, and editors, but of reading in snatches
that could reach out to the journeymen and to the spouses and daughters
helping to hang up the freshly printed sheets. Thus one Michel Blanc, a
simple pressman in Lyon in the late 1530s, knew enough of Marot's poems,
which were printed in his shop, for his son to remember later how he had
been "brought up in his youth on Marot." Possibly men may sometimes have
taken books into the tavern for reading. As for the women, they surely did
some of their reading aloud among their own sex; an example might be the
Life of Saint Margaret, with prayers for the pregnant and the parturient.

But the most innovative reading groups were the secret Protestant assemblies on feast days or late at night in private homes—innovative among

other reasons because they brought together men and women who were not necessarily in the same family or craft or even neighborhood. Thus a 1559 assembly in Paris included a goldsmith's journeyman from the Gâtinais, a university student from Lyon, a shoemaker's journeyman, and several others, all from different parts of the city. An early conventicle in the town of Saintes, organized by two poor artisans in 1557, had access to one printed Bible, from which passages were written down for discussion. Encouraged by Deuteronomy 6:7 to speak of God's law, however small their learning, the artisans scheduled written exhortations every Sunday by the six members who could read and write. Like the heretical linen-weavers of Cambrai, with their printed Bible in the fields, these Protestants read, talked, sang, and prayed.

In short, reading from printed books does not silence oral culture. It can give people something fresh to talk about. Learning from printed books does not suddenly replace learning by doing. It can provide people with new ways to relate their doings to authority, new and old.

Nor should printing be viewed merely as purveying to the *menu peuple* the science of university graduates, the doctrine of the religious, the literary production of the educated, and the orders of the powerful. Artisans, tradesmen, and women composed themselves a few of the books they read.* To be sure, some such persons had in the fourteenth and fifteenth centuries quietly authored manuscripts—of craft secrets, of mechanical inventions, of poems. But the authors had failed to become widely known and, with the exception of outstanding figures like the literary Christine de Pisan, their works were not reproduced later by the presses.

But now many individuals without the ordinary attributes expected of an author in the later Middle Ages get their books printed—and they have an audience. Their tone might range from the confident ("I've tested sundials for a long time") to the apologetic ("Excuse my unadorned language . . . I am not Latin"), but they are sure that their skills, observations, or sentiments give them something distinctive to say. Like the learned writer, they imagine varied publics for their work: their own kind and those on a higher level. Like the learned writer, they present themselves to the unknown buyers of their books in proud author portraits quite different from the humble donor picture characteristic of the medieval manuscript. Thus Milles de Norry,

---

*Anonymous city lore and song, like peasant sayings, found their way into print, as did innumerable stories and poems in which artisans and servants were the actors (such as *Le caquet de bonnes Chambrieres, declarant aucunes finesses dont elles usent vers leurs maistres et maistresses*, printed at Lyon about 1549). The authorship of such material and its relation to actual popular life and sources are such complex problems that we cannot consider them here.

previously a modest reckonmaster in Lyon, gazes from his 1574 commercial arithmetic, fitted out with a ruff and a Greek device.[38]

This widening of the circle of authors had diverse causes besides printing, but it was given some permanence by the new form of publication. Now practicing apothecaries get into print, like Pierre Braillier of Lyon, who dared to attack *The Abuses of Ignorance of Physicians,* and Nicolas Houel of Paris, who encroached on the physicians' field by writing on the plague and who published a treatise on poor relief as well. Now surgeons write on their art and even on medicine (and we must remember that they are still considered *gens mécaniques* in the sixteenth century, despite the gains of some of them in learning, status, and wealth). Ambrose Paré's first book appears in 1545, when he is a mere army surgeon and master at the Hôtel-Dieu in Paris; and at least nineteen other surgeons have vernacular texts printed from the 1540s through the 1580s. Sailors publish accounts of their travels to the New World. Poems come out from a cartwright in the Guyenne, a wine merchant in Toulouse, and a trader in Béthune, the last including a "Hymn to Commerce."

The most self-conscious artisan-author, however, was the potter Bernard Palissy. To the readers of his important dialogues on chemistry and agriculture he says that some will think it impossible that "a poor artisan . . . destitute of Latin" could be right and ancient learned theorists wrong. But experience is worth more than theory. If you don't believe what my books say, get my address from the printer, and I will give you a demonstration in my own study. What we see here is not merely fresh communication between craftsman and scholar (much discussed by historians of science), and between practice and theory (the participants in Palissy's dialogues); we see also a new kind of relation between an author and his anonymous public.*

---

*This formal invitation from the author for direct response from readers is found in other printed books as well. It is the product of a situation in which the author expects that a large number of unknown readers will be seeing his work in the near future and will be able to locate him easily. (It goes well beyond the practice of the medieval author who, as John Benton has informed me, either urged his readers to write improvements on the manuscript or—more likely—anathemized readers and scribes who tampered with his text, but who did not invite correspondence.) Robert I Estienne asked readers of his *Dictionnaire Francoislatin* to send him any works he might have omitted that they found in Latin authors and "good French authors," as well as to correct any faults they found in his definitions of hunting terms (Paris: Robert I Estienne, 1549, "*Au lecteur*" and 664). Both the physician Laurent Joubert and the bibliophile François de La Croix du Maine asked for information from their readers, as we will see below. Authors may also have received unsolicited letters: Ambrose Paré asked young surgeons using his *Oeuvres* (1575) to let him know graciously of any faults they might find rather than slander him. The reckonmaster Valentin Mennher did not especially want to hear

Another entrant into the ranks of authors was, of course, the self-educated scholar-printer. Elizabeth Eisenstein has rightly stressed the novelty of this figure, who combined intellectual, physical, and administrative forms of labor.[39] Indeed, it was not only men like Badius, the Estiennes, Gryphius, and the de Tournes who had such a creative role; lesser masters and even journeymen could shape the content of the books they printed. Sometimes their names are appended to prefaces; sometimes, as with the proof-reader Nicolas Dumont, it is only by luck that we catch a glimpse of their work as authors. A native of Saumur, Dumont was so busy preparing and correcting copy in Paris in the years 1569 to 1584 "that he scarcely had time to breathe." Yet he sometimes got hold of a press and printed pamphlets; he translated various works from Latin to French; and, in particular, he composed little news stories about Henri III's doings in France and Poland, the seizure of Tunis from the Turks, and other current happenings. Whether he presented his stories as "letters" from unnamed gentlemen observers or as anonymous eyewitness accounts, Dumont in many ways anticipated the reporter of the periodical press.

Female writers also appeared in print in noticeable numbers—more than twenty had some reputation. Mostly they came from families of gentlemen or lawyers, were involved in humanist circles, and published poems or translations. Their works still show signs of womanly modesty: they are dedicated to other women ("because women must not willingly appear in public alone, I choose you for my guide"); they address themselves to "female readers"; they defend themselves against the reproach that silence is the ornament of women. A few of them transformed the image of the author even more: Louise Labé, the ropemaker's daughter, whose appeal to women to publish we heard at the opening of this essay (and contemporary evidence indicates that many wellborn women did shyly keep their poems in manuscript); Nicole Estienne, printer's daughter and physician's wife, whose verses on "The Miseries of the Married Woman' had two editions; and the midwife Louise Bourgeois. Once midwife to the poor of her Paris neighborhood, later midwife to the family of Henri IV, Bourgeois wrote on her art, believing herself the first woman to do so. Her wide practice, she claimed, would show up the mistakes of Physicians and Surgeons, even of Master Galen himself. She looks out with poise from her engraving at the reader, this skilled woman who corrected men, publicly and in print.

---

from readers about the mistakes in his arithmetic texts: "Please just make corrections on the page rather than by useless words." The errors in a 1555 Lyon edition of his work were the printer's fault, not his *(Arithmetique Seconde par M. Valentin Mennher de Kempten* [Antwerp, Jean Loc, 1556], f. Z viii^r).

Finally, groups among the *menu peuple* sometimes spoke to the public collectively through the press. The *compagnonnages* of the journeymen of Lyon and Paris, as we have seen, printed the brief that they presented to the Parlement of Paris in 1572. This document raised a dozen objections to a royal edict on printing and attacked the journeymen's employers as tyrannical and avaricious oppressors, who worked them to poverty and illness. Their employers answered, also in print, that the journeymen were debauched conspiratorial "monopolists," trying to reduce their masters to servitude and destroy the industry. A printed protest was used again in Lyon in 1588, when master printers and journeymen were on the same side against the merchant-publishers, who were ignoring them in favor of the cheaper labor of Geneva. Here are precocious examples of artisans trying to influence literate public opinion in a labor dispute.

Groups also tried on occasion to influence public opinion in regard to political matters. Here I am thinking of the urban Abbeys of Misrule, festive societies of neighborhood or craft, which directed their charivaris and mockery not only against domestic scandals but against misgovernment by their betters. For a long time, the Abbeys had left their recreations unrecorded; but in the sixteenth century they began to print them. Thus readers outside Rouen could learn about the 1540 Mardi Gras parade at that city—with its float bearing a king, the pope, the emperor, and a fool playing catch with the globe—and could ponder its mocking verses about hypocrisy in the church, about how faith was turning to contempt (*foy* to *fy*) and nobility to injury *(noblesse* to *on blesse)*. In the Lyon festivals of the 1570s through the 1590s, the Lord of Misprint tossed printed verses to the spectators and subsequently published the scenarios, with their complaints about the high cost of bread and paper, about the fluctuations in the value of currency, and especially about the folly of war in France.

This body of pamphlet literature, small and ephemeral though it is, suggests two interesting things about the relation of printing to the development of political consciousness. First, though most early polemical literature disseminated outward and downward the political and religious views of persons at the center (whether at the center of royal government or at the center of strong resistance movements like the Huguenots and the Holy Catholic League), it occurred to some city people on the margins of power to use the press to respond. Second, the addition of printed pamphlets to traditional methods for spreading news (rumor, street song, private letters, town criers, fireworks displays, bell-ringing, and penitential processions) increased the *menu peuple's* stock of detailed information about national events. In the 1540s, the Rouen festive society could count on spectators and readers knowing the facts of local political life, but references to national or European events were usually general and even allegorical. By the end of the century in Lyon, however, the Lord of Misprint could expect that his audience would also recognize joking references to recent sumptuary legislation and to controversial decisions of the Parlement of Paris.

Readers may be thinking that these varied works authored by the *menu peuple* were such a tiny fraction of the total printed corpus of sixteenth-century France that no educated contemporary would have paid attention to them. In fact they were noticed, favorably and unfavorably. The visionary bibliographer François de La Croix du Maine, who built up a library of thousands of volumes and who sent out printed requests all over Europe for information about authors, was happy to include most of the people and books we have been considering here in his *Bibliotheque* of 1584.* He made no critical exclusions: Nicole Estienne and Nicolas Dumont are set in their alphabetical places just as are Pierre de Ronsard and Joachim du Bellay in his "general catalogue" of all authors, "women as well as men, who had written in our maternal French."

We also have a reaction from a humanist and poet deeply concerned about the character of French culture. As a member of the Pléiade, Jacques Peletier had devoted himself to the vernacular tongue and had also celebrated the printing press:

> Ah . . . one can print in one day
> What it would take thirty days to say
> And a hundred times longer to write by hand.

High quality in vernacular publication would be guaranteed, so he had argued hopefully, by right and clear Method—right method for ordering poetry, mathematics, medicine, music, even spelling. But what would happen now that all kinds of people were publishing books? In an ironic anonymous

---

*Thus among sixteenth-century authors either writing in French or translating into French, La Croix listed 110 physicians, but also 25 surgeons (22 of whom had works in print) and 9 apothecaries (8 with works in print). He included 40 female writers from the end of the fifteenth century to 1584 (at least 16 had works in print, as far as he knew); Christine de Pisan, composing her *City of Ladies* around 1405, seems to have been aware of no other contemporary female authors.

In 1579 at Le Mans, La Croix had 350 copies printed of the initial statement of his project, including his request for information about or from authors. He received six answers. He repeated the request in the 1584 edition of the *Bibliotheque,* this time remembering to suggest ways in which mail might reach him at Paris (*Premier volume de la Bibliotheque du sieur de la Croix-du-Maine* [Paris: Abel l'Angelier, 1584], *"Preface aux lecteurs"* and 523, 529, 538–39).

essay, he urged every village, every curate, every trader, every captain to write his piece; every parish, every vineyard must have its historian. *"Ecrivons tous, sçavans et non sçavans!"* And if we do badly? Well, never mind. Our books can be used by the ladies who sell toilet paper at the Paris bridges.

How indeed could the learned control not only aesthetic quality but also true doctrine and science if just anyone could get books printed, and if these books were being made available by the press in the vernacular to large numbers of ill-educated city people? The central book in the religious debate was, of course, the vernacular Bible, and for several decades the doctors of theology (strongly backed by secular law) tried to defend their monopoly on its interpretation by denying the right of the uneducated to read it. The debate was sometimes face to face, between doctor of theology and craftsman: "Do you think it's up to you to read the Bible," asked the Inquisitor in a Lyon prison in 1552, "since you're just an artisan and without knowledge?" "God taught me by His Holy Spirit," said the craftsman. "It belongs to all Christians to know it in order to learn the way to salvation."[40]

The debate also took place in print. "God does not want to declare his secrets to a bunch of *menu peuple*," said the great Jesuit Emond Auger. "Intoxicated by I know not what phrases from the Apostles, badly quoted and even worse understood, they start to abuse the Mass and make up questions." Understanding comes not from "a bare and vulgar knowledge of the words," but from the special vocation of those who have studied.[41] A young Protestant pastor answered: the pope and his doctors of theology forbid the Bible to everyone but themselves, because they know that once their lives and doctrine are examined by the Word of God, they will have to give their goods to the poor and start working with their hands. They permit a poor craftsman to read a book on love or folly, to dance or play cards, but they see him with a New Testament in his hands and he is a heretic. But our Lord has commanded us "Search the Scriptures." And the early Fathers exhorted the people—craftsmen, women, and everybody in general—to read it in their houses and often, and especially before going to sermons so they could understand them. The pastor ends up reminding his readers that reading *alone* was not the path to true doctrine. The Protestant method for guaranteeing orthodoxy was in the last instance censorship and punishment; but in the first instance it was *the combination of reading with listening to a trained teacher.*

Ultimately, despite the triumphs of the Counter-Reformation in France, the doctors of theology had to abandon their position, in fact if not always in public. Force simply would not work. What had guaranteed the clerical monopoly two hundred years before had really been a limited technology and the Latin language. Already at the end of the fourteenth century, vernacular Bibles, Biblical digests, and picture books were being used by lay families here and there. Once the first presses were installed in France, the stream of French Bibles and Bible versions began without waiting for the Reformation. No legislation, no inquisition, no procedures of censorship could stop the new relations between reading, listening, and talking that had grown up among city people—relations which Catholic humanists as well as Protestants had been ready to encourage. After the 1570s, it became legal for a French Bible—a Catholic revision of the Genevan Scripture approved by the Theology Faculty of Louvain—to circulate in France. In cheap, small format, the New Testament had some success among Catholic laymen in the cities.[42]

What was needed to maintain Catholic orthodoxy was a mode of control more suited to printing than an archaic form of sacerdotal monopoly and more effective than censorship. In 1524, a Franciscan religious who was translating and commenting a Book of Hours for a circle of noblewomen pointed the way. Everyone is admitted to preaching, no matter how unlearned, said Brother Gilles; need seeing words be more dangerous than hearing them? The answer was to make the bare text safe by clothing it with orthodox exposition. The Jesuits were to go on and fix the meaning of a devotional text by an accompanying standardized religious picture or emblem. By 1561 in Lyon, the Jesuit Possevino paid for the printing of orthodox little booklets and distributed them free in the streets. By the late sixteenth century, the Catholic laity had a growing body of spiritual literature *in which the eye was guided by exposition and illustration.*

A similar though less intense debate occurred over the dissemination of medical information to laymen. Vernacular *Regimens against the Plague* and collections of remedies for ill health and women's disorders were old genres; printing did no more than increase their numbers. In the 1530s, however, doctors of medicine began to publish translations of Greek medical texts and of Doctor Guy de Chauliac's fourteenth-century Latin treatise on surgery, as well as systematic examinations of medicine and surgery in French for the specific use of surgeons' journeymen, "who have begged us to do it," "whose ignorance must be dispelled," and "who are today more studious than many physicians." These books were used by the young surgeons who attended occasional lectures and dissections given by physicians at the Hôtel-Dieu at Lyon, special courses at the Faculty of Medicine at Montpellier, and the classes supported by the surgeons' confraternity of Saint-Côme at Paris; they were used also by older surgeons in the cities who wanted to improve their skill.[43] The next step was the publication by doctors of medicine of new regimens of health and medical advice on child-rearing in the vernacular, very often dedicated to women.

The arguments used in defense of these editions, offered by Catholic humanists and Protestants alike, resemble those used in defense of vernacular Bibles and doctrinal literature. As printers pointed out that Saint Jerome had translated the Bible into a vernacular, so the physician Vallembert pointed out in his 1565 pediatric manual that Galen and Avicenna had written in their vernacular. An English medical popularizer spoke against his critics in the very terms that the early Protestant Antoine de Marcourt had used against the engrossing "merchants" of the Faculty of Theology: "Why grutch [grudge] they phisike to come forth in Englysche? Wolde they have no man to know but onley they? Or what make they themselves? Marchauntes of our lyves and deathes, that we shulde bye our healthe onely of them, and at theyr pryces?" A French work by the Protestant Laurent Joubert makes the comparison explicit: those doctors of medicine who say that it is wrong to teach people how to maintain their health are no better than doctors of theology who deprive them of spiritual food. To those who objected to instructing surgeons in French, Joubert's son answered that good operations could be performed in any language, and that misunderstanding of a Latin text was as possible as misunderstanding of a French one ("should we burn all Latin books because of the danger that some clerk will misinterpret the law therein?"). And anyway, if we are willing to read books aloud to surgeons' journeymen, why not put them in French? "Must we put a lower value on the living voice than on the written paper?"

Laurent Joubert's volumes are especially useful for a study of the new relations between groups of people and between cultural traditions facilitated by printing. For twenty-five years he had been trying to stamp out false opinions in medicine, and in 1578 he decided to compile a new kind of book—*Erreurs Populaires* about health and medicine from conception to grave that he would collect and correct. "Popular errors" came from several sources, he explained: from weaknesses in the soul and human reasoning; from ignorant oral traditions, especially those of midwives; and from people's having heard too much from physicians and having a crude understanding of it. It seems to me, however, that as the sense of the errors in peasant lore was sharpened for the learned by the printing of that lore (as we have seen above), so the printing of all kinds of vulgar regimens, traditional books of secrets, and remedies created for Joubert the concept of general errors and made them accessible to correction.

In any case, in Volume One he got through conception and infancy, demonstrating, for instance, that it was *not* true that male children were born at full moon and female children at new moon and that it *was* true that at certain times of night or monthly period one could be sure of conceiving a male. He then told his readers that he would wait to publish Volume Two until they had had a chance to send him more popular errors. They could just address him at the University of Montpellier, where he was Chancellor of the Faculty of Medicine. Dr Joubert received 456 sayings and queries from readers within a year, which he duly published and, where possible, corrected or explained in Volume Two.

Joubert's *Popular Errors* illustrates the central paradox in the impact of printing on the people. On the one hand, it can destroy traditional monopolies on knowledge and authorship and can sell and disseminate widely both information and works of imagination. It can even set up a new two-way relationship between author and anonymous audience. But printing can also make possible the establishment of new kinds of control on popular thought. To quote once more the physician and translator Pierre Tolet, "If you want a servant to follow your orders you can't give them in an unknown tongue." Joubert's goal and that of the other popularizers was not to eliminate the distinction between expert and inexpert or to weaken the profession of medicine. It was to raise the surgeons from their "routine illiterate practice" while defining their field to keep even the most skillful of them under the authority of the physicians. It was to raise the people to a better understanding of how to take care of themselves while convincing them more effectively to obey the doctor's orders.

On the whole, it seems to me that the first 125 years of printing in France, which brought little change in the countryside, strengthened rather than sapped the vitality of the culture of the *menu peuple* in the cities—that is, added both to their realism and to the richness of their dreams, both to their self-respect and to their ability to criticize themselves and others. This is because they were not passive recipients (neither passive beneficiaries nor passive victims) of a new type of communication. Rather they were active users and interpreters of the printed books they heard and read, and even helped give these books form. Richard Hoggart, in his remarkable study of working-class culture in present-day England *(The Uses of Literacy)* has found a salty, particularistic, resourceful layer of culture existing along with a "candy-floss," slack, uniform one. If this is possible in the twentieth century, with its powerful and highly competitive mass media and centralized political institutions, all the more readily could the sixteenth-century populace impose its uses on the books that came to it. Oral culture and popular social organization were strong enough to resist mere correction and standardization from above. Protestantism and certain features of humanism converged with printing to challenge traditional hierarchical values and to delay the establishment of rigid new ones. Economic control of publishing was not concentrated in the houses of great merchant-publishers, but was shared by a variety of producers. Monopolies in knowledge had broken down but had not been replaced by effective political and religious censorship and by the theory and laws of private property in ideas.

If in a different context printing may lead the people to flaccidity, escape, and the ephemeral, in the sixteenth century the printers' journeymen could claim with some reason that printing was "the eternal brush which gave a living portrait to the spirit."

Notes

1. Robert Mandrou, *De la culture populaire aux 17e et 18e siècles. La bibliothèque bleue de Troyes* (Paris, 1964), 9–10, 18, 22. Geneviève Bollème, "Littérature populaire et littérature de colportage au 18e siècle," in *Livre et société dans la France du XVIIe siècle* (Paris, 1965), 65, and *Les almanachs populaires aux XVIIe et XVIIIe siècles. Essai d'histoire sociale* (Paris, 1969), "Avant-propos." See also Marc Soriano, *Les Contes de Perrault. Culture savante et traditions populaires* (Paris, 1968), 480–81.

2. Louis B. Wright, *Middle-Class Culture in Elizabethan England* (Ithaca, N.Y., 1958 [1st ed., 1935]), 18. Mandrou, *Culture populaire,* 19–20, 162. Bollème, however, has expressed some doubts about *whose* worldview is revealed in almanacs and other popular literature.

3. A. H. Schutz, *Vernacular Books in Parisian Private Libraries of the Sixteenth Century, according to the Notarial Inventories,* University of North Carolina Studies in the Romance Languages and Literatures 25 (Chapel Hill, 1955), 39, 78, n. 85. Albert Labarre, *Le livre dans la vie amiénoise du seizème siècle. L'enseignement des inventaires après décès* (Paris, 1971), 274. Bollème admits to the wide range in the social background of readers of almanacs in the seventeenth and eighteenth centuries *(Almanachs,* 15).

4. Schutz, *Vernacular Books,* 34 (Amaud de Villeneuve, to whom the *Tresor des povres* was attributed), 81, n. 137. E. Coyecque, *Recueil d'actes notariés relatifs à l'histoire de Paris et de ses environs au 16e siècle* ("Histoire generale de Paris," Paris, 1924), no. 106.

5. Mandrou, *Culture populaire,* 162–63. Noel Taillepied, *Psichologie ou traité de l'apparition des esprits* (Paris, 1588), chap. 6.

6. Jean-Paul Sartre, *Qu'est-ce que la littérature?* (1948), cited by Robert Escarpit in his valuable essay "Le littéraire et le social," in R. Escarpit, ed., *Le littéraire et le social. Eléments pour une sociologie de la littérature* (Paris, 1970), 18.

7. J. R. Goody, ed., *Literacy in Traditional Societies* (Cambridge, 1968). Elizabeth L. Eisenstein, "Some Conjectures about the Impact of Printing on Western Society and Thought: A Preliminary Report," *Journal of Modern History* 40 (1968), 1–56, and "The Advent of Printing and the Problem of the Renaissance," *Past and Present* 45 (Nov. 1969), 19–89, and (with T. K. Rabb), "Debate: The Advent of Printing and the Problem of the Renaissance," *Past and Present* 52 (Aug. 1971), 134–44, and "L'avènement de l'imprimerie et la Réforme," *Annales ESC* 26 (1971), 1355–82. For

a study of popular culture that uses a "relational" approach, see M. Agulhon, "Le problème de la culture populaire en France autour de 1848," Davis Center Seminar, Princeton University (May 1974). For a critique of some of the techniques used by social historians in the study of books and literary culture in the eighteenth century, see R. Darnton, "Reading, Writing and Publishing in Eighteenth-Century France: A Case Study in the Sociology of Literature," in Felix Gilbert and S. R. Graubard, eds., *Historical Studies Today* (New York, 1972), 238–50.

8. Lucien Febvre and Henri-Jean Martin, *L'apparition du livre* (Paris, 1958), 285–86, 173–237; Henri-Jean Martin, *Livre, pouvoirs et société à Paris au XVIIe siècle (1598–1701)* (Geneva, 1969), 319–26. N. Z. Davis, "Publisher Guillaume Rouillé, Businessman and Humanist," in R. J. Schoeck, ed., *Editing Sixteenth Century Texts* (Toronto, 1966), 72–77. Schutz, *Vernacular Books,* 31–73 (first appearance of craftsmen and small merchants among book-owners in the 1520s); Coyecque, *Recueil,* nos. 270, 588. Roger Doucet, *Les bibliothèques parisiennes au XVIe siècle* (Paris, 1956), 171–75 (lists names and occupations of book-owners in 194 Parisian inventories after death from 1493 to 1560). Out of 94 inventories from the years 1540–60, 10 percent relate to persons below the level of the commercial and legal elite. Calculating from Martin's analysis of Parisian inventories after death in the seventeenth century *(Livre, pouvoirs et société,* 492), we get roughly 10 percent of the book collections in the hands of lesser merchants, barber-surgeons, painters, and craftsmen.

9. Roger Vaultier, *Le folklore pendant la guerre de Cent Arts d'après les lettres de rémission du trésor des chartes* (Paris, 1965), 106. Bernard Guenée, *Tribunaux et gens de justice dans le bailliage de Senlis à la fin du moyen age (vers 1380–vers 1550)* (Paris, 1963), 277–78, 317. Michel Devèze, *La vie de la forêt française au XVIe siècle* (Paris, 1961), 2:112–13.

10. Emmanuel Le Roy Ladurie, *Les Paysans de Languedoc* (Paris, 1966), 345–47. Yvonne Bézard, *La vie rurale dans le sud de la région parisienne de 1450 à 1560* (Paris, 1929), 249–52, 185–86. Guenée, *Tribunaux,* 187–93. Jacques Toussaert, *Le sentiment religieux en Flandre à la fin du moyen age* (Paris, 1963), 60–66. M. Gonon, *La vie quotidienne en Lyonnais d'après les testaments, XIVe–XVIe siècles* (Paris, 1968), 54, 54, n. 2 (none of the testaments that prescribe the placing of children in school are from peasant parents). Bernard Bonnin, "L'éducation dans les classes populaires rurales en Dauphiné au XVIIe siècle," in *Le XVIIe siècle et l'éducation,* supplement to *Marseille* 88 (1972), 63–68. (I am grateful to Daniel Hickey for calling this article to my attention.) A major new study of literacy in France from 1650 to the twentieth century is now under way by François Furet. Isaballe Guérin, *La vie rurale en Sologne aux XIVe et XVe siècles* (Paris, 1960), 231, n. 5. Coyecque, *Recueil,* nos. 4078, 4806, 5380. The seventeenth and eighteenth centuries were periods when rural schools spread significantly. E. Campardon and A. Tuetey, eds., *Inventaire des registres des insinuations du Châtelet de Paris pendant les règnes de François 1 er et de Henri II* (Paris, 1906), no. 735. ADR, B, Insinuations, Testaments, 1560–61, ff. 9r-10v; Henri and Julien Baudrier, *Bibliographie lyonnaise* (Lyon, 1895–1912), 9, 306.

11. No books are mentioned in the reviews of household possessions and wills made by Bézard, *Vie rurale;* Guérin, *Vie rurale;* Gonon, *Vie quotidienne;* and Raveau, *Agriculture.* Note the remarkably infrequent mention of books in notarial acts in the rural Mâconnais even in the seventeenth through nineteenth centuries (Suzanne Tardieu, *La vie domestique dens le mâconnais rural préindustriel* [Paris, 1964], 358, 358, n. 2).

12. Prices taken from inventories after death in Labarre, *Livre,* 274, n. 20. Coyecque, *Recueil,* nos. 196, 96. The evaluation of Books of Hours varies considerably, depending on illustrations and bindings. The prices attributed to the same books when found in quantity in printers' stock are lower, the *Trésor des povres* at about eight deniers the volume (115s. 6d. for 165 copies) and the *Calendrier des bergers* at about six deniers the volume (69s. for 150 copies) in an inventory of 1522 (Doucet, *Bibliothèques,* 102, nos. 134, 150). Presumably these are wholesale prices for books that might not yet have been bound.

13. Martin, *Livre, pouvoirs et société,* 319–20. When the Sire de Gouberville acquired books for his little library at the manor of Mesnil-au-Val in Normandy, they were purchased in Paris and Bayeux (A. Tollemer, *Un Sire de Gouberville, gentilhomme campagnard au contentin de 1553 à 1562* [Paris, 1972], 204–9). In the 1570s and early 1580s, the bibliophile François de la Croix du Maine found it much harder to acquire books in Le Mans and vicinity than in Paris. It seems unlikely that books were sold at the Beaucaire fairs a century earlier.

14. On the variety of speech and dialect in sixteenth-century France and the growing separation between written and spoken language, see F. Brunot et al., *Histoire de la langue française des origines à 1900* (Paris, 1905–53), 1:xiii–xiv, 304ff; 2:174–75.

15. Bollème points out that the *Shepherd's Calendar* did not become part of the peddlers' literature, in a cheap edition, until the mid-seventeenth century *(Almanachs,* 40). Yet she sees the intended public for the work as always the peasants ("L'auteur qui, symboliquement, ne sait pas écrire donne au lecteur qui ne sait pas lire le moyen de sa conduire mieux selon la sagesse naturelle . . . Le Berger parle au berger, au laboureur, au paysan"—16). I am suggesting, however, that the initial public for the work was not the peasants ("Who wants to have knowledge of the heavens . . . like the shepherds without letters [can have it]. It is extracted and composed from their calendar and put into letters so that everyone can understand and know it like them"). *Cy est le compost et kalendrier des bergiers nouvellement reffait* [Paris; Guy Marchant, 1493], f. h vii^v).

16. L. Petit de Julleville, *Histoire du théâtre en France. Les mystères* (Paris, 1880), 1:373–74. Arnold Van Gennep, *Manuel de folklore français contemporain* (Paris, 1943), 1.1:209.

17. Petit de Julleville, *Théâtre,* 1:384. Coyecque, *Recueil,* no. 4470. Perhaps the Saint Victor referred to here is Victorinus, the rhetorician and teacher of Jerome, who, while still a pagan, had a statue made to him in the Forum. The tale of the three-year-old martyr and his faithful martyred mother Julithe (d. 230) was well known in France, where numerous villages were named after him. He is included

in the *Golden Legend*. See also G. Hérelle, *Les théâters ruraux en France . . . depuis le XIVe siècle jusqu'à nos jours* (Paris, 1930).

18. F. Lesure, "Eléments populaires dans la chanson français au début du 16e siècle," in *Musique et poésie au XVIe siècle,* Colloques internationaux du CNRS, Sciences Humaines 5 (Paris, 1954), 169–75. Patrice Coirault, *Recherches sur notre ancienne chanson populaire traditionelle* (Paris, 1927–33), 82–83. *Notre chanson folklorique* (Paris, 1942), 158–64.

19. Vaultier, *Folklore,* 111–12; Mandrou, *Culture populaire,* 18; André Varangnac, *Civilization traditionelle et genres de vie* (Paris, 1970), 96–97, 209; Tardieu, *Vie domestique,* 154–62. Maurice Agulhon, "Los Chambrées en Basse Provence: histoire et ethnologie," *Revue historique* 498 (1971), 359–60.

20. The *veillée* at which these tales are told is supposed to have occurred not in 1547, but in the youth of one of the peasants. E. LeRoy Ladurie, "Mélusine ruralisée," *Annales ESC* 26 (1971): 604–6. On women as storytellers, see, for instance, Soriano, *Contes de Perrault,* 79.

21. French editions of Aesop: Lyon, 1490 and 1499, prepared by the Augustinian Julien de Macho; new rhymed edition by Guillaume Corrozet, Paris, 1542 and after. Greek and Latin editions: Elizabeth Armstrong, *Robert Estienne, Royal Printer* (Cambridge, 1954), 97. Germaine Warkentin, "Some Renaissance Schoolbooks in the Osborne Collection," *Renaissance and Reformation* 5, no. 3 (May 1969): 37. Urban ownership of Aesop: Labarre, *Livre,* p. 208; Schutz, *Vernacular Books,* 72–73. Editions of the *Roman de la Rose* in its "ancient language": fourteen between 1481 and 1528 in Paris and Lyon; three prose versions "moralized" by Jean de Molinet, 1500–1521, four editions between 1526 and 1538 in the translation attributed to Marot. No further editions until 1735! (Clearly the *Roman* did not become part of the peddlers' literature.) On these editions, on interest in the *Roman* among poets, and on Marot as probable translator, see Antonio Viscardi, "Introduction," in *Le Roman de la Rose, dans la version attribuée à Clément Marot,* ed. S. F. Baridon (Milan, 1954), 11–90. Urban ownership of the *Roman,* Labarre, *Livre,* 210; Schutz, *Vernacular Books,* 67; Doucet, *Bibliothèques,* 87, n. 39. I am grateful to F. Howard Bloch, Joseph Duggan, and John Benton for suggestions on this subject. Though many medieval manuscripts remain of the *Roman de la Rose*—some 300—they are unlikely to have circulated among the peasants in this form. There is a short version of the *Roman* in manuscript, with much of the philosophical material omitted (E. Langlois, *Les manuscrits du roman de la Rose. Description et classement* [Lille, 1910], 385–86). Here again there is no evidence that these excisions were made to prepare it for reading to peasants.

22. O. Douen, "La Réforme en Picardie," *BSHPF* 8 (1859), 393. Crespin, *Martyrs,* 2: 468–69; P. Chaix, *Recherches sur l'imprimerie à Genève de 1550 à 1564* (Geneva, 1954), 194. Bernard Palissy, *Recepte véritable par laquelle tous les hommes de à France pourront apprendre à multiplier et augmenter leurs thrésors,* in *Oeuvres complètes* (Paris, 1961), 104–5.

23. On the carter Barthélemy Hector: *Livre des habitants de Genève,* ed. P.-F. Geisendorf (Geneva, 1957), 55; H.-L. Schlaepfer, "Laurent de Normandie," in *As-*

pects de la propagande religieuse (Geneva, 1957), 198; Crespin, *Martyrs,* 2:437–38. On the peddlers in the Lyonnais, ADR, B. Sénéchaussée, Sentences, 1556–59, Sentence of July 1559. Two of them, the dressmaker Girard Bernard, native of Champagne, and the shoemaker Antoine Tallencon or Tallenton, native of Gascony, purchased books from Laurent de Normandie a few months before their arrest (Schlaepfer, "Laurent de Normandie," 200).

24. See, for instance, Marcel Cauvin, "Le protestantisme dans le Contentin," *BSHPF* 112 (1966): 367–68; 115 (1960): 80–81. Le Roy Ladurie, *Paysans,* 348–51. For a picture of Protestant congregations in the seventeenth century in which individual *laboureurs* play their part, see P. H. Chaix, "Les protestants en Bresse en 1621," *Cahiers d'histoire* 14 (1969): 252–54.

25. Chaix, *Recherches sur l'imprimerie,* 120–22; Eugénie Droz, "Le calendrier genevois, agent de la propaganda" and "Le calendrier lyonnais," in *Chemins de l'hérésie* (Geneva, 1970–74), 2:443–56; 3:1–29. See also Jean Delumeau, "Les réformateurs et la superstition," *Actes du colloque l'Amiral de Coligny et son temps* (1972) (Paris, 1974), 451–87. The Protestant *Calendriers* were not the first to use historical material. A 1550 *Heures de Nostre Dame a l'usage de Romme,* published by Magdaleine Boursette, includes dates in its calendar: the death of the scholar Vatable, the Concordat of Leo X and Francois I, the birth of Henri II, etc. (Paris, 1550).

26. Vinson, *Essai,* nos. 3–4; L. Desgraves, *L'imprimerie à la Rochelle 2. Les Haultin* (Geneva, 1960): 1–3. The only other example I know of French Protestant publications in regional dialect is the catechism in "bernois," published by Pierre du Bois at Pau in 1564 at the request of Pastor Merlin for the "catechistes de ce pays de Bearn" (Schlaepfer, "Laurent de Normandie," 205, n. 1).

27. Crespin, *Martyrs,* 2:438. The publisher of Protestant propaganda sometimes shared part of the risk with the peddler, contracting, for instance, that if the books were seized within a two-month period by the "enemies of the Gospel," the *libraire* would bear all the loss (Schlaepfer, "Laurent de Normandie," 199, n. 10; Chaix, *Recherches,* 59).

28. N. Weiss, "Vidimus des lettres patentes de François 1er, 1529," *BSHPF* 59 (1910), 501–4; LeRoy Ladurie, *Paysans,* 380–404; Bézard, *Vie rurale,* 289–90; V. Carrière, *Introduction aux études d'histoire ecclésiastique locale* (Paris, 1936), 3:319–52. S. Gigon, *La révolte de la gabelle en Guyenne* (Paris, 1906); G. Procacci; *Classi sociali e monarchia assoluta nella Francia della prima metà del secolo XVI* (Turin, 1965), 161–73, 213–30; Choppin, *Oeuvres* (1662–63), 3:22 *("la multitude des Rustiques de la Guyenne, qui alloient tumultueusement armée de villages en villages en l'an 1594").* Jean Moreau, *Mémoires . . . sur les Guerres de la Ligue en Bretagne,* ed. H. Waquet (Archives historiques de Bretagne, 1; Quimper, 1960), 11–14, 75–76. A. Le M. de La Borderie and B. Pocquet, *Historie de Bretagne* (Rennes, 1906), 5:173–81; Henri Drouot, *Mayenne et la Bourgogne. Etude sur la Ligue (1587–1596)* (Paris, 1937), 1:39–55; 2:291–92. Claude de Rubys, *Histoire veritable de la ville de Lyon* (Lyon, 1604), 430–31; Daniel Hickey, "The Socio-Economic Context of the French Wars of Religion. A Case Study: Valentinois-Doios" (Ph.D. diss., Dept. of History, McGill University, 1973), chap. 4; L. S. Van Doren, "Revolt and Reaction

in the City of Romans, Dauphiné, 1579–80," *Sixteenth Century Journal* 5 (1974): 72–77. See also Madeleine Foisil, *La révolte des Nu-Pieds et les révoltes normandes de 1639* (Paris, 1970), 178–83, on nicknames and organization of the Nu-Pieds.

29. Jean-Pierre Seguin, *L'information en France de Louis XII à Henri II* (Geneva, 1961), 52.

30. The Lyon analysis is based on a study of hundreds of contracts in ADR, 3E, for the decades of the 1560s and 1570s. LeRoy Ladurie, *Paysans,* 333, 347, 882.

31. LeRoy Ladurie, *Paysans,* 333. According to André Bourde, in a lecture given at the University of California at Berkeley in December 1972, it was only in the course of the seventeenth century that French made important gains among the patriciate of Marseille, while the people continued to speak Provençal.

32. The Amiens figures are calculated by me from the data given in Labarre, *Livre,* 118–26 and 62–104. I have defined the "artisanal" group slightly differently from M. Labarre for purposes of this paper; that is, I have *excluded* from my count the unskilled workers included on 124–26 and *added* some of the goldsmiths, butchers, etc. that Labarre has categorized with the "*classe marchande.*"

33. Labarre, *Livre,* 260–63. Coyecque, *Recueil,* nos. 3768, 3791. A one-book library in Lyon in 1563 in a room rented by a mason's helper from a miller's daughter: "*une bible en francois.*" A five-book library in Lyon belonging to a merchant with a lot of paintings and furniture: "*Le livre des croniques, Les ordonnances des privileges des foyres de Lyon, Les troys miroirs du monde, La premiere partie de nouveau testament, Une Bible en francoys*' (ADR, 3E7179, ff. 467^r–68^r, 576^r–77^v).

34. The relation of prices to wages and purchases is, of course, rough:

Book	Price, place, date
Jean de Vauzelles, *Police subsidaire . . . des povres*	5 deniers, Montpellier, 1535
Livre d'arismetique	1½ deniers wholesale, Paris, 1522
Jacques de Bourbon, *Prinse . . . de Rodes*	3 sous, Paris, 1547/48
La bible des Noelz	2 sous, Paris, 1547/48
Philippe de Commines, *Les croniques du roy Loys unze*	5 sous, Paris, 1547/48

Sources: L. Galle, "Les livres lyonnais," *Revue du Lyonnais,* 5th ser., 23 (1897): 341; Doucet, *Bibliothèques,* 92, 119, 118, 126.

In the 1520s in "normal" years at Lyon, a loaf of *pain farain* cost 5 deniers. In the 1530s and 1540s, a pair of children's shoes might cost 4s. 6d.; a pound of candlewax, 2s. Painters' journeymen and printers' journeymen had wages roughly equivalent to 8s. per day in the 1540s; journeymen and workers in the building trades, about 5–6s. per day.

35. Schlaepfer, "Laurent de Normandie," 207: 4s. per copy of the New Testament, 16°. Presumably this is a wholesale price. Bibles and New Testaments varied enormously in price depending on format, illustration, etc. An illustrated New Testament in an Amiens Library in 1564 was estimated at 5 livres (Labarre, *Livre,* 311).

36. Coyecque, *Recueil,* no. 588. Medieval university students often used manuscripts as security for loans. Crespin, *Martyrs,* 2:430.

37. Henri Hauser, *Ouvriers du temps passé* (5th ed.; Paris, 1927), 82–85. Hauser points out how often regulations against night work were violated. Even when they

existed, they prohibited work after 8, 9, or 10 P.M. In 1539, the Lyon printing ateliers ran till 10 P.M.; in 1572, they closed at 8 or 9 P.M.

38. For further information on de Norry and the commercial arithmetic, see N. Z. Davis, "Mathematics in the Sixteenth Century French Academies: Some Further Evidence," *Renaissance News* 11 (1958), 3–10, and "Sixteenth-Century Arithmetics on the Business Life," *Journal of the History of Ideas* 21 (1960): 18–48.

39. Eisenstein, "Advent of Printing," 68.

40. Crespin, *Martyrs*, 1:527.

41. Eugénie Droz, "Bibles françaises après le Concile de Trents," *Journal of the Warburg and Courtauld Institutes* 18 (1965): 213.

42. E. Delarueile et al., *L'Eglise au temps du grand schisme et de la crise concili-aire (1378–1440)* ("Histoire de l'Eglise depuis les origins jusqu'à nos jours," 14; Paris, 1964), 2:712–21. Droz, "Bibles françaises," 222. See also Martin, *Livre, pouvoirs et société*, 102–4.

43. On this process, see Brunot, *Histoire de la langue française,* 2:36–55; Howard Stone, "The French Language in Renaissance Medicine," *BHR* 15 (1953): 315–43; V.-L. Saulnier, "Lyon et la médecine aux temps de la Renaissance," *Revue lyon-naice de médecine* (1958): 73–83; C. A. Wickersheimer, *La médecine et les médecins en France à l'époque de la Renaissance* (Paris, 1906), 128–78. Alison Klairmont of the University of California at Berkeley is considering these subjects anew in her doctoral dissertation on the medical profession in sixteenth-century France.

6   ORAL CULTURE AND THE
DIFFUSION OF REFORMATION IDEAS

Robert Scribner

I

A feature of the German Reformation which has always fascinated historians is the speed with which new religious ideas were so widely spread throughout Germany, precipitating within a few months what became one of the major social and intellectual upheavals in European history. Since the sixteenth century, it has been a historical commonplace that this was largely a result of the impact of printing. The printed word provided the vehicle for an un-stoppable momentum towards religious reform, so that the views of Luther and other Reformers became accessible to a mass reading public almost as soon as they were written. This reading public formed a new and powerful public opinion, the dynamic force behind the Reformation movements of the 1520s.[1] Pursuing this conviction, some Reformation historians have recently turned to the enormous production of printed pamphlets, tracts and sermons as the best sources available to trace this diffusion process, regarding them as a unique means of access to the ideas and issues motivating the religious movements of sixteenth-century Germany.[2]

Such views should be regarded with scepticism for a number of reasons. First, although the importance of printing is undeniable, to understand fully the rapid diffusion of Reformation ideas, the effects of printing must be seen in broader perspectives. To concentrate on the printed word alone directs our attention too narrowly at the small, if growing, élite of the literate, those with the ability and desire to read. It ignores the vast numbers of the illiter-ate and semi-literate, perhaps as many as ninety per cent of the population. To be illiterate did not mean, of course, that one was beyond the reach of the printed word. There is clear evidence that most villages would have contained at the very least one or two persons—perhaps the village priest or village officials—able to read and write, who could relay the Reformation message to nonreaders.[3] However, this involves a more complex process of transmission, which cannot be recaptured through study of the printed word

Reprinted from Robert Scribner, "Oral Culture and the Diffusion of Reformation Ideas," *History of European Ideas* 5 (1984): 237–56. Copyright 1984 with permission from Elsevier.

alone. Indeed, study of printed sources may even tell us very little about how the literate received their information about the Reformation, telling us more about their authors than about the response of their readers.[4]

To understand the diffusion of Reformation ideas, we must set printing in the context of the whole range of information media available to, and used by, people of that age. Besides the printed word, there were visual forms such as popular woodcuts, participational forms such as popular festivals, and above all, forms of oral communication such as the sermon, hymn-singing, and mere word-of-mouth transmission of ideas. I have set out elsewhere both a broader argument for the need to examine the interaction of these media with the printed word, and studied two of them in the popular woodcut and Carnival.[5] Here I want to concentrate on oral modes of diffusion and to ask how they influenced the nature of "Reformation public opinion."[6] In sixteenth-century Germany oral transmission was still the primary mode of communication, in which information was received by face-to-face contact within small communities. Even the printed word was most often mediated by the spoken word, by reading aloud to oneself, by reading aloud to others, or by discussion of things in print. Public and private discussions were probably the most frequent means of transmitting ideas, while pride of place as the major formal means of communication must go to the pulpit, from which most public announcements were proclaimed.

There is ample evidence of the power of the pulpit as the major means of mass communication. The religious reform was first and foremost a powerful preaching revival. The first act of any community which developed an interest in the new ideas was to request a preacher to proclaim the "pure Word of God." It was not held to be sufficient to read printed tracts or even the Bible: the desire was to *hear* the word. Indeed, for Protestants "hearing the Word" became virtually a third Sacrament alongside Baptism and the Lord's Supper. Communities cared enough about this to pay out of their own pockets to support a preacher if no benefice was vacant and to put considerable pressure on magistrates who were reluctant to provide or permit such a preacher. The ejection of an acceptable preacher by unsympathetic magistrates could lead to rebellion or riot. The power of the preacher as communicator was such that most authorities wished to have a man who conformed to their ideological viewpoint, and they regarded with suspicion any preacher who insisted that magistrates themselves were not above reformation.[7]

The sermon in itself was no distinguishing feature of the Reformation movements; preaching, and especially popular preaching in the vernacular, had been going through a revival for at least a generation before. What was different was the scope and intensity of the Reformation preaching revival, as well as its emphasis on the Bible as the source of religious truth. Yet the sermon had certain inbuilt limitations as a means of spreading new ideas. In its traditional form, it was largely a one-way process, presupposing a passive, if receptive, audience. It depended on this audience accepting its content as convincing and authoritative. However much a preacher could have relied on a general desire for religious knowledge abroad at that time, traditional preaching would not in itself have created the ferment and upheaval that characterised the Reformation as a mass movement.[8] Of course, much depended on the style, zeal, and personality of the preacher; but more importantly, the Reformation sermon broke away from traditional patterns in both form and content.

First, it was often released from the confines of the church building. During the early days, many Reformation preachers found themselves without a church in which to preach. Either they were unbeneficed, or had been refused permission to use a local church. Instead they turned to preaching outdoors, in churchyards or fields, and indoors in private homes. Such informal circumstances freed both preacher and hearers from the constraints of the formal sermon and heightened receptiveness by creating a freer atmosphere for the exchange of ideas. Printed propaganda for the Reformation presented this aspect of the evangelical sermon as a radical departure from older patterns. In broadsheets and book illustrations, the Reformation sermon is shown as something demanding active participation by the congregation, which is depicted following the preacher's text in a book or gesturing as if in discussion with him. Attenders at Catholic sermons, by contrast, are shown as passive, detached, and uninterested.[9]

It was the irregular nature of such preaching that attracted attention. In Delitzsch in Albertine Saxony, the schoolmaster Johannes Zymler held an unscheduled sermon in the churchyard before his school on the last Sunday of August 1522. He preached from an open window to a great crowd and clearly intended to provoke some open response from his audience, for he claimed that he had done it "in the manner of a disputation."[10] The same was true when laymen, and occasionally women, turned to preaching, not to mention the various wandering preachers who turn up so frequently during the early years of the Reformation. If no church was available, they were prepared to preach anywhere they found a willing audience. Michael Reutter, a wandering preacher in the Mark Brandenburg, put what was probably their typical point of view: that the Word of God could just as well be proclaimed in the marketplace as in church. But because it departed so far from the traditional norm, magistrates were highly suspicious of such irregular preaching, regarding it as socially dangerous, indeed close to sedition. Even authorities sympathetic to the new ideas preferred to regularise the position and behaviour of evangelical preachers.[11]

The content of Reformation preaching was also often a matter of shock and great scandal to those hearing it for the first time. A good example is Michael Reutter's preaching in the Lower Lusatian town of Sommerfeld between May 1524 and April 1525, as reported to the Bishop of Meissen. Reutter preached that no one had been correctly baptised for four hundred years because total immersion had not been used; that the best form of absolution was when one person forgave another; that ten mortal sins were committed daily in the Mass; that priests should be whipped if they did not cease to blaspheme and "crucify Christ" in this manner; that those who attended such Masses should be outlawed, because they "martyred God"; that the Sacrament was not a sacrifice, but a sign, testament, and pledge for those weak in faith; that the entire community should fall on its knees to pray for such weaklings (in this way, the report asserted, he effectively prohibited taking the Sacrament and did not receive it himself); that the bishop was triply perjured, and that if one put a tonsure on an ass and anointed its paws (*sic*), it would be no less consecrated; that fasting was forbidden and meat-eating allowed; and that no feast days should be observed, not even Sunday, when one was permitted to work after the sermon, as on any other day.[12]

Whether such preaching was deliberately designed to scandalise its hearers but was nonetheless grounded in a deeper and sounder theology is unclear. Perhaps the reporters noted only statements used for dramatic effect and ignored their wider context. However, the case reveals the shock-wave such ideas created among traditional believers within the community in which they were proclaimed. The shock-effect was heightened by the dress of the new preacher, who had given up his tonsure and clerical garb and wore a long red coat, fashionable shoes, and a red Scotch beret.[13] The sense of upheaval created by such preaching was further accentuated by a more radical break with the traditional sermon, the practice of interrupting and answering back the preacher.

This practice doubtless had two origins. On the one hand, an unacceptable preacher (that is, one who did not preach the "pure Word of God') was contradicted, either by heckling or by disrupting his sermon. In Ulm in 1524 a Catholic preacher who tried to open a sermon in the minster with a prayer to the Virgin was driven from the pulpit by the shouts of the congregation, which abused him as a carnival puppet. In Regensburg, the town council complained in 1524 of interjections and disturbances during sermons and of attempts to dispute with the preacher. In Augsburg, the Cathedral preacher Kress was repeatedly interrupted in 1525, and in Basel the practice reached such levels in 1528 that the town council forbade public contradiction of preachers.[14] On the other hand, the congregation became used to interrupting or, on another view of it, participating in evangelical sermons. In places where the Reformation was officially adopted, the authorities then had to reimpose the discipline of the passive congregation. In Saxony in 1532, Luther attacked interruptions of sermons as the work of "sneaks and hedge-preachers," and the Saxon church ordinance of 1533 expressly prohibited anyone speaking to the preacher while he was in the pulpit. Anyone who did not understand the preacher was to consult him in private afterwards, when he would "instruct" the questioner on the point at issue.[15]

In this way, the Reformation sermon provided stimulus to discussion and elaboration of the Reformation message, as hearers challenged the preacher to expand further on his text. In Ulm in 1530, for example, the preacher Conrad Sam was interrupted by a member of his congregation as he was finishing the sermon. The man later accosted Sam on his way home, and the two became involved in a long and passionate discussion over religion, which reached such heights that the incident was reported to the town council as a potential cause of disturbance.[16] This kind of passionate exchange of ideas was continued in private conversations, fostered especially by another form of communication of great importance, discussion and explanation of a text. This invited a far more active participation from hearers than the sermon, and seems to have arisen naturally from the custom of reading aloud.

II

Reading aloud, rather than silent scanning of the text, seems to have been the more usual form of reading for the sixteenth century. Writers of early Reformation pamphlets were aware that their works would be mediated through hearing. Many expressly suggested that their "readers" should have works read aloud to them. Thus, one pamphlet of the early 1520s told the "reader" who could not read what it had to tell about the Antichrist that he should go to a brother who could read, who would then read to him the Epistles of St Paul.[17] Some works, such as those by Eberlin von Günzburg, one of the most popular authors of cheap tracts, seem to have been deliberately written for reading aloud. Colporteurs adopted the practice by reading out the titles of the works they offered for sale, and sometimes there were extempore public readings of Reformation works, as in Nuremberg in 1524, when a clerk named Erasmus Wisperger read out one of Carlstadt's works on the market square.[18]

Discussion from or about books was a very common way of acquiring new religious ideas. Reformation pamphlets frequently depict situations in which several persons discuss the contents of a printed work, and one pamphlet of 1522 actually exhorted its reader to pass it on to another person and to discuss it with him or her.[19] We can cite some clear evidence for how this worked in practice. Johann Bornheinrich, a leather worker in Salza in Albertine Saxony, possessed a copy of the Bible and other (presumably Lutheran) books, from which members of his family and friends heard readings in 1523–25.[20] A sugar maker from Halle admitted in 1525 that whatever new matters he found in Lutheran books he tried to pass on to others, while a man called Dhoner, arrested in Pirna in that year for saying that the Lutherans were right and all the others wrong, claimed to have heard it from his son and others who read Lutheran books.[21] Especially interesting is the case of Thomas Adolff of Speyer, who in 1533 was concerned about his inability to lead a Christian life. He went to Martin Leubel, a neighbour who seemed to have no difficulty in this regard, and the two men read and discussed the Bible together, by which means Thomas was converted to Anabaptism.[22] All these examples show the printed word as part of a wider communication process, mediated through personal contacts and the spoken word—sometimes, as in the case of those to whom Dhoner spoke in Pirna, at two removes from the original ideas in print.

Some occasions of oral transmission came close to discussion circles, of which we have a good example from Cologne in 1528. Here a number of folk met half a dozen times or more in the houses of two citizens, where they sat over drinks, and read and discussed the Bible. The owner of one of the houses testified that they had come about because several citizens had approached him over disputes they had about the Gospel. He had tried by this means to instruct them according to his understanding of it.[23] Such meetings were frequent in Ulm in 1523–24, when the town council complained of them as furtive gatherings.[24] In Regensburg, following attempts to dispute with the preacher during sermons in 1534, the town council complained that discussions about religion now went on in quiet corners.[25]

These meetings were probably more ad hoc and unstructured than the term "discussion circle" implies, but they often helped initiate the formal beginnings of the Reformation in a town. In 1521 the Dominican Jakob Strauss came to Hall in Tyrol, where he gave readings from St. Matthew's Gospel to local priests, and gained such a reputation by this that the town council asked him to preach.[26] In 1529 an ex-Dominican dressed as a peasant turned up at a village outside the wall of Göttingen, where his preaching ability was discovered through private conversation. A series of small meetings followed, in which the participants grew from a handful to over two dozen, and these began to consider how a more open form of preaching might be brought about.[27] Such encounters, often prior to "hearing the Word" in a sermon or to discovering it in print, were as important as either print or the sermon in spreading Reformation ideas. Even where they occurred after hearing a sermon or reading a pamphlet, they doubtless played an important role in sifting and internalising those ideas. This was especially true where they took place in a more informal atmosphere, which loosened tongues and enabled discussion to flow freely.

There were many such occasions in the daily life of the time, both public and private. Sebastian Rost, a clerk at the monastery of Thamsbruck in Saxony, took Lutheran books to spinning bees and tried to talk folk there into accepting the ideas they contained.[28] Albrecht Steinbrück of Salza heard a sermon by a former monk and invited him to dinner for further discussion, after which the preacher stayed overnight in his host's house.[29] The dinner table was a common occasion to discuss the new ideas. In Leipzig in 1525 a number of guests at dinner with Andreas Camitianus, clerk of the jurors' court, discussed the sacrificial nature of the Mass and whether the peasants killed in the recent revolt were martyrs for the Gospel.[30] In 1525, the mayor of Torgau had a judge, a preacher and a Franciscan doctor of theology to dinner, where they discussed the nature of the Gospel and Holy Scripture. The discussion eventually became so acrimonious that the preacher mentioned it from the pulpit.[31]

Next to such essentially private conversations, the most common place for discussions about religion was the inn. Heinrich von Kettenbach commented in 1523 that many better sermons were delivered in the inns of Ulm than in church, and in Basel this seems literally to have been the case, for in 1524 there were complaints of persons who preached out of books in the inns.[32] In 1539 a Cologne Anabaptist arranged to meet another in an inn, hoping through this contact to get hold of certain books he sought. Anabaptists seem to have met frequently in inns in Cologne in the 1530s, as they did in Augsburg in the 1520s.[33] No doubt, this venue was less suspicious than meeting in private houses, where they would appear as a dangerous conventicle. But not all discussions about religion took place among those already committed to the Reformation. Inns were also the place where casual encounters occurred, in which people made firsthand personal acquaintance with unorthodox ideas.

A pamphlet of 1524 describes how an "evangelical Christian" (that is, a supporter of the Reformation) meets a Jew in an inn, where they fall to discussing religion. The Christian produces an illustrated broadsheet, which he uses to explain Reformation doctrines to the Jew. The author of the pamphlet is allegedly the barkeeper, who was so impressed with the conversation that he decided to have it printed for the benefit of all its readers.[34] The incident is probably a literary fiction, but at least one purpose of the pamphlet is to encourage Reformation believers to imitate the "evangelical Christian" in like circumstances. But there was little need for such literary exhortation: nonliterary evidence shows that these kinds of encounter were common. A baker from Franconia was arrested in 1525 for expressing heretical opinions in a Munich beerhouse.[35] Thomas Prass was arrested in Leipzig for abusing the Catholic preacher Johann Joss as a "fool, knave and heretic" while Prass was in a drinkshop.[36] Not dissimilar from such inn-talk was the case of Andreas Camitianus of Leipzig and his companions, who said that they had engaged in merry talk about religion when at their local church-ale.[37]

The inn, the spinning bee, the church-ale, and the dinner table provide a natural home for rumour and gossip, and we can see something of how rumour was used to spread unorthodox ideas through some examples from Cologne in the late 1520s. Johann Brenich was interrogated in 1527 about irreverence towards the Virgin Mary. He testified that he had been drinking in pleasant company when someone raised the question of whether the Virgin had borne two children after the death of Jesus. It was said that this was being preached elsewhere in the south of the country. Another witness stated that he had been in Wurttemberg, sitting in an inn, when he heard a Carthusian say such things about the Virgin. When he returned to Cologne, he reported this to Arnt Huntzeler, who in turn passed it on to Johann Brenich.[38] The indirect nature of rumour is well illustrated here—it always comes at best second- or thirdhand, and the Carthusian in Wurttemberg may well have been passing it on himself from an earlier "source."

The persistence of rumour and the curiosity it generates can also be illustrated from Cologne examples, for the story turned up again in 1529. Thomas Schlossmecher and others of his company had been heard claiming in beerhouses and wine bars that the Virgin had borne two sons after Christ. Schlossmecher testified that he had not said this himself, but had been told it by a Wilhelm Schlossmecher, who said that he had read it in a book. Thomas had then sought to read about it for himself. There had been some earlier gossip about the Virgin, in 1526.[39] A weaver named Hans von Hesse, who had a reputation for Lutheran views, had been asked by his master what he thought about the Virgin, and Hans himself while drinking with others had asked a certain Peter from Frankfurt what was held about the Virgin in his part of the country.[40]

Discussions about religion were also held at the workplace, or at least in the context of work: that is, when not in the actual workshop, perhaps in the guildhouse or guild tavern, where artisans relaxed after work. In our Cologne examples Hans von Hesse and his master probably discussed religion at work, and Thomas and Wilhelm Schlossmecher may have been professional namesakes. Jacob Hurling, a baker in Basel, discussed religion with his apprentices during a holiday feast in 1524.[41] Sebastian Tuschler, the baker arrested for heresy in Munich in 1525, had heard heretical views from his master in Schwatz in Tyrol. He had heard from him views on the Sacrament, and the master had read out from a book that the Virgin was a woman like any other, that she could not intercede for anyone, and that one should honour her for her son's sake or not at all.[42] There were professional ties between the group of Lutherans around Johann Bornheinrich in Salza in 1523–25. Johann was a leather worker, perhaps a shoemaker; his son Jacob was apprenticed to another member of the group, Albrecht Steinbrück; a third member, Melchior Weigandt, was a cobbler.[43] The way in which entire guilds in many cities declared themselves to be supporters of the Reformation suggests that discussion at work was common. Most noticeable is how often weavers turn up as carriers of the new ideas, possibly because of their geographical mobility, but almost certainly because their work rhythm, like that of leather workers, lent itself to discussions on the job.

Another important, but largely neglected means of spreading ideas through discussion was through the circle of friends and/or kinship. These are frequently identified in the sources by the terms *Gesellschaft, Freundtschaft* and *Verwandtschaft,* and this seems to be what was meant in the cases of Johann Brenich and Thomas Schlossmecher, who were both drinking "in company" during the incidents about which they were questioned.[44] In Salza, Claus Heusener was said to have drunk regularly and kept much company with Melchior Weigandt.[45] One circle of suspected heretics in Leipzig sat together daily over brandy.[46] The circle of friendship merged imperceptibly with that of kinship. The "sect" around Johann Bornheinrich is an interesting example. Through Johann's Bible-reading, his three sons, Jacob, Wolf, and Franz, were led to Reformation belief. Another member of the circle, Albrecht Steinbrück, was Johann's son-in-law and the brother-in-law of Melchior Weigandt, an unsurprising merging of kinship and professional connections.[47]

Kinship connections were also highly important among people converted to Anabaptism in Franconia and Thuringia during 1527. In one group in Konigsberg (Franconia), Thomas Spiegel, a carpenter of Ostheim, brought his brother to meetings. The cabinetmaker Ekarius from Coburg was rebaptised with his wife and servant, while his wife was also the sister-in-law of another Anabaptist.[48] Three brothers from Utzing in Upper Franconia, Hans, Veit, and Martin Weischenfelder, were all baptised, along with the wives of Veit and Martin and Martin's maid-servant. At the same time two other women and their daughters were rebaptised. Hans Weischenfelder himself baptised Michael from Kuptz, along with his wife, daughter, and son.[49] Also baptised with their wives were the tailor Hans Hutener of Ziegendorf, Thomas Tischer of Sangershausen, Cunrad Friedrich, and Veit Pickarten of Etzleben, Peter Weiger of Schillingstadt, and the tailor Andres, whose daughter was also baptised.[50] These cases indicate the importance of discussion between those with close personal ties, such as husband and wife, close relatives, or household members. It is epitomised in the case of

Klaus Hofman of Erfurt, rebaptised with his wife and servant, who "talked his wife into the baptism," to which she had agreed on the condition that it was not a deception.[51]

There are also cases where relatives tried to dissuade people from their rebaptism. Georg Fuchs from Erfurt was baptised with his wife in 1527 and subsequently went to visit first his sister in Penig, near Leipzig, and then his brother in Meissen, perhaps with the intention of winning them to his new faith. The brother, however, was greatly displeased and left at once.[52] Cunrad Friedrich of Etzleben went to his brother in Schillingstadt for advice, and the brother tried to dissuade him from his decision.[53] Anstad Kemmerer of Halle was consorting with Anabaptists in Eisleben and took along his brother Georg to a meeting. Georg was unconvinced by their arguments, and Anstad then rethought his own position and attempted to sever the connection.[54]

Another important mode of oral communication was singing, whether of ballads or hymns. It displays the same kind of symbiotic relationship with printing as other forms discussed above. Many pamphlets and broadsheets were written in rhyme and were clearly intended to be sung or at least recited.[55] This was a common means of advertising their contents, the colporteur singing through the titles to a well-known melody, or chanting the rhyming titles aloud. In Magdeburg in 1524, for example, a poor weaver tried to sell a collection of Luther's hymns by singing them aloud in the market square. In Lübeck a blind beggar did the same by singing from house to house in 1529, and in Brandenburg in 1524 a number of wandering apprentices sang Lutheran songs to travellers in the inns.[56] Thomas Murner tried to match this with anti-Reformation songs, giving an anti-Lutheran ballad to a poor blind singer to have it spread abroad.[57]

The ballad served several functions in the diffusion of Reformation ideas. First, it passed on news about recent events, exemplified by several ballads from around 1520 which recounted Luther's progress since his first attack on indulgences.[58] Second, it was used to hurl scorn and derision at the orthodox clergy, and many towns had to prohibit the singing of offensive songs against the clergy in their streets. Ulm was typical, the town council issuing mandates against the practice in 1523 and 1524, apparently to little effect, for it was still complained of in 1527, when a number of folk held a "sing-in" in the Franciscan church.[59] In Schneeberg, officials opposed to the Reformation were attacked in ballads in 1525, while in Erfurt a ballad was composed to celebrate the first attack of the Erfurt Reformation against the clergy, the Parson Storm of 1521.[60]

A third use of the ballad was to disrupt Catholic services and mock church music. In Wittenberg, on Christmas eve 1521, a crowd of people burst into the parish church, extinguished the lights, and sang secular ditties to disturb the service.[61] In Lübeck in 1530 the singing of Lutheran hymns was used to drown the *Salve Regina* and as a protest against Catholic doctrine following sermons in the cathedral.[62] In Göttingen in 1529 weavers disrupted a procession held to beseech divine intervention against the sweating sickness. They first tried to drown out the chants of the Catholic clergy with a German psalm, then turned to a parody of the liturgical chant *Ora pro nobis*, by chanting *Ohr ab, zum Thor aus*, loosely translated as "Shut up and clear out!"[63]

This was the fourth use of singing, as a form of witness to evangelical belief. The 1529 incident was the first public act of the evangelical community in Göttingen and effectively proclaimed its existence to the whole town. Singing had played a significant part in forming this community from the beginning, for we are told that the Reformation first began to take root there through the influence of Luther's German psalms and hymns. Various weavers had learned to sing and love these in other towns such as Goslar, Magdeburg, and Braunschweig, and they began to sing them privately at home. Thus, they learned to question the usefulness of masses, requiems, and the Catholic clergy in general.[64] Hymn-singing, as occurred here, and in similar circumstances in Lübeck, both formed the community and shaped its sense of evangelical solidarity. The arrest of the weaver who sang Luther's hymns in Magdeburg in 1524 provoked a mass demonstration of evangelical witness, as two hundred citizens marched to the town hall to demand his release from prison.[65]

III

This broader view of the diffusion of Reformation ideas should lead us to rethink our understanding of how "public opinion" developed during the Reformation. Far too often this has been too closely linked to the direct impact of printing, which is seen to have effected a dramatic shift in opinion formation. Before printing, information was exchanged and opinions shaped through personal interaction in a small communal setting. Printing, it is argued, changed this situation radically, creating a public opinion comprised of thousands of individuals silently scanning the printed page, all linked by the additive effect of independently receiving the same message.[66] There is much to be said for this view. Late-medieval Germany often had limited possibilities for the expression of public opinion. Free assembly was often restricted, and expression of dissent allowed only within a structure of careful institutional controls.[67]

Yet there is a danger of overdrawing the picture, of distorting the speed of change through our knowledge of and interest in later developments. Printing took longer than we realise to achieve a fully liberating effect on opinion formation. The traces of oral transmission which embedded themselves in early printed texts were as likely to obscure as to clarify opinions.[68] Censorship could also be remarkably effective where it was carefully and vigorously applied. A 1521 broadsheet attacking Jerome Emser, one of Luther's most forceful critics, published in a print run of 1,500 sheets but seized from the printer's shop, has survived in no extant copy.[69] Thomas Murner's *On the Great Lutheran Fool* of 1522, one of the most skillful pieces of Catholic anti-Lutheran propaganda, was effectively banned in Strasbourg in its first edition. The very rare second edition had to be put together from remnants of the first and published anonymously by the original printer, but it achieved no wide circulation.[70] The extent and influence of censorship in the first half of the sixteenth century has scarcely been examined in any detail, but Cologne began active censorship of books as early as 1487. Other towns set up strict censorship rules in the early 1520s: Augsburg and Zurich in 1523, Basel in 1524. In Nuremberg, the town council ran a tight and effective censorship, intimidating printers and publishers by fines, confiscations, and imprisonment and encouraging some authors to self-censorship.[71]

On the other hand, we can trace clear articulations of a vigorous popular opinion through many of the pre-print forms of communication discussed so far: through phenomena such as popular festivals, irregular assemblies, spontaneous demonstrations, anonymous pasquinades, popular ballads, and the forms of oral culture, above all through rumour. A recent study of late-fifteenth-century Franconia has shown the creation of an effective form of public opinion by means of rumour. Where we can follow through the sources the development of a spontaneous public opinion, it is found expressed as much through pre-print modes as it is through the medium of the printed word. This is scarcely surprising in terms of modern understanding of the complexity of communication processes. Printing may have supplied a uniform message to an abstract and widely dispersed target audience, but its message still had to be decoded at local level, in the small communities in which it was received, where it was subject to a whole range of "environmental" influences.[72]

Indeed, "public opinion" formation can be more readily understood at this local level than in terms of a large and abstract sphere. "Public opinion" is no more than the frame of mind of those people who constitute a "public," essentially all those concerned with an event or situation and likely to become involved with its consequences. As it is seen by some sociologists, this frame of mind is formed by personal interaction among the people who constitute a localised "public," as they seek to make sense of, and to internalise, the different information available about the matter of concern. This is part of a process of achieving a consensus which reaches beyond individual viewpoints to form a collective outlook, and which in the long run enables the people concerned to engage in concerted action. The process may be set in motion by formal or informal means of communication, but in its most important stage it is personal and localised, dependent on oral communication. For this reason, principally oral forms of communication, especially rumour, play a central role in creating "public opinion."[73]

Viewed in this way, "public opinion" is a complex and many-sided phenomenon. It can be stratified socially and geographically and influenced by a wide range of mediating factors and conditions. In an age of poor transport communications, geographical stratification was important enough to warrant our special attention. In the Germany of the 1520s we can discern three levels: local, regional, and transregional. At local level, public opinion was created not only by rumour, gossip, and private discussion, but also by "scandals," public incidents which set the community talking. Incidents of this kind were public abuse of preachers, disruption of sermons or church services, or desecration of images. The propaganda value of such incidents was considerable, since they incited to imitation: they were forms of agitatory communication. Acts of public witness, such as public hymn-singing or attendance at unauthorised sermons had a similar effect on opinion formation.[74]

The regional level involved a slightly more impersonal sphere of activity, those areas beyond the local community in which people moved about naturally in pursuit of daily economic and social activities. This sphere is constituted by a regional marketing pattern, with natural movement between town and country and between market and marketing region. The transregional level is really only an enlarged version of this regional sphere, linking region to region through the natural channels along which trade and travellers passed. At both of these levels, the printed word was spread no more quickly than the spoken word, for books must always be carried by people, who can pass on ideas as quickly and as effectively from person to person as can print. The oral carriers of new ideas were often the same middlemen who carried the books: at regional level, the peasant attending a local market or urban fair, the hawker and pedlar, the local official; at transregional level, carriers, merchants, colporteurs, wandering artisans or journeymen (especially weavers), travellers, and wandering preachers.[75] The last are of considerable importance for the wider diffusion of Reformation ideas but have scarcely been investigated. There are many striking examples of such wandering preachers, one of the most notable being Johann Maurer, a doctor who began to preach in the streets of Strasbourg in 1522. He travelled the triangle Strasbourg-Basel-Freiburg (in itself a large natural marketing area), with two dozen companions, preaching to the peasants as he went, before being apprehended in Württemberg in 1524.[76]

Such middlemen carried books and ideas and set in motion the chain reaction of discussion and opinion formation within the context of oral culture. Indeed, the multiplication effect usually attributed to the printed word was just as much a product of the spoken word. This is seen in the case of Hans Häberlin, a lay preacher from the village of Wiggensbach near Kempten, who was arrested in 1526 for unauthorised preaching. Häberlin had heard Lutheran sermons in Kempten and in Memmingen, and as a result purchased a copy of the New Testament to read himself. Anything he did not understand, he took to the Lutheran preacher in Kempten, who instructed him and showed him how to read the New Testament. When Häberlin began to preach for himself in Wiggensbach, he attracted an audience from twenty parishes in the vicinity, and by the time of his arrest was preaching to almost eight hundred peasants assembled in a field. This example shows what is called the "multi-step flow of information," in which information passes over a medium of communication to an "opinion leader," who then passes it on further.[77] Here the Kempten preacher is a first-step "opinion leader," passing on information received from elsewhere; Häberlin is the second step, transmitting the information further to an audience as large as could have been reached had he put his ideas into print, but with greater local effect and immediacy.

We can better understand the interrelation between the three geographical levels of opinion formation if we examine the most striking example of a movement inspired by the new religious ideas, the German Peasants' War. The central idea of a biblically inspired demand for social justice is contained in the Twelve Articles, the major manifesto of the rebellious peasants. Their influence on the formation of a transregional sphere of opinion can be traced through the various areas where they were adopted as the chief peasant demands: the southwest, Franconia, the duchy of Württemberg, the Rhine Palatinate, the prince bishopric of Speyer, Thuringia, and in the Erzgebirge between Saxony and Bohemia. There were two dozen editions, spread over fifteen printing locations, as far removed from their place of origin in Memmingen as Regensburg in the southeast, Magdeburg, Erfurt, and Zwickau to the north, and Breslau in the east.[78]

This transregional impact, however, is only explicable by their impact at regional and local level. In central Germany, for example, they were recommended from one band of rebels to another. The "Evangelical Christian League" in the Thuringian Forest wrote to their "evangelical Christian brothers" of the town of Ilmenau in April 1525, offering them an alliance and declaring that they had established a brotherhood "according to the contents of the Twelve Articles."[79] The rebels of Fulda made it their main purpose to achieve implementation of the Twelve Articles and influenced their adoption by Hersfeld and Hammelburg.[80] In the county of Henneberg, twelve villages in turn accepted the Twelve Articles in what looked like a snowball effect.[81]

A number of informative examples enable us to trace more closely the way in which the Articles were diffused at local and regional level. First, there had to be cheap copies readily available. One peasant bought his copy in Merseburg for twopence.[82] Another peasant, from Ffockendorf in the district of Borna in Albertine Saxony, purchased a copy during the Easter holiday at Pilsnig.[83] Cuntz Rudolf of Merxleben probably heard of the Articles first by word-of-mouth, for he asked another peasant to purchase a copy for him in the town of Langensalza, stating that he and others interested in them would be willing to hold whatever they contained.[84] One Saxon parson passed his copy on to a colleague, while a man from Neustruppen, near Pirna, brought the Articles back from the mining town of Joachimsthal, after having heard them read out elsewhere.[85] These were not always printed copies. The parson at Alt-Beichlingen, a village near Kolleda in Albertine Saxony, met a journeyman in a village inn, who had a handwritten copy which he gave to fellow drinkers to read. Possessing a copy did not necessarily mean agreeing with the Articles: this journeyman said that he disagreed with them; however, he still served as an agent of their distribution.[86]

Once someone had a copy of the Articles, their contents were often passed on further by word-of-mouth. Most frequently, they were read out aloud to various gatherings. The Articles were brought to Neustruppen from Joachimsthal by a brother of the village judge, perhaps out of curiosity, for a copy of the 24 Joachimsthaler Articles was also brought with them. The Articles were then read out in public by the local clerk.[87] In Merxleben, a group of rebel leaders produced a book containing the Articles (presumably, along with other items), which were then read out by the sexton to the community assembled on the market. Afterwards, one of the ringleaders asked that those who were willing to stand by the Gospel, the Word of God, and the Articles as read should raise their fingers in oath.[88] Asmus Wolf from Gerstungen said he had read the Articles in the nearby forest, and had then read them out to numerous others, including forest workers. His copy came from a miller's son, who carried them in his sleeve.[89] In Eisenach, the Articles were read out in the town hall by the captain of the rebellious peasants.[90]

The desire to read or hear the Articles read seems to be related to the reputation they had already gained even before they were seen or heard, as in the case of Cuntz Rudolf of Merxleben. In Schmalkalden, they were invoked as evidence of the excessive grievances endured by the common people[91] and sometimes appear to have been invested with almost canonical authority. They were used in Eisenach to settle a dispute between the Lord of Volckershausen and his peasants, when the town, acting as mediator, brought both parties to agree to live according to their contents.[92] In Halle, one of the ringleaders, Hans Möller, held up a printed copy of the Articles, with the claim that they should be looked to in order to know how to behave.[93] In Neustruppen, their status was attested by the village judge and clerk laying them in the statute book.[94] This status was greatly enhanced by rumour. In Fulda, it was said that the Bishop and his co-adjutor approved their contents; and one peasant in Borna had heard that there were imperial letters in Altenburg containing the Twelve Articles, thus implying the Emperor's approval. However, the strongest foundation of their authority was the belief that they were grounded in Scripture and in accordance with the Word of God. This was shown clearly in those cases, as in Merxleben, where the rebels agreed to uphold the Twelve Articles and the Gospel as though they were mutually dependent causes.[95]

It has been argued that the application of Reformation principles to social grievance transformed the protest movements of 1524–26 from mere peasant revolts into a biblically justified revolution.[96] The way in which this grew from being a theoretical possibility to being viable public opinion and then to inspiring concerted action was clearly a complex process of diffusion. It did not occur without the printed word, but it depended on the printed manifestoes being received and spread over time throughout the many layers of oral culture. This is close to Vora's spiral model of the diffusion of concepts, involving the recurrent interaction of many elements in the communication process: the source, different channels of diffusion, the message, the environment, the receiver, and the varying effects of the message.[97] A crucial feature of such interaction was the way in which the printed word was mediated through the spoken, and for this reason the process of communication was very open-ended.

Indeed, what is most striking about the evidence that can be gathered from discussions in private homes, pubs, market squares, and streets of German towns and villages is the open-endedness of popular reception of Reformation ideas. We find testimony of the honest desire of ordinary people to seek spiritual advice wherever they could find it and of the simple faith with which they received such advice. This comes out with some poignancy in two instances. The first is that of Thomas Adolff of Speyer, mentioned earlier, who was dissatisfied with his own useless and wasteful life and was led to approach Martin Leubel because he seemed to have no difficulty in this regard. The same desire for instruction and better religious knowledge is seen in the case of Alexander Brichsen, citizen of Ulm, who in 1530 fell into discussion at his home with an Anabaptist. Uncertain about whether to have his newborn child baptised or not, he went to consult the town preacher about his doubts. The latter responded in a manner that could hardly be called pastoral, denouncing the unfortunate Alexander from the pulpit as a hedge-preacher.[98] This shows the curiosity and hesitancy with which ordinary people responded to new ideas, but it also reveals their absence of preconceptions about which ideas were more or less theologically sound than others, about which were more or less "acceptable."

All historians interested in the diffusion of ideas attempt to trace their impact in the personal thoughts, emotions, and values of ordinary people. It is the argument of this article that we shall be unable to do so if we concentrate only on the printed word and ignore such apparently trivial material as street-corner gossip or private conversation, the very stuff of daily life. Popular printed literature is an invaluable source, if used with the appropriate methodological caution, but we shall not understand the reception of the Reformation (or even of the printed word) by concentrating on print alone. To believe so involves a double misconception. It misunderstands the nature of printing's impact on a predominantly oral culture; and it makes fundamental mistakes about communication processes, by believing that concentration on the transmission of ideas provides an adequate grasp of their reception. It is always a methodological mistake for the historian to rely on one type of source to the exclusion of others. This awareness should inform our research strategies and lead us to search as wide a range of records as possible. Only in this way can we adequately reconstruct how the Reformation was diffused among the entire German people, literate, semi-literate, and illiterate.

Notes

This article is a revised and considerably expanded version of a short paper first delivered to the Past and Present Annual Conference 1979 on "The Transmission of Ideas in Early Modern Europe c. 1350–1700." A slightly different version in German was presented to the Tübingen Symposium on "Flugschriften als Massenmedium der Reformationszeit" in 1980, which has been published in the conference proceedings (see note 5). I have repeated a few paragraphs of this German version here.

1. A view most forcefully stated recently by E. L. Eisenstein, *The Printing Press as an Agent of Change,* 2 vols. (Cambridge, 1979), esp. chap. 4.

2. See S. Ozment, "The social history of the reformation: What can we learn from pamphlets?," in H. J. Köhler, ed., *Flugschriften als Massenmedium der Reformationszeit* (Stuttgart, 1981), 171–203, esp. 202; B. Moeller, "Stadt und Buch. Bemerkungen zur Struktur der reformatorischen Bewegungen in Deutschland," in W. J. Mommsen, ed., *Stadtbürgertum und Adel in der Reformation* (Stuttgart, 1979), 29–39.

3. Examples are given later in this article. On literacy in Germany, see R. Engelsing, *Analphabetentum und Lektüre. Zur Sozialgeschichte des Lesens in Deutschland zwischen feudaler und industrieller Gesellschaft* (Stuttgart, 1973), 6–38, esp. 34.

4. On the complexity of mass communication and the varied theories involved in its study, see D. McQuail, *Mass Communication Theory* (London, 1983), esp. 126–27, on the inherent contradictions of studying media content as a social and cultural indicator. See also M. B. Cassata and M. K. Asante, *Mass Communication: Principles and Practices* (New York, 1979), parts 1–2.

5. R. W. Scribner, "Flugblatt und Analphabetentum. Wie kam der gemeine Mann zu reformatorischen Ideen?," in Köhler, 65–76; R. W. Scribner, *For the Sake of Simple Folk: Popular Propaganda for the German Reformation* (Cambridge, 1981); "Reformation, carnival and the world turned upside-down," *Social History* 3 (1978): 303–29.

6. The importance of oral dissemination has been noted in other Reformation contexts; see Estèbe, "Vers une autre religion et une autre Eglise (1536–1598)?" in R. Mandrou, *Histoire des Protestants en France* (Paris, 1977), 47–50; M. Mullett, *Radical Religious Movements in Early Modern Europe* (London, 1980), 18. For Germany, it has been relatively ignored until recently; see R. Wohlfeil, *Einführung in die Geschichte der deutschen Reformation* (Munich, 1982), esp. 123–32. Wohlfeil's book, which appeared after this article was written, shares a number of the general views it will advocate.

7. Discussed at further length in R. W. Scribner, "Practice and principle in the German towns: Preachers and people," in P. N. Brooks, ed., *Reformation Principle and Practice: Essays in Honour of A. G. Dickens* (London, 1980), 95–117, esp. 112ff. On the sacramental status of "hearing the word," see Eisenstein, 374; and B. Moeller, *Deutschland im Zeitalter der Reformation* (Göttingen, 1977), 125.

8. For discussion around these points, see Eisenstein, 374ff.; Moeller, "Stadt und Buch"; R. W. Scribner, "'How many could read?' Comments on Bernd Moeller's 'Stadt und Buch,'" in Mommsen, 44–45; B. Moeller, "Einige Bemerkungen zum Thema: Predigten in reformatorischen Flugschriften," in Köhler, 261–68. A good deal of this latter contribution by Moeller is taken up with a refutation of my 1979 comments, although he ignores the comments in the 1980 conference paper. His arguments about the importance of studying printed sermons fail completely to deal with the nature of oral culture or with the nature of communication processes.

9. Scribner, *For the Sake of Simple Folk*, 196–200.

10. F. Gess, ed., *Akten und Briefe zur Kirchenpolitik Herzog Georgs von Sachsen*, 2 vols. (Leipzig, 1905, 1917), 1:348. Other examples in Scribner, "Practice and principle," 107ff.

11. Gess, 2:98 n.; Scribner, "Practice and principle," 112ff.

12. Gess, 2:97–98.

13. Ibid., 97.

14. Stadtarchiv Ulm, *Ulmiensien* 5314, fol. 20r; Stadtarchiv Regensburg Eccl. I, 1, 36 (14 September 1534); Stadtarchiv Augsburg Literalien (27 July 1525), cited by P. Broadhead, "Internal politics and civic society in Augsburg during the early Reformation, 1518–37" (Ph.D. thesis, University of Kent, 1981), 114; F. Roth and E. Durr, *Aktensammlung zur Geschichte der Basler Reformation* (Basel, 1937), 3:50.

15. M. Luther, "Von den Schleichern und Winckelprediger," *Werke* (Weimar

edition), vol. 30/3, 518–27, esp. 522; E. Sehling, ed., *Die evangelischen Kirchenordnungen des XVI. Jahrhunderts* (Leipzig, 1902), vol. 1/1, 187.

16. Stadtarchiv Ulm A 5325 (31 July 1530).

17. *Ain schoner dialogus von zwayen gutten gesellen Hans Tholl und Claus Lamp,* in O. Schade, *Satiren und Pasquille aus der Reformationszeit* (Hannover, 1857), 2:128. For an excellent discussion of how this influenced early Reformation pamphlets as means of communication, see J. Schmidt, *Lestern, lesen und lesen hören. Kommunikationsstudien zur deutschen Prosasatire der Reformationszeit* (Bern, 1977), esp. part A, 128.

18. M. Rössing-Hager, "Wie stark findet der nichtlesekundige Rezipient Berücksichtigung in den Flugschriften?" in Köhler, 77–137 (with further examples of pamphlets suggesting they should be read aloud on 77, n. 1); H. Zschelletzschky, *Die "drei gottlosen Maler" von Nürnberg* (Leipzig, 1975), 24.

19. *Diss biechlein zaygt an die weyssagung von zukunfftiger betrubnuss* (Augsburg: Hans Schönspergur, 1522), fol. A2ᵃ.

20. W. P. Fuchs, ed., *Akten zur Geschichte des Bauernkriegs in Mitteldeutschland* (Jena, 1942; reprinted, Aalen, 1964), 2:652.

21. Ibid., 744, 676, respectively.

22. Stadtarchiv Speyer I A 492, fols. 14–15.

23. Historisches Archiv Köln, Ref. 1, fol. 16.

24. Stadtarchiv Ulm, Ratsprotokolle 7, fols. 390, 407, 430.

25. Stadtarchiv Regensburg, Eccl. I. 1, 76 (11 June 1535, with reference to the earlier mandate).

26. D. Schönherr, ed., *Franz Schweygers Chronik der Stadt Hall 1303–1572* (Innsbruck, 1867), 80–82.

27. F. Lubecus, *Bericht über die Einführung der Reformation in Göttingen im Jahre 1529* (Göttingen, 1967), 17.

28. Gess, 2:441; and for further details on Rost, Fuchs, 712.

29. Gess, 2:264; Fuchs, 881.

30. Gess, 2:317–19.

31. Fuchs, 68.

32. *Ein Sermon Henrichs von Kettenbach zu der loblichen Statt Ulm zu seynem valete,* in O. Clemen, ed., *Flugschriften aus den ersten Jahren der Reformation* (Leipzig, 1908), 2:107; F. Roth and E. Dürr, eds., *Aktensammlung zur Geschichte der Basler Reformation* (Basel, 1921), 1:91.

33. Historisches Archiv Köln, Ref. 14, fol. 2, and cf. Ref. 15 of 1534 for other evidence of Anabaptists meeting in inns. On Augsburg, Broadhead, 90, 146.

34. Scribner, *For the Sake of Simple Folk,* 6, 212.

35. H. Rankl, "Gesellschaftlicher Ort und strafrichterliche Behandlung von 'Rumor,' 'Empörung,' 'Aufruhr' und 'Ketzerei' in Beyern um 1525," *Zeitschrift für bayerische Landesgeschichte* 38 (1975), 564.

36. Gess, 2:618.

37. Ibid., 317.

38. Historisches Archiv Köln, Verf. und Verw. G 310, fols. 105–6.

39. Ibid., Ref. 1, fol. 17.

40. Ibid., Verf. und Verw. G 205 (Thurmbuch), fols. 37–55.

41. Roth and Dürr, 1:94.

42. Rankl, 564.

43. These links can be assembled from Fuchs, 651–52, 881; Gess, 2:257, 264; J. K. Seidemann, "Das Ende des Bauernkrieges in Thüringen," *Neue Mitteilungen aus dem Gebiet historisch-antiquarischer Forschungen,* 445.

44. Schlossmecher: *bey anderen syner geselschafft,* Historisches Archly Köln, Ref. 1, fol. 17; Brenich: *in gueder geselschafft,* ibid., Verf. und Verw. G 310, fol. 105.

45. *Vill gesellschaft und zeche gehapt,* Fuchs, 889.

46. Gess, 2:314.

47. Fuchs, 651–52, 889; Gess, 2:263–64, 543; Seidemann, 445.

48. P. Wappler, *Die Täuferbewegung in Thüringen von 1526–1584* (Jena, 1913), 228–32.

49. Ibid., 239–40, 279, 281.

50. Ibid., 243, 257, 270, 277, 287.

51. Ibid., 265.

52. Ibid., 270–71.

53. Ibid., 277.

54. Ibid., 258–61, passim.

55. For example, *Ein kurz gedicht, so nüwlich ein thurgowischer Pur gemacht hat,* in Schade, 2:160–64; or U. Schade, *Ainn new gedicht, das da spricht nach des Luthers ler* (1521), British Library 11519.dd.20 (3). See also R. W. Brednich, *Die Liedpublizistik im Flugblatt des 15. und 16. Jahrhunderts,* 2 vols. (Baden-Baden, 1974–75), who argues for the interdependence of oral and printed transmission of songs in this period, 1:12ff.

56. M. Luther, *Werke. Kritische Gesamtausgabe* (Weimar, 1923), 35:419; W. Jannasch, *Reformationsgeschichte Lübecks* (Lübeck, 1958), 273; P. Steinmüller, *Die Einführung der Reformation in die Kurmark Brandenburg durch Joachim II* (Halle, 1903), 20.

57. P. Merker, ed., *Thomas Murner. Deutsche Schriften,* vol. 9 (Leipzig, 1918), 33.

58. P. Wackernagel, *Das deutsche Kirchenlied von der ältesten Zeit bis zu Anfang des XVII. Jahrhunderts* (Leipzig, 1870), vol. 3, nos. 454–55.

59. Stadtarchiv Ulm A 3680, fol. 148, 150; Ratsprotokololle 8, fol. 40.

60. Gess, 1:122. O. Clemen, ed., *Flugschriften aus den erstem Jahren der Reformation* (Leipzig, 1907), 1:369–76.

61. N. Muller, *Die Wittenberger Bewegung 1521 und 1522* (Leipzig, 1911), 133.

62. Jannasch, 283.

63. Lubecus, 15ff.

64. Ibid., 14.

65. Brednich, 1:87.

66. On this contrast, Eisenstein, 129ff., although her own approach is more complex. The more recent interest in the Reformation as a dramatic turning point in opinion formation dates from the influence of McLuhan, but the notion has a

longer history: see, for example, K. Fischer, *Deutschlands öffentliche Meinung im Reformationszeitalter und in der Gegenwart* (Berlin, 1874); W. Bauer, *Die öffentliche Meinung und ihre geschichtliche Grundlagen* (Tübingen, 1914), 75ff., and "Public opinion," *Encyclopaedia of the Social Sciences* (New York, 1933), 12:672; K. Schottenloher, *Bücher bewegten die Welt* (Stuttgart, 1951), 1:198–200.

67. R. W. Scribner, "Sozialkontrolle und die Möglichkeit einer städtischen Reformation," in B. Moeller, ed., *Stadt und Kirche im 16. Jahrhundert* (Gütersloh, 1978), 57–65, esp. 61ff.

68. On this point see the thoughtful comments of Schmidt, 66–68.

69. M. Luther, *Werke* (Weimar edition), Briefwechsel, 2:268.

70. P. Merker, *Thomas Murner. Deutsche Schriften,* 9:40–43.

71. On Cologne, O. Zaretsky, *Der erste Kölner Zensurprozess* (Cologne, 1906); on Augsburg, Zurich, and Basel, Brednich, 1:287–88; for examples from Nuremberg on control of the broadsheet press, T. Hampe, *Nürnberger Ratsverlässe über Kunst und Kunstler im Zeitalter der Spätgotik und Renaissance* (Leipzig, 1904), nos. 1378, 1380–81, 1444, 1446, 1454–55, 1459 (for only the years 1522–41).

72. On Franconia, E. Schubert, "'Bauerngeschrey.' Zum Problem der Öffentlichen Meinung im spätmittelalterlichen Franken," *Jahrbuch für fränksiche Landesforschung* 34/35 (1975), 883–907; on communication processes, Cassata and Asante, chaps. 3–4; McQuail, chaps. 6–7. Wohlfeil's notion of "Öffentlichkeit," 123–24, also seeks to take account of this problem.

73. See Bauer, 670; H. Blumer, "The mass, the public and public opinion," in B. Berelson and M. Jonowitz, eds., *Reader in Public Opinion and Communication,* 2nd ed. (New York, 1966), 46–48; R. L. Rosnow and G. A. Fine, *Rumour and Gossip: The Social Psychology of Hearsay* (New York, 1976), 76–80; T. Shibutani, *Improvised News. A Sociological Study of Rumour* (New York, 1966), 37–40, 70–76, 129–62.

74. Scribner, "Flugblatt und Analphabetentum," 73–74; Wohlfeil, 123ff.

75. On marketing patterns and middlemen, there has so far been no applications in the area of communication of ideas. For theoretical relations, see A. Everitt, "The marketing of agricultural produce," in J. Thirsk, ed., *The Agrarian History of England and Wales* (Cambridge, 1967), vol. 4, chap. 8; G. W. Skinner, "Marketing and social structure in rural China (Part I)," in J. M. Potter, M. N. Diaz, and G. M. Foster, eds., *Peasant Society: A Reader* (Boston, 1967), 63–98; E. R. Wolf, *Peasants* (Engelwood Cliffs, N.J., 1966), 40–48. Fundamental for Germany are R. Kiessling, "Stadt-Land-Beziehung im Spätmittelalter," *Zeitschrift für bayerische Landesgeschichte* 40 (1977), 829–67; E. Meynen, ed., *Zentralität als Problem der mittel-alterlichen Stadtgeschichtsforschung* (Cologne, 1979); T. Scott, "Bemerkungen zum Begriff 'Gemeiner Mann': das Stadt-Land Verhältnis zur Zeit des Bauernkrieges," in *Die Bauernkriege und Michael Gaismair, Veröffentlichungen des Tiroler Landesarchivs* (Innsbruck, 1982), 2:289–92.

76. Calwer Verlagsverein, *Württembergische Kirchengeschichte* (Calw, 1893), 267; W. Vogt, "Zwei oberschwäbische Laienprediger," *Zeitschrift für kirchliche Wissenschaft und kirchliches Leben* 6 (1885), 416.

77. On Häberlin, Vogt, 540–42; on multi-step flow and opinion leaders, Cassata and Asante, 14–15.

78. P. Blickle, *The Revolution of 1525* (Baltimore, 1981), 58–67, esp. 58ff.; G. Vogler, "Der revolutionäre Gehalt und die räumliche Verbreitung der oberschwäbischen zwölf Artikel," in *Historische Zeitschrift* 4 (1975), 209.

79. O. Merx, ed., *Akten zur Geschichte des Bauernkriegs in Mitteldeutschland* (Leipzig, 1923; reprinted, Aalen, 1964), vol. 1/1, 292.

80. G. Franz, ed., *Akten zur Geschichte des Bauernkriegs in Mitteldeutschland* (Leipzig, 1934; reprinted, Aalen, 1964) vol. 1/2, 422 (Fulda), 368 (Hersfeld), 404 (Henneberg).

81. Ibid., 430–31, 434–35.

82. Fuchs, 463.

83. Ibid., 566.

84. Ibid., 594.

85. Gess, 2:691, 323 n.

86. Ibid., 303.

87. Ibid., 323 n., 349–51; Fuchs, 547.

88. Fuchs, 649.

89. Ibid., 650.

90. Franz, 657.

91. Ibid., 372.

92. Ibid., 656.

93. Fuchs, 745.

94. Gess, 2:349–51, passim.

95. Franz, 421, 423; Fuchs, 568.

96. Blickle, 129.

97. See Cassata and Asante, 70.

98. Stadtarchiv Speyer I A 492, fols. 14–15; Stadtarchiv Ulm [1753/1], fol. 8.

7 THE LITERACY MYTH?
ILLITERACY IN SCOTLAND, 1630–1760

Rab Houston

The story of Scottish education and literacy has reached the status of a legend. In view of Scotland's palpably superior attainment of basic literacy in the mid-nineteenth century compared to England, and because of Scotland's long history of national legislation on educational provision, it has been claimed that Scotland became a highly literate country at an early date.[1] Like eighteenth-century Sweden, Scotland has become a reference standard for early modern societies.[2] Influenced by more than a hint of romanticism and historical nationalism, some historians have been anxious to show that the exhortations of the Calvinist church combined with national legislation during the seventeenth and eighteenth centuries to produce one of the most literate of all pre-industrial societies. In seventeenth- and eighteenth-century Scotland education was said to be widely available and open to both sexes and all social groups, the best schools effecting "a wide diffusion of education to every class in society."[3] This has been linked to the allegedly egalitarian nature of Scottish society, a nation where social divisions were relatively unimportant, and where education "opened the door, or at least set it ajar" for social mobility.[4] Through all this historians have concentrated on educational provision and school curricula, reliable figures on the attainment of literacy among the Scottish population being almost totally absent.[5] "Wide generalizations have been made on narrow grounds and judgements have swung violently from extremes of praise to equally uncritical condemnation,"[6] but it has perhaps been too readily accepted that Scotland enjoyed substantially superior progress in literacy compared with other countries. Statistics on the social, sexual, and geographical distribution of literacy in seventeenth- and eighteenth-century Scotland are badly needed to test some of these assertions and to assess whether the experience of Scotland was indeed "dramatically different" in her progress towards near-universal literacy in the mid-nineteenth century.[7] Moreover, analysis of these aspects can further advance understanding of the reasons behind literacy and of its social

Reprinted from Rab Houston, "The Literacy Myth? Illiteracy in Scotland, 1630–1760," *Past and Present* 96 (1982): 81–102, by permission of Oxford University Press and the author.

importance. In addition there are a number of significant implications for the study of Scottish society as a whole.

The criterion of literacy used here is the admittedly imperfect but generally accepted one of ability to sign one's name on a document. The crudity of this index is well known.[8] It reduces a continuous variable to a dichotomous one and tells us nothing about facility in writing more than simply one's name. Because reading was taught before writing, and since girls were much less likely to pass beyond the stage of learning to read and sew,[9] the measure may understate the reading ability of women much more than men. This may also be true of poorer children of both sexes who only stayed long enough at school to learn to read the Bible.[10] In the early nineteenth century George Robertson believed that ordinary people "have always . . . been laudably ambitious of giving their children a decent education, and would be ashamed if they could not at least read the English language."[11] Yet it appears from early nineteenth-century evidence that sign-literacy did indeed form a rough midpoint in the spectrum of literate skills, most European countries following "the orthodox Catholic pattern of a close connection between reading and writing."[12] At the same time ability to sign represents a "universal, standard and direct" criterion which allows comparison between regions and socioeconomic groups as well as over time.[13] Which sources provide us with quantifiable evidence of literacy thus defined?

Two sets of material are available which afford the necessary information about sign-literacy. For the mid-seventeenth century there are a handful of surviving subscriptions to the National Covenant of 1638 and the Solemn League and Covenant of 1643 which offer evidence on adult male literacy in local communities, and which can be compared with English Protestation Oath subscriptions of 1642. Depositions of witnesses at the High Court of Justiciary, the highest Scottish criminal court, meanwhile afford detail on occupationally specific literacy over a longer time span—roughly from the mid-seventeenth century to the mid-eighteenth.[14] At best, depositions provide the name, marital status, age, occupation and residence of the witnesses plus an indication of whether or not they could sign their own names.

Ostensibly a "defensive bond," the National Covenant of 1638 was used as a political instrument to unite Scotland behind Presbyterianism. It was so phrased as to possess broad popular politico-religious appeal,[15] and by all accounts it was received with considerable approbation.[16] The 1643 Solemn League and Covenant was intended specifically to ensure support for the English parliamentary cause if the English and Irish churches were made Presbyterian, and penalties for non-subscription were severe.[17] Few of these documents survive, and fewer still are usable for analysis of literacy. Those considered below conform to certain rather strict criteria: a set of subscriptions collected in a short space of time within a delimited geographical area such as a parish and known to cover a uniform section of the population (adult males).[18]

One additional problem afflicts analysis of Scottish literacy: the fact that personal subscriptions of any kind (but marks more than signatures) are not always included in the documents. Instead notaries public generally attested to inability to write, making it clear nevertheless that the illiterate persons had been given the opportunity to sign for themselves. For the literate the phrase *sic subscribitur* ("Thus subscribed") may be used, followed by either a holograph or transcribed signature. Personal subscription was not legally necessary.[19]

II

Based on the few Covenants fulfilling these requirements, Table 7.1 provides the first firm figures on adult male illiteracy in mid-seventeenth-century Scotland. Most of the usable Covenants shown on the map (Figure 7.1) relate to parishes in lowland Scotland, but they do provide a valuable selection of contrasting economic types. Considerable variations exist even between parishes in each of the two categories in Table 7.1, but some broad patterns emerge. While a number of factors might influence literacy levels, parishes have been grouped in Table 7.1 according to the most obvious difference between them: whether they are urban or rural. Among rural parishes geographical location appears to make little difference to literacy among adult males. The upland parishes of Gartly, Legerwood, and Borgue do have above-average illiteracy, but are not unique, being matched by Dundonald, Kilmany and Edzell—all mixed agricultural communities close to market centres.[20] Newbattle's relatively low illiteracy may indicate the influence of highly developed agriculture and relatively numerous craft and trade occupations plus extractive industries in the economically and socially precocious area around Edinburgh. It is unfortunate that only one Covenant survives for a highland parish—Gartly—since we are unable to assess the importance of the highland/lowland division said to have been of fundamental importance in Scottish society.[21]

Despite these variations the mean illiteracy for the rural parishes is about 80 per cent, fully 30 per cent higher than for those parishes with a significant urban component. It is true that "most burghs were mere villages"[22] in early modern Scotland, and in fact most of the "rural" parishes did have a burgh charter of some kind. We must however distinguish between "real" and "paper" burghs and the level of commercial activity within them. The six burghs with substantially lower levels of illiteracy were commercially better developed and possessed appreciable occupational diversification.

This socioeconomic pattern provides the most likely explanation of the superior literacy of Scottish towns in the mid-seventeenth century. Burghs were designed to foster trade, and their privileges included the right to have craftsmen and tradesmen practising in them. Active towns would therefore possess proportionately greater numbers of people in literate occupations such as merchants, craftsmen and professionals.[23] In the Edinburgh parish, for example, the poll tax records of the 1690s show that of 323 taxpayers not

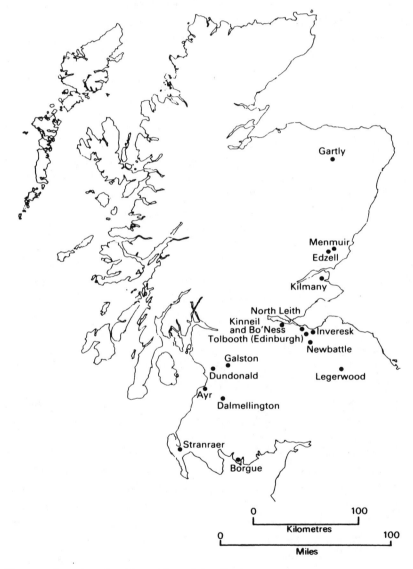

Figure 7.1. Location of parishes with surviving Covenants.

Table 7.1. Adult male illiteracy in Scotland, 1638–43

Urban parishes	(i)	(ii)
Ayr, Ayrshire	386	46
Inveresk, Midlothian	707	52
Kinneil and Bo'Ness, West Lothian	303	53
North Leith, Midlothian	357	51
Stranraer, Wigtownshire	183	52
Tolbooth (Edinburgh), Midlothian	729	32
Rural parishes		
Borgue, Kirkcudbrightshire	217	87
Dalmellington, Ayrshire	222	81
Dundonald, Ayrshire	222	83
Edzell, Forfarshire	211	90
Galston, Ayrshire	335	70
Gartly, Aberdeenshire	170	83
Kilmany, Fife	210	89
Legerwood, Berwickshire	150	82
Menmuir, Forfarshire	54	70
Newbattle, Midlothian	383	76
Forfarshire	1,058	76
Total	5,897	

Sources: In alphabetical order, the Covenants used here: Ayr, National Library of Scotland, Edinburgh (hereafter N.L.S.), Adv. MS.20.6.17b. (there is a transcript in *Ayr Advocation*, 8 Oct. 1874: N.L.S., Adv. MS.20.6.17a); Borgue, Scottish Record Office, Edinburgh (hereafter S.R.O.), SP13/160; Dalmellington, J. Scotland, *The History of Scottish Education*, 2 vols. (London, 1969), 1:49; Dundonald, S.R.O., CH2 104/1, fos. 146–50; Edzell, New College Lib., Mound, Edinburgh; Galston, in the kirk session register for 1638–44, in the keeping of the minister, the Manse, Galston; Gartly, S.R.O., SP13/161; Inneresk, N.L.S., Adv. MS.20.6.18; Kilmany, S.R.O., "File T258" (photographic copy); Kinneil and Bo'ness, New College Lib.; Legerwood, Edinburgh Univ. Lib., LaIII 229/1; Menmuir, N.L.S., MS.3279; Newbattle, Museum of the Society of Antiquaries, Queen St., Edinburgh, OA19; North Leith, New College Lib.; North-West Edinburgh, N.L.S., Adv. MS.23.3.16; Stranraer, R. Mitchison, *Life in Scotland* (London, 1978), 45; Forfarshire, N.L.S., Adv. MS.34.5.15.

Note: Column headings are:

(i) Total number of subscribers to the National Covenant of 1638 and the Solemn League and Covenant of 1643.

(ii) Number of illiterate expressed as a percentage.

described as servants or wives and children 7 per cent were lairds, 26 per cent professionals and 54 per cent craftsmen and tradesmen (of whom 43 per cent were merchants).[24] In rural areas the comparable proportions would be closer to 2 per cent, 1 per cent and 20 per cent respectively.[25] Edinburgh's very low illiteracy, like its unusually skewed occupational structure, made it unique in seventeenth-century Scotland.

We cannot, however, neglect the role of schooling as a possible explanation of observed variations in illiteracy, scanty though the evidence is. Dealing with officially established schools only, all the towns had burgh schools from at least the late sixteenth century onwards. At the same time it is generally accepted that the quality and quantity of education was best in the burghs in the pre-industrial period.[26] However we cannot ignore the fact that early modern towns drew a significant proportion of their population from rural areas, especially in periods of rapid urban expansion such as that experienced by early seventeenth-century Kinneil and Bo'Ness.[27] These people may not have been educated in the towns. As towns continued to grow the quality of education may have improved, but the ratio of places to children often worsened. Nor can variations among the rural parishes be related conclusively to the presence or absence of schools.

There was no official parish school at Kilmany even in 1658, which perhaps explains its high illiteracy,[28] but this was also true of the low illiteracy parish of Newbattle.[29] The proximity of Newbattle to the town of Dalkeith, and its relatively diversified occupational structure are a more likely explanation of its lower illiteracy. At Galston meanwhile the precentor or schoolmaster received only a pittance for keeping school in the early seventeenth century "in respect of the small number of bairnes."[30] Dundonald certainly had a viable school from 1605[31] but could only manage one in five literate adult males. The connection between schooling and sign literacy is by no means clear. Instead the importance of prior economic development is strongly suggested.

Some tentative estimates of national illiteracy levels for adult males in mid-seventeenth-century Scotland can be made from these figures. Given that perhaps 5–10 per cent of the Scottish population in 1640 lived in towns sufficiently large to decrease overall literacy from "rural" levels[32] a very approximate estimate of 75 per cent illiteracy emerges. This is likely to represent a minimum level since those failing to subscribe the Covenants were probably among the poorest, most transient, and thus least literate sections of local communities.[33] At the same time the highlands and islands are heavily underrepresented in the sample and are likely to have been even more illiterate than lowland rural parishes. This rough assessment places Scotland some 5 per cent behind contemporary England, but it seems likely that the gap was wider. It is, however, clear that if Scotland was to become a more literate country than England because of the influence of the Calvinist church and a national school system it did not do so until after the middle of the seventeenth century. This confirms the general suspicion of historians that the kirk was not strong enough to force the pace of literacy in the early seventeenth century. What was its role in the following century?

III

Depositions allow us to consider in more detail the profile of illiteracy among the Scottish population between the mid-seventeenth and late eighteenth centuries. Disaggregating literacy levels not only helps to provide a sounder basis for national estimates, but also allows consideration of the place of literacy and education in the alleged distinctiveness of Scottish society. At the same time it permits analysis of the likely relative impact of economic, social, and religious factors on literacy attainment in pre-industrial Scotland. It turns out that the role of education and religion was severely tempered by identifiable socioeconomic constraints.

Witnesses deponing before the High Court of Justiciary were cast up in a largely random way, constrained however by the type of case, the desire for deponents whose "social credit" was well established, and a number of flexible criteria which excluded those whose judgement was felt to be suspect. The breakdown of witnesses by sex, occupation, and residence makes it clear that they were not a representative cross-section of the society as a whole: women, for example, formed only 18 per cent of all deponents, some groups such as professionals (notably surgeons) are massively over-represented, while the sample is biased towards town dwellers and towards those from the lowlands. Men and women living in Edinburgh and Glasgow, for example, form roughly a third of all deponents, and a further third came from other towns. The former figure is wholly out of proportion with the distribution of population shown in Webster's census of 1755: only some 6 per cent lived in the two biggest cities.[34] Proportions for town dwellers were more in line with the 25 per cent of the population who lived in these in 1775. Fortunately depositions allow us to control for these biases.

Work on illiteracy in England has elaborated a clear picture of differences between socioeconomic groups, a pervasive hierarchical structure of illiteracy which is demonstrated in all sources between the sixteenth and nineteenth centuries.[35] In Scotland as in England the most striking feature is the markedly lower literacy attainment of women compared to men. Over the whole period men were 28 per cent illiterate while women were 80 per cent illiterate. Table 7.2 breaks this down by decades. For men the most rapid improvement seems to have occurred around the third quarter of the

seventeenth century, illiteracy dropping from over a half to one third, though
the mid-seventeenth-century figures may be suspect. There was a slow but
continuing fall until 1700, after which relative stagnation sets in at 20–25
per cent illiterate. There is some sign of a gradual improvement in female
illiteracy, but the progress was not uninterrupted and the relative changes
were comparatively modest. Throughout the period women lagged far behind men in their aggregate literacy levels and did not participate in any of
the significant improvements enjoyed by men. The impact of educational
advances and religious exhortations on female illiteracy seems to have been
comparatively slight. Education might theoretically be open to both sexes,
but males were much more likely to do well out of it than females.

Table 7.2. Male and female illiteracy in Scotland, 1650–1760

	Male		Female	
	(i)	(ii)	(i)	(ii)
1650s–60s	152	56	4	100
1670s	246	34	31	87
1680s	437	33	43	88
1690s	362	27	79	81
1700s	250	24	99	85
1710s	340	22	87	80
1720s	344	21	79	75
1730s	271	24	64	72
1740s	122	21	38	76
1750s	111	22	56	77
Totals	2,635		580	

Sources: High Court of Justiciary material from S.R.O., JC6/1–14, JC7/1–30 (High Court
minute books).
Note: Column headings are the same as in Table 7.1.

These figures present only the most skeletal outline of literacy trends and
must be qualified by more detailed consideration of the impact of various
factors in influencing aggregate levels. Important variations in aggregate
male and female illiteracy existed, for example, between different regions of
Scotland. (See Table 7.3.) The regional breakdown is admittedly crude but
conforms to the broad geographical areas often used in analysis of Scottish
society.[36] Edinburgh, easily the largest and most important urban centre in
Scotland around 1700, was kept separate to discover whether a literacy profile
similar to that in contemporary London existed. At this heavily aggregated
level, the superiority of Edinburgh males and females in literacy attainment
is clear, being matched only by those from the borders and southwest. The
latter area was a hotbed of radical religion in the seventeenth century, a force

which may have pushed illiteracy down. At the same time it is likely that the economic backwardness of this region may have been exaggerated, pastoral farmers giving instead the impression of being closely interested in markets. At around 25–30 per cent, overall male levels for the rest of lowland Scotland are remarkably consistent given the variety of occupations found in the different regions. Women living in the area north of the Highland Line were not especially illiterate, but among men there is an obvious difference which suggests more strongly than Covenant evidence the existence of a socially distinct region. It seems likely that factors such as economic necessity were more important in promoting superior female urban literacy than was the impact of education or religion. Thus areas where the Calvinist church was strong, and where educational provision is known to have been good—Fife for example[37]—do not stand out from the north where both were less so.

Table 7.3. Male and female illiteracy in regions of Scotland

	Male		Female	
	(i)	(ii)	(i)	(ii)
Edinburgh	577	15	170	71
Lothians	306	26	117	84
North	393	46	42	90
Fife, Stirlings, Angus	362	28	100	89
Western lowlands	442	26	71	80
Borders and south-west	190	18	40	70
Unknown	365	33	40	83
Totals	2,635		580	

Note: Sources are the same as in Table 7.2. Column headings are the same as in Table 7.1.

Consideration of differences between occupational groups among male and female deponents can refine analysis of variations between regions and change over time. Occupation and status terms have been grouped to conform with David Cressy's broad categories, numbers being too small to allow detailed study of any but a handful of individual occupations.[38]

The evidence presented in Table 7.4 raises a number of points of interest. As in England, the occupational hierarchy of illiteracy is clear. Landowners, the acknowledged leaders of society, joined professional men as the most literate groups, their near-total literacy marking them off from the rest of society. Below these élite groups comes the large and heterogeneous one of craftsmen and tradesmen, a category which obscures large variations in illiteracy. Merchants were, for example, only 2 per cent illiterate, but at the other end of the range, weavers were close to 40 per cent. The high literacy of merchants, who form a large proportion of the craft and trade group, is a significant bias lowering the overall illiteracy of this category.

Table 7.4. Occupational illiteracy of males and females in Scotland

	Male		Female	
	(i)	(ii)	(i)	(ii)
Lairds	213	1	23	35
Professionals	472	2	23	26
Craftsmen and tradesmen	695	16	153	71
Farmers	127	28	14	86
Labourers and servants	366	50	195	89
Rest	108	45	12	75
Unknown	654	49	160	92
Totals	2,635		580	

Note: For females the occupations are mostly those of their fathers or husbands. Sources are the same as in Table 7.2. Column headings are the same as in Table 7.1.

What of other sections of the population? In a predominantly agricultural society the small number of deponents whose occupation is given as "tenant" or "farmer" is suspicious. This may be a reflection of the predominance of town dwellers among deponents. More likely, however, is that in a society where the division of labour was relatively unmarked and where dual occupations were common, any designation other than an agricultural one was preferred in order to distinguish the deponent. This is clearly true of cottars and subtenants among whom purely agricultural pursuits were so uncommon in the lowlands that poll tax assessments of the 1690s might single out members of these groups as "cottar no trade."[39] Alternatively an agricultural designation may have been seen by the clerk of the court as a form of "default" occupation. Farmers fall slightly behind crafts and trades, a pattern similar to the relative position of yeomen and craftsmen/tradesmen in northern England.[40]

Those working for wages and/or keep form the final grouping which allows us to control for the effects of social status. The term "servant" was used promiscuously of any employee, ranging from a living-in agricultural labourer to a writer's clerk or a gentleman servant. Its vagueness is shown when we consider that servants to lairds and professionals were nearly 20 per cent illiterate, whereas those working for farmers or craftsmen were over 70 per cent. The predominance of servants in the servant and labourer category makes it appear that this group were much more literate than their English contemporaries, but it should be noted that among more directly comparable groups labourers and workmen were 82 per cent illiterate (N = 50) over the whole period, a figure very much in line with English labourers.[41] The wide usage of "servant" tends to distort the true profile of "working-class" illiteracy.

Though women are usually treated as a homogeneous group in literacy analyses irrespective of their marital status, age, or the occupation of their husbands or fathers, this can disguise interesting variations in their literacy achievements. Widows and indeed older women generally were much more literate than their single or married counterparts, while daughters, wives, and widows of lairds and professionals were appreciably more literate than women associated with other occupational or status groups. Craft- and trade-associated women held an intermediate position. Female servants—almost the only designation enjoyed by women in their own right, but one tendered problematic by its life-cycle specific nature—were 90 per cent illiterate. It is clear that a hierarchy of literacy based on status, age, and residence existed similar to the one distinguished above for men.

These figures make it plain that literacy was distributed among the population of early modern Scotland in a hierarchical fashion. We cannot compare this ranking with contemporary descriptions of the Scottish social order as has been done for England[42] since none exist, but it is clear that occupation and social status had a powerful impact on levels of illiteracy. Education might be open to both sexes and all social classes in theory, but in practice women and the lower social classes were heavily discriminated against either in curriculum or in access to education and its duration. If we assume that formal education was the most important influence promoting sign-literacy across the social spectrum (and this is by no means certain), it is clear that while the notion of "universal education" may be demonstrable in terms of widespread educational provision, the evidence of illiteracy shows that it fell far short of being total. Literacy was firmly related to economic need and to the existing social structure.

Using 1700 as a crude dividing line, and leaving aside landowners and professional men who were nearly all literate, changes over time among representatives of occupational groups which formed the bulk of the population can be considered. (See Table 7.5.) Tenant farmers, the backbone of Scottish society in the early modern period, did not see any appreciable improvement in their literacy levels, staying at roughly 30 per cent illiterate over the whole period, but among labourers and servants there was a modest fall in illiteracy from 62 percent to 49 per cent. For crafts and trades the level was nearly halved from 23 per cent to 13 per cent. Improvements in literacy among those participating in and exposed to the economic advances taking place in this period are clear. Perhaps the combined effect of better education and economic change was to enhance the literacy of the middling, non-agricultural sections of society, while for the lower echelons and the agricultural sector the effects of both were felt much less and rather later. The connection between economic change and literacy is likely to be more complex than is sometimes assumed. Only labourer/servant and craft/trade-related women deponed in sufficient numbers to allow analysis; neither experienced more than a slight fall in illiteracy between the two broad time periods.

Table 7.5. Occupational illiteracy of males and females over time

	Male				Female			
	1650–99		1700–60		1650–99		1700–60	
	(i)	(ii)	(i)	(ii)	(i)	(ii)	(i)	(ii)
Lairds	124	1	89	2	4	50	19	32
Professionals	199	3	273	1	11	36	12	17
Crafts and trades	216	23	479	13	28	75	125	70
Farmers	27	30	100	28	1	100	13	85
Labourers and servants	141	62	225	49	46	94	149	87
Rest	42	67	34	35	4	50	8	88
Totals	749		1,200		94		326	

Note: Sources are the same as in Table 7.2. Column headings are the same as in Table 7.1.

Breakdowns over such long time periods reveal basic structures, but may disguise the timing of important shifts. Unfortunately, however, decadal changes can only be studies for male craftsmen and tradesmen, and labourers and servants. For both these groups the sharpest fall in illiteracy came around the third quarter of the seventeenth century, though the trend may be distorted by small numbers in the first decades. (See Table 7.6.) Thereafter labourers and servants maintained a level of illiteracy fluctuating around 50 per cent and did not participate in the second major literacy gain shown

Table 7.6. Illiteracy of male craftsmen and tradesmen, and labourers and servants over time

	Craftsmen and Tradesmen		Labourers and Servants	
	(i)	(ii)	(i)	(ii)
1650s–60s	17	47	18	89
1670s	32	28	24	71
1680s	79	23	51	45
1690s	88	17	48	67
1700s	46	22	46	52
1710s	97	22	42	52
1720s	138	12	58	47
1730s	113	8	44	45
1740s	53	13	24	46
1750s	32	3	11	67
Totals	695		366	

Note: Sources are the same as in Table 7.2. Column headings are the same as in Table 7.1.

Table 7.7. Male and female illiteracy in different communities of residence over time

	1650s/1660s		1670s		1680s		1690s		1700s		1710s		1720s		1730s		1740s		1750s	
	(i)	(ii)	(i)	(ii)	(i)	(ii)	(i)	(ii)	(i)	(ii)	(i)	(ii)	(i)	(ii)	(i)	(ii)	(i)	(ii)	(i)	(ii)
Males																				
Edinburgh/Glasgow	35	51	37	24	73	19	104	15	68	9	111	13	121	6	81	10	59	12	19	11
Other towns	23	26	71	23	110	19	92	23	68	16	112	20	109	13	76	11	30	23	35	17
Villages	44	73	80	56	156	44	112	41	97	38	96	39	72	46	108	44	30	37	49	29
Females																				
Edinburgh/Glasgow	1	100	13	85	18	72	25	64	22	73	32	69	30	73	13	46	20	70	21	86
Other towns	2	100	10	100	10	100	18	72	17	65	27	85	21	71	32	66	2	50	11	64
Villages	1	100	5	80	12	100	30	100	51	98	24	92	23	83	18	100	16	88	22	73

Note: Sources are the same as in Table 7.2. Column headings are the same as in Table 7.1.

among crafts and trades in the first quarter of the eighteenth century. Variations in the composition of the labourer/servant group associated with small numbers for some decades explain the short-term fluctuations in levels.

Disaggregating these figures provides further valuable insights into the dynamics of literacy in early modern Scotland. As noted above, the deponent sample is heavily biased towards those living in towns and cities—a factor which turns out to have an important bearing on levels of illiteracy. Table 7.7 shows that for both men and women, experience of living in a town or city was associated with appreciably higher levels of literacy. In most time periods Edinburgh and Glasgow dwellers were the most literate groups, while those living in other parishes with economically active towns followed close behind. Those living in rural areas were generally more illiterate. To some extent this may be due to a "compositional effect"—more people in literate occupations living in towns. However, Table 7.8 shows that even within delineated occupational groups rural males were less literate than those living in towns and cities, the contrast being most clear between Edinburgh and Glasgow and the rural areas.

Table 7.8. Occupational illiteracy of males in different communities of residence within Scotland

	Edinburgh and Glasgow		Other Towns		Villages	
	(i)	(ii)	(i)	(ii)	(i)	(ii)
Lairds	12	0	36	0	69	4
Professionals	198	0	181	1	62	8
Craftsmen and tradesmen	176	10	301	17	105	32
Farmers	12	33	16	0	88	36
Servants and labourers	110	36	74	58	127	65
Rest	48	38	10	50	7	57
Unknown	42	29	108	30	402	55
Totals	698		726		360	

Note: Sources are the same as in Table 7.2. Column headings are the same as in Table 7.1.

A similar profile is shown among the wives, widows, and daughters of craftsmen and tradesmen and among women servants. The gap between Edinburgh and Glasgow and the other towns is most obvious for craft- and trade-related women: the experience of living in a town appears to have been less important in enhancing literacy for lower-class females, and in rural areas the socially determined difference all but disappears. At this level it is clear that discrimination was based on sex rather than social status. (See Table 7.9.) The gaps for craft and trade women are 13 per cent and 14 per cent respectively, but for labourer/servant women the nearly identical city and town level is only 8–9 per cent clear of rural dwellers. Once again identifiable secular forces modify the impact of religion and education as forces promoting literacy.

Table 7.9. Occupational illiteracy of females in different communities of residence within Scotland

	Craftswomen and tradeswomen		Servants	
	(i)	(ii)	(i)	(ii)
Glasgow/Edinburgh	61	57	75	88
Others towns	54	70	54	87
Villages	36	94	52	96
Totals	151		181	

Note: Sources are the same as in Table 7.2. Column headings are the same as in Table 7.1.

Using only those occupational groups with sufficient numbers for reliable statistical analysis, we can further advance our understanding of the relative importance of variables in promoting literacy. (See Table 7.10.) As well as being biased by community of residence, aggregate illiteracy levels are weighted by those living in the lowlands. Indeed the area of Scotland within which a deponent lived apparently influenced literacy levels. Edinburgh, the largest and most important urban centre in Scotland before the mid-eighteenth century, shows very low levels for both groups in Table 7.10, though the gap between Edinburgh and "non-metropolitan" Scotland is bigger for labourers and servants. Illiteracy levels in the western lowlands are depressed by the presence of Glasgow deponents, though the explanation for low illiteracy in the borders—admittedly based on relatively small numbers and dominated by Dumfries and other town dwellers—is less clear. Among craftsmen and tradesmen the north does not stand out as particularly illiterate, but this is the case with labourers and servants. This uniformity among the middling sections of society is at least suggestive of their relative lack of dependence on educational or religious influences promoting literacy compared with the lower social echelons. For both groups exposure to metropolitan life seems to have been much more important. The relationship between residence and literacy differs then according to social class, and again the impact of education and of the kirk's exhortations seems to have been tempered and deflected by existing socioeconomic divisions within Scottish society.

Refining the aggregate figures in Table 7.2 places us in a much stronger position to assess literacy levels in mid-eighteenth-century Scotland for comparison with contemporary England.[43] In the past historians have not resisted the temptation to produce national estimates of literacy on the basis

Table 7.10. Illiteracy of male craftsmen and tradesmen, and labourers and servants in different regions of Scotland

	Craftsmen and tradesmen		Labourers and servants	
	(i)	(ii)	(i)	(ii)
Edinburgh	195	11	93	38
Lothians	103	19	56	63
North	74	22	53	72
Fife, Starlings, Angus	109	23	47	60
Western lowlands	147	17	46	46
Borders and southwest	47	6	11	55
Totals	675		306	

Note: Sources are the same as in Table 7.2. Column headings are the same as in Table 7.1.

of very little evidence. Even with a range of firm figures the steps from depositions to national estimates are taken hesitantly. Because of the compositional effect we cannot accept the aggregate male and female figures reproduced in Table 7.2. Instead it is safer to consider the likely occupational composition of the population of Scotland in various areas and communities of residence, and to link this to their literacy attainments. Taking lairds and professionals as 3 per cent of the population in 1750, with 0 per cent illiteracy, crafts and trades as 20 per cent (15 per cent illiterate), farmers as 32 per cent (30 per cent illiterate), plus servants and labourers as 45 per cent (50 per cent illiterate)—figures which allow for the residential factors influencing occupationally specific literacy levels—we can produce a reasonable estimate of around 35 per cent. This is slightly better than the English national average at this time, but very much in line with the northern counties.[44] If we take into account the underrepresentation of truly highland deponents in the sample—nearly half Scotland's population lived here even in the mid-eighteenth century—it is likely that overall levels in Scotland and England were even closer. We must also raise the illiteracy of women from the level of approximately 75 per cent shown in Table 7.2 to allow for occupational and residential biases. An estimate of at least 85 per cent can be made, a figure which places Scottish women far behind the approximately 60 per cent illiteracy of their mid-eighteenth-century English counterparts.

IV

We are then faced with a number of important implications. Firstly, whatever the merits of the often acclaimed Scottish education system, it could not produce levels of literacy higher than in the north of England where a voluntary system prevailed. In Scotland as in England, voluntary schools were probably much more important in enhancing literacy. It is now safer to assert that Scotland was "one of the best educated countries in Europe,"[45] but we must also recognize that Holland, northern England, and Sweden were probably as good. If schools were important in promoting literacy it is significant that the two different systems of Scotland and England could produce such similar results. A higher proportion of Scots may have been able to read than was true of other countries, but judged by the respected criterion of ability to sign there is no reason to believe that Scotland enjoyed greatly superior progress in literacy. Keeping one eye on Sweden where near-universal reading ability was achieved almost entirely without the use of schools,[46] we may become still more sceptical about the importance of state legislation, which many early nineteenth-century educational reformers pointed to as vital for improving mass literacy in England.

There are additional implications for understanding the role of Protestantism as a force for change in society. Lockridge has argued that in New England, Scotland, and Sweden "a strong, widespread and homogeneous Protestantism carried the society into public action to ensure basic education, and thereby carried men into universal literacy."[47] Again we must doubt whether this view really does apply to Scotland, where the kirk was anxious that both sexes and all social classes should benefit. Egil Johansson has shown for Sweden that where "economic needs are what primarily directs the events" differences between sexes, between occupational groups, between town and country, and between regions remain substantial.[48] This is exactly the situation prevailing in seventeenth- and eighteenth-century Scotland. If pedagogic pressure was the main force such differences would be ironed out. This had happened in Sweden and New England by *circa* 1800,[49] but in Scotland as in England secular needs plus the religious "push" factor were constrained by the availability of education and socially specific differences in the cultural relevance of literacy. We can perhaps speculate that Calvinism was the force which drove countries otherwise lacking the benefits of economic development, for example, which might promote literacy. Scottish education did produce higher literacy levels for some occupational groups such as craftsmen and tradesmen than obtained in contemporary England, but for women and the lower social levels among males this is not the case.[50] Perhaps the most that can be said is that at its best Scottish education could produce superior results to English, but that overall there was little to chose between the systems. Various influences have differing impacts on literacy according to sex and social class, but with the exception of these variables there is no generally satisfactory explanation of differences. The similarity in illiteracy levels between Scotland outside the highlands and the northern counties of England does hint at the existence of a cultural zone with a community of attitudes which may have encouraged literacy. Local regional and social differences were determined by broadly cultural reasons rather than by national boundaries. Certainly the southwest of Scotland had a strong tradition of radical Protestantism, but this is not true of the north of England, while the tradition was less strong in the eastern borders. Finally, we can propose that the advance of Scotland to its clearly preeminent literacy in the mid-nineteenth century is likely to have been concentrated in the late eighteenth and early nineteenth centuries.

It is then simply untrue that Scottish education "effected a wide diffusion of education to every class in society."[51] If we accept the evidence of sign-literacy, we cannot maintain that there were equal opportunities in education. We must therefore qualify assertions about the role of education as a solvent promoting social mobility and as a contribution to the allegedly fluid and egalitarian society of "backward" Scotland compared to its more market-oriented, socially stratified neighbour.[52] This egalitarianism is seen as being founded on equality of opportunity in education, a notion which is based on a few prominent but atypical examples of "lads o' pairts" and which fails to recognize the barriers created by the underlying socioeconomic inequalities in Scottish society. In any case, the social mobility afforded by education to the lucky few was usually only to the level of schoolmaster or minister—positions of heavily circumscribed social, economic, and political power compared to that enjoyed by the land owners. Literacy may actually have strengthened rather than diminished socioeconomic inequality during the pre-industrial period.[53] Poorer children, where they were retained at school at all,[54] tended to be engaged in learning a range of practical skills such as stocking-making in a society "where more hands are still wanting"[55] and where the emphasis was on broadly "moral" education: inculcating habits of obedience, diligence, and industry.[56] Education's aim was less the broadening of the mind than the prevention of religious and moral ignorance. As a corollary of this it is worth questioning exactly what a school was[57]—an aspect of the history of education not properly considered in some of the more eulogistic writings on Scottish education. As far as women are concerned, their persistently high illiteracy may in some way have been related to the continuation of patriarchal dominance in Scottish society.

At the same time we may ponder the origins of this myth of Scottish society. While early nineteenth-century commentators such as Malthus and Brougham pointed to the superior education of the Scottish peasantry as a way of justifying increased public expenditure on education in England,[58] the notion of educational opportunity as a significant element in making Scotland an egalitarian society may have been propagated and refined in later periods. Is the myth, for example, a form of historical escapism from the shortcomings of society and education in twentieth-century Scotland? Is it simply a hangover from the sort of values which the Victorian bourgeoisie used to justify their social position and their dominance of educational provision?[59] A number of points are clear. Not only has the means by which literacy was attained by individuals been considered too superficially, but its usefulness to individual and society has perhaps been too readily assumed. There are also implications for the comparative study of economy and society in Scotland and England. Hitherto Scotland has been seen as a thoroughly distinctive nation, Scotland and England being treated by historians as virtually discrete entities and being considered largely in isolation as a means of discovering aspects peculiar to each. Scotland for its part is seen as something of a curiosity on the social and geographical periphery of Europe. The argument of this article has been that while Scotland may have been special in some respects, too often the nature and extent of these have been misconstrued. Systematic comparison of Scotland with other countries, plus analysis of shared characteristics, may ultimately prove more fruitful in counteracting the view of some historians who, like early travellers there, see Scotland as "a kind of *terra incognita* . . . a half-mythical country, where strange things might exist which it was irrational to look for in any place nearer home."[60]

Notes

I should like to acknowledge the comments and advice given by Rosalind Mitchison, Roger Schofield, Christopher Smout, Ian Whyte, Keith Wrightson, and Tony Wrigley.

1. L. Stone, "Literacy and Education in England, 1640–1900," *Past and Present*, no. 42 (Feb. 1969), 126–27; T. C. Smout, *A History of the Scottish People, 1560–1830* (Glasgow, 1972), 421–50, provides an excellent concise analysis of Scottish education in the eighteenth century.

2. For example, K. A. Lockridge, *Literacy in Colonial New England* (New York, 1974), 99–100.

3. H. M. Knox, *Two Hundred and Fifty Years of Scottish Education, 1696–1949* (Edinburgh, 1953), 10.

4. R. M. Mitchison, *Life in Scotland* (London, 1978), 46; A. A. Maclaren (ed.), *Social Class in Scotland Past and Present* (Edinburgh, 1976), introduction, 1–4, provides a concise and critical exposition of this view.

5. Studies of Scottish educational provision are legion. Among the better examples are J. M. Beale, "A History of the Burgh and Parochial Schools of Fife from the Reformation to 1872" (Ph.D. thesis, Univ. of Edinburgh, 1953); A. Bain, *Education in Stirlingshire from the Reformation to 1872* (London, 1965); W. Boyd, *Education in Ayrshire over Seven Centuries* (London, 1961); J. Scotland, *The History of Scottish*

Education, 2 vols. (London, 1969); J. C. Jessop, *Education in Angus* (London, 1931); J. Craigie, *A Bibliography of Scottish Education before 1872* (London, 1970). Apart from Stone's estimates of actual levels for local areas some figures can be found in Beale, "Schools of Fife," 99–100, 340; *The Justiciary Records of Argyll and the Isles, 1664–1742,* ed. J. Cameron and J. Imrie, 2 vols. (Stair Soc., xii, xxv, Edinburgh, 1949–69), 2:x.

6. W. Ferguson, *Scotland, 1689 to the Present* (Edinburgh, 1968), 198.

7. Stone, "Literacy and Education in England," 127.

8. Criticisms are summarized in P. Collinson, "The Significance of Signatures," *Times Lit. Supplement,* 9 Jan. 1981, 31. On the shortcomings of signing ability as a criterion of literacy, see G. G. Simpson, *Scottish Handwriting, 1150–1650* (Edinburgh, 1973), 10–12; R. K. Webb, "Literacy among the Working Classes in Nineteenth Century Scotland," *Scottish Hist Rev.* 33 (1954), 104–5; L. Auwers, "The Social Meaning of Female Literacy: Windsor, Connecticut, 1660–1775," *Newberry Papers* 77-4a (1977), 8; D. Cressy, *Literacy and the Social Order* (Cambridge, 1980), 42–61; R. S. Schofield, "The Measurement of Literacy in Pre-Industrial England," in J. Goody (ed.), *Literacy in Traditional Societies* (Cambridge, 1968), 318–19, 323–24. On the connection between reading and writing abilities, see F. Furet and J. Ozouf, *Lire et écrire* (Paris, 1977), 19–28; E. Johansson, *The History of Literacy in Sweden in Comparison with Some Other Countries* (*Umeå Educ. Repts.* 22, Umeå, 1977), 66. For the implications of literacy, see J. Goody and I. Watt, "The Consequences of Literacy," in Goody, *Literacy in Traditional Societies,* 27–68; H. Graff, *The Literacy Myth* (New York, 1979), passim; C. M. Cipolla, *Literacy and Development in the West* (Harmondsworth, 1969), esp. 11–36.

9. M. Spufford, "First Steps in Literacy: The Reading and Writing Experiences of the Humblest Seventeenth-Century Spiritual Autobiographers," *Social Hist.* 4 (1979), 407–35; Scotland, *Scottish Education,* 1:99, 109.

10. Beale, "History of the Burgh and Parochial Schools of Fife," 338–39.

11. G. Robertson, *General View of the Agriculture of the County of Midlothian* (Edinburgh, 1793), 27.

12. Johansson, *History of Literacy in Sweden,* 66.

13. Schofield, "Measurement of Literacy in Pre-Industrial England," 319.

14. See sources to Tables 7.1 and 7.2. Other sets of depositions exist but are less reliable. See R. A. Houston, "Aspects of Society in Scotland and North-East England, c1550–c1750: Social Structure, Literacy, and Geographical Mobility" (Ph.D. thesis, Univ. of Cambridge, 1981), 137–45, 171–218.

15. G. Donaldson, *Scotland: The Shaping of a Nation* (Newton Abbot, 1974), 190.

16. J. K. Hewison, *The Covenanters,* 2 vols. (Glasgow, 1908), 1:270–71, 388.

17. J. D. Mackie, *A History of Scotland,* 2nd ed. (Harmondsworth, 1978), 215; Hewison, *Covenanters,* 1:386–88; J. H. Pagan, *Annals of Ayr in the Olden Time, 1560–1692* (Ayr, 1897), 25.

18. Mitchison, *Life in Scotland,* 43, discusses the sorts of men subscribing the Covenants in more detail. This is also considered in Houston, "Aspects of Society in Scotland and North-East England," 389–401.

19. Court procedure is described from actual cases, and from J. I. Smith, "Criminal Procedure," in *An Introduction to Scottish Legal History* (Stair Soc., 20, Edinburgh, 1958), 426–48; *The Acts of the Parliament of Scotland,* 2 vols. (London, 1814–24), viii, 88; G. Mackenzie, *The Laws and Customes of Scotland in Matters Criminal* (Edinburgh, 1678), 442–45, 527–43. There was a stress on written procedures in Scottish courts, especially in capital trials.

20. Compare the distribution of Covenant parishes on the map (Figure 7.1) with that of market centres in I. Whyte, *Agriculture and Society in Seventeenth-Century Scotland* (Edinburgh, 1979), 182, 188.

21. I. Carter, "Marriage Patterns and Social Sectors in Scotland before the Eighteenth Century," *Scottish Studies* 17 (1973), 51–60; W. Camden, *Britannia,* 9th ed. (London, 1695), 885: "With respect to the manners and ways of living, it [Scotland] is divided into the High-land-men and the Low-land-men. These are more civilized and use the language and habit of the English; the other more rude and barbarous, and use that of the Irish. . . ." By the mid-nineteenth century the Registrar-Generals' reports show lowland Scotland far superior in sign-literacy compared to England. Literacy is also firmly related to region in nineteenth-century Scotland: Sutherland, Ross and Cromarty, and Inverness were highly illiterate, but the borders and southwest, Kinross, Kincardine, and the northeast lowlands were extremely literate. Like the industrial counties of Lancashire and Cheshire, Lanarkshire, Renfrewshire, and Ayrshire were the least literate lowland counties. *First Detailed Annual Report of the Registrar-General of Births, Deaths, and Marriages in Scotland* [for 1855] (Edinburgh, 1861), xxi–xxii; *Twenty-Second Annual Report of the Registrar-General of Births, Deaths, and Marriages in England* [for 1859] (London, 1861), vi.

22. Donaldson, *Scotland,* 241; B. P. Lenman, *An Economic History of Scotland, 1660–1976* (London, 1977), 34; I. H. Adams, *The Making of Urban Scotland* (Montreal, 1978), 57; ibid., 278–82, gives a list of burgh creations.

23. Adams, *Making of Urban Scotland,* 24–26. See deposition evidence below. Furet and Ozouf, *Lire et écrire,* 351, present a similar reason for higher urban literacy in France. Graff, *Literacy Myth,* 67–68, notes that literate persons were prominent in nineteenth-century Scottish emigration to Canada. R. S. Schofield, "Dimensions of Illiteracy, 1750–1850," *Explorations in Econ. Hist.* 10 (1973), 447–49, shows that in Bedfordshire in 1750–1850 increased literacy occurred most in parishes with a large proportion of non-agricultural occupations.

24. Scottish Record Office, Edinburgh (hereafter S.R.O.), E70/4/6, Tolbooth poll tax.

25. M. Flinn (ed.), *Scottish Population History* (Cambridge, 1977), 193.

26. Scotland, *Scottish Education,* 1:71–89; J. Grant, *A History of the Burgh and Parish Schools of Scotland,* 1, *Burgh Schools* (Glasgow, 1876); D. Withrington, "Education and Society in the Eighteenth Century," in N. T. Phillipson and R. Mitchison (eds.), *Scotland in the Age of Improvement* (Edinburgh, 1970), 169–99.

27. On the importance of migrants to the population of towns, see E. A. Wrigley, "A Simple Model of London's Importance in Changing English Society and Economy, 1650–1750," *Past and Present* 37 (July 1967), 44–70. On the growth of

population at Kinneil and Bo'Ness, see Adams, *Urban Scotland,* 51, 55; Lenman, *Economic History of Scotland,* 21.

28. J. A. DiFolco, "Aspects of Seventeenth-Century Social Life in Central and North Fife" (Ph.D. thesis, Univ. of St. Andrews, 1975), 126–27.

29. *Report on the State of Certain Parishes in Scotland made to his Majesty's Commissioners for Plantation of Kirks etc.* [1627] (Maitland Club, Edinburgh, 1835), 87.

30. Anon., *History of Galston Parish Church* (Paisley, 1909), 36–37; Scotland, *Scottish Education,* 1:63.

31. Scotland, *Scottish Education,* 1:60; J. H. Gillespie, *Dundonald: A Contribution to Parochial History* (Glasgow, 1939), 496–508; Mitchison, *Life in Scotland,* 44. The size of parish and location of the school relative to geographical barriers within the parish may have been important in determining the effective availability of education.

32. Whyte, *Agriculture and Society,* 9; Donaldson, *Scotland,* 241; Adams, *Urban Scotland,* 57, for estimates of the proportions of the population living in burghs.

33. See n. 19 above. Cressy, *Literacy and the Social Order,* 72, estimates approx. 70 per cent adult male illiteracy in the early 1640s.

34. J. G. Kyd, *Scottish Population Statistics* (Edinburgh, 1952). It is essential to recognize the fact that Scottish parishes were generally much bigger than their English counterparts, and that the proportions living in "town" parishes are not the same as those living in towns.

35. Cressy, *Literacy and the Social Order,* passim; Schofield, "Dimensions of Illiteracy," 450.

36. Flinn, *Scottish Population,* 102–6.

37. Beale, "History of the Burgh and Parochial Schools of Fife," passim.

38. Cressy, *Literacy and the Social Order,* 118–41. Occupational groupings: *Lairds*— those with "of" before their place of residence indicating ownership of land there, esquire, lord, "Mr.," portioner. *Professionals*—military officer, surgeon, apothecary, doctor of physic, writer, writer to the signet, clerk, postmaster, excise officer, court officer, court messenger, notary public, sheriff, minister, schoolmaster, factor, bailie, grieve, advocate. *Craftsmen and tradesmen*—watchmaker, cordwainer, wright, stabler, cutler, merchant, tailor, weaver, glover, maltman, salter, burgess, baxter, carrier, barber/wigmaker, goldsmith, coppersmith, plasterer, slater, smith, litster, dyster, walker, brewer, skipper, miller, mason, tanner, cabinet-maker, glazier, fleshers, saddler, quarrier, vintner, alehouse-keeper, change-keeper, cooper, chapman, candlemaker, stationer, printer, bookbinder, skinner, sugar boiler, locksmith, painter, ropemaker, whalebone cutter, staymaker, lorimer, shopkeeper, tobacco spinner, joiner, hatmaker, pewterer. *Farmers*—tenant, farmer, gardener. *Labourers and servants*—servant, herd, workman, labourer, coal-worker, cottar, seaman, boatman, hind. *Rest*—soldier, musician, piper.

39. For example, S.R.O., E70/8/8. E70/13/7, E70/13/5.

40. Cressy, *Literacy and the Social Order,* 119–21; Houston, "Aspects of Society in Scotland and North-East England," 239, 241.

41. Cressy, *Literacy and the Social Order,* 119–21, shows labourers 78–100 per cent illiterate (mainly in the period before 1660). Houston, "Aspects of Society

in Scotland and North-East England," 239, 241, using assize depositions, shows 78 per cent illiteracy among labourers in the north of England between 1640 and 1750.

42. Cressy, *Literacy and the Social Order,* 126–30.

43. Schofield, "Dimensions of Illiteracy," 445, estimates approx. 40 per cent illiteracy among adult males in *circa* 1760.

44. Unpublished figures provided by the Cambridge Group for the History of Population and Social Structure show mean illiteracy of 34 per cent in the four northernmost counties in the third quarter of the eighteenth century. For the nineteenth century, see Schofield, "Dimensions of Illiteracy," 444; T. W. Laqueur, "The Cultural Origins of Popular Literacy in England, 1500–1850," *Oxford Rev. Education* 2 (1976), 256–57.

45. Stone, "Literacy and Education in England," 135; Cressy, *Literacy and the Social Order,* 176–83, gives comparative figures for various countries in the early modern period.

46. Johansson, "History of Literacy in Sweden," passim.

47. Lockridge, *Literacy in New England,* 100. M. James, *Family, Lineage, and Civil Society* (Oxford, 1974), 104, argues that literacy spread downwards through the society of northern England because of the "Protestant concern that all should have access to the written Word of Scripture."

48. Johansson, "History of Literacy in Sweden," 76, 34.

49. Ibid., 76; Lockridge, *Literacy in New England,* 75–84.

50. Cressy, *Literacy and the Social Order,* 146, shows crafts and trades in Norfolk and Suffolk during the 1720s as 34 per cent illiterate (these are mainly rural) but London and Middlesex were only 8 per cent illiterate. Women (ibid., 144) in Norfolk and Suffolk were 74 per cent illiterate in the same decade, 44 per cent in London and Middlesex. Figures in the text above show Edinburgh and Glasgow women fluctuating around 70 per cent during the first half of the eighteenth century, with a level of 73 per cent illiterate in the 1720s. Numbers are too small to analyse craft and trade illiteracy in different communities of residence in Scotland over time. Reworked material from Houston, "Aspects of Society in Scotland and North-East England," 234–52, shows that city-dwelling women in northern England (Newcastle, Durham, York, Carlisle) were 59 per cent illiterate in 1725–50, while city craftsmen were 11 per cent illiterate (28 per cent in all types of community lumped together). Note that this is at an earlier period than the mid-eighteenth-century Scottish estimates. R. A. Houston, "The Development of Literacy: Northern England, 1640–1750," *Econ. Hist. Rev.,* 2nd ser., 35 (1982), 199–216.

51. Knox, *Two Hundred and Fifty Years of Scottish Education*, 10.

52. Maclaren, *Social Class in Scotland,* introduction, 1–2.

53. Graff, *Literacy Myth,* passim.

54. Beale, "History of the Burgh and Parochial Schools of Fife," 338–39; Bain, *Education in Stirlingshire,* 126; Scotland, *Scottish Education,* 1:90. In the early nineteenth century Alexander Somerville's sister "went no more to school than that quarter [year], having to go to the fields to help to work for the family bread": A. Somerville, *Autobiography of a Working Man,* 2nd ed. (London, 1951), 15.

55. A. Law, *Education in Edinburgh in the Eighteenth Century* (London, 1965), 42. Many kirk session registers mention poor children being "educated" in manufactures: S.R.O., CH2 471/10 (9/6/1707), and CH2 424/13, fos. 445, 464.

56. This was plainly the aim of paternalistic landowners such as Sir John Clerk of Penicuik, who was always keen to improve the tractability, "honesty," and productivity of his coal-workers. One project tried in the 1690s and 1700s was to encourage them to learn to read both by blandishment and financial incentives. S.R.O., GD18/695, fos. 67–68, and GD18/1007/1. Coal-workers can be seen as the first "industrial" workers. Graff, *Literacy Myth,* 228–33, argues that the real value of literacy to economic development was the training it provided for the work discipline of industrial life.

57. See J. S. Hurt, "Professor West on Early Nineteenth-Century Education," in M. Drake (ed.), *Applied Historical Studies* (London, 1973), 94.

58. I am grateful to Professor T. C. Smout for this point.

59. Again Maclaren, *Social Class in Scotland,* introduction, 1–9, provides clear insights.

60. P. H. Brown, *Early Travellers in Scotland* (Edinburgh, 1891), ix.

8 FIRST STEPS IN LITERACY: THE READING
AND WRITING EXPERIENCES OF THE HUMBLEST
SEVENTEENTH-CENTURY SPIRITUAL AUTOBIOGRAPHERS

Margaret Spufford

The spiritual autobiographies of the seventeenth century include the first subjective accounts, written by men from the countryside from yeoman parentage or below, of childhood, education, the importance of literacy, and the importance that their religious convictions had for them. They therefore contain first-hand accounts, or rather fragments of accounts, of the amount of education available and its effects, by the relatively humble. They thus provide insight into the effects of literacy which is not provided by any other source.

There are very, very few of these accounts, and those which do exist suffer from the disadvantage of the *genre*. The spiritual autobiographers were Puritans and dissenters,[1] and therefore were socially slanted in whatever way Puritans and dissenters were socially slanted. They must also be considered even more atypical than Puritans and dissenters in general, because the urge to write autobiography in itself defines an exceptional man.[2] Lastly, even within the whole group of autobiographers, those who bothered to set the stage for their spiritual experiences within any framework of place, parentage, and education were exceptional again. Most of them simply launched into the account of the work of God in their souls which was the purpose of their writing, without even the slightest account of their age, the region of England, or the social group from which they came. There is no means of knowing whether those who do give some detail of parentage or education were drawn to do so by temperament and were equally representative of the whole group of autobiographers whatever its social composition.

However, it is interesting, despite all these *caveats*, that those among the autobiographers who do bother to describe their social backgrounds were drawn mainly from just those groups in rural society which were most liter-

Reprinted from Margaret Spufford, "First Steps in Literacy: The Reading and Writing Experiences of the Humblest Seventeenth-Century Spiritual Autobiographers," *Social History* 4 (1979): 407–35, with the permission of Taylor and Francis, http://www.tandf.co.uk/journals. © Margaret Spufford, 1979.

ate, had more educational opportunity, and also provided most converts to
Quakerism than any other in some areas.[3] They were largely yeomen's sons,
together with some wholesalers. They did not come exclusively from this
sort of background, however. I have concentrated more here on the few who
were either born in less prosperous circumstances, or who lost their fathers
before their education was completed, and so abruptly descended the social
scale, and, as they describe their surroundings, give us some account of the
less literate world below the level of the yeoman. It is, therefore, the least
typical of the autobiographers who are discussed most fully here.

Despite the problem of typicality the autobiographers present, it seems
entirely fair to assume that this group gives the reader some insight into
the range of opportunities and experience in seventeenth-century England
which was open to other, non-Puritan boys from similar social backgrounds.
This account is therefore based on their experiences. Some of this group
of autobiographers were only able to attend school for a very short time,
and their accounts of the stage of proficiency in reading or writing they had
reached by six, seven or eight years old give a very useful guide to the time
it took to learn to read and write in the seventeenth century and the ages
at which it was customary to acquire the different skills. The incidental
description of these autobiographers of their different social worlds and
range of contacts also gives an impression of the diffusion of literate skills
at different levels of seventeenth-century society.

The ability to sign one's name[4] has been conclusively shown to be tied to
one's social status in Tudor and Stuart East Anglia,[5] for the simple reason
that some degree of prosperity was necessary to spare a child from the labour
force for education as soon as it was capable of work. So literacy was economically determined. Between 1580 and 1700, 11 per cent of women, 15 per
cent of labourers, and 21 per cent of husbandmen could sign their names,
against 56 per cent of tradesmen and craftsmen and 65 per cent of yeomen.
Grammar school and, even more, university education was heavily socially
restricted, and only sons of yeomen from amongst the peasantry had much
chance of appearing in grammar school or college registers.[6] This somewhat
gloomy picture fails to stress the small but significant groups of signatories in
even the most illiterate social groups who were able to write their names. It
dwells on grammar and university education to the exclusion of the patchy,
sporadic, but very real elementary education available in Tudor and Stuart England.[7] At the same time, Cressy admits, "we do not know whether
the acquisition of literacy was exclusively the product of formal elementary
schooling, or at what stage in a person's life he learned, or failed to learn, to
write the letters of his name." The experiences of the spiritual autobiographers throw a great deal of light on just these problems.

Because the acquisition of reading and writing skills was socially strati-fied, I have organized this account in ascending order, starting with the poorest. Viewed from this angle, those yeomen's sons whose fathers could support them through a university education appear highly privileged, and I have in fact ignored them in favour of those autobiographers whose experi-ences represent those of that part of society which is outside the cognizance of historians working from college admission registers. The evidence is of course impressionistic. It is the qualitative evidence which puts at least some flesh on the quantitative skeleton of literacy provided by the signatures. It illuminates a murky and ill-defined world in which grammar schooling was practically irrelevant and yet reading and writing skills were sought after.

Useful though it is, such a discussion of basic "literacy" which attempts particularly to gain an impression of the diffusion of the ability to read, and the period of schooling necessary to acquire the ability, necessarily comprehends very different degrees of the skill under one heading. Is one inquiring, Schofield asks, about the ability to read a simple handbill, a lo-cal newspaper, or the works of John Locke?[8] Here, inevitably, I find myself discussing under the heading "reading ability" a Wiltshire labourer who could read *Paradise Lost* with the aid of a dictionary, the Gloucestershire shepherds who could sound out words to teach an eager boy to read, and a blind thresher in Yorkshire who made a name for himself as a "famous schoolteacher" whose pupils probably learnt to "read" by rote learning only. It is obvious that completely different levels of fluency and skills are involved, but there is no way of distinguishing them. The problem can only be stated. I have deliberately let the autobiographers speak for themselves wherever possible. Since the point is to demonstrate that very limited educational opportunity did not debar at least a few people, who may of course have been highly exceptional, from the development of interests involving liter-ary skills, the way in which men who left school at six, seven, or nine later expressed themselves on paper is in itself meaningful.

Before working through the experiences of the autobiographers from the poorest upwards, it is useful to consider the specific information the autobiographies give us about the length of time it took some of them to acquire the skills of reading and of writing. This provides a background which makes it easier to assess the probable effects of the limited educational experiences of the poorer children. The seventeenth-century educationalists suggested that in the country schools, children normally began at seven or eight. Six was early. This fits well, on the whole, with the experience of the autobiographers, who learnt to read with a variety of people, mostly women, before starting writing with the "formal" part of their education at seven, if they got that far.[9]

A bright child was able to learn to read in a few months in the seventeenth century, although so much must have depended on intelligence, the sort of teacher available, and the size of group he was in, that it is difficult to generalize. Oliver Sansom, born in 1636 in Beedon in Berkshire, wrote: "When I was about six years of age, I was put to school to a woman, to learn to read, who finding me not unapt to learn, forwarded me so well, that in about four months' time, I could read a chapter in the Bible pretty readily." Latin and writing began at seven. John Evelyn, the diarist, began his schooling earlier, at four, when he joined the village group to begin the "rudiments" in the local church porch. But he was not "put to learn my Latin rudiments, and to write" until he was eight. James Fretwell, eldest son of a Yorkshire timber-merchant, born in 1699, began lessons earlier still.

> As soon as I was capable of learning [my mother] sent me to an old school-dame, who lived at the very next door . . . But I suppose I did but continue here but a few days, for growing weary of my book, and my dame not correcting me as my mother desired, she took me under her pedagogy untill I could read in my Bible, and thus she did afterwards by all my brothers and sisters . . . And as my capacity was able, she caused me to observe what I read, so I soon began to take some notice of several historical passages in the Old Testament.

He was admitted to the small grammar school of Kirk Sandall,

> my dear mother being desirous that I should have a little more learning than she was capable of giving me . . . where [the master] placed me amongst some little ones, such as myself . . . when he called me up to hear what I could say for myself, he finding me better than he expected, removed me higher, asking my mother if she had brought me an Accidence, which I think she had; so she had the pleasure of seeing me removed out of the horn-book class, which my master at first sight thought most suitable for me.

The master's assumption was not surprising. James was then aged four years and seven months. He was obviously precocious. Other precocious children's achievements were also recorded because they were unusual. Oliver Heyward married the daughter of a Puritan minister who had learnt both to read and to write fluently before the normal age in the 1640s. "She could read the hardest chapter in the Bible when she was but four years of age" and was taught to write by the local schoolmaster "in learning whereof she was more than ordinarily capable, being able at six yeares of age to write down passages of the sermon in the chappel." Anne Gwin of Falmouth, daughter of a fisherman and fishmerchant, born in 1692, likewise "took to learning very Young, and soon became a good Reader, viz. when she was but about Three yeares and a Half old, she wrote tolerably well before five." The biographers of these girls recognized their unusual forwardness; it seems safer to use Oliver Sansom as a specific example of the time it took normal children to learn to read.

The autobiographers give the impression that, unless their schooling had already been broken off, they were reading fluently by seven at the latest, even if, like young Thomas Boston, who "had delight in reading" the Bible by that age and took it to bed at night with him, "nothing inclined me to it but . . . curiosity, as about the history of Balaam's ass."

Writing began with Latin, if a grammar school education was in prospect, whether the boy began this stage of his education at seven like Oliver Sansom, at eight like John Evelyn, or at four like the forward little James Fretwell. It is even more difficult to find evidence on the time it took to master the second skill than the first. Yet one piece of very precise evidence does survive.

Alderman Samuel Newton of Cambridge kept a diary from 1664 to 1717. It contains very little personal information, amongst the accounts of corporation junketings and funerals of prominent persons. But on 12 February 1667, Alderman Newton wrote: "On Tuesday was the first time John Newton my sonne went to the Grammar Free Schoole in Cambridge." In October the same year, between a note on the assembly of parliament and a family baptism, appears an entry in a child's hand:

> I John Newton being in Coates this nineteenth day of October Anno Domini 1667 and not then full eight yeares old, wrote this by me
> John Newton.

There is no paternal comment on this entry, but Alderman Newton must have shared his son's satisfaction in the new achievement to allow the entry to be made. Obviously, to the seven-year-old John, the new skill of writing, which had taken six months to acquire, was a matter of as much pride as his emergence into manhood in his newly acquired breeches.

It seems likely, as a rule-of-thumb guide, that children who had the opportunity to go to school until they were seven were likely to be able to read. Those who remained at school until eight were likely to be able to write.

If it took the autobiographers, who may have been exceptionally gifted, four to six months to learn to read, and they began to acquire the skill at various ages from four to six, it seems reasonable to double this learning period to allow a margin of safety for less intelligent or forward children.[10] A working hypothesis would then be that children who had the opportunity of going to school would have learnt to read by seven. Similarly, since the autobiographers normally began the writing part of their curriculum at seven, and it took John Newton six months to write a good hand, it seems reasonable to double this period also and suggest that the ability to write was normally acquired by eight.

If these hypotheses are accepted, it follows from the evidence collected by Cressy on occupational differences in ability to sign, showing that only 15 per cent of labourers and 21 per cent of husbandmen as against 65 per cent of yeomen could sign, that these percentages roughly represent the proportion of those social groups which had the opportunity for schooling between seven and eight. Nothing could show more clearly that the economic status of the parents was the determinant of schooling,[11] along, of course, with the existence of some local teaching. The children of labourers and, to a lesser extent, of husbandmen, were needed to join the labour force as soon as they were strong enough to contribute meaningfully to the family economy.

It is difficult to conceive that they could have made a real contribution before six. The case of Thomas Tryon, whose father urgently needed his son's earnings, but still sent him to school from five until he was nearly six, bears this out. So does the literary evidence of Thomas Deloney, who was himself a weaver, who wrote in one of his extravagant novels glorifying the clothing trade in 1599 of a golden age in the past when "poor people whom God lightly blessed with most children did by meanes of this occupation so order them that by the time they were come to be six or seven years of age, they were able to get their own bread." John Locke, who was by no means unacquainted with the realities of childhood, recommended as a commissioner of trade concerned with encouraging linen-manufacture in Ireland in 1696 that families without estate of 40/-[six pence] a year should be compelled to send their children of both sexes aged between six and fourteen to spinning schools. There they should work a ten-hour day. Parents should be free to send four- to six-year olds also, if they so chose. The element of choice disappeared at six; obviously, to Locke, this was the viable age to start work.[12]

Further evidence for a starting age of six or seven comes from workhouse regulations of the sixteenth and seventeenth centuries governing the ages at which children could be set to work. These seem particularly likely to be reliable, since a municipal workhouse was very unlikely not to try to profit from children's labour if it were possible to do so. Westminster workhouse, in 1560, sent its children over six, but not yet twelve, "to wind Quills for weavers."[13]

The Aldersgate workhouse, in 1677, admitted children of from three to ten, and its founder wrote "as to young children, there is nothing they can more easily learn than to spin linen, their fingers, though never so little, being big enough to pull the flax and make a fine thread." At the time, in 1678 and 1681 when he wrote, he had "some children not above seven or eight years old, who are able to earn two pence a day."[14] In 1699, the Bishopgate workhouse was established for all poor parish children over the age of seven. They were to be employed from seven in the morning until six at night, with an hour off for dinner and play, and two hours' instruction in reading and writing.[15] This workhouse, which was, incidentally, a humane one by contemporary standards, was obviously run on the assumption that its children could all work these hours. It is highly significant, therefore, that it did not admit children under seven. It looks very much as if seven was thought to be the age at which a child could cope with a full working day and start to earn a wage which began to be significant.[16] It was also the age at which Tudor parents had a statutory duty to see that their sons practised regularly at the butts, that is, were strong enough to begin to be thought significant in the adult world of the militia. Obviously, rural children could only be regularly employed in areas where textile industries provided the kind of outwork performed by these city orphans. In many areas, their opportunities for work were likely to be more seasonal and more along the lines described by Henry Best. His "spreaders of muck and molehills" were for the most part women, boys, and girls, and they were paid 3*d.* [pence] a day for the "bigger and abler sort" and 2*d.* a day for the "lesser sort." Obviously a child was started at work before seven if there was a great need, as the cases of Thomas Tryon and the Westminster workhouse children show.

If seven were indeed the age at which a child could earn significant wages and was regarded as an embryonic member of the militia as well as the workforce, it also seems to have been the age at which reading had probably been mastered but writing not yet embarked on. If this conclusion is true, it is an important one. It indicates that reading skills, which unfortunately by their nature are not capable of measurement, were likely to have been very much more socially widespread in sixteenth- and seventeenth-century England than writing skills, simply because the age at which children learnt to read was one at which children of the relatively poor were not yet capable of much paying labour and were therefore available for some schooling. The restriction of writing ability to a small percentage of labourers' and husbandmen's sons, and its much wider spread amongst the sons of the yeomanry, is at once explained. Reading skills are likely to have been very much more diffused. It was, of course, the ability to read (and not the ability to write) that laid the way open to cultural change.

The argument can, of course, be started the other way round. We know that 15 per cent of labourers' sons could sign their names and presumably could read; we know that a much higher proportion of yeomen's sons could do so. We therefore know that economic necessity is likely to have been the factor that limited the opportunity to learn. It seems that a boy was physically strong and co-ordinated enough to contribute to the family budget in a significant way at some age between six and eight. The crucial question is whether this point was nearer six or nearer seven. On the answer to this, as well as the local availability of schooling, depended the number of boys, from different occupational backgrounds, who could read.

No identifiable autobiographer was fathered by an agricultural labourer, although at least one autobiographer became an agricultural labourer. Thomas Tryon, of the autobiographers who identified their backgrounds, came from the poorest home, and he certainly had the most prolonged struggle to get himself an education. He was born in 1634 at Bibury in Oxfordshire and was the son of a village tiler and plasterer, "an honest sober Man of good Reputation; but having many Children, was forced to bring them all to work betimes." Tilers and plasterers were building craftsmen, and as such were more prosperous than agricultural labourers, but the purchasing power of their wages was very low in the early seventeenth century.[17]

The size of the family did much to dictate educational opportunity, for obvious reasons. Again and again, only children or those from small families amongst the autobiographers appear at an advantage. Despite his numerous siblings, young Thomas was briefly sent to school. "About Five Year old, I was put to School, but being addicted to play, after the Example of my young School-fellows, I scarcely learnt to distinguish my Letters, before I was taken away to Work for my Living." This seems to have been before he was six, although his account is ambiguous. At six young Thomas Tryon was either not strongly motivated, as he obviously thought himself from his mention of the importance of play, or he was not well taught. Yet it is worth remembering that he was removed from school to work at about the age Oliver Sansom began to learn. His failure to learn to read was going to take great determination to repair.

His contribution to the family economy began immediately and he obviously took tremendous pride in his ability to contribute: "The first Work my Father put me to, was Spinning and Carding, wherein I was so Industrious and grew so expert that at Eight Years of Age I could Spin Four Pound a day which came to Two Shillings a Week." He continued to spin until he was twelve or thirteen, but by the time he was ten "began to be weary of the Wheel" and started to help the local shepherds with their flocks on Sundays, to earn a penny or twopence on his own account. When his father wished to apprentice him to his own trade he obeyed very reluctantly, for by this time he was determined to become a shepherd. "My Father was unwilling to gratifie me herein . . . but by continually importuning him, at last I prevailed, and he bought a small number of Sheep; to the keeping and management whereof, I betook myself with much satisfaction and delight, as well as care." But now, at last, at the age when his most fortunate contemporaries were about to go to University,[18] the desire for literacy gripped Thomas. It is worth quoting his account of the way he managed to satisfy it in full.

> All this while, tho' now about Thirteen Years Old, I could not Read;
> then thinking of the vast usefulness of Reading, I bought me a Primer,
> and got now one, then another, to teach me to Spell, and so learn'd
> to Read imperfectly, my Teachers themselves not being ready Read-
> ers: But in a little time having learn't to Read competently well, I was
> desirous to learn to Write, but was at a great loss for a Master, none
> of my Fellow-Shepherds being able to teach me. At last, I bethought
> myself of a lame young Man who taught some poor People's Children
> to Read and Write; and having by this time got two Sheep of my own,
> I applied myself to him, and agreed with him to give him one of my
> Sheep to teach me to make the Letters, and Joyn them together.

The difficulty Thomas found in learning to write, as opposed to learning to read, seems very important. Although his fellow shepherds, as a group, were not "ready" readers, they did, again as a group, possess the capacity to help him to learn to spell out words. He was not dependent on only one of them to help him. But although these Gloucestershire shepherds could read, they could not write at all. A semi-qualified teacher was called for, and it took some effort to find him.

Thomas Tryon eventually went to London as an apprentice. His addiction to print continued. He made time to read by sitting up at night for two or three hours after his day's work was finished. His wages went on education. "Therewith I furnished myself with Books, paid my Tutors and served all my occasions." He was particularly interested in the art of medicine, which he defined as the "whole study of Nature," and within that, astrology, which he defined as the "Method of God's government in Nature . . . [which] ought no more to be condemned because of the common abuse of it, than Reli-gion ought, because its so commonly perverted to Superstition, or made a Cloak to Hypocrisie and Knavery." Even after his marriage at thirty-five, he remained an incurable self-improver and then took music lessons.

> About Five and Thirty Years, I attempted to learn Musick and hav-
> ing a natural propensity thereto, made a pretty good progress on the
> Base-viol, tho' during the time of my learning, I . . . stuck as close to
> my working Trade, as ever before; so that I could only apply an Hour
> or Two to Musick, taking my opportunities at Night, or in a morning
> as best I could; and the time others spent in a Coffee-house or Tavern,

I spent in Reading, Writing, Musick or some useful Imployment; by
which means I supplyed what I could the defect of Education.

His written works which reflected his own range of interests included *The
Country Man's Companion, The Good Housewife Made a Doctor, Dreams
and Visions, Book of Trade, Friendly Advice to the People of the West Indies,
A New Method of Education* and, most surprisingly of all, *Averroes Letter to
Pythagoras.* It is a remarkable publication list for a boy who left school at
six before he could read.

When Thomas Tryon came to write down his "Principles" for the religious group he founded, his own experiences, including his battle for literacy, were directly reflected in them. In his "Laws and Orders proper for
Women to observe," he wrote, amongst various rules for the upbringing of
children which were, on the whole, remarkably sane and tolerant:

At a Year and a Half or Two Years old, shew them their Letters, not
troubling them in the vulgar way with asking them what is this Letter,
or that Word; but instead thereof, make frequent Repetitions in their
hearing, putting the Letters in their Sight. And thus in a little time,
they will easily and familiarly learn to distinguish the Twenty Four
Letters, all one as they do the Utensils, Goods, and Furniture of the
House, by hearing the Family name them. *At the same time,* teach your
Children to hold the Pen, and guide their Hand; and by this method,
your Children, un-accountably to themselves, will attain to Read and
Write at Three, Four, or Five years old . . . When your Children are
of dull Capacities and hard to Learn, Reproach them not nor expose
them, but taking them alone . . . shew them the Advantages of Learning, and how much it will tend to their advancement.

His advocacy of flash-cards has a strangely modern ring about it, as does
his suggestion of teaching writing at the same time as reading. His assumption that the teaching of reading is the natural function of the mother, is an
interesting one, particularly since several of the autobiographers were in fact
taught to read by their mothers. The few literate women in seventeenth-century society may well have had a disproportionately large influence.

A boy from a husbandman's background, rather than a skilled labourer's,
was more likely to be lucky enough to be spared from work for long enough
to gain a rudimentary education, although his education was likely to be
constantly interrupted by more pressing agricultural business. Thomas Carleton described the situation of such a boy very well.

I sprang of mean (though honest) Parents according to the flesh, my
Father being a Husbandman, in the County of Cumberland, I (accord-

ing to his pleasure) was educated sometimes at School, sometimes with Herding, and tending of Sheep, or Cattel, sometime with the Plow, Cart, or threshing-Instrument, or other lawfull labour.

This background of sporadic schooling enabled him, when the spiritual need took him, to "give myself to reading and Searching of the Scriptures." Intermittent educational experience like this was probably typical of the fifth of the husbandmen[19] who were lucky enough to get as far as learning to write their names.

John Bunyan, the best known of all the seventeenth-century dissenters, came of poor parentage, although his parents were more prosperous or their family less numerous than Thomas Tryon's. He never had to struggle for a basic education as Tryon did. His father held a cottage and nine acres in Bedfordshire. This was barely adequate for subsistence. He eked out a living by tinkering rather than by wage-labour and so is classifiable either as a husbandman on his acreage, or as a poor craftsman on his trade. Despite their relative poverty, Bunyan wrote "notwithstanding the meanness of . . . my Parents, it pleased God to put it into their Hearts to put me to School, to learn both to read and write." He was fully conscious of having had educational advantages which exceeded his parents' social position.

Amongst the autobiographers who described their parentage only Baxter and Bunyan also confessed to the reading of cheap print as a childhood sin. The yeoman's son, Richard Baxter, listed amongst his early sins committed about the age of ten, "I was extremely bewitched with a love of romances, fables and old tales, which corrupted my affections and lost my time." He also gives a very rare glimpse of a chapman at work in the 1630s: "About that time it pleased God that a poor pedlar came to the door that had ballads and some good books: and my father bought of him Dr. Sibb's *Bruised Reed*."

Bunyan is also likely to have got his reading matter from the chapmen, either at the door or at market. Elstow, where he was brought up, is two miles from the county-town of Bedford, which was not a large enough provincial town to have a bookshop in the seventeenth century. Moreover, the reading matter he describes is chapman's ware. He was much more specific than Baxter about his tastes in his youth. He wrote, "give me a Ballard, a News-book, *George* on Horseback or *Bevis of Southampton,* give me some book that teaches curious Arts, that tells of old Fables; but for the Holy Scriptures, I cared not. And as it was with me then, so it is with my brethren now." The implication is plain that either Bunyan's relations or his peer group were, at the time Bunyan was writing in the 1660s, commonly readers of the ballads and chapbooks which Bunyan himself avoided after his conversion.

Bunyan's reading seems to have left some mark on him.[20] *Bevis of Southampton* was a typical, breathless, sub-chivalric romance in which adventure follows adventure in quick succession. The hero's mother betrays his father to death and marries his murderer. Her son first escapes and keeps his uncle's sheep on a hill near his father's castle, then is sold into slavery to the "paynims." There he refuses to serve "Apoline" their god, kills a gigantic wild boar, is made a general over twenty thousand men, and wins the love of the princess. Alas, he is betrayed and thrown into a dungeon with two dragons who quickly get the worst of it. He is still able to kill his jailer, after seven years on bread and water, and runs off with the princess and a great store of money and jewels. He is next attacked by two lions in a cave, meets "an ugly Gyant thirty foot in length and a foot between his eyebrows," defeats him and makes him his page, and kills a dragon forty foot long. He then has the heathen princess baptised, and after numerous further adventures invades England, avenges his father's death, marries his paynim lady, and is made Lord Marshall. There is no attempt at characterization, and the whole piece of blood-and-thunder writing seems aimed at pre-adolescent or adolescent males; very successfully, if Bunyan's testimony is to be believed. Although his own writing was very far removed from this, some of his imagery does seem to have come from his early reading. The lions Christian met by the way, the description of the monster Apollyon and the cave where the giants Pope and Pagan dwelt, all owe something to it, as perhaps, does Giant Despair himself. It is worth remembering also that Bunyan's own voluminous output was surely aimed at the rural readership he knew in the villages around Bedford amongst which he had his ministry. He knew his readership was familiar with the giants, lions, dragons, and battles of the chapbooks, just as it was with the cadences of the Authorized Version.

Arise Evans, who came from the Welsh border, was born in 1606 or 1607. His father was a good deal better off than either Bunyan's or Tryon's and sounds indeed like a prosperous yeoman, or even a minor gentleman, from his son's description:

> My father being a sufficient man of the Parish did entertain the Curate always at his Table, and gave him a little Tenement of Land to live upon; and by reason of this kindness to the Minister, which had but small allowance from the Parson of the Parish, that had all the Tithes. The Minister was diligent to do my father's family what good he was able: and as soon as I began to speak plain, I was put to school to him.

But when Arise was only six, his father died.

A surprisingly large number of autobiographers who give any factual details of themselves at all dwell on the deaths of one, or both, of their parents. It seems that as many as one eighth of children may have lost their fathers by the time they were seven, the age at which I suggest they might have learnt to read, but not to write.[21] The death of the father leaving a young family always meant that the family economy collapsed. A son still at school usually left, either to earn his living, or to help his mother. Frequently he seems to have slithered down the social scale permanently; it is for this reason that some account of the life of a farm labourer survives. It was written by a boy who was at grammar school until his father's death, but who became an in-servant in husbandry after his mother's remarriage. The death of the mother involved less economic hardship, but often considerable psychological distress for the child. Historical demographers have so far emphasized infant mortality rates a good deal more than parental mortality rates. It seems that the social and personal consequences of as many as one child in eight losing its father when it was seven or less, were considerable and deserve more attention.

The death of Arise Evans's father involved both economic and psychological hardship for him; indeed, it seems from his autobiography that the trauma involved could well have been one of the causes of his later emotional unbalance and rather dubious visions. He had thought that he was his father's favourite child. Certainly his father had shown great pride in his ability to read aloud and had shown him off to visitors.

> It was not long before I attained to reade English perfectly, to the admiration of all that heard me: and because I was so young and so active in learning, all concluded that God had designed me for some great work . . . But . . . death takes away my father before I was seven years old, and now he forgets me at his death, that was his delight a little before; and making his last Will, he leaves a Portion to all his children by name, and to many of his kindred . . . But I was not so much as mentioned in his Will, nor any thing left for me, so that I came soon to know the folly of vain confidence in man . . . After this I was taken from school, when I had learned the *Accidence* out of Book, but never came to *Grammar*, or to write.

Arise never tells us how or when he did learn to write. Certainly, he had no opportunity at the normal age. At eight when he should have learnt to write, he was apprenticed to a tailor, far younger than usual. He retained from his brief period of education until some time in his seventh year a passion for the written word which he was hardly ever able to satisfy. One of the stories he tells dramatically illuminates this thirst for information and for books which he would satisfy at the cost of enormous personal discomfort, if only it were possible. At twenty-two he set off, like so many others, to work his way to London.

> And at Coventre I wrought and stayed a quarter of a year, by reason
> of an old Chronicle that was in my Master's house that showed all
> the passage in Brittain and Ireland from Noahs Floud to William the
> Conquerour, it was of great volume, and by day I bestowed what time
> I could spare to read, and bought Candles for the night, *so that I got
> by heart the most material part* of it.

This desire for information, together with the problems of even finding
time to absorb it during the working day, or a source of light to read it by at
night, seems to have been common to all largely self-educated working men
at all periods. The physical difficulties the autobiographers encountered
in the seventeenth century were fundamentally the same as those of their
nineteenth-century heirs.[22]

Thomas Chubb, like Arise Evans and Thomas Tryon, was a boy from
a rural background who moved to town, although in his case the town was
Salisbury, not London. Also, like Arise Evans, the death of his father affected his prospects, though not so seriously. He was the son of a maltster
of East Harnham, born in 1679. His father died when he was nine, leaving a
widow and five children, of which he was the youngest. He wrote of himself
in the introduction to a lengthy work on the Scriptures.

> The Author was taught to read English, to write an ordinary hand, and
> was further instructed in the common rules of arithmetick; this educa-
> tion being suitable to the circumstances of his family and to the time
> he had to be instructed in. For as the Author's mother laboured hard,
> in order to get a maintenance for herself and family, so she obliged her
> children to perform their parts towards it. Accordingly, the Author
> was very early required to perform such work and service as was suit-
> able for his age and capacity; so that he had neither time nor means
> for further instruction than the above mentioned.

When he was fifteen, in 1694, he was apprenticed to a glover in Salisbury.
It is not certain from his account that he left school at nine, on his father's
death, but it seems probable, since he would then have had two years in
which to learn writing and elementary arithmetic. He had obviously attended one of the schoolmasters who was so frequently licensed in visitation
records to teach "to read, write and caste an accompte."[23] He was never intended, or never had the chance, to embark on a grammar school curriculum.
After he had served his apprenticeship, he became a journeyman but was
handicapped as a glover by his weak sight. So, after 1705 he lived with, and
worked for, a tallow-chandler. He served in the chandler's shop, and made
gloves part-time only. He never married, and it sounds as if his experience
of poverty after his father's death had influenced him heavily in this:

The Author . . . [judged] it greatly improper to introduce a family into the world, without a prospect of maintaining them, which was his case; such adventures being usually attended with great poverty . . . And tho,' according to the proverb, God does not send mouths without sending meat to fill them; yet our Author saw, by daily experience, that meat to some was not to be obtained but with great difficulty. And as to trusting to providence, in such cases, the Author . . . did [not] find, that providence interposed to extricate it's . . . dependents out of their difficulties.

Thomas Chubb gives an account of the way his first tract came to be published. The fascination of this lies not in the account of the tract itself, but the way it reveals his own habits of written composition since his boyhood and the literary activities of a whole group of young men like himself in Salisbury.

When the reverend Mr. Whiston published his historical preface to those books he entitled *Primitive-christianity revived* . . . about 1711, that preface happened to fall into the hands of the Author and some of his acquaintance, who were *persons of reading* in Salisbury; and as some of his friends took part with Mr. Whiston in the main point controverted, viz. the single supremacy of the one God and the father of all; so some were against him, *which introduced a paper-controversy betwixt them.* And as the Author's friends were shy of expressing themselves plainly and fully upon the question, but chose rather to oppose each other by interrogations; so this appeared to the Author a way altogether unlikely to clear up the case, and bring the point debated to an issue . . . he was naturally led to draw up his thoughts upon the subject in the way that he did, as it appeared to him a more probable means of bringing the controversy to a conclusion. And this the Author did without . . . even a thought of it's being offered to publick consideration, but only for his own satisfaction, and for the information and satisfaction of his friends in Salisbury, to whom then his acquaintance was confined; *he having accustomed himself from his youth to put his thoughts into writing,* upon such subjects to which his attention had been called in; . . . thereby to arouse and satisfy himself, and then commit them to the flames, *which had been the case in many instances.* The Author . . . arranged his sentiments on the aforementioned subject . . . it was exposed to the view and perusal of his acquaintance . . . some of whom approved the performance, . . . but others thought the contrary, and this induced a controversy in writing betwixt the Author and some of those who thought differently . . . and several letters and papers passed betwixt them.

Eventually one of Chubb's friends took the manuscript he had composed on this latest occasion to Whiston himself to ask for his opinion. Whiston had the manuscript published, and so the work of the Salisbury journeyman first reached the printed page.

He had a cool, rational, exploratory cast of mind. He was a theist who denied the divinity of Christ and looked with a critical eye on the Scriptures.

> This collection of writings has been the parent of doctrines most dishonourable to God, and most injurous to men; such as the doctrine of absolute unconditional election and reprobation, of religious persecution and the like . . . Besides, this book, called the holy Bible, contains many things that are greatly below, and unworthy of, the Supreme Deity . . . That [God] should . . . approve of, or countenance, such malevolent desires as these, "Let his children be fatherless and his wife a widow; let his children be continually vagabonds, and beg . . . let his posterity be cut off, and in the generation following let their name be blotted out." I say that such trifling observations, and such malevolent desires as these, should be considered as the offspring of God, is playing at hazard indeed.

His collected works, which included a treatise on "Divine Revelation in General, and of the Divine Original of the Jewish, Mohometon and Christian Revelation in Particular" ended with a typical statement: "in what I have offered to the world, I have appealed to the understandings, and not to the passions of men." His achievement is not as startling as Thomas Tryon's, but the vivid image of this urban artisan, too poor to marry and support a family, a part-time journeyman-glover with bad sight, a part-time assistant to a chandler, weighing out candles in the shop and at the same time ordering his thoughts to commit them to paper for his own pleasure, or that of his friends, in their next "paper-controversy," is a fascinating one. This lively, literate atmosphere of serious debate on theological subjects amongst the journeymen who were "persons of reading" in early eighteenth-century Salisbury was, of course, urban, but Thomas Chubb participated in it, and apparently led it, from an education in a rural hamlet which taught him to read, write, and count, probably all before his tenth year, in the 1680s.

Shortly before Chubb began to write for publication in the second decade of the eighteenth century, Stephen Duck, the first of the eighteenth-century poets of the countryside to come from a humble rural background himself, was born at Chorlton St. Peter, at the northern edge of the Salisbury Plain. His education was exactly similar to that of Thomas Chubb; he learnt to read and to write English and the "arithmetic [which] is generally join'd with this Degree of Learning." His first biographer, Joseph Spence, wrote that he was not taken from school until he was fourteen, which sounds improbably late. His father was able to set him up on a small-holding after he left school, but after its failure he made his living as a day-labourer. His great opportunity for self-improvement came when he made friends with a man who had acquired two or three dozen books while in service in London. Amongst these were seven of Shakespeare's plays, Dryden, Virgil, Seneca, Ovid, the *Spectator*, and Milton's *Paradise Lost*, which Duck read twice with the aid of a dictionary before he could understand it. He relied extensively on his memory, just as Arise Evans had done. When he first read Pope's *Essay on Criticism*, he memorized almost the whole of it overnight. The verses in the *Spectator* first triggered him into composing his own poetry. His own personal experience of day-labour and his absorption with these literary models and their vocabulary lay behind his most original poem, *The Thresher's Labour*.

Even though we are now considering a period in the 1720s, Stephen Duck's ability to read Milton, Dryden, and Shakespeare and his ability to compose his own verses are invaluable evidence of the degree of literacy a basic seventeenth-century education could bestow. Of course, this day-labourer, like his older contemporary in Salisbury, the chandler's assistant, was a highly exceptional man. Nevertheless, he demonstrates the literate skills a boy from a poor rural background could develop, given an education until eight or nine in the seventeenth-century basic subjects, reading, writing and simple arithmetic.

Josiah Langdale was the first of the autobiographers considered here whose background was prosperous enough for long enough to bring him within reach of a grammar school education. He was born in 1673 in the village of Nafferton in the East Riding and went to school "after I grew up," as he wrote. His labour was not required until the death of his father, before he was nine. Then his mother found his labour essential to the family economy. Like Tryon, he took great pride and pleasure in his skills, which in his case were specifically rural, not industrial.

> I then was taken from School, and being a strong Boy, of my Years, was put to lead Harrows and learn to Plow, Also, in the Summer Time, I kept Cattel (we having in our Country both Horses and Oxen in Tethers) and moved them when there was Occasion with much Care, for I loved to see them in good Liking. In those Days, both when I followed the Plow and kept Cattel in the Field, I was religiously inclined . . . I had not time for much Schooling, being closely kept to what I could do in our way of Husbandry, yet I made a little Progress in Latin, but soon forgot it; I endeavoured however, to keep my English, and could read the Bible, and delighted therein . . .

I now being about Thirteen Years of Age, and growing strong, did my Mother good service; having attain'd to the knowledge of ordering my Plow, and being expert in this Employment could go with Four horses, and plow alone, which we always did except in Seed time; I very much delighted in holding the Plow, It being an Employment suitable to my Mind, and no Company to disturb my Contemplation, therefore I loved it the more, and found by experience that to have my mind inward and to contemplate the Ways and Works of God was a great Benefit and Comfort to me.

Josiah's inclinations were not all devotional, however, and he was much drawn towards dancing, which was an important adolescent pastime in Nafferton. He gives the only account I have seen of the way this important leisure activity was learnt in the countryside. At this point his account becomes confused, for he seems to have learnt dancing after school at night, before he was fourteen, even though he had left regular school, and lost his Latin before he was nine. It sounds as if he attended sporadically when agricultural routine allowed it, after his ninth year. Just possibly the schooling that included Latin, before this, had been outside Nafferton, unless country masters able to teach grammar also frequently taught dancing at night.

Dancing took much with the young People of our Town . . . Much Evil was committed at this School . . . The Dancing Master was a Fidler and Jugler, and after we broke up School every Night he went to play his Tricks. I did not learn many Dances before it became an exceeding Trouble to my Soul and Spirit . . . After some time my Playfellows would entice me to Feasts, where young men and women meet to be merry . . . and such Like was I invited to, under a Pretence to improve our Dancing.

Josiah's fortunes changed again when his mother remarried after seven years of widowhood and no longer needed him. At that point the fifteen-year-old became an in-servant in husbandry. His spiritual search continued and was fed by an influential close friend in his second year as a servant. His account of his friend shows just how limited seventeenth-century literacy could be.

After I was come to my new Master, he had a young strong Man that was his Thresher, but he was blind, and had been so for about Twenty Years, who had lost his Sight when about Ten Years of Age; He was never Taught further than the Psalter as I have heard him often say; yet this Man taught our Master's Children, and afterwards became a famous Schoolmaster . . . He was a Man of great Memory, and of good Understanding.

If reading could be taught by the blind, the role of memorization and rote-learning must have been very great indeed.

Josiah's description of his conversations and recreations with this friend gives some insight into the world of this literate pair of labourers in the 1680s, and the astonishingly cool and appraising round of sectarian sermon-tasting they indulged in, and their worries about the necessity of the sacraments, which held them back from Quakerism for some time. Their opinions were based on Bible reading.

> We would walk out together on First-Day mornings in the Summertime several Miles a-foot, to hear such Priests as were the most famed for Preaching; and as we walked together we should have such Talk as was profitable. One Time as we were coming home from hearing one of the most famous and learned of these Priests in our Country, Well, said he, Josiah, I am weary with hearing these Priests, they are an idle Generation, they cannot be Ministers of Jesus Christ; This Sermon that we heard to Day I heard this man preach some years ago; as soon as he took his Text I thought how he would manage it, and accordingly as I thought he would go on so he did—I do not know, said he, what People to join in Society with—I have looked in my Mind over the Church of England, Presbyterians, Baptists and the Quakers, and do say the Quakers excel all people in Conversation . . . but, said he they do not use Baptism and the Lords Supper . . . So, as I followed my Business, which was mostly Plowing, serious thoughts began again to flow afresh in upon me . . . We Two would often go on First Day Mornings into the Field, taking a Bible with us, and there we would sit down together, and after I have read a while, we have sat silent, waiting with Desires in our Hearts after the Lord.

The blind thresher and the literate ploughman had possibly become in-servants for the same reasons that their education had been disrupted, in one case the accident or disease that had caused blindness, in the other the demographic accident of parental loss. But there must have been a constant trickle of semi-literate people into agricultural labour for just these reasons, and although this literate pair in Yorkshire were probably unusual, they were certainly not unique. Richard Baxter's first "stirrings of conscience" in about 1630 in rural Shropshire were prompted by "a poor day-labourer" in the town who normally did "the reading of the psalms and chapters" in church, and who lent Baxter's father "an old, torn book . . . called *Bunny's Resolution*," which influenced young Richard. These examples of literate labourers may be taken to represent the 15 per cent of labourers between 1580 and 1700 who could sign their names.[24] We may firmly deduce from the evidence of the order in which reading and writing was taught, and the experience of the autobiographers given above, that those who could sign their names could all read. The existence of this literate group amongst agricultural labourers is one of the reasons which leads me to stress the magnitude of the change in English society between 1500 and 1700. It proves my contention that illiteracy was everywhere face to face with literacy, and the oral with the printed word. Schofield suggested some time ago that "there were probably groups in the population, such as agricultural labourers in certain parts of the country, which were entirely cut off from any contact with the literate culture."[25] Cressy recently concurred. Although he conceded that the presence of even one reader amongst a group of rural labourers could act as a significant bridge to the literate world, he feels that "normally these ordinary people were indifferent to the political and religious controversies which exercised their betters."[26] Langdale's account of lively debate scarcely bears him out. I think the combination of the existence of a measurable proportion of labourers able to sign over a period of time, combined with the amount of cheap print in circulation, combined again with the brief impressions I am able to gather from Langdale, Baxter, and Thomas Tryon's group of reading shepherds, justifies the disagreement. It seems, from the life expectancy for adult males in the seventeenth century, and the proportion of children who lost their fathers early, that there was a constant slithering down the social ladder. The steady trickle of semi-educated orphaned boys into apprenticeship and into service was one of the ways largely illiterate groups came to contain "literate" members in the sixteenth and seventeenth centuries.

All the autobiographers quoted so far either come from too poor a background, or suffered too much from their father's early death, to go to grammar school. The next group of men come from yeomen or trading backgrounds, and their education was interrupted by their fathers at an appropriate point in time when they had absorbed as much as would be of use. They were never intended for the universities. A third of the autobiographers who identified their social backgrounds and their educational experiences fully became apprentices at fourteen.[27] Here is a very important correction to a view of seventeenth-century education based on university entrants alone. Such a view necessarily completely neglects the flow of boys from the schools into the various trades. The evidence of the autobiographers suggests this flow was very considerable. The boys involved came from a tremendous social and economic range.

George Trosse of Exeter was the son of a prominent lawyer who had married the daughter of a merchant who had twice been Mayor. George shone at grammar school, and his master objected when he was removed at fifteen "having a mind to be a Merchant." Alderman Newton of Cambridge certainly took great pride in his son's intellectual achievement, or he would not have allowed him to celebrate his new skill of writing at seven by making an entry in his own diary; but proud as he was of this grammar school product, he apprenticed him to a dry-salter at fourteen. The boys concerned were not merely sons of townsmen, however. The autobiographies contain ample evidence of the degree of magnetism exerted by the towns. London was, of course, preeminent. The autobiographies provide a mass of evidence on the formative effects of their apprenticeships then and the Puritan meetings and occasions they then attended. Their backgrounds were as diverse as the distances they travelled to get there. Arise Evans had walked across country from Wales, Thomas Tryon from Gloucestershire. William Crouch was the son of a substantial yeoman of Hampshire, and his father's early death and the Civil War combined deprived him of both his inheritance on the land which he expected from his father's will and also the grammar school education he regarded, with some justification, as his right as a yeoman's son. He also ended up, after much wandering, as a London apprentice. Benjamin Bangs, son of a prosperous Norfolk yeoman who died when he was a small child, has a similar history, except that he was more humbly apprenticed to a local shoemaker and ended in London more by accident than design.

The provincial towns also drew in boys from rural backgrounds. Thomas Chubb was only one of the boys who went to Salisbury. The fanatic William Dewsbury was apprenticed to a clock-maker in Leeds at thirteen, specifically because he wanted to explore Quakerism and knew he could do so there. William Edmundson, yet another orphan, the youngest of six children, of a Westmorland family whose mother died when he was four, his father when he was eight, also lost his portion under his father's will. He was apprenticed to a carpenter and joiner in York. George Bewley was a second-generation Quaker, born in Cumberland in 1684. He attended a school about a mile from home until he was twelve, when he was sent to board with an uncle to attend a school twenty miles away. This sounds like a grammar education. At fourteen, he was sent as apprentice to a Quaker linen-draper in Dublin. His parents kept in touch with him by letter, and more interesting, his sister, the eldest child, frequently wrote him long letters also. Apart from these boys from the country apprenticed to masters in provincial towns, many others were simply apprenticed to local craftsmen in their own area. The outstanding example is, of course, George Fox, the Leicestershire weaver's son apprenticed to a shoemaker. The main utility of a seventeenth-century education, judging from the autobiographies, was to prepare boys for an apprenticeship. A university education beginning for some of the autobiographers at about fourteen was a highly specialized and rare type of apprenticeship preparing boys for the Church.

Boys who came from slightly more prosperous backgrounds than those just described or who had not been precipitated down the social ladder by their father's death, sons of wholesale traders and yeomen, were given a grammar education to an appropriate level of usefulness, before being claimed from school by their fathers. Some of them were simply sons of yeomen, being prepared for the activities and lives of the more prosperous farmers who acted as local officials in their areas, with no thought of a university training. Grammar education often seems to have been assumed by such people, university education was not. The next group of autobiographers gives some insight into the social world of the yeomen and its expectations.

James Fretwell, who was born right at the end of the seventeenth century, came from a family of yeomen and traders, timber merchants, horse-breeders and dealers, carpenters and brasiers. James's father, who was born in the 1670s, went to grammar school, but his father removed him to "put him to his own business" after "he had learn'd so far as my grandfather thought was needful." He was a substantial timber-merchant. The family pattern was repeated. James went to grammar school before he was five. Because this school was five miles away it was too far for such a small child to walk, although he began by trying it, so he was boarded out during the week with a widow who lived near the school. The autobiographers were commonly boarded out like this, to get over the problems of accessibility caused by scattered schools. Between five and fourteen, James and his younger brother went to three separate schools and were boarded with three different families. It is just possible from his account that the availability of relatives or ex-servants with whom to board the children dictated the change of school. By the time he left the second, at thirteen, he "had made an entrance into Greek." When he was fourteen, his father "thinking I had got as much of the learned languages as would be of service to a tradesman . . . thought it time to learn something which was more immediately related to the qualifying of me for business: therefore he sent me to Pontefract, to learn to write and to accompt." He was taught by a Quaker linen-draper, who kept a school which was partly run by his apprentice who "was a good penman." James, who was fluent in Latin and had had two years Greek, seems to have been astonishingly uncertain of his writing. Again, the separation between the two skills is emphasized: "I had learn't some little to write before, but nothing of accounts that I remember. Here it was that I got what learning I have of that kind. I went through most of the rules of vulgar arithmetick and decimal fractions, with some little of practical geometry." Then James, like his father before him, left school. There was never any thought of university for him.

Oliver Sansom had been born over sixty years earlier, at Beedon in Berkshire, and was also the son of a timber-merchant, who had married a yeoman's daughter. His educational experiences closely paralleled James Fretwell's. He began later. At seven, he was sent to board with an aunt to learn "latin, and writing." He had another change of schools at ten, but "stayed not long there, my father having occasion to take me home to keep his book, and look after what I was capable of in his business, which was dealing in timber and wood." Oliver Sansom's autobiography, together with that of the Quaker John Whiting of Somerset, gives the most insight into the literate yeoman world of the seventeenth century. It was a world in which the ability to read was assumed, without question. The very un-self-consciousness of the incidental remarks that give away the manner in which literate skills were used in everyday living, amongst wives and daughters as well as friends, are revealing of the way in which literacy was an accepted skill. Oliver Sansom "took great delight, even in my tenders years, in reading the Holy Scriptures, and other godly books which I met with." When he married, his wife was "of a good yeomanry family and had been brought up in a sober and suitable way of education . . . I walked as before, in great seriousness of mind, and spent much time in reading good books, the holy Scriptures more especially; with which my wife and her relations, as well as my own, were greatly affected." Oliver's autobiography includes a whole series of letters written to his wife during his lengthy series of imprisonments. More important, when he had smallpox he adjured his wife, "I desire thee not to venture to come to me, until thou hear further from me, but let me hear from thee as often as thou canst." His wife's sister also wrote to him in prison. In 1670 he wrote, "I would have thee remember me dearly to thy sister, and let her know that I received her letter and was sweetly refreshed in the sense of the love of God which is manifested in and through her."

Oliver Sansom's father had bought him a "copyhold estate" at Boxford, near Newbury, after his marriage, and he settled down to lead the life of a yeoman farmer. He had one serving man to help him, so his acreage cannot have been very large. But he was a person of consequence in the neighbourhood, well liked by his neighbours despite his Quaker beliefs. On one of his releases from prison after a two-year spell, "many of my neighbours came running to welcome me home." Indeed, in 1665, a situation reminiscent of pure farce arose when the priest spent an evening searching for the tithingman and the village constable to break up a Quaker meeting at Sansom's house. He failed to find them, because they were at it. This same priest was responsible for an event which reveals more of Sansom's assumptions about literacy than any other. In 1668, he embarked on a public tirade against Sansom, at the Court Leet of Boxford and Westbrook, when he accused him of denying the Trinity and the Sacraments, and made a long clamourous speech against me, using many bitter, reviling words. And not satisfied with that, he in his fury with his own hands plucked my hat from my head two several times, in the presence of all the people . . . thus he spent much of the time until he went to dinner, endeavouring . . . to make me a gazing-stock to the whole assembly.

Oliver Sansom was very upset, obviously partly because the Leet contained "the chief men of three or four parishes." He objected to being made a spectacle in front of such a group. His immediate redress to re-establish his credit and defend himself was to write a paper of rebuttal. "This little Paper, I fastened to a post in the middle of the great hall where the court was kept, *that it might be seen and read of all those present.*" He took it down after "it had stuck there some time and was pretty well viewed." His implicit assumption was that "the chief men of three or four parishes" could, and did, read, so that his paper of defence was as good a means of answering the charges against himself and re-establishing himself in their eyes as the speech he apparently lacked the opportunity to make.[28]

John Whiting of Naylsey in Somerset was born in 1656, the son of a convinced Quaker yeoman "having a competent estate in the same parish, where my ancestors lived for several generations." Despite the early deaths of his father, his mother, and then his stepfather, this estate was evidently considerable enough to keep John at school. He does not tell us at what age he left. He was certainly still there at twelve and may have been there until fourteen. He went to grammar school, along with the sons of the local minister, but there was never from his writing any suggestion of his going on to university. At nineteen he left his guardian and took up active farming, which was frequently disrupted by imprisonment for his beliefs.

Whiting's autobiography is in itself the most compelling piece of evidence that he shared the assumption of that other yeoman, Oliver Sansom. Unlike all but a very few of the autobiographies, it is a piece of work of which parts can still be read for their intrinsic interest. Whiting was a sober, shrewd, and perceptive observer. He noted his own reactions as a child when his conscience impelled him to put Quaker beliefs into practice and "the plain language also cost me very dear, it was so hard to take it up, that I could have gone miles about rather than to have met some of my relations to speak to them." He noted the shocked reactions of the prisoners who watched Jeffries's retribution for Monmouth's rebellion, and recorded "they forced poor men to hale about mens quarters like horse-flesh or carrion, to boil and hang them up as monuments of their cruelty." He inserted potted biographies of the other Friends he talked about, and they frequently come off. His gossip is interesting too, as when he wrote of a proclamation from Elizabeth

Bathhurst's pen in 1679: "This treatise was so extraordinary, both for depth of matter and expression that some would not believe it was written by her, being but a weakly maid, though it was known to be her own writing." His considering, unhysterical cast of mind comes through very clearly, and it is no surprise that he continued to hold local office in his parish, where he was overseer of the poor in 1679, despite his Quakerism, which had first cut him off from his peer group when he reluctantly gave up playing with the other boys after school at night when he was twelve.

Although the quality of his autobiography is the best testimonial for John Whiting's education, there is plenty of other evidence in it for the importance that reading held for him. Of course, he read "the scriptures of truth, which I diligently read as well as fireside books" as a boy. He also produces evidence on the remarkable degree of organization reached by the Quaker book trade. In one of his imprisonments he remarked incidentally, "I had a parcel of friends['] books, etc., come down from London, as I used to have . . . and the carrier left them, as he used to do for me, at Nerberryinn." His reading spread wider than the Bible and sectarian propaganda though; he refers to Eusebius and to Bishop Burnet.

All the autobiographers touched on so far were without benefit of university education. Another third of those who identified both their social backgrounds and their educational experiences did go on to university. Most, though not all, of them came from more prosperous yeomen, small gentry, merchant, and ministry backgrounds. I have not considered them here, because their experiences are more familiar[29] than the struggle to acquire basic literary skills displayed by the poorest autobiographers. These boys appear from the worm's eye view of the humbler autobiographers as an educational élite. But to summarize their circumstances as "prosperous" or "privileged" is of course relative. To the Chubbs and Tryons of seventeenth-century society, they were indeed privileged; but the plight of Henry Jessey, who in 1623 at Cambridge had 3*d.* a day for his "provision of diet" and spent some of this on hiring the books he could not afford to buy, demonstrates just how relative this "privilege" was. The most succinct description of the physical difficulties of finding privacy and quiet in which to work which were suffered by boys from humble background acquiring an education is provided by Thomas Boston. His father, who was a maltster, could put him through grammar school; but at the end of it Thomas spent two years trying to find notarial work or raise the fees for university somehow. In that time he battled to keep up his Latin, and re-read his Justinian "the malt-loft being my closet."

The general impression given by the autobiographers is that boys from non-yeoman backgrounds quite frequently had a year or two's sporadic education, but it was often broken off before seven either by family needs or demographic mishap. Those boys who were fortunate enough to be supported at school until fourteen divided into two groups. Some went into apprenticeships; some to the universities as an apprenticeship to the Church or to teaching. The latter almost all came from yeomen, or more prosperous, families.

Oxford and Cambridge had nothing to do with the "literate" worlds of the Yorkshire labourers Langdale and his friend Hewson, and the Wiltshire labourer Stephen Duck; the Gloucestershire shepherds who taught Tryon to read; the Bedfordshire small craftsman John Bunyan, whose tastes in reading changed; the urban artisans with rural educations, Tryon, Chubb, and Crouch; and the more assured and confident Berkshire and Wiltshire yeomen, Sansom and Whiting. Much more important, only Langdale, Sansom and Whiting amongst them owed anything to the grammar schools. The picture they jointly convey is one of a society in which a boy even from a relatively poor family might have a year or two's education up to six or seven. If he was at school until seven he could read; if he was at school until eight or at the latest nine, he could write. Either way, he would be able to make sense of whatever cheap print the pedlars brought within his reach. Either way, his mental environment had undergone an enormous and very important change.

There is, of course, no real conflict between recent work stressing the social restrictiveness of grammar and university education in Tudor and Stuart England and the glimpses the autobiographers give us of the spread of elementary skills, particularly reading, amongst the very humble. Yet emphasis on the first, however well justified, gives an incomplete picture unless it is tempered by the second. It is particularly incomplete in view of the likelihood that boys below the level of yeomen were quite likely to learn to read, since reading was taught at an age when they could earn little, whereas writing was commonly taught at an age after the meaningful earning lives of such boys had begun. An account of "literacy" based on the only measurable skill, the ability to sign, necessarily omits this possibility that reading was a much more socially diffused skill than writing. Since the psychological and social changes brought about by the spread of reading skills were very great, the evidence of the humbler autobiographers of their acquisition of reading skills ought to be taken into account, if a balanced picture of the effects of the combined spread of cheap print and elementary education in the sixteenth and seventeenth centuries is to be obtained.

Additional note on the influence of "literate" women

"Literate" by definition implies the ability to write. It seems quite likely, however, that many schooldames taught reading who could not themselves write, and who also escaped the episcopal licensing procedure. Bishop Lloyd compiled a very detailed shorthand survey of the small market town and parish of Eccleshall in Staffordshire in which he himself had a seat, in 1693–98. It contained the names of no less than one man and five women whom he described as "schoolteachers," as well as a visiting "writing master" who came twice a year for six weeks.[30] Not a single one of these people appears in the diocesan records at all, although Eccleshall is, admittedly, a peculiarity. (I am much indebted to Dr. Alan Smith for this information.) Four of the five women were wives of day-labourers and of small craftsmen. This is a social group of women, who have completely escaped observation. They may have played a very important part in preliminary education, as the frequency with which authors, from Dr. Johnson down to Oliver Sansom and James Fretwell, refer to their schooldames who taught the first steps, shows. This runs counter to David Cressy's suggestion that "since women were rarely educated themselves, it is unlikely that they played a great part in expanding the literate public."[31] The autobiographies do contain a number of examples of mothers teaching reading, however. They included mothers like Benjamin Bangs's mother, daughter of a Hertfordshire clergyman married to a Norfolk yeoman, who was left widowed with nine children in the mid-1650s. She was obliged to sell the farm as soon as the oldest children were old enough to be put to service, but the youngest three she kept at home "under her Care and Instruction . . . We were all indeed indifferently well brought up both in reading and writing; and although we of the younger sort were most behind, yet we were able to signify our Minds to one another by our Pens."[32] Of more interest socially than this example of a woman spreading literate skills downwards socially through demographic accident are those of women who could not themselves write, who deliberately fostered reading skills. Oliver Heywood's mother, wife of a Lancashire fustian-weaver, seems only to have been able to read. As a young girl, after her conversion in 1614, she "took her bible with her and spent the whole day in reading and praying." Later her son went with her to Puritan exercises and sermons. Afterwards he wrote, "was in some measure helpful to her memory by the notes of sermons I took." He regularly sent her notes of sermons when he went up to Cambridge, and as an old woman she meditated on these: "it was her constant course in the night when she lay waking to roll them in her mind, and rivet them there." She took great pains over her children's education: "She was continually putting us upon the scriptures and good bookes and instructing us how to pray . . ." and this work extended outside her own family. "It was her usual practice to help many poor children to learning by buying them bookes, setting them to schoole, and paying their master for teaching, whereby many a poore parent blessed god for help *by their children reading*" (my italics).[33]

Notes

1. I should like to thank Dr. Roger Schofield for reading and commenting on this piece. I am also very grateful to Miss Sandy Harrison for collecting details from those autobiographies I could not myself see. The autobiographies have been extensively discussed in Owen C. Watkins, *The Puritan Experience* (1972), and Paul Delaney, *British Autobiography in the Seventeenth Century* (1969). Neither man is particularly interested in literacy, or the social origins of the humble auto-biographer; indeed, the latter work includes the quite mistaken statement: "Before 1700, no autobiographies by agricultural labourers or yeomen are known" (142, n. 25). Thirty-one of the 141 autobiographers whose works I have been able to examine describe the social status of the autobiographer's parents and give some fragmentary details of the autobiographer's education. (Watkins, 241–59, lists au-tobiographies, and I have used this list as my base.) In addition, five more of the autobiographers give some information on their education alone, and another dozen on their background alone. I have used this information to help build up a picture of the age at which reading and writing were taught. I have also used the diaries of men born in the seventeenth century of non-gentle rural origin, and, for good measure, the educational experience of the early eighteenth-century day-labourer poet Stephen Duck. Much of this material is reused in Chapter 2 of *Small Books and Pleasant Histories: Popular Fiction and Its Readership in Seventeenth-Century England* (1981).

2. It is possible that the Quaker autobiographers were less exceptional, for the Quakers seem to have had an entirely deliberate policy of using print for evangelism and polemic. Quaker autobiographies are therefore much the most common. For the whole subject of humble autobiographers, see David Vincent's forthcoming study of the autobiographies of working men in the first half of the nineteenth century, *Bread, Knowledge, and Freedom* (1981). I am very much indebted to Dr. Vincent for draw-ing my attention to the relevance of the seventeenth-century autobiographer to my work. His second chapter discusses both the seventeenth-century autobiographers and the eighteenth-century "uneducated poets" as forerunners of the nineteenth-century working-class autobiographers and was my point of departure.

3. R. T. Vann, *The Social Development of English Quakerism, 1655–1755* (1969), ch. 2.

4. The whole question of the use of signatures to provide a measure of the dif-fusion of literary skills over time, and of the crucial relationship of writing ability to reading ability, is discussed in R. S. Schofield, "The measurement of literacy in pre-industrial England," in J. R. Goody (ed.), *Literacy in Traditional Societies* (1968), 318–25, and "Some discussion of illiteracy in England, 1600–1800" (unpub-lished). A part of the latter has appeared as "Dimensions of illiteracy, 1750–1850," *Explorations in Economic History* 10, no. 4 (1973), 437–54. I am very grateful for Dr. Schofield's permission to use the unpublished, definitive discussion of the relationship between signing and reading ability.

5. David Cressy, "Educational opportunity in Tudor and Stuart England," *His-tory of Education Quarterly* (Fall 1976), 314, and "Literacy in seventeenth-century

England: More evidence," *Journal of Interdisciplinary History* 8, no. 1 (Summer 1977), 146–48. Also *Historical Journal* 20 (1977), 4–8.

6. Cressy, "Educational opportunity," 309–13.

7. Ironically, in view of his recent care to stress restricted access to education in "Educational opportunity," the best survey of elementary educational facilities and their effects is in David Cressy, "Education and literacy in London and East Anglia, 1580–1700" (Ph.D. thesis, Cambridge University, 1972), which lists all schoolmasters appearing in the Dioceses of London and Norwich and shows them relatively well provided with masters in rural areas in the 1590 and early seventeenth century. Alan Smith, "A study of educational development in the dioceses of Lichfield and Coventry in the seventeenth century" (Ph.D. thesis, University of Leicester, 1972), and "Private schools and schoolmasters in the Dioceses of Lichfield and Coventry," *History of Education* 5, no. 2 (1976), shows that in these dioceses there were more unendowed schoolmasters teaching in more places between 1660 and 1700 than in 1600–1640. This might, of course, indicate merely an improvement in the records. On the other hand, it may indicate that the periods when most elementary education was available differed in different parts of the country. In this case, Cressy's periodization of improvement and stagnation in literacy rates does not necessarily apply to the whole country.

8. Schofield, "Measurement of literacy in pre-industrial England," 313–14, and "Some discussion of illiteracy in England, 1600–1800."

9. See Cressy, *Education in Tudor and Stuart England* (1975), 70–72.

10. This coincides well with the expectations of the early nineteenth-century monitorial schools, in which a child was expected to learn to read in eleven months. Schofield, "Measurement of literacy in pre-industrial England," 316.

11. *Pace* Peter Clark, who suggests that my argument that "the husbandman who depended entirely on familial labour was probably . . . unable to afford the loss of labour which his child's school attendance entailed . . . is stronger in the context of higher education than in the case of primary instruction. It does not take into account those many *longeurs* in the agricultural year . . . when parents were probably quite happy to send a noisy son out to school for a month or so." Peter Clark, *English Provincial Society from the Reformation to the Revolution: Religion, Politics and Society in Kent, 1500–1640* (1977), 191. The acquisition of the ability to sign was certainly normally acquired young, probably between seven and eight, and Cressy's evidence shows quite conclusively that economic status determined education to this level.

12. Extract from *Board of Trade Papers,* printed in H. R. Fox Bourne, *The Life of John Locke* (London, 1876; reprinted, Aalen, 1969), 366.

13. Alice Clark, *Working Life of Women in the Seventeenth Century* (1919), 131. In the 1640s unskilled agricultural labourers were earning 12*d.* a day. Joan Thirsk (ed.), *Agrarian History of England and Wales,* vol. 4, *1560–1640,* 864. This rate was the same as that for building labourers, which remained constant at 12*d.* a day until just after 1690. E. H. Phelps Brown and Sheila V. Hopkins, "Seven centuries of building wages," in E. M. Carus-Wilson (ed.), *Essays in Economic History* 2 (1962),

172–73 and 177. These children were earning a sixth of a man's wage. Exceptionally skilled children, like Thomas Tryon, could earn a third of a man's wage at eight.

14. I. Pinchbeck and M. Hewitt, *Children in English Society* (1969), 1:161.

15. Ibid., 154–56.

16. Ibid., 10.

17. Thirsk, *Agrarian History of England and Wales,* 865. In 1586 in London their day-wages without food had been fixed at 13*d.* a day, along with masons, coopers, and glaziers under the Statute of Artificers. This compared with 9*d.* a day for "common labourers." R. H. Tawney and Eileen Power (eds.), *Tudor Econ. Documents,* vol. 1 (1924), 369–70.

18. The autobiographers whose parents were prosperous enough to enable them to go to university quite frequently went as early as fourteen. This conflicts with Cressy's findings that the mean age for entry to university was sixteen ("Education and literacy") and bears out the suggestion that the autobiographers were probably an exceptionally gifted group.

19. The term "husbandman" can be misleadingly used in a literary sense. Otherwise, it normally describes the group of farmers with medium-sized farms between fifteen and fifty acres who were becoming increasingly rare in arable areas in the seventeenth century. The plotting of values of the goods of men described as "husbandmen" by their neighbours who drew up their inventories shows this quite clearly, although the range of values of husbandmen's goods is wide and will overlap considerably with the bottom of the range of values of the more prosperous "yeomen's" goods. Margaret Spufford, "The significance of the Cambridgeshire Hearth Tax," *Cambridge Antiquarian Society* 55 (1962), 54, n. 3.

20. When Mrs. Leavis wrote of the literary inadequacy and emotional poverty of twentieth-century mass fiction in 1939, she was unaware of the existence of the voluminous chap-literature of the seventeenth and eighteenth centuries, the content of which would have provided her with an apt comparison with modern best sellers. She wrote of Bunyan's prose as if only the *Authorised Version* was available to form his style, and of the cultural contacts of working-class men up to the 1850s as if only the *Bible,* the *Pilgrim's Progress, Paradise Lost,* and *Robinson Crusoe,* with works by Addison, Swift, Goldsmith, and so on, were on the market. "No energy was wasted, the edge of their taste was not blunted on bad writing and cheap thinking," Q. D. Leavis, *Fiction and the Reading Public* (1939), 97–102, 106–15.

21. In eighteenth-century France, about one-eighth of children had lost their fathers by this age, and by fourteen, the age at which apprenticeship normally seems to have started, a quarter of children had lost their fathers. Calculated from Harvé Le Bras, "Parents, grand-parents, bisaieux," *Population* (1973), 34. I am told by the Cambridge Group for the History of Population and Social Structure that these figures should apply to seventeenth-century England.

22. Vincent, chap. 5.

23. Although it seems that there was no hard and fast distinctive line drawn between a schoolmaster licensed to teach "reading, writing and arithmetic" and one licensed to teach "grammar." At one visitation a man might well be licensed

to teach grammar, who had previously been licensed to teach reading and writing, and vice versa. It does not seem as if there was a clear distinction, in the small "private" schools which were both so numerous and so impermanent in the seventeenth century, between "English," or "petty" schools, and grammar schools. The masters probably taught according to the aptitudes of the different children, the desires of their parents, and the length of time the children could be spared for education from the labour force, as well as their own ability and training. The flexibility frequently found in seventeenth-century education is indicated by the licenses to Thomas Orpe, *literatu,* "to teach boys in English as well as in Latin as long as they were able" at Norton, Salop, in 1695. Alan Smith, "Private schools and schoolmasters in the Dioceses of Lichfield and Coventry in the seventeenth century," *History of Education* 5, no. 2 (1976), 125; Margaret Spufford, *Contrasting Communities* (1974), 187.

24. Cressy, "Educational opportunity," 314.

25. Schofield, "The measurement of literacy in pre-industrial England," 313.

26. David Cressy, "Illiteracy in England, 1530-1730," *Historical Journal* 20, no. 1 (March 1977), 8–9.

27. Eleven of the thirty-one, including six of the nine orphans.

28. A similar situation of course already existed a century earlier amongst at least a group of the yeomanry. C. J. Harrison, "The Social and Economic History of Cannock and Rugeley, 1546–1597" (Ph.D. thesis, University of Keele, 1974), 118–23, demonstrates the social importance of the court Leet meeting and also the legal capacities and attitudes, and network of correspondents, of a sixteenth-century yeoman farmer. He himself, although technically untrained, acted as both under-steward and steward of the manor, advising his lord on legal affairs in Staffordshire. A small group of such men regularly acted as legal advisors and representatives of the other peasantry in the manor court.

29. Cressy, "Educational opportunity," passim. To him, of course, yeomen's sons at university appear a minority, sober and straitened group. This, as an overall view, is undoubtedly correct.

30. Transcripts of the Survey of the Township of Eceleshall, 1697, and the Parish of Eccleshall, 1693–98, complied by N. W. Tildesley (1969) in the William Salt Library, Stafford.

31. *Thesis cit.*, 179–81.

32. Benjamin Bangs, *Memoirs of the Life and Convincement* (1757).

33. *The Rev. Oliver Heywood, B.A., 1630-1702: His Autobiographies, Diaries, Anecdote and Event Books*, ed. J. Horsfall-Turner (1882), 1:42, 48, 51.

9   THE HISTORY OF LITERACY IN SWEDEN

Egil Johansson

The reading tradition in Sweden and in Finland

It has been difficult in the past to make the history of Swedish literacy known and accepted in other countries. A typical statement on this matter was made by Carl af Forsell in his *Statistik över Sverige (Swedish Statistics)*, 1833, which is full of useful information:

> Most foreign geographies and statistical works, e.g. those of Stein, Hassel, Crome, Malte Brun and others, maintain that the lower classes in Sweden can neither read nor write. As for the first statement, it is completely false, since there is not one in a thousand among the Swedish peasantry who cannot read. The reason for this is principally the directives of Charles XI that a person who is not well acquainted with his Bible should not be allowed to take Holy Communion and that a person who is not confirmed should not be allowed to get married. One might nowadays readily add that, in order to be confirmed, everyone should be able to prove that, besides reading from a book, he also possessed passable skills in writing and arithmetic. Even if in other respects the cottage of the farmer or the crofter gives evidence of the highest poverty it will, nevertheless, nearly always contain a hymn-book, a Bible, a collection of sermons and sometimes several other devotional manuals. The English Lord Chancellor, Brougham, said in Parliament on May 1st 1816, that in the previous six years 9,765 couples had been married in Manchester among whom not a single person could either read or write. According to the *Revue Encyclopedique* of October 1832, 74 adolescents out of a hundred in the northern departments of France could read, whilst in the western ones it was 12 out of a hundred, and in the whole country only 38 out of a hundred.

Af Forsell rejects indignantly foreign opinions about the low status of literacy in Sweden at the same time as he strikes back by referring to low figures for England and France. The problem is still of interest. It is still difficult for

From Egil Johansson, *The History of Literacy in Sweden, in Comparison with Some Other Countries*, Educational Reports no. 12 (Umeå, Sweden: Umeå University and School of Education, 1977), 2–42. Reprinted with the permission of the author.

foreign observers to understand what has happened in Sweden, owing to the special nature of the Swedish and Finnish reading tradition.

Firstly, the ability to read gained ground much earlier than the ability to write, whereas these two abilities have followed each other closely in most other countries. Secondly, people were persuaded to learn to read by means of an actual campaign initiated for political and religious reasons; in the reign of Charles XI the Church Law of 1686, for example, contained a ruling concerning general literacy.

Thirdly, this reading campaign was forced through almost completely without the aid of proper schools. The responsibility for teaching children to read was ultimately placed on the parents. The social pressure was enormous. Everybody in the household and in the village gathered once a year to take part in examinations in reading and knowledge of the Bible. The adult who failed these examinations was excluded from both communion and marriage.

These are the distinctive features that af Forsell points to as being traditionally Swedish. He hints, moreover, by referring to the large number of books, at the literate environment in these poor households. His statements are, of course, too optimistic in their generalizations about the ability to read as a whole. But his argument is typical of the dilemma, which still prevails, of presenting the Swedish tradition internationally.

This dilemma is such as to make one more voice necessary. This very distinctive reading tradition was, as it happens, also observed by foreign travellers. The Scottish evangelist John Patterson writes about his trip to Sweden in 1807–8:

> From Malmoe I paid a visit to my friend, Dr. Hylander, in Lund, made the acquaintance of the bishop and some of the professors, and enlarged my knowledge of Sweden. As Dr. Hylander had a parish not far from Malmoe, I one day went with him to attend an examination of his parishioners. It was held in a peasant's house, in a large hall, where a goodly number were collected. The people, old and young, answered the questions put to them readily in general; those who were deficient in their knowledge were severely dealt with, and exhorted to be more diligent. On the whole the exercise was calculated to be useful. It was a pleasing circumstance that all could read. Indeed, this may be affirmed of the inhabitants of all the northern Protestant Kingdoms; you seldom meet one above ten or twelve who cannot read, and the most of them write their own language; yet at the time now referred to, there was nothing like what we have in Scotland, a provision for the education of the people by means of parochial schools. The parents were the teachers of their children, till they reached the age of fourteen

or thereabouts, when they attended the pastor or his assistant, to be prepared for confirmation and being admitted to the Lord's Supper. And as no person can be confirmed till he can read and repeat his catechism, or, until confirmed, can give his oath in a court of justice, or get married, a great disgrace is attached to not being able to read; indeed, one who cannot read is nobody in the eye of the law. This state of things has its advantages, as far as education is concerned; but, alas! it has its disadvantages, as it admits all to the enjoyment of religious privileges, and thereby tends to make a nation of religious formalists. After the examination was over, all the heads of families sat down to a sumptuous dinner provided for the occasion, and which gave me a little more insight into Swedish society among the peasantry. I was much pleased with the whole, and thanked my friend for the opportunity then offered me of seeing more of the people.

Patterson commented approvingly on education for the masses in Sweden. The ability to read was a general accomplishment. School instruction did not, however, exist in the same way as in Scotland. Parents were instead responsible for the teaching of their children. The result was supervised by means of a system of examinations held by the clergy, which, however, according to Patterson, led to a certain degree of religious formalism. Thus, the various features of education for the masses in Sweden were also observed by Patterson.

Another traveller, the German ecclesiastical historian Friedrich Wilhelm von Schubert, had the same impressions as Patterson during this tour of Sweden and Finland in 1811. He observed that the ability to read gained more ground after the first decade of the eighteenth century. Von Schubert has, as a matter of fact, presented one of the most detailed descriptions of the custom of church examinations in Sweden and Finland.

The reading tradition in Sweden and Finland is also a problem for af Forsell's successors in the field of statistics today. The difficulty of comparing Sweden and Finland with other countries has, in reality, increased over the years.

Since the Second World War the accepted model has been to regard it as necessary that reading and writing should follow each other closely, that formal school instruction should be almost the only conceivable teaching method, and that economic models should provide us with a decisive explanation of a functioning literate environment. A general ability to read in a poor, pre-industrial, agrarian, developing country like Sweden or Finland seems a sheer absurdity. The notion that the ability to read gained ground much earlier than the ability to write is completely foreign to this approach.

A typical expression of this contemporary outlook on the ability to read is given in the treatment of literacy in the Finnish censuses of 1880–1930. The figure for the adults who could neither read nor write was, according to these censuses, constantly lower than 2 per cent. These figures constituted, as late at the 1930s, no major problem for the statisticians in the League of Nations. They quoted the number of illiterate people in Finland in 1930 at 0.9%.[1]

The Finnish authorities were, however, already at this time worried by inquiries about the meaning of these figures. As a result of this, the next census included unfortunately no information about cultural attainment because of obscurities when making international comparisons.

After the war UNESCO's statisticians were even harsher.[2] Those who were only able to read were classified as illiterate. The figure for the number of adult illiterates in Finland in 1930 was thus 16 instead of 1 per cent. For earlier periods, this figure was much higher. It was 29 per cent for 1920, 45 per cent for 1910, and 61 per cent for 1900. The corresponding figure for 1880 was as high as 87 per cent. The contrast is glaring in comparison with Patterson's and von Schubert's observations of the Swedish and Finnish educational tradition.

But these contemporary UNESCO observers were also uncertain about the interpretation and use of the Finnish figures. An argument with the Finnish statisticians was described in a report published in 1957. Both sides were equally confused. The Finnish group tried to include those who were only able to read with those who were able to write even if they had not been passed by the clerical examiners.[3]

Such an adjustment to the contemporary definition of literacy need not, however, necessarily be the only way of escaping the dilemma of the Finnish figures. The way out of this dilemma might instead be to accept the reading traditions on Sweden and Finland as historical reality and then adjust the concept of literacy according to that. This alternative has been attempted in this chapter.

Theoretical starting points: Two patterns of analysis

Thus, to make a population literate requires some form of organized instruction or a number of literacy campaigns. This is true of all times and all countries. The ability to read and write became universal in the West only during the final years of the nineteenth century after the consolidation of compulsory schooling. The same result is aimed at in the developing countries today by means of large-scale literacy campaigns.

Such *purposeful educational measures* always follow a typical pattern. The breakthrough of literacy is characterized by great differences—education gaps—between the age groups. The younger ones are, to a larger extent, subject to teaching. The total literate growth is concurrent with the changeover of generations. The illiterate generations die away. The coming generations are made literate by means of education. The population will thus gradually become literate. This pattern is typical both of the past and of today and is the result of strong teaching measures. It is also, of course, part of this pattern that in the end there are no noticeable differences between occupational groups, sexes, town and country, etc. All this is obvious. The observations indicated are, nevertheless, extremely useful for testing and defining various stages of literacy in a population.

This first pattern, however, gives place continually to another, which is characterized by prevailing differences amongst a population as regards *the demand and need for* literacy. These differences are principally defined by social and economic conditions. Differences primarily appear between various occupational groups. Some occupations are very dependent on active literacy. A literate environment is obtained in these occupations without any particular teaching campaign. The teaching requirements are supplied through private or limited social initiatives. Characteristic features appear here, too, with differences remaining to the very last between occupational groups, sexes, town and country, etc. To trace and observe this pattern as well has proved to be profitable when analysing the development of literacy.

For want of better terms I usually call the two patterns of analysis *push* and *pull* patterns. The former is explained by means of systematic teaching measures irrespective of, e.g., regional and social differences. The spontaneous learning motives are in the latter case explained by just such differences in environment as have been mentioned above.

Both patterns of analysis will be used below to analyse the historical source material for Sweden and Finland.

The European background

Several factors helped to pave the way for a more widespread reading ability in Europe from the sixteenth century onwards. Printing made it technically possible to produce books. The growth of nation states accentuated the need for books which would be available in the various national languages. But it was the Reformation which stimulated the popularization of reading. The individual was now expected to acquaint himself with the words of the Scriptures in his own native language.

These events are illustrated, for example, by the rapidly increasing number of translations and editions of the Bible. From the earliest history of the Church there had been versions of the Bible in about ten of the ancient civilized languages, among them Greek, Syrian, Coptic, Latin, and Gothic. In the late Middle Ages, attempts were made at translating the Bible into the western national languages. These translations were most often based on Latin. The art of printing and later the Reformation increased the importance of these translations. The Bible was printed in its entirety in German in 1466, in Italian in 1471, in French in 1487, in Dutch in 1526, in English in 1535, in Swedish in 1541, and in Danish in 1550. By this time the New Testament and other parts of the Bible had, as a rule, already been translated and printed. Luther's version of 1543 of the complete Bible from the original languages, Hebrew and Greek, appeared in no less than 253 editions during the lifetime of the translator.

To start with, the translations of the Bible were important principally for church services and sermons. It was not until the seventeenth century that the ability to read, which had been aimed at by the reformers, gained more ground among the masses. Thus, a clear difference rapidly appeared between Protestant and non-Protestant Europe. Whereas in Catholic and orthodox Southern and Eastern Europe there were still very few people who could read—less than 20 per cent—there was a dramatic increase in Protestant Central and Northern Europe. An intermediate position was held by Northern Italy and parts of France with a certain literate tradition since the Middle Ages, at least in the commercial towns.

The ability to read was perhaps most widespread in Iceland with its unbroken literary heritage. But figures for England, Scotland, and the Netherlands also show that many people were able to read in these countries as well, perhaps more than 50 per cent. In Protestant Europe it can be estimated that about 35–45 per cent of the population could read at the turn of the century in 1700.[4] The reading campaign was now in full swing in Sweden and in Finland as well. This campaign was, as a matter of fact, carried out very thoroughly in these two countries, which will be shown in the following.

The world of the "Hustavla"

The full emergence of the Reformation

Trends in Sweden corresponded closely to those in Europe. Here, too, the Reformation had led to demands for popular education. More of the Scriptures were now supposed to be read and known in church and at home. Oral instruction could not, however, by itself fulfill the increasing requirements for knowledge during the seventeenth century. Reading from a book was now an indispensable skill for everybody. Sweden did not in this respect, differ very much from other Protestant countries.[5]

The ideas of the Reformation were, in reality, put into effect by the united efforts of the whole country. The work of national reconstruction was followed up during the seventeenth century by an extensive education of the people, which showed itself in various kinds of laws and regulations; for the dioceses this took the form of resolutions from clerical conferences and diocesan regulations, and for the whole country there were ecclesiastical and parliamentary resolutions. A number of proposals concerning Church law regulations for popular instruction were brought up. They led to the Church Law of 1686, which clearly manifested the development.

The Church Law contained rulings about general literacy. It said, e.g., that children, farm-hands, and maid-servants should "learn to read and see with their own eyes what God bids and commands in His Holy Word." The expression was typical of the Reformation. Every individual should "with his own eyes" see and learn the meaning of the Bible. The object of this reading was to make the individual conscious of Christian faith and life, the latter being most important. Christian life would demonstrate faith in a social order combining every aspect of existence in what has been called "the world of the 'Hustavla.'"[6]

The world of the "Hustavla"

The collection of words from the Scriptures in the "Hustavla" lay down the guiding principles for the whole society, for clergy and parishioners in the spiritual or teaching order, for the authorities and subjects in the political order, and for master and servants in the household or the economic order. Everybody was given duties and rights in a reciprocal system where everyone had to fulfill his obligations.[7] Figure 9.1 is an attempt to illustrate the social outlook of the "Hustavla."

Everybody lived, according to the code of the "Hustavla," in a three-dimensional system of social relations. The figure can be made concrete by means of the following examples.

1. The king was sovereign in the political, listener in the spiritual, and head of the family in the economic order.

2. The clergyman was correspondingly subject, teacher, and head of the family.

3. The master was subject in the country, listener in the congregation, and head of the family in his house.

4. The rest were, generally speaking, subjects, listeners, and household members.

The system was, thus, strongly patriarchal. The father figure recurred in the home, in the congregation, and in the national economy. The master with his family, the vicar with his parishioners, and the father of the people with his subjects made up the same pattern of joint responsibility and reciprocal obligations.

But this interplay also had its tensions. The ideological and political responsibilities did not coincide. The Church guarded its sole right to teach

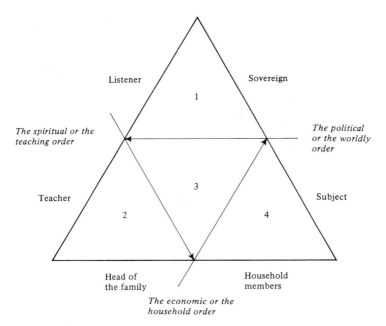

Figure 9.1. Outline of the threefold interplay of forces in "the world of the 'Hustavla.'"

and instruct. The king was, in church, only a listener, however distinguished he might be. But it was exactly in his capacity as the most distinguished of members that the king tried to assert the influence of the State over the Church. One sees this tension in the ideas of the Reformation with regard to the spiritual and the worldly domains. Both were of God. The worldly domain was God's indirect or "improper" means of maintaining the social order with the help of laws and authorities. The spiritual domain was God's direct or "proper" influence by means of his word on the individual so that a "new individual would daily prove himself," in the words of the Catechism.[8]

The tension in the household order was abolished. The head of the family was both sovereign and priest in his house. He was the teacher and the up-bringer, influenced by the activities of the teaching order in the parish.

The spiritual or the teaching order

The activities of the spiritual or teaching order were to a large extent determined by the lives of the Church and the parish. The bishop, assisted by consistory and rural deans, ruled the dioceses. Locally, the clergymen served as parish "teachers" by means of their sermons, instruction, and examinations. This spiritual education was supplemented by the healing of souls and church discipline. It was the duty of the parishioners as "listeners" to become more and more acquainted with the message of the Church and put it into practice. The divine service was increasingly used as a means of education. Sermons on the Catechism, e.g. in dialogue form between parish clerk and clergyman, were one way of improving collective learning. Questions on the sermon with the parishioners sitting on their benches, or gathered in the sanctuary together with the other members of their district, was another way of teaching and checking the learning process at the same time. Those who failed their examinations could be excluded from Communion and thus from the right to marry, since sufficient knowledge and understanding of the Scriptures was of fundamental importance for the household order as well. The duties of the clergymen were consequently extended to include calling on the parishioners in their homes and yearly examinations.

The economic or the household order

The economic or the household order functioned within the villages and in the homes. The quotations from the Bible concerning the mutual dependence between husband and wife, parents and children, master and servants took up most of the space in the "Hustavla." Except for the purely economic functions of work and everyday life, the household was also, just like parish life, characterized by sermons and instruction. Psalm-book and Bible texts were supposed to be used daily at family prayers. The older members of the family were supposed to give the children a programmed education, based on the Catechism. The clergyman was a teacher in the parish, and the master was in a corresponding way supposed to be responsible for devotion, instruction, and examination in his house. He had also the authority to bring up children and servants with "a reasonable amount of chastisement." The congruence between the teaching and household order was striking. Home life was strongly influenced by congregation life on workdays and holidays alike.[9]

Church services and instruction went side by side in the village. This was at least true of Norrland with its vast woodlands, where the villagers gathered for prayers and reading on Sundays when they did not attend church. The meetings alternated from house to house as did most often the task of reading the texts and sermons. Detailed directions are given in a separate church ordinance for Norrland, dating from the beginning of the seventeenth century.

> Likewise on Sundays or respective holy days in the Church year the clergy shall hold the daily lessons, together with Holy Scripture and Christian prayers and psalms, and also examine and instruct young persons. Residents of the outlying villages shall come to the homes of in-

dividuals who are already able to read and thereby hear the lessons and devotions which such persons are required to read aloud to them.

The ordinance also stated that "all young boys, who might be thought capable of reading from a book, shall come to the church and there learn to read and sing."

Such village reading is known from the early seventeenth century. It formed the basis of the well-known so-called "reading movement" which at times came to be opposed to new books and new regulations within the Church. From this we get a documentation of the social environment in villages and homes which developed in the world of the "Hustavla."

The political or the worldly order

Political life in its popular form was shaped within village communities and parishes. Within the village there were the village council and the village assembly, meeting a couple of times every year to decide upon the common interests of the village, such as sowing and the harvest, the tending of cattle, fencing, the management of forestland and mills owned in common, etc. The village community came together at the annual village feast and at weddings and funerals where the villagers always turned out in full force. The yearly examinations and examination feasts fitted well into this tradition.[10]

An extremely old form of popular self-government was preserved at the parish meetings, where the parishioners, gathered under the guidance of their vicar, made decisions about common problems such as church building, poor relief, and popular instruction. The life of the individual was also taken up at the parish meetings, where there was a local administration of justice, something unique to Sweden. Trials could be held for such misdemeanours as Sabbath-breaking, swearing, or drunkenness. Particular care was taken to watch over public morals with, among other things, regulations concerning betrothals and marriages. Marriages had to be contracted publicly in church. New households had to be sanctioned by the parishioners.[11]

Six or twelve representatives were chosen to carry out the resolutions of the parish meeting and to watch over general order. They were, together with the local vicars and the church-wardens, the governors of the parish. They were supported by elected supervisors in the outlying villages.

The parish assembly most often also chose the vicar, even if he then had to be appointed by the bishop or the king. It also appointed electors for the general election of representatives from the peasantry to the Swedish Riksdag (Parliament). The electors came together according to jurisdictional districts (in Dalarna within the country administrative division and in Norrland within the assize division) and appointed the representatives from the peasantry to the Swedish Riksdag for the parliamentary sessions every three years. The number of members from the peasantry was about 150 at every Riksdag during the seventeenth and eighteenth centuries. There was a rapid turn-over of representatives. About one third were chosen for one parliamentary session, another third were chosen for two, and only 10–15 per cent were chosen for five parliamentary sessions or more. These figures apply to the latter part of the eighteenth century.[12]

Some 80 representatives for the burgesses were elected in the towns in a corresponding way by the magistrates and the burgesses. The ecclesiastical estate was made up of the bishops and of elected clerical representatives, 51 members in all. The nobles, on the other hand, had personal representation for their class. Some three hundred nobles could be assembled at the same time for proceedings in the Riksdag.

Each of these classes or estates, however, cast only one vote when all the estates voted. The power of the peasantry to assert their position increased, and this has been partly explained by the fact that more and more of them were learning to read. This was the way power was divided between subjects and the authorities in the political order from the village community to the Riksdag in the world of the "Hustavla." The increasing book-learning provided important inner strength for all the functions of society.

The reading campaign around 1700

The functional need for reading ability: Books

Persons in the world of the "Hustavla" required deep ideological insight in order to be able to function properly. The liturgy and instructions concerning devotions and continued education in church and at home were taken up principally in the Psalm-book.[13]

Ever since the first editions in the 1530s the Psalm-book contained, besides psalms, the Bible texts of the ecclesiastical year, the Catechism with Luther's explanations, the "Hustavla," and prayer for home and church.

The Psalm-book of 1695 contained 413 psalms, some of them very long. The first 21 psalms were "catechetical psalms," corresponding to the five articles of the Catechism. Then followed psalms 22–112 with biblical motifs from the Book of Psalms, and from the texts of the ecclesiastical year in psalms 113–215. The remaining half of the psalms were didactic psalms for everyday life, morning and evening psalms, etc. One of the most noteworthy psalms was number 260, "The Golden ABC." Each of the 24 verses began in turn with the letters of the alphabet.

After the psalms in the Psalm-book of 1695 followed the texts of the ecclesiastical year, the Small Catechism, the "Hustavla," the Athanasian Confessional Creed, David's seven Penitential Psalms, prayers for everyday use, and the regulations for baptism, marriage, and congregational services. The volume also included a long and penetrating discourse on how to interpret and obey the Christian doctrine.

This Psalm-book appeared in at least 250 editions and in 1.5 million copies up to the introduction of the new Psalm-book in 1819. The parishioners were recommended to sing from the book in church. The rhythm was marked by this: Long pauses between the verses were supposed to allow time for reading the next one. These pauses in church music were later to puzzle music theorists.[14]

More widespread than the Psalm-book were the special editions of the Catechism, including the ABC-book, the text of the Catechism, Luther's explanation, additional expositions with questions, answers and words from the Scriptures. A number of editions of this kind were circulated during the seventeenth century with an ever increasing content.

Most widespread was the Catechism of 1689 with the expositions of Archbishop J. Svebilius. It included the text of the Catechism, Luther's explanation, Svebilius's expositions (including 303 questions and answers, and Scriptural passages), daily prayers, the "Hustavla," the seven Penitential Psalms, additional questions for young people, bridal couples, and finally J. Arndt's rules for Bible-reading in the home.

Both the exposition in the Psalm-book mentioned above and the references in the Catechism to the Bible reader stressed the importance of active and engaged reading and its application to life.

The Catechism was regarded both as a book of devotion and as a compilation of Scriptural content. The Bible editions themselves were too expensive. It was not until the nineteenth century that the Bible became a common feature in the home.

The initiative from above

The Catechism and the Psalm-book became the most important works in the household during the seventeenth century. They manifested, together with the Church Law of 1686, the edicts, which applied to everyone, stipulating a fully developed Church education for the masses.

There were also, apart from the Church Law, other ordinances applicable to the whole country. A royal decree of 1723 constrained parents and guardians to "diligently see to it that their children applied themselves to book reading and the study of the lessons in the Catechism." Neglect could lead to payment of fines used for "the instruction of poor children in the parish." Such penalties give a good picture of the initiative from above on a central level. It was in the dioceses that theory became practice.[15]

The Conventicle Edict of 1726 had a similar significance. It was best-known for its prohibition of the pietistical conventicles with their devotional meetings outside the confines of the family household. Such spontaneous meetings were in themselves signs of increasing commitment to individual reading and devotion. But they were not to be included in the instruction in the teaching and household order. In the place of such conventicles, the edict recommended and stressed regular family prayers in the home, but only for the family household.

Popular instruction was also often prescribed at diocesan level, in diocesan decrees, and in resolutions passed by the clergymen's assemblies. Instruction was to be organized by the diocesan authorities. The local responsibility was placed on rural deans, vicars, and parish representatives. The initiative from above was completed by long and harsh examinations by the bishop and the rural dean at their visitations in the parishes. The recurrent instruction and examinations of the clergy enabled the Catechism to spread to the villages and homes.

The horizontal diffusion

The reading ability campaign in Sweden was carried through almost completely without the aid of proper schools. There were "school masters" in the parishes in, for example, Skåne and Gotland. The parish clerks and other assistants were also in some parts of the country made responsible for the instruction of the children. But the main responsibility lay with the parents in the home. This, too, was one of Luther's original ideas. The master was, in the household order, responsible for education in the same way as the clergyman was in the parish. The idea of the "general priesthood" made the household order into something of a teaching order as well.[16]

A number of ABC-books with instructions for learning were published during the seventeenth century.[17] Behind these instructions one finds the pedagogic ideas of Wolfgang Ratke and Amos Comenius. Ratke's *Didactica* was translated into Swedish in 1614. Comenius's first Swedish version of *Didactica Magna* appeared in 1641 and *Orbis Pictus* in 1683. Ratke and Comenius were both consulted about the educational problems in Sweden. The latter also visited Sweden twice in the 1640s.[18]

The reading instruction recommended in the ABC-books was the synthetic alphabetic method. The children were to learn the names of the letters first and then gradually learn to combine them into syllables and words. The following instruction at a visitation in Norrbotten in 1720 provides a good illustration of this form of instruction.

> The Rural Dean admonished the parish organist and others in the congregation involved in the instruction of young people to inculcate a

firm knowledge of the lettered alphabet before proceeding with lessons in spelling. In like measure, they should not begin with basic reading before they have instructed the children in the correct and proper art of spelling. Furthermore, they should not impose any memorization exercises on the children before each is able to read directly from all books used in instruction. With respect to the first exercise in memorization, they should take heed that the children do not add or remove any letter of the written text but rather that they faultlessly follow each letter verbatim. Similarly, a child should not be allowed to recite the second lesson before the first is securely fastened in his memory. From the very beginning the children shall have become accustomed to reading clearly and diligently and to making firm observance of each sentence to its very end. Furthermore, they shall have become fully aware of the text which they are reading and heed its utterance as if they heard it spoken by another. In this manner the children should gradually acquire a firm grasp of the textual meaning and content and be able to articulate such in words other than those given in the text. In like measure, they shall answer with their own words to the questions posed them in the text.

The instruction is typical. It corresponds well to leading thoughts of the time. Learning should pass from what was concrete for the eye, via memory, to a complete understanding and application.

It was possible to spread reading ability and catechetical knowledge horizontally because of strong social pressure. It was important to make progress within households and village communities. Those who were already able to read were supposed to instruct those who could not. Successes and failures became known at the recurring examinations.

But it would be wrong to say that everything was a matter of compulsion in the Swedish reading campaign. Family prayers and village reading led many people to feel a need for religion. One sign of this was Pietism, that was just breaking through. Another were the "readers" in Norrland. Insight into both the difficulties and successes of the campaign is obtained from the Church examination registers, forming part of the most noteworthy heritage from the time when Sweden was a major European power in the seventeenth century.

The Church examination registers

Popular instruction as organized by the Church has been extremely well documented in Sweden and in Finland.[19] Progress in reading and Catechism knowledge was noted in special examination registers. The existence of these sources is in itself a strong verification of the above-mentioned campaign.

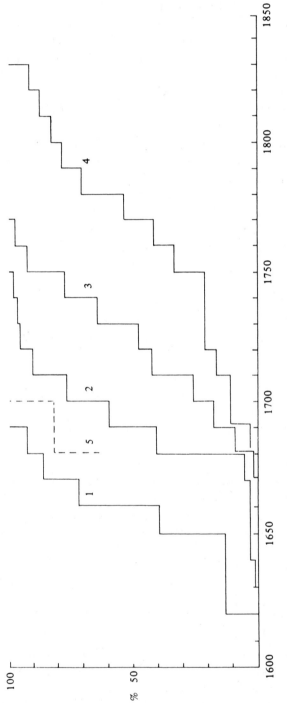

Figure 9.2. Percentage of deaneries in various dioceses within which at least one Church examination register is known to have been begun, at various points in time. (For the diocese of Lund, a second line gives special catechism registers.) Urban areas are excluded ($N = 170$). *1*, the diocese of Väster-hås ($N = 15$); *2*, the dioceses of Härnösand, Uppsala, Strängnäs, Karlstad, Växjö, and Visby ($N = 77$); *3*, the dioceses of Linköping, Kalmar, Skara, and Göteborg ($N = 54$); *4*, the diocese of Lund ($N = 24$); *5*, the diocese of Lund, catechism registers ($N = 24$). *Source:* files for the Church archives. Division of deaneries and parishes according to the 1805 deanery tables.

It will be convenient to divide up the oldest examination registers on the basis of dioceses and deaneries as a first illustration, since popular instruction was enforced vertically from the dioceses, via the rural deans and the vicars, and thence out to the people (Figure 9.2).

The dioceses differ considerably from one another. The diocese of Västerås has the oldest examination registers. Some of them date back as far as the 1620s. From this decade there are at least some examination registers still extant for every deanery in this diocese. In the surrounding dioceses, Karlstad, Strängnäs, Uppsala, Härnösand, and, in the south, in Växjö and Visby, examination registers have been preserved for most of the deaneries since before 1720. The work in connection with the Church Law of 1686 is clearly reflected in the many registers from the 1680s. In the dioceses of Linköping, Kalmar, Skara, and Göteborg there are examination registers dating from 1750 for the majority of the deaneries. The diocese of Lund is the exception, with a very early series of yearly so-called Catechism registers from the 1680s and a considerably later collection of actual examination registers. The latter are in reality so recent that the last 25 per cent of the deaneries only have examples from the nineteenth century. These sources consequently illustrate the date of the origin of the oldest preserved examination register for every deanery. This indicates the pace of the enforcement of popular instruction, where diocese and deanery make up hierarchic units. The difficult historical problem of judging to what extent the preserved source material is also the original one and the oldest is to some degree made easier because of these figures.

Some idea of the proportions of the historical problem with the archives can be gained by examining how the oldest preserved examination registers are distributed over the parishes (Figure 9.3). The order between the dioceses is the same. The majority of the parishes in the diocese of Västerås have examination registers dating back to before 1750. The other dioceses have examination registers from the latter part of the eighteenth century, and the diocese of Lund from the beginning of the nineteenth century. As for the parishes, the diocese of Lund once again has Catechism registers which are well ordered and date back to the final decades of the seventeenth century. These registers were, however, used at only one examination. New ones were made up for every new examination. They have been preserved, and there is a wide distribution over the parishes.

The Church examination registers were, on the other hand, used for many examinations, sometimes over many years. They were taken along on examination rounds which were often very long in the more extensive parishes of the country. They were subject to hard wear, damp, and fire damage and ran the risk of getting lost in many different ways. It should also be noted

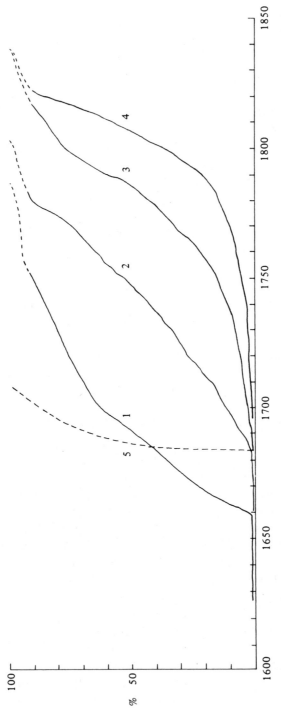

Figure 9.3. Percentage of parishes in various dioceses in which a Church examination register is known to have been begun, at various points in time. (For the diocese of Lund, a second line gives special catechism registers.) Urban areas are excluded ($N = 2,373$). For grouping of dioceses 1–4 and 5, see Figure 9.2. *Source:* files for the Church archives. Division of deaneries and parishes according to the 1805 deanery tables.

that in the beginning the examination registers did not have the same status as the older Church records, such as the registers for births, marriages, and deaths. It was not until the eighteenth century that their official importance increased as bases for census registration and as sources for the work of the Old National Central Bureau of Statistics, after 1749.

It is still uncertain to what extent the original examination registers have actually been preserved. Extensive studies are required to reduce this uncertainty. The already existing surveys nevertheless confirm the activities of the clerical authorities for a more widespread popular education after the end of the seventeenth century. An examination register from Tuna in Medelpad will be taken as a typical example of this.

An example: The reading campaign in Tuna in the 1690s

The Church Law of 1686 led to the setting up of organized examination registers in an increasing number of parishes. Tuna in Medelpad is one of them. Its oldest preserved examination register extends over the years 1686–91 (Figure 9.4).

The parish was at this time divided into six examination districts (rotes). The first pages are, unfortunately, missing in the register. The first district is, therefore, not complete and is omitted from the following analysis. Three hundred ninety-seven persons over the age of six are noted in the other five districts. The youngest children are not noted until they have been examined. This is already an illustration of the examining function of the register. The parishioners are arranged according to district, village, and household. The social position is stated for every individual within the household: husband, wife, son, daughter, maidservant, farmhand, lodger, etc. Age, reading marks, and Catechism knowledge are, together with names, noted in special columns. The latter take up most of the space, with ten columns for various types of knowledge: the words of the text, Luther's explanation of the five articles, prayers, the "Hustavla," and specific questions. It is typical that these last three or four columns are never filled in this first register even if they are always drawn up. They indicate the increasing knowledge of the Catechism acquired because of an increase in reading ability. They bear witness, in their own way, to an intensified teaching campaign. Reading and Catechism knowledge are noted with judgements in plain language, e.g. "intet"—*cannot* read, "begynt"—has *begun* to read, "lite"—can read *a little,* "någorlunda"—can read *acceptably,* and "kan"—*can* read. "*Cannot* read" and "*can* read" are presented separately in the following tables. "Has *begun* to read" is the most frequent of the other marks. It was used principally for children and young people. As regards Catechism knowledge, this report only indicates the number of Catechism items that had been learnt. A sketch of the material is presented in Table 9.1

Village	The fourth district: Farmer, Wife, Children, Servants	Age	Can read from a book	Simplic. Partes Catech.	Dialogus cum explicatione	Symbolum cum explicatione	Orat. Dom. Cum explicatione	Baptism cum explicatione	Sac. Caena cum explicatione	Confessions of sins	Prayers	The "Hustavla"
Alstad	Jacob Eriksson	62	Can	Can	Can	Can	Can	Can	Can			
	(Wife) Ingeborg Eriksdotter	40	Cannot	Can	Accept	Badly	Can	Can				
	(Son) Erik Jacobsson	14	Begun	Can	Can	Can	Can		Can			
	(Daughter) Britta Jacobsdotter	16	Begun	Can	Can	Can	Can	Can	Can			
	(Son) Jacob Jacobsson	10	Begun	Can	Can	Can	Can	Can	Can			
	(Daughter) Karin Jacobsdotter	12	Begun	Can	Can	Can	Can	Can	Can			
	(Daughter) Anna Jacobsdotter	7	Begun									
	(Aunt?) Elin Eriksdotter	66	A little	Can	(died)							

Figure 9.4. The family of Jacob Eriksson in the parish of Tuna in the fourth examination district and in the village of Alstad. Page 12 in the Church examination register for 1688–91. The family includes parents, five children, and an elderly lodger, probably an aunt. The columns indicate age, reading ability and, on one hand, knowledge of the words of the Catechism (Simplic. partes) and, on the other, knowledge of the five articles together with Luther's explanation (cum explicatione). Room is also left for confession, prayers, and the "Hustavla." At a later examination (in the Church examination register for 1696–98), all children, except Anna, have been given higher grades in reading in that "begun" has been altered to "can" read. *Source*: Tuna, Medelpad, Church examination register, 1688–91, p. 12.

Table 9.1. Reading marks and Catechism knowledge in Tuna, 1688–91 (*N* = 397)

Columns about memorization (Catechism item)	Reading marks				
	No note	"Cannot"	"Has begun,"etc.	"Can"	*N*
6–8	1	12	27	74	114
5	1	21	35	52	109
1–4	3	30	37	43	113
No note	14	20	20	7	61
Total	19	83	119	176	397

A total of about three-quarters of the population were given reading marks ('began," etc., or "can'). Reading and Catechism knowledge are highly correlated. Most of those who got a high score in memorization also had high reading marks. The reverse is, on the other hand, not equally clear. The highest score in reading is not necessarily an indication of the highest degree of Catechism knowledge. This illustrates the previously mentioned order of learning. Reading was supposed to precede memorization.

This observation is even more obvious for those who have no marks. Nineteen persons have no reading marks, and for 61 persons there are no notes for Catechism knowledge. Of these, 14 persons have no marks whatsoever. They have perhaps never been examined at all, since 5 of them are six-year-old children, whereas 4 of them are over sixty years of age. Only one of the two marks is missing for 52 persons. And 47 of these were examined in reading, but not in memorization. The reverse applies only to 5 persons. This is also a proof of the high priority given to reading instruction. The fact that several persons were given the mark "*cannot* read" does not contradict this. Quite the contrary. Reading from a book was given most attention and emphasis at the examinations. This was the typical situation of teaching and examination just before the break-through of reading in a parish. It becomes clearer when the two marks are divided according to age. Twelve persons are omitted from this and the following tables, since there is no information concerning their age (Table 9.2).

All the dramatic events in a newly started reading campaign are depicted in the table. It is clear from the column for "cannot" that nearly half of the oldest cannot read, and one-fifth of the middle generation cannot read, whereas almost no one in the youngest group is illiterate. The learning process in itself is indicated in the next column, "has begun," etc. Most of the youngest are in the midst of the process of learning to read. On the other hand, the time for learning has passed for the oldest ones. They either lack ("*cannot* read") or possess reading ability ("*can* read"). Their results may, nevertheless, give us an idea of the preliminary stages in the reading campaign. Knowing how

Table 9.2. Reading marks in Tuna, 1688–91, related to age. Percentage figures ($N = 385$)

			Reading marks			
			"Has begun,"			
Age	No note	"Cannot"	etc.	"Can"	Total	N
>60	9	43	7	41	100	(42)
51–60	0	47	13	41	100	(32)
41–50	5	35	20	40	100	(40)
31–40	0	21	37	42	100	(43)
26–30	3	20	31	46	100	(39)
21–25	2	13	22	63	100	(59)
16–20	3	16	26	55	100	(38)
11–15	2	2	46	50	100	(50)
<11	12	5	62	21	100	(42)
Total	5	21	30	44	100	(385)

little reading ability changes at a mature age, the oldest persons provide an indication of the number of people who were able to read, e.g., a quarter of a century ago. That is, they represent reading ability in the 1660s, which at that time would have been approximately 40 per cent and would thus have increased in the 1690s to over 70 per cent. The youngest children have not been included. Such a calculation also illustrates the dramatic change to a purposeful campaign for reading ability. The picture becomes even clearer when the material shows how the earlier Catechism memorization is outdistanced by reading. A division of Catechism knowledge according to age will, however, be presented first (Table 9.3).

Table 9.3. Catechism knowledge in Tuna, 1688–91, related to age. Percentage figures ($N = 385$)

				Number of parts of the Catechism					
Age	No note	1	2	3	4	5	6	7–8	Total %	N
>60	24	0	7	7	7	29	26	0	100	(42)
51–60	6	6	0	16	9	41	22	0	100	(32)
41–50	8	3	15	8	5	30	33	0	100	(40)
31–40	12	2	0	9	7	28	42	0	100	(43)
26–30	13	5	13	8	10	33	15	3	100	(39)
21–25	10	5	10	3	12	27	30	2	100	(59)
16–20	8	0	8	16	8	24	37	0	100	(38)
11–15	4	8	14	6	14	22	30	2	100	(50)
<11	48	5	2	0	5	21	19	0	100	(42)
Total %	15	4	8	7	9	27	28	1	100	(385)

It is conspicuous how evenly the Catechism items are distributed over the age groups, apart from the youngest who, so far, have not shown a very large amount of knowledge. For half of the youngest there is no note at all. The same is true of one-quarter of the oldest persons. The table gives an impression of stagnation. This shows how far the old education standard had reached with mainly oral instruction and memorization. Only three persons (1%) have gone beyond the old standard of Luther's explanations. These three belong, typically enough, to the younger generation. More people are waiting to learn all the articles of the Catechism. Some of the ten columns, drawn up in the examination register (Figure 9.4), are waiting to be filled in. But this requires a more widespread and more widely used reading ability. This process has begun, as becomes quite clear when reading marks and Catechism knowledge are put together in age groups (Table 9.4).

Table 9.4. Reading marks and Catechism knowledge in Tuna, 1688–91, related to age. Percentage figures (N = 385)

Age	No note in Catechism knowledge		Catechism knowledge		Total %	N
	Not able to read	Able to read	Not able to read	Able to read		
>40	11	2	36	51	100	(114)
16–40	6	4	13	77	100	(179)
11–15	2	2	2	94	100	(50)
<11	17	31	0	52	100	(42)
Total %	8	6	17	69	100	(385)

Here, too, the older and the younger differ a lot from each other. Among the oldest, both those who are able to read and those who are not able to read have marks in Catechism knowledge. If one examines the number of Catechism items one will, however, discover a difference in that those who are able to read among the oldest persons also have a more extensive knowledge of the Catechism. For example, in the age group 41 years and older, 32 persons got the highest Catechism score, i.e., a note for 6 items. Three-quarters of these 32 persons are also able to read. Those having marks in both reading and Catechism in the age range 16–40 are as many as 77 per cent. In the second youngest age group they are as many as 94 per cent. The children, 6–11 years, finally, once more illustrate the progressive educational campaign. Nobody obtained marks in memorization first, whereas 31 per cent have, on the other hand, obtained marks in reading first. A more detailed table strengthens these impressions (Table 9.5). Five out of the eleven children in the 6–7 age group got marks neither for reading nor for the Catechism. They are here, just as in Table 9.4, regarded as not able to read. The sequence of learning is here clearly illustrated. It passes from "has begun" reading to catechetical knowledge; one cannot come to the latter without the former.

Table 9.5. Reading marks and Catechism knowledge in Tuna, 1688–91, related to ages 6–13 (N = 68)

Age	Reading marks				
	"Cannot" No notes in Catechism	"Has begun" No notes in Catechism	"Has begun" 1–8 items in Catechism	"Can" 1–8 items in Catechism	Total N
12–13	0	0	8	12	20
10–11	2	3	9	8	22
8–9	1	5	7	2	15
6–7	5	5	1	0	11
Total	8	13	25	22	68

A typical feature of the patterns of analysis has, thus, been found in the material for Tuna. The sudden advent of the reading campaign is seen in the educational gaps between the older and the younger generations. Another typical feature is that differences between the sexes, for example, become less obvious. The reading mark "can" was obtained by 54 per cent of the men over 50 and by 33 per cent of the women. The corresponding percentage figures for the youngest, 20 years and younger, are 44 and 41 per cent respectively. A levelling-out is in progress. Women often have higher scores than men later on in the eighteenth and nineteenth centuries.

The increasing number of women who were able to read directs our thoughts to home instruction as it is depicted in literature and art, with either the mother or the father instructing the children in the home. To what extent did the children in Tuna have literate homes as early as the 1690s? A sample in the third and fourth examination district provides an answer to this question. Out of 16 families with children who were 16 years old and younger there is only one family where both the parents are illiterate. Both parents are able to read in 10 families. It is hardly possible to discover any difference in the children's standard of reading, since this is more likely due to age, as has already been indicated. The newly started reading campaign is thus further confirmed. It was possible to fulfill the demands placed on all the younger people to learn and use the printed word, provided that the required pedagogic measures were taken.

Reading ability in Tuna was tested primarily with the aid of the first pattern of analysis, starting from purposeful educational measures. The development of reading is characterized by obvious differences in grades between the generations. It also appeared in its pedagogic aspect with, principally for the children, an intensified learning-to-read stage preceding Catechism knowledge.

The second model of analysis with differences in environment, e.g., between families, has already been suggested. A knowledge of the letters of the alphabet, however easy it may be to acquire, does not spread spontaneously within a given environment. The generation gaps and the differences between the sexes among the older people also suggest this. Instruction and learning had to be provided, though not necessarily at great cost and in large quantities, but to a sufficient degree to make the basic skills of reading functional in an environment which was becoming more and more literate.

Systematic studies of the reading campaign

The Church examination registers provide an enormous field for research. The research has, however, in spite of many sporadic efforts, not obtained a firm grasp of these sources with regard to their contents and usefulness for the judgement of the distribution of reading ability. The development of methods has taken two directions within the project. The first is an integrated system of information, keeping together the total amount of information in the Church archives of a certain parish over a long period of time. This method has been adopted and fulfilled in the interdisciplinary project *Demografisk Databas* (Demographic Database).[20] The other method that has been developed within the project aims at structuring and organizing the varied notes on reading ability and Catechism knowledge in the examination registers.

The distribution of reading ability is seen as a centrally directed campaign. On the basis of this, certain hypotheses are made, in their turn leading to a defined methodology for the use of the sources. The contents of the examination register for Tuna were described in detail in the preceding section. It was, among other things, stressed that the age distribution of literacy is an important indicator of the pace of change. Change can, thus, best be seen through a comparison *between* the generations. All the youngest become literate. Many of the oldest remain illiterate. But as the older people die away, there are a growing number of literate persons in a population. Earlier differences in reading ability between the sexes, between different social groups, between town and country, between various regions, etc., also at the same time become less pronounced. The earlier characteristics of reading ability in the West thus disappear. This reading ability used to be very low and was largely preserved by the immediate economic and cultural needs of the community.

Two different patterns of analysis thus become evident. In the first one, the age distribution is decisive for the analysis. The generation gaps will be the most expressive factor. The social gaps provide the explanations in the second pattern. It is, nevertheless, of vital importance to take both patterns of analysis into consideration in every examination. They always complement each other. They are, of course, equally valid for the studies of the educational explosions of today.

These observations lead to the hypothesis that the reading marks in the examination registers in their initial stage are primarily to be correlated with the year of birth. This leads to a very simple methodology. The marks are distributed on birth cohorts, irrespective of when the examinations were carried out. This means that the same "generations" can be compared in different registers and between different parishes. The methodology will consequently also allow a certain amount of prediction of the past and the future on the basis of the time for a certain examination.

The methodology can be illustrated with the results from some preliminary studies. Table 9.6 presents reading ability in Tuna, Möklinta, and Skellefteå c. 1700. The years of birth for Möklinta are given in the examination register. The indications of age have, for Tuna and Skellefteå, been converted into years of birth. The total number of people who could read in the three parishes was, according to the registers, somewhere between 66 and 85 per cent. The results will, if distributed by decades of birth, show a great degree of similarity. Generation gaps can be discerned, with marked leaps in the process. A graph illustration (Figure 9.5) is even more explicit. The time axis indicates the measurements and the time of birth for the individuals. The curves represent a projection for every cohort back to its decade of birth. There is a great degree of similarity between the three parishes. The difference in time between the first and last measurement is still as great as thirty years. The advantage of this methodology is obvious. It will now be possible to make comparisons between various times and areas.

The methodology can be taken even further if there are results for several measurements in the same parish. Age, for example, is indicated in the Catechism registers for 1702, 1731, and 1740 for Skanör. The total number of persons able to read increases during this time from 58 to 92 per cent. The difference in 1702, with 67 per cent for the men and 49 per cent for the women, has been completely levelled out by 1740. The women have, by this time, even out-distanced the men to a certain degree with 93 per cent of the women and 91 per cent of the men literate respectively.

The result, however, becomes even more remarkable when reading ability in Skanör is projected back and forth in time on the basis of the different measurements. In Figure 9.6 the three results for 1702, 1731, and 1740 are related back in time to the respective periods of birth, and also between the

Table 9.6. Reading ability in Tuna, 1691, in Möklinta, 1705, and in Skellefteå, 1724, related to year of birth. Percentage figures (N = 385, 1,410, and 1,489 respectively)

	Reading ability		
	Tuna 1691	Möklinta 1705	Skellefteå 1724
Year of birth	%	%	%
–1619	—	21	—
1620–29	48	27	—
1630–39	54	36	—
1640–49	60	53	48
1650–59	79	61	58
1660–69	81	65	69
1670–79	90	80	79
1680–89	83	89	86
1690–99	—	89	92
1700–10	—	—	97
Total	74	66	85

Source: The Church examination registers.

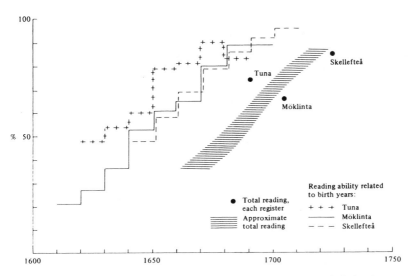

Figure 9.5. Reading ability in Tuna in 1691, in Möklinta in 1705, and in Skellefteå in 1724 according to the Church examination registers. In total (74, 66, and 85 per cent, respectively) and related to date of birth. Percentage figures. (See also Table 9.6.)

measurement dates, to composite age groups common to all three. The total increase in reading ability is drawn as a line between the measurements. The slope of the line corresponds to the retrograde projection of reading ability distributed on birth cohorts. Such a projection anticipates apparently fairly well the total reading ability some thirty years later. The simple conclusion is of course that the total reading ability of a population at a certain time is represented by the reading ability of the middle generation. This obvious rule of thumb is just as useful for the ample census material of later times for reading ability. The intensity of the education of older people must of course also be observed, since it can affect the validity of the rule.

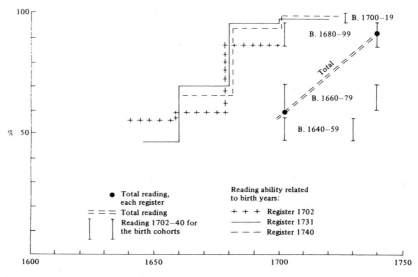

Figure 9.6. Reading ability in Skanör in 1702, in 1731, and in 1740 according to the Catechism registers. In total (58, 81, and 92 per cent, respectively) and related to date of birth. Percentage figures.

Another confirmation of the usefulness of the method is finally given in a projection of reading ability for the birth cohorts in Tuna, Möklinta, and Skellefteå. The shaded area in Figure 9.5 indicates such a projection. In other words, it indicates the total growth of reading ability in the three parishes.

Such projections of birth cohorts need not of course be used when there is a fairly long series of measurements for the same parish. This is, however, not often the case because of gaps in the material. The methodology described above is then a useful complement. It is being tried out on a sample of parishes and examination registers for the whole country.

The reading campaign in the Dioceses Västerås and Visby: Part results for a sample of parishes from the whole country

The hypotheses and the methodology presented above have created opportunities for decisive research work on the hitherto completely confusing material of the Church examination registers. The project has been awarded grants which have made it possible to plan and carry out a systematic study of a random sample of examination registers from parishes over the whole country. The parishes in every deanery have been arranged and numbered according to the deanery tables of 1805. One or two parishes for every deanery have then been selected with the aid of a table of random numbers. A division has been made into town and country parishes. Only the country parishes have been worked on so far; this is also where 90 per cent of the population lived up to the middle of the nineteenth century.

Because of the differences between the dioceses, the sample was processed diocese by diocese. The result for the diocese of Västerås will be our first example (Figure 9.7). The fifteen deaneries in the diocese of Västerås are each represented by a parish chosen at random. The earliest register with both reading marks and information about age has been studied for every parish. There is, unfortunately, information about age in only six of the parishes before 1750, but after 1750 the number of measurements increase. In seven parishes the first useful registers have been checked against later registers. This means that a total of 23 examinations can be presented. The sources of error are, of course, numerous. There are, for example, some obscurities in a number of registers. That is why the doubling of some registers mentioned above has served as a check-up. Great pains have been taken to avoid the same persons appearing several times at any one measurement. That is why, if possible, only the last examination in every register has been studied.

Since some parishes in the diocese of Västerås were very densely populated, a sample of persons has been made within the registers. This, too, has been made at random. The total population will, of course, be brought into the final report. The result for the diocese of Västerås seems to be unambiguous. Both the notes for separate examinations and a projection of the birth cohorts by two or three decades illustrate a very distinct reading campaign *c.* 1670–1720. The conclusions are verified in many ways; e.g., by the contemporary examination documents and by biographical data. They have also been verified in literature.[21]

There are also results for the diocese of Visby, although the examination registers studied for this diocese are much more recent—from 1750 onwards. The result is, nevertheless, comparable to the result for Västerås. All examination registers in the selection show a total reading ability of more than 80

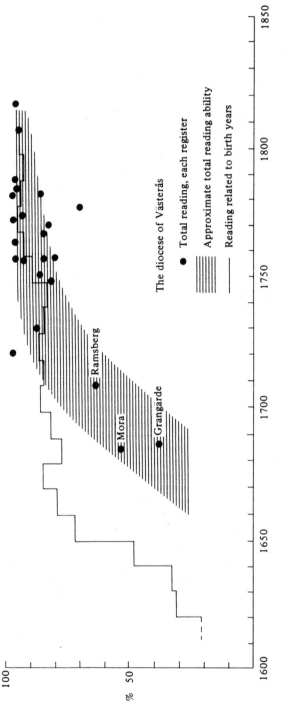

Figure 9.7. Reading ability in the diocese of Västerås according to the Church examination registers in a random sample of parishes. In total and related to time of birth. The population is about 15 years of age and older. Sample: 15 parishes, 23 church examination registers. Percentage figures ($N = 4,371$).

per cent. A retrograde projection of birth cohorts also indicates a high degree of similarity with the diocese of Västerås. The conclusion is that the actual reading campaign took place before 1750 in Gotland as well, which can also be tested on some registers from the beginning of the eighteenth century. These registers do not appear in the sample for the diocese of Visby.

These preliminary conclusions must now be tested and tried out for other dioceses as well. But at least they demonstrate the suitability of the programme by means of a sample for the whole country. The results must, of course, also be combined with other contemporary source material. They must also be compared to other relevant research results, e.g. in literature and in anthropology. The quality of the reading acquired as a result of the Swedish literacy program must also be studied. Later in the program, when the reading ability acquired in the initial campaign was to be consolidated, and deepened, in the population, the quality of reading came to be the subject of detailed markings in the examination records.

Summary of the spread of literacy in Sweden

The project has so far presented a general survey of the spread of literacy in Sweden. This can be visualized by means of a figure (Figure 9.8). The shaded areas indicate hypotheses about literacy. The hypotheses concerning reading are primarily based on the Church examination registers. The hypotheses for writing are based on school statistics and on the information concerning literacy of convicts and army recruits, and the census of 1930. These sources also verify the big difference between reading and writing till well into the nineteenth century.

This difference is, in reality, very important. It must be regarded as an established fact that general reading was achieved without formal school attendance. Swedish home instruction was so successful that those who only received home instruction were, in reality, regarded as able to read in the official statistics. This cannot be explained without returning to the rigorously controlled reading campaign, which started two centuries earlier.

The final stage of home instruction can easily be tested even today. Old people can tell you about parents and relatives who almost certainly could read printed letters but, on the other hand, could not write more than possibly their own names. These people had, as a rule, never attended school. Such "illiterates" also exist in literature, e.g. Ida, the wife of *Raskens* in the novel by Vilhelm Moberg of the same name, or the father of Ivar Lo-Johansson, "Analfabeten" (*The Illiterate*).

If this difference between reading and writing in Sweden is accepted, it will facilitate the use of the Swedish material when comparisons are being made with other countries.

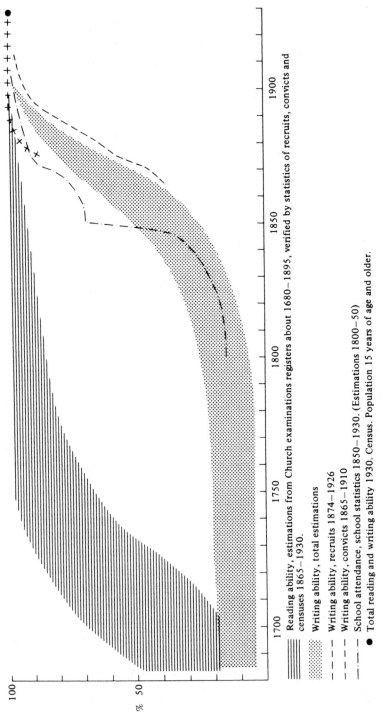

Figure 9.8. Reading and writing traditions in Sweden, about 1680–1930. Preliminary results of current research. Population about 10–15 years of age and older. Schoolchildren about 6–15 years of age. Percentage figures.

Reading ability, estimations from Church examinations registers about 1680–1895, verified by statistics of recruits, convicts and censuses 1865–1930.

Writing ability, total estimations

– – – Writing ability, recruits 1874–1926

– – – Writing ability, convicts 1865–1910

–·–·– School attendance, school statistics 1850–1930. (Estimations 1800–50)

● Total reading and writing ability 1930. Census. Population 15 years of age and older.

Some conclusions

The history of Swedish literacy provides some experiences that can also be applied to the problems of the current literacy debate.

1. The two patterns of analysis have been quite useful. The first evaluates strictly controlled mass campaigns with a political or an ideological background designed at a rapid pace and increase to bring about widespread literacy. According to the second pattern of analysis permanent differences are observed between sexes, occupational groups, town and country, etc., which reveal that economic needs are what primarily direct the events.

2. But this also contradicts the modern opinion that literacy is primarily (and solely) part of the so-called modernization process, where industrialization, urbanization, political participation, etc., make up the inevitable framework. To accept an early reading tradition in a pre-industrial, agrarian, developing country like Sweden is an important contribution towards dissolving some of the most difficult problems in this formula for Western modernization.

3. This formula also states that reading and writing always follow each other closely. The acceptance of the Swedish and Finnish material will release the literacy debate from one of its most difficult positions. A modified literacy concept must then be taken seriously with revaluations of functioning semi-literate environments.

4. This early reading tradition in Sweden also strongly emphasizes the importance of engaging the whole population in the literacy process. An informal learning process where everyone helps everyone else is cheap and provides effective co-operation between home and school, where the home and the family provide the primary educational context.

5. The Swedish material also stresses the importance of the political will for the literacy campaign. This was also strongly emphasized, e.g., in the Declaration of the Persepolis Literacy Conference in 1975.

6. Warnings were also issued in Persepolis against the so-called postliterate problem in the West. The gravity of these warnings has made itself felt in Sweden, too. A modern society does not spontaneously maintain literacy at the highest level. New directions for emphasizing the basic skills of reading and writing must be issued in the schools.

7. Finally, the Swedish tradition illustrates the fact that the ability to read must not be an end in itself. "To read the word or to read the world" was a striking theme in Persepolis. Everything was, in the Swedish tradition, concentrated on comprehending, understanding, and putting the word into practice in everyday life. Reading was not to be an end in itself; it was instead a question of experiencing the total environment of life and society. "To read the world of the Word" could be the surviving message of the old Swedish reading tradition.[22]

Notes

1. *Aperçu de la Démographie des divers Pays du Monde 1929–1936* (The Hague, 1939), 28.

2. UNESCO, *Progress of Literacy in Various Countries* (Paris, 1953), 88.

3. UNESCO, *World Illiteracy at Mid-Century* (Paris, 1957), 29.

4. Carlo Cipolla, *Literacy and Development in the West* (London, 1969), 61.

5. For Swedish progress see *Svenska folkskoland historia* (History of the Swedish elementary school), 1–3 (Stockholm, 1940–42), W. Sjöstrand, *Pedagogikens 2–3*: 2 (History of education) (Lund, 1958–63); C. I. Sandström, *Utbildnigens idéhistoria* (History of the ideology of education) (Stockholm, 1975); and for older literature, see references in Egil Johansson, *En studie med kvantitativa metoder av folkundervisningen i Bygdeå socken 1845–1873* (Study with quantitative methods of popular education in the parish of Bygdeå, 1845–1873) (Umeå, 1972).

6. Johansson, *En studie*, 76–80. The "Hustavla" (a religious plaque which was hung on the wall) was a supplement to Luther's *Small Catechism*. It consisted of specific Bible verses arranged according to the traditional, Lutheran doctrine of a three-stage, social hierarchy—*ecclesia* (church), *politia* (state), and *oeconomia* (home or household). These selections of Scripture outlined the Christian duties and obligations which each stage in this hierarchy owed to the others—i.e., priests/parishioners (teachers/pupils), rulers/subjects, heads of families (parents)/children and household servants.

7. H. Pleijel, *Husandakt, husaga, husförhor* (Family prayers, caning, and church examinations) (Stockholm, 1965), and references in this work.

8. For the conflict regarding Consistorium generale in the seventeenth century, see e.g. Y. Brilioth, *Svensk kyrkokunskap* (Knowledge of the Swedish Church) (Uppsala, 1946), 96.

9. For family prayers, home instruction, and caning, see Pleijel, *Husandakt*.

10. O. Isaksson, *Bystämma och bystadga* (Village council and village laws) (Uppsala, 1967), 252ff.

11. R. Gullstrand, *Socknarnas självstyrelse i historick belysning* (The autonomy of the parishes in a historical perspective) (Stockholm, 1933).

12. E. Alexanderson, *Bondeståndet i riksdagen 1760–1772* (The farmers in the Swedish Riksdag 1760–1772) (Lund, 1975), 41–46.

13. Pleijel, B. Olsson, and S. Svensson, *Våra äldsta folkbocker* (Our oldest population registers) (Lund, 1967).

14. B. Widén, "Literacy in the Ecclesiastical Context," in E. Johansson (ed.), *Literacy and Society in a Historical Perspective: A Conference Report*, Educational report no. 2, Pedagogiska Institutionen, Umeå Universitet (Department of education, University of Umeå), 1973, 38.

15. Johansson, *En studie*, 80–81, Royal Decree of 1723.

16. Each of the five articles in the Small Catechism is introduced with the words "huru man må det ungt folk enfaldeligen förehålla" (how easily to explain it to young people).

17. J. Naeslund, *Metoden vid den första läsundervisningen* (learning-to-read instruction) (Umeå, 1956), 20ff.; I. Wilke, *ABC-bücher in Schweden* (Stockholm, 1965).

18. R. Wagnsson, *ABC. Var folkundervisning från medeltid till enhetsskola* (ABC. Our popular education from the middle ages to the comprehensive school) (Malmö, 1955), 33, 49, 66.

19. E. Nygren, "Våra kyrkoarkiv" (Our church archives), *Tidskrift för det svenska folkbildningsarbetet* (The journal of Swedish popular education) 1922, 15–36, A. Sandberg, *Linköpings stifts kyrkoarkzvalier* (The Church archives for the diocese of Linköping) (Lund, 1948), and R. Swedlund, *Kyrkarkiven i länsarkivet i Österund* (The Church archives in the County archives of Österund) (Lund, 1939).

20. E. Johansson and S. Åkerman, *Demografisk Databas* (Demographic database) (1973): The material for Fleninge (1975), the material for Svinnegarn (1976).

21. S. Rönnegård and U. Lundberg, *Folkundervisningen i Leksand och Forshem* (Popular education in Leksand and Forshem). *ÅSU* (Annual reports of the history of Swedish education), vol. 115 (Falun, 1966), 11.

22. The complete report can be ordered from the author, Umeå University, S-901 87 Umeå, Sweden. New publications in English on the reading tradition in Sweden are forthcoming.

10 GROWTH OF LITERACY IN COLONIAL AMERICA: LONGITUDINAL PATTERNS, ECONOMIC MODELS, AND THE DIRECTION OF FUTURE RESEARCH

Farley Grubb

Literacy underwent revolutionary growth in northwestern Europe during the seventeenth and eighteenth centuries. This revolution coincided with other dramatic changes in European society, such as the industrial, demographic, agricultural, political, and religious revolutions (Deane 1969: 20–84). While the relationships between literacy and these other revolutions are not fully understood, their association is apparent, and many potential influences exist (Cipolla 1969; Cremin 1970; Graff 1981: 232–60; 1987a, 1987b; Jensen 1986: 114–28; Maynes 1985: 117–31; Mitch 1984, 1988; Sanderson 1983; West 1978). The transplantation of European society across the Atlantic brought the literacy revolution to the American periphery. While numerous studies have shown that colonial America participated in this expansion of literacy, the common longitudinal patterns of literacy growth across the various regions and populations of colonial America have received less attention.[1]

The accumulation of literacy studies over the last 30 years has made possible the examination of common patterns of growth in colonial literacy, as well as systematic comparisons with European literacy. The evidence from these studies is organized here to investigate regional similarities in the growth paths of colonial literacy and to explain how conditions and constraints peculiar to colonial America altered these growth paths from that of northwestern Europe. In particular, the evidence is used to explore the general pattern of temporary declines in colonial literacy which followed initial European settlement, a pattern called here "creolean degeneracy."

Implicit economic models have been frequently used to explain the growth in literacy. However, a consensus on the dominant explanation for the growth of colonial literacy has not emerged. These implicit models are made explicit here and used to analyze the common patterns of growth in colonial literacy, in particular the nonlinear pattern of creolean degeneracy found in the evidence. By making the models explicit, the implications of alternative economic explanations are made apparent. These explicit models are used to suggest directions for future research on colonial literacy that may resolve the debate over competing causes of the peculiar growth paths of colonial literacy, including the creolean degeneracy in literacy.

Literacy estimates

Numerous studies have measured literacy in selected areas of colonial America and Europe during the seventeenth and eighteenth centuries. The usual method of quantifying literacy is to measure the percentage of people in a population who could sign their names. Signature literacy is the only universal, standard, and direct measure available for the colonial period which provides a substantial quantity of evidence. Although a dichotomous measure, the ability to affix a signature is believed to correspond to a middle range of literacy skills or roughly to the ability to read fluently (Craig 1981; Cressy 1980: 1–19, 42–62; Lockridge 1974: 7; Schofield 1968; Soltow and Stevens 1981: 3–6).[2]

Tables 10.1 and 10.2 present the evidence from these studies for adult male literacy, organized by country or colony, time period, and urban versus rural location.[3] Because different sources of evidence possess different potential biases and because sample sizes vary, comparisons of the patterns of literacy across these studies cannot be exact. For example, signature evidence gathered from wills, deeds, petitions, or jury lists is thought to overstate a population's literacy, possibly by different degrees.[4] However, the similarity of the evidence among the colonial studies, particularly over the growth paths of individual colonial subregions, suggests that comparing the longitudinal patterns across colonial regions may be done with some confidence. If the cross-sectional biases are relatively constant over time, then the longitudinal pattern will be relatively unbiased; that is, the slope and change in slope of the estimated pattern over time will be the same as the true underlying pattern in the population.

Given the above caveats, several observations can be made about the common patterns of literacy growth. First, differences in urban versus rural literacy were significant throughout Europe and the colonies. Urban areas were systematically more literate, though rural areas were beginning to close the literacy gap by the end of the eighteenth century. The differential was 10 to 25 percentage points. A positive correlation between population density and literacy has been noted or measured in other studies (Graff 1987a, 1987b; Lockridge 1974; Soltow and Stevens 1981).

Table 10.1. Studies of colonial adult male literacy, 1650–1840

Location, years	Percentage literate	Sample size	Evidence source
I. RURAL AREAS			
New England			
1650–70	55.0	500	wills
1705–15	64.0	750	wills
1758–62	78.0	1,000	wills
1799–1829	75.0	395	army enlistees
Windsor Dist., NH			
1755–1830	91.3	10,289	all records
Pennsylvania			
Chester County			
1729–44	74.3	253	wills
1745–54	72.6	285	wills
1755–64	69.4	288	wills
1765–74	73.4	338	wills
1840	>99.0	57,515	census
Lancaster County			
1729–44	63.4	93	wills
1745–54	60.1	168	wills
1755–64	64.6	260	wills
1765–74	63.4	388	wills
1729–64	60.0	80	wills in German
1765–74	66.3	95	wills in German
New York, New Jersey, Pennsylvania			
1799–1829	60.0	574	army enlistees
Maryland			
Baltimore County			
1768	80.0	2,030	petitions
Virginia			
1600s	54.0	2,165	jury lists
1600s	60.0	12,445	deeds, depositions
1705–62	66.0	467	wills
1762–67	68.0	648	wills
North Carolina			
Perquimans County			
1661–95	67.0	51	deeds
1696–1721	57.0	187	deeds
1722–47	64.0	306	deeds
1748–76	79.0	435	deeds
South Carolina			
1729–65	80.0	—	deeds, wills

II. URBAN AREAS

New England

Boston

1650–70	77.0	100	wills
1705–10	74.0	200	wills
1758–62	82.0	150	wills

Grafton

1747	93.0	95	all records

New York

New York City (Dutch)

1675–98	74.8	254	all records
1706–38	92.6	95	all records

New York City

1699–1703	90.9	44	wills
1701–2	83.7	766	petitions
1760–75	87.3	110	wills

Albany

1654–1775	79.0	360	—

Pennsylvania

Philadelphia

1699–1706	80.0	40	wills
1773–75	81.6	98	wills
1798–1840	72.0	930	merchant seamen

Virginia

Elizabeth City

1693–99	75.0	190	deeds, depositions
1763–71	91.0	177	all records

III. POINT OF ENTRY (immigrants)

English servants

1683–84	41.2	590	contract register
1718–59	70.3	2,693	contract register

German immigrants

Radical Protestants

1727–45	71.3	334	loyalty oaths

Other Protestants

1727–45	63.4	6,600	loyalty oaths
1746–56	72.1	12,525	loyalty oaths
1761–75	80.0	4,536	loyalty oaths

French immigrants

1632–63	62.2	—	—
1680–99	44.1	—	marriage register

Sources: Beales 1978: 98; Cremin 1970: 533–43; Gallman 1988: 574; Galenson 1979: 79; Gilmore 1989: 120; Grubb 1987; Jensen 1986: 225; Kilpatrick 1912: 197, 228–29; Lockridge 1974: 24, 77; Moogk 1989: 467; Soltow and Stevens 1981: 37–38, 50–52; Strassburger 1934; Tully 1972: 304.

Notes: Radical German Protestants were ships with Dunkers, Schwenkfelders, and Moravians present. Other German Protestants were Lutheran and Dutch Reformed. The German immigrant evidence is for Pennsylvania arrivals, and the French immigrant evidence is for Canadian arrivals.

Table 10.2. Studies of European adult male literacy, 1633–1840

Location, years	Percentage literate	Sample size	Evidence source
I. COUNTRIES			
England			
1641–42	30	9,428	loyalty oaths
Suffolk County			
1696	47	10,056	loyalty oaths
1754–1800	62	—	marriage register
Nine parishes			
1754–79	57	1,896	marriage register
1780–1809	57	2,543	marriage register
1810–40	58	4,596	marriage register
Scotland			
1638–43	36	5,897	loyalty oaths
1650–60	44	152	Depositions
1690–1710	76	952	Depositions
1740–50	78	233	Depositions
1800	90	—	—
Rural France			
1686–90	19	—	marriage register
1740–59	36	—	marriage register
1760–89	42	—	marriage register
1790–1809	45	—	marriage register
Continental Europe			
Protestant			
1700	40–45	—	—
Catholic			
1700	20–30	—	—
East Prussia			
1750	10	—	—
1765	25	—	—
1800	40	—	—
Rural Belgium			
1778–92	60		
Sweden and Finland			
1800	80	—	—
Italian Piedmont			
1800	45	—	—
Netherlands			
1800	70	—	—
Geneva countryside			
1800	60	—	marriage register

Germanic areas			
1800	55–60	—	—
Castile, Spain			
1800	10–15	—	—
II. TOWNS AND CITIES			
England			
Norwich			
1633–37	44	494	Wills
London			
1641–44	78	609	loyalty oaths
Chester, Bridgewater			
1642	50	1,728	loyalty oaths
Seven towns			
1754–62	67	—	marriage register
1799–1804	70	—	marriage register
Netherlands			
Amsterdam			
1630	57	—	marriage register
1680	70	—	marriage register
1730	76	—	marriage register
1780	85	—	marriage register
Urban France			
1740–59	59	—	marriage register
1760–89	66	—	marriage register
1790–1809	73	—	marriage register
Germany			
Schriesheim			
1800	80	—	Bürger list
Koblenz			
1800	86	—	marriage register
Geneva			
1800	90	—	marriage register
Brussels			
1820	57	—	—

Sources: Cipolla 1969: 20–22, 61–64; Craig 1981: 170; Cressy 1980: 72–74, 100–107, 181; Gawthrop and Strauss 1984: 53; Graff 1987b: 195, 223; Houston 1982: 86–90; Maynes 1985: 15–18, 126; Schofield 1973: 445; 1989; Stone 1969: 100–104.

Notes: The French estimates are averages for 76 departments. In the English estimates, the reconstituted nine parishes were Ash, Austrey, Bottesford, Bridford, Dawlish, Gedling, Morchard Bishop, Odiham, and Shepshed, and the seven towns were an unweighted average of the estimates for Penzance, Oxford, Northampton, Nottingham, King's Lynn, Bristol, and Halifax.

Second, the level of literacy was higher in the colonies than in Europe.[5] Of all European countries perhaps only Scotland surpassed America in literacy by 1800. Not only had the European literacy revolution been transplanted to the American periphery during the colonial period, but colonial literacy had somehow leaped past that of northwestern Europe. Not only was the United States born wealthy (Jones 1980), it was born literate. Nevertheless, while the levels of colonial literacy were relatively high, the long-run trend appears to be slightly steeper in northwestern Europe, both in urban and rural areas. European literacy was catching up to American literacy by the nineteenth century.

Finally, while literacy levels did vary across the colonies, high levels of literacy were distributed much more evenly across the colonies than across Europe. High levels of literacy in the colonies were not confined to New England, nor were they just a product of Puritan motives or produced selectively by New England schooling legislation (Graff 1987b: 163–72, 249–57; Lockridge 1974: 72–101). Nor were they confined to English-speaking populations, as can be seen from the Pennsylvania German evidence. The levels and patterns of growth in literacy were similar across the rural areas of New England, Pennsylvania, Virginia, and North Carolina and similar across the urban areas of Boston, New York, Philadelphia, and Elizabeth City, Virginia. Mass literacy (defined here as over 70% literate) was achieved early in urban areas and increased little through the eighteenth century. Literacy in rural areas increased until mass literacy was achieved by the middle of the eighteenth century.

Causes of high initial levels of colonial literacy

What caused the high initial level and long-run growth of colonial literacy is still a matter of debate. There are two potential sources of high colonial literacy: above-average literacy of immigrants and above-average transmission of literacy to American-born colonists. Most literacy studies do not distinguish between European and American-born colonists, and there are no studies which measure literacy only for the latter. How the education of American-born colonists influenced overall colonial literacy has not been disentangled from the influence of immigrants on colonial literacy. The history of colonial literacy would be enhanced if future studies distinguished European from American-born colonists in the evidence.

Direct evidence on the literacy of European immigrants suggests that immigration was an important force in shaping colonial literacy patterns. The literacy of three immigrant populations, English indentured servants, German colonists arriving in Pennsylvania, and French-Canadian immigrants, has been measured at the point of entry into the colonies. These immigrant groups were more literate than their European home populations and were comparable in literacy to the colonial populations they entered (see Tables 10.1 and 10.2). English indentured servants went predominantly to the Chesapeake region (Galenson 1981: 220–23). Their 70% literacy rate compares well with the Virginia rate of 68%. German immigrants to Pennsylvania were 70% to 80% literate between 1750 and 1775, whereas German residents of Lancaster County, Pennsylvania, were 66% literate.[6] While limited in coverage, these three studies of immigrant literacy support the view that immigration per se may have been one of the important causes of high initial levels of colonial literacy, because of the disproportionate propensity of literate Europeans to migrate to America (see also Graff 1987a, 1987b: 163, 170, 251; Grubb 1987; Lockridge 1974: 5, 46–48, 74–75, 78, 82, 1981: 190, 193).

Explaining the long-run trend in colonial literacy, however, requires incorporating the relative influence of American-born colonists. Over time, the proportion of American-born in the colonial population rose, and thus the evidence used to measure colonial literacy would be increasingly dominated by the literacy of this group. Variation in the timing and rate of increase in the proportion of American-born in the colonial population might explain regional differences in long-run literacy patterns.

How the literacy of immigrants compared with or influenced that of their American-born offspring is unclear. Few studies measure the extent to which literacy was transmitted from immigrant parents to their American-born children during the seventeenth and eighteenth centuries. The transmission of literacy could occur through two avenues: literate parents could teach their children to read and write, or parents, regardless of their own literacy, could provide their children access to instruction by others, such as at a local church or formal school or at work, through the child's servant or apprentice contract.

Two studies have measured the literacy both of parents and of their children, among German immigrants to Pennsylvania (Grubb 1987: 74) and among families in Shepshed parish, England (Levine 1979). These studies find a positive and statistically significant correlation between the literacy of parents and the literacy of their offspring. However, the correlation is less than 1.[7] Some children of literate parents failed to learn to read and write, and many children of illiterate parents nevertheless learned to read and write. These findings suggest that if the intergenerational transmission of literacy depended solely on literate parents teaching their children to read and write, or if providing instruction outside the family, whether at church, school, or work, became more difficult, as during a migration to the colonial frontier, then the level or growth of literacy in subsequent generations might degenerate.

Measuring the ability to affix a signature or measuring how this ability correlated between parents and their children does not reveal whether that ability was learned at home, at work, at church, or at a formal school. Measuring signature literacy reveals little about the methods available or the methods actually used by parents to transmit literacy to their children. Nor do these measurements reveal whether the social and economic circumstances which enabled parents to acquire literacy were still present when their children were of educable age. In a world where formal schooling was not always available, the transmission of literacy from immigrant parents to their American-born offspring may have been difficult and certainly was less than automatic. The history of colonial literacy would be greatly enhanced if future research were directed towards the quantitative significance of the different mechanisms of literacy transmission.

The nonlinear trend in regional colonial literacy

The long-run growth of colonial literacy was not smooth. Underlying the positive trend were spells of retrogression. In newly settled areas literacy started high. As these areas developed, literacy declined, but it soon recovered and eventually surpassed the initial level. A few scholars have noted creolean degeneracy in literacy for isolated places and times in colonial America (Bailyn 1960: 78–83; Knauss 1918: 74). Typically, some obstacles to literacy transmission from immigrants to subsequent generations of colonists are assumed to have caused temporary declines in literacy. However, this nonlinear pattern has not been seen as a phenomenon affecting all colonial regions, nor has it been systematically measured.[8]

Quantitative evidence of this nonlinear pattern exists for several colonies (see Figure 10.1). Soltow and Stevens (1981: 34–37) found such a pattern between 1640 and 1760 for the regions of Maine, New Hampshire, and Essex County and Hartford County, Massachusetts. Literacy started high, 60% to 70%, then declined by as much as 20 percentage points by 1680, and finally recovered to initial levels by 1710. Because immigration to New England declined precipitously after the middle of the seventeenth century, the decline in literacy may represent some retrogression among American-born New Englanders from the literacy level of their immigrant parents.

Tully (1972) found a nonlinear pattern for the rural counties of Chester and Lancaster, Pennsylvania. Literacy declined by 3 to 5 percentage points between 1729 and midcentury and then recovered to the 1729 level by 1774. Gallman (1988: 574) found a similar pattern for Perquimans County, North Carolina. In the decades after initial colonization, literacy declined by over 10 percentage points. It recovered to initial levels by the middle of the eighteenth century.

Percentage Literate

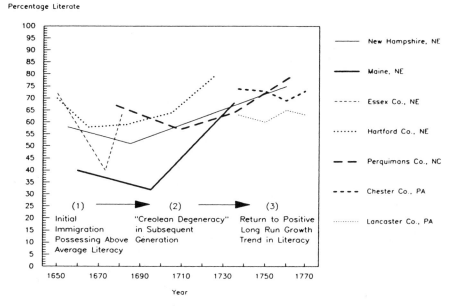

Figure 10.1. Patterns of regional literacy growth in rural colonial America.

Only one study attempts to measure colonial literacy by where literacy was acquired. Kilpatrick (1912: 197) separated the New York City Dutch population between 1675 and 1738 into men who spent their school-age years in Europe and men who spent them in America. In 1675 the American group was 38 percentage points less literate. The literacy differential steadily declined until by 1698 the two groups had similar literacy rates. Kilpatrick's evidence is consistent with the nonlinear patterns in Figure 10.1 and suggests that the cause involves differences in European and American education.

The nonlinear patterns of literacy growth in Figure 10.1 are consistent with the creolean degeneracy hypothesis. Typically, a township, county, or subregion was first settled by European immigrants, but subsequent population growth was dominated by American-born colonists. This pattern of population growth, coupled with the observed decline in literacy after initial settlement, implies that European immigrants failed to transfer their above-average literacy to their American-born children. Therefore, as the share of American-born children in a county's population increased, the average measured literacy of the county's population would temporarily decline before resuming positive long-run growth.

While the quantitative estimates in Figure 10.1 are consistent with the creolean degeneracy hypothesis, they are not conclusive proof of creolean degeneracy. They do not directly measure the literacy of immigrant parents and then compare it with the literacy of their American-born offspring, nor do they show whether literacy was initially acquired in Europe or in the colonies.

A simulation of overlapping generations illustrates that the observed non-linear trend in literacy could be attributed to creolean degeneracy.[9] Suppose the literacy of a county's population is measured at four 30-year intervals, from initial colonization by European immigrants in 1700 until 1790, using signatures on wills. Let each interval represent a new generation who are 30 years of age at the date of measurement, let each new generation be twice the size of the preceding generation, let population growth after initial colonization be only through indigenous increase, and for each generation let a random 25% sign wills at age 30 and the remaining 75% survive to sign wills at age 60. Acquisition of literacy is assumed to be complete by age 30 for each generation. Finally, let European immigrants be 70% literate, first-generation American-born 50% literate, second-generation American-born 70% literate, and third-generation American-born 80% literate. These conditions simulate the relevant features of the evidence (see Figure 10.1), namely, that immigrants were relatively literate, the proportion of American- to European-born in the population rose over time, colonial population density rose over time, and among American-born children literacy rose across generations.

For example, suppose 100 European immigrants who are age 30 and 70% literate arrive in 1700. Of this group, 25% sign wills in 1700, so that the measured literacy of the population in 1700 is 70%. In 1730, 200 first-generation American-born residents, who are age 30 and 50% literate, and 75 European immigrants, who are age 60 and 70% literate, are present. Of this group, 25% of the first generation sign wills and all 75 remaining immigrants sign wills, so that the measured literacy of the population in 1730 is 62%. In 1760, 400 second-generation American-born residents, who are age 30 and 70% literate, and 150 first-generation residents, who are age 60 and 50% literate, are present. Of this group, 25% of the second-generation sign wills and all 150 remaining first-generation sign wills, so that the measured literacy of the population in 1760 is 58%. The same algorithm produces a measured literacy of the population in 1790 of 74%. Thus, literacy follows the nonlinear pattern over time, falling from 70% in 1700 to 62% in 1730, then to 58% in 1760, and finally rising to 74% literate by 1790.[10]

Qualitative evidence from contemporary observers in several colonies is also consistent with the nonlinear pattern of literacy growth and with the creolean degeneracy explanation of that pattern. For example, Bailyn (1960) provided accounts of educational decline on the New England frontier following initial colonization in the late seventeenth century. From this evidence Bailyn concluded that the high cost of schooling on the frontier left the responsibility of transmitting literacy to the family, and the family failed to maintain literacy levels.

Similar accounts can be found for German communities in Pennsylvania for the middle of the eighteenth century. In 1747, Henry M. Muhlenberg (1942, 1:140–41), head of the Lutheran church in Pennsylvania, wrote in his diary:

> I had on several occasions been urged to visit a number of Lutherans who lived in the northwestern mountains 46 miles from my house. The people there are making a poor and precarious living and lack both bodily and spiritual nourishment. Some of them are growing up wild and hence have no further interest in churches and schools. I arranged . . . for a grant of a small tract of land for a church. On this land they were to build a wooden schoolhouse or church and, if in time they became able to support a schoolmaster, the children at least would be given some help.

Gottlieb Mittelberger (1960: 46–47), a German teacher and pastor visiting Pennsylvania between 1750 and 1754, commented:

> In Pennsylvania preachers receive no salary or tithes. Their total income is what they get annually from their church members, and that sum varies a good deal. Schoolteachers are in the same situation. Many hundreds of children, however, are unable to go to school partly because of the extent of forest land they would have to traverse. Thus many planters lead a rather wild and heathenish life. The situation of rural churches and schools is similar. In general, churches and schools are located only in those places where several neighbors or church members live close together.

The problem of educating American-born Germans was also debated in the Pennsylvania German press. For example, Christopher Sauer's *Almanac*, published in Philadelphia in 1752, presented a debate between a new German settler and an old Pennsylvania German inhabitant (reprinted in Weber 1905: 17):

> NEW-COMER: A matter that is of very great importance to me is, that, in Germany, one is able to send his children to school to have them instructed in reading and writing. Here it is well nigh impossible to get such instruction; especially, where people live so far apart. O, how fortunate are they who have access to a good teacher by whom the children are well taught and trained!
>
> INHABITANT: It is true. On that account many children living on our frontiers grow up like trees. But since the conditions are such that few

people live in cities and villages as they do in Germany it is natural that one meets with certain inconveniences. Where is there a place in this world where one does not meet with some objectionable feature during his natural life?

NEW-COMER: But this is an exceptional want, for if children are thus brought up in ignorance it is an injury to their soul's welfare,—an eternal injury.

Muhlenberg, Mittelberger, Sauer, and other members of the German-American immigrant community thought that schooling their offspring was more difficult on the American frontier than obtaining their own schooling was in Europe when they were children. On the American frontier, family instruction was usually the only option for transmitting literacy from parent to child, and it proved inadequate for maintaining literacy levels. Without access to formal schooling, children on the frontier grew up "wild," "like trees." Thus, the American-born offspring of German immigrants were in danger of literacy degeneration.

The quantitative and qualitative evidence which describes regional non-linear trends in colonial literacy is wide-ranging, emerging from many different colonial regions. However, it is also fragmentary, composed of small samples and less than comprehensive in its coverage of colonial regions. The evidence appears to support a nonlinear growth path only in rural areas and not in urban areas. More evidence needs to be gathered to firmly establish the extent and character of these nonlinear literacy patterns. Finally, the current evidence is consistent with but does not conclusively prove creolean degeneracy as the cause of the nonlinear pattern. However, the evidence is strong enough to support creolean degeneracy as a working hypothesis for future research into colonial literacy. The history of colonial literacy would be enhanced if future studies measured these nonlinear patterns and did so in such a way that the location and method of acquiring literacy might be discerned.

A supply versus demand model of colonial growth literacy

The evidence can be used to explore the causes of the nonlinear trend in colonial literacy and to develop models to guide future research. The difference in literacy between rural and urban areas suggests that changes in population density may have influenced literacy trends. European migration to the colonial frontier represented a dramatic change in the surrounding population density and therefore may be an important factor. Differential literacy between immigrants and their American-born children may also be an important factor. The combination of these two influences could produce a nonlinear literacy trend. For example, immigrants may have come from a more densely populated environment, in which the costs and benefits of acquiring literacy differed from what their children experienced on the colonial frontier. These different costs and benefits may have led immigrant parents to transmit a lower level of literacy to their children in America than what they had acquired as children in Europe. If so, colonial literacy started out relatively high because immigrant literacy was high. The failure of immigrant parents to transfer literacy to their American-born offspring temporarily lowered colonial literacy. Finally, as American-born colonists came to dominate the population, measured literacy was dominated by the long-run rise in literacy in subsequent generations.

A positive correlation between population density and literacy has been noted in several studies, but exactly how rising population density causes literacy to increase is less clear (Graff 1987a, 1987b; Lockridge 1974; Soltow and Stevens 1981). Typically, the arguments in the literature have used an implicit supply-and-demand discussion to relate changes in population density to changes in literacy. Literacy is thought of as a market: some individuals demand it and others supply it. Changes in population density shift either the entire demand schedule or the entire supply schedule of literacy, per given cost of acquiring literacy, and thus the quantity of literacy acquired by the population changes.

Whether rising population density leads to higher literacy through a shift in the demand schedule or through a shift in the supply schedule has remained unresolved. The literature has used these economic ideas loosely, without formulating explicit models. Typically, supply and demand shifts are mentioned simultaneously, without much discussion of the possible contradictions or alternative implications of a supply explanation versus a demand explanation.[11] Discovering whether population density works through shifts in supply or in demand is important for understanding the causes of growth in literacy, for tracing its ramifications for other aspects of economic and social life, and for assessing its benefits in the colonial economy. The implicit models in the literature are made explicit here, and their implications are systematically explored.

What makes economic theory empirically useful is that supply and demand schedules do not shift by themselves or for no reason. Observable parameters shift these curves, and typically a given parameter shifts only the demand curve or the supply curve, not both. For example, changes in income shift the demand curve but not the supply curve; changes in technology shift the supply curve but not the demand curve. Population density is an atypical parameter in that it may affect either the supply or the demand curve. This possibility gives rise to two different models of how changing population density affects the literacy market, the demand model, and the supply model.

The two alternative models, presented in Figure 10.2, are drawn to illustrate the nonlinear trend in colonial literacy. The initial position, Demand$_1$ or Supply$_1$, represents the conditions experienced by immigrant parents when they were children of educable age in Europe. The second position, Demand$_2$, or Supply$_2$, represents the conditions experienced by immigrant parents with regard to educating their American-born offspring. The final position, Demand$_3$ or Supply$_3$, represents the conditions experienced by subsequent generations of American-born children.[12]

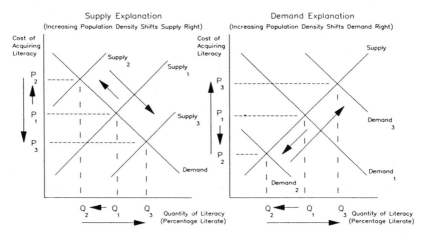

Figure 10.2. Supply-and-demand model of colonial literacy decline and growth caused by changes in population density.

Both the supply model and the demand model are drawn to trace the same longitudinal pattern in the quantity of literacy illustrated in Figure 10.1: starting from high initial levels at Q$_1$, literacy temporarily declines to Q$_2$ and then finally rises past the starting level to a long-run higher level at Q$_3$. Immigrants arrived in America with Q$_1$ literacy, but because they left a densely populated Europe for a sparsely populated America, demand and/or supply shifted left to Q$_2$ for their American-born children. Finally, as population density in America increased over time, demand and/or supply shifted right and returned literacy to higher levels at Q$_3$ for subsequent generations of Americans.

The demand model typically assumes that rising population density increased the demand for literacy by increasing its commercial value or by increasing the need to socialize the young politically and religiously. The benefits of being literate increased with the frequency of commercial transactions and social intercourse, which is assumed to increase with population density. Literacy also helped in the development of other trade skills which may have been more important in urban areas (farmers are assumed to have little commercial need for literacy). Temptations and vices are assumed to become relatively more available as population density increases. Thus, as population density rose, parents would demand relatively more literacy for their children to maintain social control or to provide their children with social and marketable skills. The demand model argues that the different levels of literacy between urban and rural areas were caused by differences in the relative demands for literacy rather than by differences in the relative costs (supply) of literacy. Over time, as population density rose, the commercial value of literacy rose or the need for social control rose, and thus the demand for literacy shifted right, causing long-run growth in literacy (Craig 1981: 157–68; Cremin 1970: 545–59; Cressy 1980: 88–95; Gilmore 1982, 1989; Graff 1987a, 1987b: 249–51; Lockridge 1974: 43–108; 1981: 183–98).

Shifts in the demand for literacy caused by changes in population density might explain the nonlinear pattern in colonial literacy. For example, German immigrants to Pennsylvania came from a relatively dense population environment, where literacy had a relatively high commercial value. Thus, they had a high level of literacy because they had a high demand for literacy when growing up in Germany, $Demand_1$. On moving to the colonial frontier, they entered a less dense population environment, where literacy had a relatively low commercial value. Therefore, immigrants were overeducated, given the value of literacy in their new environment. Given the lower commercial value of literacy on the colonial frontier, and hence a lower demand for literacy, immigrant parents would transmit a lower level of literacy to their American-born children than they possessed, $Demand_2$. Finally, as population density rose, the commercial value of literacy would rise, and hence the demand for literacy among subsequent American-born generations would rise, returning society to a long-run growth path in literacy, $Demand_3$.[13]

Some support for the demand explanation comes from the positive correlation between literacy and both wealth and occupation found in cross-sectional evidence (for example, see Beales 1978; Cremin 1970; Cressy 1980; Graff 1987b; Lockridge 1974; Tully 1972). The observed rural-urban literacy differential might be caused by income or wealth differentials rather than by population densities. If the acquisition of literacy is thought of as a consumption activity rather than an investment activity, and given a positive income elasticity of demand for literacy, then secular increases (or decreases) in income or wealth shift the demand schedule out (or in), causing the population's literacy level to rise (or fall).

This interpretation of the demand model has two problems. First, the estimated correlations between wealth and literacy relate the wealth and literacy of the same individual. Because individuals acquire literacy long before their occupation and wealth are determined, this evidence suggests that any causality flows from literacy to wealth rather than from wealth to literacy. Literacy would appear to be more an investment good than a consumption good. To estimate the effect of wealth on the demand for literacy, future studies should compare the wealth of parents with the literacy of their children, other things being equal. Second, the nonlinear trend in colonial literacy is difficult to explain as demand shifts driven by changes in income or wealth. Such an explanation of creolean degeneracy in literacy leads to the conclusion that the wealth of immigrants in America was significantly below the wealth their parents possessed when they were children in Europe. Evidence on income and wealth differentials, and the fact that immigration flows remained positive, suggests that this scenario is unlikely (Jones 1980; Perkins 1988: 1–18, 212–40).

In contrast, the supply model assumes that rising population density increased the quantity of literacy by lowering the supply cost of acquiring it. Costs are assumed to have declined with population density because of economies of scale in the provision of education. One teacher, one schoolhouse, one lesson could accommodate several students as easily as one student. The economies of scale would spread the fixed initial costs of the schoolhouse and teacher over several students and thus lower the unit cost for each student. In other words, as population density rose and group instruction became feasible, the average cost per student would decline over some limited range. Thus, the short-run supply of literacy would shift to the right as population density increased.

These economies of scale would be exhausted quickly in the city. Therefore, falling education costs caused by rising population density were more salient in the countryside or on the frontier; they had little continuing impact in urban areas. The initial difference in literacy levels between urban and rural areas would have been caused by the difference in the cost of education rather than by differences in the demand for literacy (Bailyn 1960: 78–84; Cremin 1970: 517–43; Gilmore 1982, 1989; Graff 1987b: 249–51; Lockridge 1974: 43–108; Soltow and Stevens 1981: 39–42).

Shifts in the supply of literacy might explain the nonlinear pattern of colonial literacy. For example, German immigrants to Pennsylvania grew up in a relatively dense population environment in Germany, where the cost of acquiring literacy was relatively low, $Supply_1$. On moving to the colonial frontier, they entered a less dense population environment and consequently experienced a relatively high cost of transmitting literacy to their American-born offspring, Supply$_2$. The higher cost of acquiring literacy on the frontier led immigrant parents to transmit a lower level of literacy to their American-born children than they had acquired as children in Germany. As population density in America increased, the cost of education declined, shifting the supply curve to the right and returning society to a long-run growth path in literacy for subsequent generations of Americans, Supply$_3$.

Although rising population density may have affected literacy through shifts both in supply and in demand, discovering the dominant effect is important for interpreting the impact of literacy on colonial America. If the demand model is dominant, then the high initial levels of colonial literacy were of little benefit to the colonial economy. Immigrants were overeducated. Resources used to acquire literacy prior to emigration were wasted, because literacy was of little value on the colonial frontier. Creolean degeneracy in literacy would represent no loss to colonial society. Maintaining the literacy levels of the overeducated immigrants in subsequent generations would involve investing in skills (or in social control) that had little value relative to other frontier activities.

By contrast, if the supply model is dominant, then the high initial levels of colonial literacy were a net wealth transfer from Europe to America. Immigrants acquired useful skills at low cost in Europe and then brought them to the American frontier, where learning them would have cost more. Creolean degeneracy in literacy would represent a productive loss to the economy as subsequent generations had to adapt to a higher cost of acquiring literacy than their immigrant parents faced prior to leaving for America.

Testing the supply versus demand models

Although the movements in the quantity of literacy are similar for both the supply and the demand models, the two explanations differ in regard to the movements in the cost of acquiring literacy (see Figure 10.2). If rising population density shifted the demand curve for literacy to the right, then the cost of acquiring literacy would be bid up. Alternatively, if rising population density shifted the supply curve to the right, then the cost of acquiring literacy would fall. Therefore, the dominant explanation of the nonlinear pattern in colonial literacy can be determined through measuring movements in the cost of acquiring literacy. If the cost were initially higher in Europe than on the colonial frontier and subsequently rose in the colonies over time, then the demand explanation would dominate the supply explanation. If the cost were initially lower in Europe than on the colonial frontier and subsequently fell in the colonies over time, then the supply explanation would dominate the demand explanation.[14]

While measuring changes in the cost of literacy would be the simple way to discover whether changing population density affected literacy more through shifts in supply or through shifts in demand, quantitative evidence on chang-es in the cost of acquiring literacy is not readily available. Research on the expansion of literacy in the seventeenth and eighteenth centuries has largely ignored cost measurements in favor of quantity measurements. One of the strengths of the supply-and-demand model is that it shows that gathering more quantitative evidence on signature literacy cannot by itself answer some of the important questions involving the causes and consequences of the growth in colonial literacy. Future research should be directed towards measuring changes in the cost of acquiring literacy. Estimation of the cost of literacy should include not only the direct costs of tuition, books, and teacher salaries but also the opportunity cost of the lost work time that students, instructors, and parents experienced during the education process.

Part of this new research should include studying shifts in methods of transmitting literacy from parents to children, because the method chosen might affect the overall cost of literacy. Currently, the portion of literacy acquired at home, at work, at church, or at school is not known. Finding quantitative evidence on the cost of acquiring literacy and on the methods used to transmit literacy in the colonial period may seem impossible, but then so was finding significant quantitative evidence on signature literacy for the colonial period 30 years ago. As with the accumulation of quantitative evidence on signature literacy, it may take 30 years and many new disserta-tions to develop adequate evidence on the cost and methods of transmitting literacy in the colonial period.

Several research directions might prove fruitful, such as estimating the threshold settlement size for setting up a full-time school, estimating the greatest distance a student could travel and still maintain school enroll-ment, or taking ranges of estimates of schooling fees, building costs, and labor costs and estimating the minimum enrollment needed to support a full-time school, and then using demographic information on age struc-ture to estimate the threshold settlement size needed to support a full-time school. Developing and expanding alternative evidence, for example, from contract labor markets, might also be useful for estimating education costs. For example, Grubb (1988: 599) found that the cost of acquiring employer-provided education through an indentured servant contract for German children in Pennsylvania was a 22% increase in contract length, independent of productivity differences relating to age.

Developing and expanding alternative evidence might also be useful for estimating the method used to transmit literacy. For example, servant con-tracts negotiated in Philadelphia for the children of German immigrants fre-quently stipulated the method of education to be provided by the employer. Out of 243 contracts in the servant records housed in the City Archives of

Philadelphia (1771–73) for male German children, 33.3% stipulated the provision of some kind of education. Given that adult German immigrants in the 1770s were 80% literate (see Table 10.1), this relatively infrequent stipulation is consistent with the creolean degeneracy hypothesis. The rural-urban difference in literacy is also present in this evidence. Among servants going to Philadelphia masters, 39% had education stipulated in their contracts, whereas among servants going to masters in the surrounding countryside, 28% had education stipulated in their contracts. However, this evidence on creolean degeneracy and rural-urban differentials by itself does not reveal whether the underlying causes were supply- or demand-driven.

What is interesting in this servant evidence, and illustrative of the new directions research in colonial literacy should take, is that the method of providing education was also stipulated in the servant contracts. Parents would want to choose the method of education which was the least costly to their child's employer, because the cost of the education was paid by their child through additions to his or her contract length. Thus, by choosing the least costly method of education for that employer, the parent also reduced the labor time needed by their child to acquire literacy. In the contract evidence, parents either specified a number of months of formal schooling or required only that reading and writing be taught (informal education), leaving the method of instruction up to the employer. The ratio of formal schooling to informal instruction in the contracts which stipulated education was systematically higher for children going to Philadelphia employers than for children going to employers in the surrounding countryside, .5 compared with .1. This comparison implies that formal schooling was less costly in the city than in the surrounding countryside and thus supports a supply-dominated explanation of the nonlinear trend in colonial literacy.

Finally, qualitative evidence might help sort out the demand and supply explanations. While the conclusions based on the opinions of contemporary observers must remain tentative, this evidence would appear to support the supply model as the dominant explanation. For example, the German community in colonial Pennsylvania repeatedly stressed the higher cost of schooling on the colonial frontier relative to Europe. They related the cost difference to relative population density (see the quotes above).

There appears to be less qualitative evidence which indicates that literacy was not in demand on the frontier. The colonial countryside was not a subsistence economy. Trade, exchange, and production for the market permeated the rural landscape (for example, see Jensen 1986: 79–91; Rothenberg 1981; Schweitzer 1987). It is not certain that the commercial value of literacy, and hence the demand for literacy, was necessarily lower in the countryside. Therefore, a supply-dominated explanation would appear to be more consistent with the quantitative and qualitative evidence than a demand explanation.[15]

Conclusion

Colonial America was a literate society by European standards. The accumulation of physical and human capital may have been part of the same process that was rapidly propelling Americans from frontier backwardness to competitiveness with the economies of western Europe. The rise of mass literacy may have affected the cultural, political, and economic direction of the new nation (for example, see Cremin 1970: 359–75, 545–59; Cressy 1987; Gilmore 1989; Jensen 1986: 114–28; Knauss 1918; Steele 1986; Tully 1972). However, the path to mass literacy was neither simple nor direct. Both quantitative and qualitative evidence suggests that local or regional literacy growth was nonlinear. While this nonlinear pattern appears to have been a general phenomenon across the colonies, more research is needed to establish its extent.

The causes and economic consequences of the nonlinear pattern of literacy growth are less clear. Changes in population density and the dynamics of transmitting literacy from immigrant parents to American-born offspring appear to be important factors. The evidence is consistent with the creolean degeneracy hypothesis. Colonial immigrants were more literate than their European home populations. However, on the colonial frontier, immigrant parents failed to transmit their high level of literacy to their children. Finally, as colonial populations became dominated by American-born colonists, literacy growth returned to a positive long-run growth trend.

Why colonial literacy should have behaved in this fashion is also unclear. The quantitative evidence on signature literacy is consistent with both a supply and a demand explanation. Further progress on these issues calls for a change in research strategies. The previous emphasis on gathering quantitative evidence of signature literacy should be redirected towards gathering quantitative evidence of the changing cost of acquiring literacy. Evidence on costs will help solve the problem of whether changes in the quantity of literacy was supply- or demand-driven. Finally, research should be redirected towards gathering quantitative evidence of the methods of transmitting literacy. The choice of method, such as informal education at home or work versus formal education at school or church, will help explain how colonists reacted to changes in the cost of acquiring literacy and changes in the value of being literate during the colonial era.

Notes

Earlier versions of this article were presented at the History Seminar, University of Delaware, and at the Mellon (PARSS) Seminar on Work and Population at the University of Pennsylvania. The author wishes to thank the participants in these seminars and David Galenson, Henry Gemery, Claudia Goldin, Lynn Lees, David Mitch, Erik Monkkonen, and anonymous referees for helpful comments on earlier drafts.

1. Most quantitative studies have concentrated on estimating cross-sectional variance in literacy within a given population. Quantitative measures of literacy for the seventeenth and eighteenth centuries were positively correlated with population density, wealth, occupational status, and religion (Cressy 1980: 104–41; Lockridge 1974: 13–27; Galenson 1979; Schofield 1973: 450; Stone 1969; Houston 1982). In many cases, these correlations have been interpreted as causes of variation in literacy across societies. As these societies moved towards mass literacy in the late eighteenth century, many of these correlations were weakened or eliminated. The study here will focus on common longitudinal patterns in literacy across societies or colonies rather than on cross-sectional patterns found within societies.

2. This correspondence between reading and writing was less strong in Sweden (Johansson 1981).

3. The study here will be confined to adult male literacy. While there are studies of adult female literacy (for example, see Auwers 1980; Gilmore 1989), they are too few, with sample sizes that are too small, to allow examination of common longitudinal patterns across colonial regions or to allow adequate comparison with northwestern Europeans. Studies of literacy among children and young teens are virtually nonexistent.

4. Probated wills tend to be drawn from the segment of the population with higher occupational status and greater wealth. Because literacy is positively correlated with wealth and occupation, signature evidence from wills may overstate literacy in the general population. However, probated wills also measure literacy late in life, when literacy skills may have deteriorated due to feebleness or senility. The net direction of the bias is unclear, but the wealth bias has usually been assumed to dominate. Recently, however, tests for wealth biases in samples of colonial probated wills have shown the bias to be insignificant (Main and Main 1988: 29–34). Deeds, petitions, and depositions suffer from double counting of some groups in the population, typically the more literate, and also generate inconsistent evidence for some individuals. For more discussions of the biases in the evidence and other measurement problems, see Beales 1978: 94–95; Cremin 1970: 575–76; Cressy 1980: 105–8; Gallman 1987; Lockridge 1974: 7–14, 133, 152; Soltow and Stevens 1981: 38, 207; Tully 1972: 304.

5. The typical sources of signature literacy are different between the colonies and Europe. Probated wills are the most common evidence used for the colonies, and marriage records are the most common evidence used for Europe. The relative direction of any biases is unclear. Probated wills may overrepresent the wealthy and higher occupational groups, which tended to be more literate relative to the population measured by marriage records. However, probated wills also measure literacy late in life, when it may have declined (see note 4), relative to when marriage records measure literacy. In addition, the average age difference between those signing wills and those marrying, some 25 years, may understate the relative superiority of colonial literacy to that of Europe, other things being equal. In a given

year, signers of wills should be older on average and thus members of an earlier, less literate generation than signers of marriage registers. Given a positive long-run trend in literacy, this age difference will understate the relative literacy of a given population in a given year when evidence from wills is used rather than evidence from marriage registers. My best guess is that correcting for these biases will not change the relative literacy ranking by region or country. See also notes 1 and 4.

6. Because the measured estimates of literacy for colonial populations mix European and American-born evidence, the difference between immigrant literacy and American-born literacy may be greater than indicated in Table 10.1. The French-Canadian evidence is less supportive and harder to evaluate regarding this pattern. English indentured servants, in general, were low in the occupational hierarchy. Clearly, since they could not pay the £10 that passage to America cost, they possessed relatively little wealth. Given that literacy is positively correlated with wealth and occupational status, the relatively high levels of literacy among English indentured servants suggests that the migration process positively selected colonists in the New World from the literate in the European population. The German evidence from Lancaster County, Pennsylvania, was based on wills and was thought to be biased high (Tully 1972: 305). The German immigrant evidence was relatively complete and so no representative biases exist. Therefore, German immigrant literacy may have exceeded resident colonial German literacy by an even greater margin than indicated in Table 10.1 (Grubb 1987: 66).

7. In Grubb's study, among Germans who had emigrated to Philadelphia between 1727 and 1775 a sample of 192 fathers with 252 adult sons (above age 16) was taken. The average age of the fathers was 50 and the average age of the sons was 20. The signature literacy of fathers and their sons had a correlation coefficient of .42. It was significantly different from 0 at the .0001 level, a t statistic of 6.39. The proportion of literate fathers with all literate sons and illiterate fathers with all illiterate sons was 69%.

8. Nonlinear patterns are found only when literacy is measured at frequent intervals and only when samples are confined geographically, such as to counties. For example, Lockridge (1974) did not find a nonlinear pattern in his estimates for New England (see Table 10.1). However, his estimates are too infrequent and taken from too wide a geographical area. His sample points span the nonlinear pattern and thus miss the intervening decline in literacy, as suggested by the more recent estimates of Soltow and Stevens (1981).

9. While this exercise is less ambitious than a fully specified computer simulation model, the point of the simulation, namely, that under reasonable conditions creolean degeneracy may explain the nonlinear literacy trend, can be made with this simple two-generation overlapping simulation. Thirty-year intervals are used because acquisition of literacy was usually complete by age 30 and few individuals survived to age 90.

10. The calculation of the population's literacy in this simulation model for 1700 is (100 × .25 signing wills × .7 literate)/(25 signing wills) = .7 literate; for 1730, [(200 × .25 signing wills × .5 literate) + (100 × .75 signing wills × .7 literate)]/(125 signing wills) = .62 literate; for 1760, [(400 × .25 signing wills × .7 literate) + (200 × .75

signing wills × .5 literate)]/(250 signing wills) = .58 literate; and for 1790, [(800 × .25 signing wills × .8 literate) + (400 × .75 signing wills × .7 literate)]/(500 signing wills) = .74 literate. In the actual historical environment there are several complicating factors abstracted from in this simulation, such as the possibility of continued stochastic additions of European immigrants to a given frontier region as well as stochastic migrations of American-born offspring into or out of that region.

11. Changes in the observed quantity of literacy in a population should not be equated with changes in the demand for (or supply of) literacy. This equation represents a classic error of economics, namely, confusing movements along a demand (or supply) schedule with shifts in the entire schedule. A shift in demand or supply represents an entirely new schedule of quantity of literacy per cost of acquiring literacy. Similarly, changes in parameters, such as population density, which affect supply (or demand) conditions cannot be interpreted as movements along the given supply (or demand) curve, because the supply and demand curves are plotted only with cost and quantity on the axes. Population density is not plotted along one of the axes. Changes in parameters which are not plotted along one of the two axes must be interpreted as shifts in the entire supply (or demand) schedule.

12. It should be noted that $Demand_1$ and $Supply_1$ represent the position of potential immigrants in Europe and not the average position for the whole European population. Immigrants to America were more literate than their European home populations (see Tables 10.1 and 10.2). In addition, while Q_2 is below Q_1 in Figure 10.2, it is not necessarily below the average literacy of their respective European home populations. In other words, creolean degeneracy would not necessarily lead to lower literacy levels in America than in Europe. The overall supply and demand for literacy in America may have been higher than the overall supply and demand for literacy in Europe for a number of reasons, such as relatively high religious fervor; a relatively high proportion of land ownership, which required knowledge of property rights and accounting techniques; a relatively high proportion of literate adults, who could then teach literacy to children; and so on.

13. Alternatively, one could argue that German immigrants came from a relatively dense population environment in Europe where the demand for literacy was high because social control of one's children—keeping them away from vice and competing religious doctrines—was important, $Demand_1$. On moving to the colonial frontier, these German immigrants entered a less dense population environment, where vice and competing religious doctrines were less of a threat. Therefore, immigrants were overeducated, given the value of literacy in their new environment. Given less need for social control on the colonial frontier, and hence a lower demand for literacy, immigrant parents would pass on a lower level of literacy to their American-born children than they possessed, $Demand_2$. Finally, as population density in America rose over time, the need for social control would also rise, and hence the demand for literacy among subsequent American-born generations would rise, returning society to a long-run growth path in literacy, $Demand_3$.

14. The opposite cost predictions of the supply and demand models illustrate the different possible impacts of literacy on the colonial economy. If literacy increased because the supply curve shifted right, then the economy gained in literacy without

sacrificing as many resources as previously. Expansion of literacy was accompanied by the freeing of resources which could be put to other productive uses. The initial creolean degeneracy in colonial literacy represented an economizing reaction to the increase in the real costs of literacy, which were draining the productive resources of the immigrants. Alternatively, if literacy increased because the demand curve shifted right, then the economy had to sacrifice more resources than previously to produce the higher desired literacy level. Resources were withdrawn from other productive uses in the economy to produce the higher literacy. The initial creolean degeneracy in colonial literacy represented a reaction in the colonies to the lower value of literacy, which freed educational resources for employment elsewhere during initial settlement.

15. This is not to say that demand factors were never important. For example, the difference in literacy between radical Protestants, mainstream Protestants, and Catholics is probably best explained as a difference in the demand for literacy, in terms of the strength of the desire to read the Bible for oneself. However, the emphasis in the qualitative evidence on the religious value of literacy presents another problem for the demand model. The connection between rising population density and increasing demand for literacy comes in part from the assumed higher commercial value of literacy in urban areas. However, other components of the demand for literacy, like religious motives, may work in the opposite direction. The religious demand for literacy may have been lower in urban areas because access to churches and pastors was easier there than in frontier areas, other things being equal. In town, unlike on the frontier, a person had ways of hearing God's Word other than reading the Bible. Religious revival and awakening in the colonies was important in the countryside.

References

Auwers, L. (1980). "Reading the marks of the past: Exploring female literacy in colonial Windsor, Connecticut." *Historical Methods* 13: 204–14.

Bailyn, B. (1960). *Education in the Forming of American Society*. New York: W. W. Norton.

Beales, R. W., Jr. (1978). "Studying literacy at the community level: A research note." *Journal of Interdisciplinary History* 9: 93–102.

Cipolla, C. M. (1969). *Literacy and Development in the West*. Baltimore: Penguin Books.

City Archives of Philadelphia (1771–73). "Record of indentures of individuals bound out as apprentices, servants, etc. and of German and other redemptioners in the Office of the Mayor of the City of Philadelphia, October 3, 1771 to October 5, 1773."

Craig, J. E. (1981). "The expansion of education." *Research in Education* 9: 151–213.

Cremin, L. A. (1970). *American Education: The Colonial Experience, 1607–1783*. New York: Harper and Row.

Cressy, D. (1980). *Literacy and the Social Order*. Cambridge: Cambridge University Press.

———. (1987). *Coming Over: Migration and Communication between England and New England in the Seventeenth Century*. New York: Cambridge University Press.

Deane, P. (1969). *The First Industrial Revolution*. Cambridge: Cambridge University Press.

Galenson, D. W. (1979). "Literacy and the social origins of some early Americans." *Historical Journal* 22: 75–91.

———. (1981). *White Servitude in Colonial America*. Cambridge: Cambridge University Press.

Gallman, R. E. (1987). "Two problems in the measurement of colonial literacy." *Historical Methods* 20: 137–41.

———. (1988). "Changes in the level of literacy in a new community in early America." *Journal of Economic History* 48: 567–82.

Gawthrop, R., and G. Strauss (1984). "Protestantism and literacy in early modern Germany." *Past and Present* 104: 31–55.

Gilmore, W. J. (1982). "Elementary literacy on the eve of the industrial revolution: Trends in rural New England, 1760–1830." *Proceedings of the American Antiquarian Society* 92: 87–178.

———. (1989). *Reading Becomes a Necessity of Life*. Knoxville: University of Tennessee Press.

Graff, H. J., ed. (1981). *Literacy and Social Development in the West*. London: Cambridge University Press.

———. (1987a). *The Labyrinths of Literacy*. London: Falmer.

———. (1987b). *The Legacies of Literacy*. Bloomington: Indiana University Press.

Grubb, F. (1987). "Colonial immigrant literacy: An economic analysis of Pennsylvania-German evidence, 1727–1775." *Explorations in Economic History* 24: 63–76.

———. (1988). "The auction of redemptioner servants, Philadelphia, 1771–1804: An economic analysis." *Journal of Economic History* 48: 583–603.

Houston, R. (1982). "The literacy myth? Illiteracy in Scotland, 1630–1760." *Past and Present* 96: 81–102.

Jensen, J. M. (1986). *Loosening the Bonds: Mid-Atlantic Farm Women, 1750–1850*. New Haven, CT: Yale University Press.

Johansson, E. (1981). "The history of literacy in Sweden," in H. J. Graff (ed.), *Literacy and Social Development in the West*. London: Cambridge University Press: 151–82.

Jones, A. H. (1980). *Wealth of a Nation to Be*. New York: Columbia University Press.

Kilpatrick, W. H. (1912). *The Dutch Schools of the New Netherlands and Colonial New York*. Washington, DC: U.S. Government Printing Office.

Knauss, J. O., Jr. (1918). "Social conditions among the Pennsylvania Germans in the eighteenth century, as related in German newspapers published in America." *Pennsylvania German Society* 28: 1–217.

Levine, D. (1979). "Education and family life in early industrial England." *Journal of Family History* 4: 368–80.

Lockridge, K. A. (1974). *Literacy in Colonial New England*. New York: W. W. Norton.

———. (1981). "Literacy in early America, 1650–1800," in H. J. Graff (ed.), *Literacy and Social Development in the West*. London: Cambridge University Press: 183–200.

Main, G. L., and J. T. Main (1988). "Economic growth and the standard of living in southern New England, 1640–1774." *Journal of Economic History* 48: 27–46.

Maynes, M. J. (1985). *Schooling in Western Europe*. Albany: State University of New York Press.

Mitch, D. (1984). "Underinvestment in literacy? The potential contribution of government involvement in elementary education to economic growth in nineteenth-century England." *Journal of Economic History* 44: 557–66.

———. (1988). "The rise of popular literacy in modern times and its explanation." Unpublished manuscript, Economics Department, University of Maryland, Baltimore County, Catonsville.

Mittelberger, G. (1960). *Journey to Pennsylvania in the Year 1750 and Return to Germany in the Year 1754*, trans., and ed. O. Handlin and J. Clive. Cambridge, MA: Harvard University Press.

Moogk, P. N. (1989). "Reluctant exiles: The problems of colonization in French North America." *William and Mary Quarterly*, 3rd ser., 46: 463–505.

Muhlenberg, H. M. (1942). *The Journals of Henry Melchior Muhlenberg*, trans. T. G. Tappert and J. W. Doberstein. 3 vols., Philadelphia: Muhlenberg.

Perkins, E. J. (1988). *The Economy of Colonial America*. New York: Columbia University Press.

Rothenberg, W. B. (1981). "The market and Massachusetts farmers, 1750–1855." *Journal of Economic History* 41: 283–314.

Sanderson, M. (1983). *Education, Economic Change, and Society in England, 1780–1870*. London: Macmillan.

Schofield, R. S. (1968). "The measurement of literacy in pre-industrial England," in J. Goody (ed.), *Literacy in Traditional Societies*. Cambridge: Cambridge University Press: 311–25.

———. (1973). "Dimensions of illiteracy, 1750–1850." *Explorations in Economic History* 10: 437–54.

———. (1989). "Fertility, nuptiality, and mortality according to literacy: 1754–1840." Unpublished manuscript, Cambridge Group for the History of Population, Cambridge, U.K.

Schweitzer, M. M. (1987). *Custom and Contract: Household, Government, and Economy in Colonial Pennsylvania*. New York: Columbia University Press.

Soltow, L., and E. Stevens (1981). *The Rise of Literacy and the Common School in the United States*. Chicago: University of Chicago Press.

Steele, I. K. (1986). *The English Atlantic, 1675–1740: An Exploration of Communication and Community*. New York: Oxford University Press.

Stone, L. (1969). "Literacy and education in England." *Past and Present* 42: 68–139.

Strassburger, R. B. (1934). *Pennsylvania German Pioneers*. 3 vols. Norristown: Pennsylvania German Society.

Tully, A. (1972). "Literacy levels and educational development in rural Pennsylvania, 1729–1775." *Pennsylvania History* 39: 301–12.

Weber, S. E. (1905). *The Charity School Movement in Colonial Pennsylvania*. Philadelphia: George F. Lasher Press.

West, E. G. (1978). "Literacy and the industrial revolution." *Economic History Review* 31:369–83.

11 DIMENSIONS OF ILLITERACY IN ENGLAND, 1750–1850

Roger S. Schofield

Recently an increasing number of economists have begun to consider education as a process of human capital formation and to view expenditure on education in terms of private and social investment.[1] This perspective leads naturally to the question of the contribution of education to economic growth, and economists of education have not been slow to appreciate the relevance of the English experience during the eighteenth and early nineteenth centuries.[2]

Unfortunately, the study of education in this period is much less advanced than the study of economic growth. Most accounts rely on inferences drawn from the history of the development of educational institutions and from the history of the popular press, buttressed by a few contemporary and modern studies of the literacy of a limited number of groups. The present consensus is that educational opportunities expanded during the period 1750–1850, so that by 1840 between 67% and 75% of the British working class had achieved rudimentary literacy. Some writers believe that the growth in the middle of the period was not great and point to a halt in educational advance at the turn of the century,[3] while others have discerned a particularly rapid growth in literacy in the first few decades of the nineteenth century.[4] All agree that there was considerable variation: regionally, between town and countryside, and between different occupational groups.

International comparisons of modern literacy rates and stages of economic development suggest that a 40% literacy rate may be a minimum threshold, and an increasing literacy rate a necessary condition, of economic growth.[5] The evidence at present available shows that England had crossed the 40% threshold by 1840, but it is not yet clear whether or not this had happened before 1750. However, the apparent coincidence of economic growth with a rise in literacy during the period seems to confirm the usefulness of regarding education as an investment in human resources, which brings both direct economic benefits in the form of increased productivity and indirect economic benefits in the form of the replacement of a traditional set of values by another set, sometimes characterized as "modern," or even "rational."

Reprinted from Roger S. Schofield, "Dimensions of Illiteracy in England, 1750–1850," *Explorations in Economic History* 10 (1973): 437–54, © 1973, with permission from Elsevier.

In this paper I shall avoid the larger cultural issues raised by this last proposition. Instead, I shall review the present evidence for the course of literacy in the period 1750–1850, present some fresh evidence, and suggest some implications for the relationship between literacy and economic growth in the period.

I

Arguments from changes in the volume and nature of popular publications to changes in the level of literacy enjoyed by the population at large are particularly insecure. First, there is no necessary relationship between the volume of production and the size of readership, because the number of readers per copy cannot be assumed to have been constant either over time or between publications. Second, changes in both the volume and the nature of publications may have been influenced by many factors other than changes in the level of literacy: for example, technological innovations such as the steam press, or changes in fiscal policy such as the many different rates of stamp duty charged in newspapers in the eighteenth and early nineteenth centuries. But arguments from the increase in educational facilities (the founding of the Charity Schools in the eighteenth century, the Sunday Schools in the 1780s, and the monitorial, industrial, and workhouse schools in the early nineteenth century), although frequently advanced, are also fraught with danger. Some of these schools, notably the Charity and the Sunday schools, were more concerned to impart a moral and religious training, and for them instruction in literacy was a secondary consideration. All schools had great difficulty in securing attendance. Early nineteenth-century surveys showed time and again that the number of children enrolled at school was no guide to the number actually receiving instruction.[6] This was partly because, with the exception of the Sunday schools and some of the institutional schools, fees had to be paid, for despite the large number of ostensibly free schools, very few genuinely free places were available. Education was therefore in direct competition with other goods for cash expenditure. It was also in competition with earning capacity, for the early nineteenth-century surveys also show that even in the case of free schools attendance slumped when employment was available.

Thus, the difficulty with indirect measures of literacy, such as the volume of popular publications and the supply of education, lies in the intervention of other variables; but direct measures of literacy also have their drawbacks. The early nineteenth century, particularly the 1830s and 1840s, witnessed a rash of educational, cultural, and moral surveys, made by a wide range of interested parties, many of which investigated the ability of different sections of the population to read and write, often in considerable detail.[7] Unfortunately, the restricted date span precludes their use for a study of literacy over a long period, and their great variety and frequent inexplicitness about the standards of reading and writing being measured make comparisons between them difficult. This is the same problem facing the student of literacy rates in the developing world today, who finds on closer inspection that "able to read" has been defined and measured differently in each country. Indeed, most modern investigations, like most of the early nineteenth-century surveys, rest on answers to questions about literacy rather than on direct tests. Thus, they measure people's beliefs about their literary abilities as expressed to a stranger, not the existence of these abilities. Clearly, if literacy is associated with high status, the dangers of misrepresentation are considerable.[8] For example, in a survey of literacy in East Pakistan in the mid-1960s a sample of rural cultivators was asked whether they could read a newspaper. Fifty-seven percent claimed that they could, but subsequent testing revealed that 15% in fact either could not read at all or could only stumble through the text without comprehension. The level of ability amongst the 42% who really could read also varied widely: about a half of them could only read slowly but with comprehension, while a half (or 22% of the sample) could read fluently.[9] In England in the period 1750–1850, as in East Pakistan in the mid-1960s, there was a wide range of reading ability, and in such a situation the proportion of the population reported as being "able to read" clearly depends on the level of skill taken to comprise reading ability.

Ideally, therefore, measures of literacy should be both standard and direct. For pre-industrial England in the late eighteenth and early nineteenth centuries there is only one measure which satisfies these two conditions: the ability to sign one's name. Although at first sight this is not a particularly meaningful literary skill, it has the advantage of giving a fairly "middle-range" measure of literacy in this period. This is because, ever since the sixteenth century, school curricula had been so phased that reading was taught before writing, and the intermittent nature of school attendance thus ensured that large numbers of children left school having acquired some reading ability, but little or no ability to write. In this period, therefore, the proportion of the population able to sign was less than the proportion able to read and greater than the proportion able to write. Early nineteenth-century evidence suggests that the proportion of the population claiming a basic level of reading ability may have been half as much again as the proportion able to sign, and that the proportion able to sign roughly corresponded with the proportion able to read fluently.[10] It also confirms that more people could sign than could write, but this was occasionally denied in the early nineteenth century, for the advocates of state education used the proportion of spouses unable to sign the marriage register as a stick with which to beat the defenders of private education, who consequently made valiant efforts to discredit it as a measure of literacy. Their argument was that many people who could write were inhibited from signing their names by the solemnity of the marriage ceremony or out of feeling for an illiterate spouse. However, such people would presumably have been accustomed to holding a pen and would in consequence have made firm marks. Yet the numbers of such marks in the marriage registers are very small, and are unlikely to have had more than the most marginal effect on literacy rates based on the ability to sign. Another, and contrary, objection which is sometimes brought against the use of marriage register signatures as a measure of literacy is that some people signed who could neither read nor write. Children today may be capable of this trick; but it is *a priori* unlikely in pre-industrial England, given the phasing of instruction in reading and writing, the lack of writing materials in most homes, and the very few occasions in a lifetime in which a signature or mark was required. In practice, such a signature would be ill-formed through inexperience of both pen and letters, but such signatures are rare in this period.

A further advantage of the ability to sign as a measure of literacy is that it is available for a large number of people and thus makes possible comparisons both over time and between residential and occupational groups. The source for this wealth of information is the series of marriage registers kept by the Church of England, for since 1754 the law recognized as valid only those marriages which were registered in the Anglican registers and signed by the parties and two witnesses.[11] The register evidence therefore relates to the 90% or so of the population who were ever married, and measures their ability to sign largely when they were in their mid-20s, some 15 or so years after leaving school.[12] For the period from 1839 to 1914 the Registrar General has published in his *Annual Reports* the numbers and proportions of men and women able and unable to sign their names.[13] Figure 11.1 shows the national annual illiteracy rates (percentages unable to sign) of men and women over this period, plotted on a semi-logarithmic scale to facilitate comparison of rates of change at different periods. The achievement of the second half of the nineteenth century is remarkable: the percentage of men unable to sign fell from just over 30% in 1850 to 1% in 1911, and the percentage of women unable to sign fell from just over 45% in 1850 to 1% in 1913. The fastest rate of improvement was amongst those marrying after about 1885, or leaving school after about 1870. The improvement between about 1850 and 1885 (i.e., school-leavers between about 1835 and 1870) was less rapid, and the rate of improvement between 1840 and 1850 (school-leavers of 1825–1835) was markedly slower still.

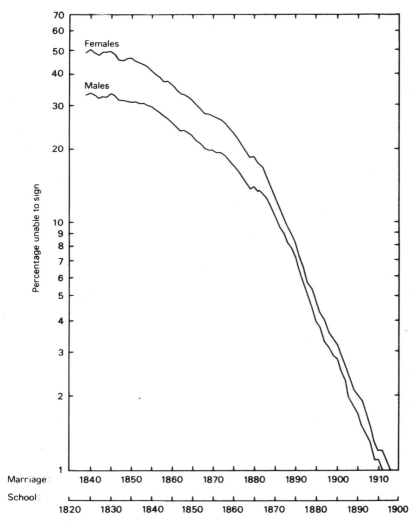

Figure 11.1. Annual percentages of males and females unable to sign at marriage, England and Wales, 1839–1912. *Source*: Registrar General of England and Wales, *Annual Reports*.

Since the marriage register evidence is available from 1754, it should be possible to extend the Registrar General's series back another 85 years. An informal attempt to do this was made as early as 1867 by a member of the Royal Statistical Society, who collected information from 26 rural and 10 urban parishes for three periods: 1754–1762, 1799–1804, and 1831–1837.[14] This tiny and haphazard sample of 36 from a population of some 10,000 parishes features in most modern discussions of the course of literacy during this period. Since 1867 a number of local studies have been made,[15] and signatures and marks in other sources, such as wills and marriage licenses, have been used to supplement the marriage register material. These sources, however, present considerable difficulties; wills were commonly made *in extremis* and consistently overstate the percentage unable to sign, while marriage by license was attractive not only to high status groups but also to the more literate in each status group, so that evidence drawn from marriage licenses consistently understates the percentage unable to sign.

One aspect of literacy in this period which is quite clear from the Registrar General's figures based on the marriage registers is a marked geographical variation in the percentage unable to sign. In 1839, the first date for which these figures are available, the metropolitan area of London is the most literate "county," with 12% of males unable to sign, followed closely by three counties near the border with Scotland, all with under 20% unable to sign. The next best group, with 20–30% unable to sign, comprises a string of counties on the northeast coast, together with Devon and Dorset. The worst two groups, with 40–55% unable to sign, are Wales and the West Midlands with Lancashire, and a belt of counties stretching from East Anglia through the home counties to Wiltshire. The midland and most of the southern coastal counties comprise an intermediate group, with 30–39% unable to sign. Thus in 1839 the proportion of males who were illiterate at marriage was three times higher in Bedford and Hertfordshire than in Northumberland, Cumberland, and Westmorland. But the Registrar General's figures for Registration Districts, which are available from 1842, show that local variation within a county was even greater than this. Thus, the national estimates of illiteracy for the period before 1838 presented in the current literature, which are based on very small numbers of parishes, are subject to large sampling errors, and accordingly little confidence should be placed in them.

II

The task of obtaining trustworthy figures and of studying this extraordinary variation in illiteracy rates can only be achieved either by making a full enumeration of all marriages registered between 1754 and 1838, or by drawing a properly designed sample. The first alternative is scarcely practicable, if only because the marriages are recorded in 10,000 parish registers, most of which are still lodged in the parish chests. This geographical constraint also makes it sensible to sample marriage registers rather than individual marriage entries. Accordingly, I have drawn a random sample of 274 parishes, a figure which was calculated to produce national estimates with a standard error of about 2%, taking into account a rather strong parish clustering effect. Figure 11.2 shows the national estimates of the percentages of men and women unable to sign in each year during the period 1754–1840. The 274 parishes produced about 1,300 marriages annually in the late 1750s, rising to about 2,900 in the late 1830s. The effect of clustering on the variance of the sample estimates was greater than expected, and the standard error of the estimates in most years was about 3%. The sampling error lends a tremor to the lines on the graph, but the trends are nonetheless clear.

The percentage of women unable to sign was just over 60% in the mid-eighteenth century and improved slowly to fall to just below 50% by 1840.

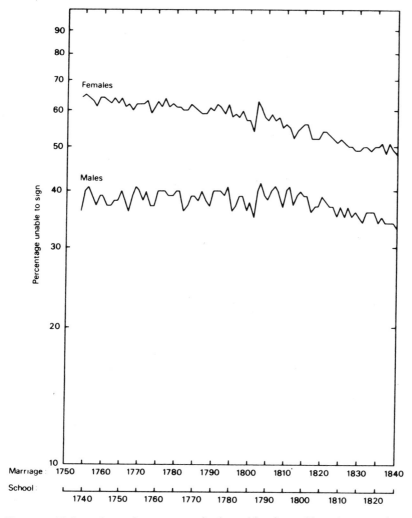

Figure 11.2. Estimated annual percentages of males and females unable to sign at marriage, England, 1754–1840. *Source*: Random sample of 274 English parish registers.

The rate of improvement after 1800 was noticeably faster than before this date, but at no time was it particularly rapid. Allowing for a 15-year lag between schooling and marriage, the quickening of improvement in female illiteracy dates from about the mid-1780s and may possibly be connected with the development of Sunday School education at this time. Male illiteracy, however, followed a somewhat different course. Far from falling throughout this period, as present accounts lead one to expect, it remained more or less stable for 50 years. Just under 40% were unable to sign until about 1795. The percentage then fell toward 1800, but rose toward 1805, and then fell again at a similar rate to that of the women to around 33% in 1840. The turning point is a little less clear for males, but it was probably between 1805 and 1815. If we assume that entry into the labor force may be taken to be the age of leaving school, then some point in the 1790s marks the date around which the literacy of entrants to the labor force may first be said to be increasing since 1740. Despite differences in scale, a comparison of Figures 11.1 and 11.2 brings out the marked contrast between the relative stability of both male and female illiteracy in this period, and the dramatic fall in the later nineteenth century.

National figures, however, as we have already observed, summarize and conceal wide variations. Ultimately, the sample results will show how far regional experiences differed from the national trend. But geographical location is only one of many factors which affect illiteracy rates. Others probably included the availability of schooling and a wide variety of social and economic variables; for example, the concentration of land ownership, the dispersion of settlement, and the occupational structure of the community. Unfortunately, information on all of the many factors likely to have influenced the local development of literacy in each parish during the period is unavailable, and the best that can be achieved is evidence for some social and economic characteristics of the sample parishes at some points during the period. An investigation has been begun into how far these characteristics, either singly or in combination, can explain differences in the levels of male and female illiteracy and differences in changes in these levels. No results are yet available for discussion, but the imperfections of the indicators which can be used make it likely that the proportion of local variation which can be explained in this way will always be small.

In the meantime something of the nature of this local variation, however, can be appreciated from a superficial examination of Bedfordshire, the worst county in England for male illiteracy in 1839, with 55% unable to sign compared to 33% nationally. A full enumeration has been made of all marriages registered in every parish in Bedfordshire in the period 1754–1844, and this has revealed an astonishingly varied picture of parishes with different combinations of high and low male and female illiteracy and of improvement and deterioration in illiteracy rates. Overall, the decadal illiteracy rate in Bedfordshire for males deteriorated from 54% in 1754–64 to 60% in 1795–1804 and then improved, with a setback in 1825–34, to return almost to its original position (55%) in the final decade studied, 1835–44. The female illiteracy rate was higher throughout; it began at 72% in 1754–64, and behaved similarly to the male rate, though it deteriorated less in the late eighteenth century, and it improved earlier and more substantially to reach 67% in the final decade, 1835–44. But not all the parishes in the county had this average experience, and so far as male illiteracy is concerned two extreme groups can be discerned: 14 parishes in which the male illiteracy rate fell by more than 10%, and 24 parishes in which it rose by more than 10% over the period. The divergent decadal male illiteracy rates for these two groups, particularly marked after 1775–84, are shown in Figure 11.3. At the level of the individual parish, female illiteracy rates in general moved parallel with the male rates, though there were some parishes in which increases in male illiteracy of more than 10% were accompanied by falls in female illiteracy.

These two extreme groups can be compared on a number of geographical, social, educational, and economic characteristics. There was little or no difference in the geographic location of the members of the two groups, nor was there any difference either in their rate of population growth or in their *per capita* expenditure on Poor Relief in the 1780s. Some of the remaining differences were weak; but, on the whole, parishes in which illiteracy *declined* by more than 10% over the period were more likely to have had an ordinary day school, but not a Sunday school, a wider dispersion of land ownership, a higher percentage of inhabitants in non-agricultural occupations, and to have expended less *per capita* on Poor Relief in the 1830s than had parishes in which illiteracy increased over the period. The parish which experienced a marked increase in illiteracy therefore tended to be predominantly agricultural, dominated by a single landlord, with little or no schooling available, and a high *per capita* expenditure on Poor Relief in the 1830s. I have reported these results informally because the small number of parishes used in the summary survey means that some of the results are barely significant statistically. There was also, naturally, considerable interaction between the social and economic variables, for example, between landlord domination and low or negative population growth, and clearly the subject of local variation in illiteracy rates deserves a more sensitive and complete exploration.

One outstanding feature of the Bedfordshire evidence was the experience of market towns, for in every case illiteracy declined during the period. This was also true of market towns throughout the country and suggests that

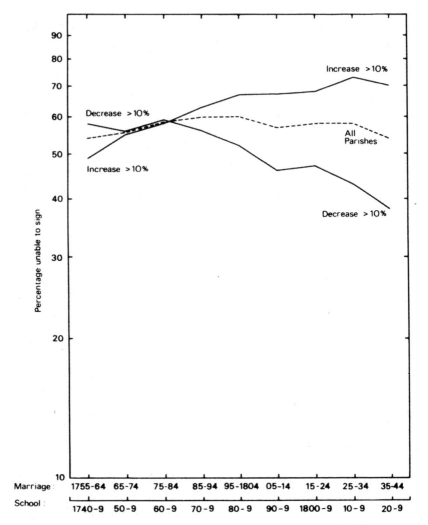

Figure 11.3. Decadal percentages of males unable to sign at marriage, Bedfordshire, distinguishing parishes in which percentages increased and decreased by more than 10%. *Source*: Parish marriage registers.

the relationship between illiteracy and occupation would repay investigation. Unfortunately, the opportunities to do this systematically are limited, for relatively few marriage registers give occupations consistently until the mid-nineteenth century. Table 11.1 shows the illiteracy rates for a number of occupational groups taken from a sample of 23 parishes whose registers give occupational descriptions throughout the period.[16]

This occupational hierarchy is one of the most consistent features of illiteracy in the past. It is to be found in all regions and at all times, regard-

Table 11.1. Illiteracy by occupational group, 1754–84 to 1815–44

	1754–84		1785–1814		1815–44	
	Sample size	%	Sample size	%	Sample size	%
Gentry and professional	68	0	170	1	204	3
Officials, etc.	20	0	43	5	94	2
Retail	19	5	94	10	150	5
Wood	137	16	361	17	448	11
Estate	29	17	66	18	87	30
Yeomen and farmers	97	19	262	18	315	17
Food and drink	57	19	189	18	277	18
Textile	41	20	83	39	38	16
Metal	60	22	170	29	301	19
Leather	78	23	232	30	320	22
Miscellaneous	81	30	129	32	130	25
Transport	154	31	462	38	549	30
Clothing	63	35	112	21	135	14
Armed forces (non-officer)	180	41	773	51	122	32
Husbandmen	665	46	560	56	123	52
Construction and mining	146	51	352	47	499	38
Laborers and servants	192	59	596	65	1,632	66
Unknown	37	24	130	25	19	26
All	2,126	36	4,784	39	5,443	35

less of the level of illiteracy. Naturally the differences between occupations vary, and sometimes categories, particularly some of the trades and crafts, exchange places. The common-sense interpretation of this hierarchy would seem to be that literacy had a different functional value in each of the occupational groups. For example, long before the mid-eighteenth century the subculture of the social élite presupposed literacy, and literacy was also essential to the economic functions of men in the professions and official positions. These groups, that is, needed to be literate in order to fulfill their economic and social roles. But others did not, for even in the mid-nineteenth century literacy was by no means indispensable in the social and economic life of large numbers of laborers. In the middle ground of different trades and crafts the superiority of occupations involving commerce and contact with the public (retail food and drink) over occupations involving heavy manual labor (construction and mining) also makes sense in terms of literacy having a different practical value to different occupational groups. Indeed, since schooling in this period involved direct cash expenditure as well as forgoing earnings, the practical utility of literacy would have been a powerful argument either for or against investing in education. For some groups the costs of this investment exceeded perceived benefits. Even in the more literate world of the late nineteenth century the abolition of school fees still left the "costs" of lost earning power to be borne, and universal investment in education was only achieved under the compulsion of the law.

III

In the late eighteenth and early nineteenth centuries a decision to invest in education was a decision to invest in the acquisition of literary skills: the ability to read and, at further cost, the ability to write. For it was primarily these two skills that were taught in the elementary schools; arithmetic and substantive knowledge were offered later and required a further cash outlay. The acquisition of literary skills, or literacy, might be desirable for three reasons: because it was essential for participation in the life of a particular social group, because it was essential for acquiring skills, or new skills, relevant to a particular occupation, or because it would lead to upward social and economic mobility. It is by and large true that in the late eighteenth and early nineteenth centuries the literate occupations had higher status and were better paid; but the early nineteenth-century educational surveys show that both the subjects children studied and the length of time they stayed at school depended on the occupation and status of their parents, which suggests that the prospect of upward mobility for their children did not lead many working-class parents to invest heavily in education.[17] How far literacy was necessary to men and women in order for them to participate fully in different walks of life in the late eighteenth and early nineteenth centuries is a large question. Literacy was clearly widespread: a majority of the population could read, and in the early nineteenth century there is plenty of evidence of a literate culture amongst large sections of the working class. The fall in the illiteracy rate amongst women from 64% in 1750 to 50% in 1850 suggests that literacy became a more important component in the life of women during the period. On the other hand, male illiteracy remained constant until the decade 1805–15. More remarkably, Table 11.1 shows that in many occupations illiteracy actually rose during the later eighteenth century and that in the early nineteenth century some occupations were still less literate than they had been in the mid-eighteenth century.

Perhaps no great emphasis should be laid on these figures, for they come from a small number of parishes for which information on occupations is available throughout the period. Yet they at least suggest the possibility that for many males in a variety of occupations literacy did not become more essential as a cultural skill during this period. They might also suggest that, with the conspicuous exception of the clothing and construction trades, literacy may have been no more essential for acquiring economic skills and techniques in the early nineteenth century than it had been in the mid-eighteenth century. Yet technical developments involved thousands of people in learning a multitude of new practical skills. An attempt was made in the eighteenth century to provide practical instruction for the poor in Charity Schools, but although this scheme proved to be greatly to the tastes of the times, it had to be abandoned as uneconomic.[18] For most children in the late eighteenth and early nineteenth centuries, school remained a specialized institution for the instruction of literary skills. Consequently, few children were regular in attendance, and few remained at school for more than 1½ years.[19] Practical economic skills were therefore learned within the context of the household and work-group, as part of a comprehensive process of socialization, of which apprenticeship is a well-known, but formalized example.

Thus, insofar as economic growth in this period entailed the acquisition of a large number of practical skills by a growing proportion of the population, developments in literacy and education were probably largely irrelevant to it. And, insofar as economic growth resulted from the increased productivity of labor brought about by the shift from domestic to factory production, literacy and education were also probably largely irrelevant, for many of the new industrial occupations recruited a mainly illiterate work force, so much so that many industrial communities were markedly more illiterate than their rural neighbors.[20] This contrast has been attributed to a collapse of education in these rapidly growing urban areas, but a large proportion of the work force had moved to these towns after having been educated elsewhere. Thus, urban migration in this period was not only occupation-specific; it was also literacy-specific. This is made clear by the opposite effect, namely, the superior literacy of market and county towns over the surrounding neighborhood. For these communities contained a high proportion of occupations concerned with distribution and exchange, which required the ability to keep the records, and thus presupposed literacy. Indeed, such an intersectoral shift in occupational structure accompanying economic growth may perhaps account for the positive correlation between literacy and economic development in present-day economies.[21] Inferences sometimes drawn from this association are that an illiteracy rate of about 60% is a threshold above which economic growth is unlikely, and that an improvement in literacy is a necessary precondition or concomitant of economic growth. The English experience in the century from 1750 to 1850 may perhaps be taken to cast some doubt on the utility of positing universal relationships between literacy and economic growth. Although it is true that the national male illiteracy rate had crossed the 60% threshold before 1750, the female rate only crossed it definitively around 1795, and female illiteracy was very high in areas of high female industrial employment; for example, it was still 84% in Oldham in

1846.[22] Nor does the static nature of male illiteracy both nationally until the decade 1805–15 and in several occupational groups until the mid-nineteenth century lend much support to the notion that an improvement in literacy necessarily precedes stability, and the marked contrast between the literacy of commercial classes and the illiteracy of much of the industrial labor force suggests that for England, at least, the usual causal relationships between literacy and economic growth might profitably be reversed. In this alternative perspective the reduction in illiteracy in nineteenth-century England would appear more as a cultural change brought about by economic growth than as one of the causes of growth.

Notes

The research underlying this paper is supported by the Social Science Research Council.

1. For example, see M. Blaug, *An Introduction to Economics of Education* (London: Allen Lane, 1970).

2. C. A. Anderson and M. J. Bowman, eds., *Education and Economic Development* (London: F. Cass, 1966), chs. 17, 18, 20.

3. Anderson and Bowman, *Education and Economic Development,* 350.

4. L. S. Stone, "Literacy and Education in England 1640–1900," *Past and Present* 42 (1969): 109.

5. M. J. Bowman and C. A. Anderson, "Concerning the Role of Education in Development," in *Old Societies and New States,* ed. C. Geertz (New York: Free Press of Glencoe, 1963), 247–49, reprinted in *Readings in the Economics of Education,* ed. M. J. Bowman et al. (Paris: UNESCO, 1968).

6. For example, the survey of education in Westminster in 1837–38 reported that school attendance in winter was down to between a quarter and a half of the number of children enrolled. Second Report of a Committee of the Statistical Society of London, appointed to enquire into the State of Education in Westminster, *Journal of the Statistical Society of London* 1 (1838): 193–215.

7. These surveys have been well summarized and discussed in R. K. Webb, "Working Class Readers in Early Victorian England," *English Historical Review* 65 (1950): 333–51, and *The British Working Class Reader, 1790–1848* (London: Allen & Unwin, 1955), ch. 1.

8. For example, a survey of education in Newcastle-upon-Tyne in the late 1830s reported, "In making such enquiries our agent was universally regarded as interfering with what they thought he had no concern and they gave answers which he knew in the majority of cases to be false." William Cargill, Esq., and a Committee of the Educational Society of Newcastle, "Educational, Criminal, and Social Statistics of Newcastle-Upon-Tyne," *Journal of the Statistical Society of London* 1 (1838): 355–61.

9. H. S. Schuman, A. Inkeles, and D. H. Smith, "Some Social Psychological Effects and Noneffects of Literacy in a New Nation," *Economic Development and Cultural Change* 16 (1967): 1–14.

10. Compare the figures cited by Webb, "Working Class Readers" and the figures given in the Registrar General's *Annual Reports*. See also the opinions of an educational inspector of the time: J. F. Fletcher, "Moral and Educational Statistics of England and Wales," *Journal of the Statistical Society of London* 10 (1847): 212. Signatures as measures of literacy are discussed more fully in R. S. Schofield, "The Measurement of Literacy in Pro-Industrial England," in *Literacy in Traditional Societies,* ed. J. Goody (Cambridge: Cambridge University Press, 1968).

11. Only Jews, Quakers, and members of the royal family were exempt; 26 George II c. 33, usually known as Lord Hardwicke's Marriage Act.

12. A rough idea of the proportion of the population never marrying and thus escaping observation in the marriage registers is given by the proportion of the age group 50–54 that was still unmarried. In 1851 11% of men and 12% of women were unmarried in this age group. These figures do not represent exactly the proportions of men and women never marrying, because although over 99% of all first marriages took place before either partner had reached fifty years of age, it was probably not the case at this period that the mortality of single people below the age of fifty was equal to that of married people. See Great Britain, *Parliamentary Papers,* vol. 88 (1852–53), "1851 Census of England and Wales," pt. 1, cci; and Registrar General of England and Wales, *Annual Report of Births, Deaths and Marriages* (1851–52), viii. Information of sufficient quality on the distribution of ages at marriage is first available in 1851. In this year 73% of all bridegrooms and 70% of all brides were between 20 and 29 years old. A further problem lies in the double-counting of further marriages of widows and widowers, especially if the risk of widowhood and the propensity to remarriage prove to have been social-class specific. In 1851, 14% of the bridegrooms and 9% of the brides were widowers and widows respectively (Registrar General, *Annual Report* [1851–52], viii).

13. Registrar General, *Annual Report* (1839–40).

14. W. L. Sargant, "On the Progress of Elementary Education," *Journal of the Statistical Society of London* 30 (1867), 80–137.

15. For local studies see, for example, W. P. Baker, "Parish Registers and Illiteracy in East Yorkshire," *East Yorkshire Local History Society* 13 (1961), and R. C. Russell, *A History of School and Education in Lindsey* (Lindsey County Council Education Committee, 1965). For the use of marriage licenses, see L. Stone, "Literacy and Education."

16. The parishes are Cheshire: Chester St. Mary; Cornwall: Budock; Derbyshire: Littleover; Devonshire: Eggesford, St. Paul's Exeter, Kentisbeare, Ottery St. Mary, Plymstock, Wembury; Hampshire (I.O.W.): Brightsone; Lancashire: Caton, Overton, Pennington, Walton-on-the-Hill; Lincolnshire: Thurlby near Bourne, Cherry Willingham; Northumberland: Earsdon; Nottinghamshire: East Drayton; Oxfordshire: Horley; Rutland: Bisbrooke; Somersetshire: Dunster, Staple Fitzpaine; Suffolk: Woodbridge.

17. For example, see the survey of education in Westminster cited above, *Journal of the Statistical Society of London* 1: 193–215.

18. "The struggle between the disciplines of labour and literature for the control of the Charity School curriculum ended in the defeat of labour. If success had crowned

the efforts of the working Charity Schools the history of elementary education in the British Isles would have followed a different course." M. G. Jones, *The Charity School Movement* (Cambridge: Cambridge University Press, 1938), 95.

19. For example, see the survey of education in Westminster cited above, *Journal of the Statistical Society of London,* 1: 193–215.

20. This is visible both in the sample parishes and also in the data printed by the Registrar General in his *Annual Reports.* Since this paper was written, an investigation of the ability to sign in Lancashire has confirmed for a key industrializing area some of the national results presented here. In particular, literacy was found to be *declining* in Lancashire in the later half of the eighteenth century "down to about the 1820s or 1830," and the author concluded that "the English industrial revolution cannot be seen as one nourished by rising educational standards at least at the elementary level." Michael Sanderson, "Literacy and Social Mobility in the Industrial Revolution in England," *Past and Present* 56 (August 1972), 75–104.

21. Bowman and Anderson, "Concerning the Role of Education in Development."

22. Registrar General, *Annual Report* (1846).

12 "WE SLIPPED AND LEARNED TO READ": SLAVE ACCOUNTS OF THE LITERACY PROCESS, 1830–1865

Janet Cornelius

Despite the dangers and difficulties, thousands of slaves learned to read and write in the antebellum South. Few left traces of their accomplishments, but 272 ex-slaves who told how they learned to read and write during slavery provide insight into the literacy process within the slave community. For slaves, literacy was a two-edged sword: owners offered literacy to increase their control, but resourceful slaves seized opportunity to expand their own powers. Slaves who learned to read and write gained privacy, leisure time, and mobility. A few wrote their own passes and escaped from slavery. Literate slaves also taught others and served as conduits for information within a slave communication network. Some were able to capitalize on their skills in literacy as a starting point for leadership careers after slavery ended.

Historians of education have drawn a distinction between "Bible literacy," whose prime motive was the conservation of piety, and "liberating literacy," which facilitates diversity and mobility.[1] The majority of owners who taught slaves were concerned with Bible literacy and connected their instruction with Christian worship and catechization. The traditional nature of this teaching is shown by the number of slave owners who gave slaves religion-associated instruction in reading but not in writing, a practice which recalled the early Protestant insistence that even the poor and powerless should be able to read the word of God for themselves, but that teaching them to write would threaten the social order.[2]

The religious context for learning was as important for slaves as it was for owners; most slaves who learned to read on their own initiative did so in a religious context, demonstrating that Christian teachings and opportunities could have liberating as well as conservative results. Reading the Bible for oneself enabled a slave to undercut a master's attempt to restrict Christian teaching to carefully selected Biblical passages. Knowing how to read gave slaves opportunities to assume religious leadership within the slave community, where reading and preaching were closely associated.[3]

The present study compiles and measures evidence from former slaves on specific aspects of the literacy process: which slaves learned to read and

From *Phylon* 44 (1983): 171–86. Reprinted with the permission of the author.

write, what levels of literacy they attained, who taught them, the context in which this teaching and learning took place, and why slaves were taught or taught themselves. Two sources for evidence by former slaves who learned to read and write were used to examine literacy in the slave community. Most evidence was taken from the slave narratives gathered by the Federal Writers Project of the Works Progress Administration, as edited by George Rawick and published under the title *The American Slave: A Composite Autobiography*, in its original 19 volumes and the 12-volume Supplement 1, and in the Virginia interviews published separately as *Weevils in the Wheat: Interviews with Virginia Ex-Slaves*.[4] A reading and analysis of all the 3,428 responses by ex-slaves questioned by the Federal Writers Project interviewers as compiled in these volumes pinpointed just over 5 percent (179) who mentioned having learned to read and write as slaves.[5] In addition to the evidence from the Writers Project interviews, 93 ex-slave accounts were taken from a variety of other sources, including autobiographies and narratives by former slaves; interviews with former slaves by nineteenth-century black writers; life histories told by ex-slaves who had fled to Canada or were seeking help on the Underground Railroad; and cyclopedias compiled by black editors listing prominent black Americans, for which they submitted their own autobiographies.[6] Only two of these narratives and autobiographies, taken largely from ex-slaves in the public sphere, were written by women. However, the Federal Writers Project interviewees who learned to read and write included 67 women out of the 179 blacks interviewed for the Project who mentioned acquiring skills in literacy while they were slaves.

These two kinds of sources encompassed a broad time frame and extensive regional coverage. Since the Federal Writers Project interviews took place more than seventy years after the end of slavery, the majority of ex-slaves who talked about their experiences were small children during slavery. This was less true for the other slaves in the study. Most of the Writers Project former slaves learned to read after 1855, while two-thirds of the other ex-slaves learned to read before that date. The two kinds of ex-slave sources also represent literate slaves in different regions of the South. The Writers Project was weighted towards the Old South and the New South frontier states. The Border South states are more strongly represented in the other ex-slave sources. The Old South is most heavily represented overall.

Accounts by former slaves used in this study illustrate the reasons why the extent of literacy among slaves is almost impossible to measure. According to these accounts, neither slaves nor those slave owners and other whites who taught them could proclaim their activities safely. Patrols, mobs, and social ostracism faced owners who taught their slaves. One former slave even recalled whispered rumors that her master had been poisoned because he taught his slaves to read and write and allowed them to save enough money to buy land at the end of the Civil War.[7] Slaves themselves believed they faced terrible punishments if whites discovered they could read and write. A common punishment for slaves who had attained more skills, according to blacks who were slaves as children in South Carolina, Georgia, Texas, and Mississippi, was amputation, as described by Doc Daniel Dowdy, a slave in Madison County, Georgia: "The first time you was caught trying to read or write, you was whipped with a cow-hide, the next time with a cat-o-nine-tails and the third time they cut the first jint offen your forefinger." Another Georgia ex-slave carried the story horrifyingly further: "If they caught you trying to write they would cut your finger off and if they caught you again they would cut your head off."[8] None of the 272 slaves in this study actually suffered any such punishments as they learned to read and write, but some had personal knowledge that such atrocities had occurred. Henry Nix's uncle stole a book and was trying to learn to read and write with it, so "Marse Jasper had the white doctor take off my Uncle's fo'finger right down to de 'fust jint'" as a "sign fo de res uv 'em." Lizzie Williams told of "one woman named Nancy durin' de war what could read and 'rite. When her master, Oliver Perry, found dis out he made her pull off naked, whipped her and den slapped hot irons to her all over. Believe me dat nigger didn't want to read and 'rite no more." Joseph Booker's father, Albert, was charged with "spoiling the good niggers" by teaching them to read and was whipped to death when Joseph was three years old.[9]

Few such demonstrations were necessary to effectively stifle the desire to read among most slaves and to establish a mythology about the dangers of reading and writing. That former slaves remembered the atrocity stories so well from their childhood suggests that they had been tempted to learn to read, and that their parents feared that they might take advantage of an opportunity to do so. It also might give rise to speculation that the children themselves did not know how many people in a single plantation community might actually possess reading and writing skills, since the knowledge of this possession led to so much danger. The recollection of Campbell Davis, thirteen years old when slavery ended, that "us git some book larnin' mongst ourselves, round de quarters, and have our own preacher," may therefore have been true within many slave communities without the knowledge of the children. As Sarah Fitzpatrick observed from her experiences as a house servant in Alabama, many slaves could read but "de ke' dat up deir sleeve, dey played dumb lack de couldn't read a bit till after surrender."[10]

Slaves who learned to read and write were a select group. Slaves who could read included a higher percentage of urban and house slaves than was true for the slave population as a whole. While the urban population of slaves in the southern United States in the immediate antebellum period is estimated at less than 4 percent,[11] at least 16.5 percent of the former slaves who could read and write described themselves as urban. House slaves were also highly represented among the slaves who learned to read: three-fourths of the former slaves who specified their tasks during slavery described domestic duties.[12] A mitigating factor might be taken into account in observing the high number of house slaves, though: the majority of slaves studied were young children when they began to acquire the skills of reading. Young children often did house duties before they reached an age when they worked in the fields:

> (N=212)   Slaves who read before age 12. . . .   150 (70.8 percent)
> Slaves who read at age 12 or over   62 (29.2 percent)

Nevertheless, the former slaves who learned to read and write had more opportunities for learning than other slaves. Their careers after slavery provide another indication of the exceptional nature of the former slaves who learned to read and write. A large number held leadership positions in the ministry, government, and education.

Almost one-third of the slaves learned to read but not to write. However, given the lack of tools and the special dangers involved in writing, it is noteworthy that the majority of former slaves did learn to write as well as to read.

Teachers of slaves were tabulated in two ways: those who were most responsible for initiating learning (only one person was counted per slave) and those who participated in teaching slaves (more than one could be mentioned by the same slave). When the initiators of learning are compiled, the two sources of former slave evidence vary greatly. Two-thirds of the Writers Project former slaves credited whites with providing the initiative and the means for their learning to read, while well over half the ex-slaves in the other sources gave themselves the credit for initiating and obtaining their learning. Some of this disparity is due to the ways in which evidence was gathered. Living in poverty and dependent for their basic needs on the good will of others, most of the Writers Project interviewees consisted of those ex-slaves most easily found by the predominantly white interviewers. Dependent ex-slaves, hoping that the interviewers could help them collect their old-age pensions, could have inflated the helping role played by the "kind" white master or mistress.

The slaves who wrote their own autobiographies and narratives, on the other hand, were the more perceptive and gifted members of the black community, as well as the relatively more fortunate, and had more control over the information they sought to give. Those former slaves who wrote narratives for a Northern antebellum audience had good reason to minimize any role by Southern whites in their achievements. Those who wrote autobiographies after slavery understandably may have remembered their own roles more sharply and precisely than the part played by others, including whites, who may have contributed to their learning.[13] Fewer owner-taught slaves assumed leadership careers after slavery. "Stealing" their own learning and obtaining subsequent leadership positions suggests that certain talented slaves acted effectively upon their belief in the "liberating" quality of literacy.

Counting all who participated in teaching slaves to read or write, 203 whites taught or helped to teach the 272 ex-slaves. Highlighting the closed character of the plantation system, at least three-fourths of these whites were slave owners, their children, or teachers they hired. Twice as many mistresses as masters taught. Teaching was an acceptable female function; some women inherited this task as part of household management. Charity Jones' mistress taught her to read and write, along with learning to card bats and spin, weave cloth, sew, and sweep. Close association in the house between white and black women sometimes included opportunities for reading. Jane Pyatt recalled that "when I was a slave, I worked in the house with my mistress, and I was able to learn lots from her. . . . although it was against the law to teach a slave, my mistress taught me my alphabets." Betty Ivery's mistress taught her to read after the day's work was done, "long after dark."[14]

Former slaves mentioned children more than any other group of whites as their teachers. Most were the adolescent daughters and sons of slave owners or the younger playmates of slaves. Slave children often learned while accompanying their white playmates to and from school, or during studying time at night. White children taught their slave playmates secretly or without conscious violation of law or custom. Sometimes white children were more tacitly or openly encouraged by white adults, who may have allowed their children to dare to do what they could not. Henry Bruce, for example, learned from the white boy he accompanied to and from school. When the boy's aunt found out and complained, Henry's owner seemed not to care about it and did nothing to stop it; in fact, he corrected Henry's spelling. Solomon, the black overseer on a large plantation, took his little mistress Liza to school. She taught him to read, and "as she growed up she kept learning more and Solomon had married and Miss Liza would go down to his cabin every night and teach him [and his wife] some more." When his master caught Solomon with a Bible in his lap and found out Liza had taught him, he was pleased and amused and even had Solomon show off by reading the Bible to some of his friends. He was able to parade Solomon's accomplishment since he had not been personally responsible for it.[15]

White teachers hired by slave owners also participated in the learning of the slaves. Louis Watkin's owner, for example, employed a white tutor who came on Sunday afternoons to his Tennessee plantation and taught slaves to read, write, and figure. In Georgia, Neal Upson's master built a little one-room schoolhouse in the backyard of the main house, where a white teacher taught the slave children reading and writing. Harrison Beckett character-ized his teacher on a large Texas plantation as a "broke-down white man," who taught "de chillen reading and writing, and manners and behaviour, too. . . . Slaves paid other whites in the cities to help them. Occasionally men or women came to the plantations on their own volition to teach slaves. Ellen Cragin remembered an old white man who used to come out to teach her father in rural Mississippi. The old man cautioned the slave family not to tell the other whites what he was doing: "If you do [tell], they will kill me."[16]

Former slaves mentioned themselves as their own teachers more often than they named other blacks. Typically, Elijah P. Marrs explained that "very early in life I took up the ideal that I wanted to learn to read and write. . . . I availed myself of every opportunity, daily I carried my book in my pocket, and every chance that offered would be learning my A,B,Cs." Many slaves credited their parents with a role in their learning. Determined mothers taught their children, sent them to schools when available, or paid others to teach them. Fathers also figured as teachers, even when they did not live with their families. Anderson Whitted's father, for example, lived fourteen miles away from him but was allowed to use a horse to visit him and taught Anderson to read on his biweekly visits.[17]

Brothers and sisters also taught one another. The children in Henry Bruce's family shared the knowledge learned from their white playmates: "The older one would teach the younger, and while mother had no education at all, she used to make the younger study the lessons given by the older sister or brother, and in that way we all learned to read and some to write." Other family members served as teachers. Ann Stokes' cousin taught her the alphabet "in the middle ob a field unnerneath a 'simmon tree." Grand-mothers, central family figures, were mentioned as teachers. Maria Parham's grandmother, "Old Lady Patsy," took care of all the sick and also taught Maria to read. Henrietta Murray's grandmother taught a Sunday school class on her Choctaw County, Mississippi plantation and, according to Henrietta, "taught us all we knowed."[18]

Other blacks mentioned as teachers included those who shared their knowledge of reading and writing beyond their family group. These included a slave in Tennessee who would make figures and letters on a wooden pad to teach the slave boys how to read and write, and Solomon, free and "ginger cake color," who made his living carrying his slate and book from plantation to plantation in Georgia, teaching slaves "for little what they could slip him along." Teaching was hazardous for the health of the black teacher and also a terrific responsibility. Enoch Golden, known to the slaves as a "double-headed nigger" because he could read and write and "knowed so much," was said to have confessed on his deathbed that he "been the death o' many a nigger 'cause he taught so many to read and write."[19]

Slaves seldom identified specific reasons why whites taught them to read and write.[20] Only the religious context of much of the teaching by whites stands out clearly as a motivation. Often teaching was casual and depended upon the slave's proximity to the house or to white playmates or upon the whims of owners. Some slaves became the pets of the white family as tiny children, and family members thought it "cute" to see them learning the alphabet and trying to read. "Bunny" Bond's owners dressed her up and let her go to school with the white children when she was five, then laughed when she fell asleep and wanted to go home. Robert McKinley's owner gave the little boy to his favorite daughter, Jane Alice, as a present; she was very fond of little Bob so she taught him to read and write.[21]

A few slave owners obviously taught their slaves because they believed in the intrinsic value of education. Robert Laird's Mississippi owner had his slaves taught how to read and write simply because "he didn't want us not to know nothin'." The owner of Robert Cheatham's mother in Kentucky tried to carry on a family tradition from Virginia, telling his slaves, "You colored boys and girls must learn to read and write, no matter what powers object . . . your parents and your grandparents were taught to read and write when they belonged to my forefathers and you young negroes have to learn as much."[22]

Sometimes whites taught for pragmatic reasons. Washington Curry's father was a doctor, and Curry recalled that "there were so many folks that came to see the doctor and wanted to leave numbers and addresses that he had to have someone to tend to that and he taught my father to read and write so that he could do it." Adeline Willis's mistress taught her the letters on the newspapers and what they spelled so she could bring the papers the whites wanted. Simpson Campbell's "Marse Bill" taught some of his slaves reading and writing so he could use them "booking cotton in the field and such like."[23]

Religion, however, was mentioned by former slaves more often than any other context in which teaching by whites took place. On the plantations and in cities, according to ex-slave accounts, owners built churches and schoolhouses and hired teachers or conducted worship and Sunday school themselves, where they perpetuated the original function of the Sunday school as the inculcator of literacy as well as religion. Squire Dowd's mistress taught such a class on a North Carolina plantation; so did Mollie Mittchell's and Easter Jones's owners on plantations in Georgia. Near Birmingham, Alabama, Andrew Goodman's "Marse Bob" built his slaves a church, where a nearby slave, "a man of good learnin'," preached to them on Sundays; then on Sunday afternoons, Marse Bob taught them how to read and write, telling his slaves "we ought to get all the learnin' we could."[24]

These owners felt their slaves should be able to read the Bible, but many hoped to shield their slaves from the liberating aspects of literacy. One measure of the conservative nature of "Bible literacy" is the level of learning attained by ex-slaves under white, religiously inspired teaching. Whites who taught slaves in a religious context taught reading only and not writing more frequently than other whites. Owners expressed sentiments about the virtue of reading but not of writing. Henry Bruce's owner was "glad his Negroes could read, especially the Bible, but he was opposed to their being taught writing," and Bruce did not learn to write until after slavery ended. Elijah Marrs's owner said that he wanted all the slave boys to learn how to read the Bible, but that it was against the laws of the state of Kentucky to write (though this was untrue). Marrs said, "we had to steal that portion of our education."[25]

Slave-initiated learning took place in a different context than that of white-initiated learning; slaves depended more on opportunity and desire. Therefore, urban slaves and household slaves were in particularly favorable positions to obtain their own learning. Many domestic workers were taught to read by whites, but more than a third of the household slaves taught themselves or tricked others into teaching them. Belle Caruthers's duties, for example, were to fan her mistress and to nurse the baby: "The baby had alphabet blocks to play with and I learned my letters while she learned hers." Moses Slaughter's mother, the housekeeper, would say to the owner's daughter, "Come here, Emily, Mamma will keep your place for you," and while little Emily read, "Mamma Emalina" followed each line until she too was a fluent reader and could teach her own children.[26]

In the cities, alert apprentices like teenage Noah Davis, bound out to learn boot- and shoemaking in Fredericksburg, made the most of their chances. Davis saw his employer write the names of his customers on the lining of the boots and shoes which he gave out to be made; Davis imitated him and could soon write his name. Benjamin Holmes, apprentice tailor in Charleston, studied all the signs and all the names on the doors where he carried bundles and asked people to tell him a word or two at a time. By the time he was twelve, he found he could read newspapers. Frederick Douglass made friends with white boys he met in the Baltimore streets and converted those he could into teachers by exchanging bread from his house for lessons. He learned to write by watching ship's carpenters write their letters for shipping lumber and by copying lessons secretly from the master's son's books when the family was out of the house.[27]

Whether in urban or rural areas, slaves created innovative solutions to the problems of tools for reading and writing and finding the time and place to use them. Slaves "borrowed" books from their owners, or bought them with their treasured small savings if the purchase did not arouse suspicion.[28] They made their own writing materials and used planks to write on, or practiced writing in sand.[29] Slaves used weekends or Sundays to learn to read and write; many studied at night. Ex-slaves told Fisk University interviewers that they slipped old wooden planks into the house, and they would light them and sit down at night and read from the light of the fire. W. E. Northcross had been warned by his master that if he were caught with a book he would be hung by the white men of his Alabama community, so Northcross carried some old boards into his house to make a light by which to read secretly. This was a hazardous undertaking, as he recalled: "I would shut the doors, put one end of a board into the fire, and proceed to study; but whenever I heard the dogs barking I would throw my book under the bed and peep and listen to see what was up. If no one was near I would crawl under the bed, get my book, come out, lie flat on my stomach, and proceed to study until the dogs would again disturb me." Former slaves were proud of conquering opposition to their learning. Jenny Proctor triumphantly told how her community of several hundred slaves under a particularly oppressive regime rose to the challenge of restrictions against books: "Dey say we git smarter den dey was if we learn anything, but we slips around and gits hold of dat Webster's old blue back speller and we hides it 'til way in de night and den we lights a little pine torch and studies dat spellin' book. We learn it too."[30]

Given the very real dangers involved in learning to read and write, what lay behind slaves' "insatiable craving for some knowledge of books," as Lucius Holsey put it? Some former slaves attributed their high valuation of reading and writing skills to their owners' resistance. Their desire to learn, along with their belief that such skills could greatly expand their world, was augmented by the fact that these skills were withheld. Henry Morehead's owners objected to his attending night school in Louisville, because school "would only teach him rascality." Morehead resented the use of that word, and his owners' resistance persuaded him to use his own money and time for school. Frederick Douglass claimed that he owed as much to the bitter opposition of his master as to the kindly aid of his mistress in learning to read: "I acknowledge the benefit of both."[31]

Slaves were aware of the promise of literacy as a path to mobility and increased self-worth. Claims about literacy's intrinsic and practical value, espoused by educational reformers in England and the northern United States had an impact even in the South. An interesting interpretation of this message came from a poor white boy who assured the enslaved Thomas Jones that "a man who had learning would always find friends, and get along in the world without having to work hard, while those who had no learning would have no friends and be compelled to work very hard for a poor living all their days." Lucius Holsey, who was the son of his master and who identified in many ways with the white world, "felt that constitutionally he was created the equal of any person here on earth and that, given a chance, he could rise to the height of any man," and that books were the path to proving his worth as a human being.[32]

Former slaves who learned on their own initiative mentioned the religious context for their learning more than any other factor. Since many of the former slaves who wrote their own narratives and autobiographies were ministers, many attributed their desire for learning to their religious aspirations. One-third of the Federal Writers Project interviewees whose learning was slave-initiated also specified a religious context for their learning to read and write.

To many slaves, the religious context for learning provided a chance for leadership; the ministry was the chief outlet for such ambition, and the literate preacher served as a leader of the black community both during and after slavery. Preachers recalled that they first wanted to learn to read after their conversion and their desire to preach. Peter Randolph's account of his conversion was typical: "After receiving this revelation from the Lord, I became impressed that I was called of God to preach to the other slaves . . . but then I could not read the Bible, and I thought I could never preach unless I learned to read the Bible."[33] The ability to read and write also obtained other advantages for slaves, including privacy. Sarah Fitzpatrick pointed out that if a slave wanted to court a girl and could not write, his master had to write his love letter for him, so "anytime you writ a note white folks had to know whut it said."[34]

Slave narratives reinforce the connection between reading and preaching. Rhiner Gardner recalled that "if there chanced to be among the slaves a man of their own race who could read and write, he generally preached and would, at times and places unknown to the master, call his fellow slaves together and hold religious services with them." On many plantations, such as that near Beaufort, South Carolina, where Melvin Smith was enslaved, "the preacher was the onliest one that could read the Bible." Former slaves recalled their belief that "white people taught their niggers what Bible they wanted them to know" only, and saw the literate black preacher as their key to unlocking the Bible's power. The preacher's high status is exemplified by Byrd Day, whose fellow slaves valued his ability to read and write so highly that they bought him a Bible so he could read it to them, and they farmed his patch of ground for him so that he could spend his nights studying the Bible.[35]

The preacher and the religious authority often became teacher too. Slaves learned to read and write in Sunday schools operated by black preachers and teachers. When Frederick Douglass was hired out to a Maryland farm, he began a Sunday school and "devoted my Sundays to teaching these my loved fellow-slaves how to read." At one time his class numbered over forty pupils of all ages. Austin Butler, Virginia Harris's preacher on a Louisiana plantation, tried to teach other slaves the alphabet during Sunday school, since "he was a man with learning." In Tennessee, James Southall recalled that "all our cullud preachers could read de Bible," and that they taught any slaves who wanted to learn.[36]

Slaves who learned to read and write were exceptional people who used their skills in literacy in exceptional ways. Some gained mobility: in Mary Colbert's Athens, Georgia, slave community those slaves who could read and write were usually chosen to travel with their master, so that if anything happened to him they could write home. At least five of the former slaves in this study used their ability to write to escape from slavery, including James Fisher, who wrote passes which got him safely across the border from Tennessee.[37]

Literate slaves also helped other slaves. Milla Granson, for example, learned to read and write in Kentucky, was moved to Natchez, and established a midnight school there, where she taught hundreds of fellow slaves to read. Slaves who could read were often furnished with newspapers stolen or purchased by other slaves, and former slaves recalled the roles played by literate slaves in the spread of the news of the war and the coming of freedom. In Georgia, for example, Minnie Davis's mother stole newspapers during the war and kept the other slaves posted as to the war's progress. Cora Gillam's uncle was jailed until the Union soldiers came because he "had a newspaper with latest war news and gathered a crowd of fellow Mississippi slaves to read them when peace was coming."[38]

After slavery, many of the blacks who learned reading and writing skills as slaves used their learning in public leadership positions, including famous "men of mark" like Frederick Douglass and "women of mark" like Susie King Taylor; founders and presidents of black colleges such as Isaac Lane and Isaac Burgan; scholars and writers like W. S. Scarborough and N. W. Harlee; and businessmen like Edward Walker of Windsor, Ontario. Government officeholders included Blanche K. Bruce, U. S. Senator from Mississippi, and Isaiah Montgomery, who with his family founded the black colony of Mound Bayou, Mississippi. Forty-five of the former slaves became ministers either during or after slavery: they served congregations or traveled circuits, assumed bishoprics or other positions in church hierarchies, or became missionaries, like Thomas Johnson, evangelist to Africa and the British isles. Literate slaves opened schools immediately after the war, including Sally Johnson, taught by her owners at the academy where she served as a nurse, and Celia Singleton, who taught her own school in Georgia two years after freedom.[39]

Some of these community leaders were taught by whites, but the connection between slaves who seized learning for themselves and their subsequent public leadership careers suggests that the belief by slaves in the liberating aspects of literacy as a form of resistance was not unfounded.

Table 12.1. Decade of birth of ex-slaves, by source

Decade of birth	Federal Writers Project interviewees		Other ex-slaves	
	N	Percentage	N	Percentage
1800–30	11	6.1	41	44.1
1831–40	39	21.8	19	20.4
1841–50	66	36.9	16	17.2
1851–59	63	35.2	17	18.3
Totals	179	100.0	93	100.0

Table 12.2. Decade when learned to read, by source

Decade when learned to read	Federal Writers Project interviewees		Other ex-slaves	
	N	Percentage	N	Percentage
1820–35	1	0.8	23	27.4
1836–45	9	7.0	18	21.4
1846–55	33	25.8	15	17.9
1856–65	85	66.4	28	33.3
Totals	128	100.0	84	100.0

Table 12.3. Regional location of slaves when they learned to read, by source

Region	Federal Writers Project interviewees		Other ex-slaves	
	N	Percentage	N	Percentage
Border South (Ky., Tenn., Mo., Md., Del., D.C.)	27	15.1	33	35.5
Old South (Va., N.C., S.C., Ga.)	68	38.0	43	46.3
New South (Miss., La., Ark., Fla., Ala., Tex.)	84	45.0	14	15.1
Totals	179	100.0	90	100.0

Table 12.4. Postslavery careers of ex-slaves, by source

Careers	Federal Writers Project interviewees		Other ex-slaves	
	N	Percentage	N	Percentage
Leadership (ministry, education, govt.)	27	15.1	64	68.8
Other (skilled trades, domestic, farm or day labor)	21	11.7	3	3.2
Careers after slavery not specified	131	73.2	26	28.0
Totals	179	100.0	93	100.0

Table 12.5. Levels of literacy attained while slaves, by source

Level of literacy	Federal Writers Project interviewees		Other ex-slaves	
	N	Percentage	N	Percentage
Learned "letters" (knowledge of alphabet to some spelling)	30	16.8	5	5.4
Learned to read but not to write	40	22.3	34	36.6
Learned to read and write	94	52.5	45	48.3
Learned to read, write, cipher, some grammar	15	8.4	9	9.7
Totals	179	100.0	93	100.0

Table 12.6. Owner- versus slave-initiated learning, by source

Initiators of learning	Federal Writers Project interviewees		Other ex-slaves	
	N	Percentage	N	Percentage
Owners	144	81.3	33	35.5
Slaves	33	18.7	60	64.5
Totals	177	100.0	93	100.0

Table 12.7. Contexts for owner-initiated teaching, by ex-slave source

Context	Federal Writers Project interviewees		Other ex-slaves	
	N	Percentage	N	Percentage
Owner-initiated teaching in a religious context*	63	43.7	13	39.4
Owner-initiated teaching in context other than religious	5	3.5	2	6.1
Owner-initiated teaching in unspecified context	76	52.8	18	54.5
Totals	144	100.0	33	100.0

*Criteria for religious context for owner-initiated teaching: (1) owner or agent taught slaves to read as part of religious instruction or Sunday school; (2) owner or agent taught slaves to read the Bible; (3) owner insisted on or encouraged religious worship as well as reading and writing by slaves in one or more of the following ways: (a) provided church on premises; (b) encouraged slaves to hold their own services; (c) paid black or white preacher for them; (d) accompanied them to church in nearby town or city; (e) held daily worship service or Bible reading.

Table 12.8. Contexts for slave-initiated teaching, by ex-slave source

Context	Federal Writers Project interviewees		Other ex-slaves	
	N	Percentage	N	Percentage
Slave-initiated teaching in a religious context*	11	33.3	25	41.7
Slave-initiated teaching in context other than religious	2	6.1	8	13.3
Slave-initiated teaching in unspecified context	20	60.6	27	45.0
Totals	33	100.0	60	100.0

*Criteria for religious context for slave-initiated teaching: (1) slave was taught by slave preacher or teacher as part of religious instruction or Sunday school; (2) slave stated that he/she decided to learn in order to read the Bible and/or preach the Gospel.

Notes

1. Kenneth A. Lockridge attributes the initial rise in mass literacy in the Atlantic world to "intense Protestantism," whose primary purpose was "pious conformity." Lockridge, *Literacy in Colonial New England: An Enquiry into the Social Context of Literacy in the Early Modern West* (New York, 1974), 98–100. Harvey Graff notes that the early 19th-century American public school movement fostered traditional Protestant morality; its architects were clergymen, its publicists were the religious press, and its major goals included the inculcation of morality. Graff, *The Literacy Myth: Literacy and Social Structure in the Nineteenth-Century City* (New York, 1979), 28, 314–15. For a definition on the "liberating" aspects of literacy, see Graff, 20; and Lawrence A. Cremin, *Traditions of American Education* (New York, 1977), 32–35.

2. For the teaching of reading but not writing in religious education in 17th-century Sweden, see Daniel P. Resnick and Lauren B. Resnick, "The Nature of Literacy: An Historical Exploration," *Harvard Educational Review* 47 (August 1977): 374. For a similar practice in late 18th- and early 19th-century England, see Michael Sanderson, "Literacy and Social Mobility in the Industrial Revolution in England," *Past and Present* 56 (August 1972): 81; John McLeish, *Evangelical Religion and Popular Education: A Modern Interpretation* (London, 1969), 95; Philip McCann, "Popular Education, Socialization, and Social Control: Spitalfields, 1812–1824," and Simon Frith, "Socialization and Rational Schooling: Elementary Education in Leeds before 1870," both in *Popular Education and Socialization in the Nineteenth Century*, ed. Philip McCann (London, 1977), 11–12, 81–82.

3. Northern observers during and immediately after the war noted that the former slaves considered learning to read almost a religious act. One Northerner on the Sea Islands described black children reciting the alphabet over a grave at a funeral in ritualistic style, and numerous missionaries commented upon the freed slaves' great desire to read the Bible. Lawrence W. Levine, *Black Culture and Black Consciousness: Afro-American Folk Thought from Slavery to Freedom* (Oxford, 1977), 156; *American Missionary* (Magazine, c. 1850) 5: 11, 257.

4. Charles L. Perdue Jr., Thomas E. Barden, and Robert K. Phillips, eds., *Weevils in the Wheat: Interviews with Virginia Ex-Slaves* (Charlottesville, 1976); George L. Rawick, ed., *The American Slave: A Composite Autobiography*, 19 vols. (Westport, Conn., 1972) (hereafter cited as Rawick); Supplement, Series 1, 12 vols. (Westport, Conn., 1977). Supplement cited in notes is Series 1; Series 2 (Westport, Conn., 1979) is used for text correction only and is thus not cited in notes.

5. For purposes of tabulating slaves who learned to read and write, I have read all the narratives and used those accounts of former slaves who told of learning or being taught to learn their "letters" or to "read" or to "read and write." Only those former slaves who were personally taught, or whose close relative such as a mother or father or a specific acquaintance were taught were tabulated; accounts of slaves who reminisced that "all the slaves were taught to read and write" were not included in the tabulations of the 272 slaves in this study.

6. Octavia V. Rogers Albert, *The House of Bondage; or, Charlotte and Other Slaves* (New York, 1890; reprint ed., 1972); Sam Aleckson, *Before the War, and after the Union: An Autobiography* (Boston, 1929); *Aunt Sally; or, The Cross the Way of Freedom* (Cincinnati, 1858); John W. Blassingame, *Slave Testimony: Two Centuries of Letters, Speeches, Interviews, and Autobiographies* (Baton Rouge, 1977); Charles Octavius Boothe, *The Cyclopedia of the Colored Baptists of Alabama: Their Leaders and Their Work* (Birmingham, 1895); Levi Branham, *My Life and Travels* (Dalton, Georgia, 1929); Hallie Q. Brown, *Homespun Heroines and Other Women of Distinction* (Xenia, Ohio, 1926); Henry Clay Bruce, *The New Man: Twenty-Nine Years a Slave, Twenty-Nine Years a Free Man* (York, Pa., 1895; reprint ed., 1969); Edward R. Carter, *Biographical Sketches of Our Pulpit* (Atlanta, 1888; reprint ed., 1968); Daniel W. Culp, ed., *Twentieth Century Negro Literature* (Naperville, Ill., 1902; reprint ed., 1969); Noah Davis, *A Narrative of the Life of Rev. Noah Davis, a Colored Man, Written by Himself, at the Age of 54* (Baltimore, 1859); Frederick Douglass, *Narrative of the Life of Frederick Douglass* (Boston, 1845); Benjamin Drew, *The Refugee: or, The Narratives of Fugitive Slaves in Canada Related by Themselves* (Boston, 1856); Orville Elder and Samuel Hall, *The Life of Samuel Hall, Washington, Iowa: A Slave for Forty-Seven Years* (Washington, Iowa., 1912); Elisha Green, *Life of the Rev. Elisha W. Green* (Maysville, Ky., 1888), Laura Haviland, *A Woman's Life-Work* (Chicago, 1887); Lucius Holsey, *Autobiography, Sermons, Addresses, and Essays* (Atlanta, 1898); Louis Hughes, *Thirty Years a Slave* (Milwaukee, 1897); Thomas L. Johnson, *Twenty-Eight Years a Slave,* 7th ed. (Bournemouth, England, 1909); Thomas Jones, *The Experience of Thomas Jones, Who Was a Slave for Forty-Three Years* (Boston, 1862); Isaac Lane, *The Autobiography of Bishop Isaac Lane* (Nashville, 1916); Elijah P. Marrs, *Life and History of the Rev. Elijah P. Marrs* (Louisville, Ky., 1885; reprint ed. 1969); A. W. Pegues, *Our Baptist Ministers and Schools* (Springfield, Mass., 1892); Gustavus D. Pike, *The Jubilee Singers and Their Campaign for Twenty Thousand Dollars* (Boston, 1873); Peter Randolph, *Sketches of Slave Life* (Boston, 1893); William J. Simmons, *Men of Mark: Eminent, Progressive and Rising* (Cleveland, Ohio, 1887; reprint ed., 1968); William Still, *The Underground Rail Road* (Philadelphia, 1872); Susie King Taylor, *Reminiscences of My Life in Camp* (Boston, 1902; reprint ed., 1968); Alexander Wayman, *Cyclopedia of African Methodism* (Baltimore, 1882).

7. Rawick, Alabama, 6:212–14; Texas, 5 (3): 121. Contrary to popular belief, there were few specific laws against owners teaching their slaves. By the 1850s, the legal codes of only four Southern states—North and South Carolina, Georgia, and Virginia—prohibited the teaching of individual slaves to read and write, and Virginia's law did not ban owners from teaching their own slaves. North Carolina, *Revised Statutes,* 1837, 209, 578; 1854, 218–19; George M. Stroud, *A Sketch of the Laws Relating to Slavery* (Philadelphia, 1856), 58–63; *Code of the State of Georgia* (Atlanta, 1861), 1878–79; *Digest of the Laws of Georgia* (Philadelphia, 1831), 316–17; *Code of Virginia* (1849), 747–48. Alabama had passed a law in 1832 prohibiting the teaching of slaves or free blacks, and it had appeared in the *Digest of the Laws in Alabama* in 1843, 543, but is not in the *Code of the State of Alabama*, 1852. Similarly,

Louisiana's law fining or imprisoning "all persons who shall teach any slave" to read or write, passed in 1830, appeared in a digest of its laws published in 1841, but did not form part of its 1856 revised Black Code, though other provisions of the same act did (*Louisiana Digest of Laws*, 1841, 521–22; *Louisiana Revised Statutes*, 1856, 54.) Mississippi revised its slave code in 1831 to prohibit blacks from exercising functions of ministers unless on the premises of a slave owner with his permission, but did not ban teaching of slaves to read. (*Code of Mississippi*, 1798–1848, 534.) Other states, including Maryland and Missouri, banned public assemblages of blacks for religious or educational purposes, but did not penalize individuals teaching individual slaves or free blacks to read or write. (*Maryland Code*, 1860, 462; *Missouri Laws*, 1847, 103–4; *Missouri Revised Statutes*, 1856). Moreover, slave owners tended to disregard any laws which seemed to interfere with their management of their own slaves, preferring to think of their plantations as kingdoms in themselves, where each planter "exercises in his own person, all the high functions of an unlimited monarch," to quote Whitemarsh Seabrook in his *Essay on the Management of Slaves* (Charleston, 1834), 15.

8. Rawick, Oklahoma and Mississippi, 7:78–79; Georgia, 13 (4):305.

9. Rawick, Georgia, 13 (3):144; Mississippi, Suppl., 10 (5): 2337; A. W. Pegues, *Our Baptist Ministers and Schools*, 62–63.

10. Rawick, Texas, 4 (1): 286; Blassingame, *Slave Testimony*, 643.

11. Claudia Dale Goldin, *Urban Slavery in the American South, 1820-1860: A Quantitative History* (Chicago, 1976), 12. House slaves, or slaves engaged in domestic tasks such as cooks, housemaids, gardeners, stewards, and coachmen, are estimated by Robert Fogel and Stanley Engerman to have comprised 7.4 percent of male workers and about 20 percent of women workers. Fogel and Engerman, *Time on the Cross: The Economics of American Negro Slavery*, 2 vols. (Boston, 1974), 2:37–43.

12. Census interviewers in most countries ask respondents whether they can read or write; no tests or other ways to measure "functional literacy" have yet been agreed upon. See Harvey Graff, "Literacy Past and Present: Critical Approaches in the Literacy-Society Relationship," *Interchange* 9, no. 2 (1978): 8–9. Resnick and Resnick, 371, note that expectations in literacy range from the ability to write one's name to "the ability to read a complex test with literary allusions and metaphoric expression and not only to interpret this text but to relate it sensibly to other texts."

13. While legitimate concerns are felt about the validity of both kinds of sources used in this study—each group is select rather than representative, and former slaves in each group were addressing a particular audience for particular purposes—the two kinds of sources present the researcher with a body of testimony about slave life which cannot be obtained elsewhere, and so have been used extensively in studies of slavery and the slave community. For discussions of the strengths and weaknesses of each kind of source and comparisons of their validity, see David Thomas Bailey, "A Divided Prism: Two Sources of Black Testimony on Slavery," *Journal of Southern History* 46 (August 1980): 381–404; Blassingame, *Slave Testimony*, xxxii–lxii; William L. Van Deburg, *The Slave Drivers: Black Agricultural Labor*

Supervisors in the Antebellum South (Westport, Conn., 1979), 77–94; Paul Escott, *Slavery Remembered: A Record of Twentieth Century Slave Narratives* (Chapel Hill, 1979), 3–17; Thomas Webber, *Deep like the Rivers: Education in the Slave Quarter Community* (New York, 1978), 26.

14. Rawick, Mississippi, Suppl., 8 (3): 1195–96; Perdue, 234; Rawick, Oklahoma, Suppl., 12:354–56.

15. Bruce, 25–26; Rawick, Oklahoma, Suppl., 12:298–300.

16. Rawick, Indiana, Suppl. 2, 2 (1):224; Arkansas, 8 (2): 44.

17. Marrs, 11; *Aunt Sally,* 74–75; Johnson, 5; Simmons, 235.

18. Bruce, 45; Rawick, Missouri, 11:333; Mississippi, Suppl., 9 (4): 1674, 1610.

19. Branham, 10; Rawick, Arkansas, 8 (2): 20; Georgia, 13 (3): 212.

20. Evidence for white motivations for teaching slaves has been limited in this study to accounts by former slaves. For white accounts of teaching slaves to read, see Moncure D. Conway, *Autobiography, Memories and Experiences of M. D. Conway,* 2 vols. (Boston, 1904; reprint ed. 1979), 1:5–7; Susan Dabney Smedes, *Memorials of a Southern Planter* (Baltimore, 1888), 79–80; Nehemiah Adams, *A South-Side View of Slavery* (Boston, 1854), 56–57; Frederika Bremer, *Homes of the New World,* 2 vols. (New York, 1853), 1:499; Mary Chesnut, *A Diary from Dixie* (New York, 1929), 292–93. For connections between the Southern white mission to evangelize slaves and slave owners who taught their slaves to read the Bible, see Janet Cornelius, "God's Schoolmasters: Southern Evangelists to the slaves, 1830–1860" (Ph.D. dissertation, University of Illinois, 1977), 263–87; Milton Sernett, *Black Religion and American Evangelicalism* (Metuchen, N.J., 1975); Albert Raboteau, *Slave Religion* (New York, 1978), 209–318. Southern churchmen proclaimed that the literacy law was constantly being violated and was practically a "dead letter," thereby encouraging owners to follow their own consciences. Petitions on Slavery, South Carolina State Archives, Columbia; *Biblical Recorder,* Nov. 9, 1844; James Henley Thornwell, *A Sermon Preached* . . . (Charleston, 1850), 47; Richard Fuller and Francis Wayland, *Domestic Slavery Considered as a Scriptural Institution* (New York, 1845), 160; William E. Clebsch, ed., *Journals of the Protestant Episcopal Church in the Confederate States of America* (Austin, Tex., 1962), 10–12.

21. Rawick, Arkansas, 9 (3):311; Arkansas, 8 (1):197–98; Indiana, 6:131.

22. Rawick, Mississippi, Suppl., 8 (3):1292; Indiana, Suppl., 5:45.

23. Rawick, Arkansas, 8 (2):84; Georgia, 13 (4):163; Texas, Suppl. 2, 3 (2):612.

24. Rawick, North Carolina 14 (1):268; Georgia, 13 (3):134; Georgia, Suppl., 4 (2):350; Texas, Suppl. 2, 5 (4):1522.

25. Bruce, 25–26; Marrs, 15.

26. Perdue, 187; Rawick, Indiana, Suppl., 5:48; Mississippi, 7 (2):365; Indiana, Suppl., 5:197.

27. Noah Davis, *Narrative of the Life of Rev. Noah Davis,* 17; Gustavus D. Pike, *The Jubilee Singers,* 57–58; Douglass, *Narrative,* 58–59.

28. Slaves named Webster's speller more often than any other book as the tool used for their initiation into reading. Distributed in millions of copies, its use was a tribute to the persistence of the nineteenth-century student, since it was a small

book with small print and few illustrations or other enticements to attract the beginning reader. While more secular then earlier spellers had been, the "blue back" still emphasized religious precepts and spiritual and moral virtues along with its syllabic exercises. Noah Webster, *The Elementary Spelling Book* (Cincinnati, 1843), esp. 26, 29, 69.

29. Rawick, Mississippi, Suppl., 9 (4):1664–65; Thomas Jones, 15; Lucius H. Holsey, *Autobiography*, 16–18; Blassingame, *Slave Testimony*, 131; Rawick, Arkansas, 10 (6):332; Arkansas, 11 (7):185; Drew, *The Refugee*, 97; Blassingame, *Slave Testimony*, 45; Rawick, South Carolina, 2 (2):50.

30. Rawick, Fisk University, *Unwritten History of Slavery*, 18:57; Alabama, 6:300–302; Texas, 5 (3):213.

31. Holsey, 16; Drew, 180–81; Douglass, 65.

32. Jones, 14; Holsey, 16–18.

33. Randolph, 10–11.

34. John B. Cade, "Out of the Mouths of Ex-Slaves," *Journal of Negro History* 20 (January 1935): 330; Rawick, Georgia, 13 (3):291; Arkansas, 10 (6):190; Boothe, *Cyclopedia of the Colored Baptists of Alabama*, 69–70.

35. Douglass, 70; Rawick, Mississippi, Suppl., 8 (3):940; Oklahoma, 7:308.

36. Rawick, Georgia, 12 (1):220; Blassingame, 234, 237. At least 55 of the 625 runaway slaves (8.8 percent) who sought assistance from William Still on the Underground Railroad in the 1850s knew how to read and write, as did 15.1 percent of the runaways to Canada questioned by Benjamin Drew in 1855. Since neither Still nor Drew was particularly interested in whether the fugitives they interviewed had learned to read or write during slavery, the proportion of literate slaves among these fugitives may have been much higher. Still, *The Underground Rail Road*; Drew, *The Refugee*.

37. Blassingame, *Slave Testimony*, 643.

38. Laura Haviland, *A Woman's Life-Work* (Chicago, 1887), 300–301; Rawick, Georgia, 12 (1):257; Arkansas, 9 (3):28–29.

39. Douglass; Taylor; Lane; Simmons, 1087, 411–12; Culp, 279; Bruce; Rawick, Mississippi, Suppl., 9 (4):1538–39; Johnson, 50 ff.; Rawick, Fisk Interviews, 18:226; Rawick, Georgia, 13 (3):270.

13 SENSE AND SENSIBILITY: A CASE STUDY OF WOMEN'S READING IN LATE-VICTORIAN AMERICA

Barbara Sicherman

The influence of the printed word may well have been at its peak in late-Victorian America. It was a time of rapidly expanding education and literacy, book and magazine production, and opportunities for self-improvement. The profusion of print, and the evident hunger for it among the working as well as the middle classes, prompted official and self-appointed guardians of culture to proffer advice on how and what to read.[1] Women were integral to the culture of reading. Besides participating in self-study programs like the Society to Encourage Studies at Home, they established reading clubs and literary societies in hundreds of communities across the nation. Taking their cultural mission seriously, clubwomen and other community leaders gave high priority to establishing libraries; indeed, one source estimates that women founded 75 percent of all American public libraries.[2]

As yet we know little about the import of these activities or how women decoded what they read. Scholars who have examined the domestic novels of American antebellum women writers have variously found in them feminist messages of subversion or conservative reinforcement of the cult of domesticity.[3] While interesting as exegesis, these studies rarely consider actual reading experiences, which we know included the work of English as well as male writers; nor do they tell us how readers engaged with texts at the time.[4] Moreover, as Janice Radway has demonstrated in her study of twentieth-century romance reading, critics have been too quick to impose their own views on texts and to assume they have a universal and controlling power over readers.[5]

A study of a late-Victorian upper-middle-class, mainly female family permits us to explore how reading functioned as a cultural style and how it affected women's sense of self (subjectivity) in the past. Historians have noted the puzzling aspects of the Progressive generation of women, in particular their ability—despite growing up at the height of Victorianism, when images of "true

From Barbara Sicherman, "Sense and Sensibility: A Case Study of Women's Reading in Late-Nineteenth-Century America," in Cathy N. Davidson, ed. *Reading in America: Literature and Social History,* 201–25. © 1989 The Johns Hopkins University Press. Reprinted with permission of The Johns Hopkins University Press.

womanhood" and the sanctity of the home still dominated popular culture—to move out into the world in daring ways. A study of women's intense engagement with books suggests that many found in reading a way of apprehending the world that enabled them to overcome some of the confines of gender and class. Reading provided space—physical, temporal, and psychological—that permitted women to exempt themselves from traditional gender expectations, whether imposed by formal society or by family obligation. The freedom of imagination women found in books encouraged new self-definitions and, ultimately, the innovative behavior associated with the Progressive generation.

This study has been influenced by reader-response criticism, an approach that changes the locus of literary study from texts to readers and that emphasizes readers' ability to find their own meanings in texts.[6] Applied to historical subjects, this approach enables us to reconstruct the situational aspects of reading (the what, where, when, and how), while also casting light on individual "stories of reading" and reading as a social system. In this particular case, the Hamilton family constituted an "interpretive community," one that privileged certain texts and interpreted them according to its own codes. Within this common framework, individuals singled out books to which they attached special importance and meaning.

What follows is not a full-scale analysis of reading in the Hamilton family.[7] Rather I have attempted to identify the varied uses of reading in a highly cultured family and to suggest ways in which evidence about reading can be utilized not only in writing individual and family biography but also in understanding shared generational values and changing female subjectivity. The study suggests the need to modify assessments of how women read fictional texts. It also casts doubt on current generalizations about late-nineteenth-century reading and suggests that women's reading behavior may have diverged from that of men.[8]

I

The Hamiltons of Fort Wayne, Indiana, were an intensely and self-consciously literary family. The fortune acquired by the patriarch, a Scotch-Irish immigrant who came to the city in 1823, provided his five surviving children and eighteen grandchildren with the accouterments of the good life, including education, books, and travel. One of the city's most prominent families, Hamiltons of three generations were distinguished by their literary interests. The oldest members of the third generation, seven women and one man all born between 1862 and 1873, belonged to three nuclear families; in childhood the cousins were each others' only playmates. Two of them attained international renown: Edith Hamilton as a popular interpreter of classical civilizations, her younger sister Alice Hamilton as a pioneer in industrial medicine and Harvard's first woman professor. All had serious aspirations. Margaret and Norah had careers in education and art, respectively. Their cousin Agnes, who hoped at first to become an architect, later entered settlement work, while as young women her older sisters Katherine and Jessie studied languages and art. Allen Hamilton Williams became a physician.[9]

The family's literary tradition descended from their paternal grandmother, Emerine Holman Hamilton, a member of a prominent Indiana political family and a supporter of temperance and woman suffrage. Alice remembered her chiefly as a woman who "lost herself" in books: "She loved reading passionately. I can remember often seeing her in the library of the Old House, crouched over the fireplace where the soft-coal fire had gone out without her knowing it, so deep had she been in her book." Emerine "enthralled" her grandchildren with Scott's poems, which she rendered mainly in prose, sometimes dropping into poetry.[10] With her three daughters Emerine established a Free Reading Room for Women in 1887, which contained, in addition to magazines, newspapers, and reference books, about four hundred volumes, mainly works of "general literature and art and the best fiction." After Emerine's death in 1889, the reading room was renamed for her and became a circulating library, with an enlarged collection that included history and biography as well as children's books. In 1896, after the founding of a public library, the collection, then numbering more than four thousand volumes, went to the Young Women's Christian Association, headed by Emerine's granddaughter Agnes.[11] It is significant that although everyone in this family read passionately, it was the women who extended reading from a private pleasure to an occasion for community service. Emerine's two sons, for their part, ensconced themselves in their libraries—well stocked with port and cigars as well as books. The collection of Edith and Alice's uncle was, at six thousand or more volumes, the largest in Fort Wayne.[12]

Edith once exclaimed that she wished "people did not think us quite so terribly bookish."[13] It is difficult to see how it could have been otherwise. The cousins were inducted into the family's literary culture at an early age, their lives and happiness closely bound up with books. When the Hamiltons thought of each other, they thought of each other reading. Edith away at school wished she could fly home and watch her closest cousin, Jessie, reading (Sunday books on Sunday), while Jessie later recalled Edith at thirteen reading a book in Greek while combing her hair.[14] Alice claimed that she and her youngest sister, Norah, were not "born" readers, but "family pressure made us too into bookworms finally."[15] A father's return from business was an occasion for gift books to children, as were holidays; in her early teens, Agnes received a volume of Scott each vacation. The young women also had access to their fathers' ample libraries—except for a few "forbidden" books, of which Alice later recalled only *The Decameron*, the *Heptaméron* of Marguerite of Navarre, and Eugène Sue's *The Wandering Jew*.[16] Bookstores constituted a central focus of interest on shopping sprees in New York City with their unmarried aunt, Margaret Vance Hamilton. After 1889, the young women borrowed books from the reading room.

Reading constituted the core of the Hamiltons' education, indeed was barely distinguished from it. Edith, Alice, and their younger sisters were educated entirely at home until sixteen or seventeen, when they went to Miss Porter's School in Farmington, Connecticut (as did the cousins and the aunts). They received formal instruction only in languages, and even these were largely self-taught. Otherwise their father proceeded by having them read his favorites and by setting them research tasks in his ample reference library. He had Edith and Alice memorize all of *The Lady of the Lake*; and, in their early teens, he gave them a page of the *Spectator* to read over three times and then write out from memory. They also learned the Bible, which Alice claimed she knew better than any other book. Religion was a serious matter in this household, at least for the women, who attended the First Presbyterian Church and taught sabbath school. But Montgomery Hamilton, more interested in theology than devotional practice, taught religious texts like any others: he had Edith and Alice do research in the Bible and memorize the Westminster Catechism.[17]

Both the method of learning—reading, memorizing, and reciting—and the subject matter obviously formed an important substrate of the Hamilton women's mental landscape.[18] Exposure to the classic works of male writers connected them to an important tradition of historical writing. In his fiction and poetry, Scott opened up the imaginative possibilities of the past, while Addison explicitly sought to bring philosophical discourse to the "tea-tables," that is, to women.

Edith responded to the *Spectator* exercise by humorously announcing a literary vocation to her closest cousin, Jessie: "I flatter myself my style is getting quite Addisonian. I hope you keep all my letters; some day, you know, they will be all treasured up as the works of 'Miss Hamilton, the American Addison, Scott & Shakespeare'!"[19] Alice perceived the gender symbolism of this education, contrasting her parents' reading tastes along with differences in their temperaments and religions as markers of character. Her father, who had a passion for "clarity and definiteness," favored Macaulay, Froude, Addison, and Pope, while her mother, Gertrude Pond Hamilton, preferred *The Mill on the Floss, Adam Bede,* and Gray's *Elegy*. While noting that her father's hatred of sentimentality sometimes included his wife's "generous enthusiasms," Alice concluded that his attitude was "probably a wholesome factor in a household of women."[20]

The young Hamiltons read widely in books the Victorians designated "the best."[21] These included numerous works of history and biography—Knight's as well as Macaulay's history of England, but evidently not the American historians Bancroft and Hildreth. Fiction, which had only recently become approved intellectual fare, played a major part in their upbringing.[22] The Hamiltons were familiar with the full range of English middle-class fiction, not only George Eliot, Dickens, and Thackeray, but those they considered "old novelish," like Maria Edgeworth.[23] Scott was a favorite with three generations—Emerine and her second son, Montgomery, as well as Edith and Jessie.[24] Two points about the Hamiltons' reading preferences deserve special mention: their bypassing of the New England literary tradition so important to many intellectual families, and their penchant for British fiction; although British fiction dominated the American literary scene until the 1890s, the Hamiltons probably represent an extreme.[25] They were, however, avid readers of the magazines of Gilded-Age America, of which *Harper's* seems to have been a special favorite.

In addition to the books one expects serious Victorians to have read, a wide range of works, popular in their day but no longer in the canon, were central to the Hamiltons. These included books read in childhood and adolescence, including the Katy books by "Susan Coolidge" (which they preferred to Louisa May Alcott's) and the works of Mrs. (Juliana) Ewing and Charlotte Yonge.[26] Religious novels also absorbed them, as did the devotional literature that constituted suitable Sunday reading in this very Presbyterian family.[27] There was also an array of now-forgotten books read mainly for diversion, some verging on "trash," a designation that probably included excessively romantic or sentimental as well as lurid works. The Hamiltons accepted the category without always agreeing on its boundaries: one person's trash was evidently another's sensibility. Thus Edith noted of a book her younger sister's college friends considered trashy, "It seems to me an earnest, thoughtful book, with a high tone through it all. I do like it very much."[28]

II

There was, then, considerable freedom in the Hamiltons' choice of reading and in the range of books that mattered. There was also greater diversity in reading behavior than has been assumed. The conventional wisdom among historians of the book is that by the late nineteenth century reading had become a private rather than public activity (one that promoted individualism and isolated individuals from one another) and that there had been a shift from a pattern of intensive reading of a few books to one of extensive and presumably more passive reading.[29] Yet a number of the reading customs in the

Hamilton family suggest that these interpretations have been too monolithic in general, and that reading had a different context, and therefore meaning, for women. Chief among these practices was reading aloud, which for the Hamiltons was a pleasurable and a lifelong habit.[30] Most such occasions were informal and structured by circumstance. There might be two participants or several; texts as well as readers might alternate. At times reading aloud was a duty as well as a pleasure: parents read to children, older siblings to younger ones, adult daughters to their mothers, women to invalids. Above all, reading aloud was social.

Hamiltons of two generations for a time constituted themselves into "a sort of a reading club."[31] In richly detailed letters, Jessie described the group and other reading occasions to her younger sister Agnes, away at school between 1886 and 1888. Daily at half past four, the Hamilton cousins "went over to Gibbon" (also known as "Gibbonhour") at their Aunt Mary Williams's:

> You don't know what fun it is to go into her rooms where the dark red curtains are pulled across the windows and the lamps and wax candles are lit and spend an hour reading. Gibbon is becoming quite interesting[,] it is no longer an effort to listen. After dinner at seven we went to Aunt Marg's room to read Carlyle's French Revolution, it is splendidly written and wonderfully powerful when you can tell exactly what he is driving at. Of course the mind was not the only part refreshed, the fruit, oranges, bananas, green, purple and pink grapes made a lovely picture in a straw basket. And what do you think we did there, something that seemed to make one of my dreams suddenly to become substance—we hemmed the dish towels for the Farmington House.[32]

When someone had to be absent, the group switched to *A Bachelor's Blunder,* of which Jessie observed, "I read parts of it aloud to mamma and though it is not anything you care about as you do Thackeray or George Eliot still it is very interesting." On another occasion, *A Bachelor's Blunder* followed *King Lear.*[33] Carlyle was resumed the following winter, but on at least one occasion Jessie reported that "somehow it did not work and we rambled off to other things."[34]

The letters suggest that for Jessie, as aspiring artist, the sensuous and social aspects of the reading sessions were central to her enjoyment—the physical accompaniments, the food, the alluring rooms with their beauty and hint of mystery. A range of family business was transacted at the sessions, including sewing (in this case for the cottage in Farmington that Margaret Vance Hamilton was fixing up for her nieces), planning their vocational futures, and gossiping about absent members. Altogether there is a fluidity about this reading circle: several books are kept going at the same time, there is no rush to finish, at times the sessions even break down. Jessie's comments further suggest a receptive attitude to all sorts of books, and a lack of self-consciousness, even in this very proper family, about reading "light" fiction. Although differentiated from the classics, *A Bachelor's Blunder* is mentioned in the same breath with, and deemed worthy of substituting for, Carlyle or Shakespeare. Jessie's description of social reading reveals the playful side of Hamilton family life, a quality seen as well in their love of word games. Such playfulness can be afforded only by those who are both seriously committed to literature and secure in their position as members of a cultured class.

The multiple possibilities of reading are most fully revealed in the diaries and letters of Agnes Hamilton. The most morally earnest of the Hamiltons, Agnes was the only one inclined to worry that she spent too much time reading novels, particularly the sort designated trash. She likened her "insane passion" for reading to an addiction and attributed her indulgence to a desire to escape unpleasant family situations, a trait she thought she shared with her paternal grandmother. After completing *Our Mutual Friend* and Bulwer-Lytton's *My Novel*, she wrote, "I have resolved not to read another novel for a week, at least, and consequently I feel like a reformed drunkard."[35] But Agnes's investment in books was more than a matter of escape or obsession. At twenty-one she wrote, "I live in the world of novels all the time[.] Half the time I am in Europe; half in different parts of America; I am sober and sensible, gay and frivolous, happy or sorrowful just as my present heroine happens to be or rather as the tone of the book happens to be. I never heard of a person more easily influenced. Sunday I read Stepping Heavenward. I had not read it for years and for two weeks I could not keep it out of my mind."[36] In addition to articulating the appeal of literature to fantasy and imagination, Agnes's comment suggests that reading could be an experience of considerable intensity. After completing Kingsley's *Hypatia,* which she liked "almost as well as any book I ever read," she observed, "I cannot enjoy these books I am reading now as much as I ought for I hurry so from one to another. All the enjoyment is while I am in the midst of it. Usually when I read a splendid novel I don't touch another for months so that I go all over it again in my mind."[37] Thus, in contrast to the rather offhand character of the group sessions, the Hamiltons invested a great deal of themselves in certain books, some of which they undoubtedly approached expecting to be overwhelmed. Jessie wanted to be well before she and Agnes started reading Kingsley's reform novel, *Alton Locke,* so she could "enjoy" it fully.[38] Clearly different styles of reading coexisted, dictated in part by the nature of the book, by the occasion, and by readers' expectations.

Among the books that acquired intense emotional meaning were those read in childhood and adolescence.[39] These continued to be the stuff of Hamilton family life well into adulthood. Reading has long been recognized as a topic of absorbing interest to adolescents, especially adolescent girls.[40] For girls books have represented an important arena for shared friendship as well as a means of creating a world more satisfying than the one ordinarily inhabited, a world in which to formulate aspirations and try out different identities. The Hamiltons' continued intense preoccupation with books, including children's books, well into adulthood suggests the prolonging of behavior that would be considered adolescent today.[41] In this family at least, such deferred maturity—what Erik Erikson has called a moratorium—prolonged the period in which the women, encouraged by one another, formulated and often reformulated their vocational plans.

For the Hamilton women, reading offered the occasion for a relatively unmediated experience, exemption from artificial social conventions, and an invitation to fantasy and imaginative play. Although they rejected Society and looked down on women whose sole interest was finding a husband, they nonetheless—especially in Jessie and Agnes's family—experienced the restrictions of Victorian gentility. In a world full of social constraints, the Hamiltons associated reading with freedom and possibility. Edith once observed, "Alice and I are out of humour, because at four o'clock we must get into something stiff and go down to Mrs. Brown's to meet some people and drink some tea. What I want to do, is to take *Wuthering Heights* and go and sit down on the shore below Arch Rock. I can feel how sweet and still and cool it would be there, how smooth and misty and pale blue the water would be, and how the little ripples would break at my feet with a soft splash."[42] In a less poetic vein, reading gave the Hamiltons access to people and situations they would normally neither encounter nor countenance. Thus Agnes noted her eagerness to read *The Old Mam'selle's Secret,* "utter stuff as it is, and full of the nastiest people I should not speak to in real life."[43]

Books also gave the Hamiltons a way of ordering, and understanding, their lives. They provided a common language and a medium of intellectual and social exchange that helped the women define themselves and formulate responses to the larger world. The process started early. When Jessie went off to Miss Porter's, seven younger Hamiltons ranging in age from fourteen to six wrote a joint letter addressed to "Dear boarding school girl." Agnes and Alice, thirteen and twelve respectively, elaborated: "Do you find boarding school as nice as it was in 'Gypsy's Year at the Golden Crescent,' or in 'What Katy Did at School'? or are you homesick like the story Mrs. Stanton told in one of the 'Bessie's'?"[44] Here the Hamiltons are not only relating life to fiction, but behaving like fictional characters: the boarding school story, a staple of preadolescent fiction, often included letters from at-home relatives. In this case fiction provided both a rehearsal for future experience (for those who had not yet gone to school) and a reference point for those who had.

Books gave the Hamiltons a symbolic code and a shorthand for experience that continued throughout their lives. When cousins or sisters were geographically distant, a literary allusion captured experience in relatively few words. Thus Alice could describe a rector as "a delicious mixture of Trollope and Mrs. Oliphant and Miss Yonge" and expect to be understood precisely.[45] Only occasionally did literature fail. Edith had difficulty in fathoming Bontè Amos, an audacious but intriguing Englishwoman who belonged to the advanced Bertrand Russell set: "She is a kind of girl I have never even read of before." They took these comparisons seriously. Edith reread a novel whose heroine had been suggested as a possible model for Miss Amos, but thought the parallel inexact.[46]

As the boarding school letter indicates, reading did not foreclose experience for the Hamiltons but offered them a range of possible responses. When Agnes began her diary shortly after her fifteenth birthday, she cited three fictional models from which to choose: "There are so many different ways of commencing journals that I did not know how to commence mine, whether to do as Else did and commence by telling about every member of the family or as Kate in Stepping Heavenward did and describe myself, but I think I will do as Olive Drayton and go right into the middle of it with out any commencement."[47] Such explicit formulation of the possibility of choice suggests both the open-ended quality of reading in this family and the degree to which the Hamiltons maintained control over their reading experiences.

The Hamiltons' world was peopled with fictional characters. It was not just that as readers they were "admitted into the company and present at the conversation."[48] The fictional company was very real to them. Allen Williams at twenty-one exclaimed, "I never can get over a feeling of personal injury in never having known the Abbottsmuir children; don't you think that, after Ellen Daly and Norah, they and Polly and Reginald seem to belong especially to us?"[49] To Agnes too, characters in a favorite book "seem dear friends and I get a homesicky feeling if I cannot get hold of the book not for anything especially fine in it but just for the people."[50] Alice Hamilton in her seventies observed, "Since we saw so little of any children outside our own family, the people we met in books became real to us . . . [among them] Charlotte Yonge's May and Underwood families, who still are more vivid to me than any real people I met in those years."[51] For the Hamiltons, then, there was a reciprocal relation—a continuum—between fiction and life.[52] If fiction was a referent for people one encountered in real life, life also cast light on fiction: Alice claimed she understood Howells's women "much better" through knowing a real-life stand-in.[53] In view of the fluidity of the boundaries it is not surprising that the Hamiltons fictionalized their own lives. After being absorbed for weeks in the story of a romance between the art teacher and a student at Miss Porter's, Edith wrote Jessie, "Don't you feel as if you had got into a story book? And with Susy Sage of all people for the heroine."[54]

The tendency to fictionalize their lives was most evident at the time of Allen Williams's engagement. His fiancée, Marian Walker, a Radcliffe student preparing for a medical career, reminded Allen not only of his closest cousins, Alice and Agnes, but also of the heroines of two novels beloved by the young Hamiltons, Nora Nixon in *Quits* (1857) by Baroness Tautphoeus, a popular English writer of the 1850s and a distant relative, and Ellen Daly in Annie Keary's *Castle Daly* (1875). As Allen informed Agnes, "[Marian] is very fond of Quits! I have told her she cannot meet any of the family until she has read Castle Daly. Can you forgive her for not having done that?" To Alice he exclaimed, "Of course she is like Nora, otherwise I could not have fallen in love. And of course *Quits* is one of her favorite books."[55] The use of such preferences as a means of establishing boundaries for group membership may strike us as quintessentially adolescent, but Allen was in his late twenties. Though professing greater maturity, Alice responded in kind:

> And it just warms my heart and fills me with gladness to have the boy turning into the sort of man that I wanted him to be, to have him doing an impulsive, unpractical, youthful thing. . . . Why he talks like the heroes in Black's novels, like Willy Fitzgerald and George Brand and Frank King. I am so glad. . . . Agnes it mustn't pass over, it is too sweet and dear and fresh and cunning. . . . Would anybody believe that that introspective, slightly cynical, critical, over-cultured fellow could be so naive, so unconsciously trite, so deliciously young! . . . I think almost the funniest part is his account of the effect the announcement had on the two mothers. It is just like poor Traddles and his Sophie in "David Copperfield" and these poor children seem to take it just as seriously.[56]

Although Alice Hamilton cast Allen as a hero, there is no evidence, then or later, that she was interested in the marriage plot for herself. Allen called her an "unconscious hypocrite" for suggesting that Marian give up her medical career, since he believed his cousin cared only for her work.[57] At forty-nine Alice still gushed about a book in words similar to those she had deployed for Allen's romance: "It is just as cunning as can be and so romantic, you can't believe any hero could be so noble."[58] But her life history, like that of the other Hamilton women, makes it clear that she preferred her heroes in the covers of a book rather than at first hand; in this one case at least, the boundaries between fiction and life remained fixed. Given their assumption that women must choose between marriage and career, for the Hamiltons and other ambitious women of the era, heroes in books were safer than men encountered in life. Indeed, there was a potent antimarriage sentiment in this family. Of the eleven women of the third generation, only the youngest married; a generation younger than her oldest cousins, she did so as an act of rebellion.[59]

III

The Hamiltons' experiences of reading suggest a need to reconsider traditional assumptions about how fiction works on readers. It is usually assumed that women respond to fiction principally through the mechanism of identification with heroines, especially the heroines of "romantic" plots. Among the Hamiltons, however, it was the men who seem to have been fascinated by heroines and who took them as models of womanhood. Montgomery, for example, wrote an essay on the subject for the Princeton literary magazine and, like his nephew Allen Williams thirty years later, alluded to Baroness Tautphoeus's novels during his romance with Gertrude Pond.[60] It was other sorts of plots, plots of adventure and social responsibility, that appealed to the Hamilton women.[61] Favorite novels—even those that end with an impending marriage—provided models of socially conscious and independent womanhood. In reading *Quits*, for example, the women probably responded more to the character of the heroine than to her fate. Nora Nixon, the unaffected and generous heroine of *Quits*, is a natural woman who loves the outdoors, orders her life rationally, and does exactly what she pleases, which happens also to be socially useful. Active, worldly, and independent, she provides a striking contrast to the stereotyped domestic and submissive "true woman." Ellen Daly, the Irish heroine of *Castle Daly*, is less able to control her surroundings than Nora, but she too is unselfconscious, generous, and independent.[62]

The heroine of Charlotte Yonge's paradigmatic *The Daisy Chain* (1856) may have provided the model for real family projects as well as fantasy. In much the same manner as Jo March in *Little Women*, Ethel May is transformed from a helter-skelter tomboy and prospective bluestocking into a thoughtful and family-centered woman. In Ethel's case this is her family of origin, for she resists marriage in order to care for her father and siblings. But Ethel has a public as well as private mission and succeeds in carrying out her resolve to found a church in a poor neighborhood. Her passion for Cocksmoor had its counterpart in the Hamiltons' involvement in Nebraska, a poor section of Fort Wayne where the women and some of the men taught sabbath school. Agnes, who later worked at a religious settlement, was instrumental in persuading her own First Presbyterian Church to establish a regular church there. Ethel May's deepest commitments—her loyalty to family and religion—were also major preoccupations of Agnes's, and it is likely that she found in Ethel a model, as she did in similarly inclined women she encountered in novels and biographies.

If the Hamiltons had a penchant for socially conscious heroines, an analysis of their reading also suggests that the traditional emphasis on identification with one character is far too restrictive an approach to an experience as complex as reading.[63] Recent work reveals the possibilities of more varied interactions between readers and texts. Norman Holland insists on the organic unity of a literary work, including plot, form, and language as well as characters, each of which can influence a reader's response. Starting from the premise that what readers bring to texts is themselves, he further suggests that the reader identifies not so much with a particular character as with the total interaction of characters, some satisfying the need for pleasure, others the need to avoid anxiety. Holland's concept of "identity themes," characteristic modes of response that influence reading as well as other behaviors, is useful for historians since it provides a key to individual reading preferences that can be applied to the past.[64] Within an explicitly feminist framework, Cora Kaplan emphasizes possibilities of multiple identifications by women readers, with heroes as well as heroines.[65]

Certainly for the Hamiltons, the continuum between fiction and reality gave considerable play to the imagination. Reading provided both the occasion for self-creation and the narrative form from which they might reconstruct themselves. Given the way they peopled their lives with fictional characters and the intensity of their interactions with books, they were quite capable of reading themselves into fiction or other forms of adventure without a strong identification with a particular heroine.

Alice Hamilton offers a striking example in claiming a literary inspiration for her decision to become a physician: "I meant to be a medical missionary to Teheran, having been fascinated by the description of Persia in [Edmond] O'Donovan's *The Merv Oasis*. I doubted if I could ever be good enough to be a real missionary; but if I could care for the sick, that would do instead, and it would enable me to explore far countries and meet strange people."[66] Since *The Merv Oasis* (1882) is a work of travels and adventure, over a thousand pages in length and with no discernible missionary focus, Alice clearly drew from it what she would. The message she found there is consistent with her early preferences in fiction, among them Charlotte Yonge's novels which highlight conflicts between individual achievement and the family claim. This was a matter that deeply troubled her as a young woman, and she resolved it only when she found work that enabled her to combine science and service, thereby effecting a balance between individualism and self-sacrifice as she saw it.[67]

Edith's aspirations and literary preferences were of a different kind. There is no mention in her letters of doing good, a frequent theme of Alice's; rather there is a longing to "live" and to do great things. Often moody as a young woman, in reading she found a lifeline, a way of getting out of herself. At sixteen her favorites were Scott's *Rob Roy* (1818) and *Lorna Doone* (1869) by R. D. Blackmore.[68] The heroine of *Rob Roy*, Diana Vernon, is one of Scott's most appealing—she is an outdoorswoman, well read, outspoken, and fearless. But the characterization is unlikely to account for the novel's appeal. (Diana fades away, becoming first an obedient daughter then, in a hastily contrived ending, wife.) It is more likely that Edith responded to the settings and plots: her favorites were tales of derring-do in wild places (the Scottish highlands, the Devonshire moors) and historical settings. They might well have cast a spell on one who was herself "a natural storyteller" and who later captured the imagination of millions with her retellings of classic myths and her romantic vision of ancient Greece.[69]

In suggesting that for the Hamiltons reading reinforced a family culture that promoted personal aspiration and achievement, I am not claiming a direct cause-and-effect relationship between reading and behavior. The late nineteenth century was a time of expanding opportunities for women, without which the aspirations of various Hamiltons could not have been enacted in the way they were. What I am suggesting is that a reading culture such as the one maintained by the Hamiltons provided a means for accustoming and encouraging women to imagine new possibilities for themselves. In a supportive environment, such possibilities had a greater chance of becoming realities.

How typical were the Hamiltons? In the intensity of their involvement with books, in the degree to which their reading activity was family-centered, and perhaps too in their bypassing of the New England literary tradition, they may have been somewhat idiosyncratic. But they were at the extreme end of a continuum rather than the oddities they might at first appear to be.

Testimony to the importance of reading comes from the autobiographies of prominent women who came to maturity in the 1880s and 1890s. For many, books acquired an almost magical status, books in general as well as particular books; among the consequences attributed to specific works are religious conversion, loss of faith, choice of vocation, and the breakup of a marriage.[70] By contrast, formal schooling received little attention, an omission that is not surprising at a time when self-study was common, when the early education of even those who attended college was often informal and erratic, and when most formal learning was by recitation. The invocation of books was no doubt a convention of a cultural elite. But its frequency is itself significant and contrasts with the lack of attention to peers and formal education, both staples of more recent autobiographical narrative. The diminished religiosity of educated Victorians undoubtedly contributed to this new veneration of literature as a source of cultural authority and models of selfhood.

Books were also markers of "taste" and, therefore, ultimately of class.[71] What one read, how much, even how one read, not to mention the size of the paternal library, were important markers of cultural style in middle- and upper-middle-class homes. But love of books was not the prerogative of the wealthy alone; indeed, for many individuals raised in a religious tradition suspicious of display, a reverence for books was a way of distancing themselves from those with merely social aspirations. For women in particular, the level of a family's intellectual aspirations was more important than its bank account or social pedigree in encouraging ambition.[72]

Of course, a passion for books and other cultural artifacts could become the means by which the cultured classes insulated themselves from unpleasant realities. In a memorable passage in her autobiography Jane Addams warns against the dangers of self-culture, in particular the habit of her class of "lumbering our minds with literature," an epiphany that followed the intrusion of a literary reflection when she confronted extreme poverty. Yet Addams too fell back on the literary culture of her youth and tried to pass it on to her immigrant neighbors: one of the first public activities at Hull House was a reading group that began with George Eliot's *Romola,* a work set in Renaissance Florence.[73] In so doing, she was continuing a tradition of women's reading that had social as well as private dimensions.

Growing up in an era when the printed word was venerated, women like the Hamiltons found in books not just the messages of official purveyors of culture, though they found these too. For some, engagement with books in childhood and adolescence permitted entry into a world of fantasy that helped them formulate aspirations for themselves different from those traditional to women, and ultimately to act on them as well. Although many of the pejorative connotations of the old association of women and fiction had disappeared by the late nineteenth century, when "good" fiction had attained the status of a cultural icon, reading was still a gender-marked activity, no doubt because it seemed a relatively passive form of intellectual exercise and one that had no practical outcome. This study has tried to demonstrate that reading had more practical and positive consequences for women than has been assumed. Many found in reading an occasion that, by removing them from their usual activities, permitted the formulation of future plans or, more generally, encouraged vital engagement with the world, a world many thought would be transformed by women's special sensibilities. Women's passion for reading must then be viewed as more than simple escapism, as absorption in books has often been designated.

IV

What generalizations may be drawn from a case study such as this one? In the matter of method, a contextual study of groups of real readers permits historians to adapt the approach of ethnographers to the past. If one looks at groups of readers, it becomes clear that reading was not restricted to writers of one genre, sex, or nationality, and that both occasions for reading and particular texts developed complex symbolic meanings for specific reading communities. Further, by studying reading as behavior rather than as textual analysis, historians can peel back later layers of interpretation and come nearer to the contemporary meaning of a work. A study of past readings also permits a deeper understanding of aspirations and emotional preferences as distinct from ideology—what Raymond Williams calls structures of feeling or sensibilities.[74] These are often difficult to get at, particularly in an era when sentimentality and self-revelation were suspect, as they were in the late nineteenth century.

Substantively, a case study of this sort can cast light not only on the impact of books and the nature of reading experiences in the past, but on our understanding of these processes. The emphasis on the escapist aspects of certain kinds of fiction, indeed on the distinction between "light" and "serious" reading, seems misplaced in view of the varied and complex sorts of reading behavior that existed in the past. Reading theorists have argued that reading is not simply a passive form of cultural consumption, that something happens to readers that becomes imperative for them to understand, and that reading stimulates desire rather than simply pacifying it. The spectator role permits readers to remove themselves temporarily from the necessity to act, enabling them to use this freedom "to *evaluate* more broadly, more amply" and thus to "modify categories according to 'the way I feel about things.'"[75] There were different sorts of reading in the Hamilton family, but their experiences of reading, both social and individual, were of the sort that encouraged them to extend the range of the possible. In their interpretive community, children's books, "light" fiction, and devotional literature (fiction or nonfiction) could all play a part in the formation of one's sense of self. From this study, it is also apparent that generalizations based on assumed oppositions between modes of reading (intensive/extensive) and loci of reading (public/private) cannot be sustained.

Evidence of the sort provided by the Hamiltons makes it possible to discover how reading behavior and self-consciousness changed over time. This study suggests a link between reading and the formation of female subjectivity in a particular historical period. By so doing, I do not wish to minimize the importance of reading for women in other times and places: adolescent girls seem to have exhibited consistently greater passion for reading than their male counterparts. Nevertheless, a number of factors seem to have contributed to the empowering nature of women's reading experiences in the late nineteenth century. Books were then especially revered cultural artifacts (without serious competition from nonprint forms of entertainment) and, at a time of rapidly expanding educational opportunity, women also had freer access to them than in earlier generations. The lesser importance of formal education in children's early years may have fostered a greater degree of self-invention compared with later, more routinized educational patterns. It is likely too that the relatively informal mode of transmitting cultural values played a part in the open and playful approach to reading exhibited by the Hamiltons.[76]

Finally, the literature of the era was especially conducive to dreams of female heroism outside family life. The downplaying of sexuality in Victorian fiction and the lesser concentration on the marriage plot in girls' adventure stories encouraged women to fantasize about other sources of fulfillment, including those that gave women a large public role.[77] Novels like Charlotte Yonge's, while telling stories about the taming of tomboys, nevertheless afforded scope for female agency, albeit within a separate sphere. Books could not create a desire for female heroism where none existed in the reader. But, in conjunction with a family culture that encouraged female aspiration and education, reading could provide the occasion for perceiving one's inmost needs and wants—desires that could later be acted upon. Like earlier critics who viewed women's reading as suspect, though for different reasons, some feminist critics have recently emphasized the dangers of reading for women.[78] In the context of late-Victorian American life, however, the impact of reading was more likely to be liberating than confining.

Notes

This paper was presented at the Berkshire Conference on Women's History, June 20, 1987; comments by the other participants, Joan Jacobs Brumberg, Janice Radway, and Martha Vicinus, were extremely helpful. I also want to thank Cathy Davidson, Marlene Fisher, Martin Green, David D. Hall, and Mary Kelley for their comments; Ann Brown, Tammy J. Banks-Spooner, and Elizabeth Young for research assistance; and W. Rush G. Hamilton for permission to quote from the Hamilton Family Papers, Schlesinger Library, Radcliffe College, Cambridge, Mass.

1. On working-class reading, see Michael Denning, *Mechanic Accents: Dime Novels and Working-Class Culture in America* (London and New York, 1987). Two diverse examples of the how-and-what genre are Noah Porter, *Books and Reading, or What Books Shall I Read and How Shall I Read Them?* (1870; rpt. New York, 1883); and *List of Books for Girls and Women and Their Clubs; with Descriptive and Critical Notes and a List of Periodicals and Hints for Girls' and Women's Clubs,* ed. Augusta H. Leypoldt and George Iles (Boston, 1895).

2. On women's literary and voluntary activities, see Karen J. Blair, *The Club-woman as Feminist: True Womanhood Redefined, 1868–1914* (New York, 1980), esp. 57–71; Anne Firor Scott, "Women and Libraries," *Journal of Library History* 21 (Spring 1986): 400–405, and "On Seeing and Not Seeing—A Case of Historical Invisibility," *Journal of American History* 71 (June 1984): 7–21; and Theodora Penny Martin, *The Sound of Our Own Voices: Women's Study Clubs, 1860–1940* (Boston, 1987).

3. Cf. Ann Douglas, *The Feminization of American Culture* (New York, 1977); Nina Baym, *Woman's Fiction: A Guide to Novels by and about Women in America, 1820–1870* (Ithaca, N.Y., 1978); and Mary Kelley, *Private Woman, Public Stage: Literary Domesticity in Nineteenth-Century America* (New York, 1984). Kelley also analyzes diverse interpretations of the genre. See also Linda K. Kerber, *Women of the Republic: Intellect and Ideology in Revolutionary America* (Chapel Hill, N.C., 1980), 233–64; Dee Garrison, *Apostles of Culture: The Public Librarian and American Society, 1876–1920* (New York, 1979), 67–101; and Elizabeth A. Flynn and Patrocinio P. Schweickart, eds., *Gender and Reading: Essays on Readers, Texts, and Contexts* (Baltimore, Md., 1986).

4. An exception is Nina Baym, *Novels, Readers, and Reviewers: Responses to Fiction in Antebellum America* (Ithaca, N.Y., 1984), who analyzes contemporary periodical reviews and includes British as well as American fiction.

5. Janice A. Radway, *Reading the Romance: Women, Patriarchy, and Popular Literature* (Chapel Hill, N.C, 1984). Engaging the debate over the impact of popular cultural forms, in particular the degree to which female subjectivity is controlled by such a formulaic genre as the romance, Radway finds a restricted but authentic self-assertion both in the circumstances under which romances are read and in the meanings attached to them. Cathy N. Davidson, *Revolution and the Word: The Rise of the Novel in America* (New York, 1986), has also pioneered in developing a reader-centered approach. See also Elizabeth Long, "Women, Reading, and Cultural Authority: Some Implications of the Audience Perspective in Cultural Studies," *American Quarterly* 38 (Fall 1986): 591–612.

6. Susan R. Suleiman and Inge Crosman, eds., *The Reader in the Text: Essays on Audience and Interpretation* (Princeton, N.J., 1980), and Jane P. Tompkins, ed., *Reader-Response Criticism: From Formalism to Post-Structuralism* (Baltimore, Md., 1980), are useful introductions to reader-response theory. One of the most influential statements is Stanley Fish, *Is There a Text in This Class? The Authority of Interpretive Communities* (Cambridge, Mass., 1980). Wolfgang Iser, "Interaction between Text and Reader," in Suleiman and Crosman, *The Reader in the*

Text, 106–19, and Hans Robert Jauss, "Literary History as a Challenge to Literary Theory," in *New Directions in Literary History,* ed. Ralph Cohen (Baltimore, Md., 1974), 11–41, were also helpful.

7. I am currently engaged in a study of three generations of Hamiltons as part of a larger project on reading and gender in nineteenth-century America.

8. The work of David D. Hall provides the best point of entry into the literature on the "history of the book" in America; see especially "Introduction: The Uses of Literacy In New England, 1600–1850," in *Printing and Society in Early America,* ed. William L. Joyce et. al. (Worcester, Mass., 1983), 1–47, and "The World of Print and Collective Mentality in Seventeenth-Century New England," in *New Directions in American Intellectual History,* ed. John Higham and Paul K. Conkin (Baltimore, Md., 1979), 166–80. See also Carl F. Kaestle, "The History of Literacy and the History of Readers," in *Review of Research in Education,* vol. 12, ed. Edmund W. Gordon (Washington, D.C., 1985), 11–53.

9. The younger brothers in the cousins' families were considered "children" by the others. There was also a fourth and much younger group of cousins. On the family, see Alice Hamilton, *Exploring the Dangerous Trades* (Boston, 1943), hereafter cited as *EDT;* Barbara Sicherman, *Alice Hamilton: A Life in Letters* (Cambridge, Mass., 1984), esp. 11–32 and genealogy; and Mina J. Carson, "Agnes Hamilton of Fort Wayne: The Education of a Christian Settlement Worker," *Indiana Magazine of History* 80 (March 1984): 1–34. The representativeness of the Hamiltons is considered below.

10. *EDT,* 23–24. Emerine was evidently named for a character in *The Prisoners of Niagara, or Errors of Education* (Frankfort, Ky., 1810), a sentimental novel written by her father. Jesse Lynch Holman, a judge and ordained Baptist clergyman, later tried to buy up and destroy the work, because he thought its morals were unsound. Israel George Blake, *The Holmans of Veraestau* (Oxford, Ohio, 1943), 5–6.

11. Robert S. Robertson, *History of the Maumee River Basin* (Allen County, Ind., 1905), 2:337–40; and library file in the Indiana Collection, Vertical File, Allen County Public Library, Fort Wayne, Ind. The reading room remained a family activity: the Hamiltons donated books, and some of the young women dispensed books to patrons. It was women's space: the intrusion of a man upset Emerine's youngest daughter, Margaret Vance Hamilton, and led the librarian to fear she would be dismissed. Katherine Hamilton to Jessie Hamilton, Sunday, September 22 [1889?], Folder 133, Hamilton Family Papers, Schlesinger Library, Radcliffe College, Cambridge, Mass. (All references to archival sources not otherwise identified are from this collection.) Margaret Vance Hamilton was also active in establishing the Fort Wayne Public Library, an outgrowth of activities of the Woman's Club League.

12. Montgomery Hamilton, Alice and Edith's father, had a library of about a thousand books, many of them reference works. The collection of his older brother, A. Holman Hamilton, specialized in English, Irish, and Scottish folklore. It also included books on witchcraft, rare medieval works, tales of "low life" as well as "good" fiction for adults and young people, numerous magazines (some for children), and books on subjects like architecture that accorded with his daughters' vocational

interests. The collections of various Hamiltons are described in Robertson, *History of the Maumee River Basin,* 350–58. There are numerous book orders in the A. Holman Hamilton Papers, Indiana State Library, Indianapolis. Marybelle Burch generously provided materials from this collection.

13. Edith Hamilton to Jessie Hamilton, August 3, 1892.

14. Doris Fielding Reid, *Edith Hamilton: An Intimate Portrait* (New York, 1967), 30.

15. *EDT,* 19.

16. Ibid., 18–19. The same "forbidden" books turn up regularly in autobiographies of Progressives, along with dime novels (the latter mainly boys' reading). The term "French novel" was almost generic for racy, with Sue, Dumas, and George Sand often singled out. See Baym, *Novels, Readers, Reviewers,* 178–80, 184–86, 213. The category may have included some pornography, the most costly books ordered by A. Holman Hamilton for which prices are available; at least one was ordered by Alice's father. A. Holman Hamilton Papers, Indiana State Library.

17. *EDT,* 27–31.

18. The impact of memorization deserves study. On Miss Porter's, where a similar mode of reading and recitation prevailed, see Louise L. Stevenson, "Sarah Porter Educates Useful Ladies, 1847–1900," *Winterthur Portfolio* 18 (Spring 1983): 39–59.

19. Edith Hamilton to Jessie Hamilton, Tuesday evening [early 1882?].

20. *EDT,* 30–32.

21. Agnes Hamilton's diary, the most comprehensive source of information about the Hamilton's reading, includes lists for the years 1855–97. On Victorian culture, see Daniel Walker Howe, ed., *Victorian America* (Philadelphia, 1976), especially the essays by Howe and David D. Hall.

22. As evangelical hostility to fiction abated, even cultural conservatives praised literature for unlocking the powers of the imagination. See Porter, *Books and Reading*; and Louise L. Stevenson, *Scholarly Means to Evangelical Ends: The New Haven Scholars and the Transformation of Higher Learning in America, 1830–1890* (Baltimore, Md., 1986).

23. Agnes Hamilton to Jessie Hamilton, July 14, 1894.

24. After 1860 or so, Scott was consigned mainly to younger readers. On his popularity, see John Henry Raleigh, "What Scott Meant to the Victorians," in *Time, Place, and Idea: Essays on the Novel* (Carbondale, Ill., 1968), 96–125; and James D. Hart, *The Popular Book: A History of America's Literary Taste* (Berkeley and Los Angeles, n.d.), 68–69, 73–78.

25. Several factors may account for the family's neglect of the New England tradition. Montgomery disliked the "woolgathering of the New England school," and it is likely that other Hamiltons also disapproved of Emerson's romantic individualism. *EDT,* 31. The family's Midwestern location and prominence in the Indiana Democratic party were also important. (Emerine's brother, William Steele Holman, served sixteen terms in Congress, her father was a judge, and her son, A. Holman Hamilton, was a two-term member of Congress.) On the Holman family's political milieu, see Jean H. Baker, *Affairs of Party: The Political Culture of North-*

ern Democrats in the Mid-Nineteenth Century (Ithaca, N.Y., 1983), esp. 33–37.
On nineteenth-century American reading patterns, see Hart, *Popular Book;* on
England, Richard D. Altick, *The English Common Reader: A Social History of the
Mass Reading Public, 1800–1900* (Chicago, 1957).

26. *EDT*, 19. Susan Coolidge was the pen name of Sarah Chauncy Woolsey.

27. See Robert Lee Wolff, *Gains and Losses: Novels of Faith and Doubt in Victorian England* (New York, 1977), for a discussion of religious novels, many of them
read by the Hamiltons.

28. Edith Hamilton to Jessie Hamilton, July 14 [1889]. The book was *The Silence
of Dean Maitland* (n.d.) by Mary Gleed Tuttiett, using the pseudonym Maxwell
Gray. See also Edith Hamilton to Jessie Hamilton, September 14 [1889].

29. Burton J. Bledstein, *The Culture of Professionalism: The Middle Class and the
Development of Higher Education in America* (New York, 1976), 77–78, emphasizes
the isolating nature of Victorian reading. In "The World of Print and Collective
Mentality," 171–72, and "Introduction: The Uses of Literacy," David D. Hall accepts the intensive-extensive dichotomy, while Davidson, *Revolution and the Word,*
72–73, and Robert Darnton, *The Great Cat Massacre and Other Episodes in French
Cultural History* (New York, 1984), 249–52, criticize the claim that the intensity
of the reading experience diminished.

30. Reading aloud was also a ritual at Miss Porter's. Even in their nineties Alice
and Margaret Hamilton belonged to a reading club.

31. Agnes used the term for a group that met "every Saturday in Aunt Marge's
room, [where] we read Henry Esmond and while one reads the rest of us do our
mending or other sewing." Agnes Hamilton Diary, April 25 [1885].

32. Jessie Hamilton to Agnes Hamilton, January 9, 1887. See also Jessie Hamilton to Agnes Hamilton, January 19 and 23, 1887; and Allen Hamilton Williams
to Agnes Hamilton, June 1, 1887.

33. Jessie Hamilton to Agnes Hamilton, January 23, 1887; see also Jessie Hamilton to Agnes Hamilton, February 11, 1887. *A Bachelor's Blunder* (1886) was a
contemporary English novel by William Edward Norris.

34. Jessie Hamilton to Agnes Hamilton, March 11, 1888. See also Jessie Hamilton
to Agnes Hamilton, February 13, 1887.

35. Agnes Hamilton Diary, July 31 [1887]. See also Agnes Hamilton to Edith
Trowbridge, August 19, 1895, folder 405.

36. Agnes Hamilton Diary, May 7 [1890]. Agnes had a penchant for works like
Elizabeth Payson Prentiss's *Stepping Heavenward* (1869), a spiritual manual in
the guise of a novel. Its heroine, who is depicted as ill-tempered and selfish at the
outset, emerges as a paragon of Christian womanhood after intense suffering.

37. Agnes Hamilton to Jessie Hamilton, December 31, 1886.

38. Agnes Hamilton Diary, September 9 [1888].

39. Margaret Meek et al., eds., *The Cool Web: The Pattern of Children's Reading*
(London, 1977), offer stimulating articles on children's reading by James Britton, D.
W. Harding, C. S. Lewis, and Aidan Warlow. Useful historical works include J. S.
Bratton, *The Impact of Victorian Children's Fiction* (Totowa, N.J., 1981); Elizabeth
Segel, "'As the Twig Is Bent . . .' : Gender and Childhood Reading," in Flynn and

Schweickart, *Gender and Reading*, 165–86; F. J. Harvey Darton, *Children's Books in England: Five Centuries of Social Life* (1932; rpt. Cambridge, 1966); Mary Cadogan and Patricia Craig, *You're a Brick, Angela! The Girls' Story, 1839–1985* (London, 1986); and Gillian Avery, *Nineteenth Century Children: Heroes and Heroines in English Children's Stories, 1780–1900* (London, 1965). Edward Salmon discusses girls' and boys' reading in *Juvenile Literature as It Is* (London, 1888) and "What Girls Read," *Nineteenth Century* 20 (October 1886): 515–29. On the United States, see R. Gordon Kelly, *Mother Was a Lady: Self and Society in Selected American Children's Periodicals, 1865–1890* (Westport, Conn., 1974).

40. Lewis M. Terman and Margaret Lima, *Children's Reading: A Guide for Parents and Teachers*, 2d ed. (New York, 1931), esp. 68–84; and G. Stanley Hall, *Adolescence: Its Psychology* (New York, 1905). Terman and Lima maintain that "at every age girls read more than boys" (68).

41. Children's books were read frequently by adults in the nineteenth century. Six of the ten bestsellers in the United States between 1875 and 1895 were children's books. Hellmut Lehmann-Haupt, *The Book in America: A History of the Making, the Selling, and the Collecting of Books in the United States* (New York, 1939), 160–61. See also Darton, *Children's Books*, 301.

42. Edith Hamilton to Jessie Hamilton, Thursday [late 1890s], folder 604.

43. Agnes Hamilton to Edith Trowbridge, August 19, 1895. *The Old Mam'selle's Secret* (1868) was by the popular German romance writer E. Marlitt, the pen name of Eugenie John. Agnes had read and liked the book many years before. Agnes Hamilton to Alice Hamilton, August 10, 1881.

44. To Jessie Hamilton [early 1882], folder 385. The books, by Susan Coolidge, Elizabeth Stuart Phelps (Ward), and Joanna Hooe Mathews respectively, were published in the late 1860s and early 1870s.

45. Alice Hamilton to Agnes Hamilton [June? 1896].

46. Edith Hamilton to Jessie Hamilton [fall 1896 and December 18? 1896]. See also Sicherman, *Alice Hamilton*, 104–7.

47. Agnes Hamilton Diary, December 6 [1883].

48. Benjamin Franklin quoted in Davidson, *Revolution and the Word*, 52.

49. Allan Hamilton Williams to Bag [Agnes Hamilton], August 11, 1890. These characters are drawn from books read in childhood or early adolescence. See below for additional comments on Nora (sometimes spelled "Norah") and Ellen.

50. Agnes Hamilton to Edith Trowbridge, August 19, 1895.

51. *EDT*, 19.

52. Davidson, *Revolution and the Word*, emphasizes the continuity between the subject matter of early American novels and contemporary life; see esp. 112–35.

53. Alice Hamilton to Agnes Hamilton [postmarked November 9, 1896].

54. Edith Hamilton to Jessie Hamilton, January 31 [1886].

55. Allen Hamilton Williams to Bag [Agnes Hamilton], July 30, 1896, and to My dear girl [Alice Hamilton], August 15 [?], 1896.

56. Alice Hamilton to Agnes Hamilton, September 12 [1896]; the letter is reprinted in its entirety in Sicherman, *Alice Hamilton*, 101–4.

57. Allen Hamilton Williams to Dear child [Alice Hamilton], September 17, 1896.

58. Alice Hamilton to Margaret Hamilton, Sunday [July 7], 1918, Alice Hamilton Papers, Schlesinger Library, The book was *The First Violin* (1877) by Jessie Fothergill, which Agnes at nineteen had characterized as "a very trashy book but great fun." Agnes Hamilton Diary, July 29 [1888]. According to a report of the American Library Association in 1881, Fothergill was one the authors whose works were "sometimes excluded from public libraries by reason of sensational or immoral qualities." Quoted in Garrison, *Apostles of Culture*, 74.

59. Interview with Hildegarde Wagenhals Bowen, December 30, 1976. It is possible that the type of romantic hero admired by Alice contributed to the women's penchant for singlehood, since of course no real-life hero "could be so noble." There were also more pragmatic reasons, including the fact that the marriages in their parents' generation were mainly unhappy, and the fathers and uncles "difficult" at best. Then too, sisters and cousins discouraged each other from leaving the family; and since they stuck together, it was difficult for a young man to breach the ranks.

60. Montgomery Hamilton to A. Holman Hamilton, July 30, 1864.

61. On the appeal of certain plots, see John G. Cawelti, *Adventure, Mystery, and Romance: Formula Stories as Art and Popular Culture* (Chicago, 1976), esp. 37–50. Nancy K. Miller emphasizes the differences in the plots of female and male authors; see "Emphasis Added: Plots and Plausibilities in Women's Fiction," *The New Feminist Criticism: Essays on Women, Literature, and Theory*, ed. Elaine Showalter (New York, 1985), 339–60.

62. Although there is no evidence that Nora and Ellen were as important models of heroism to the women as they were to Allen, there are numerous references to *Quits* and *Castle Daly* in their correspondence. They named their Aunt Margaret's Farmington cottage "Happy-Go-Lucky Lodge," the home of the beloved Irish aunt in *Castle Daly*. Anne O'Flaherty, the unmarried and independent fictional aunt, had a strong sense of responsibility for her Irish tenants. Even as a college student, Edith was delighted to come across a favorable reference to *Quits* by Washington Irving.

63. See, for example, Rachel M. Brownstein, *Becoming a Heroine: Reading about Women in Novels* (New York, 1984).

64. Norman Holland, *The Dynamics of Literary Response* (New York, 1975), esp. 262–80. See also his *Poems in Persons: An Introduction to Psychoanalysis of Literature* (New York, 1973) and *5 Readers Reading* (New Haven, Conn., 1975). One need not accept Holland's exact psychoanalytic formulation to recognize the value of his approach in illuminating individual responses to literature.

65. Cora Kaplan, "*The Thorn Birds:* Fiction, Fantasy, Femininity," in *Sea Changes: Feminism and Culture* (London, 1986), 117–46. See also Janice Radway, *Reading the Romance* and "Reading *Reading the Romance*," introduction to the English edition (London, 1987).

66. *EDT*, 26. Alice also attributes the growing consciousness of social problems she and Agnes shared to reading Charles Kingsley and Frederick Denison Maurice.

Claiming "we knew nothing about American social evils," she ignores their work at the sabbath mission school in Nebraska. Alice was interested in "slumming" by age eighteen, which was probably before she read the English social theorists. This seems to have been another case of literature seeming more real than life. *EDT*, 26–27.

67. On this conflict, see Sicherman, *Alice Hamilton*.

68. Edith Hamilton to Jessie Hamilton, Thursday, July 24 [1884]. Each book contains a sympathetic Robin Hood figure, whose dubious morality is treated ambiguously.

69. Alice called her sister "a natural storyteller." *EDT*, 19.

70. See, among others, the autobiographical accounts of Florence Kelley, Mary Richmond, Mary White Ovington, S. Josephine Baker, Mary Simkhovitch, Vida Dutton Scudder, and Charlotte Perkins Gilman. M. Carey Thomas's diary provides contemporary substantiation. Thomas Papers, Bryn Mawr College, Bryn Mawr, Pa. On nineteenth-century literary culture, see Steven Mintz, *A Prison of Expectations: The Family in Victorian Culture* (New York, 1985), esp. 21–39.

71. See Pierre Bourdieu, *Distinction: A Social Critique of the Judgement of Taste*, trans. Richard Nice (Cambridge, Mass., 1984).

72. See Barbara Sicherman, "College and Careers: Historical Perspectives on the Lives and Work Patterns of Women College Graduates," in *Women and Higher Education in American History*, ed. John Mack Faragher and Florence Howe (New York, 1988), 130–64.

73. Jane Addams, *Twenty Years at Hull-House* (1910; repr. New York, 1960), 63–64.

74. Raymond Williams, *Marxism and Literature* (Oxford, 1977), 128–35.

75. James Britton, *Language and Learning* (London, 1970), 97–125; quotation, 109–10. See also Iser, "Interaction between Text and Reader," 106–19, and Jauss, "Literary History as a Challenge to Literary Theory," 35–37.

76. Paul Lauter, "Race and Gender in the Shaping of the American Literary Canon: A Case Study from the Twenties," *Feminist Studies* 9 (Fall 1983): 435–63, and Joan Shelley Rubin, "Self, Culture, and Self-Culture in Modern America: The Early History of the Book-of-the-Month Club," *Journal of American History* 71 (March 1985): 782–806, discuss the standardization of cultural fare in the twentieth century. See also Christopher P. Wilson, "The Rhetoric of Consumption: Mass-Market Magazines and the Demise of the Gentle Reader, 1880–1920," in *The Culture of Consumption: Critical Essays in American History, 1880–1980*, ed. Richard Wightman Fox and T. J. Jackson Lears (New York, 1983), 39–64.

77. On female heroism and sexuality, see Martha Vicinus, "What Makes a Heroine? Nineteenth-Century Girls' Biographies," *Genre* 20 (Summer 1987): 171–88.

78. See, for example, Patrocinio P. Schweickart, "Reading Ourselves: Toward a Feminist Theory of Reading," in *Gender and Reading*, 31–62; quotation, 41.

14 SPONSORS OF LITERACY

Deborah Brandt

In his sweeping history of adult learning in the United States, Joseph Kett describes the intellectual atmosphere available to young apprentices who worked in the small, decentralized print shops of antebellum America. Because printers also were the solicitors and editors of what they published, their workshops served as lively incubators for literacy and political discourse. By the mid-nineteenth century, however, this learning space was disrupted when the invention of the steam press reorganized the economy of the print industry. Steam presses were so expensive that they required capital outlays beyond the means of many printers. As a result, print jobs were outsourced, the processes of editing and printing were split, and, in tight competition, print apprentices became low-paid mechanics with no more access to the multi-skilled environment of the craftshop (Kett 67–70). While this shift in working conditions may be evidence of the deskilling of workers induced by the Industrial Revolution (Nicholas and Nicholas), it also offers a site for reflecting upon the dynamic sources of literacy and literacy learning. The reading and writing skills of print apprentices in this period were the achievements not simply of teachers and learners nor of the discourse practices of the printer community. Rather, these skills existed fragilely, contingently within an economic moment. The pre–steam press economy enabled some of the most basic aspects of the apprentices' literacy, especially their access to material production and the public meaning or worth of their skills. Paradoxically, even as the steam-powered penny press made print more accessible (by making publishing more profitable), it brought an end to a particular form of literacy sponsorship and a drop in literate potential.

The apprentices' experience invites rumination upon literacy learning and teaching today. Literacy looms as one of the great engines of profit and competitive advantage in the twentieth century: a lubricant for consumer desire; a means for integrating corporate markets; a foundation for the deployment of weapons and other technology; a raw material in the mass production of information. As ordinary citizens have been compelled into these economies, their reading and writing skills have grown sharply more central to the everyday trade of information and goods as well as to the pursuit of education, employment, civil rights, status. At the same time, people's literate skills have grown vulnerable to unprecedented turbulence in their economic value, as conditions, forms, and standards of literacy achievement seem to shift with almost every new generation of learners. How are we to understand the vicissitudes of individual literacy development in relationship to the large-scale economic forces that set the routes and determine the wordly worth of that literacy?

The field of writing studies has had much to say about individual literacy development. Especially in the last quarter of the twentieth century, we have theorized, researched, critiqued, debated, and sometimes even managed to enhance the literate potentials of ordinary citizens as they have tried to cope with life as they find it. Less easily and certainly less steadily have we been able to relate what we see, study, and do to these larger contexts of profit making and competition. This even as we recognize that the most pressing issues we deal with—tightening associations between literate skill and social viability, the breakneck pace of change in communications technology, persistent inequities in access and reward—all relate to structural conditions in literacy's bigger picture. When economic forces are addressed in our work, they appear primarily as generalities: contexts, determinants, motivators, barriers, touchstones. But rarely are they systematically related to the local conditions and embodied moments of literacy learning that occupy so many of us on a daily basis.[1]

This essay does not presume to overcome the analytical failure completely. But it does offer a conceptual approach that begins to connect literacy as an individual development to literacy as an economic development, at least as the two have played out over the last ninety years or so. The approach is through what I call sponsors of literacy. Sponsors, as I have come to think of them, are any agents, local or distant, concrete or abstract, who enable, support, teach, model, as well as recruit, regulate, suppress, or withhold literacy—and gain advantage by it in some way. Just as the ages of radio and television accustom us to having programs *brought* to us by various commercial sponsors, it is useful to think about who or what underwrites occasions of literacy learning and use. Although the interests of the sponsor and the sponsored do not have to converge (and, in fact, may conflict) sponsors nevertheless set the terms for access to literacy and wield powerful incentives for compliance and loyalty. Sponsors are a tangible reminder that literacy learning throughout history has always required permission, sanction, assistance, coercion, or, at minimum, contact with existing trade routes. Sponsors are delivery systems for the economies of literacy, the means by which these forces present themselves to—and through—individual learners. They also represent the causes into which people's literacy usually gets recruited.[2]

For the last five years I have been tracing sponsors of literacy across the twentieth century as they appear in the accounts of ordinary Americans recalling how they learned to write and read. The investigation is grounded in more than 100 in-depth interviews that I collected from a diverse group of people born roughly between 1900 and 1980. In the interviews, people explored in great detail their memories of learning to read and write across their lifetimes, focusing especially on the people, institutions, materials, and motivations involved in the process. The more I worked with these accounts, the more I came to realize that they were filled with references to sponsors, both explicit and latent, who appeared in formative roles at the scenes of literacy learning. Patterns of sponsorship became an illuminating site through which to track the different cultural attitudes people developed toward writing vs. reading as well as the ideological congestion faced by late-century literacy learners as their sponsors proliferated and diversified (see my essays on "Remembering Reading" and "Accumulating Literacy"). In this essay I set out a case for why the concept of sponsorship is so richly suggestive for exploring economies of literacy and their effects. Then, through use of extended case examples, I demonstrate the practical application of this approach for interpreting current conditions of literacy teaching and learning, including persistent stratification of opportunity and escalating standards for literacy achievement. A final section addresses implications for the teaching of writing.

Sponsorship

Intuitively, *sponsors* seemed a fitting term for the figures who turned up most typically in people's memories of literacy learning: older relatives, teachers, priests, supervisors, military officers, editors, influential authors. Sponsors, as we ordinarily think of them, are powerful figures who bankroll events or smooth the way for initiates. Usually richer, more knowledgeable, and more entrenched than the sponsored, sponsors nevertheless enter a reciprocal relationship with those they underwrite. They lend their resources or credibility to the sponsored but also stand to gain benefits from their success, whether by direct repayment or, indirectly, by credit of association. *Sponsors* also proved an appealing term in my analysis because of all the commercial references that appeared in these 20th-century accounts—the magazines, peddled encyclopedias, essay contests, radio and television programs, toys, fan clubs, writing tools, and so on, from which so much experience with literacy was derived. As the twentieth century turned the abilities to read and write into widely exploitable resources, commercial sponsorship abounded.

In whatever form, sponsors deliver the ideological freight that must be borne for access to what they have. Of course, the sponsored can be oblivious to or innovative with this ideological burden. Like Little Leaguers who wear the logo of a local insurance agency on their uniforms, not out of a concern for enhancing the agency's image but as a means for getting to play ball, people throughout history have acquired literacy pragmatically under the banner of others' causes. In the days before free, public schooling in England, Protestant Sunday Schools warily offered basic reading instruction to working-class families as part of evangelical duty. To the horror of many in the church sponsorship, these families insistently, sometimes riotously demanded of their Sunday Schools more instruction, including in writing and math, because it provided means for upward mobility.[3] Through the sponsorship of Baptist and Methodist ministries, African Americans in slavery taught each other to understand the Bible in subversively liberatory ways. Under a conservative regime, they developed forms of critical literacy that sustained religious, educational, and political movements both before and after emancipation (Cornelius). Most of the time, however, literacy takes its shape from the interests of its sponsors. And, as we will see below, obligations toward one's sponsors run deep, affecting what, why, and how people write and read.

The concept of sponsors helps to explain, then, a range of human relationships and ideological pressures that turn up at the scenes of literacy learning—from benign sharing between adults and youths, to euphemized coercions in schools and workplaces, to the most notorious impositions and deprivations by church or state. It also is a concept useful for tracking literacy's materiel: the things that accompany writing and reading and the ways they are manufactured and distributed. Sponsorship as a sociological term is even more broadly suggestive for thinking about economies of literacy development. Studies of patronage in Europe and *compradrazgo* in the Americas show how patron-client relationships in the past grew up around the need to manage scarce resources and promote political stability (Bourne; Lynch; Horstman and Kurtz). Pragmatic, instrumental, ambivalent, patron-client relationships integrated otherwise antagonistic social classes into relationships of mutual, albeit unequal dependencies. Loaning land, money, protection, and other favors allowed the politically powerful to extend their influence and justify their exploitation of clients. Clients traded their labor and deference for access to opportunities for themselves or their children and for leverage needed to improve their social standing. Especially under conquest in Latin America, *compradrazgo* reintegrated native societies badly fragmented by the diseases and other disruptions that followed foreign invasions. At the same time, this system was susceptible to its own stresses, especially when patrons became clients themselves of still more centralized or distant overlords, with all the shifts in loyalty and perspective that entailed (Horstman and Kurtz 13–14).

In raising this association with formal systems of patronage, I do not wish to overlook the very different economic, political, and educational systems within which U.S. literacy has developed. But where we find the sponsoring of literacy, it will be useful to look for its function within larger political and economic arenas. Literacy, like land, is a valued commodity in this economy, a key resource in gaining profit and edge. This value helps to explain, of course, the lengths people will go to secure literacy for themselves or their children. But it also explains why the powerful work so persistently to conscript and ration the powers of literacy. The competition to harness literacy, to manage, measure, teach, and exploit it, has intensified throughout the century. It is vital to pay attention to this development because it largely sets the terms for individuals' encounters with literacy. This competition shapes the incentives and barriers (including uneven distributions of opportunity) that greet literacy learners in any particular time and place. It is this competition that has made access to the right kinds of literacy sponsors so crucial for political and economic well being. And it also has spurred the rapid, complex changes that now make the pursuit of literacy feel so turbulent and precarious for so many.

In the next three sections, I trace the dynamics of literacy sponsorship through the life experiences of several individuals, showing how their opportunities for literacy learning emerge out of the jockeying and skirmishing for economic and political advantage going on among sponsors of literacy. Along the way, the analysis addresses three key issues: (1) how, despite ostensible democracy in educational chances, stratification of opportunity continues to organize access and reward in literacy learning; (2) how sponsors contribute to what is called "the literacy crisis," that is, the perceived gap between rising standards for achievement and people's ability to meet them; and (3) how encounters with literacy sponsors, especially as they are configured at the end of the twentieth century, can be sites for the innovative rerouting of resources into projects of self-development and social change.

Sponsorship and access

A focus on sponsorship can force a more explicit and substantive link between literacy learning and systems of opportunity and access. A statistical correlation between high literacy achievement and high socioeconomic, majority-race status routinely shows up in results of national tests of reading and writing performance.[4] These findings capture yet, in their shorthand way, obscure the unequal conditions of literacy sponsorship that lie behind differential outcomes in academic performance. Throughout their lives, affluent people from high-caste racial groups have multiple and redundant contacts with powerful literacy sponsors as a routine part of their economic and political privileges. Poor people and those from low-caste racial groups have less consistent, less politically secured access to literacy sponsors—especially to the ones that can grease their way to academic and economic success. Differences in their performances are often attributed to family background (namely education and income of parents) or to particular norms and values operating within different ethnic groups or social classes. But in either case, much more is usually at work.

As a study in contrasts in sponsorship patterns and access to literacy, consider the parallel experiences of Raymond Branch and Dora Lopez, both of whom were born in 1969 and, as young children, moved with their parents to the same, mid-sized university town in the midwest.[5] Both were still residing in this town at the time of our interviews in 1995. Raymond Branch, a European American, had been born in southern California, the son of a professor father and a real estate executive mother. He recalled that his first grade classroom in 1975 was hooked up to a mainframe computer at Stanford University and that, as a youngster, he enjoyed fooling around with computer programming in the company of "real users" at his father's science lab. This process was not interrupted much when, in the late 1970s, his family moved to the midwest. Raymond received his first personal computer as a Christmas present from his parents when he was twelve years old, and a modem the year after that. In the 1980s, computer hardware and software stores began popping up within a bicycle-ride's distance from where he lived. The stores were serving the university community and, increasingly, the high-tech industries that were becoming established in that vicinity. As an adolescent, Raymond spent his summers roaming these stores, sampling new computer games, making contact with founders of some of the first electronic bulletin boards in the nation, and continuing, through reading and other informal means, to develop his programming techniques. At the time of our interview he had graduated from the local university and was a successful freelance writer of software and software documentation, with clients in both the private sector and the university community.

Dora Lopez, a Mexican American, was born in the same year as Raymond Branch, 1969, in a Texas border town, where her grandparents, who worked as farm laborers, lived most of the year. When Dora was still a baby her family moved to the same midwest university town as had the family of Raymond Branch. Her father pursued an accounting degree at a local technical college and found work as a shipping and receiving clerk at the university. Her mother, who also attended technical college briefly, worked part-time in a bookstore. In the early 1970s, when the Lopez family made its move to the midwest, the Mexican-American population in the university town was barely one per cent. Dora recalled that the family had to drive seventy miles to a big city to find not only suitable groceries but also Spanish-language newspapers and magazines that carried information of concern and interest to them. (Only when reception was good could they catch Spanish-language radio programs coming from Chicago, 150 miles away.) During her adolescence, Dora Lopez undertook to teach herself how to read and write in Spanish, something, she said, that neither her brother nor her U.S.-born cousins knew how to do. Sometimes, with the help of her mother's employee discount at the bookstore, she sought out novels by South American and Mexican writers, and she practiced her written Spanish by corresponding with relatives in Colombia. She was exposed to computers for the first time at the age of thirteen when she worked as a teacher's aide in a federally funded summer school program for the children of migrant workers. The computers were being used to help the children to be brought up to grade level in their reading and writing skills. When Dora was admitted to the same university that Raymond Branch attended, her father bought her a used word processing machine that a student had advertised for sale on a bulletin board in the building where Mr. Lopez worked. At the time of our interview, Dora Lopez had transferred from the university to a technical college. She was working for a cleaning company, where she performed extra duties as a translator, communicating on her supervisor's behalf with the largely Latina cleaning staff. "I write in Spanish for him, what he needs to be translated, like job duties, what he expects them to do, and I write lists for him in English and Spanish," she explained.

In Raymond Branch's account of his early literacy learning we are able to see behind the scenes of his majority-race membership, male gender, and high-end socioeconomic family profile. There lies a thick and, to him, relatively accessible economy of institutional and commercial supports that cultivated and subsidized his acquisition of a powerful form of literacy. One might be tempted to say that Raymond Branch was born at the right time and lived in the right place—except that the experience of Dora Lopez troubles that thought. For Raymond Branch, a university town in the 1970s and 1980s provided an information-rich, resource-rich learning environment in which to pursue his literacy development, but for Dora Lopez, a female member of a culturally unsubsidized ethnic minority, the same town at the same time was information- and resource-poor. Interestingly, both young people were pursuing projects of self-initiated learning, Raymond Branch in computer programming and Dora Lopez in biliteracy. But she had to reach much further afield for the material and communicative systems needed to support her learning. Also, while Raymond Branch, as the son of an academic, was sponsored by some of the most powerful agents of the university (its laboratories, newest technologies, and most educated personnel), Dora Lopez was being sponsored by what her parents could pull from the peripheral service systems of the university (the mail room, the bookstore, the second-hand technology market). In these accounts we also can see how the development and eventual economic worth of Raymond Branch's literacy skills were underwritten by late-century transformations in communication technology that created a boomtown need for programmers and software writers. Dora Lopez's biliterate skills developed and paid off much further down the economic-reward ladder, in government-sponsored youth programs and commercial enterprises, that, in the 1990s, were absorbing surplus migrant workers into a low-wage, urban service economy.[6] Tracking patterns of literacy sponsorship, then, gets beyond SES shorthand to expose more fully how unequal literacy chances relate to systems of unequal subsidy and reward for literacy. These are the systems that deliver large-scale economic, historical, and political conditions to the scenes of small-scale literacy use and development.

This analysis of sponsorship forces us to consider not merely how one social group's literacy practices may differ from another's, but how everybody's literacy practices are operating in differential economies, which supply different access routes, different degrees of sponsoring power, and different scales of monetary worth to the practices in use. In fact, the interviews I conducted are filled with examples of how economic and political forces, some of them originating in quite distant corporate and government policies, affect people's day-to-day ability to seek out and practice literacy. As a telephone company employee, Janelle Hampton enjoyed a brief period in the early 1980s as a fraud investigator, pursuing inquiries and writing up reports of her efforts. But when the breakup of the telephone utility reorganized its workforce, the fraud division was moved two states away and she was returned to less interesting work as a data processor. When, as a seven-year-old in the mid-1970s, Yi Vong made his way with his family from Laos to rural Wisconsin as part of the first resettlement group of Hmong refugees after the Vietnam War, his school district—which had no ESL programming—placed him in a school for the blind and deaf, where he learned English on audio and visual language machines. When a meager retirement pension forced Peter Hardaway and his wife out of their house and into a trailer, the couple stopped receiving newspapers and magazines in order to avoid cluttering up the small space they had to share. An analysis of sponsorship systems of literacy would help educators everywhere to think through the effects that economic and political changes in their regions are having on various people's ability to write and read, their chances to sustain that ability, and their capacities to pass it along to others. Recession, relocation, immigration, technological change, government retreat all can—and do—condition the course by which literate potential develops.

Sponsorship and the rise in literacy standards

As I have been attempting to argue, literacy as a resource becomes available to ordinary people largely through the mediations of more powerful sponsors. These sponsors are engaged in ceaseless processes of positioning and repositioning, seizing and relinquishing control over meanings and materials of literacy as part of their participation in economic and political competition. In the give and take of these struggles, forms of literacy and literacy learning take shape. This section examines more closely how forms of literacy are created out of competitions between institutions. It especially considers how this process relates to the rapid rise in literacy standards since World War II. Resnick and Resnick lay out the process by which the demand for literacy achievement has been escalating, from basic, largely rote competence to more complex analytical and interpretive skills. More and more people are now being expected to accomplish more and more things with reading and writing. As print and its spinoffs have entered virtually every sphere of life, people have grown increasingly dependent on their literacy skills for earning a living and exercising and protecting their civil rights. This section uses one extended case example to trace the role of institutional sponsorship in raising the literacy stakes. It also considers how one man used available forms of sponsorship to cope with this escalation in literacy demands.

The focus is on Dwayne Lowery, whose transition in the early 1970s from line worker in an automobile manufacturing plant to field representative for a major public employees union exemplified the major transition of the post–World War II economy—from a thing-making, thing-swapping society to an information-making, service-swapping society. In the process, Dwayne Lowery had to learn to read and write in ways that he had never done before. How his experiences with writing developed and how they were sponsored—and distressed—by institutional struggle will unfold in the following narrative.

A man of Eastern European ancestry, Dwayne Lowery was born in 1938 and raised in a semi-rural area in the upper midwest, the third of five children of a rubber worker father and a homemaker mother. Lowery recalled how, in his childhood home, his father's feisty union publications and left-leaning newspapers and radio shows helped to create a political climate in his household. "I was sixteen years old before I knew that goddamn Republicans was two words," he said. Despite this influence, Lowery said he shunned politics and newspaper reading as a young person, except to read the sports page. A diffident student, he graduated near the bottom of his class from a small high school in 1956 and, after a stint in the Army, went to work on the assembly line of a major automobile manufacturer. In the late 1960s, bored with the repetition of spraying primer paint on the right door checks of 57 cars an hour, Lowery traded in his night shift at the auto plant for a day job reading water meters in a municipal utility department. It was at that time, Lowery recalled, that he rediscovered newspapers, reading them in the early morning in his department's break room. He said:

> At the time I guess I got a little more interested in the state of things within the state. I started to get a little political at that time and got a little more information about local people. So I would buy [a metropolitan paper] and I would read that paper in the morning. It was a pretty conservative paper but I got some information.

At about the same time Lowery became active in a rapidly growing public employees union, and, in the early 1970s, he applied for and received a union-sponsored grant that allowed him to take off four months of work and travel to Washington, D.C., for training in union activity. Here is his extended account of that experience:

> When I got to school, then there was a lot of reading. I often felt bad. If I had read more [as a high-school student] it wouldn't have been so tough. But they pumped a lot of stuff at us to read. We lived in a hotel and we had to some extent homework we had to do and reading we had to do and not make written reports but make some presentation on our part of it. What they were trying to teach us, I believe, was regulations, systems, laws. In case anything in court came up along the way, we would know that. We did a lot of work on organizing, you know, learning how to negotiate contracts, contractual language, how to write it. Gross National Product, how that affected the Consumer Price Index. It was pretty much a crash course. It was pretty much crammed in. And I'm not sure we were all that well prepared when we got done, but it was interesting.

After a hands-on experience organizing sanitation workers in the west, Lowery returned home and was offered a full-time job as a field staff representative for the union, handling worker grievances and contract negotiations for a large, active local near his state capital. His initial writing and rhetorical activities corresponded with the heady days of the early 1970s when the union was growing in strength and influence, reflecting in part the exponential expansion in information workers and service providers within all branches of government. With practice, Lowery said he became "good at talking," "good at presenting the union side," "good at slicing chunks off the employer's case." Lowery observed that, in those years, the elected officials with whom he was negotiating often lacked the sophistication of the Washington-trained union counterparts. "They were part-time people," he said. "And they didn't know how to calculate. We got things in contracts that didn't cost them much at the time but were going to cost them a ton down the road." In time, though, even small municipal and county governments responded to the public employees' growing power by hiring specialized attorneys to represent them in grievance and contract negotiations. "Pretty soon," Lowery observed, "ninety percent of the people I was dealing with across the table were attorneys."

This move brought dramatic changes in the writing practices of union reps, and, in Lowery's estimation, a simultaneous waning of the power of workers and the power of his own literacy. "It used to be we got our way through muscle or through political connections," he said. "Now we had to get it through legalistic stuff. It was no longer just sit down and talk about it. Can we make a deal?" Instead, all activity became rendered in writing: the exhibit, the brief, the transcript, the letter, the appeal. Because briefs took longer to write, the wheels of justice took longer to turn. Delays in grievance hearings became routine, as lawyers and union reps alike asked hearing judges for extensions on their briefs. Things went, in Lowery's words, "from quick, competent justice to expensive and long term justice."

In the meantime, Lowery began spending up to 70 hours a week at work, sweating over the writing of briefs, which are typically fifteen to thirty-page documents laying out precedents, arguments, and evidence for a grievant's case. These documents were being forced by the new political economy in which Lowery's union was operating. He explained:

> When employers were represented by an attorney, you were going to have a written brief because the attorney needs to get paid. Well, what do you think if you were a union grievant and the attorney says, well, I'm going to write a brief and Dwayne Lowery says, well, I'm not going to. Does the worker somehow feel that their representation is less now?

To keep up with the new demands, Lowery occasionally traveled to major cities for two or three-day union-sponsored workshops on arbitration, new legislation, and communication skills. He also took short courses at a historic School for Workers at a nearby university. His writing instruction consisted mainly of reading the briefs of other field reps, especially those done by the college graduates who increasingly were being assigned to his district from union headquarters. Lowery said he kept a file drawer filled with other people's briefs from which he would borrow formats and phrasings. At the time of our interview in 1995, Dwayne Lowery had just taken an early and somewhat bitter retirement from the union, replaced by a recent graduate from a master's degree program in Industrial Relations. As a retiree, he was engaged in local Democratic party politics and was getting informal lessons in word processing at home from his wife.

Over a 20-year period, Lowery's adult writing took its character from a particular juncture in labor relations, when even small units of government began wielding (and, as a consequence, began spreading) a "legalistic" form of literacy in order to restore political dominance over public workers. This struggle for dominance shaped the kinds of literacy skills required of Lowery, the kinds of genres he learned and used, and the kinds of literate identity he developed. Lowery's rank-and-file experience and his talent for representing that experience around a bargaining table became increasingly peripheral to his ability to prepare documents that could compete in kind with those written by his formally educated, professional adversaries. Face-to-face meetings became occasions mostly for a ritualistic exchange of texts, as arbitrators generally deferred decisions, reaching them in private, after solitary deliberation over complex sets of documents. What Dwayne Lowery was up against as a working adult in the second half of the twentieth century was more than just living through a rising standard in literacy expectations or a generalized growth in professionalization, specialization, or documentary power—although certainly all of those things are, generically, true. Rather, these developments should be seen more specifically, as outcomes of ongoing transformations in the history of literacy as it has been wielded as part of economic and political conflict. These transformations become the arenas in which new standards of literacy develop. And for Dwayne Lowery—as well as many like him over the last 25 years—these are the arenas in which the worth of existing literate skills become degraded. A consummate debater and deal maker, Lowery saw his value to the union bureaucracy subside, as power shifted to younger, university-trained staffers whose literacy credentials better matched the specialized forms of escalating pressure coming from the other side.

In the broadest sense, the sponsorship of Dwayne Lowery's literacy experiences lies deep within the historical conditions of industrial relations in the twentieth century and, more particularly, within the changing nature of work and labor struggle over the last several decades. Edward Stevens Jr. has observed the rise in this century of an "advanced contractarian society" (25) by which formal relationships of all kinds have come to rely on "a jungle of rules and regulations" (139). For labor, these conditions only intensified in the 1960s and 1970s when a flurry of federal and state civil rights legislation curtailed the previously unregulated hiring and firing power of management. These developments made the appeal to law as central as collective bargaining for extending employee rights (Heckscher 9). I mention this broader picture, first, because it relates to the forms of employer backlash that Lowery began experiencing by the early 1980s and, more important, because a history of unionism serves as a guide for a closer look at the sponsors of Lowery's literacy.

These resources begin with the influence of his father, whose membership in the United Rubber Workers during the ideologically potent 1930s and 1940s, grounded Lowery in class-conscious progressivism and its favorite literate form: the newspaper. On top of that, though, was a pragmatic philosophy of worker education that developed in the U.S. after the Depression as an anti-communist antidote to left-wing intellectual influences in unions. Lowery's parent union, in fact, had been a central force in refocusing worker education away from an earlier emphasis on broad critical study and toward discrete techniques for organizing and bargaining. Workers began to be trained in the discrete bodies of knowledge, written formats, and idioms associated with those strategies. Characteristic of this legacy, Lowery's crash course at the Washington-based training center in the early 1970s emphasized technical information, problem solving, and union-building skills and methods. The transformation in worker education from critical, humanistic study to problem-solving skills was also lived out at the school for workers where Lowery took short courses in the 1980s. Once a place where factory workers came to write and read about economics, sociology, and labor history, the school is now part of a university extension service offering workshops—often requested by management—on such topics as work restructuring, new technology, health and safety regulations, and joint labor-management cooperation.[7] Finally, in this inventory of Dwayne Lowery's literacy sponsors, we must add the latest incarnations shaping union practices: the attorneys and college-educated co-workers who carried into Lowery's workplace forms of legal discourse and "essayist literacy."[8]

What should we notice about this pattern of sponsorship? First, we can see from yet another angle how the course of an ordinary person's literacy learning—its occasions, materials, applications, potentials—follows the transformations going on within sponsoring institutions as those institutions fight for economic and ideological position. As a result of wins, losses, or compromises, institutions undergo change, affecting the kinds of literacy they promulgate and the status that such literacy has in the larger society. So where, how, why, and what Lowery practiced as a writer—and what he didn't practice—took shape as part of the post-industrial jockeying going on over the last thirty years by labor, government, and industry. Yet there is more to be seen in this inventory of literacy sponsors. It exposes the deeply textured history that lies within the literacy practices of institutions and within any individual's literacy experiences. Accumulated layers of sponsoring influences—in families, workplaces, schools, memory—carry forms of literacy that have been shaped out of ideological and economic struggles of the past. This history, on the one hand, is a sustaining resource in the quest for literacy. It enables an older generation to pass its literacy resources onto another. Lowery's exposure to his father's newspaper-reading and supper-table political talk kindled his adult passion for news, debate, and for language that rendered relief and justice. This history also helps to create infrastructures of opportunity. Lowery found crucial supports for extending his adult literacy in the educational networks that unions established during the first half of the twentieth century as they were consolidating into national powers. On the other hand, this layered history of sponsorship is also deeply conservative and can be maladaptive because it teaches forms of literacy that oftentimes are in the process of being overtaken by new political realities and by ascendant forms of literacy. The decision to focus worker education on practical strategies of recruiting and bargaining—devised in the thick of Cold War patriotism and galloping expansion in union memberships—became, by the Reagan years, a fertile ground for new forms of management aggression and cooptation.

It is actually this lag or gap in sponsoring forms that we call the rising standard of literacy. The pace of change and the place of literacy in economic competition have both intensified enormously in the last half of the twentieth century. It is as if the history of literacy is in fast forward. Where once the same sponsoring arrangements could maintain value across a generation or more, forms of literacy and their sponsors can now rise and recede many times within a single life span. Dwayne Lowery experienced profound changes in forms of union-based literacy not only between his father's time and his but between the time he joined the union and the time he left it, twenty-odd years later. This phenomenon is what makes today's literacy feel so advanced and, at the same time, so destabilized.

Sponsorship and appropriation in literacy learning

We have seen how literacy sponsors affect literacy learning in two powerful ways. They help to organize and administer stratified systems of opportunity and access, and they raise the literacy stakes in struggles for competitive advantage. Sponsors enable and hinder literacy activity, often forcing the formation of new literacy requirements while decertifying older ones. A somewhat different dynamic of literacy sponsorship is treated here. It pertains to the potential of the sponsored to divert sponsors' resources toward ulterior projects, often projects of self-interest or self-development. Earlier I mentioned how Sunday School parishioners in England and African Americans in slavery appropriated church-sponsored literacy for economic and psychic survival. "Misappropriation" is always possible at the scene of literacy transmission, a reason for the tight ideological control that usually surrounds reading and writing instruction. The accounts that appear below are meant to shed light on the dynamics of appropriation, including the role of sponsoring agents in that process. They are also meant to suggest that diversionary tactics in literacy learning may be invited now by the sheer proliferation of literacy activity in contemporary life. The uses and networks of literacy crisscross through many domains, exposing people to multiple, often amalgamated sources of sponsoring powers, secular, religious, bureaucratic, commercial, technological. In other words, what is so destabilized about contemporary literacy today also makes it so available and potentially innovative, ripe for picking, one might say, for people suitably positioned. The rising level of schooling in the general population is also an inviting factor in this process. Almost everyone now has some sort of contact, for instance, with college-educated people, whose movements through workplaces, justice systems, social service organizations, houses of worship, local government, extended families, or circles of friends spread dominant forms of literacy (whether wanted or not, helpful or not) into public and private spheres. Another condition favorable for appropriation is the deep hybridity of literacy practices extant in many settings. As we saw in Dwayne Lowery's case, workplaces, schools, families bring together multiple strands of the history of literacy in complex and influential forms. We need models of literacy that more astutely account for these kinds of multiple contacts, both in and out of school and across a lifetime. Such models could begin to grasp the significance of re-appropriation, which, for a number of reasons, is becoming a key requirement for literacy learning at the end of the twentieth century.

The following discussion will consider two brief cases of literacy diversion. Both involve women working in subordinate positions as secretaries, in print-rich settings where better-educated male supervisors were teaching them to read and write in certain ways to perform their clerical duties. However, as we will see shortly, strong loyalties outside the workplace prompted these two secretaries to lift these literate resources for use in other spheres. For one, Carol White, it was on behalf of her work as a Jehovah's Witness. For the other, Sarah Steele, it was on behalf of upward mobility for her lower-middle-class family.

Before turning to their narratives, though, it will be wise to pay some attention to the economic moment in which they occur. Clerical work was the largest and fastest growing occupation for women in the twentieth century. Like so much employment for women, it offered a mix of gender-defined constraints as well as avenues for economic independence and mobility. As a new information economy created an acute need for typists, stenographers, bookkeepers and other office workers, white, American-born women and, later, immigrant and minority women saw reason to pursue high school and business-college educations. Unlike male clerks of the 19th century, female secretaries in this century had little chance for advancement. However, office work represented a step up from the farm or the factory for women of the working class and served as a respectable occupation from which educated, middle-class women could await or avoid marriage (Anderson, Strom). In a study of clerical work through the first half of the twentieth century, Christine Anderson estimated that secretaries might encounter up to 97 different genres in the course of doing dictation or transcription. They routinely had contact with an array of professionals, including lawyers, auditors, tax examiners, and other government overseers (52–53). By 1930, 30% of women office workers used machines other than typewriters (Anderson 76) and, in contemporary offices, clerical workers have often been the first employees to learn to operate CRTs and personal computers and to teach others how to use them. Overall, the daily duties of twentieth-century secretaries could serve handily as an index to the rise of complex administrative and accounting procedures, standardization of information, expanding communication, and developments in technological systems.

With that background, consider the experiences of Carol White and Sarah Steele. In Oneida, Carol White was born into a poor, single-parent household in 1940. She graduated from high school in 1960 and, between five maternity leaves and a divorce, worked continuously in a series of clerical positions in both the private and public sectors. One of her first secretarial jobs was with an urban firm that produced and disseminated Catholic missionary films. The vice president with whom she worked most closely also spent much of his time producing a magazine for a national civic organization that he headed. She discussed how typing letters and magazine articles and occasionally proofreading for this man taught her rhetorical strategies in which she was keenly interested. She described the scene of transfer this way:

> [My boss] didn't just write to write. He wrote in a way to make his letters appealing. I would have to write what he was writing in this magazine too. I was completely enthralled. He would write about the people who were in this [organization] and the different works they were undertaking and people that died and people who were sick and

about their personalities. And he wrote little anecdotes. Once in a while I made some suggestions too. He was a man who would listen to you.

The appealing and persuasive power of the anecdote became especially important to Carol White when she began doing door-to-door missionary work for the Jehovah's Witnesses, a pan-racial, millenialist religious faith. She now uses colorful anecdotes to prepare demonstrations that she performs with other women at weekly service meetings at their Kingdom Hall. These demonstrations, done in front of the congregation, take the form of skits designed to explore daily problems through Bible principles. Further, at the time of our interview, Carol White was working as a municipal revenue clerk and had recently enrolled in an on-the-job training seminar called Persuasive Communication, a two-day class offered free to public employees. Her motivation for taking the course stemmed from her desire to improve her evangelical work. She said she wanted to continue to develop speaking and writing skills that would be "appealing," "motivating," and "encouraging" to people she hoped to convert.

Sarah Steele, a woman of Welsh and German descent, was born in 1920 into a large, working-class family in a coal mining community in eastern Pennsylvania. In 1940, she graduated from a two-year commercial college. Married soon after, she worked as a secretary in a glass factory until becoming pregnant with the first of four children. In the 1960s, in part to help pay for her children's college educations, she returned to the labor force as a receptionist and bookkeeper in a law firm, where she stayed until her retirement in the late 1970s.

Sarah Steele described how, after joining the law firm, she began to model her household management on principles of budgeting that she was picking up from one of the attorneys with whom she worked most closely. "I learned cash flow from Mr. B——," she said. "I would get all the bills and put a tape in the adding machine and he and I would sit down together to be sure there was going to be money ahead." She said that she began to replicate that process at home with household bills. "Before that," she observed, "I would just cook beans when I had to instead of meat." Sarah Steele also said she encountered the genre of the credit report during routine reading and typing on the job. She figured out what constituted a top rating, making sure her husband followed these steps in preparation for their financing a new car. She also remembered typing up documents connected to civil suits being brought against local businesses, teaching her, she said, which firms never to hire for home repairs. "It just changes the way you think," she observed about the reading and writing she did on her job. "You're not a pushover after you learn how business operates."

The dynamics of sponsorship alive in these narratives expose important elements of literacy appropriation, at least as it is practiced at the end of the twentieth century. In a pattern now familiar from the earlier sections, we see how opportunities for literacy learning—this time for diversions of resources—open up in the clash between long-standing, residual forms of sponsorship and the new: between the lingering presence of literacy's conservative history and its pressure for change. So, here, two women—one Native American and both working-class—filch contemporary literacy resources (public relations techniques and accounting practices) from more educated, higher-status men. The women are emboldened in these acts by ulterior identities beyond the workplace: Carol White with faith and Sarah Steele with family. These affiliations hark back to the first sponsoring arrangements through which American women were gradually allowed to acquire literacy and education. Duties associated with religious faith and child rearing helped literacy to become, in Gloria Main's words, "a permissible feminine activity" (579). Interestingly, these roles, deeply sanctioned within the history of women's literacy—and operating beneath the newer permissible feminine activity of clerical work—become grounds for covert, innovative appropriation even as they reinforce traditional female identities.

Just as multiple identities contribute to the ideologically hybrid character of these literacy formations, so do institutional and material conditions. Carol White's account speaks to such hybridity. The missionary film company with the civic club vice president is a residual site for two of literacy's oldest campaigns—Christian conversion and civic participation—enhanced here by twentieth-century advances in film and public relations techniques. This ideological reservoir proved a pleasing instructional site for Carol White, whose interests in literacy, throughout her life, have been primarily spiritual. So literacy appropriation draws upon, perhaps even depends upon, conservative forces in the history of literacy sponsorship that are always hovering at the scene of acts of learning. This history serves as both a sanctioning force and a reserve of ideological and material support.

At the same time, however, we see in these accounts how individual acts of appropriation can divert and subvert the course of literacy's history, how changes in individual literacy experiences relate to larger scale transformations. Carol White's redirection of personnel management techniques to the cause of the Jehovah's Witnesses is an almost ironic transformation in this regard. Once a principal sponsor in the initial spread of mass literacy, evangelism is here rejuvenated through late-literate corporate sciences of secular persuasion, fund-raising, and bureaucratic management that Carol White finds circulating in her contemporary workplaces. By the same token, through Sarah Steele, accounting practices associated with corporations are, in a sense, tracked into the house, rationalizing and standardizing even domestic practices. (Even though Sarah Steele did not own an adding machine, she penciled her budget figures onto adding-machine tape that she kept for that purpose.) Sarah Steele's act of appropriation in some sense explains how dominant forms of literacy migrate and penetrate into private spheres, including private consciousness. At the same time, though, she accomplishes a subversive diversion of literate power. Her efforts to move her family up in the middle class involved not merely contributing a second income but also, from her desk as a bookkeeper, reading her way into an understanding of middle-class economic power.

Teaching and the dynamics of sponsorship

It hardly seems necessary to point out to the readers of *CCC* that we haul a lot of freight for the opportunity to teach writing. Neither rich nor powerful enough to sponsor literacy on our own terms, we serve instead as conflicted brokers between literacy's buyers and sellers. At our most worthy, perhaps, we show the sellers how to beware and try to make sure these exchanges will be a little fairer, maybe, potentially, a little more mutually rewarding. This essay has offered a few working case studies that link patterns of sponsorship to processes of stratification, competition, and reappropriation. How much these dynamics can be generalized to classrooms is an ongoing empirical question.

I am sure that sponsors play even more influential roles at the scenes of literacy learning and use than this essay has explored. I have focused on some of the most tangible aspects—material supply, explicit teaching, institutional aegis. But the ideological pressure of sponsors affects many private aspects of writing processes as well as public aspects of finished texts. Where one's sponsors are multiple or even at odds, they can make writing maddening. Where they are absent, they make writing unlikely. Many of the cultural formations we associate with writing development—community practices, disciplinary tractions, technological potentials—can be appreciated as make-do responses to the economics of literacy, past and present. The history of literacy is a catalogue of obligatory relations. That this catalogue is so deeply conservative and, at the same time, so ruthlessly demanding of change is what fills contemporary literacy learning and teaching with their most paradoxical choices and outcomes.[9]

In bringing attention to economies of literacy learning I am not advocating that we prepare students more efficiently for the job markets they must enter. What I have tried to suggest is that as we assist and study individuals in pursuit of literacy, we also recognize how literacy is in pursuit of them. When this process stirs ambivalence, on their part or on ours, we need to be understanding.

Notes

This research was sponsored by the NCTE Research Foundation and the Center on English Learning and Achievement. The Center is supported by the U.S. Department of Education's Office of Educational Research and Improvement, whose views do not necessarily coincide with the author's. A version of this essay was given as a lecture in the Department of English, University of Louisville, in April 1997. Thanks to Anna Syvertsen and Julie Nelson for their help with archival research. Thanks too to colleagues who lent an ear along the way: Nelson Graff, Jonna Gjevre, Anne Gere, Kurt Spellmeyer, Tom Fox, and Bob Gundlach.

1. Three of the keenest and most eloquent observers of economic impacts on writing teaching and learning have been Lester Faigley, Susan Miller, and Kurt Spellmeyer.

2. My debt to the writings of Pierre Bourdieu will be evident throughout the essay. Here and throughout I invoke his expansive notion of "economy," which is not restricted to literal and ostensible systems of money making but to the many spheres where people labor, invest, and exploit energies—their own and others'—to maximize advantage. See Bourdieu and Wacquant, especially 117–20; and Bourdieu, chapter 7.

3. Thomas Laqueur (124) provides a vivid account of a street demonstration in Bolton, England, in 1834 by a "pro-writing" faction of Sunday school students and their teachers. This faction demanded that writing instruction continue to be provided on Sundays, something that opponents of secular instruction on the Sabbath were trying to reverse.

4. See, for instance, National Assessments of Educational Progress in reading and writing (Applebee et al.; and *Looking*).

5. All names used in this essay are pseudonyms.

6. I am not suggesting that literacy does not "pay off" in terms of prestige or monetary reward is less valuable. Dora Lopez's ability to read and write in Spanish was a source of great strength and pride, especially when she was able to teach it to her young child. The resource of Spanish literacy carried much of what Bourdieu calls cultural capital in her social and family circles. But I want to point out here how people who labor equally to acquire literacy do so under systems of unequal subsidy and unequal reward.

7. For useful accounts of this period in union history, see Heckscher; Nelson.

8. Marcia Farr associates "essayist literacy" with written genres esteemed in the academy and noted for their explicitness, exactness, reliance on reasons and evidence, and impersonal voice.

9. Lawrence Cremin makes similar points about education in general in his essay "The Cacophony of Teaching." He suggests that complex economic and social changes since World War Two, including the popularization of schooling

and the penetration of mass media, have created "a far greater range and diversity of languages, competencies, values, personalities, and approaches to the world and to its educational opportunities" than at one time existed. The diversity most of interest to him (and me) resides not so much in the range of different ethnic groups there are in society but in the different cultural formulas by which people assemble their educational—or, I would say, literate—experience.

Works Cited

Anderson, Mary Christine. "Gender, Class, and Culture: Women Secretarial and Clerical Workers in the United States, 1925-1955." Ph.D. diss., Ohio State University, 1986.

Applebee, Arthur N., Judith A. Langer, and Ida V. S. Mullis. *The Writing Report Card: Writing Achievement in American Schools*. Princeton: ETS, 1986.

Bourdieu, Pierre. *The Logic of Practice*. Trans. Richard Nice. Cambridge: Polity, 1990.

Bourdieu, Pierre, and Loic J. D. Wacquant. *An Invitation to Reflexive Sociology*. Chicago: U of Chicago P, 1992.

Bourne, J. M. *Patronage and Society in Nineteenth-Century England*. London: Edward Arnold, 1986.

Brandt, Deborah. "Accumulating Literacy: Writing and Learning to Write in the 20th Century." *College English* 57 (1995): 649-68.

———. "Remembering Reading, Remembering Writing." *CCC* 45 (1994): 459-79.

Cornelius, Janet Duitsman. *"When I Can Read My Title Clear": Literacy, Slavery, and Religion in the Antebellum South*. Columbia: U of South Carolina P, 1991.

Cremin, Lawrence. "The Cacophony of Teaching." In *Popular Education and Its Discontents*. New York: Harper, 1990.

Faigley, Lester. "Veterans' Stories on the Porch." In *History, Reflection and Narrative: The Professionalization of Composition, 1963-1983*. Ed. Beth Boehm, Debra Journet, and Mary Rosner. Norwood: Ablex, in press.

Farr, Marcia. "Essayist Literacy and Other Verbal Performances." *Written Communication* 8 (1993): 4-38.

Heckscher, Charles C. *The New Unionism: Employee Involvement in the Changing Corporation*. New York: Basic, 1988.

Horstman, Connie, and Donald V. Kurtz. *Compradrazgo in Post-Conquest Middle America*. Milwaukee: Milwaukee-UW Center for Latin America, 1978.

Kett, Joseph F. *The Pursuit of Knowledge under Difficulties: From Self Improvement to Adult Education in America, 1750-1990*. Stanford: Stanford UP, 1994.

Laqueur, Thomas. *Religion and Respectability: Sunday Schools and Working-Class Culture, 1780-1850*. New Haven: Yale UP, 1976.

Looking at How Well Our Students Read: The 1992 National Assessment of Educational Progress in Reading. Washington: U.S. Dept. of Education, Office of Educational Research and Improvement, Educational Resources Information Center, 1992.

Lynch, Joseph H. *Godparents and Kinship in Early Medieval Europe*. Princeton: Princeton UP, 1986.

Main, Gloria L. "An Inquiry into When and Why Women Learned to Write in Colonial New England." *Journal of Social History* 24 (1991): 579-89.

Miller, Susan. *Textual Carnivals: The Politics of Composition*. Carbondale: Southern Illinois UP, 1991.

Nelson, Daniel. *American Rubber Workers and Organized Labor, 1900-1941*. Princeton: Princeton UP, 1988.

Nicholas, Stephen J., and Jacqueline M. Nicholas. "Male Literacy, 'Deskilling,' and the Industrial Revolution." *Journal of Interdisciplinary History* 23 (1992): 1–18.

Resnick, Daniel P., and Lauren B. Resnick. "The Nature of Literacy: A Historical Explanation." *Harvard Educational Review* 47 (1977): 350–85.

Spellmeyer, Kurt. "After Theory: From Textuality to Attunement with the World." *College English* 58 (1996): 893–913.

Stevens, Edward, Jr.. *Literacy, Law, and Social Order.* DeKalb: Northern Illinois UP, 1987.

Strom, Sharon Hartman. *Beyond the Typewriter: Gender, Class, and the Origins of Modern American Office Work, 1900–1930.* Urbana: U of Illinois P, 1992.

15 "WELCOME TO THE JAM": POPULAR CULTURE, SCHOOL LITERACY, AND THE MAKING OF CHILDHOODS

Anne Haas Dyson

> Last night my mama had me singing "I Believe I Can Fly" [from the movie *Space Jam*]. She *love* that movie. She *love* that song.
> —Lakeisha, a first grader, talking to her "fake" school family of close friends

"**M**illions of kids entered a trance-like state, experiencing a gravitational pull to a movie, starring Bugs Bunny and Michael Jordan" (Klein, 1996), that is little more than a device that big money conglomerates use for "cross-promotion"—so declares one commentator on the movie *Space Jam*. "A happy marriage of good ideas . . . [that] entertains kids . . . [and] a family movie in the best sense" (Ebert, 1996), exudes a reviewer of the same film. Despite their conflicting views, both reviewers assume a common societal stance toward the media: they pay close attention to the movie as a media product and make assumptions about how that product shapes the minds and moods of children (Kline, 1993).

This is not, however, how children's minds and the media meet. When children hear voices emanating from electronic, rather than human, sources, they organize these voices in various genres (e.g., stories, raps, inspirational songs, and informational pieces) and experience them in the contexts of growing up with families and friends, as Lakeisha's comments suggest.[1]

Moreover, as I will illustrate, children appropriate the symbolic stuff of these media genres (e.g., sounds, images, ways of talking) and adapt it to their own childhood practices, including storytelling, dramatic play, group singing, and informational display. In this way, children actively participate in the production of popular culture, through their use of "the repertoire of commodities supplied by the cultural industry" (Storey, 1998, xv) for communal meaning-producing practices (Hall, 1981). This experience with media texts figures into school literacy learning.[2]

From Anne Haas Dyson, "'Welcome to the Jam': Popular Culture, School Literacy, and the Making of Childhoods," *Harvard Educational Review* 73, no. 3 (Fall 2003): 328–61. Copyright © 2003 by the President and Fellows of Harvard College. All rights reserved. Reprinted with permission. For more information, contact Harvard Education Publishing Group at (800) 513–0763.

In this article, I draw on data from my ethnographic study of the childhood symbols and practices of Lakeisha and her self-named "fake brothers and sisters." These children were a small circle of close friends, all African American first graders in a multiracial, socioeconomically diverse urban public school.

In my project, I was interested in how children made use of the landscape of voices that surrounded them. These voices enacted varied communicative practices involving different kinds of symbol systems (e.g., written language, drawing, music), different technologies (e.g., video, radio, animation), and different ideologies or ideas about how the world works. I studied the revoicing or recontextualization processes (Bauman & Briggs, 1990) through which the children borrowed from these voices in order to produce their own cultural practices. I also examined the influence of those unofficial (or child-governed) practices on their participation in official (or teacher-governed) literacy practices, especially those involving composing.

Prevalent among these voices were those of the popular media, particularly the movie *Space Jam,* which was well loved by all the brothers and sisters. This film provided fertile analytical ground for this study because it incorporates the children's three most common sources of symbolic material—sports media, songs, and animation.

I aim to illustrate three key project findings. First, that the children's use of media material was intertextually linked to their memberships in families and neighborhoods and to the forms of pleasure, power, and companionship they found there. These memberships involved children in the dynamics of age, race, and gender, among other social categories. Second, in constructing their childhood practices (e.g., storytelling, collaborative play, and singing), children engaged in complex recontextualization processes (Bauman & Briggs, 1990), borrowing, translating, and reframing media material from the communicative practices—the varied kinds of voices—that filled the landscape of their everyday lives.

Third, these recontextualization processes shaped the children's entry into school literacy. The observed children did not approach official literacy activities in their first-grade classroom as though they had nothing to do with their own childhoods. They made use of familiar media-influenced practices and symbolic material to take intellectual and social action in the official school world. Recontextualizing material across social relations (e.g., unofficial to official), symbolic tools (e.g., audiovisual to written), and ideological values (e.g., joint to individual productions) provided teaching and learning opportunities to help children become more skillful and more sociopolitically astute decision makers and communicators in their expanding social worlds.

In illustrating these three findings, I hope to portray children's experiences with popular media as integral to the formation of contemporary childhoods. Moreover, I aim to offer an alternative view of the pathways through which children enter into school literacy practices. Although literacy theory has emphasized how texts are situated within increasingly multimodal practices (New London Group, 1996), dominant views of young children's literacy development seldom include any substantive consideration of such practices (see, e.g., Adams, 2001; Whitehurst & Lonigan, 2001). Rather, they privilege idealized, print-centered childhoods that feature school-like materials and practices (e.g., bedtime stories) (Dyson, 1999). Developmental research generally has been critiqued for normalizing learning paths based on "the" middle-class child, thereby failing to account for the variable and localized "grounds on which [children] grow and seek to become somebody" (Kenway & Bullen, 2001, 3; see also Kessen, 1979). In response to all these views, I emphasize how children's developmental journeys are shaped by the social and symbolic material of their own childhoods, much of which comes from the popular media.

Background: Popular voices and literate acts

First graders Noah and Tommy are discussing the film *Space Jam* when they slip into the voices of the film's monstrous space alien (Swackhammer) and his space lackeys (the Nerdlucks):[3]

> TOMMY: We need something—looney! Looney! (*enacting the gruff voice of Swackhammer as he decides, upon seeing the Looney Tunes on his television sets, to kidnap the Toon characters to enliven his amusement park*)
> NOAH: What if they can't come? (*enacting the small voice of a Nerdluck*)
> TOMMY: Can't come!? Make 'em!

There is nothing unusual about Noah and Tommy's play with appealing voices. Research on family conversation and language development (e.g., Dore, 1989; Nelson, 1996), storytelling (Miller & Mehler, 1994), literary response (e.g., Miller, Hoogstra, Mintz, Fung, & Williams, 1993), and dramatic play (e.g., Garvey, 1990) all illustrate children's attentiveness to plot lines and character voices that are aesthetically marked, affectively charged, and allow them to assume appealing and/or powerful positions.

Indeed, this attentiveness to voices supports children's entry into language itself. Children learn words as they participate with others in their everyday practices (e.g., dressing, eating, "peek-a-boo" games) (Bruner, 1990; Nelson, 1996). To use the concepts of the language philosopher Bakhtin (1981), children re-voice those offered words, "re-accenting" them with their own intentions. In this way, children form a sense of their own agency, their own possibilities for action, as they slip into the voices that organize their social worlds, including their routine practices.

The typicality of those voices, their ways of enacting a typical social situation, indicates their generic quality. Indeed, genres can be viewed as kinds of practices (Hanks, 1996), that is, as ways of participating in the recurrent social activities of a society. These testified voices, or genres, result from the many people who have participated in similar situations, adopting certain evaluative stances toward others and the world, speaking and singing certain thematic content in structurally compatible ways (Bakhtin, 1986). Ways of telling stories (through varied media), of reporting local and national news, and of celebrating, communicating, or praying through song are all typical voices or generic texts, and yet all are made manifest through particular and unique encounters, or dialogues, between speakers and listeners, readers and writers (Bakhtin, 1981).

Textual toys in childhood spaces

Although the particularities of childhoods vary across historical time and cultural space, children all over the globe are alert to the voice-filled landscape of their everyday lives. Within that landscape, they may find textual toys—symbolic material useful for conversation, collaborative play, and group singing—in the words of human and electronic voices. Among the latter are radio deejays and singing stars, TV sports commentators and movie characters. Through an eclectic mix of appealing symbolic stuff (including both long-standing childhood rhymes and more ephemeral media materials), children engage in cultural and expressive practices and thereby produce friendships and imaginative worlds (see also Dyson, 1993, 1997; Fisherkeller, 2002; Garvey, 1990; Jenkins, 1988; Newkirk, 2002; Opie & Opie, 1959). Indeed, the cultural geographer Massey (1998) argues that youth cultures across the globe (if not particularly childhood cultures) are marked by an openness in which commercial media, however global their reach, are always localized in how youth appropriate and adapt them to their systems of symbolic meanings and social relations (see also Hall, 1981).

Particularly in the United States, the popular media has been a central aspect of childhood, at least since World War II (Douglas, 1994; Seiter, 1998; Spigel, 1998). As Spigel and Jenkins (1991) illustrate, adults' recollections of popular childhood media programs are intertextually linked not only with each other, but also with the narratives of their experiences and feelings as children growing up with family and friends (see also Fisherkeller, 1997, 2002). For Spigel and Jenkins' interviewees, a cartoonish superhero (Batman) "brought back a situational context, a scene that painted a rough sketch of places in the house, times of the day, and childhood relationships with family and friends" (134).

And so it seemed for the brothers and sisters. The voices they appropriated were from their experiences (as reported by children and their parents) as participants in media-based practices—radio deejays who joined their families' morning routines, sports show announcers who participated in Monday night football viewing, radio stars (singers, rappers) who were overheard as they accompanied older brothers and sisters out of the house, and characters in shows who had appealing roles, lines, or even powers. The children picked up and played with this textual and symbolic stuff—that is, with the literal and generic voices of all these speakers.

As I will illustrate, playing with this material involved varied kinds of textual manipulation. The children differentiated particular material, including sounds and images, from the original sources and translated it across, and re-framed it within, differing practices. These practices often had strikingly different social or symbolic dynamics. An audiovisual story experienced at home might become an occasion for verbal affiliation or even competition with peers, as children demonstrated expertise about a valued story. A song heard on the car radio (especially one viewed by children and parents as for "teenagers") might become collaborative dramatic play among peers (as in playing "radio singing stars" on the playground), or particularly appealing bits of film dialogue might be lifted for group language play. The most "liftable" material—that is, the material most easily differentiated from its original source—often called attention to itself through its performative properties of speech (e.g., rhythm, rhyme, humor, layout) (Bauman & Briggs, 1990).

As with the brothers and sisters, children in our society are likely to bring to school a sense of agency toward, and much experience manipulating, media texts. This experience may manifest itself in complex ways during school literacy activities.

Media play and written school literacy

Literacy itself can be seen as entailing the *deliberate* manipulation of symbolic material within socially organized practices. Unlike more spontaneous casual conversation, literacy is viewed as more "volitional" (Vygotsky, 1987), involving a conscious choice of signs to render meaning. Composers do not turn inward to invent these signs; they turn outward, choosing and re-accenting signs from those in circulation among public and social groups to which they have access (Bakhtin, 1981).

The transformation of old symbols to produce new meanings is basic to all symbolic activity, whatever the medium (Hanks, 1996). Moreover, any such recontextualization may entail translating material across different symbolic modes, different social expectations, and, always, different moment-to-moment interactional contingencies, as language users negotiate meanings with and for others.

In this project, the observed children were guided by their experiences with varied kinds of cultural texts, including media texts, as they entered into the new demands of school literacy. Asked to compose "a story," to write a report about "what you learned," or simply to "write whatever you want," they drew upon familiar frames of reference and, often, old textual toys (e.g., radio songs, film dialogue, sports reports, and cartoon scenes). In this way, they made new kinds of practices meaningful by infusing them with cultural knowledge and comfortable peer relations. In a dialectic fashion, the children also considered aspects of their familiar world from within the framework of new social and symbolic demands, thus potentially gaining reflective angles on experiences. Symbolic conventions, social expectations, and ideologies all were foregrounded as children considered, for example, the functional nature of drawing relative to writing, the expectations for storytelling in official contexts relative to peer or home ones, and the pleasures condoned by teachers relative to diverse significant others.

In sum, through recontextualization, children potentially could learn about the symbolic, social, and ideological "options, limits, and blends" of practices (Miller & Goodnow, 1995), which is one way to envision literacy development (for an elaboration, see Dyson, 2003). The children's appropriation and manipulation of media texts counters the common view that children's play with media texts involves mindless imitation (Levin, 1998; Seiter, 1999). Much of that play may well entail deliberate manipulation of layers of symbols (e.g., sounds, syllables, words, phrases, and speaking turns), that is, it may be quite "literate," in the sense just discussed.

This view in no way renders media texts unproblematic. Popular images appeal to children in part for precisely the same reason they may disconcert educators: they feature dominant desires and pleasures about, for example, power, wealth, and beauty, which themselves reflect interrelated societal constructions like age, gender, race, and class (Buckingham, 1993; Newkirk, 2002; Willis, 1990). But in official spaces, media-based child products can elicit varied perspectives on the worthiness of plots and points, not to mention genres themselves. Thus, they are sources for learning and, potentially, for teaching about the discursive features and politics of text (Comber, 2001; Dyson, 1997; Marsh & Millard, 2000). Before foregrounding the children and their textual processes, I briefly describe my data-set and the particular location in which the project evolved.

Locating a childhood culture: The dataset

Wenona and I are sitting outside at a picnic table beside the school when she stands up to sing one last time into my microphone. She throws her head back, stretches her arms out wide, and improvises a song that includes a reference to Michael Jordan, encoded in the name of the movie *Space Jam*. Following is a brief excerpt:

> This is the family/And this is where we live
> We are sisters and brothers and moth-
> ers and cousins and friends/ Yeah yeah
> yeah yeah yeah yeah yeah yeah
> . . .
> Space Jam [Michael Jordan] is my brother / Believe me
> He is [my brother] Christian['s] brother too
> He's Kevin cousin / Robert [my brother] is his brother too
> Everybody that's my cousin / That's his cousin [Jordan's] too

Wenona enveloped Michael Jordan into her song and, moreover, into her family, just as she did her close friends—her brothers and sisters Marcel, Denise, Vanessa, Noah, and Lakeisha. The children's self-designation as "fake" siblings was linked to the use of the label "brothers and sisters" to refer to solidarity in the African American tradition, but it was much more literal. The children engaged in elaborate narrative play, which they called "games." In these games, and the imaginary world they constituted, the children were actual siblings. Most relevant for the project, much of the children's play was informed by the media.

The brothers and sisters lived in the school's neighborhood only from 8:30 to 2:30, when they boarded a big yellow school bus to travel to a less affluent part of town. Their elementary school (K-5) was officially described as having the "greatest crosstown span" (i.e., the greatest socioeconomic mix) in this East San Francisco Bay district. Approximately half the school's children were African American, approximately one-third European American, and the rest were of varied Latino and Asian ancestries. Roughly 40 percent (112 of the 286 children attending this small urban site) qualified for free / reduced-price lunch.

I first heard of the children's classroom through Carol Tateishi, director of the Bay Area Writing Project. Knowing of my interest in children's cultural productions, including their writing and art, Carol had recommended a visit to this class. The teacher, she said, allowed much space for such production.

On an informal visit to the class, I overheard intriguing but confusing talk coming from a table filled with the children I would come to know as the brothers and the sisters. I heard talk about what "Mama said" the children should or would do after school, comments on upcoming trips to Minnesota for hockey practice and to Dallas for football, and references to "Coach Bombay," whom I assumed (incorrectly) was a day-care teacher. In addition to the talk, there was much intermittent group singing of songs I did not know but recognized as hip-hop or R&B.

Given all this activity and its evident links to popular media (e.g., sports shows and youth music), the children presented a unique opportunity to explore a contemporary childhood and its links to varied cultural material. I had come upon a semiotic gold mine and, luckily, the children, their teacher, and their parents all allowed me entry to this mine. And so my informal visit became the beginning of a formal research project. My role thus evolved from a curious visitor to a nonthreatening and familiar adult who regularly sought out the children's company. Despite my age (more than four decades older than the children) and my race (white), I became a "fake mama," or so declared Denise. However, I never disciplined, never issued directives, and seldom gave advice, unlike both the fake "Mama" conjured up only with words and the hardworking Ms. Rita, their highly experienced teacher.

The official curriculum

Rita, the children's first-grade teacher, had professional roots in the British primary schools of the 1960s. Her classroom routines and composing practices were organized in a bookend-like structure. There were whole-class times for introducing and planning tasks, reporting on progress, discussing difficulties, and sharing final products. These times acted as bookends to more child-controlled times, when children worked as members of student-led small groups, as partners, or as colleagues doing their own writing but informally talking with one another. This social organization connected children's individual and small-group efforts to the larger community and, in Rita's words, created a "little bit" of productive tension about learning. The children, she said, would think, "'We've got to get it together here, and I'm gonna be asked to tell my opinion or read my story any minute now.' It's not just the passive, teacher's-telling-you-to-do-everything."

During the course of my project, Rita's curriculum included both open-ended writing activities (e.g., writing workshop, where the children wrote and drew relatively freely, followed by class sharing) and more teacher-directed ones (e.g., assigned tasks in study units, in which children wrote and drew as part of social studies and science learning). Throughout all composing activities, though, Rita was explicit about her expectations, and straightforward and generous in her guidance. Before writing workshop time began, she might use whole-group time to brainstorm possible topics, model diverse spelling strategies, or demonstrate the complex process of monitoring a written message (stopping to recite a planned sentence, to reread what has been written, and to see what word to write next—a cumbersome procedure for the inexperienced). In social studies or science lessons, Rita first enacted new kinds of practices (like reporting what one has learned) through collaborative oral activities. For example, pairs of children might report a newly learned fact to each other, or individuals might compose and practice oral reports for parents in whole-group meetings. Although varied genres were discussed in the class (including unexpected ones introduced by the children), the most common ones included evaluative texts on one's likes or dislikes, personal experience texts on where one had gone or what one had seen, fictional stories, lists of items to remember or things to do, and reports about what had been learned.

Data collection and analysis

During the course of an academic year, I observed in Rita's class four to six hours per week, focusing primarily on the brothers and sisters. I documented the children's participation in the morning language arts period through written observations, audiotapes of child talk, and collected products. I also followed the children out to the playground for morning recess, taking notes on children's play preferences and audio recording jump-rope rhymes and radio play.

I organized my field notes around children's participation in official production events (e.g., doing a "writing workshop book" entry) and in unofficial ones (e.g., singing a radio song). Those official and unofficial events overlapped, interrupted, and sometimes peacefully accompanied each other. In analyzing the data, I aimed to untangle at least some of the intertextual threads that indexed the brothers' and sisters' actions in both official and unofficial worlds in, for example, their experiences as writing workshop students, (pretend) radio singing stars, and, beyond that, as radio consumers (or video watchers, superhero players, churchgoers, and so on). To aid in this effort, I organized a parent meeting and presented key examples of children's media use. The parents confirmed, clarified, and extended my understandings of their children's use of particular media.

I begin with an atypical classroom occurrence, the class viewing of a video—of *Space Jam*, in fact. I reconstruct that event here, illustrating the kinds of media materials the children appropriated and foreshadow the kinds of pleasurable practices those materials served. I follow this section with two more extensive ones, focusing first on how the children recontextualized media material and, in the process, constructed a shared childhood culture. Then I describe a further recontextualization of media material, examining how the children's media play shaped their entry into official school literacy.

Watching *Space Jam*

Wenona asked Rita if she could bring *Space Jam* for the class to watch as a "treat." Rita consented, and so, on the agreed upon day (one of the last in the school year), the children gathered on the rug to watch *Space Jam*. Most of the children had already seen this film. Vanessa, for example, had gone to the movie with her mother; Denise had watched the video with her brother, and Noah repeatedly viewed the video with his (blood) siblings and cousins. Thus, the "treat" did not involve viewing the unfolding of an unknown plot but, rather, participating in a familiar pleasure.

As the film began, many children started singing the lyrical "I Believe I Can Fly," which anticipates a young Michael Jordan's flying leap to a basketball net, and then the harder-edged "Welcome to the Space Jam," which accompanies a montage of a grown-up Jordan jumping to net after net in quick succession. Group singing reoccurred throughout the film-watching, as did the dramatic enactment of and play with character voices. There were certain well-known voices and lines (e.g., Looney Tune character Sylvester's "sufferin' succotash" or Tweety Bird's "I thought I saw—I *did*, I *did*"), as well as some new lines ("Girl got some skills," uttered by Michael Jordan about the girl with b-ball talent, Lola Bunny) that most children enjoyed doing.

Noah and Marcel recited much of the movie's dialogue, and Noah matched tone, pitch, and volume almost exactly. Indeed, he did not like others to say the lines if they lacked the appropriate expertise (i.e., if they "don't say it right"). Noah's irritation may not have been simply intolerance. It was hard to hear the movie when someone's voice did not blend with the characters' voices. Noah, like many children, also did not want anyone to "tell the movie" (say what was going to happen next). This was not a matter of a child spoiling the story, which most children knew, but, rather, of insulting others' intelligence. "We know!" was the appropriate response to such ostentatious behavior.

When Rita interrupted the video to clarify her own confusion about the plot, the children reacted very differently. Rita did *not* know the storyline, and the children not only tolerated but picked up on one another's retelling efforts, so eager were most to clarify the characters and their motivations and fates for Rita. Later, after the video was over, Rita talked with the children about their movie preferences ("interviewed" them, as Vanessa said), and she also discussed the distinction between "retelling" and "summarizing" and between spoiling stories for the uninformed and being, in general, boring (i.e., giving people more detailed information than they want to have).

When the video watching resumed, so too did the children's singing, playing, and brief conversational exchanges (e.g., about liked parts, about relatives with names similar to characters). In addition, children engaged in claiming identities. The boys had the only real options—even the Looney Tunes characters are mainly male, and Lola Bunny was seen as a joke (for an analysis of gender limitations in children's media, see Seiter, 1993). However, in an unusual move, no boy claimed to be Michael Jordan, and several children positioned themselves in his family.

> VANESSA: "Daddy Daddy" (*says along with Jordan's cinematic daughter who is running to greet him*). I'm his daughter.
>
> MARCEL: I'm his son.

In no other media-related play were the children observed making themselves the sons or daughters of the powerful; they *were* the powerful—the singers, football players, teenagers with access to "too fast" music (to quote Vanessa). In fact, when the children reframed material from this film outside its screen presence, the boys could become Michael Jordan (and Wenona became his sister). Perhaps the publicness of watching the film, or the visual presence of Jordan himself, eliminated any such imaginative turn. But with crayon and paper, or basketball and playground court, or in Wenona's case a microphone, there were no such limitations.

In sum, the children's responses were contingent upon the flow of images and sounds as they engaged in the treat of movie watching. The children were also involved in other practices, including group singing, knowledge display, language play, and dramatic play. This was not entirely "free" play. It was shaped by the available toys, that is, by the material to be appropriated: conceptual content (characters, both cartoon and human, and their voiced emotions and interconnected actions), communicative genres (e.g., raps and songs), technological conventions (e.g., soundtracks, visual exaggerations of human movement possibilities), and embedded ideologies (e.g., male power in physical skill, female power in physical allure, which is also exaggerated and made humorous, as is the male swooning response). The children's practices were also informed by peer expectations (e.g., not to drown out character voices with one's own). Finally, the children's responses also seemed informed by some sense of the social appropriateness of different practices in different situations (e.g., not "telling" the plot to those who already know).

In the next section, I will illustrate children's play with media material when it is not paced by an ongoing media display. In these instances, play in the classroom and on the playground offers more possibilities for children to explore their own agency and manipulate texts, and also for children's use of the media to monitor and regulate their own childhoods.

Transforming media texts into popular toys: The authoring of a childhood

WENONA (*TO MARCEL*): C'mon. Let's sing *Space Jam*. It's boring just sitting here.

Wenona and Marcel were sitting together in their first-grade classroom, working on their official family portraits. By responding to each other, they constructed a time and space in the unofficial world for their fake family. They did this by "calibrating" their actions with the rhythm of a familiar song that both deemed appropriate for the moment (Clark & Holquist, 1984).

Like Marcel and Wenona's *Space Jam* song, the children's textual toys— their appropriated symbolic material—had origins in their participation in various institutions, dominant among them family, neighborhood, and school. Through this participation, children found human and electronically mediated material to reframe in their unofficial worlds. In so doing, they authored—or brought to voice—the times and spaces of their own childhoods. In this section, I sample these resources and textual processes, featuring variations and combinations of the practices of group singing and dramatic play.

Singing childhood times and spaces

Group singing was the practice most revealing of the breadth of children's cultural landscapes. For example, children appropriated officially sung songs for their own use more than any other kind of school material. One child would loudly begin a song, like the Mother Earth song for Earth Day, and that singing would recruit other children, who would fold into the ongoing rhythm. The children also appropriated songs (like the *Space Jam* songs) first experienced in family activities, activities carried out with parental approval. More dramatically, they appropriated and played with songs that were not directed to six-year-olds but to "teenagers." They reported (and parents confirmed) that they were learning these songs primarily from radios that played in multi-age households during morning routines and school commutes, in community center offices and public parks, and in the company of adolescents—cool people whom children admired.

The children were quite aware that these songs were not intended for them. They could enact voices that suggested (and the parent session demonstrated) caregivers' concerns about the content of certain "teenager" songs and the images they connoted. When Denise drew herself as Tina Turner in high heels and a slinky gown, Vanessa said, "I'm not putting high heels on me 'cause that's too fast, Denise. That's too *fa::st.* We're only 6 and 7. And that is too fast (with definiteness). 'Cause, Denise, I'm sorry if I'm breaking your heart . . ."

As Vanessa's comments suggest, teenager music was associated in part with ideologies of age, and so, in fact, was music associated with preschool shows. Teenager music, though, had gender and racial reverberations that preschool songs did not. Consider, for example, the following scene.

The children are making Earth Day crowns, decorated with nature scenes and sayings. There is a great deal of cutting and coloring, the sort of activities that lend themselves to group singing. Elizabeth, Denny, Cedric, Marcel, Wenona, and Noah are all sitting at the same table. (Elizabeth and Denny are European American; all the others are African American.) Marcel begins singing the Mother Earth song and others join in. Then Marcel moves on to a different song, which he sings in a soul-full style:

MARCEL: Baby, baby, baby, baby / I need you so much.
(*I do not know what the song is. Wenona does though, and she joins in.*)
NOAH (*TO MARCEL*): You like *girl* songs!
MARCEL: No I don't.
NOAH: Well, how come you singing 'em?

Noah, Marcel, and Cedric move on to a hip-hop crowd pumper, a variant of which is on the *Space Jam* soundtrack:

NOAH, MARCEL, AND CEDRIC: "Put you hands in the air / Like you just don't care . . ."

Rita puts the Mother Earth tape on, and all the children sing along. She compliments the children on the time and thought they are putting into their crowns (which look very good to me, too). She suggests that they walk around the school later, wearing their crowns and singing Earth Day songs. "Cool!" says Marcel, quite pleased. He works awhile, and then has another song selection:

MARCEL: Let's sing the Barney song. "I love you / You love me / We're a happy family . . ."

Noah joins in, to my surprise, since he has criticized Marcel for his enjoyment of the Barney song. This time Wenona offers the critique:

WENONA: Why are you singing a *preschool* song?
MARCEL: Whoops. (*looking sheepish*)

As the above example illustrates, the children used group singing to construct and monitor their own progression through childhood. Their attitudes toward the music of their early years were a comment on their sense of age categories. But the music of their future—those songs for the teenage years to come—was used also to articulate gender categories (Thorne, 1993) and, less obviously, racial affiliation.

For example, when the children sang hip-hop or R&B songs rather than official school songs, a race-related pattern was clearly evident in which class members joined in the singing (a pattern not evident when children sang school songs). Moreover, the children referred to the names of forty-three popular performers or performing groups, all African American (with the exception of Cookie Monster and Barney). Listen to Vanessa's response when I ask her about the group Immature, one of whom has the nickname "Batman":

> VANESSA: Not the Batman that flies through the air / Not the Batman that lost his underwear (*as in a children's playground rhyme*) / But Batman / He Black and he fine

Playing with voices

The actual media source of the teenager music, the radio, provided a context for a form of dress-up play: radio play. A radio show became a set of diverse and interrelated practices, including interviewing, song announcing, deejay joking, and star performing. Radio play (i.e., enacting these practices) happened mainly on the playground, unlike group singing, and usually involved just girls. (The boys tended to play team sports.) In the brief excerpt below, from playground radio play, Denise interviews herself:

> DENISE: (*assuming a polite, interested tone*) Denise. Tell us why do you like to sing—and your friends?
> DENISE: (*rapping*) We want to be a star / In the store
> We want to be on stage / For our cage.

Children used different song genres for different contexts. One day Denise and Vanessa were concerned about a classmate's "spying" on them. During recess, Denise made up a rap about this situation—in my view, a perfect genre choice, given her intense irritation. Her rap contains a driving beat and an aggressive tone, and to maintain this she works to sustain a pattern of syllable stresses and rhymes. Following is just a small sample of this long rap:

> DENISE: It's called, "Why You in My Bus'ness?" (*sternly*)
> (rapping) Why you in my bus'ness?
> Cause I got you / In my far-is-mus\
> And I had you / In my char-is-mus / my bus'ness
> Why you gotta be / In the bus'ness?

In another playground performance, Denise participated in the collaborative composing of a love song; Vanessa, as lead singer, improvised the song, as Denise and Wenona sang back-up:

VANESSA: I'm gonna sing um a make-up [*improvised*] song. Y'all gonna sing with me, right?
DENISE AND WENONA: Yeah.
DENISE: What do you want us to say?
(*And when Vanessa has no particular directive to offer . . .*)
We gonna say "I love you."
WENONA: Yeah.
VANESSA: Heck no!
WENONA: Yeah.
VANESSA: No no no. (firmly)
DENISE: We gonna say, "Baby." (*definitively*)
VANESSA: No. (*equally definitively*)
WENONA: "Baby boy?" (*tentatively*)
VANESSA: OK, OK.

Having agreed, Vanessa, as lead singer, now reissues that agreement as a directive:

VANESSA: Ok. Y'all gonna say "baby boy," OK?

Then she does the count down and begins singing:

VANESSA: 1, 2, 3. (*spoken*)
No body can tell me / to tell me who I see
to tell me when I move / OO oooh

Soon the backup comes in, soft and smooth:

DENISE AND WENONA: Baby boy. (*backup*)

In radio play, then, children's actions were supported by a sense of the genre, the kind of voice, they were appropriating. That social sense allowed them to manipulate complex layers of symbols (sounds, syllables, words, phrases, and even different vocal parts); in other words, their behavior was highly literate, involving the deliberate crafting of language units. Certainly singing varied genres heightened the children's attention to the sensory qualities of words—their rhythm, volume, and pitch, for example.

The children listened to the sensory qualities of varied kinds of speaking voices, including both generic ones and individual characters' voices. The music of sports discourse was particularly appealing to Marcel (who was named after a football player, who his mother considered to be a "role model for our children").[4] Aspects of that discourse were on display when the children "played for Coach Bombay," a dramatic game based both on the film *D2: The Mighty Ducks* (Avnet, Claybourne, Kerner, & Weisman, 1994), about a co-ed hockey team coached by Bombay, and on televised football games, particularly those featuring the Dallas Cowboys.

Like radio play, Coach Bombay play involved the collaborative construction of a range of interrelated practices, in this case, all connected with sports. Among these practices was planning agendas that allowed time for children's busy lives as players for Coach Bombay, responsible students, and helpful members of "Mama's" fake family; the children planned for practice sessions, travel to various destinations, often across state lines, (pretend) babysitting for relatives, and (not necessarily real) homework. Other practices involved narrating highlights of previous games, featuring themselves, and evaluating the relative merits of teams. Sports broadcast talk itself tends to display a proliferation of time adverbs and adverbial phrases (Hoyle, 1989), and the brothers and sisters did so too, as in the following example. Although all the brothers and sisters engaged in Coach Bombay play, Marcel and Wenona were the most avid participants, and they are featured in the vignette.

Wenona and Marcel are sitting together during a morning work period. They are doing their work in the official world, but they are also doing their "work" in the unofficial world (i.e., planning their upcoming schedule):

> WENONA: You know I'm thinking about going over to [*a relative's*] house today but we gotta play games. I forgot: We playing hockey. Today we playing hockey.
> MARCEL: 'Cause we gotta play hockey. (*agreeing*)
> WENONA: In Los Angeles—no—
> MARCEL: It's in Los Angeles. (*affirming*)
> WENONA: It's in Pittsburgh *and* Los Angeles.
> MARCEL: I forgot. We gotta play Pittsburgh.
> WENONA: *In* Pittsburgh.
> MARCEL: Pittsburgh is real weak.

"*In* Pittsburgh," said Wenona, referencing a city location, not a city's team. The children sometimes played "Dallas (pause) *in* Dallas," "Minnesota (pause) *in* Minnesota," enacting the stress-in-the-middle rhythm of sports people who know what they are talking about.

Transforming media toys into drawing adventures

Sometimes media-based dramatic play centered around the flat expanse of a blank piece of paper. Such play was more conducive to performances for oneself and others than to collaboration. The most consistent visual performer was Noah, who was a cartoon aficionado. Indeed, Noah could display his cartoon knowledge by naming a long list of the "funny stuff" (i.e., the cartoons) on TV, which, he told me, "you must watch." Looney Tune characters were among his favorites, as were superhero creatures like the cartoon Godzilla.

Given a pencil and marker, Noah tended to quickly involve himself in a visual drama, always with sound effects and some kind of running narrative about, say, the cartoon Godzilla rescuing a victim, dinosaurs running amok in a park, or the Tune Squad (from *Space Jam*) playing in a basketball game. Like other children who appropriated from animation, Noah could borrow particular character images or plot scenes and enact certain common genres, like superhero stories, and discourse features of those genres (e.g., heavy use of exclamations: "AAAAH!" "Help!"). Most strikingly, he could pick up graphic conventions, like directional indicators (e.g., arrows), symbols of power (e.g., swirls or jagged lines), or movement (e.g., repeated drawing of an object to convey, for instance, a basketball moving up toward and through a hoop). Furthermore, he infused his images with salient values and beliefs about, for example, gender, power, and looking good. In Figure 15.1, Noah is a cool basketball player with his sideways cap and his brand-name sneakers. His ball, drawn repeatedly, moves through the net, and Noah dribbles away as the scoreboard adds more zeroes at the end of the number one.

Even radio stars were a source of visual play. Although heard more than seen, radio stars were visible on TV shows and videos. Readers may recall Denise's drawing of herself as Tina Turner (with Vanessa's age-related admonishment). One day Noah drew himself as a "radio star," decked out in a backwards baseball cap and a Nike shirt, singing into a microphone. The emphasis was on visual detail (never mentioned in the playground version of radio play) and so the singing itself was just rhythmically glossed:

NOAH: (*drawing*) This is me. (*to Marcel*) I got a hat. I got a hat on. I got a microphone. I'm gonna make me a microphone. Marcel, I'm gonna make a microphone. I make me a microphone. 'Cause I'm a radio star. . . . And I do, "Yeah yeah yeah yeah yeah." You want me to make you? (*to Marcel; who is laughing*) I'm gonna make you a microphone . . . I'm singing. Me and you is singing.

The play continued as Marcel requested certain kinds of apparel (a kind of drawing interaction usually engaged in by girls drawing each other) (Dyson, 1993).

Visual play involved paper and marking instruments, tools that were usually linked to an official literacy activity. Further illustration of visual

Figure 15.1

dramatic play, then, is provided in the next major section, when I turn from the unofficial to the official classroom world.

Summary: The shared pleasure of free toys

In sum, the brothers and sisters found many toys in the voices that filled their everyday lives. They were not passively absorbing the media material around them. Rather, they appropriated diverse but interrelated symbolic material from these sources and reframed it within rather traditional childhood practices, like group singing and dramatic play. In this way, they drew upon their symbolic resources to engage with each other in a tightly knit "fake" family of boys and girls, no longer babies, who were intensely involved in a busy present and anticipated a powerful, even glamorous, future.

The brothers and sisters' family was formed and sustained in school, not at home (a fact verified by their parents), and yet it was founded on a shared cultural landscape in which media materials were woven into the fabric of their lives as young children growing up in a densely packed urban area, where hip-hop popped from radios, where families tended to be "for the Raiders and . . . Dallas" too (to quote Wenona), and where racial consciousness was part of the local landscape, and the local schools, from early childhood (see Dyson, 1993, 1997) through adolescence (see Christianakis, 2002; Rubin, 2001).

In the official world, the children's teacher Rita worked to establish what she called a "classroom family," one with its own sense of interconnections, responsibilities, and practices. That family was potentially on much more fragile ground than the fake one; classroom practices and symbols traditionally are informed by curricular and instructional expectations removed from the particularities of children's relationships, pleasures, powers, and concerns (including about being, or identity, itself). And yet, as I illustrate in the next section, the brothers and sisters did not abandon one another, or their toys, as they entered into school literacy.

Adapting popular toys to meet literacy demands: The interplay of unofficial and official space

Rita has just voiced words of praise and gratitude for the class's hard work when her student Vanessa speaks up:

> VANESSA: I'm going to bring a movie to thank you guys for being so good. . . .
> I could even bring some popcorn.

Vanessa spoke up with no hesitation, slipping into her teacher Rita's appreciative gaze at "you guys" (the rest of the class). From Vanessa's vantage point, as a fellow child, this class deserved a treat: the pleasure of one of her textual toys, complete with popcorn.

In Vanessa's fake family, the brothers and sisters actively participated in their communicative practices and shared their textual toys (not to mention any literal treats one might happen to have). Becoming a member of the *classroom* family also entailed active participation and contribution, which, in the first grade, inevitably included negotiating an entry into classroom literacy practices. In so doing, the children brought themselves, their relationships, and their textual toys—that is, the particular and generic voices they manipulated in their childhood play—into their official classroom activities.

Because of their varying media preferences, the children drew differentially on these voices as they entered into school literacy. Thus, they differed in their literacy pathways, in the precise nature of the symbolic and social challenges they faced, as they grappled with the "options, limits, and blends" of familiar and new practices (Miller & Goodnow, 1995, 121). Nonetheless, all children used recontextualization processes, and it is those processes that are the focus in the following vignettes. These vignettes feature the children, with their teacher Rita in the background. Through the efforts of both children and teacher, these recontextualization processes led to a productive interplay between official and unofficial worlds.

Jamming in juxtaposed worlds: Venturing into written literacy

With Noah's deft hand in command, Bugs Bunny stretches his arm to improbable lengths and dunks the ball into the basket (stretching being a "Tuneville" possibility used by Michael Jordan in *Space Jam*). Bugs' ball goes through the basket and then down and down as Noah draws one ball after another, capturing its movement in what seems classic animation style. Noah makes Michael Jordan grin approvingly at Bugs' success. As yet another ball starts its journey, a succession of 1's, 0's, and 5's progresses along the bottom of Noah's paper, and he calls Marcel's attention to the "points." When official composing time is almost over, Noah adds a written personal experience text to his paper, reporting that he watched *Space Jam* with his cousins.

Noah originally experienced *Space Jam* with his real family as a multimodal story, complete with pictures, music score, and dialogue. Then, with fake siblings and classroom friends, Noah recontextualized and transformed that original experience into childhood practices of group singing and dramatic play. In official composing, Noah continued the local play with a media sensation through his own multimodal retelling with voice and drawn image. The writing, though, was a separate genre. It was not a story but a personal experience text that allowed Noah to fulfill the perceived expectations of school.

Initially, the children participated in most official composing events primarily by drawing and talking, just as Noah did in the *Space Jam* event. During official events, they organized symbol-making primarily around communicative practices not explicitly taught in school, that is, by childhood practices, like dramatic and visual play. The children's actions, then, indexed their unofficial world.

After drawing (a symbolic activity sanctioned by Rita), the children wrote familiar names (e.g., of family or friends) and brief textual frames, which they appropriated from the class-generated "things to write about" list (e.g., "I like . . . ," "I saw . . . ," "I went . . ."). Typically, any media appropriations consisted of names and events that could be "liked" or to which they "went," so to speak. The writing, then, was a sociolinguistic nod to the official world, "the social matrix within which the [print] discourse" mattered (Hanks, 2000, 166).

Still, despite the brevity of the written texts, recontextualizing unofficial material yielded multimodal composing productions that were hybrids, however simple they appeared. That is, they drew from and indexed different worlds (Bakhtin, 1981). For this reason, it is possible in hindsight to see the rough edges where different kinds of cultural material met and from which tensions would arise. *Symbolic* tensions, important in all the children's case histories, seem inherent in Noah's juxtaposition of a drawn story and a written personal experience. Indeed, it would seem difficult for even a highly experienced story writer to verbally translate the visceral experience of an arm stretching unexpectedly through space, a ball tracing an arc in the sky, or even a face expressing joy; exaggerated movements and facial expressions are the prime province of animation, not of words.

The children's brief efforts also suggested *social* tensions between official and unofficial worlds. For example, the "truth" in the brothers and sisters' world was a playful truth that accomplished the serious work of social connection; it was not, however, the truth assumed in the official world when a personal experience was reported. Denise and Vanessa, for instance, each wrote that they "went" to the other's house, something they never did at all (as confirmed by their parents); their official personal experiences were bits of fiction. Finally, *ideological* tensions were evident too. Noah twice wrote that he "saw a good boy." The boy was good, he told me, because he had a "water gun" (which, in his picture, was shooting bullets, a banned kind of classroom play).

These kinds of rough edges in children's work sometimes became more expansive communicative and problem-solving spaces. For this to happen, children had to orchestrate any talking, drawing, and writing within the frame of a particular practice (see Dyson, 1989). When that happened, rough edges between media and between worlds were not so easily smoothed over, as I illustrate below.

Written play with unofficial voices

"I have the movie *spec Jam* [movie *Space Jam*]. The song goes like this."

Denise's writing book entry leads up to but does not actually include the *Space Jam* song (which is, after all, quite long). Since she was too "shy," she said, to actually sing in front of people during official sharing time, her fake siblings spontaneously began to sing for her, and then with her.

As the school year unfolded, childhood practices did sometimes frame and indeed happen through writing itself. These occurrences involved both official and unofficial practices. On the one hand, over time the children's composing actions were channeled by their continued participation in official literacy practices. On the other hand, as children found school writing practices more meaningful—that is, less mechanistic, more identifiable as kinds of communicative situations—they were more likely to use their textual toys to exploit those practices for familiar childhood ends, like play, pleasure, and performance. Consider, for example, the fate of the official practice of written dialogue.

Child use of an instructional dialogue

As Rita explained to her class, she wanted them to "stick with one piece of writing" rather than moving from one brief statement to the next. To help, she sometimes would respond to their entries with written questions requiring more writing on the same topic. For example, when Vanessa wrote that she liked to sing, Rita asked what songs she liked to sing. (She liked "made up songs," as it happens.)

In so entering into their composing events, Rita disrupted the routine of individual children producing their own written text (although, clearly, her aim was to support individuals' writing). When the children appropriated this interactional structure, they reframed it within childhood practices and, in this way, official writing could become a collaborative endeavor between equals. Within these now blended events (i.e., with aspects of official and unofficial practices), the children were guided by understood communicative situations. Given this, they did in fact write "more."

For example, Vanessa reframed dialogue writing as a guessing game, a common childhood practice. "I had fan [fun]. Til [tell] me wye?" she wrote. Denise guessed, in writing, that Vanessa had stayed in a hotel [during her trip to Disneyland]. When Vanessa wrote that she did not, Denise grinned and wrote, "Well Vanessa Sary [Sorry]" (see Figure 15.2).

On another occasion, Vanessa and Denise reframed dialogue writing as written radio play. Denise became Yoyo and Vanessa became MC Lyte, both female artists who had recorded together. The girls—as artists—took turns writing excerpts from popular love songs. However, the girls took their writing books outside to the playground to do this writing and never shared their production officially, at least in part for ideological reasons. As Denise said, Rita probably wasn't "used" to this style of song. "Teen-age-er" songs were part of the children's unofficial play, even if their production involved officially valued tools and materials.

The girls' most complex composing event did not involve radio play, although it clearly evidenced aspects of that unofficial and collaborative practice as well as of the transformed official one of writing in turns. Inspired

Figure 15.2

by the *Goosebumps* television show, the girls confronted complex symbolic and social challenges as they worked to articulate an unofficial "scary" voice on paper during official writing time.

Working in their separate books, Denise and Vanessa divide their respective pages into four sections and then begin composing in different sections. In Denise's words, they are "writing a [scary] story that goes together but in different books." In her book, Denise begins in the top section of her paper, writing about one boy and two girls playing together. In hers, Vanessa skips the top section and, in the second, writes, "And a litte girl play with a litte boy but the boy was a vapyr and the boy beis [bites] her"

Vanessa stops to consult with Denise about a title:

VANESSA: What's the title going to be?

. . .

DENISE: "One Boy and Two Girls."

VANESSA: That's not good.

DENISE: What should it be then? "The Man and Two Women."

VANESSA: That's not good either.

DENISE: "The Happy Scary Thing?" (*tentatively*)

VANESSA: No. "The Thing That Make You Shiver. Things That Makes You Shiver!"

DENISE: No! (*firmly*)

VANESSA: "One Boy and Two Girls" don't make sense. (*equally firmly*) . . .

DENISE: Well, what should it be? . . . I know what it should be called. "The Vampire."

VANESSA: Ah, whatever you want. (*resigned*) Wait! It should be, "Be Careful What You Wish For."

This appeals to Denise:

DENISE: And a girl could say, "I wish I was a vampire." And she could turn into a vampire.

VANESSA: And the boy was already one.

(*DENISE WRITES AND THEN READS:*)

DENISE: "I wish I was a vampire"—. . .

VANESSA: "I said, to myself on a star." NO, "I wish to a star."

DENISE: Write yours! We won't have time to share!

Highlighting their unofficial practices as radio performers, Vanessa and Denise negotiated vocal parts and made decisions about which lines would sound good when, something that never happened in the official turn-taking practice, which was not intended to be about collaboration between equals but about instruction. Vanessa in particular deliberately searched for the right words, given her ear for the "scary story" genre. At the same time, the girls reframed unofficial media materials—textual toys—within their official concerns as dutiful first-grade writers; they made explicit references to "making sense" and to page arrangement (not only voice arrangement) and to text details like "titles" and "ends," just as their teacher Rita modeled. This blend of practices supported their composing decisions.

Denise, however, was worried about time to share—to perform for the group (well-founded worries, as it happened). So Vanessa returned to her own piece.

Vanessa rereads ("and the boy bites her") and then adds, "I yelled." She pauses when Denise reports:

DENISE: I put, "Now it is Vanessa's turn" [*to read her part of our vampire story*].

This deliberate translation into written form of Denise's heretofore un-articulated knowledge about radio play—her knowledge that coordination of turns is required for a performance—causes some tension:

VANESSA: You shouldn't've put that. (*seriously*)
DENISE: Why?
VANESSA: Now that's gonna mess up the story [*i.e., the performed story*].
DENISE: Nuh uh. [*No it won't.*] Then you gotta go [*after I go*].
VANESSA: I know! But you don't have to say it!
DENISE: OK. I'm not gonna say it. (*begins to erase*)
VANESSA: Just—

Denise is erasing, but Vanessa seems to reconsider whether "saying" and "writing" are the same thing:

VANESSA: You're just gonna show it to me. You're gonna point to it [*the line*] and show it to me, right?
DENISE: (*still erasing*) No. I'm just gonna go (*turns toward Vanessa*).
VANESSA: No. Put a little (*jerks head down*) to it. Like this. (*jerks again*) Put a little nod to it.
DENISE: OK.

What was written must be read during official sharing time—and that would disrupt ("mess up") the performance, in Vanessa's view. There were complex symbolic and social tensions embedded in the children's recontextualization of their knowledge and know-how. As those tensions surfaced, the children negotiated what was to be written, said, or communicated through gesture. They orchestrated multiple voices, supported by knowledge embedded in diverse cultural practices and social worlds. Those negotiations were sustained and guided by a sense of the social dialogue they were participating in, that is, the kind of generic voice they were jointly articulating: their collaboration would yield a "scary story," which itself was intended to be recontextualized and performed for the classroom family.

"Scary stories" were just one of various unofficial genres that helped organize children's official writing efforts; others included sports reports, play-by-play broadcasts, movie retellings, commercials, and "caps" (or dialogues with playful insults; see Smitherman, 1994, on this and other African American discourse forms). These typically appeared during open-ended writing workshop time.

Rita also introduced various genres, as earlier noted. In this aspect of the curriculum, too, there was a necessary interplay between official and unofficial worlds. As Noah illustrates below, another genre in which children mixed their official and unofficial worlds was their work on "what I learned" reports.

Learning about "what I learned"

"I know that Michael Jordan is a superstar . . ."

This is the opening line of one of Noah's longest, most complex texts. It is framed as a report on "what I know," a phrase Rita's children sometimes used as a substitute for the "I learned that" frame of an oral information report. Noah, however, was not reporting school-based learning, although his text evidenced the rich interplay of official and unofficial learning no less than did Denise and Vanessa's "scary" story.

When Rita first introduced the "what I learned" genre, she offered much explicit guidance, as earlier noted. And yet, no child seemed to view it as a recurrent, routine way of using written language, that is, as a practice that could guide and sustain child agency. For example, consider Noah's first reporting of facts.

Inspired by Marcel, who was copying the word "space" from the book *Space Case* (Marshall, 1980), Noah based his piece on a television show similarly named. He began by speaking and writing his text: "Space [pause] case [pause] ses [pause] there was." But he only wrote as far as the first three letters of "there" and then he drew (not wrote) a space ship.

"There was some stars," he next intoned, and he drew those stars.

And then, in an animated voice that soon erupted in a burst of sound effects, the space ship "blast[ed] off" unexpectedly and went "all the way into space." The person at the controls threw TNT, and there was a burst of fire power: "BLEW::::!"

As Noah became more deeply involved in his drawn space adventure, Vanessa was completing her text. She paused to reread her writing: "I learned that the movie *Star Wars* was made—"

"Twenty [years ago]," piped up Noah, sure of the next word in this oft-repeated official fact. Indeed, that fact, or its rhythm, seemed to stay in Noah's mind, because when he finished his drawing, he wrote that the "space [ship] come from 2 years." (Later he changed the 2 to 20.)

In Noah's actions, one can hear the pull of the familiar, meaningful practice of visual storytelling. That pull was evident in his speech, as the slowly paced language of a child just learning to write a voice gave way to sound effects, and it was exceedingly evident in his graphics, as awkward written forms gave way to finely drawn details. When he was done, Noah used an appropriated fact about the production of a movie to articulate in a voice more mimicked than re-accented a statement about a fictional space ship.

Noah's actions were consistent with a key assertion of this project, that to make a new activity meaningful, children situated that new activity within their landscape of communicative experiences. From their participation in the new activity over time, including any guidance, feedback, and modeling that occurred, children could differentiate the possibilities and limits of particular activities as practices—as valued, purposeful, recurrent events.

Thus, in Noah's case, achieving some sense of the school "what I learned" practice did not involve abandoning his knowledge about visual adventures. It involved recontextualizing—that is, it involved both drawing on and differentiating the symbolic and social complexities of this cultural material so central to his agency as a composer. There were, for instance, the issues of drawing's role in report writing and, moreover, of what was to be reported. If *Star Wars* could be the topic of a fact, why not a television show with which Noah was more familiar? Noah certainly regarded his show as just as worthy a topic.

Noah's first self-initiated "I learned that" genre evidenced his symbolic, social, and ideological learning about this classroom practice. The event occurred during a class study of silk worms. Right before writing time one Monday, Rita read with the class the following morning message on the white board:

> The silk worms grew a lot on the weekend.
> They ate a lot of mulberry leaves.
> Watch them as they chew. Listen to them.
> They eat, sleep, and poop.

Rita did not suggest that the children write "what they had learned about silk worms," but she did spread the containers of worms around the room, placing them in the center of work tables. And Noah sat down and wrote what he had learned: "I learned that silk worms can't eat hard leaves like regular leaves because they will die." He thus revoiced Rita's caution, reinforced by her written message, that the worms would eat only mulberry leaves (so there was no reason to keep sticking other kinds of leaves in the containers).

As was often the case with his written texts, Noah's writing was a nod to the official world. But it was a communicative one in which he seemed to reassure Rita that, yes, he knew about mulberry leaves. When she circulated by his work area, Noah told her a true story (later confirmed with his father) about how he was "fixing to get some mulberry leaves" for her, despite the uncooperative neighbor lady who shooed him away from her mulberry tree.

Noah also talked with Rita about his close observations of the silk worms. "They're scared in there," he said. "They do like this," and he lifted his head up and looked stiffly around. Implicit in his talk was a characterization of silk worms as fellow creatures whose emotions and intelligence are expressed through bodily features and movement (the qualities exploited in visual media, particularly animation).

After Rita left, Noah began an animated visual adventure at the bottom of his paper. He drew a silk worm on a large leaf. Then to convey movement, he drew zig-zagging lines, all the while making "munching" noises. Finally, he added wings, commenting that the worm had turned into a moth. Noah thus crafted his first coherent, multimedia informative text. It evidenced his instructional experiences, and also his sense of agency, and the relevance of his knowledge and know-how. Noah coordinated visual, print, and oral material to enact what he had learned, and in so doing he also coordinated narrative, or storytelling, and informative voices.

Noah's text about Michael Jordan also evidenced a coordination of voices and the translation of visual images into written prose. But even though it was produced and shared during official composing time, this text was not addressed to Rita. It was written in anticipation of sharing with peers. Noah could scarcely contain his giggles as he shared his *Space Jam* "facts," excerpted below:

> I know that Michael Jordan is a superstar. And he know that he goes on *Space Jam*. And I like when Bugs Bunny and Lola Bunny knows what to do. And she got the moves. And I know that Michael Jordan he is a ★ [star] and he gots the moves baby. And my favorite character is Taz. It's a terrible just Taz. Michael Jordan is one of my favorite men. I'm ready to jam. I saw him and his underpants . . .

Influenced by friends' decisions to write about the movie *Space Jam*, Noah had done so too, recontextualizing a diversity of particular and typified voices. Among the former were particular utterances from the *Space Jam* script and song. Among the latter were informational (e.g., "I know that . . ."), evaluative (e.g., "I like . . ."), and personal experience (e.g., "I saw . . .") voice types. Noah had moved from a place of accommodation to the official world to one of trying out and combining differentiated voices. And yet, even as he responded to Rita's official activities and guidance, he did not become an apprentice adult nor an independent child "gyns" (genius, from Bissex, 1980) rediscovering written language. Like all the brothers and sisters, he remained a child among other children who shared, among varied resources, a (conceptual) chest of media toys.

On welcoming children to the literacy jam

During the time I was knee deep in *Space Jam* data, I came upon *For the Love of the Game*, Eloise Greenfield's (1997) own rendering of Michael Jordan's capacity to fly. A literary artist, Greenfield has long recontextualized aspects of popular culture, as well as of African American traditions, in poetic narrations of children's feelings. Thirty years ago, for example, she wrote of a little girl, missing her sibling, who "thinks he's Kareem [a well-known basketball player] / And not my brother" (1972). A generation later, she wrote of two children facing the "naysayers" of everyday life; the children take inspiration from the soaring athleticism of Michael Jordan and "rise up" and play "the game of life" (1997).

Michael Jordan's image, like that of the Looney Tunes, is a commodity marketed by the commercial media and circulated through popular culture. As such, his form is available for appropriation and articulation through particular voices and diverse genres. Greenfield's appropriation of Jordan's image in *For the Love of the Game,* unlike in *Space Jam,* is mystical, not cartoonish; the mood is somber, not humorous, and the focus does not extend beyond Jordan's life with the hoops. It is an adult's, not a young child's, appropriation of a popular image.

The fluidity of popular images like Jordan's (Douglas, 1994; Hall, 2001) and students' experience analytically constructing such images are central to cultural studies and media educators' efforts to further a critical appreciation of the media. They aim to have students understand that images are indeed just that, images constructed to appeal to and shape youthful tastes for commercial ends (e.g., Buckingham & Sefton-Greene, 1994; Fisherkeller, 2000). (Such aims do not, of course, exclude children's print literature, like Greenfield's.) I have argued here that, even among the very youngest of schoolchildren, a playful and productive stance toward the media may be implicit in children's media use; that use is constitutive of children's own childhoods and, at least potentially, of their pathways into school literacy.

Just as Eloise Greenfield, like most modern authors (Bakhtin, 1981), appropriates the stuff of everyday life to craft her own voiced response to her world, so too did the brothers and sisters, albeit in less artful, less deliberate ways. Their experiences with media texts were part of the very landscape of communicative practices within which they made sense of themselves as members of families, geographic neighborhoods, and cultural communities, as gendered and racialized beings, and, indeed as children. And those same experiences, the very stuff of their childhood practices, provided the grounds on which they differentiated a place for school literacy in their lives *as children.*

The dramatic enactment of visual adventures, the enthusiastic reporting of sports results, and the collaborative play with voices evident in singing, all organized and provided the communicative purposes and cultural stuff of children's entry into official school writing. None of the children recontextualized Michael Jordan or other aspects of *Space Jam* in a somber, or inspirational way, but they did deconstruct and reconstruct the film's elements in typified voices that stretched beyond any planned curriculum for young children. In this regard, imagine a montage of the brothers and sisters: Marcel making a list of the singers on the *Space Jam* soundtrack, Denise writing the afore-mentioned announcement of the *Space Jam* song, and Noah, more a storyteller than a broadcaster, doing that visual narration of a *Space Jam* basketball game.

Drawing adventures, making lists of valued knowledge, announcing and reporting the results of sports events, composing and recalling songs, telling and retelling stories—these were just some of the literacy practices through which children recontextualized popular media texts, including *Space Jam*. Not only did the children use unofficial genres to organize their official writing efforts, they also refrained media resources with school expected voices (e.g., "I learned that . . ." to prepare the way for reporting on studied information, "I saw . . ." to suggest a personal experience).

In recontextualizing media materials across practices, the children potentially brought into awareness symbolic challenges, social expectations, and ideological tensions. For example, ideological awareness was suggested by Noah's decision to write and officially share that he "saw a good boy"; despite Noah's drawn and enacted gun-shooting scene, the boy was not bad (and, one can assume, neither was Noah) since he had a *water* gun. Such awareness was also suggested by Vanessa and Denise's decision not to share their written radio play in the official world since their teacher was not "used" to the displayed music; the music was, after all, for teenagers. In the "scary story" event, the girls also struggled quite vividly with symbolic and social tensions as they negotiated what one had to "say," "write," or communicate with gesture in a joint performance for the official sharing time practice. In a nascent way, then, they engaged in the sort of analytic work that furthers the symbolic, social, and ideological decision making involved in text work in varied media.

The brothers and sisters' media use was able to support their official school literacy because of the clear interplay between official and unofficial worlds. In Rita's curriculum, the children's alertness to voices, their propensity to try them on and make them their own, benefited from a curriculum that was "permeable" (Dyson, 1993), that made space for and productively engaged their social and symbolic—their textual—resources. Rita both opened up composing periods for children's own authoring decisions, which were heavily influenced by their colleagues (i.e., their peers), and structured those periods to introduce new ways with written words.

A curriculum permeable to children's textual resources, particularly media resources, seems especially important in classrooms serving children of economically limited means and children of color. Children who can be so described are less likely than middle-class white children to have their cultural and communicative resources recognized and built on in school (e.g., Heath, 1983; Nieto, 2002; Vasquez, Pease-Alvarez, & Shannon, 1994). More specifically, although participation in popular culture is widespread in our society, children from economically privileged and culturally dominant homes have greater access to the sorts of textual pleasures (e.g., children's literature) that index the educated classes (Bourdieu, 1984). Based on her extensive interviewing of caregivers, Seiter (1999) suggests that even pre-school teachers serving middle-class children are likely to monitor the forms of cultural marketing that enter the classroom, making a strict distinction between what are perceived as "cheap" consumer goods (like television shows) and more "high ticket items such as computers, CD-ROMs, educational materials, and books" (88). Teachers at day-care centers serving lower-income children also value such goods but may be more tolerant of, and more forthcoming about, their own popular pleasures, in part because the media seem a much less ominous factor in children's lives than, for example, poverty or parental absence.

In Rita's classroom, media use in official school contexts was much more pervasive among children from the brothers and sisters' neighborhood than it was among those from the more affluent neighborhood. Moreover, certain media sources (like the movie *Space Jam)* were uniformly and almost exclusively referenced by African American children. In this extensive use of the media and in the relationship between media use and identity, Rita's young students were similar to participants in my previous research in local schools (Dyson, 1997) and reflective of a national survey of children's media use (Rideout, Foehr, Roberts, & Brodie, 1999). That survey documented the pervasiveness of media use among American children from age two to eighteen and, even more so, among low-income and African American and Latino children.

However, a permeability to children's textual resources has not been a dominant quality of school literacy curricula. Indeed, dominant curricula tend to have an antagonistic or, at the very least, a compensatory relationship to childhoods deemed not "mainstream" (i.e., viewed as not print-centered). This relationship was evident in the beginnings of intensive political and academic attention to very young children's literacy in the turbulent 1960s (e.g., Bereiter & Englemann, 1966) and it has continued up to the present (e.g., Neuman, 2001).

One effect of the continual return to narrow conceptions of young children's literacy is the continual neglect of popular literacies (Luke & Luke, 2001) and of the textual manipulation processes through which media material is adapted to local desires and needs. As I have argued, these very processes are key to written language development and, moreover, to children's play with identity, with who they are as people of particular heritages and loyalties. Opening up classrooms to children's textual resources and literate processes means opening them up as well to the pleasures and challenges of children's everyday lives and to the multimedia of the emerging and ever-changing textual scene (Hull & Schultz, 2001). In other words, it means educators, and schools as institutions, situating themselves in this time of energetic and spirited engagement with texts of a range of symbolic and social types and, in this way, joining the children in the jam—the literacy jam.

Notes

"Welcome to the Jam" (Quad City DJs, 1996) is part of the hip-hop and R&B score for the film *Space Jam* (Falk, Ross, and Pytka, 1996). The film stars Michael Jordan, a well-known African American basketball player, the Looney Tune characters, especially Bugs Bunny and the newly introduced Lola Bunny, and a group of goofy space aliens (the "Nerdlucks"). The aliens have been sent by the vicious tycoon Swackhammer to kidnap the Looney Tunes for his failing entertainment park. The Looney Tunes challenge the diminutive Nerdlucks to a basketball game. The Nerdlucks, though, steal the basketball talent of NBA stars and become the unprincipled "Monstars." If the Looney Tunes lose, they are to become Swackhammer's slaves, forced to entertain the alien masses. So the Looney Tunes do their own kidnapping, whisking Michael Jordan to Looney Tune land and to the "Tune Squad," their basketball team. With Jordan's animation-enhanced powers, the Tune Squad wins the day, and Jordan, who at the time had left basketball for baseball, rediscovers his passion for the game.

1. "I Believe I Can Fly" (Kelly, 1996). All the children's names are pseudonyms.

2. In this article, I do not use the term *text* to refer only to a piece of writing. Rather, I am interested in texts as any organized configuration of symbols. So a film, a television show, a radio song are all examples of texts.

3. In these transcripts, a capitalized word indicates increased volume; a single slashed line inserted into a speaking turn indicates a rhythmic break; a colon after a letter indicates that the sound of the letter was elongated—the more colons, the greater the elongation. Ellipsis points inserted into a line indicate one or more omitted speaking turns.

4. Marcel's mother felt that African American sports figures were no longer useful role models for children because the popular media now delved into all aspects of their lives. Their feats on the field—potential metaphors for discipline, courage, perseverance—no longer satisfied the media. In this regard, it is interesting that the poetic *For the Love of the Game: Michael Jordan and Me* (Greenfield, 1997), the children's book discussed in this article's conclusion, portrays Jordan solely as an athlete and, as such, as a metaphor for a soaring inner spirit.

References

Adams, M. (2001). Alphabetic anxiety and explicit, systematic phonics instruction. In S. B. Neuman and D. K. Dickinson (Eds.), *Handbook of early literacy research*, 66–80. New York: Guildford.

Avnet, J., Claybourne, D., Kerner, J. (Producers), and Weisman, S. (Director). (1994). *D2: The Mighty Ducks* [Motion picture]. Burbank, CA: Walt Disney Pictures.

Bakhtin, M. (1981). Discourse in the novel. In C. Emerson and M. Holquist (Eds.), *The dialogic imagination: Four essays by M. Bakhtin,* 254–422. Austin: University of Texas Press.

———. (1986). *Speech genres and other late essays.* Austin: University of Texas Press.

Bauman, R., and Briggs, C. (1990). Poetics and performance as critical perspectives on language and social life. *Anthropological Review* 19, 59–88.

Bereiter, C., and Engelmann, S. (1966). *Teaching disadvantaged children in the preschool.* Englewood Cliffs, NJ: Prentice Hall.

Bissex, G. (1980). *GYNS at wrk: A child learns to read and write.* Cambridge, MA: Harvard University Press.

Bourdieu, P. (1984). *Distinction: A social critique of taste.* Cambridge, MA: Harvard University Press. (Original work published 1979.)

Bruner, J. (1990). *Acts of meaning.* Cambridge, MA: Harvard University Press.

Buckingham, D. (1993). *Children talking television: The making of television literacy.* London: Falmer Press.

Buckingham, D., and Sefton-Greene, J. (1994). *Cultural studies goes to school.* London: Taylor and Francis.

Christianakis, M. (2002). "Inside the digital divide: Children using computers to write." Doctoral diss., University of California, Berkeley.

Clark, K., and Holquist, M. (1984). *Mikhail Bakhtin.* Cambridge, MA: Harvard University Press.

Comber, B. (2001). Critical literacies and local action: Teacher knowledge and a "new" research agenda. In B. Comber and A. Simpson (Eds.), *Negotiating critical literacies in classrooms* (271–82). Mahwah, NJ: Erlbaum.

Dore, J. (1989). Monologue as re-envoicement of dialogue. In K. Nelson (Ed.), *Narratives from the crib* (231–62). Cambridge, MA: Harvard University Press.

Douglas, S. (1994). *Where the girls are: Growing up female with the mass media.* New York: Times Books.

Dyson, A. H. (1989). *Multiple worlds of child writers: Friends learning to write.* New York: Teachers College Press.

———. (1993). *Social worlds of children learning to write in an urban primary school.* New York: Teachers College Press.

———. (1997). *Writing superheroes: Contemporary childhood, popular culture, and classroom literacy.* New York: Teachers College Press.

———. (1999). Transforming transfer: Unruly children, contrary texts, and the persistence of the pedagogical order. In A. Iran-Nejad and P. D. Pearson (Eds.), *Review of research in education* (24:141–72). Washington, DC: American Educational Research Association.

———. (2003). *The brothers and sisters learn to write: Popular literacies in childhood and school cultures.* New York: Teachers College Press.

Ebert, R. (1996, June 12). *Space Jam* [review]. *Chicago Sun-Times.* Retrieved June 12, 2002, http://www.suntimes.com/ebert/ebert-reviews/1996/11/111505.html.

Falk, D., Ross, K. (Executive Producers), & Pytka, J. (Director). (1996). *Space Jam* [Motion picture]. Burbank, CA: Warner Brothers.

Fisherkeller, J. (1997). Everyday learning about identities among young adolescents in television culture. *Anthropology and Education Quarterly, 28,* 467–92.

———. (2000). "The writers are getting kind of desperate": Young adolescents, television, and literacy. *Journal of Adolescent and Adult Literacy, 43,* 596–606.

———. (2002). *Growing up with television: Everyday life among urban adolescents.* Philadelphia: Temple University Press.

Garvey, C. (1990). *Play* (rev. ed.). Cambridge, MA: Harvard University Press.

Greenfield, E. (1972). *Honey I love.* New York: Harper & Row.

———. (1997). *For the love of the game: Michael Jordan and me.* New York: Harper-Collins.

Hall, S. (1981). Notes on deconstructing the popular. In R. Samuel (Ed.), *People's history and socialist theory* (227–39). London: Routledge & Kegan Paul.

———. (2001). The work of representation. In S. Hall (Ed.), *Cultural representations and signifying practices* (13–74). London: Sage.

Hanks, W. F. (1996). *Language and communicative practices.* Boulder, CO: Westview Press.

———. (2000). *Intertexts: Writings on language, utterance, and context.* Lanham, MD: Rowman & Littlefield.

Heath, S. B. (1983). *Ways with words: Language, life, and work in communities and classrooms.* Cambridge, Eng: Cambridge University Press.

Hoyle, S. (1989). Forms and footings in boys' sportscasting. *Text, 9,* 153–73.

Hull, G., & Schultz, K. (Eds.). (2001). *School's out: Bridging out-of-school literacies and classroom practices.* New York: Teachers College Press.

Jenkins, H. (1988). "Going Bonkers!" Children, play and Pee-wee. *Camera Obscura, 17,* 169–93.

Kelly, R. (1996). I believe I can fly. On *Space Jam* [CD]. New York: Atlantic Records.

Kenway, J., & Bullen, E. (2001). *Consuming children: Education-entertainment-advertising.* Buckingham, Eng: Open University Press.

Kessen, W. (1979). The American child and other cultural inventions. *American Psychologist, 34,* 815–20.

Klein, N. (1996, November 18). *Space Jam* [review]. *The Toronto Star.* Retrieved June 12, 2002, from http://www.media-awareness.ca/eng/news/news/columns/space1.htm

Kline, S. (1993). *Out of the garden: Toys, TV, and children's culture in the age of marketing.* London: Verso.

Levin, D. E. (1998). *Remote control childhood? Combating the hazards of media culture.* Washington, DC: National Association for the Education of Young Children.

Luke, A., & Luke, C. (2001). Adolescence lost/childhood regained: On early intervention and the emergence of the techno-subject. *Journal of Early Childhood Literacy, 1,* 91–120.

Marsh, J., & Millard, E. (2000). *Literacy and popular culture.* London: Sage.

Marshall, E. (1980). *Space case.* New York: Dial Books.

Massey, D. (1998). The spatial construction of youth cultures. In T. Skelton & G. Valentine (Eds.), *Cool Places: Geographies of youth cultures* (121–29). London: Routledge.

Miller, P. J., & Goodnow, J. J. (1995). Cultural practices: Toward an integration of culture and development. In J. J. Goodnow, P. J. Miller, & F. Kessel (Eds.), *Cultural practices as contexts for development, no. 67: New directions in child development* (5–16). San Francisco: Jossey-Bass.

Miller, P. J., & Mehler, R. (1994). The power of personal story telling in families and kindergartens. In A. H. Dyson & C. Genishi (Eds.), *The need for story: Cultural diversity in classroom and community* (38–56). Urbana, IL: NCTE.

Miller, P. J., Hoogstra, L., Mintz, J., Fung, H., & Williams, K. (1993). Troubles in the garden and how they get resolved: A young child's transformation of his favorite story. In C. A. Nelson (Ed.), *Memory and affect in development: Minnesota symposium on child psychology* (26: 87–114). Hillsdale, NJ: Erlbaum.

Nelson, K. (1996). *Language in cognitive development: The emergence of the mediated mind.* Cambridge, Eng.: Cambridge University Press.

Neuman, S. (2001, July 27). *Access to print: Problem, consequences, and day one instructional solutions* [press release]. White House Summit on Early Childhood Cognitive Development, Department of Education. Washington, DC.

Newkirk, T. (2002). *Misreading masculinity: Boys, literacy, and popular culture.* Portsmouth, NH: Heinemann.

New London Group. (1996). A pedagogy of multiliteracies: Designing social futures. *Harvard Educational Review,* 61, 60–92.

Nieto, S. (2002). *Language, culture, and teaching: Critical perspectives for a new century.* Mahwah, NJ: Erlbaum.

Opie, I., & Opie, P. (1959). *The lore and language of school children.* London: Oxford University Press.

Quad City DJs. (1996). Space jam. On *Space Jam* [CD]. New York: Atlantic Records.

Rideout, V., Foehr, U., Roberts, D., & Brodie, M. (1999). *Kids & media @ the new millennium.* Menlo Park, CA: Henry J. Kaiser Family Foundation.

Rubin, B. (2001). *Detracking in practice: Students negotiating race, friendship, and competence in daily classroom life.* Unpublished doctoral dissertation, University of California, Berkeley.

Seiter, E. (1998). *Sold separately: Children and parents in consumer culture.* New Brunswick, NJ: Rutgers University Press.

———. (1999). *Television and new media audiences.* New York: Oxford University Press.

Smitherman, G. (1994). *Black talk: Words and phrases from the hood to the Amen Corner* Boston: Houghton Mifflin.

Spigel, L. (1998). Seducing the innocent: Childhood and television in postwar America. In H. Jenkins (Ed.), *The children's culture reader* (110–35). New York: New York University Press.

Spigel, L., & Jenkins, H, (1991). Same bat channel, different bat times: Mass culture and popular memory. In R. Pearson & W. Uricchio (Eds.), *The many lives of the Batman* (117–48). New York: Routledge.

Storey, J. (1998). *An introductory guide to cultural theory and popular culture* (2nd ed.). Athens: University of Georgia Press.

Thorne, B. (1993). *Gender play: Girls and boys in school.* New Brunswick, NJ: Rutgers University Press.

Vasquez, O., Pease-Alvarez, L., & Shannon, S. (1994). *Pushing boundaries: Language and culture in a Mexicano community.* New York: Cambridge University Press.

Vygotsky, L. S. (1987). *L. S. Vygotsky, collected works, Vol. 1: Problems of general psychology.* New York: Plenum Books.

Whitehurst, G., & Lonigan, C. J. (2001). Emergent literacy: Development from prereaders to readers. In S. Neuman & D. K. Dickinson (Eds.), *Handbook of early literacy research* (11–29). New York: Guilford Press.

Willis, P. (1990). *Common culture: Symbolic work at play in the everyday culture of the young.* Boulder, CO: Westview Press.

BIBLIOGRAPHY OF THE HISTORY
OF LITERACY IN WESTERN EUROPE
AND NORTH AMERICA

CONTRIBUTORS

INDEX

BIBLIOGRAPHY OF THE HISTORY OF LITERACY IN WESTERN EUROPE AND NORTH AMERICA

This bibliography is comprehensive in scope but makes no claims to completeness. For additional guides to the literature, see works by Graff (1981a, 1987a, 1995b), including the introduction to the 1991 paperback edition of *The Literacy Myth* (Graff, 1979/1991), Houston (2002), and Vincent (2000). For related work in the field of the history of the book, see the publications of the Society for the History of Authorship, Reading, and Publishing (SHARP).

Abrams, Philip. (1980). "History, Sociology, Historical Sociology." *Past and Present* 87: 3–16.

"Adult Literacy." (1990). Special issue, *Comparative Education Review* 34, no. 1.

Allen, James Smith. (1979). "Toward a Social History of French Romanticism." *Journal of Social History* 13: 253–276.

———. (1983). "History and the Novel." *History and Theory* 22: 233–52.

———. (1991). *In the Public Eye: A History of Reading in Modern France.* Princeton: Princeton University Press.

Altick, Richard. (1957). *The English Common Reader.* Chicago: University of Chicago Press.

Amodio, Mark C. (2004). *Writing the Oral Tradition.* Notre Dame: University of Notre Dame Press.

Amory, Hugh, and David D. Hall, eds. (2000). *A History of the Book in America.* Vol. 1, *The Colonial Book in the Atlantic World.* Cambridge: American Antiquarian Society/ Cambridge University Press.

Andersen, Jennifer, and Elizabeth Sauer, eds. (2002). *Books and Readers in Early Modern England.* Philadelphia: University of Pennsylvania Press.

Armbruster, Carol, ed. (1993). *Publishing and Readership in Revolutionary France and America.* Greenwood: Greenwood Press.

Arnove, Robert F. (1981). "The Nicaraguan National Literacy Crusade of 1980." *Comparative Education Review* 25: 244–60.

———. (1986). *Education and Revolution in Nicaragua.* Westport: Praeger.

———. (1994). *Education as Contested Terrain: Nicaragua, 1979–1993.* Boulder: Westview.

Arnove, Robert F., and Harvey J. Graff, eds. (1987). *National Literacy Campaigns: Historical and Comparative Perspectives.* New York: Plenum.

Aronowitz, Stanley, and Henry Giroux. (1985). *Education under Siege: The Conservative, Liberal, and Radical Debate over Schooling.* South Hadley, Mass.: Bergin & Garvey.

———. (1988). "Schooling, Culture, and Literacy in the Age of Broken Dreams: A Review of Bloom and Hirsch." *Harvard Educational Review* 58: 172–94.

Aston, Margaret. (1977). "Literacy and Lollardy." *History,* 62: 347–71.

Augst, Thomas. (2003). *The Clerk's Tale: Young Men and Moral Life in Nineteenth-Century America.* Chicago: University of Chicago Press.

Bailey, Peter. (1978). *Leisure and Class in Victorian England*. Oxford: Taylor & Francis Group.

Bailyn, Bernard, and John B. Hench, eds. (1980). *The Press and the American Revolution*. Worcester, Mass.: American Antiquarian Society.

Barrett, Michael J. (1990). "The Case for More Schooling." *Atlantic*, November, 78–106.

Bartoli, A. Langeli, and A. Petrucci, eds. (1978). "Alfabetismo e cultura scritta." *Quaderni Storici* 38.

Bartoli, A. Langeli, and X. Toscani, eds. (1991). *Istruzione, alfabetismo, scrittura: Saggi di storia dell'alfabetizzione in Italia*. Milan: Franco Angeli.

Barton, David. (1994). *Literacy: An Introduction to the Ecology of Written Language*. Oxford: Blackwell.

Barton, David, and M. Hamilton. (1998). *Local Literacies: Reading and Writing in One Community*. London: Routledge.

Barton, David, Mary Hamilton, and Roz Ivanic, eds. (2000). *Situated Literacies: Reading and Writing in Context*. London: Routledge.

Barton, David, and Roz Ivanic, eds. (1991). *Writing in the Community*. Written Communication Annual 6. Newbury Park: Sage.

Baumann, Gerd, ed. (1986). *The Written Word*. Oxford: Oxford University Press.

Bauml, Franz. (1980). "Varieties and Consequences of Medieval Literacy and Illiteracy." *Speculum* 55: 237–65.

Baym, Nina. (1984). *Novels, Readers and Reviewers: Responses to Fiction in Antebellum America*. Ithaca: Cornell University Press.

Besnier, Niko. (1993). "Literacy and Feelings: The Encoding of Affect in Nukulaelae Letters." In *Cross-Cultural Approaches to Literacy*, ed. Brian V. Street, 62–86. Cambridge: Cambridge University Press.

———. (1995). *Literacy, Emotion and Authority: Reading and Writing on a Polynesian Atoll*. Cambridge: Cambridge University Press.

Bhola, H. S. (1990). "Literature on Adult Literacy: New Directions in the 1990s." *Comparative Education Review* 34: 139–44.

Biller, Peter, and Anne Hudson, eds. (1994). *Heresy and Literacy, 1000–1530*. Cambridge: Cambridge University Press.

Birkerts, Sven. (1994). *The Gutenberg Elegies*. Winchester, Mass.: Faber and Faber.

Bloch, Maurice. (1989). "Literacy and Enlightenment." In *Literacy and Society*, ed. Karen Schouseboe and Moges Trolle Larsen, 15–37. Copenhagen: Akademisk Forlag.

Bloch, R. Howard, and Carla Hesse, eds. (1995). *Future Libraries*. Berkeley: University of California Press.

Boone, Elizabeth Hill, and Walter D. Mignolo, eds. (1966). *Writing without Words: Alternative Literacies in Mesoamerica and the Andes*. Durham: Duke University Press.

Bossy, John. (1970). "The Counter Reformation and the People of Catholic Europe." *Past and Present* 47: 51–70.

Botstein, Leon. (1990). "Damaged Literacies and American Democracy." *Daedalus* 119, no. 2: 55–84.

Bottero, Jean, et al. (1992). *Ancestors of the West*. Chicago: University of Chicago Press.

Boyarin, Jonathan, ed. (1993). *The Ethnography of Reading*. Berkeley: University of California Press.

Brandt, Deborah. (1990). *Literacy as Involvement: The Acts of Writers, Readers, and Texts*. Carbondale: Southern Illinois University Press.

———. (2001). *Literacy in American Lives*. New York: Cambridge University Press.

Brantlinger, Patrick. *The Reading Lesson: The Threat of Mass Literacy in Nineteenth-Century British Fiction*. Bloomington: Indiana University Press, 1998.

Briggs, Asa, and Peter Burke. (2002). *A Social History of the Media*. Cambridge: Polity.

Brodhead, Richard H. (1993). *Cultures of Letters: Scenes of Reading and Writing in Nineteenth-Century America:* Chicago: University of Chicago Press.

Brooks, Jeffrey. (1985). *When Russia Learned to Read: Literacy and Popular Literature, 1861–1917.* Princeton: Princeton University Press.

Brown, Gillian. (2001). *The Consent of the Governed: The Lockean Legacy in Early American Culture.* Cambridge, Mass.: Harvard University Press.

Brown, Richard D. (1989). *Knowledge Is Power: The Diffusion of Information in Early America, 1700–1865.* New York: Oxford University Press.

———. (1996). *The Strength of a People: The Idea of an Informed Citizenry in America, 1650–1870.* Chapel Hill: University of North Carolina Press.

Bruckner, Martin. (2006). *The Geographic Revolution in Early America: Maps, Literacy, and National Identity.* Chapel Hill: University of North Carolina Press.

Burke, Peter. (1972). *Culture and Society in Renaissance Italy.* London: Batsford.

———. (1978). *Popular Culture in Early Modern Europe.* New York: Harper and Row.

———. (1987). *The Historical Anthropology of Early Modern Italy.* Cambridge: Cambridge University Press.

———. (2000). *A Social History of Knowledge.* Cambridge: Polity.

———. (2004). *Languages and Communities in Early Modern Europe.* Cambridge: Cambridge University Press.

Burke, Peter, and Roy Porter, eds. (1987). *The Social History of Language.* Cambridge: Cambridge University Press.

Calhoun, Daniel H. (1969). "The City as Teacher." *History of Education Quarterly* 9: 312–25.

———. (1973). *The Intelligence of a People.* Princeton: Princeton University Press.

Capp, Bernard. (1979). *Astrology and the Popular Press.* London: Faber and Faber.

Carceles, Gabriel. (1990). "World Literacy Prospects at the Turn of the Century." *Comparative Education Review* 34: 4–20.

Carpenter, Kenneth, ed. (1983). *Books and Society in History.* New York: Bowker, 1983.

Casper, Scott, et al., eds. (2002). *Perspectives on American Book History.* Amherst: University of Massachusetts Press.

Cavallo, Guglielmo, and Roger Chartier, eds. (1999). *A History of Reading in the West.* Amherst: University of Massachusetts Press.

Cayton, Mary Kupiec. (1987). "The Making of an American Prophet: Emerson, His Audiences, and the Rise of the Culture Industry in Nineteenth-Century America." *American Historical Review* 92: 597–620.

Chartier, Roger. (1985). "Text, Symbols, Frenchness." *Journal of Modern History* 57: 682–95.

———. (1987). *The Cultural Uses of Print in Early Modern France.* Princeton: Princeton University Press.

———. (1989a). "Texts, Printing, Readings." In *The New Cultural History,* ed. Lynn Hunt, 154–75. Berkeley and Los Angeles: University of California Press.

———, ed. (1989b). *The Culture of Print.* Princeton: Princeton University Press. .

———. (1994). *The Order of Books.* Stanford: Stanford University Press.

———. (1995). *Forms and Meanings.* Philadelphia: University of Pennsylvania Press.

———. (1996). *On the Edge of the Cliff.* Baltimore: Johns Hopkins University Press.

Chisick, Harvey. (1980). *The Limits of Reform in the Enlightenment.* Princeton: Princeton University Press, 1980.

Cintron, Ralph. (1997). *Angels' Towns: Chero Ways, Gang Life, and Rhetorics of the Everyday.* Boston: Beacon.

Cipolla, Carlo. (1969). *Literacy and Development in the West.* Harmondsworth: Penguin.

Clammer, J. R. (1976). *Literacy and Social Change: A Case Study of Figi.* Leiden: Brill.

Clanchy, Michael T. (1979/1993). *From Memory to Written Record: England, 1066–1307.* Cambridge, Mass.: Harvard University Press; rev. ed., Oxford: Blackwell.

Cohen, Patricia Cline. (1982). *A Calculating People: The Spread of Numeracy in Early America.* Chicago: University of Chicago Press.

Coleman, Janet. (1981). *Medieval Readers and Writers, 1350–1400.* New York: Columbia University Press.

———. (1996). *Public Reading and the Reading Public in Late Medieval England and France.* Cambridge: Cambridge University Press.

Cook-Gumperz, Jenny, ed. (1986). *The Social Construction of Literacy.* Cambridge: Cambridge University Press.

Cope, Bill, and Mary Kalantzis, eds. (2000). *Multiliteracies: Literacy Learning and the Design of Social Futures.* London: Routledge.

Cornelius, Janet D. (1983). "'We Slipped and Learned to Read': Slave Accounts of the Literacy Process, 1830–1860." *Phylon* 44: 171–86.

———. (1991). *When I Can Read My Title Clear: Literacy, Slavery, and Religion in the Antebellum South.* Columbia: University of South Carolina Press.

Cranfield, G. A. (1978). *The Press and Society.* London: Longman.

Cremin, Lawrence. (1970). *American Education: The Colonial Experience.* New York: Harper and Row.

Cressy, David. (1980). *Literacy and the Social Order: Reading and Writing in Tudor and Stuart England.* Cambridge: Cambridge University Press.

Crick, Julia, and Alexandra Walsham, eds. (2004). *The Uses of Script and Print.* Cambridge: Cambridge University Press.

Cushman, Ellen, Eugene R. Kintgen, Barry M. Kroll, and Mike Rose, eds. (2001). *Literacy: A Critical Sourcebook.* New York: Bedford/St. Martin's.

Damon-Moore, Helen. (1994). *Magazines for the Millions: Gender and Commerce in the Ladies' Home Journal and the Saturday Evening Post, 1880–1910.* Albany: SUNY Press.

Danky, James P., and Wayne A. Wiegand, eds. (1998). *Print Culture in a Diverse America.* Urbana: University of Illinois Press.

———, eds. (2006). *Women in Print: Essays on the Print Culture of American Women from the Nineteenth and Twentieth Centuries.* Madison: University of Wisconsin Press.

Darnton, Robert. (1972). "Reading, Writing, and Publishing in Eighteenth-Century France." In *Historical Studies Today,* ed. Felix Gilbert and Stephen R. Graubard, 238–50. New York: Norton.

———. (1979). *The Business of Enlightenment.* Cambridge, Mass.: Harvard University Press.

———. (1982). The *Literary Underground of the Old Regime.* Cambridge, Mass.: Harvard University Press.

———. (1983). "What Is the History of Books?" In *Books and Society in History,* ed. Kenneth E. Carpenter, 3–28. New York: Bowker.

———. (1984a). *The Great Cat Massacre and Other Episodes in French Cultural History.* New York: Basic Books.

———. (1984b). "Readers Respond to Rousseau: The Fabrication of Romantic Sensitivity." In *The Great Cat Massacre and Other Episodes in French Cultural History,* 215–56. New York: Basic Books.

———. (1986). "The Symbolic Element in History." *Journal of Modern History* 58: 218–34.

———. (1990). *The Kiss of Lamourette: Reflections on Cultural History.* New York: Norton.

Davidson, Cathy N. (1986). *Revolution in the Word: The Rise of the Novel in America.* New York: Oxford University Press.

———, ed. (1989). *Reading in America.* Baltimore: Johns Hopkins University Press.

Davis, Natalie Z. (1975a). "Printing and the People." In *Society and Culture in Early Modern France,* 189–226. Stanford: Stanford University Press.

———. (1975b). *Society and Culture in Early Modern France.* Stanford: Stanford University Press.

De Certaux, Michael. (1984). "Walking in the City" and "Spatial Stories." In *The Practice of Everyday Life.* Berkeley and Los Angeles: University of California Press.

Denning, Michael. (1987). *Mechanic Accents: Dime Novels and Working-Class Culture in America.* London: Verso.

Diebert, Ronald J. (1997). *Parchment, Printing, and Hypermedia: Communication in World Order Transformation.* New York: Columbia University Press.

diSessa, Andrea A. (2000). *Changing Minds: Computers, Learning, and Literacy.* Cambridge, Mass.: MIT Press.

Dobranki, Stephen B. (2005). *Readers and Authorship in Early Modern England.* Cambridge: Cambridge University Press.

Docherty, Linda J. (1997). "Women as Readers: Visual Representations." *Proceedings of the American Antiquarian Society* 107: 335–88.

Douglas, Ann. (1977). *The Feminization of American Culture.* New York: Knopf.

Dyson, Anne Haas. (1997). *Writing Superheroes.* New York: Teachers College Press.

———. (2003). *The Brothers and Sisters Learn to Write: Popular Literacies in Childhood and School Cultures.* New York: Teachers College Press.

Edelsky, Carole. (1991). *With Liberty and Justice for All: Rethinking the Social in Language and Education.* London: Falmer.

"Education as Transformation: Identity, Change, and Development." (1981). Special issue, *Harvard Educational Review* 51, no. 1.

Eisenstein, Elizabeth. (1979). *The Printing Press as an Agent of Change: Communications and Cultural Transformations in Early Modern Europe.* 2 vols. Cambridge: Cambridge University Press.

Eklof, Ben. (1986). *Russian Peasant Schools, 1861–1914.* Berkeley: University of California Press.

Eldred, Janet Carey, and Peter Mortensen. (2002). *Imagining Rhetoric: Composing Women of the Early United States.* Pittsburgh: University of Pittsburgh Press.

Elfenbein, Andrew. (2006). "Cognitive Science and the History of Reading." *PMLA* 121: 484–502.

Engelsing, Rolf. (1973). *Analphabetentum und lekture.* Stuttgart: J. B. Metzler.

———. (1974). *Der berger als leser: Lesergeschichte in Deutschland, 1500–1800.* Stuttgart: Metzlersche.

Esrock, Ellen J. (1994). *The Reader's Eye: Visual Imaging as Reader Response.* Baltimore: Johns Hopkins University Press.

Ezell, Margaret J. M. (1999). *Social Authorship and the Advent of Print.* Baltimore: Johns Hopkins University Press.

Feather, John. (1980). "Cross-Channel Currents: Historical Bibliography and *L'histoire du livre.*" *Library* 2: 1–15.

———. (1985). *The Provincial Book Trade in Eighteenth-Century England.* Cambridge: Cambridge University Press.

Febvre, Lucien, and Henri-Jean Martin. (1958). *L'apparition du livre.* Paris: Editions Albin Michel.

———. (1976). *The Coming of the Book.* London: New Loft Books.

Ferdman, Bernardo. (1990). "Literacy and Cultural Identity." *Harvard Educational Review* 60: 181–204.

Ferguson, Eugene. (1977). "The Mind's Eye: Nonverbal Thought in Technology." *Science* 197: 827–36.

———. (1992). *Engineering and the Mind's Eye.* Cambridge, Mass.: MIT Press.

Ferguson, Margaret W. (2003). *Dido's Daughters: Literacy, Gender, and Empire in Early Modern England and France.* Chicago: University of Chicago Press.

Fernandez, James. (1988). "Historians Tell Tales." *Journal of Modern History* 60: 113–27.

Fernandez, Ramona. (2001). *Imagining Literacy.* Austin: University of Texas Press.

Finkelstein, David, and Alistair McCleery, eds. (2000). *Book History Reader.* London: Routledge.

Finnegan, Ruth. (1973). "Literacy versus Non-literacy: The Great Divide." In *Modes of Thought,* ed. Robin Horton and Ruth Finnegan, 112–44. London: Faber and Faber.

———. (1988). *Literacy and Orality.* Oxford: Blackwell.

Fleury, M., and P. Valmary. (1957). "Les progrès de l'instrucion élèmentaire de Louis XIV à Napoléon III." *Population* 12: 71–92.

Flint, Kate. (1993). *The Woman Reader, 1837–1914.* Oxford: Oxford University Press.

———. (2006). "Women and Reading." *Signs* 31: 511–36.

Fox, Adam. (2000). *Oral and Literate Culture in England, 1500–1700.* Oxford: Oxford University Press.

Fox, Adam, and Daniel Woolf, eds. (2002). *The Spoken Word . . . Britain, 1500–1800.* Manchester: Manchester University Press.

Frankel, Oz. (2006). *States of Inquiry: Social Investigations and Print Culture in Nineteenth-Century Britain and the United States.* Baltimore: Johns Hopkins University Press.

Frasca-Spada, Marina, and Nick Jardine, eds. (2000). *Books and the Sciences in History.* Cambridge: Cambridge University Press.

Freebody, Peter, and Anthony R. Welch, eds. (1993). *Knowledge, Culture and Power: International Perspectives on Literacy as Policy and Practice.* Pittsburgh: University of Pittsburgh Press.

Freedman, David. (1999). "African-American Schooling in the South Prior to 1861." *Journal of Negro History* 84: 1–47.

Freire, Paulo. (1985). *The Politics of Education: Culture, Power and Liberation.* Boston: Bergin & Garvey.

Freire, Paulo, and Donaldo Macedo. (1987). *Literacy: Reading the Word and the World.* South Hadley, Mass.: Bergin & Garvey.

Fullerton, Ronald. (1977). "Creating a Mass Book Market in Germany." *Journal of Social History* 10: 265–83.

———. (1979). "Toward a Popular Culture in Germany." *Journal of Social History* 12: 265–83.

Furet, Francois, and Jacques Ozouf. (1976). "Literacy and Industrialization: The Case of the Department du Nord." *Journal of European Economic History* 5: 5–44.

———. (1977). *Lire et écrire.* 2 vols. Paris: Editions de Minuit.

———. (1983). *Reading and Writing.* Cambridge: Cambridge University Press.

Furtwangler, Albert. (2005). *Bringing Indians to the Book.* The Emil and Kathleen Sick Lecture Book Series in Western History and Biography. Seattle: University of Washington Press.

Gagnon, Paul, and the Bradley Commission on History in Schools, ed. (1989). *Historical Literacy: The Case for History in American Education.* New York: Macmillan.

Galenson, David. (1977). "Immigration and the Colonial Labor System: An Analysis of the Length of Indenture." *Explorations in Economic History* 14: 360–77.

———. (1979). "Literacy and the Social Origins of Some Early Americans." *Historical Journal* 22: 75–91.

———. (1981a). "Literacy and Age in Pre-industrial England." *Economic Development and Cultural Change* 29: 815–29.

———. (1981b). "The Market Evaluation of Human Capital: The Case of Indentured Servitude." *Journal of Political Economy* 89: 446–67.

———. (1984). "The Rise and Fall of Indentured Servitude in the Americas: An Economic Analysis." *Journal of Economic History* 44: 1–26.

———. (1989). "Labor Market Behavior in Colonial America: Servitude, Slavery, and Free Labor." In *Markets in History: Economic Studies of the Past,* 52–96. Cambridge: Cambridge University Press.

———. (1994). "The Rise of Free Labor: Economic Change and the Enforcement of Service Contracts in England, 1351–1875." *Capitalism in Context: Essays on Economic Development and Cultural Change in Honor of R. M. Hartwell,* ed. John A. James and Mark Thomas, 114–37. Chicago: University of Chicago Press.

———. (1995). "Educational Opportunity on the Urban Frontier: Nativity, Wealth, and School Attendance in Early Chicago." *Economic Development and Cultural Change* 43: 551–63.

———. (1997). Neighborhood Effects on the School Attendance of Irish Immigrants' Sons in Boston and Chicago in 1860." *American Journal of Education* 105: 261–93.

———. (1998a). "Ethnic Differences in Neighborhood Effects on the School Attendance of Boys in Early Chicago." *History of Education Quarterly* 38: 17–35.

———. (1998b). "Ethnicity, Neighborhood, and the School Attendance of Boys in Antebellum Boston." *Journal of Urban History* 24: 603–26.

Gallego, Margaret A., and Sandra Hollingsworth, eds. (2000). *What Counts as Literacy: Challenging the School Standard.* New York: Teachers College.

Gallegos, Bernardo P. (1992). *Literacy, Education, and Society in New Mexico, 1693–1821.* Albuquerque: University of New Mexico Press.

Gallman, Robert E. (1988). "Changes in the Level of Literacy in a New Community of Early America." *Journal of Economic History* 48: 567–82.

Gamble, Henry. (2003). *Books and Readers in the Early Church.* New Haven: Yale University Press.

Garvey, Ellen Gruber. (1996). *The Adman in the Parlor: Magazines and the Gendering of Consumer Culture, 1880s to 1910s.* New York: Oxford University Press.

Gee, James. (1990). *Social Linguistics and Literacies: Ideology in Discourses.* London: Falmer.

Gee, James Paul, Glynda Hull, and Colin Lankshear. (1996). *The New Work Order.* Boulder: Westview.

Gerber, David A. (2006). *Authors of Their Lives: The Personal Correspondence of British Immigrants to North America.* New York: New York University Press.

Gere, Anne Ruggles. (1997). *Intimate Practices: Literacy and Cultural Work in U.S. Women's Clubs, 1880–1920.* Champaign: University of Illinois Press.

Gerling, Gordon, and Andrew Sum. (1988). *Toward a More Perfect Union: Basic Skills, Poor Families, and Our Economic Future.* New York: Ford Foundation Project on Social Welfare and the American Future.

Gilmore, William J. (1989). *Reading Becomes a Necessity of Life: Material and Cultural Life in Rural New England, 1780–1835.* Knoxville: University of Tennessee Press.

Ginzburg, Carlo. (1980). *The Cheese and the Worms.* Baltimore: Johns Hopkins University Press.

Giroux, Henry A. (1988). "Literacy and the Pedagogy of Voice and Political Empowerment." *Educational Studies* 38: 61–76.

Giroux, Henry A., and Harvey J. Kaye. (1989). "The Liberal Arts Must Be Reformed to Serve Democratic Means." *Chronicle of Higher Education,* 29 March, A44.

Gitelman, Lisa. (1999). *Scripts, Grooves, and Writing Machines: Representing Technology in the Edison Era.* Stanford: Stanford University Press.

Goodman, Dena. (2002). "L'ortografe des Dames: Gender and Language in the Old Regime." *French Historical Studies* 25: 191–223.

Goody, Jack, ed. (1968). *Literacy in Traditional Societies.* Cambridge: Cambridge University Press.

———. (1968/1977). "What's in a List?" In *Literacy in Traditional Societies,* ed. Jack Goody, 32–51. Reprinted in Jack Goody, *The Domestication of the Savage Word,* 74–111. Cambridge: Cambridge University Press.

———. (1977). *The Domestication of the Savage Word.* Cambridge: Cambridge University Press.

———. (1986). *The Logic of Writing and the Organization of Society.* Cambridge: Cambridge University Press.

———. (1987). *The Interface between the Written and the Oral.* Cambridge: Cambridge University Press.

Goody, Jack, and Ian Watt. (1968). "The Consequences of Literacy." In *Literacy in Traditional Societies,* ed. Jack Goody. Cambridge: Cambridge University Press.

Gough, Kathleen. (1968). "Implications of Literacy in Traditional China and India." In *Literacy in Traditional Societies,* ed. Jack Goody, 69–84. Cambridge: Cambridge University Press.

Gowen, Sheryl. (1992). *The Politics of Workplace Literacy: A Case Study.* New York: Teachers College Press.

Graff, Harvey J. (1978). "Literacy Past and Present: Critical Approaches in the Literacy/Society Relationship." *Interchange* 9: 1–21.

———. (1979/1991). *The Literacy Myth: Literacy and Social Structure in the Nineteenth-Century City.* New York and London: Academic Press. Reprinted with a new introduction. New Brunswick, N.J.: Transaction.

———. (1981a). *Literacy in History: An Interdisciplinary Research Bibliography.* New York: Garland.

———, ed. (1981b). *Literacy and Social Development in the West.* Cambridge: Cambridge University Press.

———. (1981c). "Reflections on the History of Literacy: Overview, Critique, and Proposals." *Humanities in Society* 4: 303–33.

———. (1987a). *The Legacies of Literacy: Continuities and Contradictions in Western Culture and Society.* Bloomington: Indiana University Press.

———. (1987b). *The Labyrinths of Literacy: Reflections on Literacy Past and Present.* London: Falmer.

———. (1988). "Whither the History of Literacy? The Future of the Past." *Communication* 11: 5–22.

———. (1989). "Critical Literacy versus Cultural Literacy: Reading Signs of the Times." *Interchange* 20: 46–52.

———. (1993a). "Literacy Patterns in Historical Perspective." In *Reading across the Life Span: Recent Research in Psychology,* ed. Steven R. Yussen and M. Cecil Smith, 73–94. New York: Springer-Verlag.

———. (1993b). "Literacy, Myths, and Legacies: Lessons from the Past—Thoughts for the Future." *Interchange* 24: 271–86.

———. (1994). Literacy, Myths, and Legacies: "Lessons from the History of Literacy." In *Functional Literacy: Theoretical Issues and Educational Implications,* ed. Ludo Verhoeven, 37–60. Amsterdam: John Benjamins.

——. (1995a). "Assessing the History of Literacy in the 1990s: Themes and Questions." In *Escribir y Leer en Occidente*, ed. Armando Petrucci and M. Gimeno Blay, 5–46. Valencia, Spain: Universitat de Valencia.

——. (1995b). *The Labyrinths of Literacy: Reflections on Literacy Past and Present*. Rev. ed. Pittsburgh: University of Pittsburgh Press.

——. (1995c). *Conflicting Paths: Growing Up in America*. Cambridge, Mass.: Harvard University Press.

——. (1999a). "Interdisciplinary Explorations in the History of Children, Adolescents, and Youth—For the Past, Present, and Future." *Journal of American History* 85: 1538–47.

——. (1999b). "Teaching and Historical Understanding: Disciplining Historical Imagination with Historical Context." In *The Social Worlds of Higher Education: Handbook for Teaching in a New Century*, ed. B. A. Pescosolido and R. Aminzade, 280–93. Thousand Oaks, Calif.: Pine Forge.

——. (2001). "The Shock of the '"New" Histories': Social Science Histories and Historical Literacies." *Social Science History* 25, no. 4: 483–533. (Originally delivered as the Presidential Address, Social Science History Association annual meeting, 2000.)

——. (2003). "Understanding Literacy in Its Historical Contexts: Past Approaches and Work in Progress." Special double issue, *Interchange*, ed. Harvey J. Graff, Alison Mackinnon, Bengt Sandin, and Ian Winchester, 34. nos. 2–3: 123–31.

Graff, Harvey J., and John Duffy. (2007). "The Literacy Myth." In *Encyclopedia of Language and Education*, ed. Nancy Hornberger. Vol. 2, *Literacy*, ed. Brian Street. New York: Springer.

Graff, Harvey J., Alison Mackinnon, Bengt Sandin, and Ian Winchester. (2003). "Introduction to Historical Studies of Literacy." Special double issue, *Interchange*, ed. Harvey J. Graff, Alison Mackinnon, Bengt Sandin, and Ian Winchester, 34, nos. 2–3: 117–22.

Grafton, Anthony T. (1980). "The Importance of Being Printed." *Journal of Interdisciplinary History* 11: 265–86.

Grafton, Anthony T., et al. (2002). "How Revolutionary was the Print Revolution." *American Historical Review,* 107: 84–128.

Gray, Edward G. (1999). *New World Babel: Languages and Nations in Early America*. Princeton: Princeton University Press.

Gregory, Eve, and Ann Williams. (2000). *City Literacies: Learning to Read across Generations and Cultures*. London: Routledge.

Grendler, Paul. (1989). *Schooling in Renaissance Italy: Literacy and Learning, 1300–1600*. Baltimore: Johns Hopkins University Press.

Griswold, Wendy, Terry McDonnell, and Nathan Wright. (2005). "Reading and the Reading Class in the Twenty-First Century." *Annual Reviews in Sociology* 31: 127–41.

Gross, Robert A. (1988a). *Books and Libraries in Thoreau's Concord: Two Essays*. Worcester, Mass.: American Antiquarian Society.

——. (1988b). *Much Instruction from Little Reading: Books and Libraries in Thoreau's Concord*. Charlottesville: University of Virginia Press.

——. (1989). "Printing, Politics, and the People." *Proceedings of the American Antiquarian Society* 99: 375–97.

——. (1996). "Reading Culture, Reading Books." *Proceedings of the American Antiquarian Society* 106: 59–78.

Grubb, Farley. (1987). "Colonial Immigrant Literacy: An Economic Analysis of Pennsylvania-German Evidence, 1727-1775." *Explorations in Economic History* 24: 63-76.

——. (1990). "Growth of Literacy in Colonial America: Longitudinal Patterns, Economic Models, and the Direction of Future Research." *Social Science History* 14: 451–81.

———. (1992). "Educational Choice in the Era before Free Public Schooling: Evidence from German Immigrant Children in Pennsylvania, 1771–1817." *Journal of Economic History* 52: 363–75.

Grubb, W. Norton, and Marvin Lazerson. (1982). *Broken Promises: How Americans Fail Their Children.* New York: Basic Books.

Gustafson, Sandra M. (2000). *Eloquence Is Power: Oratory and Performance in Early America.* Chapel Hill: University of North Carolina Press.

Hackenberg, Michael, ed. (1987). *Getting the Books Out.* Papers of the Chicago Conference on the Book in 19th-Century America. Washington, D.C.: Library of Congress.

Hall, David D. (1979). "The World of Print and Collective Mentality in Seventeenth-Century New England." In *New Directions in American Intellectual History*, ed. John Higham and Paul Conkin, 166–80. Baltimore: Johns Hopkins University Press.

———. (1983). "The Uses of Literacy in New England, 1600–1850." In *Printing and Society in Early America*, ed. William Joyce et al., 1–47. Worcester, Mass.: American Antiquarian Society.

———. (1992). *Worlds of Wonder, Days of Judgment: Popular Religious Belief in Early New England.* Cambridge, Mass: Harvard University Press.

———. (1996). *Cultures of Print.* Amherst: University of Massachusetts Press.

Hall, David D., and John Hench, eds. (1987). *Needs and Opportunities in the History of the Book: America, 1639–1876.* Worcester, Mass.: American Antiquarian Society.

Hall, Oswald, and Richard Carlton. (1977). *Basic Skills at School and Work: The Study of Albertown.* Toronto: Ontario Economic Council.

Harman, David. (1974). *Community Fundamental Education.* Lexington, Mass.: Lexington Books.

Harris, William V. (1989). *Ancient Literacy.* Cambridge, Mass.: Harvard University Press.

Hautecoeur, Jean-Paul, ed. (1990). *Alpha 90: Current Research in Literacy.* Quebec: UNESCO Institute for Education.

Havelock, Eric. (1963). *Preface to Plato.* Cambridge, Mass.: Harvard University Press.

———. (1973). *Prologue to Greek Literacy.* Cincinnati: University of Cincinnati.

———. (1976). *Origins of Western Literacy.* Toronto: Ontario Institute for Studies in Education.

———. (1977). "The Preliteracy of the Greeks." *New Literary History* 8: 369–92.

———. (1986a). *The Literate Revolution in Greece and Its Cultural Consequences.* Princeton: Princeton University Press.

———. (1986b). *The Muse Learns to Write.* New Haven: Yale University Press.

Haywood, Ian. (2004). *The Revolution in Popular Literature: Print, Politics, and the People 1790–1860.* Cambridge: Cambridge University Press.

Headrick, Daniel R. (2002). *When Information Came of Age: Technologies of Knowledge, 1700–1850.* Oxford: Oxford University Press.

Heath, Shirley Brice. (1983). *Ways with Words: Language, Life, and Work in Communities and Classrooms.* Cambridge: Cambridge University Press.

Hebrard, Jean. (1980). "Ecole et alphabéisation au XIXe sièle. (approche psychologique de documents historiques)." *Annales: e.s.c.* 35: 66–80.

Henkin, David. (1998). *City Reading: Written Works and Public Spaces in Antebellum New York.* New York: Columbia University Press.

Hesse, Carla. (2001). *The Other Enlightenment: How French Women Became Modern.* Princeton: Princeton University Press.

Higham, John, and Paul Conkin, eds. (1979). *New Directions in American Intellectual History.* Baltimore: Johns Hopkins University Press.

Hilliard, Christopher. (2006). *To Exercise Our Talents: The Democratization of Writing in Britain.* Cambridge, Mass.: Harvard University Press.

Hindman, Sandra L., ed. (1991). *Printing the Written Word: The Social History of Books, circa 1450–1520*. Ithaca: Cornell University Press.

Hirsch, E. D., Jr. (1987). *Cultural Literacy*. Boston: Houghton Mifflin.

———. (1988). *The Dictionary of Cultural Literacy*. Boston: Houghton Mifflin.

Hirsch, Rudoph. (1978). *The Printed Word*. London: Variorum Editions.

Hobbs, Catherine. (1995). *Nineteenth-Century Women Learn to Write*. Charlottesville: University of Virginia Press.

Hobsbawm, E. J. (1980). "The Revival of Narrative: Some Comments." *Past and Present* 86: 3–8.

Hoggart, Richard. (1958). *The Uses of Literacy*. Harmondsworth: Penguin.

Horowitz, Helen. (1992). "Nous Autres: Reading, Passion, and the Creation of M. Carey Thomas." *Journal of American History* 79: 68–95.

Houston, Rab. (1982a). "The Development of Literacy: Northern England, 1640–1750." *Economic History Review* 35: 199–216.

———. (1982b). "The Literacy Myth? Illiteracy in Scotland, 1630–1760." *Past and Present* 96: 81–102.

———. (1983). "Literacy and Society in the West, 1500–1800." *Social History* 8: 269–93.

———. (1985). *Scottish Literacy and the Scottish Identity: Literacy and Society in Scotland and Northern England, 1660–1850*. Cambridge: Cambridge University Press.

———. (2002). *Literacy in Early Modern Europe: Culture and Education, 1500–1800*. London: Longman.

Hudson, Nicholas. (1994). *Writing and European Thought, 1600–1830*. Cambridge: Cambridge University Press.

Hull, Glynda, and Katherine Schultz, eds. (2002). *School's Out! Bridging Out-of-School Literacies with Classroom Practice*. New York: Teachers College Press.

Hunter, Jane. (2002). *How Young Ladies Became Girls: The Victorian Origins of American Girlhood*. New Haven: Yale University Press.

Hunter, Michael. (1979). "The Impact of Print." *Book Collector* 28: 335–52.

Hyde, J. K. (1979). "Some Uses of Literacy in Venice and Florence in the Thirteenth and Fourteenth Centuries." *Transactions of the Royal Historical Society*, 5th ser., 29: 109–29.

Illich, Evan, and Barry Sanders. (1988). *The Alphabetization of the Popular Mind*. San Francisco: North Point.

Innes, Matthew. (1998). "Memory, Orality and Literacy in an Early Medieval Society." *Past and Present* 158: 3–36.

Isaacs, Rhys. (1976a). "Dramatizing the Ideology of Revolution: Popular Mobilization in Virginia, 1774 to 1776." *William and Mary Quarterly* 33: 357–85.

———. (1976b). "Preachers and Patriots: Popular Culture and the Revolution in Virginia." In *The American Revolution*, ed. Alfred F. Young, 125–56. Dekalb: Northern Illinois University Press.

———. (1982). *The Transformation of Virginia*. Chapel Hill: University of North Carolina Press.

Ivins, William. (1969). *Prints and Visual Communications*. Cambridge, Mass.: MIT Press.

Jackson, H. J. (2005). *Romantic Readers: The Evidence of Marginalia*. New Haven: Yale University Press.

James, Louis. (1963). *Fiction for the Working Man*. Oxford: Oxford University Press.

Johansson, Egil. (1977). *The History of Literacy in Sweden*. Educational Reports no. 12. Umeå, Sweden: Umeå University and School of Education.

———. (1981). "The History of Literacy in Sweden." In *Literacy and Social Development in the West*, ed. Harvey J. Graff, 151–82. Cambridge: Cambridge University Press.

———. (1985). "Popular Literacy in Scandinavia about 1600–1900." *Historical Social Research* 34: 60–64.

———. (1998). *Alphabeta Varia: Orality, Reading and Writing in the History of Literacy*. Festschrift in honour of Egil Johansson on the occasion of his 65th birthday. Album Religionum Umense 1. Umeå, Sweden: Umeå University.

Johns, Adrian. (1998). *The Nature of the Book: Print and Knowledge in the Making*. Chicago: University of Chicago Press.

Johnson, Richard. (1976). "Notes on the Schooling of the English Working Class." In *Schooling and Capitalism*, ed. R. Dale, G. Esland, and M. MacDonald, 44–55. London: Routledge and Kegan Paul.

Jordan, John O., and Robert L. Patten, eds. (1995). *Literature in the Marketplace*. Cambridge: Cambridge University Press.

Joyce, William L., David D. Hall, Richard D. Brown, and John B. Hench, eds. (1983). *Printing and Society in Early America*. Worcester, Mass.: American Antiquarian Society.

Justice, Steven. (1994). *Writing and Rebellion: England in 1381*. Berkeley: University of California Press.

Kaestle, Carl F. (1976). "Between the Scylla of Brutal Ignorance and the Charybdis of a Literary Education: Elite Attitudes toward Mass Schooling . . ." In *Schooling and Society*, ed. Lawrence Stone., 77–191. Baltimore: Johns Hopkins University Press.

———. (1983). *Pillars of the Republic*. New York: Hill and Wang.

———. (1985). "The History of Literacy and the History of Reading." *Review of Educational Research* 12: 11–53.

Kaestle, Carl F., Helen Damon-Moore, Lawrence C. Stedman, Katherine Tinsley, and William Vance Trollinger Jr. (1991). *Literacy in the United States: Readers and Reading since 1880*. New Haven: Yale University Press.

Kaestle, Carl F., and Maris Vinovskis. (1980). *Education and Social Change in the Nineteenth Century*. Cambridge: Cambridge University Press.

Kammen, Michael, ed. (1980). *The Past before Us*. Ithaca: Cornell University Press.

Kaplan, Steven L., ed. (1984). *Understanding Popular Culture: Europe from the Middle Ages to the Nineteenth Century*. Berlin: Mouton.

Kasson, John. (1984). "Civility and Rudeness: Urban Etiquette and the Bourgeois Social Order in Nineteenth-Century America." *Prospects* 9: 143–67.

Kates, Susan. (2006). "Literacy, Voting Rights, and the Citizenship Schools in the South, 1957–1970." *CCC* 57: 479–502.

Katz, Michael B. (1976). "The Origins of Public Education." *History of Education Quarterly* 16: 381–408.

———. (1988). "The New Educational Panic." In *America in Theory*, ed. Leslie Berlowitz, Denis Donohue, and Louis Menand, 178–94. New York: Oxford University Press.

———. (1989). *Reconstructing American Education*. Cambridge, Mass.: Harvard University Press.

Kelley, Mary. (1996). "Reading Women/Women Reading: The Making of Learned Women in Antebellum America." *Journal of American History* 83: 401–24.

———. (2006). *Learning to Stand and Speak: Women, Education, and Public Life in America's Republic*. Chapel Hill: University of North Carolina Press.

Kett, Joseph F. (1994). *The Pursuit of Knowledge under Difficulties: From Self-Improvement to Adult Education in America, 1759–1990*. Stanford: Stanford University Press.

Kett, Joseph F., and Patricia A. McClung. (1984). *Book Culture in Post-Revolutionary Virginia*. Worcester, Mass.: American Antiquarian Society.

Kirsch, Irwin S., Ann Jungeblut, Lynn Jenkins, and Andrew Kolstad. (1993). *Adult Literacy in America*. Educational Testing Service under Contract with National Center for Education Statistics, Office of Educational Research and Improvement, U.S. Department of Education. Princeton: Educational Testing Service.

Klaus-Joachim, Lorenzen-Schmidt, and Bjorn Poulsen, eds. (2002). *Writing Peasants: Studies on Peasant Literacy in Early Modern Northern Europe*. Reykjavik, Iceland: Landbohistorisk Selskab.

Kozol, Jonathan. (1965). *Amazing Grace: The Lives of Children and the Conscience of a Nation*. New York: Crown.

———. (1978a). *Children of the Revolution*. New York: Delacorte.

———. (1978b). "A New Look at the Literacy Campaign in Cuba." *Harvard Educational Review* 48: 341–77.

———. (1981). "Education as Transformation: Identity, Change, and Development." Special issue, *Harvard Educational Review* 52: 54–60.

———. (1985). *Illiterate America*. Garden City: Doubleday.

———. (2000). *Ordinary Resurrections: Children in the Years of Hope*. New York: Crown.

Krug, Rebecca. (2002). *Reading Families: Women's Literate Practice in Late Medieval England*. Ithaca: Cornell University Press.

LaCapra, Dominick. (1985a). "The Cheese and the Worms: The Cosmos of a Twentieth-Century Historian." In *History and Criticism*, 45–69. Ithaca: Cornell University Press.

———. (1985b). *History and Criticism* Ithaca: Cornell University Press.

———. (1988). "Chartier, Darnton, and the Great Symbol Massacre." *Journal of Modern History* 60: 95–112.

LaCapra, Dominick, and Steven L. Kaplan, eds. (1982). *Modern European Intellectual History*. Ithaca: Cornell University Press.

Lanehart, Sonja. (2002). *Sista Speak! Black Women Kinfolk Talk about Language and Literacy*. Austin: University of Texas Press.

Lankshear, Colin, and Moira Lawler. (1987). *Literacy, School and Revolution*. London: Falmer.

Lankshear, Colin, and Peter McLaren, eds. (1993). *Critical Literacy: Politics, Praxis, and the Postmodern*. Albany: SUNY Press.

Laqueur, Thomas W. (1976a). "Working-Class Demand and the Growth of English Elementary Education, 1750–1850." In *Schooling and Society,* ed. Lawrence Stone, 192–205. Baltimore: Johns Hopkins University Press.

———. (1976b). "The Cultural Origins of Popular Literacy in England, 1500–1800." *Oxford Review of Education* 2: 255–75.

Lee, A. J. (1974). *The Origins of the Popular Press*. London: Croom Helm.

Lehuu, Isabel. (2000). *Carnival on the Page: Popular Print Media in Antebellum America*. Chapel Hill: University of North Carolina Press.

Leith, James. (1973). "Modernization, Mass Education, and Social Mobility in French Thought." *Eighteenth Century Studies* 2: 223–38.

———. (1977). "Introduction: Unity and Diversity in Education during the Eighteenth Century." In "Facets of Education in the Eighteenth Century," ed. James Leith, Special Issue, *Studies on Voltaire and the Eighteenth Century*: 13–28.

———. (1983). "The Hope for Moral Regeneration in French Educational Thought." In *City and Society in the Eighteenth Century*, ed. Paul Fritz and David Williams, 215–29. London: Hakkert.

Leonard, Thomas. (1995). *News for All: America's Coming of Age with the Press*. New York: Oxford University Press.

LeRoy Ladurie, Emmanuel. (1978). *Montaillou: Promised Land of Error*. New York: Braziller.

Levine, David. (1979). "Education and Family Life in Early Industrial England." *Journal of Family History* 4: 368–80.

———. (1980). "Illiteracy and Family Life during the First Industrial Revolution." *Journal of Social History* 14: 25–44.

Levine, David, and Zubedeh Vahed. (2001). "Ginzburg's Menocchio: Refutations and Conjectures." *Histoire Sociale* 34: 437–64.

Levine, David P. (2005). "The Birth of the Citizenship Schools: Entwining the Struggles for Literacy and Freedom." *History of Education Quarterly* 44: 388–414.

Levine, Kenneth. (1982). "Functional Literacy: Fond Illusions and False Economies." *Harvard Educational Review* 52: 249–66.

———. (1985). *The Social Context of Literacy.* London: Routledge and Kegan Paul.

Levine, Lawrence W. (1978). *Highbrow/Lowbrow: The Emergence of Cultural Hierarchy in America.* New York: Oxford University Press.

Lindblom, Charles. (1990). *Inquiry and Change.* New Haven: Yale University Press; New York: Russell Sage Foundation.

Lindblom, Charles, and David Cohen. (1979). *Usable Knowledge.* New Haven: Yale University Press.

"Literacy, Culture, and the Dilemmas of Schooling." (1988). *Journal of Education* 170, no. 1.

"Literacy in America." (1990). *Daedalus* 119, no. 2.

Lockridge, Kenneth A. (1974). *Literacy in Colonial New England.* New York: Norton.

Long, Elizabeth. (2002). *Book Clubs.* Chicago: University of Chicago Press.

Luebke, David M. (2004). "Signatures and Political Culture in Eighteenth-Century Germany." *Journal of Modern History* 76: 497–530.

Lunsford, Andrea A., Helene Moglen, and James Slevin, eds. (1990). *The Right to Literacy.* New York: Modern Language Association.

Luria, Keith. (1986). "The Paradoxical Carlo Ginzburg." *Radical History Review* 35: 80–87.

Lyons, Martyn. (2001). *Readers and Society in Nineteenth-Century France: Workers, Women, Peasants.* London: Palgrave.

Mace, Jane. (1988). *Playing with Time: Mothers and the Meaning of Literacy.* London: University College London.

Machor, James L., ed. (1993). *Readers in History: Nineteenth-Century American Literature and the Contexts of Response.* Baltimore: Johns Hopkins University Press.

MacKenzie, D. F. (1999). *Bibliography and the Sociology of Texts.* Cambridge: Cambridge University Press.

———. (2002). *Making Meaning.* Amherst: University of Massachusetts Press.

Mah, Harold. (1998). "Suppressing the Text: The Metaphysics of Ethnographic History in Darnton's Great Cat Massacre." *History Workshop* 31: 1–20.

Main, Gloria L. (1991). "An Inquiry into When and Why Women Learned to Write in Colonial New England." *Journal of Social History* 24: 579–89.

Manguel, Albert. (1996). *A History of Reading.* New York: Viking.

Marchesini, Daniele. (1987). *L1 bisogno di scrivere: Usi dela scrittura nell'Italia modera.* Rome: Laterza.

Marcus, Steven. (1973). "Reading the Illegible." In *The Victorian City,* ed. H. J. Dyos and Michael Wolf. pp. 257–276. London: Routledge.

———. (1974). *Engels, Manchester, and the Working Class.* New York: Random House.

Martin, Henri-Jean. (1968–70). *Le livre et la civilisation écrite.* 3 vols. Paris: Ecole nationale supérieure des bibliothèques.

———. (1975). "Culture écrite et culture orale, culture savante et culture populaire dans la France d'Ancien Régime." *Journale des Savants:* 225–82.

———. (1977). "Pour une histoire de la lecture." *Revue française d'histoire du livre* 16: 583–609.

———. (1978). "The Bibliotheque Bleue." *Publishing History* 3: 70–102.

———. (1994). *The History and Power of Writing.* Chicago: University of Chicago Press.

Martin, John. (1992). "Journeys to the World of the Dead: The Work of Carlo Ginzburg." *Journal of Social History* 25: 613–26.

Martinez, Pedro Luiz Moreno. (1989). *Alfabetizacion y cultura impresa en Lorca (1760–1860).* Murcia: Universidad de Murcia.

Marvin, Carolyn. (1988). *When Old Technologies Were New: Thinking about Communications in the Late Nineteenth Century.* New York: Oxford University Press.

Maynes, Mary Jo. (1979). "The Virtues of Archaism." *Comparative Studies in Society and History* 21: 611–25.

———. (1980). "Work or School?" In "The Making of Frenchmen." Special Issue, *Historical Reflections* 7: 115–34.

———. (1985a). *Schooling for the People: Comparative Local Studies of Schooling History in France and Germany, 1750–1850.* New York: Holmes and Meier.

———. (1985b). *Schooling in Western Europe.* Albany: SUNY Press.

———. (1995). *Taking the Hard Road: The Life Course in French and German Workers' Autobiographies in the Era of Industrialization.* Chapel Hill: University of North Carolina Press.

Mayor, A. Hayett. (1981). *Prints and People.* Princeton: Princeton University Press.

McCloud, Scott. (1993). *Understanding Comics: The Invisible Art.* New York: Harper Perennial.

McHenry, Elizabeth. (2002). *Forgotten Readers: Recovering the Lost History of African American Literary Societies.* Durham: Duke University Press.

McHenry, Elizabeth, and Shirley Brice Heath. (1994). "The Literate and the Literary: African Americans as Writers and Readers—1830–1940." *Written Communication,* 11: 419–44.

McKitterick, David. (2003). *Print, Manuscript and the Search for Order.* Cambridge: Cambridge University Press.

McKitterick, Rosamond. (1989). *The Carolingians and the Written Word.* Cambridge: Cambridge University Press.

———, ed. (1991). *The Uses of Literacy in Early Medieval England.* Cambridge: Cambridge University Press.

———. (2004). *History and Memory in the Carolingian World.* Cambridge: Cambridge University Press.

McLaren, Peter L. (1988). "Culture or Canon? Critical Pedagogy and the Politics of Literacy." *Harvard Educational Review* 58: 213–34.

McNeely, Ian F. (2003). *The Emancipation of Writing: German Civil Society in the Making.* Berkeley: University of California Press.

Melton, James Van Horn. (1988). *Absolutism and the Eighteenth-Century Origins of Compulsory Schooling in Prussia and Austria.* Cambridge: Cambridge University Press.

———. (2001). *The Rise of the Public in Enlightenment Europe.* Cambridge: Cambridge University Press.

Messaris, Paul. (1994). *Visual Literacy: Image, Mind, and Reality.* Boulder: Westview.

Mignolo, Walter D. (1995). *The Darker Side of the Renaissance: Literacy, Territoriality, and Colonization.* Ann Arbor: University of Michigan Press.

Miller, Arthur I. (2000). *Insights of Genius: Imagery and Creativity in Science and Art.* Cambridge, Mass.: MIT Press.

Miller, Susan. (1998). *Assuming the Position: Cultural Pedagogy and the Politics of Commonplace Writing.* Pittsburgh: University of Pittsburgh Press.

Milner, Henry. (2002). *Civic Literacy.* Hanover: University Press of New England.

Mitch, David. (1992a). *The Rise of Popular Literacy in Victorian England*. Philadelphia: University of Pennsylvania Press.

———. (1992b). "The Rise of Popular Literacy in Europe." In *The Political Construction of Education,* ed. Bruce Fuller and Richard Rubinson, 31–46. Praeger.

———. (1999). "The Role of Skill and Human Capital in the British Industrial Revolution." In *The British Industrial Revolution: An Economic Perspective*, ed. Joel Mokyr, 2nd ed., 241–79. Boulder: Westview.

Mitchell, Candace, and Weiller, Kathleen, eds. (1991). *Rewriting Literacy*. New York: Bergin and Garvey.

Mitchell, Sally. (1977). "Sentiment and Suffering: Women's Recreational Reading." *Victorian Studies* 21: 29–45.

———. (1981). *The Fallen Angel: Chastity, Class and Women's Reading, 1835–1880*. Bowling Green: Popular Press.

Monaghan, E. Jennifer. (1988). "Literacy Instruction and Gender in Colonial New England." *American Quarterly* 40: 18–41.

———. (1990). "'She Loved to Read in Good Books': Literacy and the Indians of Martha's Vineyard." *History of Education Quarterly* 30: 492–521.

———. (1991). "Family Literacy in Early 18th-Century Boston: Cotton Mather and His Children." *Reading Research Quarterly* 26: 342–70.

———. (1998). "Reading for the Enslaved, Writing for the Free: Reflections on Liberty and Literacy." *Proceedings of the American Antiquarian Society* 108: 308–41.

———. (2005). *Learning to Read and Write in Colonial America*. Amherst.: University of Massachusetts Press/American Antiquarian Society.

Moran, Jo Ann Hoeppner. (1985). *The Growth of English Schooling, 1340–1548: Learning, Literacy, and Laicization in Pre-Reformation York Diocese*. Princeton: Princeton University Press.

Morgan, Teresa. (1998). *Literate Education in the Hellenistic and Roman Worlds*. Cambridge: Cambridge University Press.

Morris, Robert C. (1976). *Reading, Riting, and Reconstruction: The Education of Freedmen in the South, 1861–1871*. Chicago: University of Chicago Press.

Moylan, Michele, and Lane Stiles, eds. (1996). *Reading Books: Essays on the Material Text and Literature in America*. Amherst: University of Massachusetts Press.

Muchembled, Robert. (1985). *Popular Culture and Élite Culture in France, 1400–1750*. Baton Rouge: Louisiana State University Press.

Munck, Thomas. (2004). "Literacy, Educational Reform and the Uses of Print in Eigtheenh-Century Denmark." *European History Quarterly* 34: 275–303.

Murray, John. (1995). "Human Capital in Religious Communes: Literacy and Selection of Nineteenth Century Shakers." *Explorations in Economic History* 32: 217–35.

———. (1997). "Generation(s) of Human Capital: Literacy in American Families, 1830–1875." *Journal of Interdisciplinary History* 27: 413–35.

———. (2000). "Literacy and Industrialization in Modern Germany." In *The Industrial Revolution in Comparative Perspective,* ed. Christine Rider and Michéal Thompson, 17–32. Melbourne, Fla.: Krieger.

———. (2003). "Fates of Orphans: Poor Children in Antebellum Charleston." *Journal of Interdisciplinary History* 33: 519–45.

———. (2004a). "Family, Literacy, and Skill Training in the Antebellum South: Historical-Longitudinal Evidence from Charleston." *Journal of Economic History,* 64: 773–99.

———. (2004b). "Literacy Acquisition in an Orphanage: A Historical-Longitudinal Case Study." *American Journal of Education* 110: 172–95.

Neuberg, Victor. (1973). "The Literature of the Streets." In *The Victorian City,* ed. H. J. Dyos and Michael Wolff, 1:191–210. London: Routledge and Kegan Paul.

————. (1977). *Popular Literature*. Harmondsworth: Penguin.

Newbury, Michael. (1997). *Figuring Authorship in Antebellum America*. Stanford: Stanford University Press.

Newcomb, Lori Humphrey. (2002). *Reading Popular Romance in Early Modern England*. New York: Columbia University Press.

New London Group. (2000). "A Pedagogy of Multiliteracies Designing Social Futures." In *Multiliteracies: Literacy Learning and the Design of Social Futures*, ed. Bill Cope and Mary Kalantzis, 9–37. London: Routledge. Reprinted from the *Harvard Educational Review* 66 (1996): 60–92.

Newman, Charles. (1985). *The Post-Modern Aura*. Evanston: Northwestern University Press.

Nicholas, Stephen, ed. (1988). *Convict Workers: Reinterpreting Australia's Past*. Cambridge: Cambridge University Press.

Nicholas, Stephen J., and Jacqueline M. Nicholas. (1992). "Male Literacy, 'Deskilling,' and the Industrial Revolution." *Journal of Interdisciplinary History* 23: 1–18.

Nicholas, Stephen J., and Deborah Oxley. (1993). "The Living Standards of Women during the Industrial Revolution, 1795–1820." *Economic History Review,* 2nd ser., 46: 723–49.

————. (1996). "Living Standards of Women in England and Wales, 1785–1815: New Evidence from Newgate Prison Records." *Economic History Review,* 2nd ser., 49: 591–99.

Nicholas, Stephen J., and Richard H. Steckel. (1991). "Heights and Living Standards of English Workers during the Early Years of Industrialization, 1770–1815." *Journal of Economic History* 51: 937–57.

Nilsson, Anders. (1999). "What Do Literacy Rates Really Signify? New Light on an Old Problem from Unique Swedish Data." *Paedagogica Historica* 35: 275–96.

Nilsson, Anders, and Birgitta Svard. (1994). "Writing Ability and Agrarian Change in Early Nineteenth Century Rural Scania." *Scandinavian Journal of History* 19: 251–74.

Nilsson, Anders, et al. (1999). "Agrarian Transition and Literacy: The Case of Nineteenth Century Sweden." *European Review of Economic History* 3: 79–96.

Noakes, Susan. (1981). "The Development of the Book Market in Late Quattrocento Italy." *Journal of Medieval and Renaissance Studies* 11: 23–55.

Nord, David. (2001). *Communities of Journalism: A History of American Newspapers and Their Readers*. Champaign: University of Illinois Press.

————. (2004). *Faith in Reading: Religious Publishing and the Birth of Mass Media in America*. New York: Oxford University Press.

Nunberg, Geoffrey, ed. (1996). *The Future of the Book*. Berkeley: University of California Press.

OECD. (1992). *Adult Illiteracy and Economic Performance*. Paris: Centre for Educational Research and Development, OECD.

Ohmann, Richard. (1996). *Selling Markets: Magazines, Markets, and Class at the Turn of the Century*. London: Verso.

Olson, David. (1977). "The Languages of Instruction: On the Literate Bias of Schooling." In *Schooling and the Acquisition of Knowledge*, ed. Richard C. Anderson and William E. Montague. Hillsdale, N.J.: Lawrence Erlbaum.

————. (1994). *The World on Paper: The Conceptual and Cognitive Implications of Writing and Reading*. Cambridge: Cambridge University Press.

Ong, Walter. (1958). *Ramus, Method, and the Decay of Dialogue*. Cambridge, Mass.: Harvard University Press.

————. (1967). *The Presence of the Word*. New Haven: Yale University Press.

——. (1977). *Interface of the Word.* Ithaca: Cornell University Press.

——. (1982). *Orality and Literacy.* London: Methuen.

Pauwels, Luc, ed. (2006). *Visual Cultures of Science: Rethinking Representational Practices in Knowledge Building and Science Communication.* Hanover: Dartmouth College Press.

Pawley, Christine. (2001). *Reading on the Middle Border.* Amherst: University of Massachusetts Press.

Pearson, Jacqueline. (1999). *Women's Reading in Britain, 1750–1835: A Dangerous Recreation.* Cambridge: Cambridge University Press.

Pelizzari, Maria Rosaria, ed. (1989). *Sulle vie della scrittura: Alfabetizzazione, cultura scritta e istitzioni in eta moderna.* Naples: Edizioni Scientifiche Ialiane.

Perlmann, Joel, and Dennis Shirley. (1991). "When Did New England Women Acquire Literacy?" *William and Mary Quarterly* 48: 18–41.

Perlmann, Joel, Silvana R. Siddali, and Keith Whitescarver. (1997). "Literacy, Schooling, and Teaching among New England Women, 1730–1820." *History of Education Quarterly* 37: 117–39.

Peters, Kate. (2005). *Print Culture and the Early Quakers.* Cambridge: Cambridge University Press.

Peterson, Glen. (1997). *The Power of Words: Literacy and Revolution in South China, 1949–95.* Vancouver: University of British Columbia Press.

Petrucci, Armando. (1987). *Scrivere e no: Politche della scrittura e analfabetismo nel mondo d'oggi.* Rome: Riuniti.

——. (1995a). *Public Lettering.* Chicago: University of Chicago Press.

——. (1995b). *Writers and Readers in Medieval Italy.* New Haven: Yale University Press.

Phillipps, K. C. (1984). *Language and Class in Victorian England.* London: Blackwell.

Plumb, J. H. (1972). "The Public, Literature and the Arts in the 18th Century." In *The Triumph of Culture: Eighteenth Century Perspectives.* Eds. Paul Fritz and David Williams, 27–48. Toronto: A. M. Hakkert.

——. (1975). "The New World of Children in Eighteenth Century England." *Past and Present* 67: 64–95.

Poster, Mark. (1986). "Darnton's Historiography." *Eighteenth Century* 27: 87–92.

——. (2001). *What's the Matter with the Internet?* Minneapolis: University of Minnesota Press.

Prendergast, Catherine. (2002). "The Economy of Literacy: How the Supreme Court Stalled the Civil Rights Movement." *Harvard Educational Review* 72: 206–29.

——. (2003). *Literacy and Racial Justice: The Politics of Learning after "Brown v. Board of Education."* Carbondale: Southern Illinois University Press.

Purcell-Gates, Victoria. (1995). *Other People's Words: The Cycle of Low Literacy.* Cambridge, Mass.: Harvard University Press.

Rabb, Theodore K., and Robert I. Rotberg, eds. (1982). *The New History: 1980s and Beyond.* Princeton: Princeton University Press.

Radway, Janice A. (1983). "Women Read the Romance." *Feminist Studies* 9: 53–78.

——. (1984a). "Interpretive Communities and Variable Literacies." *Daedalus* 113: 49–73.

——. (1984b). *Reading the Romance: Women, Patriarchy, and Popular Literature.* Chapel Hill: University of North Carolina Press.

——. (1986a). "Identifying Ideological Seams: Mass Culture, Analytic Method, and Political Practice." *Communication* 9: 93–123.

——. (1986b). "Reading is Not Eating: Mass-Produced Literature and the Theoretical, Methodological, and Political Consequences of a Metaphor." *Book Research Quarterly* 2: 7–29.

————. (1989). "The Book of the Month Club and the General Reader: On the Uses of Serious Fiction." In Davidson, *Reading in America*, 259–84.

————. (1997). *A Feeling for Books: The Book-Of-The-Month Club, Literary Taste, and Middle-Class Desire*. Chapel Hill: University of North Carolina Press.

Raven, James, Helen Small, and Naomi Tadmor, eds. (1996). *The Practice and Representation of Reading in England*. Cambridge: Cambridge University Press.

Rawski, Evelyn. (1979). *Education and Popular Literacy in Ch'ing China*. Ann Arbor: University of Michigan Press.

"Reading Old and New." (1983). *Daedalus* 112. Special Issue, Winter.

Richardson, Brian. (1994). *Print Culture in Renaissance Italy*. Cambridge: Cambridge University Press.

Roche, Daniel. (1987). *The People of Paris*. Berkeley and Los Angeles: University of California Press.

Rollo, David. (2000). *Glamorous Sorcery: Magic and Literacy in the High Middle Ages*. Minneapolis: University of Minnesota Press.

Rose, Jonathan. (1992). "Rereading the English Common Reader." *Journal of the History of Ideas* 53: 47–70.

————. (2001). *The Intellectual Life of the British Working Classes*. New Haven: Yale University Press.

Rose, Mike. (1989). *Lives on the Boundary: The Struggles of America's Underprepared*. New York: Free Press.

————. (1995). *Possible Lives: The Promise of Public Education in America*. Boston: Houghton Mifflin.

————. (2004). *The Mind at Work: Valuing the Intelligence of American Workers*. New York: Viking.

Royer, Daniel J. (1994). "The Process of Literacy as Communal Involvement in the Narratives of Frederick Douglass." *African American Review* 28: 363–74.

Royster, Jaqueline Jones. (2000). *Traces of a Stream: Literacy and Social Change among African American Women*. Pittsburgh: University of Pittsburgh Press.

Rubin, Joan Shelly. (1983). "'Information, Please!' Culture and Expertise in the Interwar Period." *American Quarterly* 35: 499–517.

————. (1985). "Self, Culture and Self-Culture in Modern America: The Early History of the Book-of-the-Month Club." *Journal of American History* 71: 782–806.

————. (1992). *The Making of Middle-Brow Culture*. Chapel Hill: University of North Carolina Press.

Ryan, Barbara, and Amy M. Thomas, eds. (2002). *Reading Acts: U.S. Readers' Interactions with Literature, 1800–1950*. Knoxville: University of Tennessee Press.

Saenger, Paul. (1977). *Space between Words: The Origins of Silent Reading*. Stanford: Stanford University Press.

Saljo, Roger, ed. (1988). *The Written World: Studies in Literate Thought and Action*. Berlin: Springer-Verlag.

Sanderson, Michael. (1972). "Literacy and Social Mobility in the Industrial Revolution in England." *Past and Present* 56: 75–104.

Schenda, Rudolf. (1970). *Volk ohne buch . . . 1770–1910*. Frankfurt: Vittorio Klostermann.

————. (1976). *Die lesestoffe der kleinen leute*. Munich: Beck.

Schofield, Roger S. (1968). "The Measurement of Literacy in Pre-industrial England." In *Literacy in Traditional Societies*, ed. Jack Goody, 311–25. Cambridge: Cambridge University Press.

————. (1973). "The Dimensions of Illiteracy in England, 1750–1850." *Explorations in Economic History* 10: 437–54.

Schudson, Michael. (1978). *Discovering the News*. New York: Basic Books.

Schutte, Anne Jacobson. (1976). "Carlo Ginzburg: Review Article." *Journal of Modern History* 48: 296–315.

———. (1981). "Printing, Piety, and the People in Italy." *Archive for Renaissance History* 71: 5–19.

"Scientific Literacy." (1983). *Daedalus*, Spring.

Scribner, R. W. (1981). *For the Sake of Simple Folk: Popular Propaganda for the German Reformation*. Cambridge: Cambridge University Press.

———. (1984). "Oral Culture and the Diffusion of Reformation Ideas." *History of European Ideas* 5: 237–56.

Scribner, Sylvia, and Michael Cole. (1973). "Cognitive Consequences of Formal and Informal Education." *Science* 182: 553–59.

———. (1981a). *The Psychology of Literacy*. Cambridge, Mass.: Harvard University Press.

———. (1981b). "Unpacking Literacy" In *Writing: The Nature, Development, and Teaching of Written Communication*, ed. Marcia Farr Whiteman, 127–37. Mahwah, N.J.: Lawrence Erlbaum Associates.

Searle, John. (1990). "The Storm over the University." *New York Review of Books*, 6 December, 34–42.

Selfe, Cynthia L. (1999). *Technology and Literacy in the Twenty-first Century*. Carbondale: Southern Illinois University Press.

Sewell, William H., Jr. (1985). *Structure and Mobility: The Men and Women of Marseille, 1820- 1870*. Cambridge: Cambridge University Press.

Sharpe, Kevin. (2000). *Reading Revolutions: The Politics of Reading in Early Modern England*. New Haven: Yale University Press.

Sheridan, Dorothy, Brian Street, and David Bloome, eds. (2000). *Writing Ourselves: Mass-Observation and Literacy Practices*. Cresskill: Hampton.

Shor, Ira. (1982). *Empowering Education: Critical Teaching for Social Change*. Chicago: University of Chicago Press.

Sicherman, Barbara. (1989). "Sense and Sensibility: A Case Study of Women's Reading in Late-Nineteenth-Century America." In Davidson, *Reading in America*, 201–25.

———. (1993). "Reading and Ambition: M. Carey Thomas and Female Heroism." *American Quarterly* 45: 73–103.

———. (1995). "Reading Little Women: The Many Lives of a Text." In *U.S. History as Women's History*, ed. Linda K. Kerber et al., 245–66. Chapel Hill: University of North Carolina Press.

Singh, Michael Garbutcheon. (1989). "A Counter-Hegemonic Orientation to Literacy in Australia." *Journal of Education* 171: 35–56.

Siskin, Clifford. (1998). *The Work of Writing: Literature and Social Change in Britain, 1700–1830*. Baltimore: Johns Hopkins University Press.

Slights, William W. E. (2001). *Managing Readers: Printed Marginalia and English Renaissance Books*. Ann Arbor: University of Michigan Press.

Soltow, Lee, and Edward Stevens. (1977). "Economic Aspects of School Participation in the U.S.," *Journal of Interdisciplinary History* 8: 221–44.

———. (1981). *The Rise of Literacy and the Common School in the United States*. Chicago: University of Chicago Press.

Spufford, Margaret. (1979). "First Steps in Literacy: The Reading and Writing Experiences of the Humblest Seventeenth-Century Spiritual Autobiographers." *Social History* 4: 407–35.

———. (1981). *Small Books and Pleasant Histories: Popular Fiction and Its Readership in Seventeenth-Century England*. London: Methuen.

Starkey, Kathryn. (2004). *Reading the Medieval Book*. Notre Dame: University of Notre Dame Press.

Starr, Paul. (2004). *The Creation of the Media.* New York: Basic Books.

St. Clair, William. (2004). *The Reading Nation in the Romantic Period.* Cambridge: Cambridge University Press.

Stearns, P. (1991). "The Challenge of 'Historical Literacy.'" *Perspectives: American Historical Association Newsletter* 29: 21–23.

———. (1993). *Meaning over Memory: Recasting the Teaching of Culture and History.* Chapel Hill: University of North Carolina Press.

Steedman, Carolyn. (1987). *The Tidy House.* London: Virago.

Stephens, W. B., ed. (1983). *Studies in the History of Literacy: England and North America.* Educational Administration and History Monographs, no. 13. Leeds: Museum of the History of Education, University of Leeds.

———. (1987). *Education, Literacy, and Society, 1830–1870.* Manchester: Manchester University Press.

Stevens, Edward. (1985). "Literacy and the Worth of Liberty." *Historical Social Research* 34: 65–81.

———. (1988). *Literacy, Law, and Social Order.* DeKalb: Northern Illinois University Press.

———. (1995). *The Grammar of the Machine: Technical Literacy and Early Industrial Expansion in the United States.* New Haven: Yale University Press.

Stevenson, Louise L. (1990–91). "Prescription and Reality: Reading Advisors and Reading Practice, 1860–1880." *Book Research Quarterly* 6: 43–61.

Stock, Brian. (1983). *The Implications of Literacy: Written Language and Models of Interpretation in the Eleventh and Twelfth Centuries.* Princeton: Princeton University Press.

———. (1990). *Listening for the Text.* Baltimore: Johns Hopkins University Press.

———. (1996). *Augustine the Reader.* Cambridge, Mass.: Harvard University Press.

———. (2001). *After Augustine.* Philadelphia: University of Pennsylvania Press.

Stone, Lawrence. (1969). "Literacy and Education in England, 1640–1900." *Past and Present* 42: 69–139.

———. (1979). "The Revival of Narrative: Reflections on a New Old History." *Past and Present* 85: 3–24.

Stout, Harry S. (1977). "Religion, Communications, and the Ideological Origins of the American Revolution." *William and Mary Quarterly* 34: 519–41.

Strauss, Gerald. (1978). *Luther's Home of Learning.* Baltimore: Johns Hopkins University Press.

———. (1984). "Lutheranism and Literacy: A Reassessment." In *Religion and Society in Early Modern Europe,* ed. Kaspar Von Greyerz, 109–23. London: Allen and Unwin.

Strauss, Gerald, and Richard Gawthrop. (1984). "Protestantism and Literacy in Early Modern Germany." *Past and Present* 104: 31–55.

Street, Brian. (1984). *Literacy in Theory and Practice.* Cambridge: Cambridge University Press.

———. (1993). *Cross-Cultural Approaches to Literacy.* Cambridge: Cambridge University Press.

———. (1995). *Social Literacies: Critical Approaches to Literacy in Development, Ethnography, and Education.* London: Longman.

———. (2001). "The New Literacy Studies." In *Literacy: A Critical Sourcebook,* ed. Ellen Cushman, Eugene R. Kintgen, Barry M. Kroll, and Mike Rose, 430–42. Boston: Bedford/St. Martin's.

Stuckey, Elspeth. (1991). *The Violence of Literacy.* Portsmouth: Boynton/Cook.

Svenbro, Jesper. (1993). *Phrasikleia: An Anthropology of Reading in Ancient Greece.* Ithaca: Cornell University Press.

Swearingen, Jan. (1991). *Rhetoric and Irony: Western Literacy and Western Lies.* New York: Oxford University Press.

Tannen, Deborah, ed. (1982). *Spoken and Written Language: Exploring Orality and Literacy.* Norwood: Ablex.

Thomas, Keith. (1986). "The Meaning of Literacy in Early Modern England." In *The Written Word: Literacy in Transition,* ed. Gerd Baumann, 97–131. Oxford: Oxford University Press.

Thomas, Rosalind. (1989). *Oral Tradition and Written Record in Classical Athens.* Cambridge: Cambridge University Press.

———. (1992). *Literacy and Orality in Ancient Greece.* Cambridge: Cambridge University Press.

Thompson, Paul. (1975). *The Edwardians.* Bloomington: Indiana University Press.

———. (1978). *The Voice of the Past: Oral History.* Oxford: Oxford University Press.

Thornton, Tamara Plakins. (1996). *Handwriting in America: A Cultural History.* New Haven: Yale University Press.

Todd, Emmanuel. (1987). *The Causes of Progress.* Oxford: Blackwell.

Tompkins, Jane. (1985). *Sensational Designs: The Cultural Work of American Fiction, 1790–1860.* New York: Oxford University Press.

Tortella, Gabriel, ed. (1990). *Education and Economic Development since the Industrial Revolution.* Valencia, Spain: Generalitat Valencia.

Toth, Istvan Gyorgy. (2000). *Literacy and Written Culture in Early Modern Europe.* Budapest: Central European University Press.

Tuman, Myron C. (1987). *A Preface to Literacy: An Inquiry into Pedagogy, Practice, and Progress.* Tuscaloosa: University of Alabama Press.

———. (1993). *Word Perfect.* Pittsburgh: University of Pittsburgh Press.

Van Slyck, Abigail A. (1995). *Free to All: Carnegie Libraries and American Culture, 1890–1920.* Chicago: University of Chicago Press.

Vinao, Frago A., ed. (1989). "Alfabetizacion." *Revista de educacion,* 288.

Vincent, David. (1981). *Bread, Knowledge, and Freedom: A Study of Nineteenth-Century Working-Class Autobiography.* London: Europa.

———. (1989). *Literacy and Popular Culture: England, 1750–1914.* Cambridge: Cambridge University Press.

———. (2000). *The Rise of Mass Literacy: Reading and Writing in Modern Europe.* Cambridge: Polity.

Wagner, Daniel A. (1990). "Literacy Assessment in the Third World: An Overview and Proposed Schemes for Survey Use." *Comparative Education Review* 34: 112–38.

Walvin, James. (1978). *Leisure and Society.* London: Longman.

Warner, Michael. (1990). *The Letters of the Republic: Publication and the Public Sphere in Eighteenth-Century America.* Cambridge, Mass.: Harvard University Press.

Warner, William B. (1998). *Licensing Entertainment: The Elevation of Novel Reading, 1684–1750.* Berkeley: University of California Press.

Watt, Teresa. (1991). *Cheap Print and Popular Piety, 1550–1640.* Cambridge: Cambridge University Press.

Webb, Robert K. (1955). *The British Working Class Reader.* London: Allen and Unwin.

Webber, Thomas. (1978). *Deep like the Rivers: Education in the Slave Quarter Community.* New York: Norton.

Weber, Eugen. (1976). *Peasants into Frenchmen.* Stanford: Stanford University Press.

Welch, Kathleen E. (1999). *Electric Rhetoric: Classical Rhetoric, Oralism, and a New Literacy.* Cambridge, Mass.: MIT Press.

West, E. G. (1975). *Education and the Industrial Revolution.* London and Sydney: Batsford. Toronto: Copp Clark.

———. (1978). "Literacy and the Industrial Revolution." *Economic History Review* 31: 369–83.

Wheale, Nigel. (1999). *Writing and Society . . . Britain, 1590–1660.* London: Routledge.

Whiteman, Marcia Farr, ed. (1981). *Writing: The Nature, Development and Teaching of Written Composition.* Vol. 1, *Variation in Writing.* Hillsdale: Lawrence Erlbaum.

Wiles, R. M. (1968). "Middle Class Literacy in Eighteenth Century England." In *Studies in the Eighteenth Century,* ed. R. F. Brissenden, 49–66. Camberra: Australian National University Press.

———. (1972). "Provincial Culture in Early Georgian England." In *The Triumph of Culture,* ed. Paul Fritz and David Williams, 49–68. Toronto: Hakkert.

Williams, Heather Andrea. (2005). *Self-Taught: African American Education in Slavery and Freedom.* Chapel Hill: University of North Carolina Press.

Williams, Susan S. (1990). "Widening the World: Susan Warner, Her Readers, and the Assumption of Authorship." *American Quarterly* 42: 565–86.

Willinsky, John. (1990). *The New Literacy: Redefining Reading and Writing in the Schools.* New York: Routledge.

Winchester, Ian. (1978). "How Many Ways to Universal Literacy?" Paper presented to the Ninth World Congress of Sociology, Uppsala, and Seminar on the History of Literacy in Post-Reformation Europe, University of Leicester.

———. (1990a). "Beyond the Revised Standard Picture of Literacy." Paper presented to the Social Science History Association, Minneapolis, 1990.

———. (1990b). "The Standard Picture of Literacy and its Critics." *Comparative Education Review* 34: 21–40.

Wormald, Patrick. (1977). "The Uses of Literacy in Anglo-Saxon England and Its Neighbours." *Transactions of the Royal Historical Society,* 5th ser., 27: 47–80.

Wrightson, Keith, and David Levine. (1979). *Poverty and Piety.* New York and London: Academic.

Wyss, Hilary E. (2000). *Writing Indians: Literacy, Christianity, and Native Community in Early America.* Amherst: University of Massachusetts Press.

Young, Morris. (2004). *Re/Visions: Asian American Literacy Narratives as a Rhetoric of Citizenship.* Carbondale: Southern Illinois University Press.

Zambelli, Paola. (1985). "From Menocchio to Piero Della Francesa: The Work of Carlo Ginzburg." *Historical Journal* 28: 983–99.

Zaret, David. (2000). *Origins of Democratic Culture.* Princeton: Princeton University Press.

Zboray, Ronald. (1993). *A Fictive People: Antebellum Economic Development and the American Reading Public.* New York: Oxford University Press.

Zboray, Ronald J., and Mary Saracin Zboray. (2005). *Literary Dollars and Social Sense: A Peoples' History of the Mass Market Book.* New York: Routledge.

———. (2006). *Everyday Ideas: Socioliterary Experience among Antebellum New Englanders.* Knoxville: University of Tennessee Press.

CONTRIBUTORS

HARVEY J. GRAFF is Ohio Eminent Scholar in Literacy Studies and Professor of English and History at the Ohio State University, where he is developing the Literacy Studies @ OSU initiative. A comparative social historian, Graff is noted internationally for his research and teaching on the history of literacy; the history of children, adolescents, and youth; and urban history and studies, among his areas of interest. His books include *The Literacy Myth: Literacy and Social Structure in the Nineteenth-Century City*; *The Legacies of Literacy: Continuities and Contradictions in Western Culture and Society*; *The Labyrinths of Literacy: Reflections on Literacy Past and Present*; *Conflicting Paths: Growing Up in America*; and *The Dallas Myth: The Making and Unmaking of an American City*. In 1999–2000, Graff served as president of the Social Science History Association.

MICHAEL T. CLANCHY taught medieval history at the University of Glasgow from 1964 to 1985 and has been a researcher at the Institute for Historical Research, University College London, and the Warburg Institute. A legal and social historian, he is author of the popular textbook *England and Its Rulers*; *Abelard: A Medieval Life*; and *Medieval Mentalities and Primitive Legal Practice*.

ELIZABETH L. EISENSTEIN is Alice Freedman Palmer Professor of History Emerita at the University of Michigan. Known internationally for her work on the history of early printing, she is the author of many books, including, *Grub Street Abroad: Aspects of the Eighteenth-Century French Cosmopolitan Press* and *The Printing Revolution in Early Modern Europe*.

ANTHONY T. GRAFTON is Henry Putnam University Professor of History at Princeton University. His many books include a study of the scholarship and chronology of the foremost classical scholar of the late Renaissance, Joseph Scaliger (2 vols.); *Leon Battista Alberti: Master Builder of the Italian Renaissance*; *Defenders of the Text: The Traditions of Scholarship in the Age of Science, 1450–1800*; *Commerce with the Classics: Ancient Books and Renaissance Readers*; *Forgers and Critics: Creativity and Duplicity in Western Scholarship*, and with Lisa Jardine, *From Humanism to the Humanities: Education and the Liberal Arts in Fifteenth- and Sixteenth-Century Europe*. He is a corresponding fellow of the British Academy and a recipient of many scholarly awards.

NATALIE ZEMON DAVIS, a cultural and social historian of early modern France, is professor emerita of history at Princeton and currently adjunct professor at the University of Toronto. She is a pioneering exemplar of interdisciplinary cultural history. Among her best-known books are *Society and Culture in Early Modern France*; *The Return of* Martin Guerre; *Fiction in the Archives: Pardon Tales and Their Tellers in Sixteenth-Century France*; *Women on the Margins: Three Seventeenth-Century Lives*; and *Trickster Travels: A Sixteenth-Century Muslim between Worlds.*

ROBERT SCRIBNER has been University Lecturer and Reader in the Social History of Early Modern Europe at Cambridge University and is now professor of Modern European Christianity at the Divinity School of Harvard University. Among his many books are *For the Sake of Simple Folk: Popular Propaganda for the German Reformation*; *Popular Culture and Popular Movements in Reformation Germany*; *The Reformation in National Context*; and *Germany: A New Social and Economic History.*

RAB HOUSTON is professor in the School of History at the University of St. Andrews. He has published in many areas of European, English, and Scottish social history including literacy, education, mental illness, and demography. Among his books are *Scottish Literacy and the Scottish Identity: Literacy and Society in Scotland and England, 1660–1850*; *Literacy in Early Modern Europe: Culture and Education, 1500–1800*; *Social Change in the Age of Enlightenment: Edinburgh, 1660–1760*; and *Madness and Society in Eighteenth-Century Scotland.*

MARGARET SPUFFORD is a distinguished historian and a Fellow of the British Academy. She is internationally renowned for her books on early modern social history, covering religion, literacy, trade, and poverty. They include *Contrasting Communities: English Villagers in the Sixteenth and Seventeenth Centuries*; *Small Books and Pleasant Histories: Popular Fiction and Its Readership in Seventeenth-Century England*; *Figures in the Landscape: Rural Society in England 1500–1700*. In 1996 she was also awarded the OBE for services to social history and disabled students.

EGIL JOHANSSON is University Professor Emeritus at Umeå University in Sweden, where he founded the Demographic Data Base, the Research Archives, and the Department of Religious Studies. He is the author of *The History of Literacy in Sweden, in Comparison with Some Other Countries* and many pioneering historical studies in Swedish. *Alphabeta Varia: Orality, Reading and Writing in the History of Literacy: Festschrift in Honour of Egil Johansson on the Occasion of His 65th Birthday, March 24, 1998*, edited by Daniel Lindmark, collects some of Johansson's most important papers in English.

FARLEY GRUBB is a professor of economics at the University of Delaware and has published widely on economic history, immigration, labor and labor contracts, literacy, and monetary policy and currency in early America and the Atlantic world. With Susan E. Klepp and Anne Pfaelzer de Ortiz, he edited *Souls for Sale: Two German Redemptioners Come to Revolutionary America: The Life Stories of John Frederick Whitehead and Johann Carl Büttner.*

ROGER S. SCHOFIELD is director emeritus of the Cambridge Group for the History of Population and Social Structure, where for many years he worked with Peter Laslett and E. A. Wrigley, and is a Fellow of Clare College. A constitutional and demographic historian, he is the author and coauthor of several books, including *The Population History of England, 1541–1871: A Reconstruction*; *English Population History from Family Reconstruction*; and *Taxation under the Early Tudors.*

JANET CORNELIUS, was professor of history at Danville Area Community College in Danville, Illinois. She is the author of several books, including *When I Can Read My Title Clear: Literacy, Slavery, and Religion in the Antebellum South.*

BARBARA SICHERMAN is the William R. Kenan, Jr., Professor of American Institutions and Values Emerita at Trinity College. A historian of American medicine, women, and culture, she is author of *Alice Hamilton: A Life in Letters*; coeditor of *Notable American Women: The Modern Period*; and author of a series of studies of nineteenth-century American women readers.

DEBORAH BRANDT, a professor of English at the University of Wisconsin–Madison, is a well-known literacy scholar and author of *Literacy as Involvement: The Acts of Writers, Readers, and Texts* and *Literacy in American Lives.* She is the recipient of the University of Louisville Grawemeyer Award in Education, the Modern Language Association Mina Shaughnessy Prize, and the Conference on College Composition and Communication Outstanding Book Award. She is at work on a study of writing in the late twentieth- and early twenty-first-century United States.

ANNE HAAS DYSON is a professor of curriculum and instruction at the University of Illinois at Urbana-Champaign. Among her many publications are *The Multiple Worlds of Child Writers*; *Social Worlds of Children Learning to Write*; *Writing Superheroes*; and *The Brothers and Sisters Learn to Write.* Her research focuses on language and literacy development in the early childhood years.

INDEX

Page numbers in italics denote figures and tables.

Abbayes de Jeunesse, 134
Abbeys of Misrule, 148–49
ABC-book (Sweden), 248–49, 250
activist education, 31–32
Adam of Eynsham, 43
Addams, Jane, 347
adolescents, reading and, 341
adult literacy, 24–25
advanced contractarian society, 368–69
Aelfric, 51
Aesop's Fables, 135
Af Forsell, Carl, 238, 239
African Americans. *See* children, African American; school literacy; slaves
age-grading, 23, 24
agricultural manuals, 138–40
Alberti, Leone Battista, 93
Alexander, 70
Alfred, 51
almanacs, French, 127, 131–34
alphabetic literacy, 15, 21, 34
Alton Locke (Kingsley), 340
America, colonial, 3, 10; creolean degeneracy, 272–73, 280–84, 291, 295n12; economic models, 272–73, 284–89, 295–96n14; English immigrants, 278–79, 294n6; French-Canadian immigrants, 278–79, 294n6; German immigrants, 278–79, 287, 294n6; intergenerational transmission of literacy, 279–80, 285, 290; levels of literacy, causes of, 278–80; literacy estimates, 273–78; nonlinear trends in regional literacy, 280–84, 281, 292, 294n8; population density, 285–89, 286, 292, 295n12; regional differences in literacy, 273, 274–75; servant contracts, 290–91; supply vs. demand model of growth, 284–89, 295–96n14, 295nn11–13; temporary declines in literacy, 272, 280; testing economic models, 289–92; urban/rural division, 274–75, 288, 290–91; wealth and literacy, 287–88; wills, 293n4, 294–95n5
America, Victorian: constraints on women, 341; self-study, 346–47; social problems, literature

about, 340, 345, 355–56n66; true womanhood, images of, 334–35
amplification, 96–98
Anabaptism, 166, 169, 170
anachronism, 117; in conveyances, 57–58; in medieval scholarship, 45–46
analysis, patterns of, 242–43, 260–62, 269
Anderson, Christine, 372
animation, 380, 382–83, 395
Anselm, St., 61–63, 69, 71
apprentices, 322–23, 357
appropriation: by children, 379–80; of Michael Jordan, 385, 388, 406–7; sponsors of literacy and, 361, 370–75
archetypum, 116–17
Aristotle, 118
ars dictaminis, 72
Ars Minor (Donatus), 70
artisans, early modern France: as authors, 145–47; and book ownership, 142–43; literacy rates of, 141–42; reading groups, 144–45
Astrologie des Rustiques (Mizaud), 138
audience, 128; fiction, response to, 344–48; participation, 163–65; for sermons, 162–65
audit, as term, 68
Auger, Emond, 150
authors: anonymous public and, 146–47n; *archetypum* and, 116–17; artisans, tradesmen, and women, 145–47; impact of printing on, 93–94, 106, 116; physicians as, 146, 151–53
autobiographers, spiritual: boarding at grammar schools, 228–29; childhood reading ability, 209–12, 219; deaths of parents, 218–19, 220, 230, 236n21; sign-literacy, 208, 225–26; sons of yeomen, 207–9, 226–32; university students, 231–33, 236n18; women, 230–31
axioms, Scholastic, 45

Bachelor's Blunder, A, 339, 340
Bacon, Roger, 70
Bailyn, B., 282–83
ballads, 170–71

Bangs, Benjamin, 227, 233
Bathhurst, Elizabeth, 230–31
Baxter, Richard, 217, 225
Beaulieu, abbot of, 68
Beauvais, Vincent of, 118
Becket, Thomas, 51, 71
Bedfordshire, England, 306–8, *308*
benefit of clergy, 48
Béroald, François, 144
Best, Henry, 213
Beutler, Corinne, 139n
Bevis of Southampton, 217–18
Bewley, George, 227
biases, 20–21, 22
Bible: French vernacular, 136–38, 150–51; vernacular versions of, 98, 119, 242–43; wicked,
    of 1631, 86
Bible literacy, 315
Bibliothèque bleue, 127–28, 136n, 149
Billanovich, Giuseppe, 118, 124n26
Biondo, Flavio, 111, 118
births, recording, 38–39
Birunguccio, Vannoccio, 144
Bisticci, Vespasiano da, 112
Blackmore, R. D., 346
boarding school stories, 341–42
Boarstall Horn, 58
Bollème, Geneviève, 127, 156n15
Boniface VIII, 47, 66–67
Book of Hours, 132, 142, 143
book ownership, France, 129, 131–32, 142–43
books: as carriers of relationships, 128–29; chapbooks, 217–18; cost of, in early modern France,
    143–44, 156n12, 159n33; format of, 87–88; as
    revered, 349; sharing of, 143–44; as symbolic
    objects, 56–57; values and ideas in, 127–28
bookshops, 115
Bornheinrich, Johann, 165–66, 169
Boston, Thomas, 211, 231
Botstein, Leon, 19–20
Bourde, André, 159n31
Bourdieu, Pierre, 376nn2, 6
Bourgeois, Louise, 147
Bracciolini, Poggio, 102n36, 112–13
Bracton, 60–61
Braillier, Pierre, 146
Branch, Raymond, 362–64
Bray, Henry de, 42
broadsides, 112
Bruni, Leonardo, 111, 118
Bunyan, John, 217–18
Burckhardt, Jacob, 93, 102n38, 111
bureaucracy, 92
Bury St. Edmunds abbey, 42

Cade, William, 50
Calendrier. See *Grand calendrier et compost des
    bergers*
Calendrier historial, 137–38
calligraphy, 86
Calvinism, 135–36, 183, 189
capitalist industries, 86–87
Carleton, Thomas, 216–17
Castle Daly (Keary), 343, 355n62
Catechism of 1689 (Sweden), 249
censorship, 172
chansons rustiques, 134–35
chapbooks, 217–18
Charity Schools, 300, 311, 313–14n18
Charles XI, 238, 239
Charter of the Forest, 65
charters, 54–56, 61
Chauliac, Guy de, 151
Chaytor, H. J., 68
children, 3–4; and deaths of parents, 218–19, 220,
    230, 236n21; institutionalization of, 23–24; reading ability of, 209–12, 219; white, teach slaves to
    read, 319–20; in workhouses, 212–13; working
    age, 212–15, 218–19, 223–24, 235–36n13
children, African American, 11; appropriation of
    media genres by, 379–80; cultural landscapes
    and group singing of, 390–92; fake siblings of,
    at school, 385–86, 396–97; ideological awareness of, 380, 408; instructional dialogue, use
    of, 400–3; media play and literacy learning
    by, 383–84; production of popular culture by,
    379–80; recontextualization processes and,
    380, 387–88, 398. *See also* school literacy
Choppin, René, 140
Christianity, expansion of, 40–41
Chubb, Thomas, 220–22
Church Law of 1686, 239, 244, 249, 253, 255
Cicero, 40, 41, 118
civilization, condition of, 15
Clanchy, Michael T., 9
Clark, Peter, 235n11
clergy, literacy and, 39–44, 52–54
clerical work, 372–75
clerici, 40–44
Clericis Laicos (Boniface VIII), 47
clericus, 40–44, 48
cliché, as term, 96
Cnut, law of, 51
Coach Bombay play, 394
cognitive psychology, 21
Cole, Michael, 21, 36n7
collaborative language arts, 31, 400–3
college curriculum, 33
Collège de la Trinité, 141

Comenius, Amos, 250
Commelin, Jerome, 114
commonsense knowledge, 22
communities, disciplinary, 108
comparative history, 1, 3–5
compradrazgo, 360–61
consciousness, 33
Conventicle Edict of 1726, 250
Copernicus, 88
Cornelius, Janet, 10
correctors, 114–15
Counter-Reformation, 150–51
Credo, 51, 53
Cremin, Lawrence, 376–77n9
creolean degeneracy, 272–73, 280–84, 291, 295n12
Cressy, David, 191, 208, 212, 226, 233, 235n7
crises of literacy, 1–2, 12–14, 27; sponsors of literacy and, 361, 365–70; strands of, 14–16
critical literacy, 29–32, 360
critique, 33
cross-cultural interchanges, 82–85; early modern France, 140, 152–53
Crouch, William, 227
Crowland abbey roundel, 57–58
Crusius, Martinus, 114
cultural capital, 376n6
cultural literacy, 12, 13, 15, 29
cultural studies, 407
Cyriac of Acona, 118

D2: The Mighty Ducks, 394
Daisy Chain, The (Yonge), 344–45
Davis, Natalie Zemon, 9
Decades (Biondo), 111
De Humani Corporis Fabrica (Vesalius), 116
De la Mare, Albinia, 112
Deloney, Thomas, 212
Demografisk Databas (Demographic Database), 261
deskilling of workers, 357
desocialization, permanent, 30–31
developmental research, 381
Dewsbury, William, 227
dictating, 71–72
Didactica Magna (Comenius), 250
Didactica (Ratke), 250
discussion groups: German Reformation, 166–69, 176–77; spiritual autobiographers and, 224, 226
dissemination, as term, 82, 83–84
Doctrinale (Alexander), 70
documents, symbolic objects used in transfer, 55–61
domesticity, cult of, 334

Donation of Constantine, 63
Donatus, 70
Dore, Ronald, 20
Douglass, Frederick, 322–23, 325
du Bellay, Joachim, 149
Duck, Stephen, 222–23
du Fail, Noel, 131n
Dumont, Nicolas, 147, 149
Dyson, Anne Haas, 11

Eadmer, 61–63, 69, 71
East Pakistan, 301
economic development, 2, 4; education and, 299–300, 309–12; expectations and, 19–20; literacy as, 11, 19, 27, 309, 358
economic models, 272–73, 284–89, 295–96n14
economies, 376n2; differential, 364; twentieth century, 357–58
Edinburgh, 188, 190, 196–97
editing, 87–89
Edmund of Abingdon, St., 43
Edmundson, William, 227
education: as contested territory, 13–14; cost of, 300, 309–10; economic growth and, 299–300, 309–12; elementary, 25–26; as human capital formation, 299–300; institutions (1300–1500), 112; purposeful educational measures, 241–42. *See also* schools
Edward I, 47, 65
Edward the Confessor, 58
Egyptian hieroglyphs, 84
Eisenstein, Elisabeth L., 9, 147; accounts of intellectual advances, 119–20; main arguments of, 106–9; problems of method and approach, 110–13; Renaissance scholarship, view of, 117–19; secondary sources, use of, 109–10, 120
elementary/basic literacy, 15, 18–19
employer backlash, 368–69
employers, as sponsors of literacy, 372–75
Emser, Jerome, 172
England: geographical variations in literacy, 304; illiteracy rates, nineteenth century, *303*, 304–10, *305*; immigrants to America, 278–79, 294n6; market towns, 307–8; marriage registers, 301–4, *303*, 313n12; men, literacy rates, *305*, 305–7, *308*, 310; occupational hierarchy, 308–10, *309*; peasants, 50–52; pre-industrial, sign-literacy, 301–7, *308*
English Protestation Oath of 1642, 184
Erastian policies, 91, 103n41
Erikson, Erik, 341
errata, 85–86
Erreurs Populaires (*Popular Errors*; Joubert), 152–53

essayist literacy, 369
Estienne, Charles, 114, 131, 139
Estienne, Nicole, 147, 149
Estienne, Robert I., 146n
Estoire de Waldef, 69
ethnicity, 25, 26
ethnographic studies, 11
Eugeneius III, 67
Europe: American colonies, literacy and, 272, 294n6; immigrants to America, 278–79, 287, 294n6; linguistic map of, 90–91; literacy (1633–1840), 273–78, 274–75, 276–77; Sweden, background for literacy, 242–43
Evans, Arise, 218–19, 220, 227
Evelyn, John, 210
Exeter, statute of, 47
expectations, 19, 23, 26

Federal Writers Project, 316, 324
feedback effect, 97
feudal heirs, proving age of, 38–40
fiction, reader response to, 344–48
financiers, 51
Finland, 239, 241
Finnegan, Ruth, 22
flash-cards, 216
forgeries, 63
For the Love of the Game (Greenfield), 406–7, 410n4
Fothergill, Jessie, 355n58
foundationism, 25–26
Foundations of Early Modern Europe, 1460–1559, The (Rice), 120
Fox, George, 227
France, early modern, 3, 9, 105n62; people, defined, 126–27, 129–30, 159n32; reading groups, 144–45; rural literacy, 130–32; types of books, 129; values and ideas in books, 127–28; vernacular Bible and, 136–38, 150–51; women, 126, 130, 147. *See also* peasants, France; printing, early modern France
Francis, St., 63
François I, 127
Frankfurt bookfair, 115
Freemasons, 96
Free Reading Room for Women, 336
Freire, Paulo, 29–30
Fretwell, James, 210, 211, 228
Froben, Johann, 110, 113
frontiers, linguistic, 97–98
functional literacy, 12, 14, 15, 20, 331n12
Furet, François, 27

Galbraith, V. H., 48–49
genres, 207, 379–80, 382, 393

gentry, 50
geographical stratification, 173–74, 304
Gerald of Wales, 43, 44, 53, 54, 63; Innocent III, audiences with, 67–68; *Topography of Ireland*, 71
German Peasants' War, 174–75
German Reformation, 9–10, 161; content of sermons, 164; context of printing, 162; discussion meetings, 166–67; friends and kinship, role in, 169–70; geographical stratification, 173–74; hearing the Word, 162, 164, 165–66; illiteracy, 161; inns, meeting in, 167–68, 169; open-endedness of discussion, 176–77; peasants and, 174–76; preaching revival, 162–63; printed pamphlets, 163, 165–66, 167, 170, 175; public opinion, 161, 162, 171–77; public witness, 171, 173; rapid diffusion of ideas, 161–62; singing, role in, 170–71; Twelve Articles, 174–76; workplace discussions, 168–69
Germans: American-born, 283–84; immigrants to Pennsylvania, 278–79, 287, 294n6
Gilles, Brother, 151
Giovanni of Verona, 117
Giroux, Henry, 33
Glanvill, Ranulf de, 50
Glasgow, 196, 197
Godric, St., 51, 52–54
Golden Legend, 143
Goody, Jack, 22, 128
Goosebumps, 400–401
Gospel book, as symbolic object, 56–57
Graff, Harvey J., 1, 9, 29, 329n1
Grafton, Anthony T., 9
Gramsci, Antonio, 33
Grand calendrier et compost des bergers (*Shepherds' Calendar*), 127, 132–34, 156n15
Grand' Monarchie (de Seyssel), 127
graphicacy, 15
"Great Boke of Statutes," 88, 92
Great Dichotomy/Great Divide, 8, 18–19, 22
Great Seal, 57
Greek, preservation of, 90, 102–3n38
Greenfield, Eloise, 406–7, 410n4
Gregorian calendar reform, 139
Gregory VII, 41
guilds, 169
Guillemeau, Jacques, 138
Gutenberg Bible, 70
Guthlac, St., 57–58
Gwin, Anne, 210–11

Häberlin, Hans, 174
Haller, William, 105n61
Hamelin, Philibert, 136

Hamilton, A. Holman, 352n25
Hamilton, Agnes, 339, 340
Hamilton, Alice, 335–37, 343–46
Hamilton, Edith, 335
Hamilton, Emerine Holman, 336
Hamilton, Gertrude Pond, 337, 344
Hamilton, Jessie, 336, 339–40
Hamilton, Katherine, 336
Hamilton, Margaret, 336
Hamilton, Margaret Vance, 337, 339, 351n11
Hamilton, Montgomery, 337, 344, 351n12, 352n25
Hamilton, Norah, 336
Hamilton family, 335–38; antimarriage sentiment, 344, 355n59; choice of reading materials, 337–38; literary allusions, 341–43; tendency to fictionalize, 342–43, 345
Hauser, Henri, 159–60n37
hearing, 52–54; anachronisms in conveyances, 57–58; in charters, 54–55; colloquial usage of term, 68–69; in litigation, 55–56; reading and, 69–71. *See also* listening; memory; seeing
Heinsius, Nicolaas, 115
Henry I, 42, 48, 59, 61–63
Henry II, 48–50, 73
Henry III, 42, 64–65
Herbert of Bosham, 71
Hermes Trismegistus (Thoth), 84, 104n57
hermetic corpus, 84, 104n57
Heywood, Oliver, 233
Hirsch, E. D., 29
history of literacy, 1–2, 6–8, 12, 14–15; lessons from, 17–32; ongoing transformations in, 368–69; provenance of past, 32–33; repetition, 30
History of the Florentine People (Bruni), 111
Hoggart, Richard, 153
Holland, Norman, 345
Holman, William Steele, 352n25
Holsey, Luciusto, 323, 324
homo universalis, 93
Hornschuch, Jerome, 106–7, 114
Houel, Nicolas, 146
Houston, Rab, 10
Hughes, H. Stuart, 103n39
husbandmen, as term, 236n19
Hustavla, 243–48, 245, 270n6

Iceland, 243
iconography, 57–58
imagination, 33
immigrants, 4, 187, 278–79, 287, 294n6
immortality, print-made, 93–94
imperialism, 22

incunabula, 87
Index, 96
individualism, 92–94, 338
information economy, 372
Innocent III, 63, 67–68
inns, religious discussions in, 167–68, 169
Inquest of Sheriffs, 49
intellect, 22–23
interdisciplinary literacy, 31
interdisciplinary studies, 1–5
interpretive communities, 11, 335
inventions, 92
inventories after death, 131–32, 143–44
Isidore of Seville, 70

Jehovah's Witnesses, 373, 374
Jenkins, H., 382–383
Jessey, Henry, 231
Jesuits, 151
Joachimsthaler Articles, 175
Jocelin of Brakelond, 42, 68
Johansson, Egil, 10, 199
John, King, 49, 65
John of Lexington, 44–45
John of Salisbury, 43, 54, 56, 70, 72–73
Jordan, Michael, children's appropriation of, 385, 388, 406–7
Joubert, Laurent, 152
journeymen, 141, 148

kalendarium, 68
Katz, Michael, 13, 14
Kaye, Henry, 33
Keary, Annie, 343
Ker, N. R., 70
Kett, Joseph, 357
Kilpatrick, W. H., 281
king of Sweden, 244–45
kings of England, knowledge of Latin, 48–50, 72–73
kinship connections, 169–70
kleros, 40
knights, 40, 44, 50
Knights Hospitaller, 58, 60
knives, as symbolic objects, 58–60
knowledge industry, 90
Koberger, Anton, 113
Koestler, Arthur, 83
Kozol, Jonathan, 20
Kristeller, Paul O., 102n36, 112, 116–17, 123n22

Labarre, Albert, 131n
Labé, Louise, 126, 147
La Croix du Maine, François de, 149

laicus, 40–44
laity, literacy of, 44–48
Langdale, Josiah, 223–25, 226
laos, 40
Latin: as artificial language, 70; challenges to supremacy of, 47–48; clergy and, 39–44, 52–54; kings of England and, 48–50, 72–73; knowledge of among nonchurchmen, 48–54; peasants acquainted with, 51
Lauber, Diebold, 112
layci, 39
lectio, 69, 70–71
Le Fournier, André, 127
legalistic form of literacy, 368–69
LeRoy Ladurie, Emmanuel, 130, 137, 142
letters, 54, 56
Levine, Kenneth, 14
liberating literacy, 315
libraries: established by women, 334, 336; personal, 351–52n12; of private scholars, 112–13
licensing and privileges, 92
Life of St. Alban (Paris), 57
Life of St. Anselm (Eadmer), 69, 71
Life of St. Margaret, 70
Lindisfarne, Holy Island of, 58–59
listening, 67–73; in Hustavla world, 244–46; reading as, 69, 70–71. *See also* hearing
literacies, 15, 21, 30, 36n7
literacy: acquisition, 3–4, 23–25, 296n15; complexity of, 18–20; costs of acquiring, 290–91, 295–96n14; differences between Protestants and Catholics, 98, 296n15; direct tests for, 301; as economic development, 11, 19, 27, 309, 358; essayist form of, 369; as historical variable, 3–5, 16–18; hybridity of practices, 371, 399; impacts of, 8, 19; as individual attainment, 11; legalistic form of, 368–69; as manipulation of symbolic material, 383–84; as market, 285–289; mass, 24–25, 278, 292, 374; meanings of, 4–5; medieval attitudes toward, 72–73; minimal, 46–48; modern vs. medieval assessments of, 46–48; patterns of analysis, 241–42, 260–62, 269; presumption of value neutrality, 20–22; as resistance, 326, 360; restrictions on, 24; strong theories of, 5, 19; as unproblematic, 18–19; upward mobility and, 360; as valued commodity, 361
Literacy in American Lives (Brandt), 11
literacy myth, 10, 19
litteratus, meaning of, 40–44
Little Women (Alcott), 344
livery of seisin, 58, 60–61
Locke, John, 212
Lockridge, Kenneth A., 199

Longchamp, Nigel de, 40, 41
Lopez, Dora, 362–63
Lorna Doone (Blackmore), 346
Lowery, Dwayne, 365–70
Lowick, chapel of, 58–59
Luther, Martin, 108, 110, 115, 119, 165, 250; ballads about, 170–71

magical arts, 83–84, 99n11
Magna Carta, 64, 65–67, 92
Main, Gloria, 374
Mandrou, Robert, 127–28, 141
Manuzio, Aldo, 113, 115
Manuzio, Paolo, 114, 123n20
Map, Walter, 43–44, 50, 53, 67, 71
mappae mundi, 83
maps, 83, 98n5
Marcourt, Antoine de, 152
market, 26; literacy as, 285–89
marketing areas, 173–74
market towns, 307–8
Marot, Clément, 135
marriage, Sweden, 238, 239, 246, 248
marriage registers, England, 301–2, *303*, 313n12
Martin, Henri-Jean, 129
Massey, D., 382
mass literacy, 24–25, 278, 292, 374
master-printer, 108–9
maternal language, 67
Matilda (Henry I's queen), 70
Maurer, Johann, 173
McKenzie, D. F., 114
media, 382–83; children's play informed by, 379–80, 385–86, 389; written school literacy and, 383–84
Medici, Cosimo de', 84
Meditation on Human Redemption (St. Anselm), 69
memory, 52–53, 220, 223; blind teachers, 224–25; books on memory arts, 96; medieval reliance on, 38; shift from to written record, 55; symbolic objects and, 55–61; synthetic alphabet method and, 250–51
men, literacy rates in England, *305*, 305–7, *308*
mercatoris studium, 53–54
merchants, 50–54, 191
Mer des Histoires, 143
Merv Oasis, The (O'Donovan), 345
Metalogicon (John of Salisbury), 54
Middle Ages: abbreviations, 70; academic standards, decline in, 40–41, 67; attitudes toward literacy, 72–73; hearing and seeing, importance of, 54–73; laity, literacy of, 44–48; Latin, challenges to, 47–48; listening, impor-

tance of, 67–73; roles of knights and clergy, 40–44; sign-literacy, 46–47; social classes, 50–51; writing decoupled from reading, 45–46. *See also* reading, Middle Ages; writing, Middle Ages

Middle-Class Culture in Elizabethan England (Wright), 127

milites litterati, 44–45

minimal literacy, 46–48

Mittelberger, Gottlieb, 283

Mizaud, Antoine, 138

mnemonic devices, 96, 104–5n59, 144

modernization, 2–3, 26–28, 87, 269

Momigliano, Arnaldo, 111

Montfort, Henry de, 46

Montfort, Simon de, 46

moral literacy, 15, 329n1

mother, role in teaching reading, 216, 233

motivation, 23, 29

movies, 379; *D2: The Mighty Ducks*, 394; *Space Jam*, 379, 380, 381, 385, 388–89, 406, 410

Mowbray, Roger de, 54, 56

Muhlenberg, Henry M., 283

multi-step flow of information, 174

Murner, Thomas, 172

music: cultural landscapes and group singing, 390–91; French peasants and, 134–36; Scholastic art of, 70; singing, 170–71

narrative play, 385

National Covenant of 1638 (scallops), 184

nationalism, impact of printing on, 91, 97

nation states, 242

Natural History (Pliny the Elder), 117–18

neutrality, presumption of, 20–22

Nevill, Ralf, 43

Newman, Charles, 32

newspapers, 365–66, 369

Newton, Samuel, 211, 226

New York City Dutch population, 281

Niccoli, Niccolò de, 112

Nolhac, Pierre de, 118

Nominalists, 54

nonfunctional literacy, 12

nonliterate, inclusion of, 72

Norry, Miles de, 145–46

oaths, 57

objects, symbolic, 55–61; charter supersedes, 56–57; Gospel book, 56–57; knives, 58–60; seal as, 60

O'Donovan, Edmond, 345

Offa of Mercia, 57

Old National Central Bureau of Statistics, 255

Olson, David, 22

Ong, Walter, 66

On the Great Lutheran Fool (Murner), 172

On the Privileges of Rustic Persons (Choppin), 140

oral culture, 9, 140–41

oral testimony, 38

oral transmission, 162; rumor, 168, 172–73, 176; slaves and, 318–19; wills, 55. *See also* German reformation

Orbis Pictus (Comenius), 250

Orderic Vitalis, 71–72

Ording, Abbot, of Bury St. Edmunds, 43

Orme, N., 50

Ortelius, Abraham, 116

Orthotypographia (Hornschuch), 106–7, 114

Osbert Huitdeniers (Eightpence), 51

out-of-school literacy programs, 20

Ozouf, Jacques, 27–28

Palissy, Bernard, 146

pamphlets, 148, 163, 165–66, 167, 170, 175

Panofsky, Erwin, 117

Paré, Ambrose, 146

parents: deaths of, 218–19, 220, 230, 236n21; intergenerational transmission of literacy, 279–80, 285, 290; mother, role in teaching reading, 216, 233; role in reading instruction, Sweden, 239–40, 249, 250, 260, 267

Paris, Matthew, 42, 44–45, 57

parish meetings, Sweden, 247

Parkes, M. B., 50

Parlement of Paris, 148

Paschal II, 61–62

Pater Noster, 51, 53

paths, 14, 32

patron-client relationships, 360–61

pattern books, 144

Patterson, John, 239–40

Paulin Peyver (Piper), 42

Paul the Silentiary, 115

peasants, England, 50–52

peasants, France: festive and musical life, 134–36; inventories after death, 131–32; oral culture, 140–41; rural literacy, 130–32; *veillée*, 135–36, 140, 144; vernacular Bible and, 136–38, 150–51. *See also* France, early modern; printing, early modern France

peasants, Germany, 174–76

peasants, Sweden, 247–48

Pecham, Archbishop, 66

pedagogy, 30–31, 35n4

peddlers, 136–38, 140, 158n23, 158n27, 173

Peletier, Jacques, 149–50

people, the, 126–27, 129–30, 159n32
Persepolis Literacy Conference (1975), 269
perspective, 33
Peter of Blois, 49, 72
Peter the Chanter, 42
petits gens, 127
petits imprimaturs, 114
Petrarch, 116, 118, 123n21
Philadelphia, City Archives of, 290–91
Philip IV of France, 47
Philip of Harvengt, 41, 42–43, 44
physicians, as authors, 146, 151–53
pictorial devices, 132–33
Pirotechnia (Birunguccio), 144
Pisan, Christine de, 145, 149n
Plantin, Christopher, 113, 115, 116
Pliny the Elder, 117–18
Pliny the Younger, 117–18
Polenton, Sicco, 118
politics, preservation of text and, 91–92, 103n41
Poliziano, Angela, 118
popular, as term, 126–27. *See also* toys, textual
popular culture, 11; children's production of, 379–80, 382–83
popularizers, 151–53
popular publications, 300
population density, literacy and, 285–89, *286*, 292, 295n12
Possevino (Jesuit), 151
power awareness, 30–31
preachers, 162–64, 173–74; sermons, 162–65; slaves, 324–26
premodernity, 9, 24
Prentiss, Elizabeth Payson, 342, 353n36
Presbyterianism, 184
preservation, 89–96, 116
printing, early modern France: by Abbeys of Misrule, 148–49; active participation in, 153–54; artisans and tradesmen, 148–50; book ownership and, 129, 131–32, 142–43; *Calendrier historial*, 137–38; *Grand calendrier et compost des bergers*, 127, 132–34, 156n15; inventories after death, 131–32, 143–44; literacy in cities, 141–42; popularizers, 151–53; vernacular, 105n62, 149–53; writing of new books, 138–40. *See also* peasants, France
printing, impact of, 107–8; advancement of learning, 95–96; amplification and reinforcement, 96–98; book format, 87–88; capitalist industries, 86–87; crafts created, 141; editing and reorganizing texts, 87–89; errata, 85–86; magical arts and trade skills, 83–84; preservation, 89–96; public opinion, 171–72; standardization

and, 85–87; veneration of ancients, 94–96; wide dissemination, 82–85
printing-houses, 106–7, 113–16
Printing Press as an Agent of Change, The (Eisenstein), 9
problem-posing, 31–32
proclamation, 65
Protestant Reformation, 9–10, 107, 108, 119; early modern France, 135–38; Sweden, 242–44. *See also* German Reformation
Psalm-book of 1695 (Sweden), 248–49
Psalm-book of 1819 (Sweden), 249
Psalter, 52
Psychology of Literacy (Scribner and Cole), 21
public, 172–73
publication, process of, 116–17
public opinion: geographical stratification, 173–74; German Reformation, 161, 162, 171–77
public schools, 24–25, 329n1
publishing houses, working conditions, 144, 159–60n37
punctuation, medieval, 70
Puritans and dissenters, 207

Quakers, 208, 225, 227, 229, 230–31, 234n2
Quits (Baroness Tautphoeus), 343, 344, 355n62

radio play, 392–95, 400
Radway, Janice, 334
rationalization, 87
Ratke, Wolfgang, 250
Rawick, George, 316
reader-response criticism, 11, 335
reading: ability, 209–12, 301; aloud, 162, 165, 175, 339; built-in aids for, 87–88; community service and, 336; contextual study of, 348; as cultural style, 334, 336–37; current view of, 240–41; editing and translation during, 135; impact of printing on, 87; possibility of choice and, 342, 345–46; practical consequences of, 347–48; precedes writing, 184, 240, 301; as private activity, 338; as public activity, 338–39; taught before writing, 184, 240, 301; use of, for evaluation, 348. *See also* reading, Middle Ages
reading, Middle Ages: coupled with speaking, 46; decoupled from writing, 45–46; hearing as, 69–71; *lectio*, 69, 70–71; methodologies, 24; as physical exertion, 69; privileged over writing, 10; seeing as, 56; of world, 29–30. *See also* reading
reading clubs, women and, 334, 339–40, 347
reading groups, early modern France, 144–45

Realists, 54

realities (*res*), 54

recontextualization, 380, 387–88, 398

recovery of lost knowledge, 94–95

Regimens against the Plague, 151

Reginald of Durham, 53

Regiomontanus, 120, 125n33

Registrar General, 304, 305, 314n20

reinages, 134

reinforcement, 96–98

religion: slaves and, 321–22, 324–25; women and, 337. *See also* German Reformation; Protestant Reformation

religious drama, 134

Religious Wars, 129

remembrance, 33

Renaissance: intellectual advancement, 117–18; process of publication, 116–17; scholarship during, 117–19. *See also* printing, impact of

Renaissance Discovery of Classical Antiquity, The (Weiss), 111

research: databases, 3, 261; early nineteenth century, England, 300–301; on impact of printing, 88–89; mid-nineteenth century, England, 303–4; qualitative measures, 282–84, 290, 291; quantitative measures, 3, 273, 281–82, 290; random sampling, 304–5; 1970s and 1980s, 2–3

resistance, literacy as, 326, 360

resistance movement, early modern France, 148

Resnick, Daniel P., 331n12, 365

Resnick, Lauren B., 331n12, 365

Respublica litteratum, 97–98

retelling, 388

Reutter, Michael, 163, 164

revolutionary consciousness, 30

Rice, Eugene F., Jr., 120

Richard, lord of Harlestone, 42

Richard, sheriff of Hampshire, 49–50

Richardson, H. G., 49

Rishanger, 66

Rizzo, Silvia, 123n22

Robert, *miles ille litteratus*, 44–45

Robertson, George, 184

Rob Roy (Scott), 346

Roger, bishop of Salisbury, 43

Rollos, Richard de, 54

Roma Instaurata (Biondo), 111

Romance of Horn (Master Thomas), 69

Roman de la Rose, 135, 157n21

Roma Triumphans (Biondo), 111

Ronsard, Pierre, 149

Rosicrucians, 96

Rouen festive society, 148–49

Royal Statistical Society, 303

Rudel, Jaufre, 64

Ruelle, Jean Il, 135–36n

rumor, 168, 172–73, 176

sailors, as authors, 146

Sale, William de la, 39

Salutati, Coluccio, 112, 118

Sam, Conrad, 165

Samson of Bury St. Edmunds, 42, 68

Sansom, Oliver, 210, 211, 228–30

Sarton, George, 85, 95

Sartre, Jean-Paul, 128

Sauer, Christopher, 283–84

Sayles, G. O., 49

scandals, 173

Schofield, Roger S., 10, 209, 226

scholar-printer, self-educated, 147

school literacy, 3–4, 21–25; adapting popular toys for, 397–406; children's appropriation of, 379–80; classroom curriculum, 386–87; data collection and analysis, 387–88; drawing and, 394–96; media play and, 383–84; performance concerns, 402–3; permeable curriculum, 408–9; "what I learned" reports, 404–6; written literacy, 398–99. *See also* children, African American; education; parents; schools

schools, 235n7; boarding out, 228; boarding school stories, 341–42; Charity Schools, 300, 311, 313–14n18; early modern France, 141; licensing of teachers, 236–37n23; literacy acquisition equated with, 3–4; modern assumptions, 53; nationalism and, 91; opened by ex-slaves, 326; public, 24–25, 329n1; Scotland, 188, 198–200; Sunday Schools, 300, 360, 371, 376n3; urban, 28–29; women as teachers, 232–33; workhouse, 300. *See also* education

Schucan, Luzi, 112

scientia litteratum, 40

Scientific Revolution, 107, 108, 109, 119–20

Scott, Walter, 337, 346

Scottish literacy, 10, 278; burghs, 185–88; England compared with, 183, 188–89, 198, 199–201; female illiteracy rates, 189–90, *190*, 193, *194*, *195*, *197*, 198; highland/lowland division, 185, 191, *191*, 198, *198*, 203n21; literacy, problems of analysis, 183–85; mid-eighteenth-century illiteracy levels, 197–98; mid-seventeenth-century illiteracy levels, 184–96; nineteenth-century literacy levels, 183, 199–200; occupation, illiteracy by, 191–94, *192*, *194*, *195*, *196*, 205n50; schools, 188,

Scottish literacy (*continued*)
198–200; sign-literacy, 184–85, 193; socioeconomic bias, 189–97; socioeconomic patterns, 185–88, *186*, *187*, 204n38; urban/rural division, 185–88, *187*, *195*, 196, 197; women and, 189–90, *190*, 193, *194*, *195*, *197*, 198

scribes, 46

Scribner, Robert, 9–10

Scribner, Sylvia, 21, 36n7

seal (*signum*), 46–47, 50, 52, 55, 57, 60

Searle, John, 12–14

seeing, 54; anachronisms in conveyances, 57–58; in litigation, 55–56. *See also* hearing

Seiter, E., 409

self-study, 30–31, 53, 346–47; sponsors of literacy and, 363–64

sergeants, 141–42

sermons, 162–65

Serres, Olivier de, 139n

servants, as term, 192

Servius, 118

Seyssel, Claude de, 127

Shepherdesses' Calendar, 132

Shepherds' Calendar. See *Grand calendrier et compost des bergers*

Shor, Ira, 30–32

Sicherman, Barbara, 10–11

sign-literacy: colonial America, 273, 280, 290; early modern France, 142; medieval era, 46–47; pre-industrial England, 301–7, *308*; Scotland, 184–85, 193; spiritual autobiographers, 208, 225–26, 232, 235n11

Simon, Richard, 119, 125n32

slaves, 360; apprentices, 322–23; Bible literacy vs. liberating literacy, 315; black teachers for, 320–21; dangers in teaching, 316–18, 330n7; escapees, 325, 333n36; household, 317–18, 322, 331n11; literacy as path to mobility, 323–24, *327*; motivations to teach, 321–22, *328*, 332n20; oral and written histories, disparities in, 318–19; owners as teachers, 316–17, *327*, *328*; preachers, 324–26; religion and, 321–22, 324–25; siblings as teachers, 320; slave-initiated learning, 322–25, *327*, *328*; statistics, *326*–27; as teachers, 325; urban/house, literacy rates, 317–18; white children teach to read, 319–20; white teachers for, 320; writing and, 318, 322

social science literature, 2

Society to Encourage Studies at Home, 334

Solemn League and Covenant of 1643 (Scotland), 184–85

Soudek, Josef, 112

Space Jam, 379–80, 406, 410; children's appropriation of, 381, 385, 388–89

speaking: business and, 63–64; legislation by proclamation, 65; privileged over writing, 63–65; writing vs., 54–55, 61–67. *See also* voices

speech, properties, 383

Spence, Joseph, 222–23

Spigel, L., 382–83

sponsorship of literacy, 11; appropriation and, 361, 370–75; concept of, 359–61; employers and, 372–75; literacy crisis and, 361, 365–70; obligation toward, 360; stratification of opportunity and, 361–65, 370; teaching and, 375–76; twentieth century economies and, 357–58

sports discourse, 393–94

sports figures, 385, 388, 406–7

sports media, 380

Spufford, Marbury, 10

St. Albans abbey, 58

St. David's, 63, 67

St. Jerome's Psalter, 52

St. Mary's priory (Monmouth priory), 56–57, 59

standardization, Renaissance era, 85–87

standardized tests, 15, 361

standards, 13, 14; Middle Ages, 40–41, 67

statistics, 240–41

Statistik över Sverige (Swedish Statistics; Af Forsell), 238

steam press, 357

Steele, Sarah, 371–75

Steinberg, S. H., 90–91

Stephen of Bulmer, 58–59

Stepping Heavenward (Prentiss), 342, 353n36

stereotypes, 96, 97

Stevens, Edward, Jr., 368–69

stewards, 54

"Storm over the University, The" (Searle), 12–14

strong theories of literacy, 5, 19, 26

Stuckey, Elspeth, 20

summarizing, 388

Sunday Schools, 300, 360, 371, 376n3

supply vs. demand model of growth, 284–89, 295–96n14, 295nn11, 12, 13

Svebilius, J., 249

Sweden, 3, 10, 199; confirmation, literacy required for, 238, 240; economic/household order, 246–47; European background for literacy, 242–43; foreign observers of, 238–40; Hustavla, 243–48, *245*, 270n6; marriage, literacy required for, 238, 239, 246, 248; parents, role in reading instruction, 239–40, 249, 250, 260, 267; political/worldly order, 247–48; Protestant reformation in, 242–44; reading tradition in, 238–41; royal decree of 1723, 249; spiritual/teaching order, 245–46. *See also* Sweden, literacy campaign

Sweden, literacy campaign: age differences, 257–64, *258*, *259*, *260*; analysis, patterns of, 242–43, 260–62, 269; Church examination registers, 251–55, *252*, *254*; conclusions, 269; functional need for reading ability, 248–49; horizontal diffusion, 250–51; initiative from above, 249–50; summary, 267, *268*; systematic studies of, 261–64; Tuna, Möklinta, and Skellefteå, 262–64, *263*, *264*; Tuna register, 255–61, *256*, *257*, *258*, *259*, *260*, *263*; Västerås and Visby, 265–67, *266*; by year of birth, *263*, *264*, *266*. *See also* Sweden

Swedish Riksdag, 247–48

symbol systems, 380, 383–84

synthetic alphabet method, 250–51

table of contents, 88

Tacitus, 97

Tateishi, Carol, 385

Tautphoeus, Baroness, *343*, 344

teaching, dynamics of sponsorship and, 375–76

technology of the intellect, 22

tensions, symbolic, 399, 408

Theatrum Orbis (Ortelius), 116

Theodosian Code, 131

Theology Faculty of Louvain, 151, 152

theory, 17

Thermopylae, references to, 97

Thomas, Master, 70

Thomas of Eccleston, 68

Thompson, John W., 48

Thresher's Labour, The (Duck), 223

Tolet, Pierre, 153

Tony, Robert de, 38–40

Topography of Ireland (Gerald of Wales), 71

toys, textual: adapting for literacy demands, 397–406; cultural landscapes and, 390–92; drawing and, 394–96; radio play, 392–94, 400; shared pleasure of, 396–97; transformation of, 390–97

translators, Renaissance era, 94

Tresor des povres, 127, 132

Trosse, George, 226–27

Tryon, Thomas, 212, 214–16, 227

Tuna, Sweden, 255–61, *256*, *257*, *258*, *259*, *260*, *263*

Twelve Articles, 174–75

typography, 86

Ugolino, Cardinal, 67–68

UNESCO statistics, 241

unions, literacy and, 366–68

universality, 22–23

University of Paris, 131

urban literacy, 27–29, 273

urban/rural division: colonial American literacy, 274–75, 288, 290–91; Scottish literacy, 185–88, *187*, *195*, 196, 197

Uses of Literacy, The (Hoggart), 153

Valete, as term, 54–55

Valla, Lorenzo, 117, 118

veillée, 135–36, 140, 144

vernacular, 60, 67, 105nn62, 63; Bible, versions of, 98, 136–38, 150–51, 242–43; linguistic map of Europe, 90–91; printing in early modern France, 105n62, 149–53

Vesalius, Andreas, 116

Victor, St., 134, 156–57n17

Virgil, 118

visual literacy, 21, 162, 404–5

Vitalis, Orderic, 42

voices: electronic, 379; radio play, 392–94, 400; re-accenting, 381–82; recontextualization of, 380; written play with unofficial, 399–400. *See also* speaking

voices (*voces*), 54, 56

von Günzberg, Eberlin, 165

von Schubert, Friedrich Wilhelm, 240

Vora, 176

Vostet, Jean, 139–40

Walker, Marian, 343

Walter, Hubert (archbishop of Canterbury), 42, 54, 63

Walter of Bibbesworth, 39

Ware, prior of, 55–56

Watkins, Owen C., 234n1

weavers, 169

Webster's speller, 323, 332–33n28

Wecheleu (hermit), 53

Weevils in the Wheat: Interviews with Virginia Ex-Slaves, 316

Weiss, Roberto, 111

West Acre chronicle, 38–40

White, Carol, 371–75

Whiting, John, 229, 230–31

William of Astle, 58, 60

William of Well, 68

Williams, Allen Hamilton, 336, 342

Williams, Mary, 339

William the Conqueror, 55

wills, 46, 55, 293n4, 294–95n5, 304

Winchcombe abbey cartulary, 54

Winchester, Ian, 18

witnesses, 55–61

women: classic male authors and, 337; in England, literacy rates among, *305*, 305–7, 310;

women (*continued*)
ex-slaves, 316; and formation of subjectivity, 349; in France, 126, 130, 147; intense engagement of, with books, 335, 340–41; libraries established by, 334, 336; literary inspiration for career choice by, 345–46; middle-class, 10–11; and permissible feminine activities, 374; and preaching, 163; and reading clubs, 334, 339–40, 347; and religion, 337; as schoolteachers, 232–33; in Scotland, literacy rates among, 189–90, *190*, 193, *194*, *195*, *197*, 198; social constraints on, 341; and spiritual autobiographers, 230–31; in Sweden, literacy rates among, 260; writing ability among, lack of, 232–33
woodcuts, 133, 162
workhouses, 212–13
world, reading the, 29–30

Wright, Lewis B., 127
writing, 10, 11, 22; and classroom curriculum, 386–87; collaborative, 31, 400–403; learning, 213, 215; slaves and, 318, 322; union activity and, 367; women's lack of ability, 232–33
writing, Middle Ages: abbreviations, 70; decoupled from reading, 45–46; as dictating, 71–72; as physical exertion, 69; speaking vs., 54–55, 61–67; as symbolic object, 57–58; as unreliable, 63–64
writing studies, 358
written literacy, 398–400

Yonge, Charlotte, 344–45, 349
youth cultures, 382

Zymler, Johannes, 163